THE CRISIS OF GENOCIDE

From the years leading up to the First World War to the aftermath of the Second, Europe experienced an era of genocide. As well as the Holocaust, this period also witnessed the Armenian genocide in 1915, mass killings in Bolshevik and Stalinist Russia, and a host of further ethnic cleansings in Anatolia, the Balkans, and Eastern Europe. *The Crisis of Genocide* seeks to integrate these genocidal events into a single, coherent history.

Over two volumes, Mark Levene demonstrates how the relationship between geography, nation, and power came to play a key role in the emergence of genocide in a collapsed or collapsing European imperial zone—the Rimlands—and how the continuing geopolitical contest for control of these Eastern European or near-European regions destabilised relationships between diverse and multifaceted ethnic communities who traditionally had lived side by side. An emergent pattern of toxicity can also be seen in the struggles for regional dominance as pursued by post-imperial states, nation-states, and would-be states.

Volume II: Annihilation covers the period from 1939 to 1953, particularly focussing on the Second World War and its aftermath, the Holocaust and its lasting impact, and the latter part of the Stalinist regime. Levene demonstrates that while the attempted Nazi mass murder of the entirety of European Jewry represents the most thoroughgoing and extreme consequence of efforts aimed at political and social reformulation of the Rimlands' arena in particular, the accumulation and concentration of genocidal violence against many 'minority' groups would suggest that anti-Semitism or racism alone is insufficient to provide a comprehensive explanation for genocide.

Mark Levene is Reader in Comparative History at the University of Southampton, and in the Parkes Centre for Jewish/non-Jewish Relations. His writing ranges from Jewish history to genocide and anthropogenic climate change, including, most recently *History at the End of the World? History, Climate Change and the Possibility of Closure* (co-edited with Rob Johnson and Penny Roberts, 2010). He is founder of Rescue! History, and co-founder of the Crisis Forum. The two volumes of *Crisis of Genocide* continue a multi-volume project—begun with *The Meaning of Genocide* and *The Rise of the West and the Coming of Genocide* (2005)—to chart the history of genocide in the age of the nation-state.

Annihilation

The European Rimlands 1939–1953

MARK LEVENE

OXFORD
UNIVERSITY PRESS

OXFORD
UNIVERSITY PRESS

Great Clarendon Street, Oxford, OX2 6DP,
United Kingdom

Oxford University Press is a department of the University of Oxford.
It furthers the University's objective of excellence in research, scholarship,
and education by publishing worldwide. Oxford is a registered trade mark of
Oxford University Press in the UK and in certain other countries

Published in the United States of America by Oxford University Press
198 Madison Avenue, New York, NY 10016, United States of America

British Library Cataloguing in Publication Data
Data available

Library of Congress Cataloging in Publication Data
Data available

ISBN 978–0–19–968304–8 (Hbk.)
ISBN 978–0–19–879177–5 (Pbk.)

For
Daniel, Adam, and Karen

'In the end moral and political truths have to be proved *on the body*, because this mass of nerve and muscle and blood is what we are.'

Pat Barker, *The Eye in the Door*

Contents

List of Maps

A Brief Note on Languages and Transliteration

This study's geographical focus is on regions of once great ethnic and linguistic complexity. Across many languages, this author has thus opted for names as commonly cited in standard works. While the aim is to be consistent, it is not to render, for example, Polish or Czech names as if they were Russian, or, for that matter, English. Readers should be able to spot the differences soon enough. Place names, however, are that much more problematic in the sense that what, for example, in 1914 might have been referred to by the politically dominant group as Lemberg, by 1919 had become Lwów, and then again, by 1945, Lviv. Our response has been to use the most appropriate name at any given time, at least with reference to the linguistic group which named the place as such. But sometimes we offer a second name in brackets, especially where, at that given time, another group (referred to in the text at that point) had its own alternative appellation for the place in question. There is also an issue of nomenclature where a group's self-designation is not the same as that used often pejoratively by others. The obvious example here is 'gypsy', which we use when we are referring to the negative appellation by those outside the community, while opting for 'Roma' as our standard ascription. The general point is that if some of this may read ambiguously, it is because ambiguity was built into the historical predicament in question.

Map 1. The Rimlands in the Era of the Molotov–Ribbentrop Pact, 1938–41

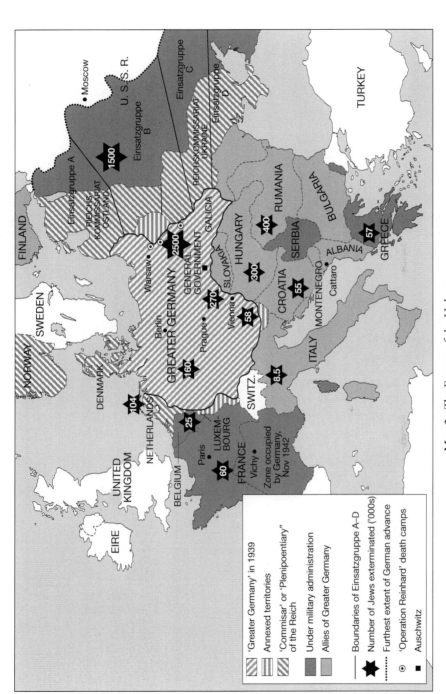

Map 2. The Europe of the Holocaust

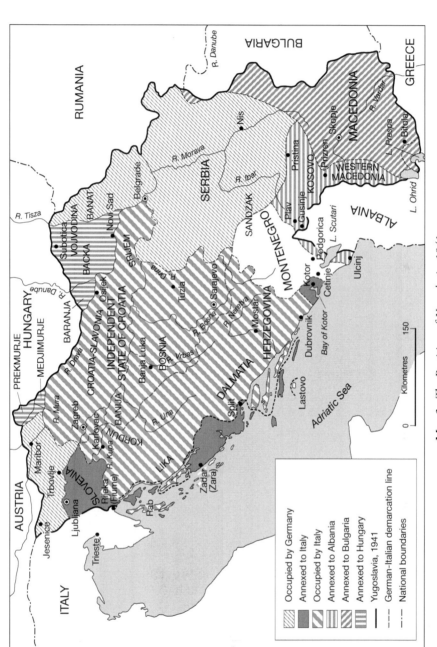

Map 3. The Partition of Yugoslavia, 1941

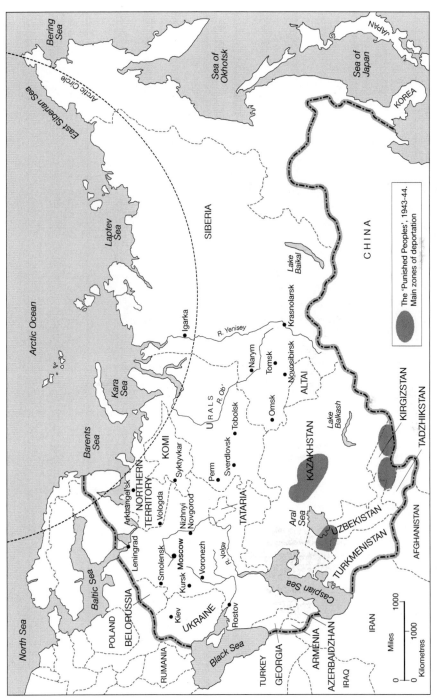

Map 4. The Russian Heartland, Dumping Ground of Peoples: Stalin's Reality, Hitler's Imagination

The 'Punished Peoples', 1943–44.
Main zones of deportation

German expellees   Polish expellees   Polish resettlers from Central Poland

Other peoples (see accomapnying notes)

Territory lost by Germany   Territory gained by Soviet Union

Boundaries in 1939   Boundaries in 1945

(A) Czech resettlers within Czechoslovakia
(B) Ukraine deportees within Poland (150,000)
(C) Belorussian expellees from Poland to Soviet Union (33,000)
(D) Poles originally deported to Siberia and Central Asia
    returning to Poland, 1939 to 1941 (266,000)
(E) Ukrainian expellees from Poland to Soviet Union (482,000)

Map 5. The Final Ethnic Cleansing of the 'Lands Between', 1944–8

Introduction

In Volume One of *The Crisis of Genocide* we set out the historical and geographical parameters of a sequence of European and near-European genocides, or genocidal violence, spanning the period 1912–53. In the Introduction to Volume One we spelt out why this incidence was most prevalent and persistent in regions at the edge of the 'advanced' nation states of the western parts of the Continent and more precisely in the western rim of what had been the great 'world' empires of Russia, Austria, and Ottomania. From 1912 onwards, beginning with the inter-state conflicts in the Balkans, these empires began to buckle under the strains of what rapidly turned into the Great War, precipitating, in each case, internal collapse from late 1917 to the end of 1918. The ensuing chaos throughout the collapsed imperial polities is a well-known story. What we sought to demonstrate in Volume One, however, was how something more specific about the shattering of the imperial zones contiguous with the more advanced polities of the West—or, put in more world-system terms, the zones of interface between metropolis and semi-periphery—brought in its wake not just chaos but genocide. Further to this line of argument we proposed that these shatter zones should be understood not only in terms of discrete countries but transnationally, and as a whole.

The term we used in Volume One and continue to use in Volume Two for these regions is 'the rimlands'. In part this is question of emphasizing their geopolitical precariousness and vulnerability as indicative of their place within the fundamentally changed relationship *between* a more hegemonic West and a weakened semi-periphery. It also translates into a further geopolitical distinction articulated by the British geographer Sir Halford Mackinder, between these regions and what he designated to be a Eurasian, more specifically Russian, 'Heartland'. But critical to the formulation, too, is the historically embedded ethnic heterogeneity of these rimland zones. Under imperial, especially late imperial, rule, negative distinctions and attitudes on the part of the state against specific ethno-religious communities had sometimes manifested themselves in discrimination and persecution. In some rare instances, these tendencies turned genocidal. In the changed or changing circumstances of post-1912 imperial collapse and reformulation, the potential for state violence against ethnic groups (as recognized by the Raphael Lemkin, creator of the term genocide), became much more pronounced. In those parts of the rimlands whose reformulated political future was given international shape and recognition by the Western powers at the 1919 Paris Peace Conference (PPC), the victory of the national imperative ensured the division between ethnic 'majorities' and 'minorities'. We charted the attempt to regulate and manage this implicitly toxic relationship through the Minorities Treaties. Yet the general failure of this 'New Europe' to find grounds for social reconciliation between dominant and lesser *ethnies* ensured that most parties thenceforth increasingly sought communal security through the existence of or aspiration to their own sovereign and homogeneous nation states. A sustained explosion of inter-ethnic violence in late Ottoman Turkey, beyond the immediate reach of PPC protagonists but in which the liberal West was heavily implicated, led to its official involvement in the 'Lausanne' exchange of populations, which became an important precedent for the further 'unmixing of populations'. Broadcast as a successful, non-violent model of how this could be done, Lausanne in fact disguised the actual circumstances of late Ottoman ethnic cleansing while offering legitimation and cover for a much more intensive range of post-1939 genocidal deportations, as to be discussed in Volume Two. More generally beyond Western reach, attempts at post-imperial reformulation undertaken by a post-Ottoman Republic of Turkey and a post-tsarist USSR suggested the degree to which both social and ethnic homogeneity were now perceived as domestically progressive and modern, not to mention a necessary method for strengthening both state and society within the context of—or as a bulwark against—a dominant Western liberal system.

Granted, early Soviet experiments in *korenizatsiia* (indigenization) implied a recognition of ethnic (but not religious) plurality within the state, though, rather significantly, by giving national labels to all such entities. Under Stalinist rule, however, Bolshevik revolutionary violence of the civil war period returned with a vengeance, directed not only against class enemies but, increasingly, against 'national' entities. The consequences included the terror-famines, especially in the Ukraine (the *Holodomor*) and Kazakhstan, as well as a range of 'national operations' which became increasingly fundamental to the Great Terror/*Ezhovshchina*. If this underscored the nature of Stalin's personal paranoia, we also suggested in Volume One a renewed convergence with the geopolitical anxieties of late tsarism, centring as they very precisely did on the rimlands. By similar token, the effort at national homogenization of the late Ottoman state under the Committee of Union and Progress (CUP)—whose most fundamental genocidal outcome was the destruction of the Armenians (*Aghet*) and Syriacs (*Safyo*)—continued to be pursued with vigour by the formative and later ensconced Kemalist republic against not only Christian Greeks, but fellow Muslim Kurds. Indeed, the continuity between its actions in the 1920s and 1930s is emphasized right at the outset of this volume, with the genocidal assault on Dersim: the final action in this particular anti-Kurdish sequence.

One imperial entity, of course, which had no post-Great War recovery or reformulation was Austria-Hungary. The possibility that such a trajectory might have been encompassed under the aegis of an also 'imperial' Germany—Austria's own senior partner in the Great War Central Powers combination—was denied under the terms of the PPC. Critical to our argument in Volume One was the degree to which not only Germany but all the major participants in the Great War were in collective, psycho-cultural and social, as well as statist terms, destabilized by this monumental European catastrophe. And we also charted how this destabilization found one critical outlet through confabulations of Jewish responsibility for the war, thus further emphasizing how, in crisis conditions, elite-led geopolitics has the capacity to intermesh with psychopathological tendencies towards projection. In 1918, however, when the German war effort itself collapsed, Judaeophobic myths became central to much of the post-Wilhelmine national narrative as to what had gone wrong. This necessarily coincided with the Bolshevik ascendancy in Russia and an international revolutionary threat widely, yet entirely erroneously, perceived as 'Jewish'. The drive towards a reformulated German hegemony in Central Eastern Europe (thus, Habsburg and Hohenzollern empires combined), and from that the aspired-for conquest of the east *through* the rimlands—as enunciated by German nationalists and then given palpable form through the Hitler-led Nazi takeover and dismantling of the Weimar state—carried with it a view of geopolitical struggle in which the idea of an international Jewish conspiracy was not just incidental, but central. Our last chapter of Volume One, 'Anti-System Two: The Emerging Hitler State', also demonstrated how other peoples, most notably Roma, could be marked down for destruction through the racial 'science' which underpinned the Nazis' radicalized urge towards social and ethnic homogeneity. However, at the chapter's conclusion it was the way the specifically Jewish incubus interacted with Hitler's agenda for the emasculation of both the Western system and Soviet anti-system which brought to us our 1938 endpoint.

*

Whereas Volume One covered twenty-six years of rimlands' devastation and genocidal violence, the final phase of the sequence, as presented here in Volume Two, telescopes the pattern into a fourteen-year equivalent. That in itself suggests a greater, more complete intensity to what happened in this phase: necessarily with the Second World War the major frame of reference, and with the Holocaust at the very epicentre of the discussion. However, just as consideration of the *Aghet* alone would be insufficient to understanding the totality of genocide or its wider significance in the period 1912–38, so here in the period 1939–53, deliberating only on the Holocaust, even over and beyond its Germanocentric aspects, would be to equally fail in our task. This volume is thus organized into two parts, the four chapters of Part One charting the different pulses of rimlands' genocidal violence, against both Jews and non-Jews, which immediately preceded or accompanied the Second World War. Part Two's further two chapters survey genocidal violence in the war's aftermath, leading towards the effective expurgation of the rimlands.

The stricture against treating the Jewish catastrophe purely through the prism of Nazi assault is perhaps particularly germane to our first chapter, 'The Second Crisis of the Rimlands'. This implicitly posits that even were we to consider the Jewish fate alone we would need to do so within a wider context of Nazi, Soviet, and Western interactions, not to mention those of other state and societal protagonists. But, by further implication, it was not just renewed European war which lit the touchpaper for a wholly more catastrophic wave of exterminatory violence against Jews and non-Jews, so much as the preceding reconfiguration of the 'Lands Between' rimlands zone, which the Nazi–Soviet Pact of August 1939 heralded. At the core of this first chapter, thus, is the fate of Poland and its *peoples*, under both Soviet *and*

Nazi occupation. To be sure, it is from the Polish perspective rather than the Jewish that the two-sided aspects of liquidation are at their most emphatic: the consequences of Nazi, SS-organized elitocide in the so-called AB extraordinary pacification campaign demanding cross-reference with NKVD massacres exemplified by Katyn and the 1940–1 deportations to the Soviet east. A paradox of the Polish Jewish situation under Nazi rule, by contrast, was Hitler's failure to have the Jews—and indeed those from already conquered or absorbed territories elsewhere in Central Europe—equally removed into the Soviet sphere. The unresolved nature of the 'Jewish question' thus, over and beyond the more obvious genuinely geopolitical wartime equation, became a further factor in Hitler's resolve to smash the Soviet Union, making space in this 'Heartland' not only for Germans to inhabit but also for Jews and other unwanted rimland peoples to be eructed into its far, uninhabitable wastes.

Chapter Two thus hinges on the further *failure* of Hitler's agenda, this time in the form of his inability to defeat the Soviet Union and the manner in which, as the military campaign unravelled, a series of stage-by-stage Jewish *genocides* emerged, initially against Soviet rimland Jews, then against the entirety of European Jewry. Even so, the trajectory of European-wide Jewish destruction involved mass deportation to various specific extermination sites in the 'Lands Between'. Yet just as the Nazi war on the Jews had as a corollary, if not always in an obviously linear fashion, a Nazi war on the Roma, so it had too a whole set of corollaries in the anti-Jewish behaviour of other satellite states and societies operating under Nazi aegis. Chapter Three particularly seeks to demonstrate how 'the Holocaust' was very much more than a German affair. Indeed, the European anti-Jewish reach of the 'Final Solution' and the way this played into Nazi, more precisely SS, geopolitical assessments of the war's ultimate outcome, was closely mirrored in the initial efforts of many satellite states, rimland and otherwise, to get rid of some or all of their own Jews—and Roma—followed by equally convoluted (and sometimes quite contradictory) efforts to retreat from total Jewish destruction. The fourth and final chapter in Part One, 'War of All against All', then seeks to demonstrate how, out of the conditions of the failing Nazi war, a whole set of *other*, non-Jewish mass murders and ethnic cleansings in the rimlands emerged. To be sure, a great swathe of rimlands mass killings, notably in Belorussia, were a consequence of a lethal, if ultimately pyrrhic, Nazi counter-insurgency strategy. But critical to our reading is how weakening Axis control in both 'the Lands Between' and the Balkans provided opportunities for weak state, shadow state, or sub-state players (Ustasha, Chetniks, Ukrainian Insurgent Army—UPA—et al.) to conduct their own genocidal campaigns against unwanted minorities in what rapidly descended into 'wars of all against all'.

The very virulence of these struggles practically ensured that just as in 1918, Great Power-determined general 'peace' did not constitute an end to the struggle for the rimlands, nor to the potential for genocide. But our second and final Part of this volume offers a key distinction. The extension of Soviet power, by way of the Red Army, far into these regions, ensured that any national reordering would be at Moscow's behest rather than the West's. Chapter 5 charts how Stalin accomplished this in the now expanded 'domestic' realm of the USSR by extinguishing, through deportation, the national existence of a whole series of peoples on its southern rim, and pulverizing the movements for independence in the 're-liberated' Baltic and Ukrainian territories initially absorbed by dint of the Nazi–Soviet Pact. This implicit Russifying process, however, had its apotheosis in the projected deportation of Soviet Jewry to the east. It was Stalin's intended (albeit at his death aborted) reckoning with the Jews, not Hitler's, we argue, which brings the specifically Jewish element of our overall narrative to its terminus. That said, the expansion of the power of the USSR beyond its borders also carried with it a major new impetus towards the homogenization of the rimlands. This final attempted homogenization is the subject of our sixth and final chapter. Set against the ostensible success of Lemkin's contemporaneous efforts to outlaw genocide within the framework of the newly formed United Nations, Soviet diktat in the east ensured that violently accomplished deportations, ethnic cleansings, and population exchanges of entire societies were the order of the day. *And with Western acquiescence.* To be sure, there remained unfinished business, in Yugoslavia and parts of the Caucasus most particularly. But what had been a traditional, ethnographically mixed mosaic of rimland societies in 1912, by the late 1940s had been almost entirely replaced—at the behest of political elites at both national and international levels—with a landscape of *modern*, monocultural nations. With genocide as intrinsic and fundamental to the achievement.

PART ONE

RENEWED EUROPEAN CATACLYSM

1

The Second Crisis of the Rimlands

SETTING THE SCENE

'Who still talks nowadays of the extermination of the Armenians?'[1] Attributed to Hitler in a secret speech made to German army chiefs on 22 August 1939, this apparently throw-away line has become well known as testament to the Führer's murderous anti-*Jewish* intentions. Neatly shortened for more general consumption into 'who remembers the Armenians?', the minor problem that the attribution—as reported by Louis Lochner, the Berlin bureau correspondent of the Associated Press—came at second or third hand, is generally overlooked. So, too, is the fact that its source seems to have been notes taken by one of the senior officers at the meeting secretly *opposed* to Hitler's plans. In other words, somebody who might have had an interest in embroidering such notes. Whatever the truth on that score, there is a further significant irony about Hitler's purported assertion. It does not appear to have been about killing Jews as such—but 'men, women and children of *Polish* race and language'. On that score, we might be less surprised. This was, after all, little more than a week before Hitler's invasion of Poland, precipitating the outbreak of the Second World War. In all probability, Hitler *did* say something to this effect. At the very least its approximate veracity can be confirmed because around this time there were a number of other recorded occasions when Hitler spoke about his exterminatory intentions.[2] Many of these remarks include reference to Jews. But at this juncture they were *primarily* about Poles.

Are these opening remarks, in this second volume of our study, designed to undermine genocide scholarship's standard focus on the period 1939–41 as critically one of prelude to the Holocaust? On one level, absolutely not. That focus is not only necessary but vital, given the extreme lengths to which the Hitlerian regime went thereafter to wipe out European Jewry in its totality. And attempting to understand the preliminaries to that sequence—with due deference to those who have already meticulously charted and analysed the course—is something we cannot abstain from here. But having introduced a wider Polish dimension to the genocidal possibilities inherent in Hitler's drive to world war, is even this sufficient to our task? The very date of Hitler's speech, practically on the verge of the signing of the Nazi–Soviet non-aggression pact, ought to remind us of the particular circumstances under which Poland's fate was decided. German invasion from the west not only precipitated, within brief weeks, a Soviet corollary from the east, but exposed to international gaze some inkling of a mutual project—over and beyond that of a

simple promise that Germany and the USSR would not go to war with each other
for the next ten years.

The arrangements, entered into by foreign ministers Ribbentrop and Molotov,
included a secret protocol—not admitted by the USSR until 1990—for the carve-up
of the core 'Lands Between' zone of the rimlands into Nazi and Soviet spheres. For
genocide scholars this ought to have a special poignancy, if for no other reason
than that the initial territorial division cut across Lemkin's own home province of
Białystok.[3] The ruthless involvement of Stalin in the Polish carve-up, of course,
does not of itself prove Soviet complicity in, or co-responsibility with, Nazi exterminatory motives or schemes. After all, from a historical perspective the partition
of Poland was nothing new. Germans and Russians had connived at the same in
the late eighteenth century. The difference between 1795 and 1939 was that, in the
latter case, Hitler was effectively acting for the *two* previous imperial German powers: Austria *and* Prussia. And while on the earlier occasion the geopolitical machi-
nations of the predatory powers were—as one would expect—indicative of the will
to violence, nobody remembers the 1795 suppression of Poland, or its immediate
aftermath, for anything we might call genocide.

This chapter, however, proposes that consideration of the 1939 partition and *its*
genocidal implications cannot happen through a purely Germanocentric lens.
Indeed, if we were minded to apply Lemkin's own understanding of genocide as
'a coordinated plan of different actions aiming at the destruction of the essential
foundations of the life of national groups', including 'the disintegration of the[ir]
political and social institutions',[4] this would be a particularly fitting description of
Soviet rule in Poland. Though not just in Poland. As Baltic and other peoples
further south in 'the Lands Between' found themselves forced, as a consequence of
the Nazi–Soviet protocol, into the latter's embrace, the Lemkinian terminology
would be equally applicable. At stake here is not simply a competitive matter of the
numbers of fatalities in the respective German and Soviet spheres, to the time of
Barbarossa—there were more on the Soviet side. The issue, rather, is whether, and
to what degree, the Soviet purpose in the absorbed (in Soviet minds, 'reabsorbed')
lands was disintegrative of discrete communities. Or, to put it a different way, supposing Lemkin had known the full facts, or alternatively had been writing his
wartime study of genocide without reference to the Western Allied accord with
Stalin from 1941, might not his study have been called 'Axis *and* Soviet Rule in
Occupied Europe'?

To be sure, this is a counterfactual supposition. The reason for posing it is in
order to beg some further uncomfortable questions. The way, in retrospect, that we
get round the problem of the German–Soviet modus vivendi is to remind ourselves
of what came after: the explosion of *German* exterminatory violence against Jews,
Soviet POWs, and other peoples in the USSR. From this perspective, and with the
knowledge that the modus vivendi came to an abrupt end, the only historical
issues that matter are the staging-post elements towards what came subsequently.
These elements in themselves help to conveniently deflect any notion of the Soviets
as genocidal perpetrators. The hindsight view thus screams out to us the provisionality of the Nazi–Soviet accord; and in the process it blinds us to seeing it in

terms of its own moment—as something suggestive if not of permanence, then certainly of semi-permanence.

One might consider the plausibility of this argument, in critical part, by reference to the deeper historical record. The Molotov–Ribbentrop Pact was an attempt to restore the imperial continuity of the rimlands ruptured in 1918–19 by the 'illegitimate' intrusion of the Western-imposed 'New Europe'. And by uniting the two great surviving post-imperial polities who were the losers in that earlier process—this time not as opponents but as joint, anti-system protagonists—one might read the Pact as an attempt to remove from the rimlands not only the virus of nation-statism, but also of the Western-cum-North Atlanticist hegemony from which the virus had originated. What this interpretation clearly lacks is a recognition of the radicalized nature of the transformed Russian and German states under their respective Soviet and Nazi masters. Whereas in their traditional guise, imperial administrators in Berlin or Petersburg may have looked upon their non-dominant national communities with benevolence, indifference, or utter disgust, notions that such communities could be collectively reordered, or spatially relocated to somewhere else at the far reaches or even *beyond* the imperial domains, were rarely, if ever, entertained. Violence may have been fundamental as an instrument of control, while policies of socially engineering the populations of a region to favour the dominance of one ethnic group against another were certainly, towards the fin de siècle, contemplated—this, after all, was a key feature of Bismarck's 'Polenpolitik' in the 1880s.[5] But to go beyond that to systematic, even wholesale, elimination—as, for instance, enacted by the tsarist regime against the Circassians in 1864—was to move towards something not only seemingly novel but, even within the corridors of power, viewed as being of an extreme and controversial nature.[6] By contrast, not only were the Soviets *as well as* the Nazis hypersensitive to the 'national question', but each sought to resolve the 'problem' by exactly such methods of terror-based mass coercion, as if this was the standard, entirely correct procedure for the purpose.

What is thus striking about the period of the Pact is the degree of synergy between the two contracting parties which, though geared towards a seeming restoration of the rimlands to the imperial status quo ante, did so on the back of a largely *revolutionary* agenda of national group pulverization. The attempted evisceration of the Poles, developed from September 1939, would have been inconceivable in 1795. To be sure, Nazis and Soviets mostly undertook this process in separate but parallel compartments. But there was also, as we will see, recognition and acknowledgement of the other's interests in the process. This was especially the case in the matter of the Volksdeutsche. The potential for a mass violent eruption of ethnic Germans from the Russian side of the rimlands had reared its head in the early crisis of the Great War. Hitler's decision to resettle those caught on the Soviet side of the 1939 demarcation within the greater German sphere can be interpreted as clear awareness of their likely fate under Stalin. Equally, however, it might be read as remarkable feat of cooperation between the two sides—as sealed by a further secret protocol—to resolve the issue for once and for all.[7]

As recent studies have made abundantly clear, it was this 'peaceful' 1939–40 Nazi evacuation of the Volksdeutsche that proved to be both the catalyst for and pivot around which the entirely more violent eructions of *other* peoples in Hitler's recently acquired eastern sphere were to revolve.[8] And as the acute geographical limitations of these attempted population reorderings *within* the German sphere intensified so, in turn, this helped precipitate the breakdown of the accord *without*. Again, we might choose to read this outcome narrowly as proof of the underlying fragility and hence provisionality of the Nazi–Soviet Pact. But equally we might treat its breakdown as more broadly indicative of the unfinished business which began in 1919 with the attempted but now aborted Western efforts at Versailles to impose a post-imperial order in the rimlands. The new moment of semi-periphery crisis, twenty years on from then, cannot, thus, be reduced solely to the relationship—ephemeral or otherwise—between the two anti-system giants, or to their efforts alone to expunge a 'chaotic' ethnic rimlands diversity in favour of their own mercilessly ordered, brave new worlds.[9]

To be sure, the political liquidation of Poland from two sides, followed by the subsequent deportations and killings of Poles and a wider range of population groups in both Nazi and Soviet spheres remains this chapter's central focus. Of necessity, this requires us to consider a little more fully the main agents in this process, most particularly the SS in its various guises on the one hand, and their alter egos in the NKVD on the other. That logically *does* take us to a further consideration of the specifically Jewish dimension of the second rimlands crisis. While this may seem a dreadfully familiar foretaste of the 'optimal' genocide soon to come, looked at through the broader geopolitical context of 1939–41 it also lends itself to some further uncomfortable conclusions about what the Nazis were actually seeking in this period as their avowed final solution to the European Jewish question. But then, that broader geopolitical context involved a range of other state, or would-be state, actors in the rimlands. Even sometimes at their last gasp these may have been lesser actors with much more confined room for manoeuvre than either Nazis or Soviets. However, as the pre-war crisis escalated, some of them too were thinking of, sometimes even acting out, limited versions of extreme, exterminatory violence against subordinate communities as the route out from their own perceived atrophy. Perhaps, counter-intuitively, we need to begin not with the Pact itself, but a review of this wider rimlands scene on the cusp of world war and catastrophe.

NATIONAL POLITICS, GEOPOLITICS, AND THE GROWING INCIDENCE OF RIMLANDS' VIOLENCE

Hitler may have said words to the effect of 'Who remembers the Armenians?' But then who actually knows that what happened to another set of peoples, from the same eastern Anatolian region twenty-three years on from the *Aghet*, was yet another case of genocide? What was done by the Turkish state to the various Alevi, Zaza-speaking, Kurdish tribes of the Dersim region defies any other terminology. Indeed, it is, at least in our rimlands zones, the only definitive but immediate pre-war example. Certainly, how many of the estimated 65,000 to 70,000 inhabitants of the mountainous, ravine-strewn plateau from the south of the Sivas to Erzurum highway were annihilated in the military campaigns of 1937, and more specifically 1938, is difficult to ascertain.[10] What is undoubted is that, once begun, no mercy whatsoever was shown. Whether the Dersimi tribes had, or had not, participated in the initial scratch rebellion against Ankara rule, and whether or not they had surrendered themselves to the fake amnesty proffered by the military in early spring 1938, the killings were prosecuted systematically and without discrimination. One local Kurdish historian pulling together various sources, including oral testimonies, many years later, offers this summary of the final stages of the campaign:

> In the spring of 1938, the government offered amnesty to all who would surrender their arms. The Karabal, Ferhad, Pilvank, Sheykh Mehmedan and Karaca tribes, who responded to this call, were entirely annihilated. In a later stage, they also killed most of the Kureyshan tribe of Mazgirt district, the Yusufan and Bakhityar tribes, not sparing women, old men and children. They were killed en masse, in many cases by the bayonet. Towards the end of summer, the Hormekan, Kureyshan and Alan of Nazimiye district, and part of the Bamasuran of Mazgirt were also annihilated by poison gas bombs as well as by bayonets. Their corpses were doused with kerosene and set alight.[11]

Of course, this is a single retrospective report by a highly partisan nationalist, writing under the pseudonym of Dr Şivan. One of the problems of piecing together what actually happened in Dersim in 1937–8 is not only the paucity of documentary or other evidence-based material but the lack of detached contemporary witnesses to corroborate what is available from the Kurdish nationalist sources. Nevertheless, enough information exists, as demonstrated by the social anthropologist Martin van Bruinessen, to confirm that, in their essentials, Dr Şivan's account and that of Nuri Dersimi, another Kurdish participant in the early stages of the rebellion, are correct. These include detailed reports in an official military history of the campaign, photocopies of which van Bruinessen was able to see long after its limited publication had been withdrawn and copies had ostensibly been destroyed.[12] Equally, the British consul in Trabzon—from the information he had amassed at the time—was able to offer a clear summary of what had taken place: 'Thousands of Kurds including women and children were slain; others, mostly children were thrown into the Euphrates; while thousands of others in less hostile areas, who had first been deprived of their cattle and other belongings, were deported to vilayets in central Anatolia.'[13] The picture at the core of the military offensive, however, is of unadulterated and unforgiving atrocity: of *aghas* and their retainers tortured and then brutally killed; of women and children burnt in haylofts— on specific occasions doused in kerosene and set alight; and of other instances, where they were bricked up in caves and these then set alight. There appear to have been instances where surrendering communities who had survived the artillery fire and aerial bombing of their towns or villages were then lined up and machine-gunned to death. And then, there were specific instances where the women and girls of the Kureyshan and Bakhtiyar tribes threw themselves from the high cliffs of the Munzur and Parchik ravines to avoid what they certainly would have perceived as a worse fate from the Turkish soldiery. When the British consul noted, 'It is now stated that the Kurdish question no longer exists in Turkey', he was simply reprising the revengeful Turkish press slogan of the day (recalling the Roman general Scipio's destructon of Carthage): '*Delenda est Darsim*'.[14]

Ankara's commitment to this being a final reckoning with the Kurdish problem is indubitable. At least three army corps were committed to the campaign, and these included heavy artillery and aircraft. This recalls, on the one hand, the earlier Turkish military drives against Kurdish insurgencies and, on the other, the Red Army campaigns especially of the early 1920s, directed towards the annihilation of zones of remaining anti-Bolshevik independence, whether in the Caucasus, Central Asia, or Tambov. From a military perspective, the very nature of the Dersim campaign must provoke questions as to how much the Kemalists were replicating, or building on Soviet 'best practice'—after all, Moscow was more than simply Ankara's nominal ally—or, perhaps, seeking to 'learn' from other 'small wars' of the period, most obviously that conducted by the Italians in Abyssinia. Reports of the use of poison gas in the Dersim operation, though unsubstantiated, would strongly suggest a Turkish willingness to follow, for instance, what had been a projected tool in Tukhachevsky's destruction of the *Antonovshchina*, just as much later, perhaps, Saddam's more extensive use of gas against Iraqi Kurds—most infamously against the town of Halabja—might suggest that Baghdad's military planners, amongst other things, had been reading earlier Turkish manuals. Only a historian with a more precise knowledge of military doctrine, development, and interstate exchanges of training and practice could offer more concrete advice on these matters.

Yet what is clear about the specifics of the Dersim offensive is how much it followed the contours of colonial-style military massacre, and the degree to which such campaigns made no discrimination at all between combatants and non-combatants. In the British quelling of the Chimurenga, in the 1890s, surviving women and children had been consciously suffocated or burnt to death in caves. In the Russian subjugation and then extirpation of numerous Circassian tribes from the north-west Caucasus, thirty years before that, the wholesale massacre of women and children isolated in ravines or valleys had been par for the course. Like them, like the Hereros, so too the Dersimi tribes were relentlessly terrorized, pursued, and exterminated, not necessarily until every last one of them was dead but certainly until their ability to be viable as an ongoing and independent community had been extinguished.

But if this, then, *is* genocide, it does rather beg the initial question: why is this important case so poorly integrated into today's comparative genocide studies? The issue cannot be entirely a spatial one: in other words, a product of the backwater nature of eastern Anatolia, given the prominence of the geographically congruous Armenian example. In temporal terms, one might wish to excuse a wider 'international' (in other words, Western) lack of interest in the event, on account of more immediate points of concern. In 1937 the Spanish Civil War was raging. A year later, in addition to its horrors, Western media was fixated on first the Austrian, then Sudeten, crises. The highpoint of the Dersim paroxysm, from spring to autumn 1938, was exactly coterminous with these two events.

This is not to suggest that what Turkey did on the wider international stage was of no consequence for the West. On the contrary, when it came to Ankara's major foreign affairs effort of this time—spurred on by an ailing Kemal—towards getting France to 'return' the *sanjak* of Alexandretta (at the southernmost tip of our rimlands zones) from the Mandate of Syria to Turkey, the issue had the potential to spark a direct Franco-Turkish conflict. That the mandatory power, supported by Britain, was prepared to concede on the matter, despite the fact that only 38 per cent of the population of the *sanjak* was Turkish, tells us just how desperate both Paris and London were to avoid either war with Ankara or the excuse for its alignment with the Berlin–Rome axis. The further fact that the route to resolution of the matter involved the French authorities in Alexandretta turning a blind eye to cross-border Turkish 'rent-a-crowds' intimidating the populace in order to arrive at the necessary Turkish majority in elections for the region's newly inaugurated autonomous parliament—the obvious prelude to its acclamation of unity with Ankara—also speaks volumes about the Versailles victors' abandonment of minority rights. The outcome speaks for itself: when in late June 1939, Alexandretta joined Turkey as the province of Hatay, tens of thousands of Armenians as well as Arabs, whether orthodox Muslim, Nusayri (Alevi), or Christian, fled south into Syria and the Lebanon.[15]

Paris and Londons' desertion of the Alexandretta communities can be read as a straightforward consequence of appeasement. After all, this is also the moment of British tergiversation on its internationally binding commitment to the Jewish National Home in Palestine. Yet while such heavily geopolitically informed acts carried with them Western liberal regret, even shame, it is difficult to glean similar sentiments evinced on behalf of the Dersimi tribes. If Czechoslovakia, in 1938, was Neville Chamberlain's 'far away country of which we know nothing', then clearly Dersim might as well have been on the moon. Which would suggest that the way *its* peoples' fate fell down a memory black hole in Western consciousness—more or less remaining there to the present day—was not just the result of cynical geopolitical ploys. The failing was of a more deeply cultural kind.

For Ankara, the whole of Kurdish-dominated eastern Anatolia was an embarrassment, a throwback to the sort of backward, feud-ridden tribal society, to which Turkification was the state's unyielding riposte. And all the more reason why Dersim, the last region of the new republic, as one American diplomat had put it, operating 'within the fatherland but outside the law',[16] was such an affront to its sensibilities. Yet Ankara's position on the matter represented no more than a feedback loop to a Western understanding of what politically constituted modernity. Within *its* bounds no society or community could be allowed to operate at one remove to integrated market relationships, centralized tax systems, or as if the very territorial resource base from which they derived sustenance belonged to them, rather than being subject to the imperatives and diktats of the developmentalist body politic. Yet this was exactly the Dersimis' sin. They lived in what Ernst Bloch would have called a 'non-synchronous contradiction',[17] eking out a meagre living from their flocks of goats and sheep, from horticulture and silviculture, and, where these proved insufficient, as increasingly they did in a degraded environment, from raiding each other or non-tribal communities adjacent to the massif. Nobody in the West was going to empathize particularly with this violent, chief-led lawlessness, or, for that matter, the Dersimis' inertial lifestyle. Contemporary leftists might have been able and willing to relate to Basques or Catalans as progressives who were part and parcel of an anti-fascist republican front in Spain. And there appear to have been those within the Kurdish movement who sought to make Dersim's simmering resistance to Ankara's iron grip more palatable to Western sympathies by propounding its objectives as nationalist, or otherwise aligned to the more overtly modernist and radical aims of Armenian parties still seeking a revolutionary toehold in eastern Anatolia.[18]

However, if these efforts were likely to have little resonance with the West, for Atatürk and his entourage they were received as nothing less than proof of an irremediable recidivism. The very fact that Dersim Alevis had been conspicuous in their offering of refuge and protection to many fleeing Armenians in 1915 was historically dubious enough: the failure of their tribal leaders to give wholehearted cooperation to Kemal in the critical eastern Anatolian-focused phase of the Turkish independence struggle in 1919–20 doubly so. Was it the latter which Ankara could never forgive? Or the former, with its resonances of Armenian cultural sympathies, even similarities? Historically, ethnographically, and linguistically, there was a degree of Armenian osmosis with Alevi Kurdish society in the Dersim region.[19] Yet, actually, there was no grand narrative of Dersimi alignment. They had fought against Armenians as well as Russians in the latter stage of the Great War. To some considerable extent they had involved themselves, too, in the Koçgiri and then Shaikh Said revolts. That said, the Dersimi had not thereby demonstrated their consistent loyalty to or even general comprehension of the Kurdish nationalist cause.[20]

All along, however, what stood out about the region for Ankara was not just its continuing association with unruliness, banditry, religious reaction, or even revolt. It was rather its degree of independent, even truculent *particularisms*. And this went against the very grain of Atatürk's route to modernization, proclaimed as national, secular, *and* populist by Ankara: to have a region which refused to participate in this given universe of obligation and did so, moreover, with gun in hand, was simply too much for the regime to countenance. Not only did it represent an actual barrier to the country's internal reordering—by way of a ludicrously idealized notion of an all-embracing homogenized Turkishness—but it equally signified to the wider world Ankara's inability to genuinely arrive at its aspired-for goal. If, thus, the Dersimi could not be dragged, kicking and screaming, into the embrace of Turkish citizenship or, failing that, could not be pacified to the point where they could then be forcibly dispersed and fragmented as a group, or groups, in the wider population, then the only alternative was to find a pretext for their destruction.

In part, this already existed. Growing Dersimi opposition to the 1934 resettlement law and, more particularly, to the designation the following year of the region as special Zone Four,[21] which could be closed off from the rest of the country and its population evacuated, was cited by Ankara as a casus belli. In fact, the charge was unfounded. In November 1936, Kemal declared in parliament that Dersim was Turkey's most important internal problem.[22] The region was placed under military government with full powers of martial law, and a programme of road and bridge building, accompanied by a network of police posts, initiated. Military roads had been the last act in the British subjugation of the Scottish Highlands nearly two centuries earlier; while the German project to bisect Hereroland with a railway line a mere thirty-odd years before, in south-west Africa, had been one of the final triggers to indigenous rebellion there. In Dersim, by contrast, only five out of a hundred of the region's tribes appear to have joined the religious leader, Seyit Riza, in overt defiance. The resettlement law carried with it draconian punishment, including summary execution where resistance was encountered. And when the initial rebellion was scotched in autumn 1937 and Seyit Riza and the other ostensible leaders rapidly executed, most of the tribes readily opted for the proffered amnesty. This proved, however, only to be a subterfuge for the mounting of the major, much more systematic phase of the military campaign, geared towards the tribes' obliteration.

*

From where we stand now looking back to Dersim, two things come across as particularly noteworthy. The obvious one is Ankara's determination to make a clean sweep of the perceived problem. The interior minister of the time, Şükrü Kaya, spoke of the region as a 'disease' and, thus, the need for 'radical treatment'. No amount of hedging such public statements with promises of 'civilized methods' to arrive at the required result could disguise the regime's intent to do its worst.[23] That this was of a genocidal order was recognized at the time by the most pertinent observers. The British consul in Trabzon explicitly compared it to what had happened to the Armenians in 1915.[24] But the second point relates exactly to that foreign awareness and the fact that nobody, publicly or diplomatically, intervened. Remember, this was, in interstate terms, peacetime with the League of Nations still extant. Five years earlier, a very similar sort of state military action, the Assyrian affair, had been brought to a halt faced by British censure.[25] While most of the survivors or descendants of the Hakkâri community—that other notable obstacle in the way of Turkish nation state-building—had thus been spared across the Iraqi border, the destruction of the Dersimi on the Turkish side proceeded with unalloyed impunity.

Should we read this as evidence of the outstanding *success* of Kemalist genocide, even of a Turkish *Sonderweg*? Kemal's dream of Turkish recognition as a member of, if not total integration within, the Western state system was not troubled by the Dersimi affair. On the contrary, the destruction or dispersal of Dersim's people, the administrative reordering of its borders—most of it, henceforth, in the thoroughly toponymically Turkified province of Tunceli—stands as a tangible and long-lasting monument to the leader who died within weeks of its final subjugation. While a Hitler or Himmler's evocation of a Genghis Khan massacring his way across Central Asia carries through today as further proof of their crazed mental condition,[26] nobody much in the West questions Kemal's obsession—at least not in the same way—with similar Turkic warriors of the steppe. As for what actually happened in Dersim, it is passed over in nearly all standard Western texts, either in silence or in the briefest and most opaque of commentaries.[27] Yet Dersim's airbrushing serves to reinforce the Kemalist point of the exercise. Until 1981 there was no further politico-military challenge to Ankara's authority from eastern Anatolia. The Kurdish question ostensibly ceased to exist. Insofar as this study is concerned, it brings to an abrupt closure any further analysis of Turkey as a proactive component of the rimlands' crisis.

Of course, the Kurdish question had neither been extinguished nor resolved. Rather, it remained latent until it burst into renewed life—and, with it, a new dialectic of state versus community violence—in the 1980s. But the fact that Ankara under Kemal and his successor, Ismet Inönü, had dared to act as they had done—where others might have only dreamed of doing so—again would seem to underscore the notion that Turkey was a special case.

*

Throughout the wider rimlands the urge to deal with troublesome minorities once and for all was becoming, in the late 1930s, an almost constant establishment refrain. Polish exasperation at a burgeoning Ukrainian nationalist insurgency in the *kresy* was being expressed by the post-Piłsudskian regime of the Colonels with increasingly violent countermeasures.[28] In Yugoslavia, the bitter long-term struggle between Albanians and Belgrade—centred on the upper Drenica valley—was also leading to ever-more draconian state measures designed to terrorize, punish, and ultimately get rid of the 'problem' population. As earlier suggested, in Volume One, the nature of Yugoslav and Turkish counter-insurgencies against Albanians and Kurds respectively, had historical and contemporary parallels. However, nobody in Belgrade (or, for that matter, Warsaw) was prepared to act in quite the forcibly unilateral fashion that Ankara had done. We know full well from the records of the Serbian Cultural Club that, informally, all the talk was of how Albanian removal might be accelerated—with extreme violence as its most appropriate instrument. If this was intended to constitute a softening-up process, what the Stojadinović administration actually opted for in 1938 (that is the year of Dersim) was an agreement which would see 40,000 Albanian families formally resettled in Turkey. The agreement only broke down for lack of funds to enable its completion.[29]

Thus, the Yugoslav preference for organized Albanian removal would suggest not some replication of the Turkish precedent, but more a return to the standard Western-endorsed one by way of Lausanne. The only flaw with this argument is that by 1938 what the purveyors of the Western 'system' had to offer in the form of power-brokerage in 'New Europe' disputes was largely irrelevant. Versailles was in shreds, as was its Minorities Treaties' subtext. It was the *anti*-system players who were now largely calling the shots. As Vaso Cubrilović, a leading adviser to the Yugoslav government—and otherwise infamous for being one of the conspirators in the assassination of Archduke Franz Ferdinand—put it to the Serb Cultural Club in 1937:

> When it is possible for Germany to force tens of thousands of the Jews to emigrate, for Russia to transfer millions of people from one part of the continent to another, a world war will not break out just because of some hundreds of thousands of displaced Arnauts [Albanians].[30]

Of course, few in the 'New Europe' were actually proposing to follow a Stalinist lead. But the irony is that when, after the Nazi dissolution of the rump Czech state in March 1939, Germany became the undisputed hegemonic player in the region, its role as arbiter in the subsequent round of post-Versailles border rectifications did *not* lead to the immediate jettisoning of the Lausanne model. On the contrary, when, in succeeding months, indeed into the war itself, the Nazis sought to ensure oversight, especially of Rumanian borderland displacements in northern Transylvania and southern Dobrudja—the former favouring an irredentist Hungary, the latter, an irredentist Bulgaria—their involvement was seen by the respective parties 'as simply an extension of the League of Nations Minority Commission'.[31] This is hardly to downplay the much more overt, not to mention shrill, baying for blood which, picking up on the Nazi domestic cue, was now becoming the defining feature of burgeoning Eastern European ultra-nationalist parties. It is, thus, doubly ironic that the violent rampage of a small, and otherwise now almost entirely forgotten example of this type of grouping—the Sich Guard, who were seeking at the eastern extremity of Czechoslovakia to create a Carpatho-Rus republic—provided the goad to an attempted reassertion of Prague's authority in the region, then an excuse for Hungarian intervention, and, finally, part of the pretext for Germany's spring overthrow of the Czech polity.[32]

All this is to underscore how oddly paradoxical were the months leading to war in the 'Lands Between'. Overtly fascist groupings such as Szálasi's Arrow Cross in Hungary, or Codreanu's Iron Guard in Rumania—with altogether larger popular constituencies than Volozhin's Sich Guard—were certainly dreaming at this time of the massacre of their 'enemies', Jews in particular. The Iron Guard would infamously demonstrate their worst desires when they went on their own spectacular anti-Jewish killing spree in Bucharest, in January 1941. Significantly, however, this came at a moment when they were making one last desperate, in fact failed, bid for state control.[33] Equally, the non-fascist, army-led administration of Marshal Antonescu, who put them down and monopolized Rumanian power thereafter, would have no compunction about initiating its own anti-Jewish *genocide* once Operation Barbarossa had begun. But that further underscores the fact that it was not necessarily how far towards the fascist end of the authoritarian spectrum incumbent or would-be state actors in Eastern Europe were which determined their proclivity to minority extirpation, but rather a matter of timing and context. In late 1938, or early 1939, there was no lack of elite politicians and military men who were thinking long and hard about how they might get rid of their unwanted minorities, Jews in particular. But none amongst them dared to cross the line—at least *not yet*—into a call for open season.

The obvious alternative route was to put an occupational and economic squeeze on the Jews in order to make their existence untenable. The regimes in Hungary, Rumania, Poland, and the Baltic states, all with the Nazi precedent in mind, moved towards various forms of draft or actual legislation of this type.[34] But the obvious problem with tormenting any communal group in this manner was that it did not necessarily lead to getting them out of the country. As the Nazis had already discovered to their cost, the wealthiest, most dynamic, and capable of the community might find ways and means of obtaining visas for somewhere else, while the poorest and most wretched were most likely to remain in situ—even potentially, in the process, becoming a financial burden on the state. There also remained a certain risk for these regimes in that too closely emulating the German model might be taken by the French and British as an unacceptable snub to what remained of *their* hegemonic order. Thus when Octavian Goga, a new fascist-leaning Rumanian prime minister, in early 1938, declared that he intended to dispense with Versailles-guaranteed Jewish citizenship rights, and that those henceforth made stateless would have to leave the country, London and Paris interpreted this as a Bucharest move towards the Nazi sphere and promptly put pressure on King Carol to have him dismissed.[35]

This hardly stopped 'New Europe' leaders from searching for a formula by which the goal of Jewish eviction might still be achieved; it simply meant that they were increasingly open to a much wider range of formerly 'unthinkable' options. In the spring and summer of 1939, for instance, the Polish Colonels began to secretly train and arm members of the ultra- Zionist Irgun and Betar movements, with the aim of the latter mounting an invasion of British Palestine. The obvious implication was that this would open up the territory to mass Polish Jewish immigration.[36] In 'normal' times such a proposition would have seemed not only bizarre but hare-brained. It also happened to involve a convoluted subterfuge, as, at the very same time as the Colonels were organizing what amounted to an anti-British *conspiracja*, one of their number, the foreign minister, Beck, was basking in the glory of having wrested from the British a 'blank cheque' guarantee to come to Warsaw's assistance in the event of *any* German threat to Polish independence.[37]

Yet, strikingly, Polish efforts to be shot of their 3 million Jews of a more public nature were also, by degrees, drawing Britain, as well as France, into their diplomatic manoeuvres. Again, the notion that the French island of Madagascar could be requisitioned as some sort of refuge, or, more bluntly, 'reservation', for rimland Jewry proved a chimera once a three-man commission—with French approval—had investigated and offered its negative findings on the possibility.[38] Yet the British Foreign Office, in the summer of 1939, most probably at Roosevelt's prompting, went one step further in stating that His Majesty's Government would be prepared to consider this and other settlement projects, providing other governments were prepared to follow suit.[39]

The intimation of some comprehensive multilateral agreement to eliminate the Jewish presence from the rimland arena, in whole or in part, was music to most 'New Europe' political ears. The then Hungarian prime minister, Béla Imrédy, some months earlier, had called for a 'Europe-wide solution of the Jewish question'.[40] But such statements were not just evidence of growing frustration at the Jewish presence, or of a wish-fulfilment (mirroring that of progressive Turks) to achieve economic nationalism through some grand expropriation of middleman 'wealth'. They also represented a geopolitical shift. The formerly notably anglophile Imrédy was, through his words, signalling his intention to bring Hungary closer into the German sphere. When the newly independent Slovakia—that is, independent entirely at German behest—galvanized by the threat of Jews fleeing into the country from the

Subcarpathian Rus, used the occasion to set up its own Central Office for the Solution of the Jewish Problem in Slovakia,[41] it, too, was recognizing (and affirming) the new shape of ethnic politics in a once separate Austro-Hungarian orbit that was now firmly under the aegis of a single German imperium.

That Whitehall, in the summer of 1939, was prepared to negotiate with Hitler about East European populations and places, even while, publicly, it was supposed to be standing up to him, is again indicative of a Western acknowledgement of the shift in the European balance of power. That this involved efforts to appease the Nazis by reviewing possible Jewish removals to unlikely places such as British Guyana, or French Madagascar, from this perspective should be no more surprising than British willingness to sponsor a possible population exchange of the mixed communities of Danzig and the Polish Corridor, in the interests of a general peace.[42]

But here lay the rub. While the Western states were prepared (however unenthusiastically) to consider Jews and other rimland 'minority' peoples as necessary pawns in a wider geostrategic game, for Hitler they—the Jews—were themselves the *fundamental* players in the game. If even before the Prague debacle the Allies were moving towards their more publicly belligerent stance against further German aggression towards Poland or other states in the rimlands' arena, then, for the Führer, it was self-evident that plutocratic Jewry was behind the effort. If London, Paris, and Washington were also recalcitrant about coming to an arrangement on any 'final solution' of the Jewish question in Central and Eastern Europe—that is, mass removal—then that too proved that these same plutocrats were seeking to spike Hitler's wider *Raumpolitik*. To consider how this Hitlerite projection of some Western-cum-Jewish nexus helped drive Nazi policy towards mass Jewish annihilation we need to say a little more in the final section of this chapter, 'The insoluble problem: getting rid of the Jews'. But the critical point thus far is this: Hitler's conviction that it was the hidden hand of international Jewry behind Western governments which was leading him into a military conflict with them dovetailed with a different set of raw information proffered by Hjalmar Schacht and other hard-headed advisers. This clearly stated that—autarchic hegemony or no in Mitteleuropa—Germany's poor foreign currency reserves, and lack of general economic stability including massive inflationary pressures, plus a basic insufficiency of energy and mineral requirements for intended armaments production, all pointed towards the rapid unravelling of Germany's fortunes in any war with the Allies.[43] The 'Jewish' threat from the *West* was clearly compounded in Hitler's mind by the fact that his whole operating strategy for war was geared towards the destruction of the Jew Bolsheviks in the east, opening up the vision of a great racially-informed Teutonic overlordship in the Russian 'Heartland'.

This is not to suggest that there was no expectation of some eventual showdown with the Western Allies—Hitler's programme, after all, was predicated on the breakup of the Western hegemonic system and its replacement with a single, German-dominated one.[44] A two-front conflict, however, was unthinkable. It conjured up exactly the nightmare scenario which had brought Germany to its knees in the First World War. And not just for direct military reasons. All Germans were haunted by the memory of starvation, as the Allied blockade had finally kicked in. Victory against Russia in 1918 had come too late to turn the tables on that. All of which determined that, caught between a rock and a hard place, the Nazis would have to do some radical thinking outside of the box to arrive at a way of extricating themselves from their immediate dilemma. Hitler's invasion of Poland was originally set for 26 August 1939. The actual delay of six days was a consequence of something which seemed at the time to be quite unprecedented, not to say quite inconceivable: an alliance with the Soviets.

*

What is relevant to us here is less the occasion of the Nazi–Soviet Pact and much more its significance for the fate of the peoples of the 'Lands Between'. Even so, the sheer fact of the Pact requires us to be reminded of just how extraordinary this event was in world-historical terms. Viewed through an ideological prism—and, after all, these were not only the two *ideological* regimes of the twentieth century par excellence, but standing in polar opposition to one another—any mutually supportive relationship between them ought to have been impossible. Violence marked every turn in the struggle between German ultra-nationalism and international communism from 1918 onwards, most recently in the Spanish cockpit. The whole notion of an anti-fascist front, beloved of leftist radicals throughout Europe and beyond, was predicated on Moscow's leading role fighting Franco, Mussolini, *and* Hitler. Only the iron internal discipline of Western communist parties aligned to the Comintern could disguise the mortification and disbelief within their ranks on the announcement of the Pact.

But, on other grounds, where ideology merged with geopolitical considerations, a Nazi–Soviet understanding also seemed counter-intuitive. Hitler saw the USSR as a threat not only because it was supposedly 'Jewish'-dominated but because its rapid drive to industrialization threatened to put a spoke in the wheel of Germany's own thrust for European hegemony. Or, put yet more crudely, the sheer trajectory of anticipated Soviet tank production determined, perhaps even predetermined, a German strategic thinking geared towards getting in its *Flucht nach vorne*—its preemptive strike—before its realization. Equally, this suggested that, put into the even larger geopolitical equation of defeating the (Western) system, there could be no room for two competing anti-systems. Sooner or later one would have to either withdraw or, more likely, be eliminated from the game. What thus makes the events of August 1939 that much more paradoxical is that in beating a path to the Kremlin's gate—against all his political, racist, not to mention Judaeophobic, 'sensibilities'—Hitler was acknowledging that, for the time being at least, Germany was the weaker anti-system competitor. Indeed, the very success of its unchallenged march across Habsburg Central Europe over the previous eighteen months, in now finally coming up against the buffers of Anglo-French refusal to countenance any more, highlighted the degree to which Germany was henceforth dependent on Russian food, fuel, and other basic supplies if it was to wage war against Britain and France. In others words, what has been described as 'the diplomatic bombshell of the century'[45] might more keenly be read as an act of German desperation in the face of its own geopolitical overreach.[46] In turn, this paved the way for a potentially huge extrusion of Soviet power into Europe—beginning with direct territorial aggrandizement in the rimlands.

However, if we were to take as our starting point for the Pact the agreement to carve up the rimlands—*pace* the fact that this involved major, including ongoing, concessions by Hitler to Stalin—the Nazi–Soviet relationship, instead of looking simply peculiar or lopsided, begins instead to make much more *sense*. Both partners, after all, believed intrinsically in their ability to reshape geographical and human entities to their will. The institutional, social, and cultural obliteration of what was already there in the rimlands, in favour of new socially engineered 'arrangements', would not have caused either to blanch at the prospect.[47] On the contrary, as both Nazi and Soviet polities were founded on ideas of transcendent historical destiny, the fundamental instrument of which was violence, the notion that each would strive for unfettered scope of action in its respective sphere would have been entirely anticipated—and acknowledged—as 'normal' by the other. One might quibble that there was no cult of violence per se in the USSR, as there was in Nazi Germany. And one might wish to protest further against any congruity between the two by iterating that communism stood in principle for the Promethean liberation of humankind, not its hierarchical ordering and subjugation on spurious racial grounds. Yet Soviet practice against perceived or real social or ethnic enemies, especially as it reached its peak in the late 1930s, was as ruthless, as cynical as anything the Nazis could muster. Indeed, judged by a straightforward inventory of fatalities to 1941, Stalinist excess vastly exceeded that of its Nazi rival.[48] Ironically, it was exactly this ruthlessness which made for some admirers among the Nazi elite, not least Goebbels, who was inclined to read Stalinism as national Bolshevism, while others, including Goering, would have given their hind teeth for the sort of Stalinist command economy which Nazi 'polycratic' tendencies largely denied.[49]

But again, one might interject that this is to miss the essential historical point. When the Nazis and Soviets reached their August accord, they were not simply re-establishing the close working relationship between Moscow and Berlin which had characterized their efforts to overcome the political and military isolation imposed by the Western Allies in the 1920s. Rather, the significance of 1939 lay in the degree to which it recalled an earlier epoch of German–Russian geopolitical understanding, which had arguably reached its apotheosis in Bismarck's Dreikaiserbund between Germany, Russia, *and* Austria in the 1880s. To be sure, central to the German thinking then had been insurance against the possibility of an attack from France. But viewed more precisely in terms of domestic interests, the alliance reiterated the empires' aversion to the spread of Slavic nationalism in the 'Lands Between'. Given that Russian interests were geared towards the support of exactly such movements in the residual Ottoman Balkans, there was clearly an inherent contradiction here. But viewed solely through the prism of the more northern rimlands zone, the emperors knew full well what they had in common: an absolute abhorrence of any return to a pre-1795 situation. Or, put again more pointedly, a situation in which the fulcrum of political and cultural power in the rimlands lay not in the Russian or German capitals but in Warsaw.[50]

The principle of a German–Russian cooperation geared towards the subordina-tion of the peoples of the 'Lands Between', was thus in itself nothing new. What was—through the ratcheted up, ideologically-informed German and Russian revi-sionism of Hitler and Stalin—was the practice of national (majority and minority) liquidation.

LIQUIDATING POLAND

That Nazis and Soviets connived with each other to destroy Poland as a political entity is explicit from the secret protocol of the 23 August Pact. At the end of September a new set of arrangements between them confirmed that they would work with each other to suppress any 'Polish agitation' affecting the other's territory.[51] By that juncture Poland had been militarily crushed by the Germans in the west, and invaded by the Soviets in the east, as far as the agreed demarcation line on the river Bug. Twenty years on from her resurrection as a sovereign state, Poland, the major Allied-sponsored creation of the 'New Europe', had again ceased to be.

Should we interpret the very loss of political power—in the context of the 1939 defeat—as the key factor opening up the population to the potentiality of geno-cide? More disturbingly, perhaps, does this suggest that the Poles, through their leadership's maladroit political behaviour in the lead-up to the catastrophe, were, in some sense, *protagonists* in their own national fate?[52] Again, the very fact that Warsaw, earlier in the year, had eschewed overtures from Hitler to join an anti-Soviet alliance and had chosen instead to gamble on what turned out to be useless Western guarantees of support in the face of Hitler's subsequent megaphone threats, does suggest politically suicidal tendencies whose nearest parallel might be Serbian truculence in the face of Vienna's German-backed July 1914 ultimatum. Both sets of behaviour indicate a ready resort to martyrology, almost as if in accept-ing a picture of the world as conflict-ridden, the only thing to do when faced with the military consequence is to embrace it as a religiously ordained sacrifice.[53]

Czech behaviour, in the face of similar disaster, would seem to offer some sober-ing contrast. They too had been abandoned by the West in their hour of need—in fact twice: the first time during the Sudeten crisis, the second when the Nazis had marched into Prague. The difference was that the Czechs at that point had not attempted to physically oppose the fait accompli and, over the course of the next six years—indeed until May 1945—made no further collective attempt to overtly defy Nazi rule. The only notable exception, leading to the assassination of Hey-drich, in May 1942, was not at the instigation of the puppet Czech administration in Prague but of Beneš' 'government-in-exile' in Britain. The result, certainly at that point, was an act of Nazi revenge which, in its massacre and obliteration of the villages of Lidice and Ležáky, amounted to a genocide in miniature.[54] Heydrich's death also provided a further Nazi pretext for accelerating the mass deportation of Czech Jewry. In its face, the Czechs, again, were largely passive bystanders, even if what they were witnessing proved, in fact, to be only a subtext in the now much larger programme of mass Polish Jewish extermination. But the dilemma at the heart of this comparison is whether general Czech passivity—in other words hunkering down and attempting to survive the Nazi storm—was what ultimately protected them (Jews and Roma apart) from the sort of repeated exterminatory assault which was visited on the Poles.[55] After all, the Nazis held the Czechs in more or less the same degree of racial contempt as all Slavic peoples, the Poles included. Moreover, if the Czechs had fought in defence of their territory—as they had had every intention of doing *before* the British-inspired Munich debacle—the Nazis would almost certainly have used this as justification for the same sort of retributive exaction that they visited on the Czechs' northern neighbours.

Must this leave us to conclude that Czech (though not necessarily Slovak) avoidance of the worse Polish fate was due as much to luck as good design? It is a subject to which we will return briefly in Chapter 4. What is definite is that it was Poland, not Czechoslovakia, which provided the initial test bed for Nazi mass killing—and Lemkinian nightmare. And the one factor producing this result was not simply Poland having gone to war with Germany and being defeated, but its having gone to war as, in the eyes of its adversary, an 'illegitimate' state–society. We have previously described this sort of warfare as of a Type Two category, in which Geneva Convention-informed restraints on what can and cannot be done in the course of such a conflict are consciously dispensed with by the side which solipsistically considers itself 'legitimate' and 'civilized'. On its own, this ensured that the initial Nazi military assault on the Poles followed contours of atrocity closer to that of earlier colonial conflicts engaged in by Western states against Third or Fourth World peoples. But what is equally significant for us is the aftermath. In having been unequivocally crushed militarily the institutional and socio-legal membrane which, in normal times, would have protected the ordinary people of the now defeated polity from the worst excesses of arbitrary state power had been effectively stripped away. In itself that would be most likely to have led to further resistance—just as in colonial struggles, particularly those which developed a national character. Necessarily, however, because the struggle was now of a subaltern, stateless community against a powerful (and ruthless) state, this posed the likelihood of a further War Type Three, that is, not only without restraint but with the communal resisters, or indeed non-resisters, exposed to a much greater genocidal potentiality from the occupying state power.[56]

In the discussion of this issue in *The Meaning of Genocide* it was emphasized that such a situation does not have to lead to genocide. Rather, it is heavily contingent on the behaviour and intentions of the dominant state protagonist. And it is noteworthy that in the early weeks of the Nazi invasion and conquest of Poland a question mark still lay over whether Hitler's intentions were ultimately geared towards the compete extirpation of 'Polishdom'. Initially it seems that he might still have been prepared to contemplate some sort of continued 'controlled' autonomy—if only to make a diplomatic opening to belligerents opposing him in the West—or, perhaps, again, as a way of developing a form of joint Nazi–Soviet condominium over Polish space.[57] If there had been a decision of this kind, it is conceivable that a trajectory of amplified mass violence might yet have been moderated. But the fact that *national* 'extirpation' became thereafter the firm order of the day puts to one side any further insinuation that the Poles themselves had something for which to answer. On the contrary, if we want to understand the driving forces towards the subsequent Polish paroxysm we need rather to contemplate not only the Nazi animus against them, but the Stalinist one.

*

German angst about an emerging Polish national consciousness and the potential threat this posed to the integrity of those parts of the rimlands historically under Prussian control, as we have suggested in Volume One, predated the Great War. Schemes during the 1914–18 era to scotch the threat, once and for all, included the proposal to create a hundred-kilometre frontier strip to the east of the old German–Russian border from which all the Polish inhabitants would be compulsorily removed. It was Wilhelmine defeat which put paid to these earlier plans.[58] In the aftermath of the Great War, the boot, indeed, was on the other foot. Far from the eastern marches being 'repopulated' with a human wall of German settlers, some three-quarters of a million ethnic Germans became refugees from the new Poland. The majority fled to Weimar Germany but some were literally pushed: the victims, in particular, of the Polish post-war insurrections in Upper Silesia through to 1921. The fact that *Freikorps* units operating in the region had failed to avert this localized disaster would, in 1939, be essential grist to Germany's vengeful mill. The *Freikorps* themselves were not held responsible for the earlier failure. Rather, a seething revanchist anger at the loss of German territory was directed against the 'treacherous' Poles: an anger kept at an almost constant boil by the various ultra-nationalist refugee associations.[59] Their repeated accusations of Polish persecution of the remaining 1 million of their countrymen still living across the border simply fuelled a much wider cultural-cum-racial outrage at the notion of civilized Teutons subordinated to a primitive, even savage, Slavic people. The fact that the Western victors of 1919 had allowed this to happen, and had even, following the plebiscite over Upper Silesia, ignored its people's majority vote to remain with Germany—sanctioning instead the takeover of its industrial eastern upper part by Warsaw—underscored German reasons for hating the Polish 'monstrosity born of Versailles'.[60]

There is irony, of course, in that one of Hitler's first acts on the international stage was to sign a non-aggression pact with Poland. Nazi goodwill to Warsaw seemed to continue into early 1939 when it picked up the long-sought-after prize of Czech Teschen—thanks to the Nazi-sponsored carve-up of Prague's remaining domains. There seemed even to be a nod and a wink to the Poles that they might be cut into any deal Berlin could arrive at with London or Paris for taking over one of their African colonies as a mass reservation site for East and Central Europe's Jews.[61] All these signs of ongoing, even comfortable, Polish–German accord, however, collapsed as soon as it became clear that the Colonels were neither going to conform to Hitler's role for them as little anti-Soviet allies, nor show enthusiasm for their new proposed satellite status by dutifully accepting whatever territorial concessions (in and around the free port of Danzig, in particular) the Führer demanded of them. We can read Hitler's rapidly ensuing decision to prepare for Poland's destruction as symptomatic of a megalomaniac's incandescent rage at having been crossed. Yet behind the madness was also method: singularly chilling method. When Hitler spoke of eliminating Poland 'as a political factor for the next several decades', as he did, in March, to Field Marshal von Brauchitsch, the Wehrmacht's overall commander, or in terms of destruction of Poland's 'living force', as recorded by General Halder at the infamous August conference,[62] he was not simply speaking of a dismantling of the machinery of the Polish republic. What he actually meant was the physical annihilation of the leading elements of Polish national society. Or, put more succinctly: elitocide.

Who was included in this Nazi warrant for mass murder? Security Service (*Sicherheitsdienst*, SD) head Reinhard Heydrich, who claimed to be tasked with the remit directly from Hitler, had a rather opaque formulation for who these Poles might be: those 'hostile to the Reich and German people'.[63] In practice, this meant those at a national and local level who believed in the idea of the Polish people and were themselves prepared, through their words and actions, to make this into a living reality. It was no coincidence that, in the following months and years, it was teachers, priests, academics, military officers or ex-officers including NCOs, professionals and administrators, business people, members of political parties, or of the residual aristocracy—in other words, either the most educated and articulate members of Polish Catholic society or those who saw themselves as 'natural' leaders—who were most repeatedly targeted. These were the people—primarily, though not necessarily exclusively, male—who would probably be the kernel of resistance to German rule and of any attempt to restore a Polish state, which the Nazi aim from that point on was to absolutely deny. There was a figure, at least according to the minutes of a critical meeting Heydrich held with his leading Einsatzgruppen operatives on 21 September, for how many Poles would be eliminated: 3 per cent. There was an already SD-formulated initial blacklist with 61,000 Polish and Jewish names on it. And indeed, at an earlier meeting with Einsatzgruppen commanders in late August, Heydrich had imparted oral instructions as to just how 'extraordinarily radical' the liquidation order was intended to be. If any commander had any doubt as to what was expected of them all they had to remember was Heydrich's terminology: *Flurbereinigung*, fundamental cleansing.[64]

This, then, was not a Hitler programme for the physical liquidation of *all* Poles but rather, in the focused Lemkinian sense of genocide, a plan to disintegrate them as a people, by eliminating their national 'masters'.[65] If we take this to be the foundation of the Nazi policy, later statements, for instance by Reichsführer-SS Himmler, in March 1940, that the aim was to ensure that 'all Poles disappear from the world', become entirely consistent with his further memorandum to Hitler two months later, in which he envisaged them as an 'ethnic mush'.[66] To put it tersely, Heydrich, having done his business, would then hand over to his senior line manager, Himmler, whose own task was to turn the residue of Poles, as now duly designated 'unpeople', into helots: ripe for service, removal, or death as the Nazi racial state demanded of them. Or such, at least, was the aspiration.

The immediate challenge was one of implementation. Necessarily, Heydrich could only carry through with *Flurbereinigung* on the back of, or more exactly perhaps under the cover of, the Wehrmacht's military success. His accelerated summer task was, first of all, to improvise a special strike force which would effectively carry through the project. But equally challenging was to do this in such a way that lines of demarcation between army and security police were clear and understood. But that in itself raised some further thorny questions. This was not just a matter of these Einsatzgruppen being technically subordinate to the military command. There was a further question of presenting to the army chiefs a rationale for the SD operation—codename Tannenberg—which would at the least appear legitimate and consonant with the laws of war as understood for conflicts between recognized sovereign states. The Wehrmacht may have found its own way of inter-preting the Hague and Geneva Conventions with elasticity. But it had not yet, in 1939, dispensed with them, as it would do in the invasion of the Soviet Union two years later. At least until defeated and—paradoxically—handed over to civil rule, Poland could only be fought and subdued according to the recognized rule book. Or so thought the Army High Command. Was there an element of subterfuge, then, when Heydrich or his immediate SD subordinates meeting with General Wagner, the army's senior officer tasked with liaising with them, presented Opera-tion Tannenberg as essentially a 'security' operation?[67] Behind the lines of the advancing military offensive there could indeed be insurgents and guerrillas seek-ing to (once again) stab German forces 'in the back'. Was it not appropriate, from the perspective of pure 'military necessity', that special forces should be on hand to combat, arrest, and, where appropriate, dispatch such threats?

Or was it that nobody in the High Command had quite grasped, or wanted to grasp, the implications of what Heydrich was proposing? To be sure, there was something unprecedented about an operation of this sort. Heydrich had no blue-print. The very act of putting together a coherent team for Operation Tannenberg was itself of a highly improvised and ad hoc nature. The original four operational groups—Einsatzgruppen der Sicherheitspolizei (special task forces of the security police)—mustered from the SD, Gestapo, and Security Police (Sipo), were soon supplemented by others, including one which, in bearing the name of its com-mander, Udo von Woyrsch, suggested its own autonomous set of directives. Indeed, the unit made quite a reputation for itself for the atrocities it subsequently com-mitted both in its immediate Silesian zone of operation and a few weeks later when it massacred 500 to 600 Jewish men further to the east at Przemyśl, on the old Austro-Russian border. This was the single largest massacre of the Polish campaign. That other Einsatzgruppen units also figured prominently in the roll-call of Polish and Jewish mass murder in September 1939 should not, perhaps, surprise. Most of the commanders were specifically selected for their roles because of their previous experience in the *Freikorps*. Some of them, like von Woyrsch, were rimland refu-gees, Silesian or otherwise, with their own implicit reasons for wanting to exact revenge against Poland and Poles.[68]

Yet at this point any reading of the estimated 20,000 Polish non-combatant deaths by individual or mass execution in the course of Case White (the September military campaign)[69] as primarily the consequence of Heydrich's Operation Tannenberg directives begins to look rather ragged. Not only was there a range of other units, over and beyond the 4,000-plus men in the Einsatzgruppen, which were mobilized or hastily thrown together for counter-insurgency efforts. Waffen-SS Death Head companies from the concentration camp system and Order Police battalions were also supplemented by *Volksdeutscher Selbstschutz*, that is, paramilitary units created from ethnic Germans in Poland. And there was the *Freikorps Ebbinghaus*—formed at the behest of the army for operations in Upper Silesia. Yet even taken together these do not account for all the atrocities of the month. Many Wehrmacht units, including the Secret Field Police certainly, but also front-line troops, were protagonists.[70]

What this information does is undermine a clear picture of focused intent—with Heydrich's Operation Tannenberg at its centre—by bringing into play a contingent aspect to the killing more reminiscent of German military behaviour in Belgium and northern France at the beginning of the Great War. Indeed, what is particularly striking about many of the atrocities committed in the early days of September 1939 is how much they were induced by exactly the sort of 'guerrilla psychosis' which had plagued large swathes of Moltke's 1914 army. German intelligence, in fact, anticipated that there would be fierce resistance by irregular Polish units designed to slow down or sabotage any Wehrmacht advance—especially in the highly contested regions of the Polish Corridor and East Upper Silesia. These assessments proved accurate. But having been fired upon by snipers in the rear of the recognized front, or having heard stories of comrades having their throats cut while in bivouac, a fearful animosity against the Poles appears to have become common fare within the German ranks. Just as in 1914, so here again, a whole population was reified into not just 'cruel and cunning' but 'inhuman' and 'degenerate' enemies who would stop at nothing to visit violence on an 'honourable' German soldiery. If these visceral feelings were born of a form of projective self-justification similar to that which had led junior commanders to line up old men, women, and children in Belgium and execute them as *franc-tireurs*, there was, however, an additional factor in the Polish case which turned the German soldier's fear into the potential for unadulterated rage.

The Polish Corridor, at the north-western limits of the 'Lands Between', was populated by ethnic Germans and Poles as well as those who fell between the two stools or, as in the case of many Silesians, did not offer firm allegiance to either Warsaw or Berlin. Among the Volksdeutsche, however, many of those already covertly organized into *Selbschutz* units awaited the signal from across the border to rise up and liberate themselves from the Polish yoke. Which, given the opportunity, many did by organizing their own, locally significant, killing sprees. Warsaw, however, had its own contingency plans for this eventuality, including the rounding up of some 10,000 to 15,000 suspected insurgents who were to be force-marched, as hostages, further east. Some of these men were actually killed en route. But something more briefly spectacular occurred in Bydgoszcz (Bromberg) on 3 September—the day France and Britain declared war on Germany. Here a premature rising by the local *Selbschutz* precipitated a massacre of some thousand Volksdeutsche men and boys by retreating Polish troops. Soon thereafter the German army entered the city and, in a joint operation with Einsatzgruppe IV, proceeded over the following week to summarily execute at least a thousand Poles. Part—though not all—of the revenge operation was at Hitler's direct behest.[71]

Back home in Germany, Goebbels' propaganda machine also sprang into action to amplify the scope of the original Polish atrocity into the 'Bloody Sunday' massacre of 5,400 (his figures) fellow countrymen. But one might argue that the army rank and file, or at least significant parts of them, from this time on needed neither Hitler nor Goebbels to be convinced that they were indeed fighting a *Volkstumskampf*—a 'peoples' war; that the Poles were in every way the primitive *Untermenschen* that they had historically been portrayed as, and that doling out summary punishment, including the massacre of whole communities and the razing of villages, in lieu of finding actual insurgents, was perfectly justified.

This, clearly, was not the whole picture. The scale of military atrocity against surrendered combatants and non-combatants alike was not of the order visited on Russia and the Balkans from late spring or early summer 1941. Nor were there army orders, as there were at the later date, effectively shielding soldiers from punishment. Indeed, some of the more senior and traditionally 'correct' commanders tried to rein in those units who had committed some of the most egregious offences, invoking, in some instances, court martial. Yet, at the same time, the Army Command's highly dubious interpretation of the Hague Convention on the taking of hostages specifically allowed officers down the chain of command to execute them in place of insurgents. Some senior commanders, moreover, of their own volition instituted their own tariff in instances where Germans had been killed—the execution of ten Poles (or Jews) for every Wehrmacht soldier providing one ominous precedent—while Himmler waded in with his own orders to the SS that *all* suspects should be summarily shot on the spot. What we have, therefore, is a highly dichotomous picture. On the one hand, the Army High Command found itself at odds with a type of warfare (i.e. War Type Two) over which it seemed to lack control. This perhaps was its critical objection to the atrocities: it made for a situation where there was a breakdown in military discipline, undermining its own sense of authority and legitimacy in the eyes of outside, more specifically in this case US, onlookers. But if this led to efforts by a limited few to distance themselves from the Einsatzgruppen 'cleansing' operations and even, in a handful of cases, to personal protests to Hitler—one limited if belated Brauchitsch victory was the recall of von Woyrsch—on the other hand, there were clearly senior officers in the field quite willing to cooperate or assist in such operations, or, of their own initiative, conduct mass executions in defiance of army regulations. Such was the case of the Ciepielów massacre, when 300 surrendered Polish soldiers were machine-gunned to death—the worst, though very far from an isolated, occasion of this kind.[72] Moreover, all dispute on such matters appeared to be brought to a definitive end in early October when, with Poland surrendered, Hitler closed the book on any notion of court martials, by offering a comprehensive amnesty to offenders.

Was this, in fact, the green light for a resumption of Heydrich's *Flurbereinigung*? The very fact that German-controlled areas of Poland were soon handed over from military to civilian rule meant, ironically, that the last defence the Polish population had against the untrammelled terror of the SS had evaporated. With the shift came, too, a termination of military jurisdiction over the security apparatus. In mid-October Heydrich celebrated by ordering the liquidation of the Polish leadership within the following two weeks.[73] He was fancifully as well as boast-fully running ahead of himself. It was not until 6 November that the Gestapo accomplished the first truly symbolic act in response to his command, when they arrested the entire 183-strong faculty of the ancient Jagiellonian University in Cracow. All were deported to Sachsenhausen. Shortly afterwards, 1,700 priests were sent to Dachau. A message to any Poles who might think of fighting on, this was also an unequivocal shot across the bows of the Western Allies, who, having failed to come to Poland's assistance *militarily* in its hour of need, were now being forcefully made to watch as Hitler acted with complete impunity in his Greater Reich. By the end of December, the execution death toll had reached some 50,000, both Poles and Jews. It included 107 Poles rounded up on the streets of Wawer, near Warsaw, on 27 December, and then shot in reprisal for the killing of two German soldiers.[74]

But if Heydrich believed he was simply carrying out the Führer's writ, complica-tions were rapidly looming which pointed, on the one hand, to a dramatic exten-sion of the cleansing method; on the other, to its supersession by more immediate and pressing concerns. In major part the impetus for the sea-change came from Stalin. What amounted to his diktat to Berlin on 20 September—a mere three days after the Soviet march into eastern Poland—to the effect that Moscow would not entertain the existence of any residual Polish state but only a straightforward 'fourth partition' of the country, was itself reinforced a week later when further negotiations over the territorial boundaries of what was now a burgeoning Soviet rimland sphere threw up the fate of the Volksdeutsche within it. The subsequent Nazi–Soviet agreement on the immediate 'repatriation' of some estimated half a million mostly ethnic German farmers posed the obvious question: where would they be settled? The man who insisted to Hitler that he could find the answer was Himmler who, in addition to his role as Reichsführer-SS and chief of the German police, now had himself grandiosely designated *Reickskommissar für die Festigung deutschen Volkstums*—Reich Commissioner for the Strengthening of Germandom (RKF).[75] Himmler's remit to bring the ethnic Germans home created in turn a greater urgency to consolidate the Polish conquests as regions ripe for rapid 'Ger-manization'. Those already provisionally earmarked for direct incorporation into the Altreich would also be the ones which would integrate the incomers. But these happened to be already densely inhabited by majority populations which were not ethnic German but Polish. The discrepancy was especially marked not so much in the relatively smaller districts which were absorbed into Silesia and East Prussia, but the two completely new *Gaue* carved out of the Polish Corridor as Danzig-West Prussia and Warthegau. Not only was the latter now the largest *Gau* in the Reich, but it had an overwhelmingly Polish majority. Indeed, if the avowed intention was to make all these *Gaue* 'German' then the estimated 8.9 million Poles, plus up to 600,000 Jews, within them would somehow have to be 'disappeared'.[76] More pointedly still, if room was to be made, more specifically farms provided, for the imminently incoming Volksdeutsche from the east, a substantial sum of the Polish and Jewish natives, Polish farmers in particular, would have to be 'disap-peared' fast. Himmler's first orders for deportation from the annexed territories were made on 30 October, with a million people the estimated outflow.[77] As with Operation Tannenberg, Heydrich, and his recently formed Reich Security Main Office (RHSA), were on hand to act as chief designers and organizers of the deportation process. At least it was quite clear where the deportees were going to go: there was only one place available, the residual unincorporated Polish territory centring on Warsaw now designated as the General Government. However, the programme almost immediately began to go awry.

One might be inclined to ask why. Himmler and Heydrich, after all, were still simply striving (with all the resources at their disposal) towards what they understood Hitler's expectations to be. And his most recent private statements on the matter reaffirmed that whether Poles lived or died was of little consequence to him. The Polish purpose in the new order was to be no more, nor less, than a reservoir of compulsory labour for German needs, whose level of education was to be consciously degraded so that they were unable to think or aspire beyond their subservient role. Expressed by one contemporary commentator as making of them a 'type of coolie'[78]—with all its colonial connotations—the emphasis on hyper-exploitation was further underscored by a food ration for the inhabitants of Polish cities set in early 1940 at 609 calories a day—that is, 2,100 calories below that of Germans and, hence, tantamount to a famine diet.[79] If Poles from the annexed *Gaue* were thus to be dehoused, made propertyless without compensation, and then forced onto rail cattle trucks (often in the most appalling conditions) in the direction of the General Government, where their survival would be entirely dependent on Polish charities providing them with shelter, food, and basic hygiene, so be it! The fact that those same charities were already being steadily overwhelmed by up to 12 million Polish—and Jewish—inhabitants already in need was hardly something which Himmler's RKF planners were likely to lose sleep over.[80] Especially when set against Hitler's supposed orders to Himmler in early summer 1941 for a demographically entirely reordered eastern empire, which was expected to fall under German control in the wake of Operation Barbarossa. The consequent RKF plans envisaged almost the complete expulsion of surviving Poles way out to the east[81]—a proposal which, in practice, amounted to genocide.

Yet in 1939–40 there was an internal obstacle to these social-Darwinian, zero-sum scenarios. Or, rather, two. The first was summed up in a single name: Hans Frank. The newly inaugurated civil head of the General Government was a jurist, *alter Kämpfer*, and sometime Hitler confidante. He was also vulgar, vain beyond belief, and, in his co-responsibility with SS police chief Wilhelm Krüger for the seamless range of atrocities visited on the region, an undoubted *génocidaire*.[82] It was not, then, that Frank, despite all his contradictions (or rivalry with Krüger) had a more humane side, or, by the same token, was really a sheep in wolf's clothing. Frank cared not a fig for what ultimately happened to the Poles. As for the Jews, they could literally go to hell. What drove Frank to contest Himmler and Heydrich's plans to turn the General Government into a 'dumping ground' was the fact that it was *his* fiefdom and one from which he hoped to derive personal aggrandizement and venal advantage. That, in his mind, meant an autonomous 'unity of administration'—that is, separate from the control of Reich ministries—supported by a minimally Polish-run infrastructure in order than it might operate, if for no more than in the medium term, as a going economic concern geared towards providing services, including armaments production, for the Reich.[83] In brief, his strong card against the Himmler deportation programme on the one hand, and Heydrich's brand of relentless ultra-violence on the other, was the argument that these destabilized German rule in Poland almost before it had begun.

This also provided an opening to the second drag on immediate mass murder from a further unlikely source: Goering. His remit, as Four Year Plan supremo, was to keep Germany's war production buoyant, at least to the point of keeping pace with the British (and, in the background, US) armaments effort. That required not only having an industrial workforce but being able to feed them too. Polish peasants and workers, preferably operating either in situ in the eastern *Gaue*, or as coerced labourers in the Reich itself, were thus seen by Goering as indispensable to the war effort. And he was quite willing to say so when he brought together Himmler, Frank, assorted state secretaries, plus the new Gauleiters, including Arthur Greiser for the Warthegau and Albert Forster for Danzig-West Prussia, for a high-level meeting on exactly that subject, at his East Prussian estate of Karinhall, in February 1940.[84]

The Karinhall meeting highlighted the internal contradiction at the heart of the Nazi project for Poland, and more broadly for the 'Lands Between'. Eructing from the region its non-German inhabitants could only be achieved by unmitigated and ultimately genocidal violence. Keeping those same inhabitants alive and well in order to meet the war needs of the Reich could ultimately only succeed by placating them, or even pretending that the difference between them and supposedly racially superior Germans was of no great relevance. It is significant that the hardline Nazi Forster, in his own Danzig-East Prussia fiefdom was willing to venture down this alternative path once he had recognized the impracticality of anything else. Unlike his counterpart Greiser, in Warthegau, who was at one with the security chiefs in wanting the Poles off his turf, Forster opted for the simple expedient of categorizing the majority of his *Gau*'s Poles (not, of course, his Jews: he was at one with Greiser in wanting shot of them) as *Germans*.[85] Frank's pleas to resist Himmler's further deportation plans from the *Gaue* to the General Government also seemed to bear fruit when, in the wake of Karinhall, Goering put a temporary halt to these. There would even come a time in the following year when the regime would practically give up, if not on Polish eviction from homes and farmsteads in the eastern *Gaue*, then at least on wholesale deportation.[86]

None of this was based on the grounds of some newly found Nazi benevolence towards the Poles, however. Prior to his change of tack, Forster, in the autumn of 1939, had fully taken the initiative in organizing Polish deportations from Danzig-West Prussia into the General Government. Utilizing both Einsatzgruppen and the region's *Selbschutz* as his main strike force, Forster piled on a renewed reign of vengeful terror with the aim of either directly killing or terrifying 'Polish teachers, academics, ex-officers and members of nationalist organisations' into leaving. Some 20,000 Poles are believed to have been killed in this operation. Bydgoszcz was a

particular target. But in Gdynia the results were in some ways even more spectacular, some 50,000 people, or an estimated 44 per cent of the port-city's population,
being forced into flight as a consequence of murderous local paramilitary action
highly reminiscent of Balkan and Anatolian ethnic cleansing of a quarter-century
earlier.[87] The fact that in this region a Gauleiter was prepared to discriminate
between Congress Poles (i.e. ones who had, since 1919, settled in the western
regions) and autochthonous ones (who were thereby, supposedly, *really* Germans),
against the grain of Nazi racial orthodoxy, however, no more softened the implicitly genocidal nature of what was being envisaged for the country than did Goering's plans to ship 1 million 'released' Polish POWS and other able-bodied men
and women *into* the Reich proper to service Germany's wartime labour effort.

Neither Forster's nor Goering's supposed pragmatism thus did anything to reverse
the core disintegrative aspect of Nazi Polish policy. All it provided was a further
catalyst to Polish resistance. This came to its immediate head in the late spring of
1940 when, in response to a demand from the authorities for all able-bodied subjects of the General Government aged between fourteen and twenty-five to make
themselves available for compulsory labour conscription, the vast majority predictably refused. Frank had already seen his earlier attempts to coax Polish workers to
volunteer themselves for work in Germany humiliated. He now reached out for
the only remaining tool he had at his disposal to make the Poles comply: extreme
violence. The cynically entitled *Aussenordentliche Befriedungsaktion* (AB)—Extraordinary Pacification Campaign—led to the rounding up of 3,500 political and
social activists—in other words, the embryo of the nascent Polish underground—
and then to the mass murder of the majority of them in a forest near Warsaw. In
addition to 3,000 professional criminals also targeted in this *Aktion*, up to 2,000
other Poles previously detained, mostly again from the intellectual layer of society,
were killed during the summer months, in mass executions across the breadth of
the General Government. More tellingly, perhaps, it was at this juncture that Frank
initiated, in concert with Herbert Backe, the Nazi state secretary for agriculture, a
programme of calibrated reductions in the food supply reaching the Polish
cities.[88]

Therefore, German–Polish wartime relations of violence were firmly set in train
by the events of early 1940. Indeed, the dynamic could hardly operate in any other
direction but towards more severe. This is reflected in the almost complete absence
of *ethnic* Poles willing to collaborate with the Nazis. True, there was the so-called
Blue Police, and those ready to act for venal reasons when it came (mostly later on
in the war) to handing over fugitive Jews to the authorities.[89] There was also one
very small grouping, the ultra-right Świętokrzyska Brigade, which, in the face of
the Red Army advance in 1943–4, was prepared to put itself under German military command, suggesting a very tentative parallel with other ultra-rightist collaborationists in occupied Europe who were willing to entertain the notion of a
Hitler-led anti-Bolshevik defence of the continent.[90] But nearly all other Poles,
including the mass, otherwise stridently right-wing, Endek movement, remained
firmly aligned to the Polish government-in-exile in London, the Delegatura, as
well as its underground administration at home, along with the latter's covert

military wing, the Armia Krajowa (AK). As Dr Shöngarth, head of the security police and the SD in the General Government put it at one of the many security conferences organized by Frank in 1941, *all* Poles were 'in the broadest sense of the term' resisters.[91]

Pace what was beginning to happen to their Jewish neighbours, one might thus argue that the outlook for the Poles under Nazi rule was as black as imaginable. Denied the most basic civil rights, subject to drumhead courts which could pass death sentences on them for so much as murmuring an anti-German utterance, required to toil for starvation wages, denuded of all their former national memorials and culture, not to mention refused almost everything and anything in terms of entertainment or even religious solace—as bit by bit their churches were closed down and their wayside shrines vandalized—depopulation, not to say decimation, beckoned. By the end of the war 2.8 million Polish men and women were working under duress in Germany, large numbers of them in slave labour camps. In addition to specific concentration camps, notably Dachau and Mauthausen, where they also constituted a major inmate group, vast numbers of Poles were incarcerated in the thousands of other camps on home terrain.[92] The most significant of these was the emerging complex close to the Upper Silesian town known in Polish as Oświęcim, and better known by its German name, Auschwitz. Here, in April 1940, Himmler authorized the construction of a new concentration camp, the avowed *initial* purpose of which was to terrorize the recalcitrant Poles of the region and act as a holding pen for thousands of others as they were dispatched to forced labour camps further west.[93] Further west still, the Allies' ability to come to the Poles' aid seemed to have been dealt a lethal blow with the defeat of France in the summer of 1940.

All this would seem to confirm a Lemkinian analysis of the Polish situation under Nazi rule—with or without the Jewish component—as set on a course for not just cultural but actual physical genocide. Yet one would have to intrude at this point something contradictory, even counter-intuitive. Nazi policy never properly came to rest on exactly how it viewed the General Government: was it really a '*Nebenland*', ripe for Germanization; a '*Zwischenland*', not quite as ripe for exterminatory procedure as the more overtly Slavic lands further east; or perhaps even, as it was originally designated, a protectorate, which would have put the Poles therein on a par with their Czech counterparts?[94] That aside, simply on grounds of labour policy Germany still *needed* its wartime Polish workforce. But there is something else again which serves to disrupt any one-dimensional verdict on Nazi monstrosities. The 1939–41 Soviet record in the territory of its Polish conquests was *worse*.

*

The figures as presented by Jan Gross, who has studied both occupation patterns, are stark. While in the period 1939–41 an estimated 120,000 subjects in German-occupied Poland met violent or unnatural deaths—the largest number of these Jewish—in the Soviet area the equivalent, either in situ, or as a consequence of deportation, Gross puts at 400,000. However, given that total population in the combined German area amounted to some 21.8 million, compared with only some 13.2 million in the actually larger Soviet area, Gross takes the per capita mortality difference to be one of 600 per cent.[95] Such statistical extrapolations are, of course, dependent on the accuracy of the figures provided. Norman Davies, for instance, has claimed that of 1.5 million Soviet-enforced deportees from Polish soil, half may have died unnatural deaths, thus widening the Nazi and Soviet death tolls even further. The only problem with this estimate, as Gross and other, both Polish and Russian, analysts have pointed out, is that even accepting the official Soviet archival figures of up to 327,000 deportees from the Polish east as too low, there is little evidence to suggest that the total number in the four great deportation waves from Poland, between early 1940 and June 1941, exceeded the 400,000 mark.[96] This hardly softens the deadly reality of what happened to swathes of these unfortunates, or the equally high fatality—perhaps as much as 20–25 per cent—of others mobilized for hyper-exploitative forced labour by the Soviets in the *kresy* itself.[97] It simply denotes that when figures are already large, there should be no need to exaggerate their magnitude further still.

Yet take a further consideration by Gross of the figures, this time of the number of people in the Soviet zone imprisoned during the twenty-one month period through to Operation Barbarossa, and perhaps we come closer to why the Soviet occupation of Poland truly surpassed that of the Nazis in its intensity. Add in the refugees from the German zone to arrive at a population under Soviet control of roughly 14 million: Gross estimates that of this number 1.5 million people temporarily, or more permanently, were incarcerated. Add to this, again, the probability that most of the detainees were men, and his further conclusion is that a staggering 10 per cent of all adult males were detained at some time or other during the 1939–41 occupation.[98] What, moreover, is revealing about these figures is the degree to which they dovetail with evidence suggesting a much more thorough Soviet elimination of Polish resistance than the Nazis were able to achieve. One may thus certainly make parallels, both in the way in which, at the outset of their respective campaigns, the SD and NKVD operated on the basis of blacklists to strike at particular targets and, equally, as regards the similarity between the Einsatzgruppen and the nine special NKVD operational groups tasked with these roles. Yet the NKVD blacklists had been in the process of compilation since 1925, long before the SD began their comparable task.[99] Indeed, it was not just that the NKVD were much better resourced to accomplish the elimination of a Polish elite than their Nazi counterparts: this actually was a function of an entirely more focused and sustained Stalinist-cum-Soviet aspiration to destroy both an independent Polish state and its leading political and social class.

Inevitably, this poses a further question, as to whether the Soviet anti-system was responding solely to its own self-created obsessions or in the longer shadow of its tsarist predecessor. Historically, no love was lost between Polish Catholic and Muscovite Orthodox polities. Even with the demise of the former's Commonwealth, Russian anxieties about its potential revival were linked to deeper memories of Moscow's subjugation, even occupation, by Polish forces. When Congress Poles revolted against tsarist rule in 1863, the influential Russian nationalist, Mikhail Katkov, encapsulated the matter bluntly: 'Poland as a political term is Russia's natural and irreconcilable enemy.'[100] The geographical epicentre of this two-way conflict was necessarily in the outer rimland zone—the *kresy*—in which the majority populations were Belorussian and Ukrainian peasants. The fact that there was here a traditional Polish ruling class whose economic power was not entirely dislodged by Russian overlordship after the 1790s, acted powerfully on the Soviet mind. Thus, in 1939, captured Polish officers were repeatedly taunted by their Red Army captors as *'Pan's*—Polish nobles and hence 'enemies of the people'—even though only a tiny percentage were actually of aristocratic origin.[101]

More keenly, however, Soviet anti-Polish animus did not have to rely on distant memories of a haughty nobility when the Bolshevik polity had its own truly 'never again' moment to focus its attention. In 1920, having defeated the advancing Red Army at the gates of Warsaw—the famous 'miracle on the Vistula'—Piłsudski's armies had turned the tables on the Soviets by marching far into the *kresy*, even beyond the proposed demarcation line suggested some months earlier by the then British foreign secretary, Curzon.[102] Soviet humiliation at the loss of territories that extended Polish rule to the rivers Dvina in the north and Dniester in the south, was compounded by the shame of having to confirm Polish suzerainty in the Treaty of Riga the following year. Indeed, the shame was doubly compounded for Stalin himself, who had been rebuked—possibly unfairly—by Tukhachevsky no less, for precipitating the defeat by his refusal, as effective co-commander of one of the two participating Soviet armies, to countersign an operational order.[103]

We have already seen through the example of the 1938 'Polish operation', how the Piłsudski bogey continued to gnaw at NKVD security thinking. The semi-secret Polish Military Organization—POV—founded by the future Polish leader during the First World War to recruit and train a Polish army, had been disbanded in 1921. Yet in the Soviet mindset it continued to have a chimerical hold. Even Stalin's ephemeral retreat from collectivization, signalled in his 1930 'Dizzy with Success' article in *Pravda*, can be linked to Chekist fears that peasant disturbances in the western border areas could trigger a Polish invasion.[104] Behind this repeated Polish bogey, of course, were the Western Allies. The fact that French military advisers had played a part in the 1920 Polish victory suggests a skein of truth in the Soviet nightmare vision. Yet when Molotov had spoken of Poland, at the time of his Pact-signing with Ribbentrop, as 'this ugly offspring of Versailles', he was effectively saying that the only way you could scotch the nightmare was by wiping off the map the premier Western-sponsored state of the 'New Europe'.[105]

The key problem for the Soviet leadership in September 1939 was that they had no casus belli. Even when the Red Army entered the country from the east there was no Polish state order to resist them. Logically, the relational dynamic between Poles and Soviets should have lacked the lethal component which had turned the German invasion of the country from the west into a 'peoples' war'. Yet this is exactly what the Soviets achieved. And they did so by playing the ethnic card.

The Achilles heel of the Polish victory in 1921 was in the very fact that it had delivered to Warsaw ethno-linguistic communities which, taken together, made of the overtly Polish element of the *kresy* a distinct minority. Put aside for a moment the over a million Jewish inhabitants of the region at the time of the Soviet invasion and the much smaller number of Lithuanian speakers. It was the over 4.5 million

Ukrainians, and the nearly 2 million Belorussians (compared that is, with the 5 million-plus ethnic Poles) who, in the Red Army order delivered on the eve of invasion, now became 'brothers' to be liberated from their 'enemies'.[106] To be sure, one might argue that the Polish state had a case to answer on its treatment of its non-Polish populations of the east, just as it did with regard to the Volksdeutsche on its western borders. Piłsudski's dream of a federation of Eastern peoples marching unified and together—albeit to a Polish tune—was long buried under the reality of enforced Polonization and nationalist, more especially Ukrainian, resistance, as most starkly posed by the Organization of Ukrainian Nationalists (OUN). The German onslaught provided a signal opportunity for anyone with a grievance in the *kresy* to take their revenge, with or without Soviet encouragement. Indeed, as the Wehrmacht and the Polish army fought for control of the Corridor, not only was there a widespread breakdown of law and order, especially in Volhynia, Galicia, and further north around Grodno—as peasants rushed to expropriate Polish landholdings or the OUN sought to seize institutions of state power—but, on the other side of the coin, Polish police, border guards, and paramilitaries attempted (just as they had done against suspected Volksdeutsche militants) to pre-empt destabilization by arresting thousands of nationalist suspects, or took punitive reprisals against alleged malefactors, including whole villages. Into this volatile mix—with all its resonances of the civil war that had engulfed the region in 1919—entered the Red Army, accompanied by an NKVD contingent of no less than 195,000 operatives. They knew what they were about. Their immediate purpose was to fan the flames of the inter-ethnic violence—by quite consciously giving free rein to the anti-Polish side. In fact, they went one better than that. As well as shooting on the spot significant numbers of surrendered Polish soldiers, especially officers, they not only abetted the formation of local peasant and worker militias, which were incited on grounds of 'class war' to hunt down Polish 'fascists' and 'exploiters', but freed criminals from the local prisons, giving them carte blanche to ratchet up the terror against anybody associated with the old regime.[107]

Gross speaks of this sequence as one of 'organised lawlessness'.[108] The purpose was highly calculated. By presiding over the forcible transfer of property and land from the alleged expropriators (Poles) to the expropriated (other nationalities) the Soviets ensured that the latter were bound to opt for Soviet citizenship, which the majority duly did when the question came to a consciously precipitative vote in late October 1939. As a result, Soviet-occupied Poland was duly absorbed into either Belorussian or Ukrainian SSRs.[109] More pointedly, by making so much of the population complicit in the violence committed against another part of it, the new overlords sought to bind them to a Soviet destiny. Or put another way, having made so many of them collaborators in the destruction of Polish institutional, cultural, and personal life, Moscow sought to deny them any chance of a belated change of mind in favour of their former condition. Having made their pact with the devil, retreat was out of the question. Within months, exposed to the full weight of NKVD surveillance, OUN and leading elements, political or otherwise, from the other nationality groups, would find themselves threatened with arrest, or worse, as their Polish equivalents had been. That certainly left the peasant society of the *kresy* poorly positioned to effectively resist the next major Soviet move geared towards crash collectivization.

Even so, it was the Poles who were most vulnerable to either deportation or liquidation—the main instruments of subsequent Soviet terror in the *kresy*—doubly so if they had any passing association with former Polish state power in the east. In this sense, the parallels with the Nazi elitocide are quite striking. In the western *Gaue* Polish post-1919 incomers, especially those who were given land for military service in this period were particular and immediate targets of the Nazis' own deportation drive.[110] In the east, where these *osadniki*—the great majority veterans of the 1920 war—were a much more critical feature of Warsaw's attempted interwar recolonization of the *kresy*, the Soviet effort to expunge them was altogether more systematic and ferocious. Lavrenti Beria, Ezhov's successor as NKVD chief, proposed to Stalin in December 1939 that the estimated 140,000—described as 'the bitterest enemies of the working people'—be rounded up en masse and sent to special labour settlements in the distant Urals or beyond. In this sense, to be typecast as an *osadnik* in official Soviet parlance was henceforth akin to being branded a kulak, or, perhaps even more exactly—remembering those moments in recent Soviet history when it had literally been a crime—as a Cossack.[111] As such, whether one was an old widowed mother of a settler, or a six-month-old child of one, the verdict of being a 'socially dangerous element' translated, in February 1940, into an NKVD night raid, removal by cart or lorry to a railhead, followed by a possibly several thousand mile trip by cattle car in the dead of winter, for weeks, if not months, on end.

All this, of course, was nothing new, but simply reprised the fate of so many *Soviet* communities over the previous decade. Lack of sufficient food, water, warmth, or proper hygiene on the journey, exacerbated by the most atrocious living and working conditions in the mines or forests to which these 'special resettlers' were duly assigned, took their murderous toll over the following months and years. As with their predecessors, it was not calculated extermination—simply the sort of conditions in which mass death, beginning with the old, the young, and the lame, was inevitable. The key difference about this sequence was that it was the first of its kind encompassing whole *non*-Soviet communities. Technically the regime had already got round this particular problem by making the *kresy*'s population Soviet citizens—albeit with those deported being now designated as belonging to the 'Second Category'.[112] But it could hardly hide the fact that the purpose of the exercise was to 'remove' from the scene anybody in the eastern region who might help kindle the demand for, one day, an irredentist return to a sovereign Polish state. It was no accident, after all, that in this first wave of deportees went a whole tranche of former Polish political activists and officialdom.

The issue of these people's status under international law became all the more testy when it involved a second great deportation wave in April 1940—or rather would become so when something of its ramifications became self-evident three years later. By this time the USSR was aligned with the Western Allies against Germany, and thus ostensibly an ally too of the London-based Polish government.

Caught up in the second wave were a range of people allegedly of better social or economic status, but also including the families of uniformed Poles—soldiers, gendarmes, and border guards—who had surrendered to the Soviets the previous September. Those caught in this second wave of deportation, with its heavy preponderance of women and children, were 'administratively exiled', mostly to north Kazakhstan, where, like the first wave, they suffered significant demographic collapse as a consequence of the conditions undergone. That something else was at stake, however, began to become clear during the course of 1942, when a fraction of the survivors of this ordeal were allowed to accompany the army under General Anders—reconstituted from the residual core of Soviet-captured Polish POWs— as it evacuated itself, with Soviet agreement, to British Command in the Middle East. Glaringly obvious was the acute lack of officers in the evacuation. Soviet stonewalling over their whereabouts had, by early 1943, become heavily intertwined in the minds of the London Poles with the Soviet's equal insistence that Poland's eastern borders (as effectively redetermined by the Nazi–Soviet non-aggression pact) were non-negotiable.[113] Goebbels' propaganda machine weighed in, in April 1943, with the public announcement that it had uncovered, in a forest near Katyn, the mass grave of over 4,200 Polish reserve officers who, it alleged, had been killed by the Soviets in 1940—making good the claim by bringing in a team of international experts to conduct a full forensic enquiry. As a consequence Soviet–Polish diplomatic relations promptly collapsed.

*

The story of Katyn, not to mention, until 1990, the USSR's long-standing denial of culpability, has necessarily become a cause célèbre. The very fact that a total of some 14,500 mostly Polish officers, gendarmes, and officials are now known to have been executed by the NKVD in top secret and cold blood in April and May 1940—at three sites in western Russia, one of which was Katyn—is shocking enough.[114] True, put against the broader range of Soviet maltreatment of its own people in uniform—during the course of its 1941–5 war *alone* 'some two million people, enough to form 250 divisions to fight the Germans',[115] may have been arrested and executed or worked to death in the Gulag—the scale of the Polish officer massacres might seem less remarkable. But then, not only was there a *qualitative* difference in that the Polish POWs were meant to be protected under the terms of the Geneva Convention but, at first sight, this should have presented good reason for the Western Allies to more fully consider the criminal evidence. That they chose not to do so, in fact suppressing their own reports which affirmed Soviet responsibility, and opting instead for Stalin's version of events which blamed the invading Nazis—gives us the second key component as to why Katyn has remained a subject of heated controversy to the present day.

Looked at through the prism of realpolitik, the Anglo-American wartime dissembling of the truth should hardly surprise. By 1943, Russia was as essential to winning the war against Germany as she had been in 1917. Certainly, there could be no question this time round of some alliance break-up as there had been in that earlier world war. Recognizing, moreover, that this was exactly the point of the

German propaganda campaign, the end result was that the Western Allies knowingly bound themselves closer to Stalin, even while this made them party to a Soviet version of liquidating the country which London, at least, had gone to war ostensibly to defend.[116] Indeed, to confirm the point, the very fact that Katyn became the final straw blocking off the London Poles from Moscow actually smoothed the way for Churchill and Roosevelt to come to their own geopolitical arrangement with Stalin over the very fate of the *kresy*.

However, while this narrative of Katyn's *aftermath* in terms of its international ramifications is the one which bulks large in Western consciousness, there remain questions to be answered about the killings themselves. Was Stalin's elimination of the officers a more or less preordained plan for ridding his new conquests of their former Polish elite? Take into account the fact that those killed at Katyn, as also those from another officer camp murdered in the NKVD prison in Kharkov, were primarily reservists who, in their peacetime roles, constituted the crème de la crème of eastern Polish society—engineers, lawyers, doctors, academics, and the like—and the indictment against Stalin, or at the very least his NKVD henchmen, would seem an open and shut case. One might go further and surmise that Nazis and Soviets connived in their major, synchronous acts of anti-Polish elitocide in spring 1940. Given what we now know about Soviet assistance to the German war effort in the wake of the non-aggression pact, and, by extension of that, the high-level information-sharing between Nazi and Soviet security apparatuses—including a series of joint conferences organized in Zakopane between late 1939 and early 1940[117]—the suggestion hardly seems fantastical.

Yet there is another possibility much more in keeping with the way genocidal decisions are repeatedly made at the high level: that the Katyn executions were not so much pre-planned but contingent upon a perceived crisis *at that particular moment*. Moreover, this line of explanation would have much less to do with how the Nazis were responding to their perceived security interests in the General Government and much more to do with the Soviets' own 'never again' anxieties about a revived *Western* threat to Russia. At first sight, of course, this sounds a good deal more fantastical than anything which might suggest NKVD–Gestapo collaboration. How, after all, could imprisoned Polish officers assist a Western attack on the USSR? Indeed, how can one even speak of a Western attack when, in early 1940, Britain and France had their hands full with war against Germany?

The answer lies in the peculiarity of the world war period betwixt the political destruction of Poland and the German *Blitzkrieg* against the West in mid-April 1940. These months of hiatus, or 'phoney war', were marked on the Soviet side by an unwillingness to completely close down relations with the West—a case of hedging one's bets in the event of any possible German reversal—and, on the Anglo-French side, by a hardening of their antagonism against the USSR, primarily inflamed by Stalin's military assault on the Finns, beginning in late November 1939. To this we need to return later. What matters for us here is where the Polish officers fitted into this increasingly fraught picture. On Stalin's part, the fact that towards the end of 1939 the families of Polish POWs interned in the USSR were allowed to make contact with them via the Red Cross suggests his awareness that they could be a valuable bargaining counter in any future negotiations with the Allies.[118] Western—more specifically French—anti-Soviet animus, by contrast, was translating in early 1940 into tentative military planning, both in the form of possible assistance for the Finns, via northern Scandinavia, and the more daring possibility of a diversionary attack via the Caucasus to either bomb or directly seize the Baku oil wells.[119] As we will see in our penultimate chapter, 'Stalinist Reordering: Russian Peace', this itself later fed into another bout of genocidal Stalinist anxiety about the peoples of *that* region. Where the *London* Poles came into the immediate picture, however, was in the notion that the Allies would assist in the formation of a Polish brigade who might participate in these operations (Polish national consciousness actually having its own romantic affinity with rebel nineteenth-century Caucasian Mountaineers). Perhaps significantly, according to NKVD agents in the POW camps not only were the officers therein well apprised of these developments, but there was at least some discussion of how, given the opportunity, they would join these efforts 'to make war on the Soviet Union'.[120]

Two strands thus coalesced to inform Beria's top secret memorandum presented to the Politburo on 5 March 1940, calling for the officers' liquidation. The first is Soviet awareness that France and Britain were on the point of directly supporting the Finns in their war with the Soviets, and intended to use a Polish contingent.[121] In fact, the offer of assistance came just too late to save the Finns from suing for peace terms, which, in turn, made of the issue of the POWs as hostages against the possibility of Western intervention an irrelevance. Or, briefly if cynically put, Beria's, or, more precisely, Stalin's death sentence on them was because they no longer served as pawns in the wider geopolitical game. The second strand is both altogether more chimerical yet at the same time tersely enunciated in Beria's memorandum. In it, the officers are charged as 'sworn enemies of Soviet power filled with hatred of the Soviet system' who are 'just waiting to be released in order to enter actively into the battle against Soviet power'. Cited also in the memorandum were several counter-insurgency organizations operating in the annexed Polish regions in which, according to Beria, the former Polish army and police officers were playing 'an active guiding role'.[122]

The notion of Polish POWs running counter-insurgency rings from inside their camps, or breaking out of them and running amok in the Russian forests, sounds ludicrous. Just about as ludicrous as Hitler's nightmare vision of Jews in camps, out of camps, or wherever, striking at German forces in the rear. Yet, just as for Hitler the distorted memory of such an eventuality bringing the Nazi state crashing down was cemented to the calamitous ending of the Great War, so, in a similar sense, was Stalin informed. Nikolai Tolstoy, for one, has insisted that Stalin lived 'in real fear of an internal collapse of the Soviet regime similar in suddenness to that which engulfed the Provisional Government of Kerensky in 1917'.[123] The fact that it was the Bolsheviks themselves—in other words, a consciously small but vanguardist insurgency—who had made this happen would have only reinforced the internal security argument that a group of determined conspirators was quite capable of overthrowing the Soviet polity. In 1917, moreover, the Bolsheviks had not even been operating with direct foreign support. Within a year *Czech* POWs (formerly from the Austro-Hungarian army), who had been reconstituted into a military legion in Russia but were on the point of evacuating it to join the Allied war effort in the West, were instead practically determining the course of the Russian civil war along the Trans-Siberian railway, much of which they had overrun. The Czechs, from seemingly nowhere, had become the spearhead of foreign 'imperialist' intervention.[124]

Could it be this sort of worst-case scenario which informed Stalin's Politburo rubber-stamped fiat for Katyn? If we are looking at the event through the prism of the then recent *Ezhovshchina* the answer must surely be affirmative. Here, yet again, was Stalin striking out at real or imagined—internal or external—counter-revolutionary enemies, with the order executed by almost identical and precise NKVD procedures. The result was the highly secret transport in batches of not only the 14,500 reserve officers, policemen, and other uniformed agents of the former Polish state, to their dead-of-night execution and mass burial, but the parallel execution of a further 7,300 non-uniformed Polish 'counter-revolutionaries' held in NKVD custody in what was now western Ukraine and Belorussia.[125]

But if this speculation is correct and we ought to view Katyn, therefore, as an example of a very specific, targeted, and essentially gendered killing—the Soviet self-justification for which was the perceived threat of a Western-inspired, Polish-led insurgency—we are all the more left with a conundrum. We have already asserted that mass casualties as a result of the Soviet part-occupation of Poland were—until Operation Barbarossa—worse than under their Nazi counterparts. Yet we are equally proposing the exceptionality of the Katyn episode. How can both positions be valid? The answer can only be found in the distinction between Soviet and Nazi first principles, even while their separate practices veered towards the same outcomes.

The difference is first revealed in the survival of some 400 of the Polish officers in the Soviet POW camps. These were the ones who had been willing to cooperate with the NKVD interrogations the previous winter and, having been spared the majority fate, later in the war were mostly integrated into the 'free' Soviet-sponsored Polish army under General Berling. Stalin's overall intention, thus, was not to exterminate this officer elite simply because it was an elite, nor purely on the grounds that its composition were (mostly) *Polish*. By the same token, one might propose that Stalin had no intrinsic issue with the continued existence of General Sikorski's government-in-exile in London, providing, in turn, it accepted without demur the irrevocable loss of the country's eastern provinces. That Stalin had no interest in the destruction of the Polish leadership stratum for its own sake is further emphasized by the fact that once the supposed threat from the POW camps had passed, a further 4,000 Polish officers who surrendered when Lithuania was absorbed into the Soviet sphere in mid-June 1940 were (while indicted as counter-revolutionaries) not murdered but instead transferred to labour camps in Murmansk.[126]

Yet what does this actually tell us? That Stalin only in extraordinary circumstances—albeit of self-created or confabulated crisis—opted for direct mass killings? And that this, in the Polish case, according to a confession of Vsevolod Merkulov, Beria's second-in-command, may even have been recognized—given the later upset with the Allies—as a 'fatal mistake'?[127] But that hardly negated the use of every other method of death-dealing terror and coercion in the Soviet security manual. The point, after all, was to arrive at complete dominion in the annexed rimlands. That could in part be facilitated, as we have seen, by playing the ethnic card, one immediate consequence of which was the rapid release of some 170,000 captured ethnic Belorussians and Ukrainians in the defeated Polish army who were supposedly malleable to Soviet cajolery.[128] But by the same token, that equally ensured the neutralization of anybody *else* who might challenge the seamless totality of Soviet power. Just as the SRs, Mensheviks, Trotskyites, and others who, in the 1920s and 1930s had been struck down because they represented an alternative focus of power, so now, in 1940, another self-evident focus had to be smashed to smithereens. The problem was that guilt by such association now encompassed almost anybody who had been imbued with a Polish consciousness at home, school, or workplace, in the previous twenty years.

This effectively means we come, in one sense at least, full circle. Officially, NKVD arrests might be of socially dangerous elements, most obviously people who were wealthier, or part of the former administrative class.[129] In practice, what took place throughout late 1939 and 1940 was a *political* round-up. And as the dominant former politics was that of an independent Polish nation, the focus of Soviet assault was, ipso facto, on ethnic Poles. Not all Poles, to be sure, and, in that sense, the genocidal implications remain highly ambiguous. Yet, as Gross has pointed out, 'communists do not hesitate to tamper with the biological substance of nations'.[130] A Polish peasant with two acres of land in the Zbarazh district might be as liable to arrest as a university professor from Lwów.[131] And their families too. And, of course, those of the Polish POW rank and file, they themselves having been shipped off en masse to do hard labour on Soviet military projects, while their wives and children ended up equally fighting for dear life in Kazakhstan. What thus linked the majority of these prisoners in their fates was not the likelihood of *immediate* physical execution but a place on one of the deportation transports to the east, the first two waves of which, we have already noted, were followed by another two (though by this time also including many Jewish refugees fleeing from the German zone) through to the onset of Operation Barbarossa.[132]

It was the impact of these cleansings of Polish society in the *kresy* which Lemkin would have recognized as having a genocidal quality. The deportees themselves, of course, may have died or survived, but the land they left behind, according to one Delegatura report, had become—by autumn 1940—'a large Polish cemetery'.[133] With its religious and national buildings destroyed or expropriated, its educational system entirely airbrushed out of existence to make way for Marxism-Leninism, its very institutional persona expunged along with the personalities which made it what it was, Polishdom in the east under the Soviets was as much, if not more, on the road to extinction than it was in the west under the Nazis. But with this key distinction: in the past, caught between Russia and Germany, there had always been a question of whether it was better for patriotic Poles to escape from the Russians to the Germans or vice versa.[134] In 1940, with the exception of the Jews, there was actually no contest. At the tightly controlled Soviet–German border crossings 'many Poles begged the German authorities for the permission to cross over' into their zone.[135] Arguably, they had good reason. What ultimately gave the qualitative edge to Stalin in the 1939–41 violence stakes was the one card that he held which Hitler crucially did not. Both may have sought to thoroughly reorder the rimlands, but Stalin had the whole expanse of the Russian heartland into which to remove its human detritus.

EXPERIMENTS IN POPULATION REORDERING

On 6 October 1939, in the immediate wake of Poland's political destruction, Hitler delivered a major Reichstag speech. In it he set out his intention to reconfigure ethnographic relationships in Europe on national grounds as a route to the elimination of conflict within the continent. This was hardly novel in itself. What else had Versailles been but the proposed reformulation of the Central European empires on national lines? But Hitler's speech gave notice not just of a dismantling of the redundant 1919 boundaries to suit the interests of the now Greater German Reich. The key to the resolution of all nationality issues would now be a resettlement of peoples, including cross-border resettlements, an agenda in which, Hitler assured his audience, 'Germany and the Union of Soviet Republics have agreed to support each other'.[136] In other words, ethnic communities, perhaps whole nations, would be moved around like so many pawns on a chess board until the point had been arrived at when each would be living as a single cohesive unit in its allotted space, as appropriate to its national *and* racial standing. Or again, put more crudely, the superior Germans would allot to themselves the lion's share of the available *Lebensraum* in the German sphere, with the lesser peoples getting whatever was left—as determined by their *Übermensch* superiors.

Putting aside its genocidal implications this was clearly a highly ambitious plan. Grand German resettlements of the east had been envisaged on paper in the Wilhelmine past, and at the height of Ludendorff's supremacy in the Great War were even discussed as if they were implementable programmes.[137] Where 1918 defeat had ended those aspirations, military triumph first in 1939, then in 1940, not only seemed to make them (in their revamped Nazi version) wholly plausible but with an ostensibly coherent apparatus on hand, in the form of RKF, for their practical realization. Himmler's various sub-agencies would surge ahead to determine who would be moved from where and who would replace them. Jews, Himmler insisted in his May 1940 memorandum—acidly entitled 'Thoughts on the Treatment of the Alien Population in the East'—would be eliminated from the equation altogether, through mass migration to an African colony. Certain Poles, especially children with the right racial characteristics, would be redeemed for Germandom and thus saved from the general Polish fate of deportation and/or denationalization. A graded racial register—the *Volksliste*—to characterize who was 'in' and who was 'out', with the appropriate 'scientific' screening and sifting apparatus on hand for this purpose, would ensure that no racially valuable stock went missing. Other 'minority' peoples, such as the Kashubians, or the 27,000-strong Gorals of the Tatra region, whom Himmler's racial experts had identified as quite separate *ethnies* from the Poles, would be encouraged as such.[138]

But this was the imagining, not the reality. Almost from the outset things went wrong. As we have already intimated, the very process of mass Polish and Jewish deportation from the annexed territories proved much less easy to expedite than had been anticipated. Nor was it just the issue of Frank's objections. Administrative and logistical problems mounted as the various agencies involved in the programme found their ability to act in unison compromised by their separate planning agendas and priorities. As well as turf wars there were disputes of an ideological nature, not least between the departmental units with oversight of racial selection of Poles for Germanization. The issue was not simply one of how many such Poles were 'redeemable' but, more problematically, how it was that those categorized as good German stock according to the *Volksliste* were often the most truculently 'Polish' in their behaviour.[139]

Behind all this, however, was a deeper, more intrinsic problem. Why was it that the Soviets could seemingly remove whole swathes of unwanted rimlands communities at will, while the Nazis could not? Was it because members of the NKVD were more experienced or efficient at their work than their German counterparts? Perhaps, though, the sheer numbers of detainees the NKVD were holding, initially in annexed Poland, then in the Baltic provinces, later still in the absorbed Rumanian territories, meant that they too had their problems. These included overflowing prisons and the need to requisition buildings for the excess.[140] It was not, then, the case that the Soviet security people were necessarily the better organizers though, paradoxically, they might have taught the Himmler functionaries a thing or two about forward as well as centralized planning. The order for the round-ups of the twenty-three categories of socially dangerous persons in the Baltic was, for instance, drafted in October 1939, some twenty months before it was fully put into operation.[141] But the NKVD's fundamental advantage was quite simply geographical. They could act as and when they chose in the absolute knowledge that there would always be somewhere in the vast expanse of the Russian lands 'out there' in the east to which enemy peoples could be eructed.

Indeed, the luxury of the space went hand in hand with time. The NKVD scheduling of mass rimland deportations in the same month as Operation Barbarossa, in June 1941, is thus more than simply coincident: it is deeply ironic. It shattered in an instant the Soviet advantage in mass population movements, forcing the NKVD into a spasm of otherwise unintended massacres against those still held in rimlands prisons. Up to that point it had always been the Himmler–Heydrich apparatus which had been operating on the back foot. And again, we can read this, in significant part, as a function of Stalin having seized the geopolitical advantage—an advantage, that is, over 'space', as built into the very fabric of the 1939 rimlands carve-up.

The notion that it was the Nazis who were constrained by space in 1939 when they had made all the running in their Czech and Polish conquests may sound at first quite mistaken. Yet when set against the resource requirements of war with the West—that is, the material needs of food, oil, and metals—it was clear that in the face of Allied naval blockade German sufficiency could only come from the Russian heartland. The German geopolitical experts who had imbibed the Halford Mackinder line were thus among those who were most insistent on the necessity of a Russo–German alliance.[142] Yet it was exactly the fact that Stalin had it in his gift to supply the Nazi war machine with its basic desiderata which gave him the whip hand in the territorial division of the rimland spoils. The evidence is there, in the late September 1939 negotiations in which the Germans deferred to Stalin's change of mind over the Polish carve-up: the *vozhd* conveniently handing back territory west of the Bug upon which there were too many Poles for the Soviets to digest (in other words, landing the Germans with the 'problem') and instead taking a controlling stake in the fate of Lithuania. It is there again in the Nazi acquiescence in the Soviet takeover of Finnish Karelia in the spring. And in the early summer, when Stalin took over the Baltic states, including the so-called Lithuanian tip—which, on account of its significant Volksdeutsche population, Ribbentrop thought he had previously safeguarded. Finally, the Germans, though clearly mortified, had to stand by and watch the Red Army's march into not only Bessarabia but also the northern Bukovina, which had not even been part of the pre-1914 Russian imperial domain.[143]

All of this, of course, had vast and catastrophic human consequences. To be sure, Hitler would have cared not a jot for the majority of the 20 million-plus rimlands peoples added to the USSR as a result, and only perhaps passingly for the many tens of thousands of menfolk and their families from these regions' administrative and political class (in addition to those already gone from Poland) who were the bulk of the new May–June 1941 wave of deportees to Central Asia.[144] In these circumstances many of these peoples—the Poles aside—looked to Germany as their would-be saviour. Indeed, when the German advance to the east inevitably came, many of the residual elite class from these regions were eager to assist.

There was, however, only one rimlands community which Hitler actually strove to save from the Russians: the estimated 1 million or more Volksdeutsche marooned on the Soviet side of the carve-up. Coming to an agreement which would ensure their orderly, non-violent evacuation to the west became the sine qua non of the wider territorial deal with Stalin, which, in return, he was in a position magnanimously to grant. The population movement itself could be dressed up and proclaimed to the world as a well-organized, closely supervised expedition through which Germans, lost for centuries to the Reich, were returned to the fold. It could even be trumpeted as 'Reich strengthening'—Himmler, no less, giving personal imprimatur to the notion when he greeted the last of 15,000 wagons of the great Volhynian caravan as they trundled, in freezing conditions, across the San river at Przemyśl at the end of January 1940.[145] Nothing, however, could disguise the fact that the evacuation project was, above all, an emergency measure, forced on the Nazis by the realization that if the Soviets had not taken over parts of their allotted sphere they would be doing so soon—and hence that, in the case of the Baltic Germans for instance, there was a limited time frame in which the exodus could be completed. As for the 'Option Agreements' the Nazis concluded with the USSR (and the then sovereign Baltic states about to disappear under Soviet hegemony), the degree to which this was a one-way transfer of population, and not even an exchange of populations in the Lausanne sense, was self-evident.[146] The Nazis might have entertained the idea that the deal could informally involve the removal of Jews across the San and Bug borders—both German SS and Wehrmacht certainly trying to force the issue in the late autumn and early winter of 1939. The Soviets, however, would have none of it. Nor did the agreements even involve the transfer of Volksdeutsche financial assets from the sale of their properties and valuables to assist in their resettlement on the German side. Those possessions had already been traded in advance by the German Finance Ministry for Soviet oil and foodstuffs. The notional restocking of homes, farms, businesses, tools, livestock, and household effects for those resettled would have to come instead from what Germany itself could provide. This was accomplished by taking these things from the Poles and Jews it 'expropriated, expelled, and ghettoised', calling the procedure, as only Nazis could with a straight face, 'natural restitution'.[147]

It is this awareness that Volksdeutsche resettlement was at the lethal expense of others which makes it difficult to be sympathetic to their plight or suffering. But it should not cloud our awareness that the majority were as much pawns of a geopolitical game as other, more acutely dispossessed and dislocated, communities. To be sure, the estimated 10,000 deaths in transit from the some half a million migrants of the first wave was clearly a fraction of the death rate among Jews and Poles terrorized and eructed to make way for them.[148] If, today, we think at all of the Volksdeutsche in their wartime context it is as a group who aided and abetted this process.[149] Like the Circassians in the Ottoman twilight, the ethnic Germans became the bully boys of the piece, the bitter refugees willing to take their revenge on those they were displacing. But what all this might serve to underscore is the nature of *their* physical as well as psychological trauma. One might make the rejoinder that they did not *have* to move: the ethnic German evacuation was not a compulsory transfer. In fact, some of them, including many of the Baltic Germans in particular, did try to stay put, only, for the most part, besieging the German migration bureaucracy (the *Volksdeutsche Mittelstelle*—Vomi) when they belatedly faced up to what would happen to them if they stayed.[150] Which rather suggests how limited was their actual choice in the matter.

From this perspective the Volksdeutsche were indubitably victims of the crisis: not absolute victims as Jews were to become as the crisis further unravelled—but victims nevertheless. We can certainly read this, à la Bauman, as an aspect of the relentless, modernizing urges which saw the rimlands as an untidy and dishevelled garden. In place of the 'tangled web' of ethnic relationships which characterized the historic condition there, a clean sweep would deliver clear, clean, demarcated ethnic boundaries.[151] This was far from solely a Nazi project. It was the 'New Europe', nation-state project, as it was also the Soviet project. It just happened that when push came to shove it was neither Bolsheviks nor rimlands nationalists who forced the issue for the Volksdeutsche, but their supposedly fellow Germans. The point is, of course, that for many rimland German communities, especially the peasant ones, their degree of commonality with Germans of the Reich was highly tenuous. Himmler, in the wake of the Polish takeover, might have waxed lyrical about how Teutonic blood and soil were once more coming together as they had allegedly done in pre-historic times, just as he was wont to invoke medieval flights of fancy as he set in motion his very twentieth-century plans for a streamlined—and entirely artificial—spatial reorganization of the east.[152] Meanwhile, what was truly historic about the Volksdeutsche—namely, their rooted place within the complex ethnographic mosaic of rimlands society—was on the point of being blotted out in the interests of Nazi (hence essentially *foreign*) wartime strategy.

The big picture of some grandiose Himmler-led social engineering project thus has to be set against the much more immediate headache the Nazis landed them-selves with: how to integrate, in double-quick time, hundreds of thousands of incomers in a relatively limited, and actually quite rurally *over*populated, area. Not that the Nazi response to what was now, in effect, another population 'problem' was anything but cynical. It should be noted, for instance, that one possibility completely ruled out was that the Volksdeutsche might be absorbed within the more mixed industrial and agricultural economy of the Altreich. The annexed or expanded eastern *Gaue* where the majority were instead to be settled, remained in practice another country, with policed borders between old and new Reich lands; the latter being treated, of course, as a colonized foreign space. In other words, the ethnic Germans were to be intentionally relocated on the periphery, at arm's length from metropolitan society and where they were to be consciously used—and abused—as an additional German counterweight to the indigenous Polish and Jewish components of the population.[153] No wonder that large elements of them were considered by the receiving immigration bureaucracy as recalcitrant. Having been uprooted from *Heimat* and home, a staggering 300,000 of them proceeded to fail the screening tests which would have provided them with housing and occu-pational benefits worthy of the superior racial categories of the *Volksliste*.[154] Many, anyway, found themselves incapable of adapting to their new, stressful environ-ment. As late as the winter of 1940–1, up to quarter of a million continued to languish in some 1,500 resettlement camps.[155]

But this was hardly a statement of *their* failure. The onus was on the RKF sub-agencies to find them housing, and make good their promise, to the farmers in particular, to find them suitable landholdings—usually set at the equivalent of two former Polish farms for each incoming family. But this again, critically, brings us back to the spatial limitations inherent in the Nazi–Soviet Pact. To consolidate incoming Germans from the east presupposed Poles and Jews relocating elsewhere. But as this clearly could not follow the Soviet method by which unwanted aggre-gates were shipped off to the far beyond, the next best thing could only be the reshuffling of such populations within the circumscribed range west of the Bug. As the whole point, moreover, was to strengthen a coherent ethnic German bloc, this ipso facto precluded diffusing incomers either within, or perhaps even to the outer eastern rim of, the General Government. A clear example of this thinking can be seen in the decision to evacuate a swathe of ethnic Germans in the Chełm area of the Lublin district—in other words, from the outer to the inner rim—in the first instance to make room for a proposed mass Jewish reservation. After this 'Lublin plan' had been abandoned the German resettlement continued to be carried out,

says Christopher Browning, 'for its own sake'.[156] Even so, what it equally demonstrates is that the struggle for *Lebensraum* under the shadow of the Pact could not be
conducted in the vast expanses, say, of the Ukraine—Hitler's, but not just Hitler's,
dream vision instead had to be concertinaed within the rimland 'space' available.
A crude zoning policy, Jews on the outer rim, Poles in the middle, ethnic Germans
closer to the metropolitan core was the assumed consequence. Or, put differently,
instead of Przemyśl, the historic Habsburg garrison city on the Russian border,
being the gateway to an expansive German movement of people colonization, or
alternatively people-eruction to the east, the 1940–1 epicentre of population disen-
tangling and reforming now took place much closer to Central Europe. Indeed, the
fulcrum of this heightened activity was the formerly western Polish city of Łódź: 'the
switching yard' between incoming ethnic Germans and deported Poles and Jews.[157]
Increasingly, however, it also became the locus of Nazi frustrations.

*

Łódź had been the nearest thing interwar Poland possessed to an industrial power-
house. Post-September 1939, Frank certainly assumed it would be a prize for his
General Government, its geographical position, after all, was west of the Polish centre but clearly not of the 'Corridor'. Its industrial potential, however, was exactly
what Goering's Four Year Planners would have sought to get their hands on. In addition, it had a very sizeable German population alongside that of Poles and Jews. It
also happened to be a major railway junction. Having thus been added to the territory of the Warthegau, and renamed Litzmannstadt, it was logical that the main
offices of Vomi and other agencies for resettlement and deportation should be
deployed here. Łódź thus could serve as a transit camp for those being expelled from
the Warthegau into the General Government, just as it might provide a substantial
quantity of appropriated homes for the stream of Baltic incomers. Taking the dwellings of Łódź Jewry offered one immediate expedient for this purpose, while bottling
the Jews themselves in a closed and fetid ghetto offered an entirely different
precedent—the unlikely yet grotesquely infamous outcome of which was that it
became its own mini-powerhouse of wartime production on the Nazis' behalf.[158]
    But cramming Łódź Jewry into a tight corner and then terrorizing it into work,
cunning as it was as a model for how to most efficaciously exploit a despised population, hardly resolved the immediate problem. Only a small percentage of the first
major wave of Baltic Germans could be accommodated in expropriated Jewish
dwellings, whether in Łódź or elsewhere in the annexed territories. The overwhelming occupational profile of the incomers, anyway, was agricultural, which logically
implied the expropriation not of Jewish urbanites but rural Poles. The very fact,
moreover, that Jews were being shipped into an already burgeoning Łódź ghetto
from other towns in the Warthegau rather than being *removed* en masse to the
General Government confirms that the grand deportation project, as set in motion
by Heydrich's revamped office for 'Emigration and Evacuation Matters', was simply not working.
    In the course of the period from late 1939 to early 1941 the office produced four
successive short-range plans (*Nahplane*), each with quotas running into the tens or

hundreds of thousands of Poles or—in, one case exclusively—Jews, who would be removed, primarily from the Warthegau. According to figures produced by Eichmann, chief coordinator at this point for not just Jewish but Polish expulsions too, 408,525 people from the annexed territories were deported before 15 March 1941(a figure which does not include the much larger number of Poles internally displaced).[159] Yet none of the plans came within sight of meeting their actual targets. On the contrary, the more the Łódź-based bureaucrats of the Central Resettlement Office (UWZ) attempted to recover the ground lost from the previous plan, the more the gap widened. We have already emphasized the key obstacle to successful implementation in the form of Hans Frank. But his veto on transports to the General Government was not absolute or continuous. Equally responsible for the derailment of UWZ efforts was the very complex interchange of outward expulsion and inward resettlement into which the Nazis had fatally ventured.

The Soviets, as we have seen, had no fundamental internal obstacles to their eastward deportations, notwithstanding the frequent protests from administrators in the receiving regions. The westward ones equally were Vomi's responsibility and were of no concern to the Kremlin once the transports had crossed the new international border. In neither case did the NKVD have reason to fret about the human consequences. Nor were they operating in any way reactively to crisis. In the German case, by contrast, the logistical complexity of a two-, or more exactly, three-way *internal* human freight traffic between Germans, Poles, and Jews was fundamentally shaped by the contingent aspect. Each *Nahplan* was effectively a response to the realization that another wave of perhaps Volhynian or Bessarabian inward-migration was imminent. As the priority, thus, was always the 'inward' one of bringing the Volksdeutsche 'home', all available ships, trains, and rolling stock—over and beyond the already huge requirements of the Wehrmacht—had to be apportioned accordingly. The net result was that 'outward' movement transports had to be repeatedly postponed, rescheduled, or downsized. On top of that was the simple fact that while Volksdeutsche were queuing up in an orderly fashion to be repatriated, both Poles and Jews were doing their best to avoid or escape the round-ups, and only once caught in the dragnet were screened, categorized, and then, transport permitting, either deported or ghettoized.

If this inward–outward movement was doomed to become a logistical nightmare, what further destabilized it was the SD insistence on adding to the Polish burden from elsewhere in occupied Europe. Heydrich's 'Jewish question' expert, Adolf Eichmann, at the time of the Polish invasion, still not only had a backlog of Jews from Vienna which he wanted to shift en masse, but saw in the possible creation of a vast holding area at an obscure place called Nisko on the San an opportunity to both expand and accelerate the eruction of Jews from Austria and the Protectorate, as well as from the newly annexed *Gaue*. Largely of his own volition he had begun organizing transports which passed through western Poland to Nisko, in October 1939.[160] In addition, he was eager to clear out 30,000 Roma from Berlin, Prague, and Vienna, calling a special conference of stakeholder Nazi agencies to consider the matter at the end of January 1940.[161] Predictably, Eichmann's efforts ran into a storm from both Wehrmacht and

General Government—Frank had even issued orders that he was to be arrested 'if he set foot in his domain'.[162] Goebbels committed to his diary, around this time, with not a little *schadenfreude*, 'Himmler is shoving whole peoples around at the moment. Not always successfully.'[163] But the protests did not prevent all of Eichmann's transports from reaching (or part-reaching) their destination, even if, in the case of Roma ones, the deportees ended up in conditions of absolute squalor in a camp separate to the main Łódź ghetto. One consequence was a major and thoroughly deadly outbreak of typhus.[164]

To what degree Eichmann's efforts *also* provided a goad or precedent for military and civil authorities elsewhere in the German Empire to act in a similar fashion is debatable. For instance, some of the Roma from *western* Germany who ended up in Polish work camps in spring 1940 were the victims of a very standard Wehrmacht trope that they might act as spies in the forthcoming French campaign.[165] After its successful conclusion, moreover, the Gauleiters in Alsace and Lorraine wasted no time in clearing out in the direction of France tens of thousands of Jews, homosexuals, Francophiles, and actual Frenchmen, as well as Roma, in their own *völkische Säuberung*. The desire to purify the Greater Reich of social and ethnic undesirables was clearly a top goal of all Nazi administrators, especially in 'mixed' areas (the Austrian Burgenland being another where, in particular, Roma as well as Jews were slated for removal) and especially, too, in the summer of 1940, when opportunities to put such grand designs into effect seemed to be at their zenith with the supposed imminence of victory against the Western Allies.[166]

What none of this could resolve, however, was the need to find immediate dwellings for the incoming Volksdeutsche from the east. A defeated France had no choice but accept those dumped on her from the western *Gaue*. Those same *Gaue* might also be able to take in, as a consequence, *some* ethnic German incomers. But the point of Reich strengthening was primarily to build up the German demographic majority in the *eastern* rimlands. The fact was that any further transports of unwanted human cargo from the West simply compounded not only the Łódź traffic jam but the 'absolute organizational deficiency' of its day-to-day operation.[167] Other, perhaps desperate, remedies would have to be found.

One such remedy was to free up hospitals and suchlike space in the annexed Polish territories as temporary habitation, especially for old and sick Volksdeutsche, as well as for wounded German soldiers. This is how the murder of mentally and physically disabled residents of care homes and asylums began in Poland. Of course, a covert programme of compulsory euthanasia of similar such patients in Reich institutions, including congenitally ill children, had already been moving into gear on Hitler's say-so, even before war had begun. For those adults selected as being 'unworthy of life' (according to the criteria determined by unit T-4's medical experts) the end was most likely to follow at one of six dedicated German centres to which patients were secretly transported from throughout the Reich. Here the majority were killed in specially improvised gassing units. Most sick children who were murdered, by contrast, either died through deliberate starvation, conscious drug overdoses, or lethal injection, in 'special' paediatric clinics. As is well-known, the T-4 programme officially came to an end in the summer of 1941, when sufficient leakage of what was happening behind closed doors led to an upsurge of public disquiet, especially from within the German Catholic community, as notably amplified by a pulpit denunciation from Münster's bishop, von Galen. In fact, the murder of children was not included in Hitler's subsequent official halt to the euthanasia programme. Meanwhile, the personnel involved in T-4, including the medical practitioners, were largely redeployed to other similar operations, including Aktion 14f13—the gassing of sick concentration camp inmates—and to the 'Final Solution'.[168]

All of this underscores the fact that not only were there no obvious structural inhibitors preventing German medical involvement in the mass murder of the most vulnerable in society, but Nazi doctors positively embraced such murder as an appropriate method for the realization of notions of racial hygiene. Yet euthanasia in Nazi Germany was still implemented through administrative subterfuge in order to conceal its true nature from the wider public. What happened in occupied Poland, by contrast, involved nothing by way of 'medical disguise'. Nor was it part of the T-4 operation. The linkage, at this stage, lay only in the fact that psychiatric patients were the victims. Otherwise, the primary motivation lay in ensuring the rapid 'utilitarian' resolution of Himmler's 'Reich-strengthening' problem. The Reichsführer-SS, indeed, seems to have played a critical, if somewhat ambiguous, role in the process.[169]

As early as 22 September 1939 the first mass killings of patients were carried out by the eponymous SS Eimann commando in the Szpegawski forest, near the mental hospital at Conradstein (Kocborowo), West Prussia. The commando rapidly expanded its operation to include patients from Pomeranian asylums on the German side of the border, demonstrating that when it came to disability no intrinsic discrimination existed between national groups. By December, Eimann had made institutional space for Himmler over the bodies of perhaps 10,000 former asylum inmates, killed either in the initial Szpegawski murders, or at the second Pomeranian killing site at Piasznicz, north-west of Gdynia. Other similar killings were carried out in this period by Einsatzgruppen and local *Selbschutz*. The eagerness of Gauleiters to be rid of their unwanted human burdens helped facilitate the rapid spread of the procedure far and wide into East as well as West Prussia, Pomerania, and the Warthegau. The results also set in motion something of a scramble for the evacuated buildings, involving not just Himmler's agencies but the Wehrmacht.[170]

However, it was the search for space rather than a coherent blueprint to eliminate all mental patients which determined the continuation of killings well into 1940. Experiments with mass gassing in Fort VII, Poznań, the previous November, using carbon monoxide, had been translated within two months into a facility for a *mobile* gassing unit, enabling mass death to be brought to inmates of clinics and asylums around the Warthegau, rather than vice versa. The search for space even extended outside the annexed territories to Chełm on the General Government border with the Soviets: the murder of an entire cohort of 441 patients of a hospital here in January enabling its rapid conversion into a receiving camp for the Volhynian Volksdeutsche convoy then in train.[171] The increasing institutionalization of process can be seen, too, in the way the dedicated gas unit, led by senior Einsatzgruppe officer Herbert Lange, 'rented' its services at a rate of ten Reichsmarks per head for a sustained bout of mass murder at a mental hospital in Soldau, East Prussia, from late May through early June.[172] Their new tally of some 2,000 mostly Polish but also German victims paved the way for the hospital's conversion into a central transit camp for ethnic German evacuees from Lithuania. By the summer of 1941, according to Aly and Heim, as many as 30,000 Polish, German, and Jewish mental patients had been murdered for the 'purpose of creating room for ethnic German settlers'.[173]

Yet despite all these efforts on behalf of the Volksdeutsche, the logjam between their resettlement and those who supposedly were going to make way for them, far from being resolved, had, by the end of 1940, even been admitted by Himmler himself as 'a policy fiasco'—albeit in an extraordinarily roundabout way.[174] Not only does the Reichsführer-SS appear to have been exercised by the open *manner* of the Eimann killings—possibly a factor in his growing interest in the gassing alternative—but, more damagingly for the regime, the ugly details of the deportations were being regularly reported in the neutral, more especially US, press. The forcible eviction of *German* Jews from Stettin, including the occupants of two old age homes the previous February, to make way for Baltic German incomers, and the subsequent death of over 200 of the Stettin cohort as they were marched in temperatures of -22 degrees Centigrade from Lublin to their holding camp, excited particular outrage.[175] Stalin, by contrast, was accomplishing the same and much more, but entirely without the foreign attention.

Hitler's own growing irritation with Stalin in the summer of 1940 may not have directly begun with his awareness of the degree to which the NKVD could seemingly shift (or eliminate) whole peoples at will while he could not, but this could not but at some point intermesh with his wider disenchantment with the terms of the Soviet Pact. In the spring he had been assuring Mussolini that the arrangement remained durable.[176] After the defeat of France, however, the very basis upon which the Pact was continuing to be of practical geostrategic value to both Nazi *and* Soviet parties was clearly becoming unstuck. Stalin's frantic summer and then autumn push for further territorial concessions, especially at the expense of Rumania and Bulgaria, was rather obviously his insurance policy against what was now a German imperium across Europe *integrale*.[177] But by seeking to extend domination along the whole breadth of the 'Lands Between', even as far as the Balkans, the Soviet land-grab complicated Nazi relations with their own still independent rimland protégés, the immediate consequence of which was a further round of territorial 'awards' to other interested parties, which Berlin, again, had to adjudicate. The irony is that Germany was advantaged not one iota by these new 'consequences of consequences'. So long as Britain remained undefeated, thus largely being able to enforce its naval blockade, German dependency on Russian resources remained as absolute as ever; resources which, sooner or later, would be deployed by Stalin for an attack on Germany. Stalin, after all, already controlled the 'Heartland'. But he was now better positioned that ever to use his new rimland acquisitions as a launching pad against his erstwhile collaborator.

Even against his better judgement to avoid a two-front war at all costs—the disaster scenario of the Great War—Hitler's mind was already moving in the aftermath of the 1940 neo-victory in the West towards a new military campaign which would overturn Stalin's advantage. Germany would get its retaliation in first and smash its Soviet anti-system competitor once and for all. And, in thinking through this new direction, not only the Nazi security people but other critical agencies too would once again be given free rein to both plan and pontificate on how the rimlands were going to be cleansed of their racially inferior, defective, or simply dangerous populations, and the Aryan conquest of the *Lebensraum* beyond begun.

AGENTS OF DESTRUCTION

The notable paradox is that this strategic shift represented the sidelining of the German followers of the Mackinder line. Predetermined geographical and environmental factors would be overcome by the sheer will of the German people.[178] And with that breakthrough the Nazis would be able to act as they chose. Is it in this that we should discern the truly genocidal nature of Nazism as opposed to communism? The Soviet system equally believed in the triumph of the will. But it also utterly rejected the notion that this potentiality only belonged to particular peoples by dint of their racial advantage. At no time did the Soviets, even on the cusp of total victory in 1945, conceive of a programme such as the Nazi *Generalplan Ost*, whereby whole nations would be consciously, *physically* eliminated from the territorial map. Yet this statement is itself unsatisfactory. We have already seen that in spite of the absence of racial ideology, Stalin's plans for Soviet control of the rimlands *did* involve, at the very least, the emasculation of independent nations. By the end of the war this had been translated, in the Caucasus and near-Caucasus zone, into wholesale people deportation. If there is a question here of the degree to which different mindsets nevertheless converged in terms of practice, there is equally a question of the degree to which such convergence can be found in the similarities between Soviet and Nazi institutions of state control and their respective operational behaviours.

But at this point we immediately run into a problem. The Western-language literature on the Nazis is replete with biographical information and analysis, not only of the leading SS players but of a wide array of their middle-management underlings. Adolf Eichmann is a case in point, as well he might be, given his crucial role in the organization of the 'Final Solution'. Ironically, Eichmann was himself, until the time of his post-war capture by the Israelis in 1960, hardly recognized as a figure of great consequence. He was, after all, in terms of the SS hierarchy, essentially a bureaucratic cog who largely (though far from exclusively) organized the 'emigration and evacuation' of millions from his desk in his Berlin Kurfürstenstrasse office.[179] His rise to a position of universal—and ongoing—notoriety in the roll-call of *génocidaires* is thus related not only to contemporary Western absorption with the Nazi mass murder of the Jews but, more precisely, its supposedly unique qualities. Which makes the continuing obscurity of Ivan Serov, Eichmann's nearest Soviet counterpart, explicable if not excusable. Described as 'a highly skilled mover of people and material', Serov was actually a much higher ranking and entirely more important figure in his own security apparatus than was Eichmann, rising from a position within Stalin's personal secretariat in the 1930s to become first deputy minister of state security in the wake of a major NKVD reorganization in 1941. It was his role as key architect and organizer of the Baltic deportations at that juncture, skills which were transferred to the more all-encompassing wave of Crimea and Caucasus 'evacuations' of 1943–4, which offers the clearest parallel with the director of Referat IVB4. One key disjuncture, one might add, is that while Eichmann ended his ignominious existence as the only individual ever judicially executed by Israel, for his comparable efforts Serov went on to be awarded the Order of Lenin and feted as a hero of the Soviet Union.[180]

The discrepancy between the general familiarity we have with the Nazi, and lack of it with the Soviet, person, however, should not deflect us from the wider issue at stake: namely, the essential symmetry in the relationships of SS and NKVD to their respective states. This does not require us to view them as the *same*. Nor does it immediately betoken that both apparatuses were ipso facto instruments of mass, including genocidal, murder. They *became* so by dint of their common function. Critical to this were their efforts to provide to their inner state leaderships total surveillance of society—whether metropolitan or conquered—in order both to predict and then prevent the possibility of dissent, civil unrest, or uprising. Such surveillance necessarily extended to foreign connections on the assumption that internal destabilization would be prompted, financed, or directed by external 'enemies'. Again, of itself this agenda does not necessarily close off either NKVD or SS from comparison with *other* national security outfits of the period or later, when we know that a more general trajectory towards surveillance, interference, and control of the lives of state inhabitants was becoming increasingly the norm in advanced Western polities.[181] That the USSR and Nazi Germany represented the avant-garde in this direction may simply confirm a Baumanesque verdict on their relationship to modernity. But what made Nazi and Soviet security agencies quite different from their liberal equivalents—over and beyond their disproportionate size and budgets—was the complete lack of checks and balances which might have prevented them, in time, from becoming not simply the guardians of state but the state *itself*. It was this, above all, which exercised Lemkin's analysis of the Nazis' drive to genocide as the consequence of conspiracy.[182] But this was only the case because civil society in Germany, as in Russia, had already been foreclosed by Bolshevik revolution and Nazi *Machtergreifung*. With nothing else to fill the vacuum except the pseudolegal façade of whatever laws or decrees either regime enacted, the security-cum-surveillance apparatuses became, in each case, not simply states within states—which, of course, they were—but *potential usurpers* both of remaining public space and whatever residual powers were still vested in other state institutions, including the military. As a result, whereas—again, rather paradoxically—the security apparatuses of liberal states operated essentially from the shadows to advise elected representatives who might or might not chose to take their advice, the SS and NKVD were able to act in the open (albeit on the authority vested in them by Führer or *vozhd*) as if they were the authentic defenders of both general will and common good.

For the time being, hence, the survival of Hitler on the one hand, Stalin on the other, remained the only real check on the proliferation of security powers—to the point where a complete state takeover became inevitable. This carries its own further deep irony, as the primary source of security anxieties, including those relating to the alleged mischievous behaviour or downright malice of entire social or ethnic communities, emanated from these two self-same dictators. It can only thus be speculated where the untrammelled leadership of the security apparatuses would have taken our two parallel anti-systems. It would have almost certainly involved even more rapid developmental drives to overtake a Western advantage. And at each turn the already proven NKVD and SS focus on efficiency would have had as its corollary a recognition of human worth only to the extent that it could be utilized for the achievement of precise goals. The alternative was clinical destruction. Serov's adeptness in moving *matériel* as well as people is indicative. Both were forms of cargo to which the sender had no affective attachment.

*

However, we do not need—against the grain of historical truth—to imagine what a Germany or Russia would have become had a Himmler or Beria ascended to the crown when we already have, in embryo, the critical elements of an NKVD or SS state in 1940. Nor do we need hindsight to see that each recognized their essential similitude. It is there in the degree of cooperation and even expressed warmth as the two agencies liaised and shared information in order to obliterate resistance on Polish soil in the period of the Pact.[183] And, in a more grotesque way, it is illustrated in the wake of the German capture of Simferopol in the Crimea in May 1942, when the local NKVD card-index file disastrously fell into SD hands. How did the latter react, when they discovered that the lists were of both NKVD agents-cum-collaborators *and* their suspects? They indiscriminately shot as many as they could lay their hands on from either list.[184] The compiling of meticulously organized and categorized lists of people and 'things' is, of course, a fundamental function (or arguably dysfunction) of all bureaucracies: ancient as well as modern. What made the NKVD or SS 'super'-bureaucrats was their commitment to the analysis and then application of this information in the interests of the most far-reaching goals of societal transformation: goals which were not only not negotiable but which dictated that, where resisted, those resisting were to be crushed.

In the SS case, the tendency is most keenly demonstrated by the cohort of several hundred individuals who filled the senior ranks of Gestapo, SD, and Security Police in the 1930s and went on from there, most obviously as Einsatzgruppen commanders, or SS and Police leaders (SSPF—in some cases, Higher: HSSPF) to coordinate and/or lead mass killing operations, not from their desks but directly in the field.[185] These cutting-edge *génocidaires* were certainly Nazi ideologues of the first rank. But they can neither be dismissed as unthinking dullards—which might be said of many of the Nazi *alte Kämpfer*—or simply blood-crazed thugs. Entirely more troubling, they were from a generation of younger Nazi acolytes than the original party founders, who came to adulthood mostly after the Great War; had been highly educated under Weimar, most often with social science, law, or similar higher degrees to their name; were of undoubted intellectual calibre; and, as required through their occupational training, duty-bound to think on their feet and for themselves. This may have involved the instilling of what the regime itself called an 'anticipatory obedience' in all tasks, including mass murder[186]—though more precisely, if cynically, we can express this as a penchant for what one might call optimum-goal analysis. In other words, they were expected, as Charles W. Sydnor has put it—speaking of their prime mentor, Heydrich—to use their 'executive instinct' in problem-solving and expeditiously find the 'correct', most efficacious, and decisive answers.[187] Brought together under his calculating aegis—Heydrich was very much of their generation and middle-class, if certainly meritocratic, kind—they were, in every sense, the fast-track elite of the party, perhaps even embodying, as one eminent German historian has put it, the regime's 'permanent revolution'.[188]

All these doctrinal and organizational advantages aside, there was one curious inertial drag denying the SS total power—at least on *home territory*. The German population, or rather a significant percentage of it, supported the regime. But they fundamentally did so through the person of Hitler and what they perceived he represented to themselves. The vast Brownshirt constituency, which one might characterize as the authentic mass movement phase of Nazism, was thus, to the SS, a little like what the proletarian support base for the Bolsheviks was to the emerging Stalinist security state. In both cases a somewhat inchoate if populist *sans-culotte* tendency was at odds with an increasingly institutionalized, not to say select and highly agenda-driven, technocratic formation. But whereas in Russia any truly demotic acclaim for Bolshevism had been stifled out of existence almost at birth by none other than the party leadership itself, in the Germany of 1940 the grass-roots adulation of the leader, if not necessarily of the regime, was probably as great as it ever would be. It was exactly his awareness of this relationship which, a year later, led Hitler to officially close down the euthanasia programme. In other words, Hitler viscerally, if in no other sense, recognized the immediate limits *within the Reich* on carrying through to completion the streamlined vision of the German future to which his SS elite aspired: even with the essential reduction of civil society.

That, in turn, in some critical sense, acted as goad to Himmler, while also exaggerating the onus on him, to carry out the ultra-radical elements of his programme offstage, that is, *abroad*. For example, in the summer 1939, not only did the SS empire of concentration camps on German soil actually amount to only seven such camps, but six of these were situated at the southern or eastern extremities of the Altreich. With the camp population diminished after the post-*Kristallnacht* Jewish surge to a 'mere' 25,000 or, perhaps, one hundredth of the equivalent number contemporaneously languishing and dying in the Gulag, Himmler's aim to achieve an independent revenue stream for his inner state by means of slave labour remained, at this stage, largely aspirational. True, the existence of DESt, the SS company formed in early 1938 and geared towards developing quarries, clinker works, and gravel pits, to which several of the camps were already assigned—with Mauthausen in Austria the most recent—was evidence of Himmler's intent.[189] But it was not until the Wehrmacht had pulverized Poland that the Reichsführer-SS was able to conceive of a much wider network of camps which would provide not only building materials for Germany's war effort, projected new autobahns, and monuments to Hitler's great glory, but the necessary manpower to prepare the groundwork for the 'new', racially perfected society. In this sense, even before the construction of mass extermination facilities there, Auschwitz was a key locus of interest—at once a major source of sand and gravel, and a town, as well as district, ripe for model reconstruction, and, by degrees too, an attractive location for huge laboratories, plant nurseries, and stockbreeding, which would ensure its place as '*the* agricultural research station for the eastern territories'.[190] None of this, nor the concomitant industrial development nearby, could take place without a free, plentiful—and expendable—supply of labour.

Himmler's desire to design a brave new world by way of an Auschwitz launching pad into the rimlands (and thus out of general German public view) was thus, even putting aside the will to genocide, intermeshed with hyper-exploitative purpose. The latter was made entirely admissible by racial science. No wonder the growing Auschwitz camp complex became a nexus for SS-sponsored medical institutes whose route to scientific 'excellence' included human experimentation.[191] A rigorous, forward-looking research programme, founded on the fusing of decades of German medical and scientific advance with unforgiving Nazi ideology, was as much a facet of the emerging SS inner state as were Himmler's more idiosyncratic projects such as the SS-Ahnenerbe to find the supposedly authentic, original bloodline of 'true' Aryans.[192] The wider significance, however, lies in the fact that Himmler was building up Germany's academic elite, from anthropologists to zoologists, into a genuinely interdisciplinary network whose purpose was to both legitimate the SS project and make it, in turn, utterly indispensable to the Nazi millennium. Equally telling was the geopolitical framework. Having purloined the leading geographer Prof. Konrad Meyer from the Reich's national planning authority for his own operational staff in the Office of the RKF, Himmler sought to envisage a plan for the German (re)colonization of the east, which would not only provide a detailed programme of how the entire landscape of the inner rimlands—and, with the first draft of *Generalplan Ost* in 1941, the lands beyond—would be Germanized, but which would, in effect, present to the Altreich a perfected image of itself.[193]

We might at this point prefer to read the hydra-like growth of the SS as an extension of the megalomaniac urges of an otherwise rather 'average, middle-class, paternalistic Bavarian'.[194] Or perhaps as evidence of how fanatical and crazy ideas can come to the fore in the context of a totalizing one-party state. It is evident that Himmler's personal, even kinky, fantasies of himself as a reincarnated, Slav-slaying Heinrich I, supping at a Round Table in his Wewelsburg castle with his austere peasant–warrior knights, had a political corollary in the drive to create a new SS aristocracy conceived from his *Lebensborn* programme of racially pure, yet extramarital Nordic couplings.[195] Which one might be inclined to read as something of a cul-de-sac in terms of modernist security state thinking. By the same token, the translation of Himmler's emotional longing for a rural (implicitly anti-urban) Germanic paradise into the essentially agriculturally-focused settlement specifications of the Meyer plan seem a long way off from the developmentalist ground rules which one might expect to be the basis of an anti-system challenge to Western supremacy.

Where Himmler's project can be less easily dismissed as backward-looking, however, is in its very conception of rimlands space as some giant laboratory for the future. *Generalplan Ost*, as it emerged out of its chrysalis into its stark final May 1942 form, may have carried the notion of some rural idyll in the making: communists, after all, also talked distantly of a 'withering of the state'. But what the immediate stages of project more keenly spoke of was a succession of five-year plans, each—on paper at least—minutely designed, budgeted, and audited for the purposes of a massive demographic and environmental reordering of a swathe of territory between the Baltic and the Crimea. To carry through this transformation clearly involved cleansing the space of what was already there. If, in the inner General Government zone, Frank's technocrats continued to filibuster as to the degree to which the Poles were long-term productive (or expendable) assets,[196] for the designers of the SS outer project, there were no such constraints. Meyer envisaged, phase on phase, hundreds of thousands of forced labourers from the region put to incessant work for its accomplishment. There was precedent aplenty for such practice, including Europe's—more specifically, Germany's—recent colonial past. But could it be, in this instance, that the SS were more obviously working towards an NKVD model?

*

Soviet commitment to major infrastructural and industrial build had been dependent on seemingly limitless NKVD supplies of Gulag, or related, slave labour for years. Soviet hyper-exploitation was neither directly genocidal nor very efficient. But then NKVD aspirations towards assisting in the sculpting of an ultra-modernist Soviet future seemed perfectly capable of coexisting with a messy, often vastly chaotic, waste of human resources in the process. The fact that that this resource was derived from those identified as socially dangerous, counter-revolutionary, or plain 'kulak', ensured that the NKVD saw themselves as performing a dual role: building but also correcting. The further fact that, in the winter of 1938–9, some 90 per cent of prisoners newly coming into the Gulag were *dying* primarily of cold, starvation, and disease,[197] rather suggests how the Nazi welcoming sign *Arbeit macht frei* over concentration camp entrances was even more sardonically apt for Soviet equivalents.

In the post-Pact phase, however, the NKVD was clearly having to prove its mettle as the Soviet state sought to digest at speed its rimland conquests. Vast numbers of NKVD troops in 'complete battle readiness' were deployed at the beginning of July 1940 for the Baltic task in hand. Just as the SS had begun as an armed paramilitary organization, to which large-scale, entirely militarized formations, in the form of the Waffen-SS, were an additional accretion, so an already mature NKVD had an entire panoply of specialist units to arrest, torture, deport, or liquidate perceived opponents. The Baltic operation, as organized by Serov, was utterly meticulous in its synchronization and follow through. The very compilation of its suspect lists embracing Esperanto speakers, people who had travelled abroad, hotel proprietors, and restaurateurs, alongside political activists from all parties including ex-communists, as well as state administrative, military, and police officials of all kinds, was testament enough to the assiduity of its card-indexing departments.[198] The mass round-ups throughout the three countries, incarceration, subsequent entrainment to the Gulag, or to special settlements in the case of family members, again demonstrated that Serov had micromanaged his plan of campaign to the very last detail.

However, the very scale of this operation, and the levels of violence which accompanied it, point less to a desire to fill the Gulag's depleting manpower resource base and more to another bout of heightened Stalinist panic about resisters—in this case either the newly conquered nations or their fellow *ethnies* in Russia itself— sparking off more general dissent and upheaval against the regime.[199] We have already seen how Soviet anxiety about the supposed sabotage potential of Polish officers led to the Katyn massacres. In the wake of the ultimately successful but otherwise utterly botched war against the Finns, a great swathe of returning Red Army POWs, in addition to thousands of serving officers, met the same fate.[200] The immediate consequence of the *initial* round-ups in the Baltic countries, similarly, was not the deportation of the suspects to the east but torture and, for many, their extra-judicial murder. In Estonia, for instance, of an estimated 8,000 arrested at this juncture, only a few hundred survived the initial killings, or *later* deportation. In Latvia, Tolstoy reports that of over 34,000 disappeared individuals (more than 2 per cent of the total population) in the year *before* the mass deportations got under way, more than 1,300 are known to have died in NKVD torture chambers. In Lithuania the scope and scale of the killings was reflected in the mass graves uncovered after the German invasion in the forest of Petrašiūnai, near Kovno (Kaunus). Even when the deportations primarily of women and children got under way the following June, an estimated 60 per cent of some 10,000 to 11,000 Estonian deportees alone died.[201]

The nature of the NKVD assault on human flesh and mind in these 1940 rimland subjugations in a rather obvious way reminds one, once again, not so much of a radically new security departure as of a replay of Ivan Grozny's *Oprichniki*. And that, in a critical sense, is exactly what the NKVD was: an updated version of a sixteenth-century political police force whose only role was to protect a supposedly all-powerful but paranoid tsar and quash whatever disloyalty he imagined. The inference would suggest that under Stalin, at the very least, there could be no possibility of the security apparatus becoming *the* state. Just as Ivan had got rid of some of the leading *Oprichniki* when he decided they had become too powerful, so Stalin had cut a swathe through the NKVD command structure when he had decided to call time on the *Ezhovshchina*. Nor did Stalin always defer to the agency when he wanted some important political task undertaken. It was his personal 'creatures', Dekanozov, Vyshinsky, and Zhdanov, not the NKVD's leading commissars, who were flown, or, in Zhdanov's case, transported by armoured train, into the Baltic capitals simultaneously to the Red Army takeover, in order to nominate new puppet prime ministers and then pulverize them into absolute servility. As Vyshinsky sardonically quipped to his terrified audience in Tallinn: 'everything will be done in accordance with democratic parliamentary rules ... We're not Germans'![202]

So if it was Stalin who was the master puppeteer, micromanager of state terror but also ultimate arbiter of who wielded it, why propose that the NKVD nevertheless remained the most likely signpost to the USSR's post-Stalinist future, and thus a standard, too, for Himmler's emulation? Part of the reason is very straightforward. Having convinced himself that nobody in the party, and certainly nobody in the army, could be trusted, Stalin had no choice but to keep tabs on these elites round the clock. Here, after all, were the elements of political life who might yet offer to a still restive but essentially disenfranchised populace a route map *away* from Stalinism. The regime's perpetuation, thus, by the late 1930s, had become bound up with complete dependence on a massive internal surveillance machine. The paradox involved in the 1939–40 drive into the rimlands is that this dependence was ratcheted up still further as *real* independent political and social actors presented the threat of an alternative, in place of those in the USSR proper who had already been eliminated. In conditions of self-induced crisis, therefore, Stalin may have not trusted his security chiefs any more than any other state component. But while he might dispense with them in person, he could not dispense with the machinery.

The reality is reflected in the sheer size and range of the security edifice emanating from GUGB-NKVD, the Main Administration of State Security. Like the RHSA it had its own critical intelligence-gathering and espionage units, including the Secret Political branch, Department I, and the counter-intelligence Third Department. There was also a massive separate wing in the form of the Gulag High Command and, essential to the NKVD's entire state-wide functioning, the GTU-NKVD, the Main Transport Administration. Operating within a command economy and with priority over all rail, boat, and other transport links, one can be assured that an Eichmann, if not a Himmler, would have given his eye teeth for such a facility.[203]

None of this had stopped Stalin from ordering the liquidation of not only Ezhov but nearly all the cadres most closely associated with his bloodstained tenure at the NKVD—some of whom, including Ezhov, were not finally executed until early 1940. Yet at the same time he could only carry out this 'Augean stables' exercise by bringing into play an alternative combination *within* the NKVD. Beria's Caucasian gang, as they quickly became known, were every bit as ruthless and murderous as their predecessors. Stalin would sometimes refer to Beria himself as 'our Himmler'.[204] But the very fact that Stalin had to turn to the Mingrelian and his own actually very closely interconnected Mafia-like crew underscores just how much the security apparatus was all that kept the regime from collapsing in on itself. By the same token, one major survivor of the Ezhov purge was V. M. Blokhin, the operator responsible for the hands-on executions at at least one of the three main Katyn murder sites. In fact, Major (later Major-General) Blokhin had been a sanctioned and expert state terminator since the early days of the Cheka, through which he rose to be head the imperiously entitled Kommandatura branch of the Administrative Executive Department of the NKVD-AkhV, with personal over-sight of nearly all the major wipe-outs of Stalin's most wanted enemies. He was, in short, indispensable, ensuring that when Beria requested his removal and death as part of the clean-up of the Ezhov order, Stalin refused.[205]

The perpetuation of the NKVD system and its centrality in the post-Pact period—albeit with a somewhat different set of lead players from a few months earlier—confirms that Stalin, having invested so heavily in this formula, could not now abandon it without destroying himself. It was this 'sunk-cost effect' which Beria was now able to exploit for all its worth.[206] With his brandishing of 'the exotic flattery, sexual appetites and elaborate cruelty of a Byzantine courtier in his rise to dominate first the Caucasus, then Stalin's circle, and finally the USSR itself',[207] immediate likenesses to the externally buttoned-up Himmler or the out-wardly cold and steely Heydrich do not present themselves. Yet, actually, the paral-lels between Beria and Heydrich in particular, and, by extension, their respective peer groups are worth noting. Just as with the new breed of SS police chiefs brought on by Heydrich in the 1930s, so Beria's circle, like Beria himself, were highly intel-ligent, educated individuals—of a younger post-1918 generation than the old Bolsheviks—whose professional development was *through* the security service. Their sophistication, even, in some cases, artistic sensitivities, were no more incom-patible with beating the living daylights out of 'traitors' and 'enemies', than was the case with many of their SD counterparts. Indeed, in both forces, while personal refinement was a bonus for career advancement, an unflinching commitment to, and proficiency in, extreme violence were a sine qua non.

It was Beria's ability to make Stalin's anxieties about his personal security identical with that of the state and its future which might suggest that his opportunistic, empire-building calculations were on a par with Himmler—or Heydrich's—demonstrable drives to meet the Führer's *own* agenda. Beria, of course, never achieved total power. His NKVD aggrandizement, through the advancement of his Caucasian placements, was always kept in check by Stalin. This was maintained either through the elevation of counterweights to senior position, Serov being one such, or through prising apart the administrative unity of the Beria group: the, albeit ephemeral, division of NKVD functions between an NKVD under Beria and NKGB under Vsevolod Merkulov, in February 1941, being one clear example of this disruptive tactic. A further irony in all this is Stalin's adroitness in publicly dis-tancing himself from the ethnic circle and milieu from which he himself hailed and with which he retained intimate familiarity. Beria, albeit from a distinct Mingrelian background, was a fellow Georgian; Merkulov, an Armenian associate of Beria from their time together at Baku Polytechnic in 1918. The wider Beria NKVD coterie of Georgians, Armenians, and Azeris in part testifies to how a destabilized rimland of violent, including genocidal, encounters could bring forth its own *génocidaires* in very much the same way as Germany's own 'lost territories or threatened borders' produced such a high percentage of senior SS and SD personnel.[208]

What then did Beria have which Himmler did not? Not a genuinely independ-ent power base, to be sure. But with security of the leader and of his will as the all-embracing justification for the projects Beria placed before Stalin, and simply through the fact that he was operating in an already tightly centralized command economy, Beria was arguably better positioned to take control of key sectors and programmes than the Reichsführer-SS. Advanced weapons research and development, for instance, was one particular arena, during the latter stages of the 'Great Patriotic War', where Beria's monopoly of power notably trumped a Himmler who would have liked very much to have the same. The latter, by then, certainly had large bodies of slave labour at his disposal: one major prerequisite for projects of this sort. But, as in so many areas of the still 'polycratic' state, the SS leadership was unable to wrest an absolute authority. Nor even then did Himmler have the vast spaces for major secret 'controlled environments' necessary for the testing of such weaponry, nor again, the automatic right to appropriate whatever technical cadres he needed for the job. These were exactly the sort of powers which, later on, would make Beria the leading post-war protagonist in the building of the Soviet atom bomb.[209] The great irony, of course, is that while both Beria and Himmler were utterly absorbed in their wider empire-building projects, both spectacularly missed the real security threats right under their noses. Beria might have been good at exterminating 'dangerous' rimland elites but that counted for naught if he could not forecast or, alternatively, effectively pass on to the *vozhd*, in June 1941, the fact that the Nazi–Soviet peace was phoney and German invasion imminent. But by the same token the Himmler apparatus was so fixated on providing a final solution to Hitler's chimerical obsession with 'international Jewry' that when it came to a genuine *internal* threat—the 1944 bomb plot, after all, was a product primarily of discontented *German* generals—it was only good luck and a heavy table, not security interdiction, which saved the Führer.[210]

The very fact that, as late as 1944, there remained relatively autonomous foci of power in Hitler's Germany, and that, albeit in an emasculated form, these included the Army High Command, perhaps is what ultimately gave the edge to the Soviet security apparatus as the more likely state-in-waiting. Undoubtedly, the NKVD's responsibilities for all actions in the field of people destruction (over and beyond direct war-making) were entirely more coherent, comprehensive, and clear-cut than those of its German opposite number. We might note the way, for instance, in which each German state ministry had its own *Judenreferat*, often with its own pet proposal for dealing with the Jewish question. Even on this crucial issue, an SS or, more exactly, RHSA monopoly was far from a given. Out on the Eastern and Balkan battle fronts the Wehrmacht, too, proved perfectly capable of administering its own lethal security responses to the Jews—with or without SD clearance or coordination. Clawing back authority on the question and having that rubber-stamped by Goering seems to have been one of Heydrich's major preoccupations. We can chart the preoccupation from the time of his infamous September 1939 *Schnellbrief*—setting out a hastily thrown together interim agenda for RHSA control over Polish Jewish matters—through to the altogether more absolute enunciation of his authority and plan for a European-wide solution of the Jewish question, presented to a range of officials from *other* ministries at the January 1942 Wannsee Conference.[211]

Moreover, while Himmler might repeatedly insist that that the Führer had placed upon him special tasks which only he, Himmler, could fulfil,[212] those tasks clearly did not extend into all areas where Hitler required a covert programme of mass killing. Aktion T-4, most notably, was organized under the aegis of the personal office of the Führer (KdF), its development being entrusted to its *alter Kämpfer* head, Philipp Bouhler, along with Victor Brack, its section chief and an engineer by training. Certainly, KdF was quickly drawn into complex synergies with the SS, not least as it grappled with the most efficacious method for killing large numbers of people in a confined space. At the centre of these early interactions was the criminal police, Kripo, more specifically its chemistry department, which advised Brack on the use of carbon monoxide gas.[213] And, as a subdivision of the RHSA, Kripo's actions and results were clearly interesting to Himmler, especially as these were applied to the wider (non-KdF) murder of mental patients in Poland, including those undertaken by Lange's sealed truck unit. All this ultimately fed into the 'Final Solution'. Even so, T-4 never came under Himmler's umbrella. Nor was the interaction all one way in terms of advice. Brack, for instance, elevated to an honorary position on the Reichsführer-SS staff, proposed in March 1941 that Himmler's Jewish problem might be resolved by a mass programme of 'concealed' sterilization using powerful X-rays. Some 3,000 to 4,000 Jews, Brack proposed, could be dealt with daily in this way.[214]

The fact that Brack's submission was at Himmler's request not only suggests that the question of 'what to do with the Jews' had become, for the SS leadership by this juncture, a very pressing one, but underscores the fact that, in the absence of an answer to their problem, they were ready to consult with a variety of 'experts' outside their immediate security circle.[215] More perversely, however, it points to one aspect of Himmler's mindset where utter self-deception was the consistent rule; namely, in the similarity of his agency's *methods* to those of the NKVD. 'The Bolshevist method of physical extermination of a people out of inner conviction,' he insisted, in May 1940, was 'unGermanic and impossible'. Even after he had been responsible for the death of millions, Himmler could still proclaim to SSPF cadres, in his infamous secret speech at Posen (Poznań) in October 1943, that he, and they, had remained 'decent'.[216]

It is as if there was something quite schizophrenic about the man's inner self: on the one hand, a fantasist revelling in the notion of slaughter conducted by 'hard' men; on the other, a definite sense of anxiety, even squeamishness, when faced with its messy reality. When confronted with mass Jewish execution, on the one attested occasion on which the Reichsführer-SS was present, at Minsk, in August 1941, he could hardly stand his ground.[217] The true Heinrich was neither like the NKVD specialist, Blokhin, professionally very good at his mass murdering job, nor like Eimann or Lange, operators who clearly relished the opportunity. The latter's men were referred to by a German doctor who witnessed their behaviour at Soldau, as 'the psychopaths club'.[218] The irony is that while there were senior officials of state— Backe, at the Agriculture Ministry was clearly one—who, by early 1941, were, from their desks, talking with enthusiasm of the death of millions of 'useless eaters' through starvation in a post-conquest Russia, Himmler was trying to convince himself that the Lange route, using poison gas, was a 'neater, cleaner, less upsetting way of killing large numbers of people'.[219]

The problem, whichever way a Himmler or anybody else in the SS *Apparat* chose to address mass murder, was that they could not get round the facts that sooner or later it would become very difficult to conceal what they were doing from their own home public, and that large numbers of these might have to become involved in the process itself. Particularly if, as in the case of the Jews, that meant entering into a wider population and selectively rounding-up and then removing them en masse to some 'secret' place, or places, of execution. Even assuming some 'technical fix' could be found at that point for their 'disappearance' into mid-air—which, presumably, would require a significant staff of specialist operators—the sheer removal the victims would require altogether more extensive human resources for the task. Not only would the process thus involve ordinary people, but the likelihood of it degenerating into a wholly 'unGermanic' yet, grotesquely, rather 'democratic' opportunity for gratuitous violence could hardly be discounted, not even by a Himmler.

Here then was a true conundrum for the elite SS state within the state. Would it have to recruit, like its NKVD counterpart, tens of thousands, perhaps hundreds of thousands, more personnel to do its bidding? And, if so, how could it count on all these clearly non-elite, common folk to remain silent? Or was the logical consequence of genocide that either everyone would have to be complicit in the act, or the secret state really would have to take over, lock, stock, and barrel, to enforce the silence? As for any unintended witnesses of the fact, would they also have to be embraced within this complicity? Or simply shot, as had been the fate of those who had strayed onto the site of the Katyn massacre? There was, of course, an alternative path. Why could the Jews, if they were the ultimate problem, not simply be whisked away to somewhere completely 'off the map'? It did not have to involve *directly* killing them: just, as the Soviets did with their dangerous populations, removing them to the far beyond, where nobody—that is, in the 'civilized' world—would even know, or, alternatively, care, about their demise.

THE INSOLUBLE PROBLEM: GETTING RID OF THE JEWS

However, there were by 1941 a lot of Jews to remove. For a state so intent on being *Judenfrei*, invading Poland could be adjudged a case of wilfully spiting one's face. It was, of course, not the first time in the rimlands that a polity with overweening imperial pretensions had to weigh up the advantages of conquest over the perceived disadvantages of what would come with it. Tsarist Russia had also been horrified at all the Jews it inherited at the time of the Polish partitions. The difference was that it then spent the next hundred and more years constantly prevaricating as to what it was going to do about them. There could be no question of such a postponement in the Nazi case. The problem was that having added an estimated more than 2.5 million Polish Jews to the several hundred thousand in the Altreich, Austria, and the Protectorate still to be disposed of in 1939, the regime—in then going and conquering Western Europe in 1940—simply added many hundred thousands more to the number.[220] That the writing was on the wall for all these unfortunate souls seemed already to have been clearly signalled in Hitler's infamous speech to the Reichstag on 30 January 1939. In it he chillingly prophesied:

> ... if international Jewish financiers in and outside Europe should succeed in plunging the nations once again into a world war, then the result will not be the Bolshevisation of the earth and with it the victory of Jewry but the annihilation of the Jewish race in Europe.[221]

The standard wisdom has always treated these lines as evidence of Hitler's premeditated intention to commit the Holocaust. This would seem to be rather at variance with the line taken here, that no concrete evidence exists to suggest either a blueprint or specific programme of extermination at this stage, or for some considerable time thereafter. How does one then reconcile these conflicting positions? Or is it that a closer, more contextualized reading of Hitler's speech might take us towards a different, but not usually explored, explanation: in which Hitler's fantasies about international Jewish power intermesh with his geopolitical thinking?

As we have already seen, by early 1939 a hardening of the Western position in the wake of Munich was bringing to the dictator an awareness that his chances of avoiding war with the Allies were fast receding. At stake peace not just with France and Britain. The US stance was also turning more truculent, the clearest expression of which was Roosevelt's State of the Union address four days into the new year. In this, the Nazi threat to US security was explicitly linked to its core values of democracy and religious freedom, which, in turn, could be taken as a reflection of the recent US public outcry at the events of *Kristallnacht* and its aftermath.[222]

Hitler's Reichstag speech, thus, can be taken not simply as a riposte to Roosevelt's but as an accusation directed against those who, in Hitler's mind, were the culpable party goading Roosevelt's antagonism: the Jewish financiers on Wall Street and their supposed cronies close to the president himself. That this would simply make the US leader a tool of the world Jewish conspiracy, thereby representing a further embellishment of Hitler's consistent obsession, is not what is of relevance here. What is, is that this supposed Roosevelt–Jewish capital nexus *appeared* to offer to Hitler a last chance for making a deal with the West by which war would be averted. By this reasoning, what did the 'financier' Jews want which Germany could deliver? The answer was: the evacuation of their fellow Jews from the Reich. To which the Nazi response was, in turn, 'let them have them', but with the firm stipulation that there could essentially be no bargaining about the price, and with the added proviso that the deal would have to contain guarantees ensuring that the Jews would be prevented from overturning it and so 'plunging the nations... into world war'.

Roosevelt had already made clear, in the wake of the US-sponsored international Evian conference on the Central European Jewish refugee issue, in summer 1938, that he wanted progress on the matter, and had ensured that a trusted but also highly competent friend, George Rublee, was appointed as commissioner to conduct face-to-face negotiations with the Germans. To this, Hitler responded in late 1938 by bringing back from the political cold his ex-economics minister, Schacht, to act for the German side—with, as the latter now insisted, the Führer's direct authority. With the old financial wizard in charge, the notion of some sort of *ha'avera*-style package writ large being pulled out of the hat represented the most optimistic reading of the subsequent London talks. The problem was that at the core of Schacht's remit was the expectation that the 'rich' Jews of the USA and Britain would find 1.5 billion Reichsmarks to secure a foreign currency loan for Germany. It was against this astronomical sum that the *already* sequestrated assets of Germany Jewry would be nominally offset.[223] In other words, even supposing that that sum could be found there was no guarantee that the bulk of Central European Jews who might then be released would be provided by the Germans with the wherewithal to avoid becoming charges on foreign countries—the bottom line of Roosevelt's rescue package. But then the Nazi position was not founded on Jewish emigrants' resettlement in countries of their choice. As Rosenberg put it to a meeting of the Berlin diplomatic community in February the following year, 'If the West is serious about its friendship for the Jews', then it was a matter of making up their minds in the near future as to which territory would be designated as a 'Jewish reservation'.[224] Or, to summarize: Western Jews, more exactly their charitable agencies—not Western treasuries—were being pressurized into providing not only a fantastic sum of money, money which anyway they did not possess (not least as their budgets were stretched beyond breaking point by the exigencies of the already escalating refugee crisis), in order that the Nazis might continue their drive to war while at the same time incarcerating their fellow Jews in some tropical territory such as Madagascar, where they would be held as hostages against the fact.

Faced with blackmail on this scale, it was hardly surprising that the Jewish organizations categorically refused to participate any further. Which must lead to the question: if the Nazis knew this would be the inevitable outcome why did they raise the possibility in the first place, except as some sort of subterfuge? Yet there is important evidence to suggest the Nazis, in fact, were in earnest. This is perhaps best expressed in January 1939—the time at which the negotiations were meant to get into full swing—with the creation of Heydrich's new mandate, the *Zentralstelle*, to implement central control over the entirety of Jewish emigration. But it also can be read in the shrill tones of Hitler's Reichstag speech. In the face of the negotiations having stalled, perhaps even collapsed for good, he resorted to undiluted threats. And we can take it that he did mean what he said: that part of the speech, at least, is unequivocally terrifying. However, as Yehuda Bauer, the historian who has most closely examined the significance of the Schacht–Rublee negotiations, has posited, Hitler's position does have its own internal logic.[225] For Hitler there *really* was a grand dialectic between German and Jewish power. The latter, with its supposedly bottomless wealth and infinite political penetration into the lives of great states, if it so chose, could meet Hitler's 'just' territorial demands in the east. The failure of the Western Jewish plutocrats to play ball would thus determine not just the fate of their European co-religionists but the fate of the world.

But the more immediate problem for Hitler was the discrepancy between his confabulated imagining of the Jewish stranglehold on Western politics—reflected in their supposed sabotaging of his grand evacuation scheme—and the reactions of Allied politicians themselves. That the Western powers were not reading the linkage between Jews and international relations as was Hitler is intimated in, for instance, a comment by Lord Halifax, the British foreign secretary, to a British Jewish deputation, that the plight of their Central European co-religionists was unlikely to affect or prevent 'the conduct of negotiations with the German government on matters involving peace or war'. The internal Foreign Office view on the matter was more terse still: that the position of Central European Jews in no way represented 'a British interest'.[226]

Admittedly, this was a short while before the abortive Schacht–Rublee negotiations, or Roosevelt's own push in spring 1939 to resuscitate the stalling negotiations, got under way. As a result, notwithstanding the countdown to war, the British *were* drawn into discussions on the possibilities of creating a Jewish territorial refuge in some out-of-the-way place. But by this juncture they were doing so as part of last-ditch attempts at war's avoidance, while at the same time making strenuous efforts to row back from any insinuation that they were being drawn into 'a Jews' war'.[227] In this sense, the underlying and pervading anxiety in Allied capitals from the previous world conflict—that Jews had some financial, even diabolical, pull with which to determine its onset or course—had, if not quite evaporated into thin air, then certainly become heavily muffled. And who had achieved this extraordinary feat? Hitler. Through the course of 1938 he had demonstrated that the notion of Jewish clout on the international stage was utterly illusory. Indeed, at the very moment when such projection of power might have acted as a talisman protecting actual Jewish lives in Europe, the leading Western states concluded that it was a complete irrelevance in the actual geopolitical equation. The reality is summed up in the manner in which the German ship the *St Louis* trundled back and forth across the Atlantic with a forlorn cargo of unwanted Jewish refugees during the summer of 1939, with nobody willing to accept them.[228] Indeed, European Jewry had fallen into a trap between a Western system which—for the time being at least—had broken with the notion of them as its oldest and greatest threat, and a Nazi anti-system which depended on exactly that myth as the very corner stone of its raison d'être.[229]

But if the result was that the West was not going to find a way of relieving Hitler of his Jews, while at the same time insisting on separating the 'Jewish question' from its wider geopolitical considerations, where, or to whom, could the Führer turn for answers? Going to the Russians, as he did in the late summer of 1939, should, by rights, have been unimaginable given everything that he and his fellow Nazis believed about Judaeo-Bolshevism. The fact that he did so either means that he was so desperate that he was prepared to overlook what was, in the Nazi mindset, blindingly obvious—perhaps even thereby inwardly acknowledging that 'the Jews' could not be beaten—or that he genuinely believed that Stalin had brought the Jewish–Bolshevik menace to heel. Answers to this conundrum remain elusive to this day, though perhaps one might suggest that while Jewish-Bolshevism resumed its all-encompassing role as public justification for the genocidal assault on the USSR from June 1941, the emotional fulcrum of Hitler's international Jewish power fantasy had already shifted firmly to Washington.[230]

This still, however, begs the question whether Hitler imagined that he might be able to do some sort of deal with Stalin for a mass Jewish exit in a Soviet direction, perhaps as a quid pro quo for his September 1939 agreement on the 'return' of Volksdeutsche. There is nothing in terms of documentary evidence to suggest that the subject was broached as part of the Molotov–Ribbentrop horse-trading. On the other hand, the very fact that Heydrich, in mid-September, began making on-the-hoof plans for the wholesale removal of Jews *and* Roma from the Reich area as well as Poland, suggests that he was privy to discussions between Himmler and the Führer 'of considerable significance for foreign policy'. The protocol of the meeting between Heydrich and his division heads a few days later, on 21 September, tersely states, 'The Jewish deportation into the non-German region, expulsion over the demarcation line is approved by the Führer.'[231] At this very same time both Einsatzgruppen and Wehrmacht units were attempting to drive thousands of Jews across the San into the Russian zone. The von Woyrsch-initiated massacre at Przemyśl can thereby be read as part of a conscious goad *pour encourager les autres*. Would it not follow that Heydrich's simultaneous instructions—the *Schnellbrief*—for the immediate removal of all Polish Jews to a limited number of city 'concentration points', preferably with railway junctions, was premised on Heydrich's belief that he had found a window of opportunity through which to arrive at a final solution?[232]

To be sure, there are other aspects of the instructions which should not be overlooked, not least the manner in which Heydrich's security apparatus henceforth arrogated to itself not just a monopoly of Nazi relations with the Jewish communities but the determination, through the creation of Councils of Jewish Elders, of how such communities were now to be organized to facilitate RHSA demands. One might argue that behind all this was an overriding anxiety of Heydrich to maintain his personal executive control over the implementation of a comprehensive deportation programme, the consequence of which was a spectacular overreach in terms of what was actually possible or plausible at that given moment. Behind the hastily improvised short-team planning was an extremely vague final goal. And even the short-term project for ghettoization, pending deportation, came to a rapid terminus barely more than a week after its initiation when Himmler, citing Wehrmacht objections, downgraded Heydrich's plans to 'preparatory measures' only.[233]

Was this postponement linked to Stalin's refusal to countenance a Jewish exodus across the San, or anywhere else along the demarcation boundary? What we *do* know is that the *vozhd*, in putting his signature to the revised Nazi–Soviet protocols on 29 September, handed over the very Lublin region on which the Nazis had had their sights for a Jewish 'out-migraton' eastwards. It was surely one way of reminding Hitler that the Jewish problem was his—not Stalin's. The very same day the Führer told Rosenberg that German-occupied Poland would have to be split three ways, on top of German and Polish areas: the Stalin-relinquished territory between the Vistula and Bug now being reserved for the Jews.[234] But if that, as of now, really was Hitler's intention, the whole Nazi game plan to be shot of the Jews would be back at square one. The best that could be hoped for would be some sort of geographically circumscribed reservation: something like the Cromwellian English had designated for the Irish in Connacht in the 1650s. In the modern Nazi version the reservation would become a sort of 'no man's land' between a projected 'Eastern Wall' protecting the Nazi heartland and the demarcation line with the USSR, 'at the furthest extremity of the German empire'.[235]

Connacht, however, was not a very illustrious model. Indeed, it had run into all sorts of military, logistical, and demographic difficulties from the start, with the result that it was soon abandoned.[236] Eichmann's efforts to make of his Nisko swamp the kernel of a larger reservation project proved—for not dissimilar reasons—equally futile, though not before starvation, forced labour, and murder had taken their toll 'in what was effectively an open air prison'.[237] But then it is doubtful that either Eichmann or his superiors saw Nisko as anything more than a *Durchgangslager*, a provisional passing place, out of the rimlands to somewhere far away. Could Soviet intransigence on the matter be tested a little more? Certainly, there were repeated covert efforts to force more Jews across the fluvial demarcation line—now the Bug rather than the San—until Soviet shootings of the rivers-crossers, and, more effectively, the threat to block the return of the Volksdeutsche in retaliation, slowed down and then put an end to that ruse.[238] But then, the issue was not the getting rid of a few hundred Jews here, or a few thousand there. Heydrich's men were still doing their best to remove as many of them as they could from Central Europe, even, while still possible, by illegal means, to wartime Palestine.[239] Some 20,000 Polish Jews—perhaps less than half of those who, of their own volition, sought to and were actually allowed by the Russians to cross into the Soviet zone at the official border posts—also represented a welcome deficit from the Nazi perspective.[240] There is irony, of course, in the fact that nearly all these unfortunate folk were then exiled to Central Asia, the Arctic north, or Siberia, in the third great wave of Soviet deportations from Poland, in June 1940: the survivors thus figuring among the luckiest avoiders of the Holocaust.

Critically, however, the issue for Hitler was not *simply* eructing the Jews. The whole point of the early 1939 negotiations had been to use them as bargaining counters to prevent war with the West. To have instead opted for carrying out his extermination threat at this point would have been a matter of burning his bridges back to the Allied capitals, should the chance for peace talks have materialized further down the line. Or at least that is what we must assume, given Hitler's idée fixe about London and Washington being in thrall to 'Jewish power'. The abeyance in wholesale anti-Jewish action through the first half of 1940 thus was not simply a consequence of very real logistical difficulties. By this juncture the terrorization, degradation, and dehumanization of all Jews under Nazi rule had been markedly ratcheted up several degrees; the compulsory requirement for Polish Jewry to wear a Star of David armband at all times (though not extended to those in Germany until autumn 1941) representing simply the most obvious sign of their isolation from the rest of society.[241] But the regime still had its fundamental question unanswered: how could Jewish hostage potential be converted into a lever for the unconditional acceptance of German demands by the Western powers?

The idea of using Jews in this way was a Nazi favourite. Back in 1936, Hitler and Goering had envisaged—but then changed their minds about—enacting a law which would hold German Jewry collectively responsible for any alleged individual act of sabotage against the Four Year Plan.[242] If some, or, better still, all of European Jewry could somehow be herded into a giant reservation separate from the rest of humanity, and there held as hostages against the ongoing belligerence of the West, it would be like a Nazi wet dream come true. The party applause which greeted the German Foreign Office proposal to cart off the entire cohort under their rule to France's Malagasy colony in the aftermath of her signal defeat in June 1940 was not just a matter of finishing with the Jewish European presence. It also elicited enthusiasm because it seemed to present a method for finally bludgeoning the West into submission to the odd notion of a pax Germanica. Madagascar itself, as we have already seen, was in no sense novel as an imagined space through which European anti-Semites might divest themselves of their Jewish 'problems'. But in new Nazi guise, as more particularly (and rapidly) hijacked by Heydrich's team, the proposition was to turn the island into a police state—a sort of vastly amplified Tasmania in its original convict-centred formulation—in which the captive Jews would be held under constant SD surveillance as eternal hostages against any British or US idea of reviving warlike intentions.[243]

Again, as with the Schacht–Rublee talks eighteen months earlier, the Nazis appear to have been in complete and deadly earnest. The fact that the previous Polish commission of inquiry into Madagascar's settlement potential confirmed that this was extremely limited had no bearing whatsoever on Nazi thinking. On the contrary, the limitations actually dovetailed with a vision of their new territorial scheme as the path through which European Jewry would succumb to the rigours of tropical squalor, leading to its relentless decimation. The further fact that Eichmann summoned a group of Central European Jewish leaders to a meeting in early July where they were given a twenty-four hour ultimatum to compile a list of considerations to be taken into account in the transfer of 4 million co-religionists, similarly provides a foretaste of the manner in which Jewish councils from 1941 onwards were made complicit in their own communities' destruction.[244]

The problem was that the Madagascar plan was a classic example of a *génocidaire* regime striving for the unattainable. For a start, it was predicated on being able to transport several million souls across the oceans, without military challenge, to their unwanted destination. But this was an entirely phantom notion so long as Britain, with its overwhelming sea power, remained steadfastly at war with Germany. That this was inevitable was confirmed by the Royal Air Force repulsion of the first phase of German plans for cross-Channel invasion—the so-called Battle of Britain—ensuring that, from autumn 1940, there would be neither a German-dictated peace, nor Jewish mass deportation to *outside* Europe. With the consequent collapse of the Madagascar project, expectations riding on it—not least those of General Government functionaries who were gagging for a Jewish disappearing act from their patch—were bound to take a major tumble. But it was not just Frank's interest which had been stymied. Raul Hilberg has noted that when the project collapsed, 'the entire machinery of destruction was permeated with a feeling of uncertainty'.[245] As well it might be. The perpetuation of war starkly confronted the Nazis with many imponderables. High on this list, however, was what was to become of its Jewish exit strategy.

What the Madagascar failure did, above all, was to underscore the idea that any solution would have to come through the regime's *own* devices. Or, put differently, *unless* it could find a way of breaking out of its politico-geographical straitjacket—as imposed by the Soviet Pact—it would most likely have to find that solution in the confined space of the inner rimlands. Needless to say, there had been no pre-planning for what to do with Eastern, let alone Western, European Jewry, in the event of a prolonged war. Ghettoization in Poland had never been intended as more than a temporary expedient. Actually, contra Heydrich's September 1939 orders, there were still large numbers of Jewish communities, eighteen months later, who had yet to be ghettoized. As for sustaining them within or without ghetto walls, that was supposedly a problem for the Judenräte—the SD-appointed Jewish councils—not the Germans. But when properties and homes had been sequestrated, businesses and savings appropriated, livelihoods taken away, how was any ghetto administration 'going to be able to pay for food, coal, water, electricity, gas, rent, removals of human waste, and taxes' let alone 'discharge debts to public agencies or Polish creditors'?[246] In such circumstances mass starvation, sooner or later, was bound to set in. To be sure, Jews were already designated as at the very bottom of the Polish food rationing pile: the daily intake was set at 369 calories, and hence way below anything which could sustain survival for very long.[247] The idea that 'the Jewish question' might simply solve itself through taking its 'natural course' was perfectly acceptable to large numbers of 'on the spot' German middle managers. And by the spring of 1941, when deliberate denial of food began to translate into skyrocketing death rates—ultimately, according to Hilberg, to the loss of half a million ghetto inhabitants[248]—these managers' expectations were well on the way to realization.

However, it has to be emphasized that there was no central plan for this result. The very process of ghettoization was in the hands not of Heydrich's men but a range of administrators and technocrats whose responses to the problem were var-ied, piecemeal, and improvised. They also had wider contingencies to consider: for instance, where starvation led to infectious disease, such as spotted fever, spreading epidemically across supposedly enclosed spatial boundaries into the wider com-munity. One could simply attempt to enforce the quarantine zone and shoot those who crossed it, or one could alternatively seek to ameliorate the ghetto condition by putting the Jews to work in the interests of Reich war production. This emerg-ing dichotomy between 'attritionists' and 'productionists', as Christopher Brown-ing has famously called the internal debate within the German occupying authorities, in an important sense exemplifies the post-Madagascar malaise with regard to how, where, and when a comprehensive resolution to the Jewish 'prob-lem' was going to be found.[249]

In the interim, it was clearly the administrators on the ground who were having to pick up the pieces of others' grand designs, and make the best of the situation as they thought appropriate. Nobody on the 'productionist' side of the argument was proposing to be suddenly nice to the Jews. The only real criterion was making the ghettos economically viable. To this end, those like Hans Biebow, the head of the Łódź ghetto administration from May 1940, saw opportunities to rationalize and hence maximize industrial output in a highly controlled environment, in return for the barest nutritional minimum enabling its inhabitants' survival.[250] In the other large ghettos, such as Warsaw and Cracow, there were somewhat less rigorous variations on this theme. In East Upper Silesia, an area of major industrial and mining operations, an emphasis on the systematic exploitation of Jewish forced labour came rapidly to the fore. But these Schmelt camps, named after their former police chief and SS Oberführer head, also sought to keep their workers alive. The reason is not difficult to gauge. Labour shortages, not least through the deportations of Poles from the region to the General Government, meant that local firms were willing to pay fees for the loan of Jewish workers, regardless of their relatively enfeebled condition or output.[251] To be a Jewish male or female slave worker in the Schmelt camps certainly was of little consolation in itself. But, relatively speaking, those incarcerated here were in a better place than those rounded up to work in the Lublin region under the aegis of Odilo Globocnik, another SS man, but of very different stripe to Schmelt.

The work projects in the Nazi-designated 'green frontier' area between the San and the Bug represented the extreme end of the improvized schemes most fully developed in the hiatus between Madagascar and Operation Barbarossa. In this instance, Himmler's imprint was self-evident. After the failure of the initial attempt at creating a Lublin 'reservation' by way of Nisko, the area had continued to be both a dumping ground for Jews eructed from elsewhere and a landscape in which the able, and not so able, were put to exhaustive work in a plethora of improvised camps: draining swamps, building dykes and roads as well as a huge anti-tank ditch—otherwise known as the 'Eastern Wall': again, one of Himmler's pet projects.[252] Globocnik served here as SSPF, throwing his weight around against Frank's civil authorities, but at the same time demonstrating an enthusiasm for gratuitous violence which, even by Nazi standards, was in a class of its own. This Austrian acolyte was indeed a publicly known, convicted killer but one who had been instrumental in his party's takeover of Vienna in 1938. He succeeded to the position of Gauleiter but was then removed for expropriating party funds. Thereafter, his protector was none other than Himmler who, his peculiar sense of rectitude set aside, chose to turn a blind eye to Globocnik's infelicities, recognizing in his protégé a particularly valuable tool for his SS empire-building designs.[253]

In early November 1940 Himmler secretly ordered Globocnik to develop the Lublin area 'as a self-sufficient, closed zone of SS industrial and constructive enterprises, farmsteads, and military and training installations that would serve as the basis for the expansion of SS and police power in the East'.[254] The toll on the Jewish labourers in these projects was, in essence, not very different from those already visited on Polish Jewish POWs—perhaps as many as 25,000 of whom had been worked to death by spring 1940—or, for that matter, on Jews and others by the Ober Ost military administration during the Great War.[255] But Globocnik's regime had a special edge. Brushing aside the protests of Frank's people, his SS units conducted a series of razzias in the Lublin area and surrounding districts to press-gang thousands of Jews into his camps, where death might follow from overwork, illness, or entirely unpredictable orgies of drunken shootings carried out by Globocnik's privately recruited *Selbschutz* of ethnic German guards.[256] Reading backwards from what began to happen here in late 1941, we can perhaps see in his emerging camp network, not least the one at Bełżec, a major staging post in the extermination process.

But reading backwards in this way has its problems. What Hitler wanted was a complete, comprehensive programme for European Jewish removal, far away from the German Reich where, rendered powerless, the Jews could do no harm. The various efforts in 1940 to put them to work, lethal or otherwise, had no bearing whatsoever on this ultimate goal. On the basis of the regime's forthcoming political and military objectives which were likely, in the near future, to take in both the Balkans and the Iberian Peninsula, Eichmann reviewed his Jewish statistics for the continent and accordingly revised his deportation figures upwards, in December 1940, to a staggering 5.8 million. Yet critically, he added, the relocation was to be '*to a territory yet to be determined*'.[257]

Implicit in Eichmann's statement was, again, that underlying but fundamental kink in the Nazi understanding of life, the universe, and, more immediately, the supposed Jewish grip on the Western system. Trading hostage Jews with that system as part of a bigger deal for peace had failed first in January 1939, then again in July–August 1940, when the Nazis thought they had finally—quite incorrectly—caught the Allies in their Madagascar vice. Hitler might publicly repeat his prophetic warning of what would happen to the Jews if the West did not come to heel, two years to the day from its first histrionic outing.[258] But by then the chances of undoing British resolve were rapidly waning, while Roosevelt was equally rapidly bolstering it, not least through the passing of the March 1941 Lend-Lease Act, providing Britain with all the war *matériel* it could use and, in the process, undoing any remaining pretence of US neutrality.

To beat the now almost combined forces of Anglo-American interest, and so also beat 'international Jewry', there was only one course of action left to Hitler: destroy Russia. Only thus, from Mackinderian strength, might he subdue the Allies into recognition of his world supremacy. And only with that impunity would he be able to finally, irrevocably, deal with the Jews: in the Soviet fashion, by vomiting them out to the distant corners of 'the Heartland'. As Hitler's new programme took shape in the spring, Heydrich was once again called upon to prepare the groundwork. All the vast Arctic wastes and Siberian tundra would enable him to find a solution which now really would be *final*. For good measure the rest of the Polish, Czech, and Gypsy rubbish could be entombed there too. But, first of all, the USSR had to be conquered. On that now hinged, specifically, the fate of European Jewry.

2

The Nazi Wars of Jewish—and Roma—Extermination

SETTING THE SCENE

'"What a people," whispered the old man, "these little Jews of yours. There's a devil in them."'[1]

Does there come a point in a book such as this when the supposedly detached authorial mask has to be cast off? My Jewish grandparents' families on my mother's side came from Włocławek in western Poland; on my father's, from the Volhynian region, near Kovel. From the East End of London the immigrant Levene family retained contact with their relatives in 'the old country' through to the war. At its end there was one known survivor. I didn't know these people: their names, their lives, their loves, their travails. But what happened to them at the hands of the Nazis touches me not as historian but as myself. Knowing that, can I keep a straight course, indeed, do I want to keep such a course, plotting the wider scope and sequence of rimlands genocide?

But destabilization of the wider project at this juncture also comes from another quarter. The seemingly relentless Nazi programme of European Jewish destruction has produced, in recent decades, a vast historiography of the Holocaust, the accumulated findings of which would seem to suggest no easy comparison between this and other genocides. There is the sheer magnitude of the communal death toll. Of over 8,300,000 Jews living in countries directly occupied by, or allied to the Nazis, during the course of the war, considerably over 5 million, and probably much closer to 6 million perished. The death toll includes a staggering 1 to 1.5 million children.[2] On a more localized basis the killing rate in the Rwanda genocide *is* comparable. But that bloodbath came to an end after one hundred days. The Nazi mass murder of the Jews was sustained over four years. And while one might argue that the 'Anglo' assaults, in particular on native peoples in the Americas and Antipodes, were continent-wide—though one might add over a vastly extended time frame—there is *nothing* in the annals of genocide, before or since the Nazi anti-Jewish assault, which replicates its spatial dimension across sovereign state boundaries. Not just were entire communities in this or that village, town, or city consciously and systematically blotted out of existence, but this happened throughout entire regions. In some countries, notably the Baltic states, the Jews as a physical entity practically ceased to exist. In Poland, the epicentre of European Jewish life, a communal population of 3,300,000 at the beginning of the war had, by its end, lost 85, perhaps 90 per cent of its number.[3] Much of this specific Polish Jewish catastrophe was enacted in an intense killing phase between the summer of 1942 and spring 1943. Nevertheless, the project of destruction extended far beyond the rimlands, to the far corners of a Europe where Nazi writ held sway.

It is this all-embracing aspect of the Holocaust, this desire to obliterate a ubiquitous people, and to deploy not only vast human and material resources, but considerable time, energy, and ingenuity in its accomplishment (even while Germany was fighting, and ultimately losing, its own war of survival), which has led so many of the leading exponents in the field of studies relating to it—most notably during the 1980s and 1990s but, in attenuated form, through to the present day—to resist efforts towards historically integrating it in synchronous terms, let alone within a wider history of genocide.[4] More recently, a number of thoughtful scholars have attempted to reforge Holocaust links back to colonialism, or the *Aghet*, its most obvious forerunner.[5] Yet it is difficult to muster up any direct or obvious precedent, Der Zor notwithstanding, for the industrialized conveyer belt system of mass death which epitomized 'the Holocaust' at its zenith.

Above all, it is the gas chambers, the crematoria, and the accompanying chimney stacks which have captured our—more specifically, Western—imagination. Nazism, as a consequence, has become *the* touchstone for 'evil', reiterated at every turn in a 'Holocaust industry' of documentaries, films, and a wider media, which have helped embed in popular consciousness the extraordinary, even 'unique', quality of Jewish destruction. It is not our concern here to critique this Holocaust-centric turn in our contemporary popular culture or its corresponding evolution through public memorialization on the one hand, and its centrality in school history curricula on the other. Except perhaps to comment that it has created a certain totemic, even sacred, aura around the actual 'event' which would seem to carry with it an already predetermined narrative as to what happened and how it happened, as well as why.[6] If the shorthand rendition of this Holocaust narrative reads as something done (more or less) exclusively to the Jews, its universalized message—its warning from history—is about how a society, even an advanced, 'civilized' society such as 'ours', can go to the bad if it succumbs to racial prejudice. Once set on this agreed path we may interpret the ensuing step-changes towards extermination by way of a tortuous functionalism, or transparent intentionalism, a consequence of Hitler's inner conviction, or a process of cumulative radicalization, yet sure in the knowledge of where we must inevitably end our journey: at the gates of Auschwitz.

To posit in the face of this narrative the need for a counterfactual consideration of the launching of the 'Final Solution'—as *extermination*—might thus seem not just an inappropriate but an unwarranted provocation, and especially so for those who have refuted any notion that the Holocaust can be understood or assessed according to normal methods of historical enquiry.[7] However, here we must offer our own insistence that we should approach the events beginning in the summer of 1941 through Hitler's lens; in other words, through his expectation of what Operation Barbarossa would achieve. His purposes, after all, were twofold: firstly, to dismantle the Soviet state, thus wiping out his main anti-system competitor in the heartland arena and so paving the way for the implementation of his *Lebensraum* project; secondly—and arguably much more importantly in the short term—to force the system, the *West*, to the negotiating table in order to accede to a global pax Germanica. If we start from this point, rather than from what we know with hindsight, the question we then have to ask is: had Hitler succeeded in this objective, how *then* would this have impacted on Heydrich's mandate to accomplish a comprehensive solution of the Jewish question? Would it have led to a mass eruction of European Jewry to Siberia, the Arctic, or somewhere 'colonial' equally far removed, as the Nazis had repeatedly sought throughout 1939 and 1940? Or, rather, to a speeded-up version of the killing process which actually took place? Of course, we cannot know the answer because the question *is* counterfactual.[8] The implication, moreover, that a positive military result for Hitler may have altered the direction of Jewish policy away from total mass murder is, I concede, also profoundly distasteful. Yet historically the implication is surely meaningful. At the end of Chapter 1 we argued that Operation Barbarossa was conceived as Hitler's last throw of the dice in his war against Britain, and, behind Britain, the USA. Which, in further synthesis, might read, 'Defeat Russia: win the global war against the Jews.' Interpreted through a normative 'realist' prism of international relations the statement is entirely nonsensical. The 1939–45 war waged for global supremacy was fought between blocs of advanced industrial states, just had been the case for the preceding Great War. There was *no* Jewish dimension to this geopolitical equation. Yet for Hitler no such distinction existed. The Jewish factor *was also* the geopolitical factor; which Hitler consistently and repeatedly enunciated all the way through to his final will and testament from his beleaguered bunker, at the end of April 1945.[9]

It is this absolute enmeshing of Hitler's pathological Judaeophobia into the fabric of his assessments of the ongoing state and likely course of the war—most particularly but not exclusively in the key Russian theatre—which is at the core of this chapter's explication. The desire to be revenged on 'the Jews', of course, was already thoroughly embedded in Hitler's psyche. Redemptive, visionary, apocalyptic—all these terms are appropriate—the wellsprings of his projection date back at least to 1918, and so to the even murkier waters of a Christian European self-affliction. Yet at the same time the catalysts to the actual implementation of systematic mass killing came out of precise contingencies arising from a *failing* war. The will to genocide was indeed intentional but it was also, as Jacques Burrin has purposefully developed, conditional on broad context and specific circumstance.[10]—which could be equally read as functional. One may wish to note that I am not offering anything new here, purely an interpretation on the basis of work already painstakingly developed by recent and not so recent scholarship in this most intensively studied subject arena.[11]

However, it is because of the intense, sometimes hothouse and often fractious debate surrounding this subject, and the attention this justifiably draws from a wider public, that I must clarify what I have already intimated to this point and so avoid any basis for misunderstanding. I am not proposing that had Hitler triumphed in his Russian campaign there would not have been a massive Jewish death toll as a result. That Hitler and his cohorts were intent on the spilling of Jewish blood is quite evident from the nature of Nazi policy from 1933 onwards. Indeed, the desire for a reckoning with the Jews was fundamental to Hitler's world view, dating back to the 'catastrophe' of 1918. Nor, as I have laboured to emphasize, was this desire peculiar only to him. The speed with which German and, more especially, Austrian troops in occupied Yugoslavia, from the summer of 1941, responded to local *Serb* insurgency by massacring Jews—as well as Roma—is evidence enough of a broad intentionalism. That a 'perpetrators' "never again" syndrome' could operate in this way without direct Hitlerite initiative or order further underscores the fact that what began in this way in the Balkans was quite capable of taking on a military life of its own in the even more merciless conditions of Operation Barbarossa.

But in proposing that the Nazi invasion of Yugoslavia provides a critical foretaste of the wider evolution of Jewish extermination in the east, as we do in the next, 'Balkan prelude' section of this chapter, we also aim not to lose sight of the wider geopolitical significance of this event for the course of Hitler's war. By inadvertently forcing Hitler to strike south at a time when all his focus was on the Russian campaign, the *British* plot to disrupt Belgrade's absorption into Berlin's sphere also disrupted *Fall* Barbarossa's timetable—possibly with fatal results. Our second section, 'A conscious if limited genocide', on this campaign's Jewish subtext carries through an argument about the underlying motivations of the German military—not just the SS—to be revenged on the Bolshevik–Jewish 'enemy' for the sins of 1918, as well as considering the scope for carrying out a targeted, gender-focused mass murder which the invasion opened up. In this sense, we might read the massacres of late June through July 1941 as the first in a run of Jewish *genocides*. But the supersession of this phase by something altogether more all-embracing and total, we will argue, relates much more closely to Hitler's personal realization that there would be no *ultimate* German victory in the world war. We do not propose that this realization happened all at once, nor that specific initiatives undertaken by *génocidaires* in the field—or, for that matter, at their desks—were not significant in this radicalization process. Nevertheless, in our third section, 'The shift to total genocide', we will seek to relate the step-changes by which Jewish genocide in Russia turned into a comprehensive European Jewish extermination drive, and the inexorable, and, one might propose, suicidal Nazi plunge into a truly global war arraigned against a joint USSR–USA–Britain combination.

The inference here that the sequence of German-organized Jewish killing over the next three years operated according to a wider set of, albeit crisis-ridden, responses to the war, rather than according to its own internal momentum, may, again, be read as controversial. But the Europe-wide nature of Jewish destruction, from early 1942 onwards also actually begs other difficult questions. One is purely geographical. Having been denied domination of 'the Heartland' by the Soviets, and with this the ability to deport European Jewry (and other unwanted populations) to its furthest reaches, the Nazis were forced into a default position of organizing their anti-Jewish vengeance on territory which they held. However, there was nothing which stated that the destruction of Dutch, French, Italian, Norwegian, or, for that matter, German Jews could not be accomplished on their home ground. Which makes the manner in which these communities were 'evacuated' for special treatment to the confines of the rimlands, at the very least, noteworthy. Or should we say 'evacuated' to what, in time, became the primary *European* extermination facility perched on the inner cusp of that rimland zone? Is the location of Auschwitz, or the other would-be or actual extermination camps, something which should condition our understanding of the origins and evolution of the killing process? In our fourth section, 'Genocide as "system"', we seek to situate what might be deemed an industrial 'system' of mass death within a wider historical context. In an earlier volume, we insisted that genocide cannot be a system, but is something which states *do*.[12] So, does 'the Holocaust' buck this trend, identifying it, as Bauman would argue, as 'a rare yet significant and reliable test of the hidden possibilities of modern society'?[13] Or does an analysis which focuses on a scientifically-based, rational–purposive, problem-solving *technique* of mass murder inadvertently edify a set of sordid contingencies, one of which, entirely paradoxically, involved maximization of a Jewish slave labour potential, thereby reversing the age and gender front-loading of the killing process at its outset?

To be sure, none of this is to underestimate the human and material resources which were earmarked for Jewish destruction, even, as in the case of Hungarian Jews in the summer of 1944, when this meant the denial of those resources where they were otherwise urgently needed in what by then had become a desperate war for sheer German survival. But that in itself would rather beg the question of how and, more arguably, why it was that the momentum of Jewish destruction continued to be sustained over months and years, and towards the end even speeded up, when one might have expected entropic tendencies by this juncture to have overwhelmed the exercise. Nor was it only Jews who, in 1944, were being delivered en masse to the gas chambers. In our penultimate section, 'The Roma: an additional complication', we consider the fate of the Roma under Nazi wartime rule. Was what happened to them a subset of the Jewish-exterminatory drive? Or something which perhaps needs to be understood in its own terms, perhaps even as something which more exactly fits the Nazis' claimed *racial* justification for their actions? As with the Jews, so even more with the Roma, the scope, trajectory, and actual implementation of killing seems to have become more convoluted as the war progressed towards its cataclysmic climax. And in that *Götterdämmerung*-like Nazi knowledge of coming self-destruction we perhaps have our most elusive set of questions to ask in this chapter's coda. Did the Jews remain a key element in the Nazis' geopolitical equation to the very end? Was it this which explains the chaotic attempts at cover-up of their crime, the Terezin façade, or even the more or less autonomous SS effort to try and turn the fate of the European Jewish remnant into a yet another bargaining counter, geared, this time, towards splitting the Allied camp?

One very large question looms as we attempt to assess this picture in its totality. Are we considering a sequence of events which have a coherence, even a preordained coherence, for which the terms Holocaust, Shoah, or, in the case of the Roma, *Porrajmos*, provide the necessary unifying gel? Our assumed familiarity with the terrain makes these shorthand expressions obvious endorsements of such a reading. But suppose we are really dealing with a series of less coherent, more piecemeal, perhaps not even wholly sequential mass killings? Even where they blur into each other they may also each contain elements of singularity, which might suggest that what we are actually dealing with is a series of discrete if overlapping *genocides*. And while each, again, was, in some sense, part of that wider range in the 1912–48 rimlands' sequence, each, in other respects, was not only distinct but, alone, dwarfed 'those committed by other modern genocidal practitioners against other victim groups'.[14] At the beginning of this chapter I stated my own sense of destabilization on personal as well as scholarly grounds in attempting to work through this particular landscape of mass killing, which—in my own, admittedly contradictory, shorthand—I have described as the 'ultimate genocide'. While this chapter will seek further to clarify the matter it does not anticipate closure on the destabilization.

BALKAN PRELUDE

In late March 1941, as Hitler's secret plans were moving into high gear for the projected invasion of Russia at the end of May, British and US intelligence services organized what amounted to a palace coup in Belgrade. It was a very conscious effort to disrupt Yugoslavia's absorption into the German alliance system and, equally importantly, aimed to turn the tables on German moves to create a stranglehold on Britain's growing military build-up in Greece. For a brief moment it looked, instead, as if the Belgrade coup had, in exposing the weakness of Germany's southern flank, opened up the possibility of a British move on Rumanian oilfields: the critical resource base for Berlin's assault on Russia. Indeed, even the intimation of such a move threatened to sabotage Hitler's grand design.[15] He responded with an immediate, utterly devastating if essentially improvised *Blitzkrieg* on the Yugoslav state, blasting central Belgrade itself to smithereens in a Luftwaffe strike vastly more destructive of human life than any single air operation of the war to that point.[16] With the Yugoslav rout completed in a matter of days, the British position in Greece also rapidly unravelled, the consequence of which was that, by the end of May, the entirety of the Balkan peninsula, plus the Greek islands, had fallen under Axis control.

Yet if this was unequivocally an Allied military disaster, looked at through the German prism its negative ramifications were hardly marginal. Not only had the Balkan campaign slowed up the schedule for the start of Operation Barbarossa by at least three weeks; it had also exposed a classic problem of military overstretch. Berlin might have provisionally divvied up the territory of the now defunct Yugoslav state between itself, its Axis allies, and the new Independent State of Croatia (NDH) puppet satellite, but none of this guaranteed pacification of the region, the sine qua non of the campaign in the first place. A near-spontaneous and very much grass-roots Serb uprising, beginning in late July, largely precipitated by the NDH genocidal assault on Serbs within its polity but also directed at

German rule in residual Serbian territory, underscored exactly this weakness. Compared with the intensity and scope of the struggle with Tito's Partisans in subsequent years, the summer 1941 uprising was geographically limited and strategically inchoate. But an insurgency operating in the Wehrmacht's rear just at the time when the success or otherwise of the Russian campaign was coming to its critical threshold, could hardly be ignored. Not least given that two very different military–political entities—the Serb Chetnik nationalists and the communist, all-Yugoslav-orientated Partisans—seemed to have made common cause in the armed struggle.[17]

The problem for the Wehrmacht was that, having redeployed to the Russian front the combat troops who had spearheaded the April assault, the 25,000-strong four divisions of ageing reservists, plus a handful of SD units and a police battalion assigned to the Serbian arena, were hardly sufficient in number or, necessarily, competence for the task in hand.[18] Hastily improvised *Selbschutz* regiments made little difference to the overall balance of forces. There was, however, a significant additional dimension to the trajectory of the ensuing struggle. Two of the Reich divisions hailed from the Ostmark, in other words, post-Anschluss Austria. Their deployment to Serb territory was quite conscious, and indeed entirely in keeping with Hitler's own consistent view that Austrians (himself included) knew exactly how to deal with Serb *Untermenschen*. Austrian animosity against Serbs stretched back, at the very least, to the Great War. The very fact that a major arena of the current insurgency developed in the Mačva valley area of the Sava bend, around Šabac, where, in 1914, the stymied Austrians had responded with major atrocities, simply inflamed old memories.[19] Then, as now, officers of the occupation forces responded to attacks on their men with hostage-taking and mass reprisal against civilians. In September, with an explicit remit from Hitler himself 'to restore order with the severest of measures', his newly-inaugurated plenipotentiary commanding general and fellow Austrian, Franz Böhme, proclaimed to his troops:

> Your objective is to be achieved in a land where, in 1914, streams of German blood flowed because of the treachery of the Serbs, men and women. You are the avengers of those dead. A deterring example must be established for all of Serbia, one that will have the heaviest impact on the entire population. Anyone who carries out his duty in a lenient manner will be called to account, regardless of rank or position, and tried by a military court.[20]

One might wearily comment, *plus ça change, plus c'est la même chose*. Except if the occupiers had unmasked their 'old', treacherous, and loathsome Serb enemy and desired a reckoning accordingly, why now take it out on the Jews, a community entirely marginal to either 1914 or 1941 Serb resistance? Of an estimated 80,000 in Yugoslavia at the outbreak of hostilities—some 17,000 in Serbia itself—there was, unsurprisingly, a small if significant element who were communists, or who would become so. These included a handful who rose to prominence in the Partisan struggle.[21] However, the notion that Jews were at the heart of Serb resistance to the occupiers is entirely fanciful. This was doubly the case with regard to the refugee component of the community, several thousand of whom, particularly from

Austria, were stranded in several camps—including one at Šabac—with the single purpose of escaping from Europe as quickly as possible by way of Rumanian or Yugoslav ports as soon as they could obtain the necessary permits to travel.[22] To be sure, individual foreign or Serbian Jews on Nazi suspect blacklists were rounded up and, in some instances, shot by the Einsatzgruppen who accompanied the Wehrmacht invasion. But the lack of targeted Einsatzgruppen massacres of Jews, which were so central to the Barbarossa campaign a few months later, rather suggests that there was no prior security assessment of a *specific* Jewish threat.

Certainly, once the country had been overrun, the SD apparatus got to work, rapidly issuing orders for the registration and isolation of Jews from the rest of the population. Yet it was the ruling Wehrmacht authorities themselves—without any RHSA bidding—who took the lead in terrorizing Jews. One major foretaste of what was to come was a looting and killing spree in (soon to become NDH-controlled) Sarajevo, a mere ten days after the invasion. The action, as initiated by army units, included one spectacular act of desecration when the city's great Jewish library went up in flames.[23] It proved not entirely successful in—as had been intended—arousing local Muslims' passions against their neighbours. But this did not deter the military authorities from seeking to develop a major anti-Jewish propaganda campaign in Serbia. Nor from taking over Jewish businesses and homes at will, with all the ransacking or theft of property which went with it.[24]

Nevertheless, it was with the start of the insurgency that military policy moved from the essentially exploitative to the lethal. During late July and into August, in Šabac and elsewhere, Jewish men started to be pulled out of their homes and shot in the streets in increasingly large numbers. Much of this was sheer retribution by junior commanders for comrades killed, in the absence of an actual enemy.[25] However, under Böhme's leadership from late September, as reprisal policy became more systematized, other reasons for shooting Jews started to become evident. A new tariff ordered by Field-Marshal Keitel, at the Army Supreme Command (OKW), prescribed that for every German soldier killed, between fifty and one hundred 'communists' were to be shot. Keitel was himself responding to Hitler's insistence upon collective retribution. Yet for Böhme to make the terror campaign work 'on the ground' he had to demonstrate not only that the countryside was being pacified, but that insurgents, their families, or fellow villagers were paying the price. If, instead, they decamped en masse to the hills, whom then did you kill? Interned Jews provided one obvious answer. Once those from one camp were eliminated you simply took them from another and repeated the process. As a result, throughout the autumn, Serbs in Belgrade and other major towns were presented with the strange spectacle of public executions by Austrians, very often of fellow Austrians, for 'crimes' the Serbs had supposedly committed.[26]

In this way, Jews, both native and refugee, as well as Roma for good measure (though in smaller numbers), made up a disproportionately large element of the hostages facing execution in the holding camps. The convenience of using Jews in particular for this purpose was reinforced by the fact that it meant time could be saved screening other—Serb—prisoners in order to determine whether they were communist or not. Jews ipso facto *were* communists. Again, the only problem was that this pseudo-argument was having no effect in staunching the course of the insurgency whatsoever. Some officials clearly understood why. Harald Turner, the head of the military administration in Belgrade, privately confided to a fellow SS-Gruppenführer that the Jews were the wrong target. They just happened to be available in camps to be shot.[27] Typically, and very much in line with the German administrators in Poland over the previous two years, Turner sought mass deportation to somewhere else as his preferred way of 'getting rid of' the problem. In this approach he was supported by Felix Benzler, the German Foreign Office representative in Belgrade. Between them they urged both RHSA and FO back home to accede to this course of action. To no avail. Already, in September, Eichmann had tersely advised the FO Jewish expert, Karl Rademacher—the official responsible the previous year for dreaming up the Madagascar scheme—to tell the military administrators to 'shoot'. A joint FO–RHSA delegation to Belgrade in mid-October simply reiterated the message.[28]

But then 'shooting' had been exactly what the military had been doing anyway—with or without Eichmann's advice. Set against the escalating contours of a peoples' war in the Balkans this should not perhaps surprise us. Over the course of the next three years all the participants in the struggle for control of the peninsula fought each other with merciless ferocity, seeing their own tallies of genocidal atrocity mount. At the centre of this vortex, the Wehrmacht, in their efforts to remain hegemonic overlord, enacted mass reprisal, whether in Yugoslavia or Greece, as a standard operating procedure.[29] For instance, just as Rademacher and Turner were squaring up to each other in Belgrade over what to do with the Jews, not far to the south, in the towns of Kraljevo and Kragujevac, Wehrmacht forces who had found themselves under Partisan attack responded in grand retaliatory mode. In the former, soldiers of the 717th Division, according to their own records, lined up and shot 1,736 men and 19 'communist' women. In the latter, short of the necessary quota of 2,300 to be garnered from alleged communist suspects and Jews, they seized the students from the high school and machine-gunned most of them too.[30] Clearly, Germans in uniform were not *that* particular about who they shot in reprisal, especially in the Balkans where the populace were deemed subhuman, a sangfroid attitude to the taking of life was de rigueur, and no military court was going to punish those who showed particular zeal in the offence.

But while general reprisal shootings in Serbia in the autumn of 1941 threatened all sections of the population, there remains something qualitatively different about the killings of Jews—and Roma. For a start, while General Bader, Böhme's replacement in early December, lowered the reprisal quotas—an indirect acknowledgement that Böhme's policy was both unworkable and counterproductive[31]—there is nothing to suggest this diminution was intended to be applied to the two latter groups. Assuming, that is, any able-bodied Jews or Roma were still available to be shot. Bar 500 Jewish men kept alive for ghetto maintenance and security, by early November all Jewish men on Serbian soil, and most of the Roma, who had not escaped incarceration, had been 'used up' en masse in reprisal killings. And with no German civilian or military official—neither Turner, despite his private misgivings, nor anyone up the chain of command to Field-Marshal List, the overall commander in the Balkan theatre—contested one iota that Jewish men *ought* to be eliminated. Certainly, when it came to killing women, children, and the elderly, a difference in tone began to intrude: the Belgrade command apparently claiming that such a course of action would be 'dishonourable'.[32] Yet in terms of what happened next, while the Wehrmacht were able to absolve themselves of direct responsibility, their complicity in the matter remained quite transparent.

A new SD commander, Emanuel Shäfer, directly appointed by Heydrich, arrived in Belgrade in the wake of the Wannsee Conference, in mid-January 1942, tasked with bringing the Jewish question on Serbian soil to a closure. He was assisted in this 'special assignment' by the arrival of a Sauer gas van from Germany in early March. Into this the remaining Jews were loaded daily, in batches of fifty to eighty, from their internment camp in Semlin (Sajmište)—a former industrial fairground on the Croat site of the Sava—and driven across the river through central, bomb-shattered Belgrade. Its citizenry would not have been able to see what was happening to the mostly women and children inside the van but would have become habituated to its singular journey through the city several times a day. Not after 10 May though, when the gas from the van's exhausts had done its worst and the last Serbian Jews had suffered their excruciating, collective deaths. Semlin was the only locale outside of the major killing zones in the 'Lands Between' where such a van operated. Indeed, the authorities here did not seem to be over-exercised by the transparent nature of the procedure: the van, replete with its dead cargo, continuing each of its journeys to a shooting range south-east of Belgrade, where the bodies were emptied into a mass grave. Some 85,000 Jewish people had been incarcerated in Semlin, in appalling and fetid conditions with a consequent death rate to match. The majority died in the camp; however, some 7,500 were murdered in the gas van.[33]

However, if RHSA operatives delivered the coup de grâce, what is striking is not just the degree to which the military authorities cooperated entirely in the process—to the point where Turner was actually seeking to take credit for Serbia's *Judenfrei* status later in 1942[34]—but, equally, the Wehrmacht's own volition in 'anticipating' systematic Jewish destruction before the conventionally accepted beginning of the 'Final Solution'.[35] There had been no prior blueprint for Serbian Jewish extermination; such that one might posit that the unfolding of the killings from the summer was a German military reaction to unforeseen contingencies. Yet clearly this cannot suffice as a serious explanation for the Jewish and Roma mass murders. Not only did the Wehrmacht consider it right and proper that these two unarmed groups, posing no threat to the occupying regime, should—against all the evidence—be cast in this threatening role.[36] More pointedly, they *chose* to carry out an extermination of their male component, as if they genuinely constituted such a threat. To be sure, one would then have to note one critical distinction. Having killed all the Roma men in captivity, when it came to the 300 gypsy women and children still incarcerated in Semlin in early 1942, the authorities made a point of releasing them while making no effort whatsoever to countermand or question SD orders to carry out the mass murder of the much larger number of Jewish women and children there.[37] Which might remind us that, while congruent in part, the Nazi destruction of the two peoples was neither in terms of chronology nor, necessarily, of motivation, identical.

But that begs a more specific question about Jewish extermination. If the army were not simply compliant, but active, autonomous agents in the systematic destruction of the Jews in Serbia, does this not offer a signpost to the evolution of the Jewish extermination process in Russia? Not purely as a project pertaining to Himmler and Heydrichs' security apparatus—but as a concrete expression of a broader German national will?

A CONSCIOUS IF LIMITED GENOCIDE BY WAY OF OPERATION BARBAROSSA

How could killing Jews expedite the destruction of Stalin's communist state? The question reads like something from an SS training exercise. To which the answer from the dedicated student might be manifold. Bolshevik and Jew were known to be synonymous. By killing Jews you cut off the head of the regime as well as the world system against which you were fighting. Eliminate the Jewish element and nominal popular support for communism would crumple. Hitler had said so many times himself.[38] The blow would be doubly powerful as it would help defeat not only the military enemy but the ideological one. In this way you suffocated the possibility that Bolshevism might rise again in Russia as well as in other parts of Europe which might look to it as a nucleus—a kernel—of ongoing resistance to Nazi occupation.[39]

The perspicacious student, at this point, however, might realize that implicit in the question was something more than simply the assurance of victory against the Kremlin. Victory, after all, had been denied Germany in the east in the previous Great War, not because of any defeat on the battlefield but because of what had happened in the rear, even on civilian home turf. If only on the precautionary principle, it was imperative that one should identify, isolate, and eliminate all Jewish–Bolsheviks who fell into one's hands, not only as a prophylactic against unseen attacks on one's own troops but to deny the escape, once again, of the Jews' pernicious ideas into the broader environment. Was it not they, after all, who had wrecked a Kaiser-led peace and stability for Europe by striking at Germany itself in 1918? Did these fomenters of not just racial but political disintegration not include *Ostjude* women of the Rosa Luxembourg-type, who had been at the very vanguard of the movement which had sabotaged Germany's triumph then? They would behave in exactly the same way now: unless, that is, the forces of German salvation got in their retaliation first.

Our imaginary discussion is offered as a pathway into the peculiarly bifurcated thinking prevalent within not only the Nazi security apparatus but its military command at the onset of *Fall* Barbarossa. On the one hand, the enemy was clear-cut; yet on the other, ubiquitous, yet elusive, as it reared its vengeful, insurgent head anywhere in the Wehrmacht's rear. And because Jews in this representation were the vicious aggressors, in the process making of the German soldiery potential victims, the latter became doubly justified in taking whatever measures necessary to defend themselves.

Over and beyond the fact that this was a classic self-exculpatory inversion of the truth there was, however, clearly something else here which did not compute. Hitler and his generals, in the lead-up to the campaign, had, on one level, convinced themselves that a lightening *blitzkrieg* assault would have the Soviets, just like the Poles and the French before them, spiralling towards collapse in a matter of weeks.[40] Assurance on the matter was amplified by the knowledge that the bulk of their adversary was composed of supposedly racially inferior Slavs and Asiatics. Putting aside all the other spatial, demographic, military-industrial, and geopolitical factors which might call this optimistic forecast into question, Nazi analysis narrowed down to an assumption that German willpower, aligned with the natural superiority of its people, would be the cause of success. Yet intrude the underlying 'Jewish' incubus and this rosy picture was not just destabilized but entirely turned on its head. In this alter-image of events, instead of Red Army remnants and partisans behind the lines folding up, they offered a vicious, calculated, guerrilla-style fightback: morale among German troops plummeted as casualties mounted, and the Wehrmacht, unable to deal effectively with this asymmetric 'uncivilized' warfare, found themselves bogged down in a struggle they could neither contain, nor bring to a definitive conclusion.

Read back to themselves, this dystopian vision of what might happen if preventative measures were not taken thus became a justification to conduct a war in Russia not simply outside the standard terms of the Hague and Geneva conventions, but in which *everything* was permissible. Add to that the racial element, and one had recast in modern, supposedly scientific form a justification for a war of the civilized against savages; in other words, a remit for the sort of unadulterated atrocity which we have previously characterized as War Types Two and Three. But add then a further layer in which the narrative—as Hitler himself articulated—is that of 'a conflict between two world views', in which the organizers of the Asiatic fightback are none other the 'Jewish–Bolshevik intelligentsia',[41] and one had more than simply a rationale for a targeted strike against the alleged leadership strata of the Soviet polity. Indeed, one had something entirely more potent: a basis for a rerun of the 1914–18 conflict, but this time with (supposedly) no chance of defeat.

Hitler's insistence, in his meeting with Alfred Jodl, the OKW chief of staff, on 30 March 1941, that it would be such ideological first principles which would determine the ground rules for the conquest and occupation of Russia, firmly set in place a transmission belt for the set of infamous 'special' army orders which followed. Issued in mid-May, the military jurisdiction order (*Gerichtsbarkeitserlass*, or Barbarossa-*Erlass*) did not simply cancel 'until further notice' normal court-martial proceedings against soldiers who carried out summary executions in cases of assumed or actual resistance—it positively urged the necessity of collective reprisals against guerrillas or those who harboured them. This was effectively carte blanche to commanders down to the most junior level to exterminate whole communities, innocent or otherwise; while subsequent 'Commissar Order'

(*Kommissarbefehl*) from early June singled out political commissars with the Red Army as elements particularly deserving of summary execution. Their status as POWs was to be voided, and they were either to be shot immediately or, where apprehended in the rear, to be handed over to and eliminated by Einsatzgruppen.[42]

This represented a complete demolition of accepted international norms of warfare: Hitler had already rammed home to a gathering of senior military commanders at the end of March his point about it being an ideological *Weltanschauungskrieg* as well as one which, being fought against an entirely different sort of 'criminal' enemy, necessitated exterminatory warfare—*Vernichtungskrieg*—in which there could be no place for personal scruples. The same argument was, in turn, conveyed to the troops as guidelines for their behaviour as they prepared for battle, in early June.[43] Interestingly, this was the only occasion when one of these military orders explicitly named Jews, alongside agitators, guerrillas, and other active or passive resisters, against whom 'ruthless and energetic measures' were to be taken.[44]

That said, what is striking in all these documents, in either their draft or final form, is the manner in which the Jewish bogey—commissar or otherwise—completely suffused them. Early drafts of the Barbarossa-*Erlass* are particularly revealing. A first one specifically justified summary executions of civilians by reference to 'the collapse of 1918, the subsequent period of suffering on the part of the German people and the struggle against National Socialism—with the many blood sacrifices made by this movement'. All of these things, the draft continued, 'can be traced to Bolshevik influence: and no German should forget this'.[45] A further reworking more explicitly spelt out why troops would have the right and obligation to defend themselves against what it called 'disintegrative powers' emanating from 'carriers of the Jewish–Bolshevik worldview'. The soldiers, indeed, were to be warned that this 'especially dangerous element … will use his weapon of disintegration deviously and from behind against the German military'.[46]

If, thus, fears of being attacked in the rear read like a regurgitation of the 'guerrilla psychosis' which had been so prevalent an aspect of the actual or perceived German soldiers' experience, dating back to the last war and earlier still, implicitly if not explicitly foregrounding the Jews in this equation added an entirely new dimension to it. The notion of Jews as a force of 'disintegration' or 'decomposition', which, in part, can be traced back to Hitler's own musings or public utterances on the subject, is particularly telling. Suggestive of powers which were overwhelmingly contagious but at the same time alien to the human condition, the motif conjures up a situation in which even the most resolute and steadfast of Aryan warriors might find themselves paralysed before they might effectively respond. All the more reason why members of the armed forces had to be ever vigilant and ready to strike at this reservoir of evil. Even after Jews had been entirely exterminated in whole regions of the Soviet rimlands, Wehrmacht, SD officers, and civil administrators were still invoking a Jewish fomenting force as their standard legitimization for mass reprisals in the face of partisan attack.[47] But this phobia-ridden logic serves only to underscore how the 'disintegrative' motif supplied Operation Barbarossa's planners with a pretext, indeed an alibi, for something else: taking a long-term revenge on the Jews.

Key to an unravelling of the thread backwards from 1941 to the crystallizing moment of German defeat and humiliation twenty-three years earlier, was Hitler's reference, in his *Fall* Barbarossa planning meetings and pronouncements, either to 'the Jewish–Bolshevik intelligentsia' or, in more concrete terms, to the commissars and political police within the Soviet state.[48] Here was a subject on which there was practically national elite, certainly armed forces' elite, consensus. The fact that Germany, even in the Nazi narrative, had been brought to its knees in 1918 by Jews *within* the country, made not an iota of difference to an explanation which equated those *same* Jews with their 'internationalist' parasite cousins who had taken over the tsarist state a little earlier. There was the rather inconvenient further fact, of course, that the Nazi regime had found itself quite capable of coming to an agreement with Stalin two years back. Surely, according to the Nazis' own tortuous logic, this could point only to a diminution of Jewish control over the Kremlin since the time of the revolution? And the RHSA's scrutiny of internal Soviet affairs would surely also have pointed to a radical decline in the 'Jewish' presence in the ranks—including senior ranks—of the NKVD during, or in the wake of, the *Ezhovshchina*?[49] Putting aside any discussion on whether Jews in the Soviet administration or communist party, before or after 1938, felt themselves in any way to be operating as 'Jews'—a nuanced discourse clearly beyond the bounds of Nazi epistemics—as the Nazi–Soviet Pact was consigned to the rubbish bin of history so the German military quickly fell in behind Hitler's explication of their prime 'enemy', essentially because this was consonant with what they already held to be indubitable truths.

When it came to Heydrich and Generalquartiermeister Wagner hammering out—just as previously over Poland—operational coordination between the RHSA and Wehrmacht for the course of the invasion, the latter, this time, offered no fundamental block on the former's now vastly expanded role. The Reichsführer-SS would have autonomy within the army's operation area to carry out the 'special tasks' directly assigned to him by the Führer, but with the army providing logistical support to the Security Police and, more specifically, the Einsatzgruppen to help them bring to a conclusion the struggle between the 'two opposing political systems'. In effect, the Wehrmacht was providing its own carte blanche for SS special squads to conduct mass executions as they saw fit, including of civilian population, in the rear of but as well as within the immediate combat zone.[50] Or, put another way, while the armed forces were being given the task of fighting and defeating the Red Army, the security apparatus were being deployed against the *real*, underlying enemy in order (one might add, highly paradoxically) to protect the armed forces.

None of this amounted, however, to the Wehrmacht's washing its hands of responsibility for what ensued. Operation Barbarossa, after all, was openly broadcast to the ordinary German soldier, not to mention the population back home, as a war of annihilation: not just a matter of military necessity, but because the 'truly subhuman'—including 'Asiatic' and 'Mongol'—peoples of Russia deserved to be eliminated from the space of their legitimate Teutonic successors.[51] Narrativized, too, as the culmination of a historic struggle between civilization and barbarism in which the very reference to the German medieval warrior emperor Frederick Barbarossa was intended to conjure up the righteous fury of a holy crusade,[52] all this would have been incitement enough to the young rank and file of the Wehrmacht, already heavily indoctrinated through their time in the Hitler Jugend, to be willing accomplices or active participants in the liquidation of *Untermenschen*.[53]

As the campaign got under way, one major consequence was the alacrity with which troops took it upon themselves to shoot their surrendered Red Army opposite numbers—or other alleged partisan suspects—in droves.[54] But this was hardly a spasm of stochastic atrocities by trigger-happy troops, off the rein and out of control. The front-line soldiers were doing no more than carrying out what they understood their orders to be, as transmitted down from OKW. And if that body, with its much-vaunted credentials for iron discipline, had wished such actions to be any different, the massacres would have been speedily terminated. The utterly staggering figure of some 500,000 to 600,000 POWs executed hardly suggests a military hierarchy which had any doubts about what it was allowing.[55] The majority of the mass executions were carried out not by combat troops, nor the Wehrmacht's accompanying field security police, but by Einsatzgruppen squads, Gestapo, or other SS units. But that still barely accounts for the several more million Russian POWs who were marched off to army-run, open-air transit camps where, together with interned civilian male inmates, over 2 million of their number, in succeeding months, starved to death.[56] German troops would either have seen the POWs in the early stages of their paroxysm or been directly assigned to guarding the camps. They would have understood full well the intention from on high. The scale of death cannot be put down to some unfortunate tragedy due to the logistical difficulties of fighting a major campaign *and* looking after prisoners. More precisely, lack of sufficient food for both victors and vanquished can longer be cited as mitigating evidence when it is known that local peasant women were repeatedly prevented—to the point of death—from providing sustenance at the camp perimeters. Later on, in the early winter, Keitel issued orders that food should be made available so that the *surviving* prisoners might be put to work. But by then a gendered mass murder of 'Russians'—albeit uniformed, but surrendered—had taken place: the conscious intent and enormous scale of which come arguably 'very close to the parameters' of the UN definition of genocide.[57]

Whether one accepts this conclusion or not, one thing is striking. That is, that the exterminatory violence meted out to the Soviet POWs was justified *in advance* through the claim, as in the *Kommissarbefehl*, that 'hate-inspired, cruel and inhuman treatment of POWs' would be what Soviet soldiery at the instigation of their political commissars—'the real leaders of resistance'—would inflict upon their German counterparts.[58] And it is in this utterly projective portrayal of themselves as victims, and hence symbolic of what had befallen and would once again befall the entire German nation unless they acted with decisive ruthlessness, that the military leadership returned to their chronic idée fixe.

It was against 'the bestialities which have been committed against the Germans and related races' that General von Reichenau, commander-in-chief of Army Group 6, issued, of his own volition, an infamous proclamation to his troops on 10 October. Past sins clearly weighed as much as present danger in Reichenau's mind as he urged his men to nip in the bud the Jew-plotted rebellions in the rear, yet at the same time urged that they should be 'avengers' who would bring 'just atonement' to 'Jewish sub-humanity' for the Bolshevik system that they had created and which now threatened, through 'Asiatic influence... the European cultural sphere'.[59] Reichenau's hotchpotch of claims and justifications was entirely in keeping with the Hitlerite world view. Which may explain why the Führer not only praised his order, but ensured its distribution among all combat units on the Eastern Front. On this basis we might be inclined to dismiss Reichenau as an exception amongst the generals. Here was a dyed-in-the-wool Nazi whose murderous reputation preceded him in the Polish campaign, in his order to shoot Soviet POW stragglers, and through his recent close collaboration with Einsatzgruppe C in the great Jewish massacre at Babi Yar.[60]

The problem is that Reichenau galvanized several other combat generals to issue their own, even more radical, proclamations—among them the widely celebrated yet notably 'apolitical' professional, General von Manstein.[61] He, even more than Reichenau, was of the view that 'Judaism constitutes the mediator between the enemy in the rear and the still fighting remnants of the Red Army and the Red leadership'. Like another general, Hoth, who warned that if the 'Jewish intellectuals' were not dealt with 'Asiatic barbarism'would overwhelm European culture, Manstein was quite ready to inextricably mix doom-laden prognostications with a demand for Jewish 'atonement' for perpetrating Bolshevism in the first place.[62]

The generals' proclamations came at the moment when the invasion of the Soviet Union had crystallized instead into a recognition that what was now under way was a life-and-death struggle. Operation Barbarossa, like the amended Schlieffen plan in August 1914, had shot its bolt. With no strategic reserves available, the Wehrmacht effort in the late autumn of 1941 became centred on one last desperate bid to capture Moscow and so finish the matter. Yet at this moment of overwhelming crisis, it was not Stalin, or the Red Army command, which haunted the Wehrmacht military mind. Rather, among Nazi and non-Nazi alike, it was the memory of 1918—the desire for vengeance against those held fundamentally responsible—allied to a promise to themselves that this time there would be no repeat performance of that earlier moment.[63] The mission with which their soldiers were entrusted—to show no compassion as they blotted out Jewish–Bolshevism and so saved Germany—was indeed a case of the 'perpetrators' "never again" syndrome' in full flood. There was only one problem: how were you going to get at your Jewish–Bolshevik enemy and so utterly destroy it?

*

There was in fact a further complication. When the Kaiser had sought to destroy the Herero insurgency in German South West Africa back in 1904, he had entrusted the task to his most ruthless general, Lothar von Trotha. But it was not von Trotha's military heirs who were given the remit for the destruction of the anticipated Soviet insurgency in 1941. That role was reserved for Himmler. There may have been a certain logic implicit in this, at least in a convoluted Nazi sense, over and beyond the fact, that is, that he and Heydrich already arrogated to themselves a mandate on all matters relating to the 'Final Solution'. If the Jewish–Bolshevik intelligentsia was, as the Nazi leadership kept telling itself, the backbone of the Soviet state—if, indeed, this translated into their commanding role among commissars in the Red Army and, more pointedly still, within the NKVD security and intelligence apparatus—then it surely followed that what the RHSA would be entering into, while no-holds-barred, was something akin to a symmetrical, 'like with like' struggle. In which case, it surely made sense to make serious preparations. On the one hand, this would be a matter of legitimate self-defence. On the other, it clearly became the sine qua non for the complete pacification of the country once the Wehrmacht had captured Moscow and its units had advanced as far as the A-A (Archangel to Astrakhan) line, which marked the proposed extent of German occupation in Russia. If we can empathize thus far with the Heydrich view, the purpose of assembling officers and men of the four Einsatzgruppen at the German border police training school in Pretzsch in the weeks before Operation Barbarossa, was presumably to induct them into the fine detail of their mission.

Here, however, we run into something of an evidential problem. We know that there followed an intensive round of meetings and training sessions with senior RHSA staff and other experts. We also know that the men hand-picked to command the units, such as Dr Otto Ohlendorf, the appointed head of Einsatzgruppe D, were not only absolutely dedicated to their task but considered to be of the highest intellectual calibre. All this would seem to reinforce just how essential their task was considered to be. But what exactly *was* it? The witness testimony, as supplied by Ohlendorf at the post-war Nuremberg Einsatzgruppen trial, that the units had received a comprehensive order to kill *all* Soviet Jews is now generally held to have been a subterfuge whose purpose was to demonstrate that the officers in the dock were simply following orders.[64] We know that Heydrich did deliver verbal instructions to the unit commanders in person just prior to their deployment. Significantly, however, when he followed these up with a written summary ten days into the actual operation, on 2 July, the list of those specifically to be executed referred to Comintern and communist party officials, commissars, and functionaries of all ranks, the usual range of suspected saboteurs, agitators, and so on, and *'Jews in party and state positions'*.[65]

Disarmingly, perhaps, this would seem to suggest not so much a complete break with the tasks assigned to the Einsatzgruppen squads in Poland and Yugoslavia, as simply a more focused role vis-à-vis the Soviet enemy. Even then, a question mark remains over whether Heydrich intended *only* Jewish administrative and political personnel to be killed, or whether his verbal instructions extended this mandate much more widely. One factor which might suggest that a sweep across the entire Jewish population was not contemplated, at least at this point, was the relatively limited Einsatzgruppen strength at the outset of the campaign. The various inputs from the SD, Security Police, Kripo, Order Police, and others, including technical staff, spatchcocked together (in fact, rather similarly to the Polish campaign) to

comprise the around 3,000 members of the Einsatzgruppen,[66] was hardly a sufficient force to eliminate by firing squad an estimated 5 million or more Jews spread
across the breadth of the USSR. But then there seem, too, to have been instances
where Einsatzgruppen commanders on the ground interpreted their remit rather
more cautiously than was probably expected of them by their senior line managers. The commanders of Einsatzkommando sections were certainly expected by
Himmler and Heydrich to use their initiative, yet when, on arriving in Grodno
eight days into the campaign, the two men found to their consternation that EK 9
deployed around Lida 'had so far liquidated' *only* ninety-six Jews, they complained
to the unit's Einsatzgruppe B superior, who immediately ordered a stepped-up killing rate.[67]

The Reichsführer-SS and head of the RHSA certainly played a key role in their
frequent, sometimes frenetic, visits to the front-line units to reiterate the message.[68] Even so, there was a certain ambiguity in the approach. Wary of unauthorized massacres, whether by the army or other non-Einsatzgruppen police units,
jealous of their specific mandate, and absolutely paranoid—perhaps not
surprisingly—about news of the killings being broadcast abroad, and thereby back
to the German public at home, these two prime architects of genocide were caught
between the urgency of eradicating the alleged—above all, Jewish—threat behind
the lines and the potential for massacre they had unleashed getting entirely out of
their hands. In an effort to maintain, as Browning has put it, a 'controlled escalation' of the exercise, Heydrich sought to have the Einsatzgruppen commanders
compile meticulous reports of their operations, including detailed body counts, for
edited RHSA circulation to other executive agency heads in Berlin.[69] To be sure,
some units seem to have got into the quotidian swing of mass executions more
rapidly than others. Einsatzgruppe A, operating in the Baltic, and the largest of the
formations, produced tallies far in excess of, for instance, Einsatzgruppe B, operating alongside the Wehrmacht's central drive towards Moscow and with a particular
remit to eliminate state functionaries on arrival there.[70] Broadly speaking, while
the killings began almost as soon as German forces had crossed the international
border, not until mid-July were Einsatzgruppen units reporting *single* actions, such
as the one which occurred in the Belorussian town of Slonim, with over a thousand
Jewish 'intelligentsia' eliminated.[71]

Does this mean that what was taking place on the ground in late June and early
July 1941 was somehow too embryonic and unformed really to be classed as genocide? Certainly, the executions were mostly limited to men, and then not always
exclusively Jewish men: non-Jews—overall perhaps 10 per cent of the total—could
also fall foul of Heydrich's checklist. The improvisation, even initial circumspec-
tion, with regard to killing a full cohort of arrested men also stands in contrast to
events in the early autumn when entire Jewish communities might be rounded up
and liquidated by these same Einsatzgruppen units in their thousands, or even
tens of thousands. Simply in numerical terms, it is clear that the figure of 62,805
people executed by the squads to the end of July is dwarfed by the hundreds of
thousands of Soviet Jews killed thereafter.[72] The fact that these killings included
the peremptory dispatch of thousands of Jewish Red Army POWs—a facet rather

reminiscent of the *Aghet*, in which Armenian men in uniform were early mass casualties of CUP state policy—is, as in that earlier case, an aspect of unfolding events which has either failed to register or, usually, been rapidly skimmed over in Holocaust studies.

This ought to be surprising given the manner in which the mass murder of up to 8,000 men and boys in Srebrenica in 1995 became a benchmark for genocide in more recent times. We might also note that justification presented by the Bosnian Serb perpetrators or their defence lawyers, that the murdered men represented a potential military threat, were not upheld by the Hague tribunal.[73] Could it be, however, that there remains some lingering sense that the murder of men—soldier or civilian—is less terrible than that of women or children, or, in our case, that at least their dispatch was clinically expedited by professionals without recourse to gratuitous torture in the process? The notion of the Einsatzgruppen personnel as simply conscientious, even emotionless, terminators unflinchingly carrying out orders as commanded, has come under some recent critical scrutiny.[74] Moreover, there is a particular trap in assuming that all the Jewish killings in these early weeks were carried out only by these squads. They most certainly were not. Putting aside the killings by other indigenous rimland militias or vigilantes, to which we will return in Chapter 3, a plethora of army units, Waffen-SS, other non-Einsatzgruppen-attached SD units, military field police, and especially Order Police, committed massacres—whether independently of one another, or closely coordinated.[75] In many of these cases, far from being cold, calculated acts, the participants, officers and men alike, gave free rein to their feelings about Jews with sadomasochistic relish, in the process dreaming up all manner of inventive humiliation of their victims before their gruesome, violent deaths.

One notable example is what took place in Białystok when the formerly Polish city was captured just days into the invasion. With the classic justification that they had been fired upon, men of both Police Battalion 309 and the 221st Security Division rampaged through the Jewish district, shooting indiscriminately, beating up those they could catch, and engaging in games of physical and mental torture in which their victims were required to sing, swear, dance, had their beards set on fire, and were urinated upon. The culmination of this charivari-style episode came when those who had not already been removed from the holding area in the marketplace for shooting in selected sites were driven into the main synagogue—the largest, in fact, in Poland—where, packed full and doused in gasoline, the building was both set on fire and shot at. This was indeed a holocaust. Not less than 2,000 Jewish people, including women and children, died in the 27 June inferno.[76]

Equally significant, however, is the sequel to this event. On 8 July Himmler visited Białystok, followed the next day by Kurt Daluege, head of the Order Police. On these and two subsequent days, up to 3,000 Jewish men, who had been detained and incarcerated in a makeshift camp on the outskirts of the city, were shot by members of two other police battalions, under the supervision of the SD and Security Police. Again, Himmler's imprimatur is evident. Present in Białystok to meet him were the senior military commander of the Rear Army Group Centre, the equivalent head of the Police Regiment Centre, and Erich von dem Bach-Zelewski, the HSSPF for the area: a figure whose centrality in the expansion of Jewish killing would soon bulk large. His orders on 11 July, transmitted via the Police Regiment commander, required all Jews aged seventeen to forty-five convicted of plunder to be shot, a hardly opaque way of saying 'shoot if not all then large numbers of the Jewish men you can lay your hands on'.[77] This clear insistence on accelerating the Jewish body count was also reflected in even higher figures of mass execution— of both Jews and Soviet POWs—in Minsk at this time.[78]

But if the ulterior purpose was to justify a widening of the scope of the killing, the continued emphasis on Jewish *men* carried with it an evolving frustration all of its own. We have already referred to how the mythological aura of Jews *as* Bolsheviks, dating back to 1918, was entirely at odds with the actual declining presence of Jews in political, military, and security roles in the Soviet state. Which, in itself, altered not a jot the RHSA or Wehrmacht desire to have their revenge. The problem was that the development of the USSR over the previous twenty years *had* created structural possibilities for at least a significant proportion of Russian Jewry, in the circumstances of 1941, to escape from Nazi clutches. Having removed all disabilities associated with the tsarist Pale of Settlement and given them, for the first time, equal citizenship, the communist anti-system enabled Jews, at least in principle, to abandon domicile in the moribund *shtetlach* of the rimlands and migrate internally to the big cities closer to, or in, the Russian heartland. As a consequence, by 1939, 86.9 per cent of all Soviet Jews were living in urban areas, above all in Moscow and Leningrad, the latter two of which were never captured by the Nazis.[79] Of course, this would have been of little consolation to those who had moved to other major centres of Jewish settlement, most especially Kiev, Kharkov, Dnepropetrovsk, and Odessa, which did fall. But even then this was not the whole story. Because much of the post-1917 generation of Russian Jewry had successfully assimilated into Soviet life and become an important element of its professional, administrative, and technocratic strata, these Jews would have been amongst those who were prioritized from July onwards in the state's mass evacuations to the east.[80]

Thus, geography and timing were crucial factors which determined whether Jews in this manner, or through their own volition, were able to escape. Broadly speaking, those living furthest away from the initial rapid German thrust into the *kresy*, the Baltic and western Ukraine—and hence favoured by the gradual stiffening of Red Army resistance slowing down the Wehrmacht advance—were the ones most likely to be able find transport to get out and away from danger. Consequently, perhaps as many as half of the Jews in Kiev and Zhitomir were thus able to leave in relatively good order. East of the Dnieper, which the Wehrmacht only began to cross from mid-September, the figure was over 80 per cent, in some cases even 100 per cent.[81] Einsatzgruppe B could hardly conceal its bewilderment when it reported that it was barely possible 'to maintain liquidation figures at their previous levels simply because the Jewish element is to a large extent not present'.[82] A further critical factor in this equation was one of age and gender. In places where they could leave, it was the youngest, most active members of the Jewish population who cleared out. Necessarily, this weighted the exodus heavily towards the younger men who were mobilized into the Red Army, though this would have been of little consolation if they ended up being captured. The evidence suggests that those caught and identified as Jews by the Wehrmacht suffered the most horrible abuse, violence, and degradation before death.[83] One might add that those who survived this fate would also have had slim chances of survival, given the relentless scale of Soviet military loss on the Eastern Front in the subsequent four years of war.

Statistically speaking, however, if the Nazi aim was to destroy an essentially active and, implicitly, largely male Jewish 'enemy', what actually was available to them in the summer of 1941 could be broken down into two major categories. In the first, there were the Jews of what one might call here the inner space of the 'Lands Between'; in other words, the territories absorbed by the Soviets as a consequence of the Nazi–Soviet Pact but where full Soviet assimilation was yet to take hold. This area was rapidly overrun in the initial week of Operation Barbarossa, thus preventing wholesale flight. In the second, in the outer rimlands—those parts of the former Pale which had been firmly under Soviet tutelage since late 1919—or further east still, the profile of the remaining Jewish community by the time the Germans reached them would have been skewed towards women and their children or much older and infirm people. There are some ironies of note here. One is that older Jewish people might have been less ready to flee because (against the grain of the forest-fire spread of Nazi atrocity stories) their own experience of German occupation in the Great War would have suggested to them that another bout of the same, while it be might be harsh, would not be lethal. Another is that eructing the Jews east had been the very thing the Nazis had desired but were stymied from achieving in the period of the Pact. Now, it was movement in this very direction which, for possibly up to 1.5 million Soviet rimland Jewry, offered, if not salvation, then, at the very least, a temporary respite. Finally, the very scale of this evacuation determined that the Nazi ability to strike at the supposed Jewish–Bolshevik jugular was becoming if not exactly mirage-like then certainly at one remove from the best efforts of the Einsatzgruppen.

None of this would ultimately have mattered *for the Nazis* if their timetable for their entry into Moscow and Leningrad had gone to plan. But here lay the rub. Hitler's invasion of the USSR was predicated in the first place on one enormous gamble. He knew full well from his military technical advisers that there could be no prolonged successful war in Russia, and certainly not with the Anglo-American build-up at his back. Everything was dependent, therefore, on a surprise assault of such initial weight, speed, and ferocity that his Panzer Groups would be inside the gates of Moscow within six, eight, perhaps, ten weeks. Of course, Napoleon had achieved a comparatively similar feat in 1812 but still lost the battle for Russia and, thus, ultimately, his hold on the European continent. With the largest armed force ever marshalled—3.6 million Germans and Axis allies comprising 153 divisions, and with corresponding air power to match—the optimistic, indeed hubristic, side of Hitler and his generals told them that there would be no repeat of that scenario. Nor would they end up, as in 1914–18, in a static war of attrition in which an unstaunched haemorrhage of German manpower and *matériel* would be set against the industrialized, resource-rich build-up of the powers arrayed against them. Instead, the Wehrmacht military blow at the outset would be so crushing that once the Soviet enemy was down and out, the London–Washington alignment, too, would be falling over itself to make terms with the new masters of 'the Heartland'.[84]

The first couple of weeks of the campaign confirmed the Nazi forecast to a T. On 4 July—US Independence Day—having received glowing reports of imminent victory from General Halder, chief of the army staff, a euphoric Hitler was pronouncing that the Soviets had 'virtually lost' the war.[85] The euphoria, however, proved premature. Just the day before, Stalin, whose silence up to this moment in the campaign had been ominously deafening, broadcast to the *nation*. He stated that the people would fight a patriotic struggle without mercy, in which, led by himself as supreme warlord, those who deserted or showed dereliction of duty would be dealt with, scorched earth tactics would be the order of the day, and partisan warfare would be waged behind enemy lines.[86] Was this simply the last desperate ravings of a terrified paper tiger of a leader as the Soviet edifice collapsed around him? Vast swathes of his forces continued to be annihilated in the days and weeks that followed, just as they had been beforehand. But within ten or eleven days, from the early July low point, OKW and OKH (the Eastern Front High Command) assessments of what was transpiring at the front dampened the formerly upbeat German mood. The Red Army had been pulverized but not completely routed or exterminated. On the contrary, having either fought their way out of encirclement, even where this involved conceding space, Soviet armies had, in places, regrouped and *attacked*. The situation also showed in the losses on the Wehrmacht side. German casualties by the end of July had risen to 213,000, some 15 per cent of the invasion force.[87] Worse was the logistical crisis. Not only were there no combat manpower reserves to fall back on, but the necessity to refit and resupply an army already at geographical and material overstretch were evident signs that there was no obvious Plan B if Operation Barbarossa failed. Food and fuel supplies could not be sustained if a long war was now in prospect. Nor would Germany be able to keep pace with the rate at which Soviet factories—already rapidly relocating to the Urals and beyond—could turn out new tanks and aircraft; not to mention those of the Soviets' new or soon-to-be British and American allies.[88]

For the first time in more than twenty months of almost continuous success, Hitler found his war plans not simply being militarily resisted, but in danger of reaching a dead end. And, according to the generals closest to him such as Jodl, Hitler knew full well 'that the war was lost' long before others had dared to contemplate it.[89] Even so, Admiral Canaris was, at the time, noting the nervous atmosphere in Hitler's headquarters and the wider awareness there that the campaign, instead of being concluded 'according to the rules of the game', was leading rather 'to a strengthening of Bolshevism'.[90]

It is in this context that we might consider the now shifting contours of the Jewish killing. Up to this point the Nazi war machine had been murdering Soviet Jews because its leading military and security strata accepted the Hitler view that it was both a necessary strategic subtext of the invasion, and justified retribution for

1918. The intended result was a form of extended elitocide, though the actuality of the killing tells us everything about Nazi projection and paranoia and absolutely nothing about the victims themselves. Even so, looked at through the Nazi prism, the mass murder of male Jews in June–July 1941 was clearly making no difference to the developing course of the war, or the threat of partisan attack in the rear. As for the sweetness of revenge, that was frustrated, too, by the elusiveness of the defined commissar-cum-intelligentsia enemy. Of course, officially the campaign was still on course. Russia would be defeated. Which, in turn, meant that Heydrich's comprehensive remit for a 'Final Solution'—confirmed again by Goering at the end of July—would be fulfilled.[91] But just as the armed forces chiefs were already wrestling with the knowledge that the Wehrmacht would be fighting a very different war from the one they had anticipated (and that this indeed potentially involved a *Götterdämmerung*-style conclusion), so, in the same 'real time', Hitler and his immediate entourage were equally searching for an appropriate way of translating into action their bottomless reservoir of hatred against the cosmic enemy who, yet again, had diabolically denied Germany its redemption.

THE SHIFT TO TOTAL GENOCIDE

How much importance should we attribute to the presence of Himmler at Hitler's East Prussian headquarters—the 'Wolf's Lair'—during a five-day period in mid-July? 'Himmler's appointment diary regarding Hitler and the Jewish Question', Mark Roseman informs us, is 'abbreviated and cryptic.'[92] So what actually passed between them at this moment can only be surmised. What we do know is that at a meeting of the core Nazi leadership, which Hitler addressed on 16 July (though in this case minus Himmler), the Führer went off into a grandiose flight of fancy about creating a 'Garden of Eden' in the east, only to then go on to specify all the 'necessary measures'—including shootings and forced resettlements—which would be required to arrive at a 'final settlement'. Fortunately, in Hitler's view, through ordering partisan warfare Stalin had provided the perfect pretext to exterminate anyone not just hostile but who even 'looks sideways at us'.[93] On the very next day Himmler's responsibility for all security as well as settlement policy throughout the entirety of Soviet territories was formalized by decree. On the latter score, Himmler had seemingly obtained if not quite carte-blanche political control for the east, then sufficient authority to pursue his own grandiose racial project for the 'Germanization' of the entire region. But there was also that immediate if linked priority: the supposed partisan threat. On this score, Himmler's response was to go into accelerated overdrive, with a huge build-up of SS and other forces now specifically assigned to the task.[94]

To paraphrase: the cover of an alleged behind-the-lines insurgency in the context of an actual, self-inflicted military crisis became, through the person of Himmler, the trigger for a seismic shift *towards* total Jewish genocide. But part of the problem for the Nazis writ large (and as a consequence for those studying them) is that they *already* had a programme for the 'Final Solution': mass European

Jewish evacuation. Judging from what Hitler is recorded to have said to a visiting Croatian, Marshal Slavko Kvaternik, just a few days later, nothing had essentially changed: 'Where one will send the Jews, to Siberia or Madagascar is all the same.'[95] But then Hitler repeated the same mantra on at least two occasions to members of his close circle in early 1942, that is, when the European Jewish, not just Soviet Jewish, mass murder was already well advanced.[96] Was Hitler on these later occasions simply being disingenuous, deluded, or just plain contradictory? Or might we equally read into his earlier comments to Kvaternik about the Jews being a source of bacteria which needed to be cleared out a scarcely oblique reference to the emerging—or possibly pre-existing—Nazi aim to physically obliterate them? Of course, Jews as a bacillus of social decomposition was an all too favourite Hitler trope, and Kvaternik, in July 1941, was not its only recipient.[97] Indeed, it appeared again in a conversation with a visiting foreign supporter in February 1942, with the clear implication that the correct bacteriological response was elimination. Yet this was itself not very long after Hitler had been holding forth about the Jews *leaving* Europe.[98]

Is all this simply a case of mixed messages, or further evidence that Hitler's erratic commentary is far from the best guide to the evolution of Nazi Jewish policy? Functionalist historians have, for decades, suggestively worked their way around the 'Hitler problem', not least through showing how the wider Nazi apparatus—certainly with Himmler and Heydrich at the 'centre', but also security personnel, Wehrmacht officers, and administrators at the 'periphery'—sought, where necessary, to improvise solutions in response to the growing crescendo of contingencies on the ground: the cumulative radicalization of which coalesced into a programme of extermination.[99] A recent refinement of this argument has been made by Michael Mann with regard to all manner of states which embark on what he describes as 'murderous cleansing'. This occurs, suggests Mann, as a Plan C or D, when prior planned solutions of a repressive but non-exterminatory type, or their initial adaptation, cannot be implemented due to 'the unintended consequences of a series of interactions yielding escalation'.[100] The most extraordinary aspect of the Nazi case, following the Mann model, would be the lack of any real Nazi–Jewish interaction from the latter side—the Soviet state providing the actual replacement protagonist along with the 'key unintended consequence' in its fightback against Nazi invasion. However, Mann, like successive generations of functionalists before him, still assumes a progression—in effect, a step-by-step sequence—which leads to an ultimate threshold.

Supposing, however, that the practice (rather than the model) is one where the tension between what was intended and what develops out of the contingent crisis or crises is never properly resolved, the result of which is that the prototype model and its bastard offspring (singular or plural) continue to jostle with each other for dominance against a backdrop of ongoing and highly destabilizing emergency? That might suggest that there can be no exact moment when a reformulated policy becomes fixed, or even that we cannot properly call this reformulation a 'policy' at all. This does not preclude moments of radical crisis response with long-term outcomes. Mid-July 1941 is clearly one of them, and we might firmly agree with

Browning that it constitutes a 'turning point'.[101] After that, Nazi behaviour towards Jews—certainly in Russia, and arguably more broadly still—fundamentally, irrevocably changes. But this alone does not deliver a new *coherence*. Rather, it acts as an intrusive screen to, and certainly destabilizer of, the earlier plan. But without necessarily superseding it.

We might describe this tension as one between contingent responses to the 'now' and projected, long-term planning for the 'later'. The 'later' remained technically in the hands of Heydrich, given his mandate to achieve an all-European solution of the 'problem' *at the end of the war*. That the 'later' programme was still active during the July 1941 emergency is evident both from the additional expertise brought into Eichmann's Referat IVB4 with regard to legalizing the extraction of Jews from foreign countries, and the new document of authorization Heydrich elicited from Goering to pursue 'the necessary preparations with regard to organisational, technical and material matters' for an overall solution 'within the German sphere of influence in Europe'.[102] We might, indeed, read the renewed commitment to this programme as causally related to Hitler's mid-July vituperations against the Jews, which we may surmise were also uttered in person to Himmler. Heydrich's, aim, of course, was not to have the deportations festering as some remote plan for the distant future. Stymied throughout 1940 on this very matter, his aim was, as it was that of the restive Gauleiters in annexed Poland, not to mention the Frank entourage in the General Government, to move without delay towards a rapid implementation of Jewish 'emigration' and 'evacuation'—that is, from Europe into Russia—and so make the 'later' into *'now'*. But so long as western Russia remained a battle zone, the RHSA desiderata remained on hold. In mid-August, Hitler himself reaffirmed that there would be no green light until the war was over.[103]

But if this simply confirms the fact that, in the high summer of 1941, all immediate Nazi attention was on 'Russia' *as* 'now', and thus separate from the broader Jewish deportation programme, the realization that there might be no successful conclusion to its conquest posed yet another dilemma. To date, Nazi plans for the 'Final Solution' had been predicated on the *European* Jews being eructed somewhere 'far': most obviously into the extreme Gulag-ridden outer space of 'the Heartland', or perhaps still, as Hitler indicated to Kvaternik—assuming the Western Allies could be made to submit—to somewhere on the colonial periphery. And up to this point the possibility that the course of the war might act as a barrier to this central Nazi purpose had been unthinkable. But Soviet state resistance thrust to the fore not only that possibility, but with it, its fundamental geographical premise. If the 'Final Solution' could not be resolved in the 'far' would it actually have to be enacted closer to home in somewhere 'near', most obviously in the rimlands?

Over the next few months 'now' and 'later', 'far' and 'near' operated neither as mutually reinforcing, twin-track policies, nor as ones which were bound to somehow converge at some point on the distant horizon into joined-up policy. Instead, the direction of travel was ultimately determined by the exigencies of failing war, and it was this which concertinaed the 'later' of deportations into the 'now' of wholesale extermination, not in the 'far' but the 'near'. It was this exigent aspect, too, which worked its way through into a further set of queries for the regime leadership: 'how' would the European Jews be killed, and by 'whom'? But it is debatable that, even with the Wannsee Conference in January 1942, this amounted to a firm and comprehensive clarification of the ongoing process of destruction. Only with the privilege of hindsight do we assume that there must have been some moment when it all came together into some single, definable, and finalized set of orders or instructions.[104] If it did, it is unlikely, however, that this occurred in July or August 1941. The leadership was much more fixated on the immediate *military* situation: in other words, the 'now'.

Having, on this score, been hoist by their own petard, the Nazi leadership's answer by way of redoubling the exterminatory drive against *Russian* Jewry marks the absolute vacuity of its thinking. But then, these men were fanatics and, as George Santayana said, 'fanatics always step up their efforts as the goal recedes'.[105] The flurry of new orders from 17 July included one transmitted through OKW which gave the go-ahead for Heydrich's special commandos to screen the POW camps for the removal and elimination of dangerous political elements, thus precipitating the spiralling mass murder of surrendered Red Army men.[106] But equally significant at this moment was the activation of the Kommandostab Reichsführer-SS, the 25,000-strong combination of various Waffen-SS brigades and other units under Himmler's personal, executive command, formed two months earlier.[107] With Bach-Zelewski given charge of the operation, a major part of the force was assigned to sweep the Pripet marshes, technically under the control of the Wehrmacht Rear Army Area Centre but now handed across to the Kommandostab: ostensibly to clear the region of partisans. This could be read as classic counter-insurgency, legitimized by the supposed insurgent threat close to a major communications route into the Russian interior. But over and beyond the fact that this simply deflected attention away from the decisive military engagements being fought between the Red Army and Wehrmacht further to the east, the Pripet sideshow was little more than a Himmler experiment to find out how Jews, in particular, might be liquidated under cover of a pacification exercise. Over a several-day period at the onset of August, and at almost no loss on the German side, the Waffen-SS units, supported by Order Police and regular army, killed around 3,000 'Jews and partisans'. The tally included women and children. More significantly perhaps, Kommandostab units involved in the Pripet operation were then deployed to Pinsk, the major regional centre, where over subsequent days 10,000 Jews, mostly men but also women and children, and including old people, were murdered.[108]

Was this a radical departure, or would that be to overstate the case? At the very first recorded mass killing of Jews in the course of Operation Barbarossa—on 24 June, in the Lithuanian town of Garsden (Gargždai), just across the German border from Tilsit—a woman and at least one child were among the 201 Jewish people executed by firing squad, ostensibly as a reprisal for the Wehrmacht soldiers killed and wounded in the taking of the town. Incidentally, this was not directly an Einsatzgruppe A action but one initiated by local Tilsit and Memel security police units, out of which an additional Einsatzkommando 'Tilsit' was born.

Certainly, by mid-July, this unit's tally alone had reached over 3,300 victims, including *some* women.[109]

Indeed, there was nothing to exclude females, or even minors, in principle, from the killing orders. The notion that all Jews, of whatever age or gender, were implicated in the sabotage or provocation being worked against Germany was standard Wehrmacht and security services fare. When thousands of Jews, both men and women, were killed in a Kommandostab anti-partisan 'cleansing action' more or less simultaneous to that of the Pripet region, this time in the Sluch valley area in north-western Ukraine, the commander of HSSPF Russia South, Friedrich Jeckeln, reported their crime as that of 'supporting Bolshevism and Bolshevik partisans'.[110] A flurry of similar, Einsatzkommando-perpetrated massacres, again embracing women and children, took place either at the very end of July, or early in August, in various other small towns in Belorussia, and in both Lithuania and Latvia. The justification was that these were 'pacification' campaigns.[111] By the same token, the incarceration—and then murder—of the Serbian Jewish women and children at Semlin was on the grounds that they were 'proven to be pillars of the intelligence service of the insurgents'.[112] Perhaps we can read into such orders a sort of circular Nazi apologia to the effect that, once the men had been killed, following through with 'the women and children did not appear to be a major step', or that, as 'useless eaters'—a mantra repeatedly invoked by Wehrmacht troops in the face of anticipated food supply shortages—eliminating them was the appropriate 'utilitarian' action.[113] But if the latter was true, the 'logical' next step would have been to close off the Jewish quarters and let the women and children within them starve to death, as had been the case with the majority of the captured POWs, and as would also be the case, in the following months, with other Soviet city dwellers under German occupation.[114]

But this was clearly *not* the premise upon which the Reichsführer-SS was operating. Starvation was considered too good for the Jewish families and communities. Only direct, physical murder would suffice for the crimes they had committed or would commit if allowed to survive. Looking back over the landscape of Jewish destruction from November 1943 Himmler infamously explained himself thus, in the course of a secret speech to fellow SS leaders:

> ...we know how difficult we would have made it for ourselves, if on top of the bombing raids, the burdens and the deprivations of war, we still had Jews today in every town as secret saboteurs, agitators and troublemakers. We would now have probably reached the 1916–17 stage when the Jews were still part of the body of the German nation...We had the moral right, we had the duty to our people to destroy this people which wanted to destroy us. All in all, we can say that we have fulfilled this most difficult duty for the love of our people.[115]

Judging from the tone of Himmler's retrospective self-exculpation, the notion that the shift into killing of women and children was just some incremental step-change cannot be sustained.[116] He himself, certainly, was entirely cognisant of the fact, at the time of the Pripet operation, that he was moving onto new, psychologically as well as practically unstable ground, and tried to find a formula by which he could somehow make what he was ordering less unpalatable. His verbal directive, 'All Jews must be shot. Drive the female Jews into the swamps', reeks of a mental effort to imagine the women dying but without tainting the hands of his precious fighters. It has been noted many times that Himmler was only interested in ministering to the welfare of his SS minions and worried not a jot about the mass murder of his victims.[117] But this may only be half the story. The driving into the swamps trope—repeated to, of all people, the arch-*génocidaire* Jeckeln in early 1942—was clearly one way by which Himmler tried to distance the killers from the killed, just as his post-Pripet directive to Arthur Nebe, at that point commander of Einsatzgruppe B, to look into alternative killing methods, including a refinement of the gassing technique, was another.[118] Himmler's insistent repetition, in his long-winded speeches, on the importance of his men maintaining *Anständigkeit*, a personal sense of 'decency' or 'moral virtue' in the face of their mission,[119] represents a suitable case for the psychiatrist's couch on its own.

What is without doubt, however, is that the passage from the killing of Jewish men to whole communities, as a consequence of the extended killing directive, was not a seamless one. Men of Police Battalion 322 who, up to this point, were reported by their commander to have carried out repeated executions of males, including adolescents as well as their family elders, 'smoothly and without incident', were, when it came to executions of females and their children, behaving quite differently. The first occasion on which the Battalion carried out such an order, at Kobryn, close to Brest, in mid-August, the policemen evinced varying degrees of psychological resistance, failed to shoot straight, thus exacerbating the gruesome messiness of the executions, and, as a result, began to display symptoms ranging from vomiting through sleep deprivation and stomach pains, to complete nervous collapse.[120] On another occasion in August, in the small town of Belaya Tserkov in central Ukraine, when a *Sonderkommando* unit of Einsatzgruppe C, having dispatched the men and most of the women, were about to follow through with the children, there was an altercation involving—amongst others—Wehrmacht chaplains. The dispute was eventually resolved by the general in charge, von Reichenau: in favour of the *Sonderkommando*.[121] Other Wehrmacht security officials excused such 'remedial actions' by claiming that 'the provisioning of Jewish children and infants left without parents sometimes created difficulties'.[122] On occasion, individuals in their own right protested that they could not be party to what was taking place. When the mass killings of women and children reached Semlin in Serbia by way of the Sauer gas van, the camp commandant asked for a transfer. Denied this request he then 'constructed an elaborate fiction, convincing the women that they were being transferred to another camp in Serbia'.[123]

Clearly, adjustment to the new reality was more difficult for some of those in uniform than for others, involving all manner of convoluted apologetics or denial. None of this, however, represented more than mere interruption to a standardization of procedure. To be sure, it did not happen all at once or across the entirety of the Russian zone of occupation. The role of particular individuals is noteworthy in forcing the pace. One was Jeckeln. Operating as Himmler's 'direct and personal representative',[124] he had amassed thousands of SS and Order Police, army security personnel, but also now hastily enlisted Ukrainian auxiliary police to quite consciously liquidate the Jewish communities in the path of the Wehrmacht's drive on Kiev. *Sonderkommando* units such as Sk4a under the command of SS-Colonel Paul Blobel—the perpetrators of Belaya Tserkov—readily fell in with this wider remit, though, perhaps significantly, Blobel always had on hand a plentiful supply of schnapps for his shooters, as compensation for their pains.[125] The death toll in the destruction of entire Jewish communities in the central Ukrainian belt correspondingly began to escalate exponentially from late July through the latter part of August and into early September. But no longer as a result of the Einsatzgruppen alone: the first single *Aktion* to exceed the 10,000 figure for those killed—in fact vastly so—at Kamianets-Podilsky, at the end of August, though carried out under the authority and direct supervision of Jeckeln, was largely the work of another Order Police Battalion, 320.[126]

It was not just the scale of the Kamianets-Podilsky massacre which marked it out as a major transitional event. It was also a case of location—and timing. Way back from the battle zone, close to the intersection of the pre-war Polish, Soviet, and Rumanian borders, the town was a place that had become inundated with Jewish refugees forced from pillar by post by both Hungarian and Rumanian authorities. Jeckeln's sense of urgency to have both them and their indigenous Jewish counterparts liquidated was undoubtedly driven by an awareness that the town was about to be handed over to German civil administration on 1 September. The expectation of massive German resettlement of regions, such as the Baltic, may equally have been anticipated in the very precise orders at the beginning of September for the liquidation of all Jews in Lithuania.[127] Further, south, in eastern Galicia, again by this time far from the battlefront, and in a region actually assigned for incorporation into the General Government, it was more localized concern, that there was not enough room in the planned ghetto at Stanisławów, which galvanized the regional SSPF, Fritz Katzmann, into conducting a liquidation of 10,000 'superfluous' Jews in one massive 'Bloody Sunday', in early October.[128] The Stanisławów massacre is notable less for the death toll—by this time the scale of such killings was often being reached and sometimes surpassed in the Jeckeln- or Einsatzgruppen-led massacres to the east—than for the seepage of this al fresco style of mass murder back westwards across the Nazis' own notional internal boundaries. Not only, thus, was the geographical range of the mass murder widening, but it was involving SD personnel who, to date, had been largely standing on the sidelines. Here was further indication that the security 'men on the spot' had imbibed the 'correct' script about the collective Jewish danger to the rear, or even their threat to 'food security'. Or, put in more personal terms, a cohort of supposedly responsible individuals was assured that they would not only not face internal discipline or prosecution for taking the initiative, but would be positively rewarded in terms of their career prospects through the most active and forceful interpretation of the necessary measures for dealing with the Jews on their patch. Oberführer Katzmann, soon to be elevated to Brigadeführer for his contribution to solving to the Jewish question in Galicia, certainly falls within this category.[129]

Even so, Katzmann, like the others, had to resolve issues of technique if not emotional turmoil in preparation for first-time massacres. The local security police chief for Stanislawów, Hans Krüger, assisted by conducting a smaller practice run on the nearby town of Nadworna, a few days earlier, which he then dissected with Katzmann.[130] In the wake of the Pripet operation, a joint army and SS training session in Mogilev, in late September, had considered best practice for the 'screening of population', with Bach-Zelewski and Nebe closely involved. The workshop concluded with a 'hands-on' live exercise in which 'thirteen male Jews and nineteen Jewish women were shot in cooperation with the Security Service'.[131] Meanwhile, Blobel, like Ohlendorf, fretted over shooting victims in the back of the neck—too much like an NKVD operation and, anyway, bound to reinforce feelings of 'personal responsibility'—experimenting instead with techniques such as the 'sardine method', in which batch upon batch of victims were made to lie down in a ditch and then were killed by cross-fire from above.[132] There were, of course, occasions when formalities were rapidly dispensed with. One such was the massacre at Babi Yar. Fired up by the havoc wreaked by delayed action mines laid by the NKVD, which killed hundreds of German officers and men in Kiev soon after its capture in late September, Blobel's Sk4a and Order Police units, under the direct supervision of Jeckeln, but with close Wehrmacht support supplied by Reichenau, marched the entire remaining Jewish population of the city into the nearby ravine. Here, in the space of two days—29 and 30 September—they machine-gunned to death 33,771 of them: the dead, the fatally injured, the old, and newborn dropping together, layer upon layer, into the ravine.[133]

Babi Yar, not surprisingly, has become an iconic event in Holocaust remembrance.[134] More Jewish people died in this single Nazi act of mass atrocity than on any other such occasion—though, as we will see Chapter 3, with at least one, possibly two, other atrocities committed by the Rumanians soon after exceeding it in terms of sheer numbers. But while the vengeful wrath and fury of the participants in this one episode are clearly central to its hideousness, it is entirely improbable that there would have been no mass murder of Kievan Jews had the Wehrmacht occupation of the city proceeded without incident. In the western and central Ukrainian area Einsatzkommando or Order Police battalions working to Jeckeln's command had, in the month prior to Babi Yar, already conducted mass—though not quite total—eliminations of major Jewish communities including Berdichev, Vinnitsa, and Zhitomir, and many smaller ones too numerous to list. Across the Dnieper, the process was resumed in October at Dnepropetrovsk and Kharkov, and in the following month in a briefly captured Rostov.[135] By this time, too, Einsatzgruppe D had penetrated the Crimea and was mass-murdering not only Jews but the crypto-Jewish Karaim and Krymchaks of the area.[136] Meanwhile, much of Jeckeln's forces had looped back on themselves to eradicate the historic Jewish communities of Volhynia centred around Rovno (Rivne), some of which had escaped the initial Einsatzgruppen thrust.[137]

All this might suggest that, in the course of a few months, the extermination of Russian Jewish communities had become generalized, even routine—which would make Babi Yar an extreme incident on the Richter-type scale but hardly unique.

However, the politico-military ramifications of the battle to take Kiev might remind us just how critical contingent circumstances were in fuelling the eliminationist drive. This necessarily takes us back to Hitler's centrality in its further *expansion*. Wracked by one of his periods of anxiety-induced depression in late August[138]—one domestic contributory factor to which was surely the growing von Galen-led clamour against the Aktion T-4 programme—Hitler would have felt even more intensely thwarted by the Wehrmacht failure to deliver the necessary knockout blow against the Red Army. In early September, German prospects again began looking up in response to his orders to prioritize the advance in the southern sector in the direction of the crucial oil reserves of the Caucasus—actually against the better judgement of his generals. But no sooner was this put into action than it became clear that the first immediate objective, the envelopment of the Soviet armies in the Kiev pocket, was meeting too fierce a resistance to stick to its tight schedule. A momentous victory was eventually wrested, but not until the end of September. This left little or no time for the army's Panzer units to regroup for the breakneck assault on Moscow—Operation Typhoon—which was now what Hitler gambled everything upon to bring the war to an end before the Russian winter set in.[139]

Nazi frustrations were clearly taken out on the Jews of Kiev, as throughout occupied Russia. But killing Jews could not alter the bitter truth: Hitler was running out of options. His musing about a negotiated peace with Stalin during the period of the first July crisis had never been followed through,[140] with the result that the drawing together of the Big Three Alliance against him was becoming quite palpable. The USA did not technically join the war until Japan unleashed its December attack on Pearl Harbor—in itself a rather significant decision on the part of Tokyo *not* to come to the assistance of its Tripartite ally in the Soviet theatre. But the sealing of the relationship between the USA and Britain, exemplified by the Atlantic Charter declaration in mid-August, was succeeded in early October by the opening of US 'Lend-Lease' deliveries to the USSR. Arguably much worse for Hitler in the immediate term, the drive on Moscow was dramatically repulsed two months later, almost at its very gates. A Germany ill-equipped for war on a wintertime Eastern Front, not to mention without sufficient resources to sustain it in the medium let alone longer term, could now only look forward to a war of attrition continuing into 1942 and probably well beyond.

Hitler's mindset, thus, would already have been clouded by dark thoughts of Nemesis when Stalin invoked his own little piece of retaliation against Germans on Soviet soil. The Kremlin insinuation that the ethnic German communities of the Volga region were a security threat was no more nor less than what Berlin had been saying about Jews. But the dramatic mid-September deportations of hundreds of thousands of Volksdeutsche to Siberia was not only a reminder that two could play at games of collective people punishment but may well have dredged up some of Hitler's unspoken frustrations as well as anxieties about the now thoroughly redundant Nazi–Soviet Pact. After all, German kith and kin were now being transported in conditions of immeasurable misery and danger to the Soviet east, when it was Central European Jews who *should* have been cleared off in that direction, as quid pro quo for the 'return' of the rimlands Volksdeutsche in 1939 and 1940. Or, alternatively, the Jews should have been heading in that direction *now* if Barbarossa had gone to plan. It would doubtless not have taken much for Hitler to respond affirmatively to Rosenberg's urgings that Jews from Central Europe should be deported to the east in reprisal for the Volga clearances.[141] Over the following weeks, increasingly unhinged by the military crisis engulfing them, his generals at the front would issue their own shrill, utterly projective calls for exterminatory retaliation against the Jewish–Bolshevik enemy which had resisted them. Hitler, in private, was equally consumed by notions of Jewish responsibility for German lives and losses.[142]

Even so, his tit-for-tat order to deport the entirety of the Jews from the Greater German Reich to the east could not but be a momentous one. Putting aside the logistics of where exactly they were going to be transported to, here was a complete volte-face on Hitler's commitment to only resolve *this* problem when the war itself was resolved. One might add that, so far, German, Czech, and Austrian Jewry, while they remained firmly under the Nazi cosh, were *not* being mass murdered as were their fellow Jews in Russia. Indeed, even as Operation Barbarossa was getting under way there were still small numbers of German Jews with official Nazi permits to travel, who were making their way via Siberia to safe havens in the Far East. Even more paradoxically, and bizarrely, up to 30,000 of those who remained in Berlin were filling the jobs of other skilled Germans soaked up by mobilization—in, of all areas, arms production![143]

To be sure pressures for getting rid of the Jews—and not just those in the Greater Reich area—were building up steadily from below. The German authorities in occupied France, for instance, had been interning foreign Jews in camps since May. The clamour from this quarter for the Jews' eastward removal was closely linked to the argument that 'hostage deportations' would act as an exemplary warning in the face of a growing post-Operation Barbarossa crescendo of French anti-German sabotage and assassinations—'naturally' held to be the responsibility of communists, a.k.a Jews.[144] The problem with the hostage argument, however, was that it lost all bite if everybody was deported. After all, it was by the threat, not the execution, of deportation that Hitler had sought to blackmail the West, more specifically the USA, into caving in to Nazi demands before and during the early course of the war. Peter Longerich has persuasively argued that the new wave of deportations very publicly set in train in the full glare of international, in other words, US, press coverage on the 15 October, were a shot, one might say Hitler's final shot, across Washington's bows, against its entry into the war.[145] But to hint at the concrete enactment of his prophecy of destruction in this way, while at same time blaming the US thraldom to 'world Jewry' for it, was equally to confirm that his policy of blackmail was effectively exhausted. Once begun, the deportations were evidence enough that Hitler had finally and irrevocably burnt his bridges to the Western system leaders. Indeed, with the recognition that the Americans, British, *and* Soviets were now part of the same alliance nothing prevented the collapsing, in principle, of any distinction between Nazi treatment of Soviet Jewry, on the one hand, the rest on the other.

But, arguably, this is to overstate the case. A decision had been made for the deportation of European Jewry, not its wholesale extermination. In the absence of a coherent or streamlined all-Jewish policy, there was no prescription which stated that what had been done to the Jews in Russia would now be automatically applied to the remainder. Certainly, the division between the separate compartments in which the two groups had travelled thus far—as determined by the circumstantial distinction between 'now' and 'later'—was, by late 1941, looking decidedly ragged. But by then, the realities of war in the east were intervening to ensure that whatever the actual fate of the non-Soviet Jews would be, it would be enacted not in the 'far' heartland, but the 'near' rimlands.

*

The immediate problem was that Hitler's deportation order threatened to repeat the entire logistical logjam of 1939–40 all over again. Not surprisingly, those who felt the matter most keenly were the administrators in the annexed western parts of Poland, more exactly in places such as Łódź, who were likely to receive the bulk of the deportees. During the summer their immediate challenge had been how to accommodate the latest influx of Volksdeutsche from the Bukovina and Bessarabia. Greiser had freely encouraged his advisers to brainstorm the problem, and the SD chief and head of UZW in Posen, Rolf-Heinz Höppner, had gone to the trouble of summarizing to Eichmann some of their blue-sky thinking. Supposing all the Jews in the Warthegau were put to work in a huge labour camp, the women of childbearing age sterilized, and those not capable of work killed 'by some quick-acting agent'? It would be better, opined Höppner, than starving them to death, and would, in the space of a generation, solve the Jewish problem. Fishing for Eichmann's opinion, Höppner stated that these ideas all sounded somewhat 'fantastical' though adding, 'in my view they are thoroughly practicable'.[146]

We do not know if Eichmann replied to this particular missive. What we do know is that Höppner remained in close contact with his RHSA superiors and, in a further memorandum to them in early September, asked an extremely pertinent question regarding what was 'to be done in the end with these displaced populations that are undesirable for the Greater German settlement areas. Is the goal to permanently secure them some sort of subsistence, or should they be totally eradicated?'[147] With concerns about not only space but available food clearly uppermost in the minds of the Greiser's senior technocratic staff, Höppner's question might be interpreted as an extreme example of triage-informed utilitarianism, though now with *all* Jews, including the able-bodied, potentially slated for immediate elimination. But as the trains began to roll from Central Europe in the direction of the Warthegau, the implication was hardly any longer in the realms of fantasy. Whatever the long-term solution with regard to the majority of European Jews, if some were going to be dumped on the Warthegau, those already there would have to make way for them. For the likes of Höppner, what that meant in practice was clear. Carrying it through may at this point have been a matter of improvisation—with gassing not shooting the method. However, if the initiative came from local officials, authorization for the elimination of 100,000 indigenous Polish Jews, along with the provision of the gassing vans, came firmly from Himmler.[148]

Improvised approaches of this nature assumed that Eichmann's bureau in Berlin would be able to work hand in glove with administrators on the ground, overcoming logistical difficulties as they arose. The General Government as a deportation hub—temporary or otherwise—remained, at this juncture, firmly out of bounds. 'Evacuating' the Jews deep into the Ukraine—a possibility Heydrich seems to have entertained in October[149]—was even more chimerical, with war still raging in its eastern half. There was, however, to the north, the 'pacified' area of the recently captured Soviet rimlands, which had just been handed over to civil administration as the Reichskommissariat Ostland. Here the important centres of Minsk, Kovno, and Riga were ones to which rail transports could conceivably be directed. The deportee load could thus be spread eastwards from Łódź, and, given that killings of indigenous Soviet Jews in at least two of these cities had already begun, making room for the newly arrived deportees on paper looked plausible. That said, the reaction from local officials from the Reichskommissar downwards predictably adopted the same negative tenor as had come from the administration in occupied Poland over the previous two years. In place of an easy life with plenty of scope for self-aggrandizement, the new rulers of the east found themselves landed with a logistical burden of immense proportions. What was really significant, however, was not that they were unable do anything to stop the deportations per se, but the issue at the heart of their objection: the expansion of the subsequent killing to include *German* Jews.

To say that the killing began by misadventure is to exaggerate. Some thirty-odd transports were delivered to Łódź and Minsk between mid-October and mid-November 'without incident'. But with local administrators distancing themselves, to varying degrees, from involvement in the elimination of the ghettoized Jews in the Ostland to make way for the incomers, the task fell to none other than Jeckeln, now redeployed as HSSPF for the Baltic region. However, as the planned ghetto area for Reich Jews in Riga was not yet ready when a further five transports arrived there in late November, they were re-routed to Kovno where Jeckeln, on his own initiative, had them liquidated. Himmler got wind of what had happened and telegraphed Heydrich, expressly forbidding the liquidation of the following transport from Berlin. For whatever reason, including the possibility that he had not received the message, Jeckeln had these one thousand Jews murdered on their arrival in Riga. For his pains he was personally reprimanded by Himmler.[150]

Why the fuss? There was no official objection when Jeckeln proceeded almost immediately thereafter to exterminate 14,000 of Riga's remaining Jews in the same Rumbuli pits where those from Berlin had just been murdered. Nor, looking back across the carnage of the last few months, had the massacre of foreign Jewish nationals in the occupied Soviet sphere elicited wider dismay—not, for instance, when German-speaking Memel Jews had been executed at Garsden; nor most certainly, when the much vaster numbers of displaced Jews, mostly from the Carpatho-Rus, were massacred, again by Jeckeln, at Kamianets-Podilsky. But then in both these instances, the victims were identified (correctly or incorrectly) as *Ostjuden*. What seems to have stuck in the gullet of administrators in the Ostland, not to mention back in Berlin, was the fact that the Jews from the transport killed in Riga were ones with whom *they themselves* might identify, including decorated and wounded Great War veterans, some with Iron Crosses, and others who were obviously *Mischlinge*. 'I am surely hard and prepared to help solve the Jewish question', wrote Wilhelm Kube, head of the newly inaugurated commissariat in what was now deemed White Russia, to his immediate superior, 'but men who come from our own culture are something different from the indigenous animal-like hordes.'[151] Three days later, Bernhard Lösener, the Interior Ministry's Jewish expert no less, having noted the disquiet in Berlin circles at the news from Riga, almost resigned. For all the supposed racial distinctions repeatedly touted by the regime and the incessant Goebbels propaganda which went with it, there were those, it appeared, especially of the older generation within the political, military, and administrative elite, who had not entirely imbibed Hitler's 'Jewish' discourse.[152]

By the same token, however, such reservations were clearly circumscribed by these people's own cultural prejudices. There had been no elite revolt against the killing of Soviet Jews, even, when push came to shove, women and children. The sensitivity appeared to be about identifiable *Westjuden*: cultured, cultivated, socially respectable *individuals*, who went to the opera, had nice manners, perhaps even, in former times, with whose children one might not have objected to one's own children playing. The immediate solution to the problem was to ensure that Jews of this sort were assigned to the 'special' camp at Theresienstadt (Terezin) on Bohemian—Protectorate—soil, where the pretence of Nazi concern for their wellbeing could be spun out.[153] For the rest, there was no change in the deportation programme, or what that ultimately '*now*' meant for those deported.

In this sense Riga was clearly a further break-point in the widening of the killing process, paving the way for more of the same. Certainly, Himmler was very aware of the ripples emanating from the event, but the primary lesson he took from it was again the need, which he reiterated for the 'correct' behaviour of *his* men at the killing sites, combined with concern that they should not suffer consequent psychological damage.[154] There was, too, an issue which had been bothering him since the beginnings of the summer mass murders, but became doubly significant now as the killings encompassed bona fide Europeans. How could one pursue a secret policy of wide-scale mass murder screened from public view?[155] Within a purely Russian context one might pursue the hackneyed sophistry that all Jews were partisans or their supporters. After a meeting with Hitler in mid-December 1941—that is, soon after the Führer had committed himself to a further Europe-wide expansion of Jewish mass murder—Himmler jotted down in his office diary the now all-too familiar exculpation: 'Jewish question/to be extirpated as partisans.'[156] But one could hardly apply this counter-insurgency pretext to little old ladies ordered out of their Vienna or Berlin apartments. What Himmler needed was a magic disappearing act. Fortunately for him, his technical fixers had been working around the conundrum for several months. When a new transport from Vienna arrived in Riga in February 1942 it was met by a gas van.[157]

Two such vans for the elimination of 'surplus' Jews in the Warthegau had already been in use at Chełmno, fifty-five kilometres north-west of Łódź, since

November. Dealing with the 'local' Jews in this manner was, in effect, the quid pro quo for the Łódź authorities taking in some 25,000 of the Jews (and Roma) now being scheduled for eruction en masse from Germany and the Protectorate.[158] In December the relevant technical department at the RHSA put in an order for the production of thirty more gas vans, with enhanced killing capacity. Over in Lublin, Globocnik, after consultation with Himmler, had already begun construction of a fixed extermination facility at Bełzec, using carbon monoxide as the murder agent. Personnel previously loaned by Himmler for Aktion T-4 now found their expertise and experience reintegrated into the SS mission. Gassing facilities further east, including one at Mogilev with a 'daily cremation capacity of more than 2,000 corpses', were also in a planning stage by mid-November.[159] One can trace these various developments back to meetings between Himmler and the 'men on the spot', and the Reichsführer-SS's subsequent directives in mid-October.

Recent research has suggested that arguably the most significant of these developments related to the proposed facility at Mogilev.[160] Situated in the Pripet region—where Himmler's first efforts at scaling-up the mass murder of Russian Jews had begun—Mogilev was also one of the sites where Nebe, on Himmler's orders, had conducted some of his gruesome, high summer experiments in different techniques of mass murder. In addition, Götz Aly has pointed to the town's geographical significance. With its largely ice-free, navigable position on the upper Dnieper, Mogilev was accessible for ship transports from not only the Russian hinterland but much further afield, including south-east Europe by way of the Black Sea, as well as from Central Europe. Here then was a method by which Himmler and Heydrich might truly emulate their NKVD adversaries. The building of the Dnieper–Bug Channel by the Soviets in 1940—as always in such cases with Gulag labour—provided both a model for the Nazis' own imperial slave labour ambitions and, at the same time, a highly fortuitous alternative to the logistically fraught and relatively more expensive rail method by which to transport large cargoes of human material to the point where they could be unloaded and then 'disappeared'.[161] Admittedly, Mogilev was not the Arctic or 'far' tundra wastes of their fond imagination. But it would surely suffice as a final terminus for the Jewish deportees at the distant (and, importantly in the face of any prying Western onlookers, obscure) edge of the 'Lands Between'.

With Himmler's go-ahead for what looks very much like a major extermination camp at Mogilev have we not arrived, then, at the point where an almost continuous 'policy drift' finally came to rest in a single decision? It would certainly explain why notions of a Jewish territorial reservation had, by this juncture, seemingly evaporated from high-level RHSA discourse. Yet, even taking account of the fact that the Mogilev project was abandoned almost as soon as it was begun, the overall picture of what was happening on the ground in late 1941 does not add up to a picture of streamlined coherence. For all the comings and goings between Himmler and his security police subordinates, the other extermination facilities were essentially contingent responses to local or regional logjams. Himmler himself, moreover, into early 1942, remained very unclear, and possibly even uneasy—at least according to Jeckeln—as to whether Reich Jewish transports should be shot immediately or put into prepared holding camps.[162]

Yet again, one has a sense that a collapsing of the distinction between the treatment of Reich and arguably other European Jews, on the one hand, and Soviet Jews on the other, had not been fully resolved upon. To be sure, we can see a step-by-step process at work in the autumn by which Jews in *Germany* were required to wear the yellow star, and found themselves under a clear emigration ban, while at the same time, in accordance with the eleventh amendment to the Reich Citizenship Law, being denuded of all rights to German statehood and property as they were forced onto the transports across the international border.[163] It was as if, in a perverse version of crossing the Rubicon, those sent eastwards became, in the process of travel, 'unpeopled': nothingless 'nobodies' who thenceforth could be dispensed with in the same manner as their *Ostjude* brethren.

Which begs the equally perverse question: why not dispatch them accordingly? Was it that Kube's request 'to do what is necessary in the most humane form',[164] reflected an anxiety which continued to have purchase with Himmler too—even while German Jews were being shot into ditches outside the Riga camp at Salaspils? Was it this peculiar obsession with the modus operandi of death which determined that what had begun with the 'mercy killing' of the sick and lame under Aktion T-4 was now equally justified as the *most appropriate* technique for the mass elimination of non-Soviet Jews? Is this anxiety, by the same token, the explanation for why the last remnants of Volhynian Jewry in 1942 were shot in situ and not sent to Bełzec, or Sobibor, even though the Jews of Luboml, for instance, were a mere eighty kilometres aways from these camps?[165] If there was such an invisible dividing line at the Bug, the extermination facility at Mogilev would have breached it. But then we might speculate that the rapid halt to this project was determined by the failure of Operation Typhoon, ensuring that the conveyer belt mass murder of European Jews would have to be radically repositioned, from Russia, to the 'near'. Indeed, parts of the massive crematoria intended for Mogilev were reassigned to Auschwitz, another site in the autumn of 1941 where killing experiments—this time using crystalline prussic acid on sick Soviet POWs—were being conducted.[166]

Auschwitz at this time had no pre-eminent position in a still very preliminary constellation of camps and sites for Jewish extermination. But the fact that it would become the killing facility par excellence—thereby reaffirming the geographical retreat from Russia as the location of Jewish destruction—is ever more clearly indicative of the other side to Himmler's inclination towards the gassing-cum-mass incineration technique: it provided a better chance of keeping the project behind closed doors. Again, however, one is struck by an internal contradiction. Why should the mass murder now be kept secret? Hitler had 'prophesied' all along that world war involving the USA would lead to Jewish annihilation. In mid-November, following consultation with Himmler, Rosenberg—the new minister for the occupied Soviet territories—provided a confidential but otherwise extraordinarily frank briefing to the German press, referring explicitly to the coming 'biological eradication of the entire Jewry of Europe'. Goebbels, almost simultaneously, offered a similar formulation in a German journal. Hitler himself, some ten days later, made few bones about what a victorious Germany would do to the Jews in Palestine when giving an audience to the Grand Mufti of Jerusalem.[167] If anybody in the German public sphere by this time had any doubts as to his intentions these surely would have been laid to rest after Hitler's speech to *Gaue* and party leaders on 12 December. Goebbels' diary entry offers a fairly unequivocal rendition of what Hitler said: he intended 'to sweep the floor clean. He had prophesied to the Jews that if they ever caused a world war again they would suffer extermination... *the world war is upon us* ... the *original* agents of this bloody conflict must pay for it with their lives'.[168]

It is the timing of this speech, in the wake of Pearl Harbor, and, more precisely, within twenty-four hours of Hitler's momentous and fatal decision to declare war on the USA, which has led Christian Gerlach to contend that this was the moment when Hitler's 'fundamental decision'—his *Grundsatzentscheidung*—for a comprehensive programme of European Jewish extermination was finally made and revealed.[169] The argument on one level is perfectly logical. Given that the US political administration had become, in Hitler's mind, one and the same as 'New York Jews'—and hence 'World Jewry'—any notion of keeping European Jews alive as hostages against Washington's entry into war became yesterday's irrelevance. It followed that the world war with the Allies was the same as world war with the Jews. And, as Hitler opined to Rosenberg a few days later, in the circumstances 'it should be no wonder if the consequences hit them first'.[170] It is in this context, proposes Gerlach, that we should understand the preparations for, and relevance of, the Wannsee Conference.

Given the level of concrete—if not always coherent—moves towards a generalized programme of European Jewish extermination over the previous two months, the threshold nature of the 12 December speech remains at least discussable. More tellingly, perhaps, are two aspects of the public and private statements by Hitler and other Nazi leaders around this time, which suggest not simply an acute cognitive dissonance but a profound schizophrenia. Promising the destruction of Jews in the context of his declaration of war on America was, in effect, a promise that he would take down his main enemy in his *own* destruction. In an historical moment (just) before the atom bomb, this was perhaps the nearest a state leader could come to unleashing a weapon of last resort: comprehensive mass murder as nothing but revenge.[171] Yet the schizophrenia lies in the assumption that having broadcast the promise publicly, semi-publicly, or at the very least in circumstances where it was likely to percolate into the public domain, Hitler and his entourage sought to imagine the actual *implementation* of the promise as something which could be pursued in the strictest secrecy, both from the German public and the world at large.

Would this really prove possible? British intercepts of decrypted Order Police radio communications during Operation Barbarossa meant that the Allies were already well furnished with evidence of the first genocide carried out against the Russian Jews.[172] Himmler would now have his work cut out to deflect, avoid, and cover up knowledge of the wider European Jewish genocide which, as of early 1942, was still in its early stages. Meanwhile Nazi efforts to attain the unattainable in the face of total war threw up another unanticipated complication upsetting the drive to a clearly defined programme of Jewish eradication: the need for labour.

GENOCIDE AS 'SYSTEM'

In mid-November 1941, Hinrich Lohse, head of the civilian administration in the Ostland, requested clarification from his immediate superior, Rosenberg, on the intended fate of Jewish labourers on his patch. The question happened to coincide with a heated meeting between Rosenberg and Himmler over whether administrators in the east had any jurisdiction on the Jewish question, or whether this was entirely in the hands of the security police. Lohse did not receive a formal reply for more than a month. When it came, it strongly suggested that his concern to keep alive Jewish workers essential for war production had been overruled. On the contrary, 'economic considerations', he was told, were 'to be disregarded in principle in the settlement of this problem'.[173]

Yet if this was an unadulterated statement of writ from on high, how do we explain that *some*, nearly always young and able-bodied Jewish men and women, albeit for relatively brief periods of time, continued to survive into late 1942, even 1943, under close Nazi supervision, in the ghettos and labour camps of the General Government and occupied eastern territories, even when the rest of their families and communities had been exterminated? How indeed, by the same token, was it possible, let alone conceivable, that at the end of the war there were other young Jews from other liquidated communities, notably Hungary, working in, of all places, Albert Speer's armament factories in the Reich?[174]

We might read this as simply another layer of contradiction, in turn played out in a revised version of the tension between 'now' and 'later', though this time running through to the cataclysmic end of the war. The order to kill *all* Jews 'now' found itself pitted against an entirely cynical, if pragmatic, alternative, which proposed that either in the face of labour shortage or the actual value of some Jews as skilled workers and craftsmen, comprehensive liquidation might be better put off to 'later'. We see this tension being played out in the Russian theatre as early as September 1941, when Wehrmacht officers liaising with their SD counterparts began requesting the separating out of indispensable labourers in Belorussia from mass executions. A report from Otto Rasch, the head of Einsatzgruppe C, even more forcefully proposed that, without the urban Jewish stratum of workers, 'the economic reconstruction of Ukrainian industry as well as the strengthening of the urban administrative centres will be almost impossible'.[175] It is as if the report were mimicking Ludendorff's comments as head of the Ober Ost during the Great War, as to the 'indispensable' role of Jewish middle-men in providing *matériel* for German war industries.[176] Yet the Einsatzgruppen had been the units charged in the summer with exterminating Jewish able-bodied men on the very grounds that they represented the most dangerous obstacle to the German war effort. Here then, Rasch's recommendations for 'the extensive use of Jews for labour', leading to their *'gradual* liquidation', was a complete reversal of the summer's killing order.

The women and children were now, by implication, the ones who ought to be dispensed with first, the able-bodied men kept alive, at the least for the time being, as a helot class.

The report, however, was not an anomaly but entirely consistent with guidelines set down in Rosenberg's so-called 'Brown file', for use by his Ostministerium (OMi). This was reflected too in Lohse's continued efforts to prevent 'uncontrolled' executions on his Riga patch, in which, as we have seen, he was stonewalled;[177] which again would seem to be consistent with the sidelining of OMi by Himmler's adjutants, certainly in the pursuit of Jewish and other 'security' matters in the east, just as, increasingly from this time onwards, would be the case in the General Government. Nevertheless, what the Rasch report would seem to indicate is that to understand this tension as one of security apparatus versus assorted military and ministry interests is to too readily simplify the matter. After all, despite the former's clear primacy on the Jewish question, the notion of what became known as *Vernichtung durch Arbeit* (annihilation through work) was one the RHSA also embraced, even championed.

Key evidence for this lies in the minutes of the conference held at Wannsee, just outside Berlin, on 20 January 1942. The true significance of the conference has become a major stumbling block within Holocaust studies, all the more so given that years of extensive analysis have conclusively demonstrated that what it seemed to be initiating—a programme of mass European Jewish extermination—had already begun. Which begs the question: what exactly was the point of calling a conference of senior German ministry personnel, in order to present them with, if not a fait accompli, then certainly a project already well in train?[178]

Part of the answer may crucially relate back to the man who sent out the invitations: Heydrich. Was his authoritative remit for the preparation of the 'Final Solution' somehow slipping? Nobody could deny his energy or enthusiasm for the task. His frequent visits to Einsatzgruppen units in the field in the summer of 1941 to urge them on to even greater acts of mass murder were surely proof enough of that. But then the actual 'hands-on' decision-making and execution of the remit seemed to be more and more taken over by others 'on the spot'—Jeckeln, Bach-Zelewski, Globocnik, even Himmler himself. Could it be that Heydrich felt threatened by eclipse? Or that the laurels which would undoubtedly come with the completion of the task might have to be shared by Heydrich with lesser mortals? From this perspective Wannsee might be seen as a straightforward attempt by the head of the RHSA to reassert his primacy and, with it, monopoly of the *overall* project. Indeed, it has been suggested by Gerlach that the postponement of the original meeting, scheduled for early December as a consequence of events leading from Pearl Harbor to Hitler's 'fundamental decision', gave Heydrich his signal opportunity to present his Wannsee audience with an all-encompassing programme for the 'evacuation' of the entirety of European Jewry to the 'east'.[179]

Certainly, one striking aspect of the Wannsee protocol is the country-by-country inventory prepared by Eichmann. Embracing British and Irish Jewry, the entirety of those in the USSR, Scandinavia, and the Iberian Peninsula, as well as countries either occupied, neutral, or, as in Central and south-eastern Europe, allied to the

Axis, it is quite clear from the tenor of the minutes that all of the communities subsumed within the estimated 11 million total were now intended for the chop.[180] Whether the compiling of this comprehensive wish-list can then be traced back to a Hitler decision in early to mid-December is entirely another matter, not least given that Eichmann at his trial claimed that he had prepared the inventory *before* the original, postponed meeting.[181]

Needless to say, whatever the truth on that score, the 11 million figure can only cause a chill to run down the spine, especially when we know, from Eichmann's testimony in Jerusalem, that the Wannsee minutes did not include details of the conversations between participants in which they freely talked about extermination and the methods of killing which might be utilized.[182] Scholars have often remarked on the euphemistic language of the protocol—or, as Eichmann put it, 'over-plain talk' rendered by himself into 'office language'.[183] Equally significant, one might add, was what was unsaid at the meeting—for instance, that by early 1942 the possibility of sucking in either British Jewry, outside a handful of individuals in the occupied Channel Islands, or the vast bulk of Soviet Jewry now to the lee of the Wehrmacht assault, amounted to little more than wish-fulfilment.

But then there is also a section from the transcripts which, until recently, has been assumed to be euphemism but which taken at face value offers a very different explication of how Heydrich foresaw Jewish destruction proceeding:

> In the course of the 'Final Solution' and under appropriate leadership the Jews should be put to work in the East. In large, single-sex labour columns, Jews fit to work will work their way eastwards constructing roads. Doubtless the large majority will be eliminated by natural causes. And doubtless any final remnant that survives will consist of the most resistant elements. They will have to be dealt with appropriately, because otherwise, by natural selection, they would form the germ cell of a new Jewish revival.[184]

In fact, a major project very similar to Heydrich's description was already in train, and it was almost certainly this to which the RHSA chief was alluding. *Durchgangstrasse* IV (DG IV) was an ultra-ambitious project to build a major supply route, with additional connecting spurs, from Lwów in Galicia, all the way across the Ukraine to Taganrog, at the northern edge of the Sea of Azov. At a distance of 2,175 kilometres, DG IV, thus, was much more than simply a road. Not unlike the Roman military highways, it would have a series of hubs, facilities, and depots at strategic positions all along it—plus, of course, labour camps. From these camps the slave workers would be put to work quarrying stone for the gravel and other construction material for the actual highway, and shifting it to site, plus constructing not only the road itself but the necessary drainage ditches and embankments to protect it.[185]

DG IV was got under way at its east Galician end in September 1941. Though technically the road fell under the authority of the Todt organization, itself accountable to Speer's Construction Inspectorate, for the particular benefit of the Wehrmacht, the sense of it being an SS road was quickly transparent. Not only did its proposed route dovetail with Himmler's grand settlement plans envisaged in

Generalplan Ost, for which DG IV provided a central axis, but it naturally fell to Himmler's regional HSSPF subordinates to provide and control the labour source and, as necessary, eliminate the exhausted component. Needless to say, relentless, backbreaking toil, even putting aside the intolerable conditions, near-starvation, disease, and constant terror as applied by the overseers, ensured that attrition, as anticipated by Heydrich at Wannsee, rapidly set in. Of course, all this assumes that the victims were only Jews. Clearly, especially to begin with, this was not the case. Soviet POWs were the obvious labour reservoir but the collapse of this source, one element of which was as a result of the road building itself—plus the need to protect rimlands' peasantry at a time when maintaining food supply to the Wehrmacht was becoming a critical issue—ensured that the obvious replacement source was a Jewish one.[186]

Globocnik's expanded Lublin domain, now including eastern Galicia, where Katzmann was his subordinate, particularly lent itself to this assumption. Moreover, as Lublin was designated a special SS zone, at which it was anticipated large numbers of Central Europe deportees would arrive in spring 1942, the notion of them being deployed and then 'used up' on road-building or similar projects seemed to confirm the Heydrichian logic. To be sure, the search for Jewish labour further east along the route of DG IV was already compromised by the extent to which available male Jews, in the outer regions of German control, had already been massacred. Where Jewish slave labour was in short supply district SD or Sipo staff often had to make deals with others from further afield, or with Rumanian officials in their Transnistrian zone of occupation to the south, to make up the shortfall.[187]

The obvious problem with this road-centred narrative is that it hardly equates with the much more familiar picture we have of Jewish death throughout 1942 and indeed subsequently. Does this mean that to place too much store by what Heydrich ostensibly said at Wannsee is mistaken? Or, alternatively, that treating him as somehow pivotal to the plot is itself in error? One might, for instance, agree with those who have argued that while Heydrich was good at calling high-level conferences in Berlin to assert his jurisdiction, he was actually left far behind by those in the field who were having to deal with the daily reality of what to do with Jews on their patch, whom his superior, Himmler, anyway, repeatedly reminded his H/SSPF, *ought* to be eliminated.[188] The new push for more immediate mass murder actually surfaced towards the end of the Wannsee Conference itself when Dr Josef Bühler, the General Government state secretary, in effect Frank's deputy, proposed that the solution to the Jewish question in his arena need 'not be obstructed by issues involving labour deployment' because most of the 2.5 million Jews there were 'unfit for work'. And Bühler's inference was given added weight by another delegate representing a civil administration, this time Dr Alfred Meyer, from OMi, who urged the need for 'certain preparatory measures' which should be carried out immediately in the relevant area itself though without causing alarm among the local population. Such remarks, with their nod and wink at the construction of not labour but extermination camps clearly point in a direction quite different from Heydrich's Wannsee proposals.[189] Moreover, one might argue that by this time Heydrich had other more pressing concerns to contend with. He had new duties as acting Reichsprotektor in Bohemia-Moravia—albeit these arose as a consequence of his own efforts to carve out for himself a commanding role in the east.[190] One might even go so far as to propose that ultimately Heydrich's only real contribution to the comprehensive execution of the 'Final Solution' was to bequeath his name posthumously to Operation Reinhard—the mass murder of Polish Jewry which, though accelerated after his assassination at the end of May, was already in train.

However, this verdict might too readily throw out the baby with the bath-water. Immediate results of the Wannsee emphasis on 'annihilation through work' included an early 1942 deal arrived at in Bratislava between the RHSA representative Dieter Wisliceny and the Slovak government for the deployment of 20,000 'young, *strong*, Slovak Jews'—both male and female—for work at the behest of the Reich.[191] Three things stand out immediately about this development. The first relates to the arrangement itself. The Jews offered by Bratislava were in lieu of gentile Slovak workers being demanded by Berlin from its satellite regime. After initial prevarication the RHSA took up the counter-offer, which is not surprising given that Himmler in the wake of Wannsee had authorized his concentration camp inspectorate (IKL) to expect up to 100,000 Jews and 50,000 Jewesses to replace the growing Soviet POW shortfall.[192] But equally it is the direct absorption of the Slovak Jews within the camps at Auschwitz and Majdanek—the latter an emerging king-pin in Globocnik's Lublin empire—which marks a really significant departure. The fact that the Slovak Jews were not deployed directly in camps along DG IV, nor in some grand Gulag-style drainage and reclamation scheme in the Pripet or Dnieper regions[193]—a stock-in-trade assumption from the previous autumn— strongly suggests that European Jewish deportation to the 'east', in the sense of to the Russian 'heartland', had now been completely abandoned. But over and beyond that was the fact that the Slovak Jews were not being sent to already existing ghettos—symptomatic in itself of the housing overload of earlier months out of which mass shootings had resulted. Instead, they were being sent to purpose-built camps where they could be incarcerated and minutely supervised by SS personnel. Indeed, with the transfer of the Slovak young women to Auschwitz's satellite camp complex at Birkenau, we begin to see the beginnings of the Auschwitz mass extermination 'system'.

But it is this which brings us to our third outcome and with it a notable paradox. The young women were crammed into their new barracks, shaved, and put into old Russian uniforms. And they *were* put to work, mostly on land reclamation projects around the Birkenau site. Extermination, instead, began as an almost inadvertent by-product of their arrival, applied in the first instance neither to them nor to the men sent to Majdanek, but to *other* family members. It was the opening Bratislava saw from the initial deportation to remove *whole* family units (who would, they claimed, bereft of their able-bodied elements, otherwise become a burden on the Slovak economy) which precipitated a further bi-national agreement in early March. Germany agreed to take a further 70,000 Jews, for which the Slovaks paid 500 marks per capita for the costs of deportation. In fact, one thing did not lead directly to the other. In March the Birkenau technical staff were only just in the process of converting a peasant dwelling—the so-called 'little red house'—into what was then intended as a temporary gassing facility. Schmelt Jews considered 'unfit for work' were the first group to be murdered here, while the first transports of Slovak Jewish families, meanwhile, were either sent to Majdanek where some of them too were selected for work while the remainder continued their terminal journey to the already up and running extermination facility at Bełzec. It was not until early July, when a another cottage, 'the little white house' a.k.a. Bunker 2 was ready for use as an improved facility now using prussic acid—Zyklon B—as its killing agent, that Slovak Jewish extermination really began.[194]

Even so, what was emerging from the late spring of 1942 was a sequencing of mass murder not only seemingly at odds with Heydrich's Wannsee hyper-exploitation narrative but with the foot firmly pressed down on the 'now' accelerator. 1942 was *the* year of mass Jewish death. If well over a million had perished the previous year, the death toll in this one rose to an estimated 2.7 million lives.[195] Ironically, the contribution made by Auschwitz-Birkenau to this hideosity was relatively small—perhaps 8 per cent of the total. What the Slovak precedent had confirmed was that this was a convenient killing facility to which Jews from across Europe could be expedited, whether those Jews were living under German rule, or that of puppet governments. By the end of the year large numbers of Jews from France, the Low Countries, Croatia, even Norway, as well as from Upper Silesia and Białystok, had perished in Birkenau's two bunkers.[196]

However, it was the once Pale of Settlement—the historic heart of Ashkenazi Jewry—which was the real 1942 focus of killing. In the Soviet territories under German occupation, the HSSPF were the driving force in a 'second sweep' which liquidated practically all the remaining ghettos, work camps, and communities which had survived the onslaught the previous year. In the months between August and November 1942 *alone* Himmler's own estimate (provided for Hitler's edification) of those killed in the Ukraine and South Russia, as well as the Białystok district, amounted to over 363,000 people. This, however, did not include the massacres which wiped out almost all Volhynian and Podolian Jewry in the late spring and early summer.[197] But if this sequence can be read as a continuation of the process from the previous year in which the Jews of the USSR seemed to be singularly marked down for complete liquidation, it was the conscious effort to do the same with respect to the Jews of the General Government which is the defining aspect of Jewish genocide in 1942. Or perhaps, more precisely, from mid-March 1942 to mid-February 1943, the period in which the three dedicated Operation Reinhard extermination camps, Bełzec, Sobibor, and Treblinka were attempting to operate at full tilt. During this time, notes Browning, over one-half of the Jews who died in 'the Holocaust' perished, the majority of them Polish Jews.[198] Indeed, if one wanted to home in on the killing frenzy at its high-point one would look to seven murderous weeks from late July to mid-September. This was the period when all but 70,000 of the 380,000 still surviving Jews in Warsaw were rounded up ghetto section by section. The process, undertaken according to Sipo-SD orders and initially using Judenrat and Polish police, became more unremitting and brutal as auxiliary (usually Latvian or Ukrainian) police took over. Under whoever's cosh, the victims were herded into a staging area, the Umschlagplatz, and from there packed into the first available cattle trucks for 'resettlement in the east'. In reality, that meant immediate transit to the gas chambers at Treblinka.[199]

How do we explain, after all the twists and turns of 1941, the overdrive nature of these killings? Might we be ultra-cynical and propose that on one level the mass murders of 1942 were another consequence of 'the sunk-cost effect'? Having put time, resources, and expertise into the creation of extermination facilities, not then to exploit them, and indeed enhance their efficiency as killing machines, was equivalent to a wasted investment. The only problem with this line of reasoning, as we will note further below, is that as 'technical fix' answers to the problem of eradicating lots of human beings, the extermination camp 'systems' were not markedly efficient. The 'ordinary men' of Police Battalion 101, as made famous by both Christopher Browning and Daniel Goldhagen, were put to work in the Lublin district *shooting* thousands of Jews, either because the railroad network proved inadequate to getting the local Jews to their Reinhard camp destinations, or because 'the overburdened killing machinery broke down'.[200] In Russia, practically all the killings were accomplished by such shooters, anyway. The imperative was to kill Jews; the method was not ultimately dictated.

But that again rather begs the question: why this accelerated version when Heydrich had already developed his own grotesque but somewhat more gradual 'later'-based alternative? Longerich has suggested that shortly before his death Heydrich had had a 'remarkable series of meetings within an eight day period' with Himmler which indicate not Heydrich disagreement with, but actually his enthusiastic acceptance of the latter's plans to push through a comprehensive extermination agenda.[201] In other words, founded on the Führer's firm desire now to be rid of the Jews, the notion of 'later' had simply become, by spring 1942, a compete irrelevance in Nazi *Judenpolitik*. Himmler's order six weeks on from Heydrich's death to HSSPF Friedrich Wilhelm Krüger to bring the destruction of the General Government's Jews to a conclusion by the end of the year, thus represented no fundamental derogation of the Heydrich line.[202] What it did mean, however, was that the policy drift and prevarication as to what exactly the Nazi regime meant by the 'Final Solution' had, finally, come to a terrifying end.

Moreover, Himmler's firm control of the extermination programme in the General Government itself was at this point assisted by a corruption scandal involving Frank, one critical consequence of which was that the latter had to concede the elevation of his personal arch-rival Krüger to State Secretary for Security, from which vantage point he could do exactly whatever *his* superior, Himmler, demanded in Frank's ostensible fiefdom. Again, by way of Bühler's remarks at Wannsee, there is a danger of overstating the General Government trajectory as somehow representing a victory of the 'hawk' Himmler over the 'dove' Frank. After all, the latter had been insistently petitioning Hitler to have the Jews 'deported' from his patch for the last two years, and by the end of 1941 his remarks on the matter suggest he had reached the end of his tether.[203] But as Jews clearly could not be evacuated any further eastwards (any doubts on that score being properly put to rest in early 1943 with the great Wehrmacht defeat at Stalingrad) Himmler's route to rapid in situ obliteration could be equally read almost as a favour to Frank enabling his rival to 'secure' his internal regime.

Even so, the decision for Polish Jewish mass murder did completely cut across another Nazi imperative: to keep war production at maximum level. And it just so happened that in the summer of 1942 the productionists' agenda with regard to ghettos such as Warsaw was beginning to realize exactly such expectations. One other consequence of this was that that ghetto's monthly death rate in May 1942—primarily as a result of starvation—'dropped below 4,000 for the first time in a year'.[204] In other words, *logically* speaking there were still grounds for going easy on the speed of extermination. But then there was nothing logical about the disaster Hitler was day by day driving Germany towards. Longerich has proposed that the only way we can understand 'the annihilation policy' is by seeing it as 'an integral part of National Socialist war policy, as a major factor alongside strategic, military-economic and alliance policy considerations'. But he also proposes that from 1942 onwards 'the annihilation policy also took on key functions in the regime's war policy'.[205] Perhaps one might take this argument further by suggesting that as a response to the self-inflicted crisis of war, which by mid-1942 clearly could not logically be won, the drive to transcend its limitations took the form of a *limitless*—as well as at the same time pointless—revenge on the Jews.

Yet there *still* remains the contradiction. Throughout the rimlands zone in the 'east', not to say closer to the German heartland, a patchwork of slave camps, ghettos and factories continued to practice 'annihilation through work'—or more accurately, perhaps, murder at the point where exhaustion or illness ensured that the worker was expendable[206]—even alongside the standard operating procedure. However anomalous as a result, there were hundreds of thousands of Jewish men and women labouring on DG IV, the Estonian oil shale mines, at Salispils, further west in the Plaszów camp—housing the last remnant of Cracow Jewry—in Majdanek, the Auschwitz complex, scores of satellite camps and several hundred other *Zwangarbeitslager für Juden* (ZALs) run by the military, industry, and civil administrators as well as the SS.[207] Those who were still alive in these camps towards late 1943, malnourished, weakened, and physically as well as psychologically terrorized beyond belief as they were, might still cling onto the faint hope that, as the war in the east turned in favour of the Red Army, they might yet be liberated.[208] They would have been joined in this hope by the surviving residue of ghetto inhabitants in Vilna, Białystok, the East Upper Silesian towns of Bendzin and Sosnowitz—where Jews continued to labour on the Shmelt projects—and most strikingly of all in Łódź where 90,000 coerced Jewish providers for the German war economy toiled until the ghetto was finally liquidated on Himmler's orders in August 1944, at the moment when the Soviets were indeed closing in.[209]

Should we be surprised by the ongoing nature of the discrepancy? Tens of thousands of Armenians were put to work on infrastructural and military communications projects, most obviously a section of the Berlin–Baghdad railway line before most of them, eventually, were put to death. Like the Jews, the very notion of putting Armenians to backbreaking work may well have gratified core persecutors who would have reviled them in their pre-war existence as parasitic blood-suckers. Indeed, while many Germans may have balked at the idea of total extermination, the Nazi regime may have calculated that the idea of Jews being put to strenuous manual work was something they could legitimately sell to a wider public. If it could be demonstrated that Jews were getting what they had always deserved—and large sections of the German public certainly would have endorsed that narrative—the regime had won half its battle in its efforts to make that public complicit in its even more lethal project.

That said, making either a quantitative or qualitative assessment of the degree to which Jews through slave labour represented a significant contribution to the war effort is beyond the scope of this study.[210] Most assessments agree that able-bodied Jews were deployed where other groups were not available but that given that the notional Jewish work force was much smaller than that for other national groups sucked into the camp system, their contribution could only be a relatively limited one. Jews, moreover, were usually singled out for rapid dehumanization, the most arduous and dangerous labour, and gratuitous ill-treatment. Consequently, they suffered death rates far in excess of other groups. This would suggest that their *perceived* economic value was negligible or, equally, that the point of them being there was to be worked to death as rapidly and violently as possible. However, this picture was not uniform over time or place. As we have already noted, from relatively early on in the invasion of Russia, Wehrmacht, civil adminstrators, even SS personnel, strove to preserve those they considered essential skilled Jewish workers and their families, suggesting that the standard argument that as 'useless eaters' they should be dispatched without further ado, was questioned even by Nazi ideologues. Much later on when the exigencies of total war were forcing Speer towards an attempted rationalization of military production, former strictures about Jews working not just in the Reich but even in armaments production were overturned. The result might be that while in 1944, recently deployed Hungarian Jews working not just on 'secret' construction sites, such as the 'V' weapons factories deep in the Harz mountains might have a life expectancy of weeks, those 'lucky' enough to be assigned to indoor work in arms factories included some who outlived the Nazi defeat.[211]

The emergence of this renewed utilitarian emphasis again highlights the extraordinary inconsistency not to say disjuncture in Nazi Jewish 'policy'. Of course, one might argue that nothing more complex than necessity determined the 1944 change of course, to which even Hitler gave his imprimatur. And this departure certainly did not mean Jews stopped being murdered en masse: alongside the over 100,000 Hungarian Jews put at the disposal of the German war economy, Auschwitz-Birkenau reached its peak in the conveyer-belt destruction of the several hundred thousand more considered unfit for work; this clearly following in the path of the original twin-track pattern of the Slovak arrangement two years earlier.

Yet contrast this situation with 1943 when most of the surviving Jews in the camps and ghettos in the General Government had been mass-murdered. The very notion of Jews working in installations and facilities in the Wehrmacht rear, especially where they might sabotage the war effort or incite more general revolt, had been the abiding leitmotif of Nazi security anxiety. When it came to light that hundreds of skilled Jewish labourers had been working on Hitler's secret Werewolf bunker, in the Ukrainian Zhitomir region, his own special Reich Security Police were sent in early 1942 to wipe them out before his imminent visit there. A similar operation conducted by the SD took place at Himmler's nearby Hegewald complex later in the year.[212] That the security apparatus had scoured the surrounding region to eliminate *all* Jews, for fear of their threat to the Führer's person, yet had somehow overlooked those working on his and Himmler's headquarters represents a curious, even bizarre episode in the destruction of Ukrainian Jewry.

But if no direct danger to the Nazi leadership is recorded as emanating from Jewish sources, a rising crescendo of Jewish resistance to the liquidation of the ghettos is well known. Emblematically represented by the Warsaw ghetto uprising in April and early May 1943, these putative or ephemeral revolts had no broad military purpose: they were essentially declarations by the last survivors of the rimlands ghettos of their refusal to go like 'lambs to the slaughter'. But they were almost certainly interpreted quite differently by the Nazi security elite, especially when put alongside the spate of attempted sabotage and rebellion in the extermination camps. Involving both Jewish *Sonderkommandos*—in other words, the work details who removed the bodies from the gas chambers—and other inmates who serviced the wider camps, there were organized break-outs from both Treblinka, in August, and Sobibor, in October. In both instances the rebellions were rapidly put down but not before, in the case of Sobibor in particular, hundreds of Jews had escaped. A year later, there would be too, an extraordinarily brave act by *Sonderkommandos* at Auschwitz, when they blew up and set on fire one of the crematoria.[213]

A wider German fear mixed with awe about the strike-back power of the Jews had already surfaced in common talk about the Allied bombing of German cities, as if this were a Jewish act of retribution.[214] And what logically can be seen as last-ditch acts of courageous defiance by camp and ghetto inmates were exponentially magnified by the likes of Himmler into proof of a renewed Jewish–Bolshevik onslaught on the lines of the 1918 insurgency in the rear. In which case, the only answer was to nip the rebellion in the bud and eliminate as many of the potential insurrectionists as one could, before they could spread their 'contagion'. The consequence was rapid but meticulous preparation for a final Operation Reinhard clean-up which would empty practically all the remaining camps in the Lublin slave labour heartland of the General Government. Code-named Operation Harvest Festival (*Erntefest*) the killing was put into action on 2 November and over the following day led to the mass death by shooting of 42,000 Jewish workers in the remaining main camps in and around Majdanek.[215] They could not be gassed: in response to the rebellions Himmler had already taken the precautionary step of closing down the remaining two Operation Reinhard facilities.

Was this then, the culmination of 'total' genocide, or, as Julius Streicher in *Der Stürmer* put it in Nazi-speak, later that month, the end of the Jewish 'reservoir in the East'? Donald Bloxham argues so, and certainly looking at it through the prism of a rimlands ethnographic landscape he would seem to have more than a point.[216] Bar those who had escaped to the forest and the partisans, or were in hiding under assumed gentile identities, the entire sweep of the 'Lands Between' from the Baltic to Bessarabia, and further south into the Balkans had, by Nazi diktat, been made *Judenfrei*. Of course there remained, notwithstanding persecution and up to this time partial extermination, the Jewish populations under satellite regimes in Slovakia, Bulgaria, and especially Hungary and Rumania. And there were certainly still some surviving but much smaller populations in *Western* Europe. In addition, to these populations, there were also Jews in the remaining camps, above all in and around the Auschwitz complex. But the point of geographical interest about Auschwitz was that while it might have been a place from which one looked east towards the rimlands it was equally a place where the rimlands met metropolitan Europe.

*

By a tortuous trajectory, thus, and not until quite late in the day, Auschwitz attained its position at the pinnacle of the Jew-destruction machine, utilizing both direct gas chamber extermination and indirect 'annihilation through work'. But did it amount to a 'system'? Genocide, we posited in an earlier volume, is not 'something fixed in the make-up of regimes', it is what 'different types of regimes *do*'.[217] However, could one not make an exception for a 'regime' such as Auschwitz? 'System', I read in my dictionary, is 'a group or combination of interrelated, interdependent or interacting elements forming a collective entity; a methodical or coordinated assemblage of parts, facts, concepts etc.'.[218] No condition of sustainability would seem to be required for a system to *be* a system: the ephemerality of Auschwitz, or for that matter of the Operation Reinhard camps, would not suffice to exclude them from the definition. And, of course, to make them *work*, they were dependent on a whole network of well-tried, tested, and regulated techniques, scientific processes, transport operations and bureaucratic support functions to ensure their orderly and regular functioning. Such a combination would appear to make Auschwitz not only a system, but a very modern system. As Bauman puts it:

> The most shattering of lessons derived from the analysis of the twisted road to Auschwitz is that—in the last resort—the choice of physical extermination as the right means to the task of *Entfernung* was a product of routine bureaucratic procedures: means–end calculus, budget balancing, universal rule application.[219]

Bauman, of course, rejects the notion that Auschwitz was some sort of perversion of modernity. Rather, it was in the very attempt to create a racially ordered 'brave new world' that he sees the Holocaust as one of modernity's authentic, indeed quintessential offspring. Yet in his commentary, Bauman does not seem to dispute that conveyer-belt mass murder is the logical, even inevitable terminus to which heretofore all Nazi efforts had been heading. Nor does his critique notably detract from a more general contemporary fascination with its bureaucratic and technological aspects. In a not dissimilar way Raul Hilberg's magisterial early study of the Holocaust, especially with its emphasis on card-indexing and procedural preparations for deportations from German cities, has done much to lay the foundations of our understanding of the mechanisms of destruction as an orderly, routine process. Indeed, Hilberg's attention on this score to the minutiae of not just rail-way timetabling but the methods by which the Reichsbahn's books in the process were audited and duly balanced (by RHSA sequestration of residual Jewish funds) has become practically iconic.[220]

As for the methods of mass, standardized gassing, generations of Western-educated school children have imbibed the story of the backroom technicians—men of the ilk of the SS mechanic Willy Just—who had to experiment with just how a Sauer van could be adapted, refitted, and hermetically sealed so that the carbon monoxide pumped into its 'load space' could do its work efficiently and then be further equipped with drainage facilities so that the fluids and detritus from its operation might be repeatedly flushed out. Nazi documents, such as that detailing Just's efforts on behalf of the Chełmno facility in June 1942, have a way of reinforc-ing our sense that the 'Final Solution' developed through a problem-solving which involved not only a detached and impersonal view of those who would end up as its victims but, when all is said and done, a certain perspicacity.[221] Even more is this arguably the case with regard to Kurt Prüfer, the leading engineer and designer of the furnaces supplied by the Erfurt family business Topf und Söhne for use by the SS at Auschwitz and elsewhere. Prüfer's big challenge was to calculate how bodies might be efficiently burnt in the crematoria without wasting coal. Part of what the Central SS Office of Budget and Building (SS-HHB) was concerned about was 'the most economical and fuel-saving procedure'—in other how they might save money. Prüfer's response was to experiment with different loads of bodies, and he came to the conclusion that as female corpses were more combustible than male, and younger ones more so than older ones, a scientific method of mixing the bodies was necessary. For good measure, body fat collected from funeral pyres might itself be recycled as fuel for the next round of efficient burnings.[222]

Certainly, at the time, Prüfer gained something of a reputation with his SS-HHB customers as a 'magician' of cremation.[223] But does this mean that we too, while we rightly proclaim our horror and detestation of the consequences, also have to fall in with a verdict of extermination camp technology as somehow innovative, cutting-edge, even 'clever'? A much keener assessment is on offer from Michael Marrus:

> The Topf personnel and their SS employers applied their learning to solve the murder-ers' problems, to be sure, but their work seems to be far more akin to an artisan's workshop than a scientist's laboratory. Indeed, the gruesome history of the mechanics of the death machinery recount one blunder after another, broken equipment, failed experiments and persistent malfunction.[224]

This is not to belittle German wartime technological innovation *tout ensemble*. If Auschwitz, in Marrus' view 'was hardly the equivalent of the Manhattan Project', one could still argue that the *omnicidal* potentiality of nuclear weaponry only truly came of age when the atomic science of the Oppenheimer team was coupled with the ballistic missile technology of Wernher von Braun's V-2 project.[225] The fact that V-2 was also littered with broken machinery, and the rest, en route to it becoming arguably the most fearful weapon of mass destruction to come out of the war, pre-Hiroshima, hardly detracts from its breakthrough quality in terms of rocket science.[226] The consequent assault on Antwerp and London in the last months of the European war also reminds us that Hitler's thirst for revenge was not restricted to a single Jewish 'enemy'.

By contrast with V-2's innovation one might propose that the extermination camps were in no sense novel but rather representative of an attempt to apply an older, well-tried if still certainly very modern killing technology: the purpose-built abattoir. Mechanized assembly lines for the mass butchery of animals emerged in the mid-1860s with the Union Stockyards in Chicago and Haussmann's La Villette slaughterhouse central to his grand design for a rebuilt Paris. The former was soon processing 200,000 hogs a day while the founders of the latter sought to represent it as 'the ideal slaughterhouse of the future'. Here, the supposedly humane, pain-less, hygienic but mechanized dispatch of living, highly sentient animals was assisted by a panoply of tracks, trolleys, belts, and cranes which, in turn, under-scored not only the (again supposedly) depersonalized conveyer belt nature of the process but the Taylorian separation of tasks and operations which went with it.[227] Indeed, the very manner in which the extermination camps sought to replicate with human beings the abattoir-style mass murder of animals by stop-watch, and as if the victims were simply numbered 'things', arguably represents the epitome of the Taylorian quest for the industrially organized, scientifically 'managed' and, cru-cially, emotionless working day. To be sure, the designers of Bełzec and Birkenau did not set out to develop blueprints for destruction on the basis of these preceding models. There were no gas chambers or crematoria adjoining the Union Stock-yards. But just as the way in which terrified and panicked animals were slaughtered amidst the blood of those who had come before, and in which the filth from the process turned a local river into a contagious sewer gives the lie to either the opera-tion's compassion or its cleanliness, so what equally was the essence of extermina-tion camp system was not its clinical efficiency but rather its sordid squalor and unbounded cruelty.

The true reality is illustrated by what Robert-Jan van Pelt refers to as the 'secre-tory catastrophe' at the heart of the emerging Birkenau camp at the time when the Slovak Jews began arriving en masse 'for work' in the late spring and early summer of 1942. They would find that they had been provided with precisely one wash basin for each 7,800 of them and similarly one ditch latrine for each 7,000. These facilities, moreover, were only available for use in a given half-hour period before roll-call. With an entirely insufficient supply of water to help flush the discharge straight into the Vistula, not only did the dysentery-ridden inmates end up caked in excrement and overwhelmed by the resulting stench, but the camp comman-dant, Hoess, and his officials, soon began to panic as a consequent but inevitable typhus epidemic took hold.[228] It has become rather common knowledge how Zyklon B, the prussic acid-based insecticide used originally for killing vermin in the camps came through trial, error, and a considerable dose of 'luck' to be the agent for the extermination of Jewish 'vermin' at Auschwitz. Yet, in July and August, Hoess was using tons of the stuff not to kill Jews but again for its original delousing purpose. He did so, however, in complete crisis mode. He attempted to halt the epidemic in an entirely quarantined camp, at the same time concealing from Himmler the insanitary conditions which had brought about the crisis in the first place. He also concealed from the WVHA—the successor to SS-HHB—the true reasons as to why he needed such huge quantities of Zyklon-B. The irony of ironies was that Hoess was able to get his additional supply of prussic acid by claiming that he needed the extra for the 'special treatment' of 'unfit Jews at Birkenau', the ruse involving inflating 'by more than 3000 per cent the quantities needed to do the job in the gas chambers'.[229]

This should simply underscore Marrus' view that the very modus operandi of death-camp extermination was poorly conceived, inadequately designed, thoroughly hand-to-mouth in its implementation, and hence spectacularly prone to breakdown or worse. The summer 1942 epidemic in particular highlighted the nightmare scenario for all *génocidaires*: vast numbers of untreated corpses leading to disease not only among the perpetrators but spreading rapidly to the wider population. Having Prüfer's new furnaces up and running so that bodies piling up in pits could instead be incinerated proved only a temporary respite when it transpired that the initial crematorium's smokestack could not cope with the extra capacity.[230] Around this same time the situation at Treblinka was even more chaotic. Deportees arriving there were confronted with mounds of unburned bodies in various stages of decay. Unable to deal with the daily volume of transports for 'special treatment', the camp administration, under the management of one Dr Irmfried Eberl, by the end of August was on the point of collapse, necessitating Globocnik's direct intervention to overhaul staff and procedures.[231]

Clearly, the technical and administrative problems were mostly overcome. From early 1943, Treblinka, minus crematoria but having developed a more uniform technique for the mass burning of bodies, was back on course as it worked its way through to a final estimated tally of 763,000 victims by April of that year.[232] As for Auschwitz-Birkenau, having seen at first hand the systemic flaws in the killing process its lead architects not only built new crematoria but refined their design to combine undressing rooms, gas chambers, morgues, and furnace halls into an integrated 'functional sequence'. These refinements and further functional add-ons, including a new railway spur directly into the Birkenau camp, ensured that with the closure of its Reinhard competitors, Auschwitz was *the* fit-for-purpose killing centre in the constellation of Jewish destruction. And judged purely on these criteria, it certainly came into its own with the Hungarian operation in 1944. In a mere fifty-four days between 15 May and 9 July, 437,402 deportees were 'inducted' into the camp, a significant number from there were selected for labour camps, and the rest sent directly into the gas chambers. Despite ongoing problems with one of the furnaces, the crematoria were able to cope with the five- to sixfold increase in 'cargo' over the 32–34,000 monthly average. As van Pelt and Dwork have noted, the number of people murdered in May and June 'exceeded the official incineration capacity of 132,000 corpses per month'.[233]

In other words, it is Auschwitz at its peak performance, and then after nearly two years of muddling through, that we chiefly remember in terms of its ultramodernist efficiency. This is not to dispute that there were aspects of the killing that were not only frighteningly modern but, by way of the SS obsession to turn the whole process into an ongoing cost-benefit exercise, arguably unique. Having calculated how much profit they could generate from the work of an average concentration camp prisoner who survived nine months—1,431 RM (*c.*$654)—after deducting, that is, upkeep and incineration costs, why could one not go one step further and include body parts, gold teeth, or even bones for fertilizer as 'added value'?[234] Of course, making an inventory of one's victims *financial* assets was nothing new. When, as one small example, the German authorities in Shumsk, Volhynia, drew up a list in May 1942 of the thousand wrist-watches, 5,000 gold roubles, $2000 in cash, fifty typewriters, five trucks, 500 light bulbs, and one hundred bicycles which they had filched after having shot some hostages from the residual Judenrat, they were following a behavioural pattern perfectly familiar to a Talât or a Reshid.[235] But then to move a stage on from that and consider how one might extract a use from living or dead female victims' hair, including genital hair, seemed to harp back more obviously to the sort of maximization of biotic value derived by the Union Stockyard packinghouses from animal massacre. Granted, there is no evidence that leather, soap, gelatine, or glue were derived as by-products of the Auschwitz operation as they were from the Chicago slaughterhouses. But we do know that human hair from the extermination camps was collected by the train load and then industrially processed for use in the production of felt, yarn, stockings, socks, rugs, cords, insulation material, and even the ignition mechanisms of delayed action bombs.[236]

For 'a nation obsessed with tracking, diagnosing, registering, grading and selecting',[237] as one writer puts it, none of this should particularly surprise. Whether this points to a peculiarly Germanic approach to the body in terms of its organic properties let alone its metaphysical representation is certainly open to discussion.[238] But what is more keenly observable as in line with very contemporary, Central European mentalities is the manner in which the victims' material or physical assets were *recycled* for the German war effort. And to this one might acerbically add that this was, in the circumstances and leaving aside all ethical considerations, a perfectly logical thing to do. Germany, after all, was fighting a total war of national life and death. Stripped of their possessions and clothes in the 'changing rooms' adjacent to the gas chambers, where in their nakedness they were—mostly unknowingly—to be murdered, the victims' intimate valuables were no longer of any personal use but of considerable benefit to those, for instance, such as resettled Volksdeutsche, whom the regime considered worthy of assistance. As for all the victims' jewels, gems, hard currency, and other monetary items, these were (supposed) to accrue to the state forthwith. The emergence of a system in which, at its high point, up to 2,000 Jewish male and female prisoners in Auschwitz meticulously sifted through, ordered, and stored these goods is highly indicative of the importance the camp authorities gave to this effort.[239] The storerooms themselves famously became known to the prisoners as 'Canada', conjuring up untold riches but lacking the other more subtle allusion to native dispossession.

However, there was—hardly surprisingly—an even more lurid underside to the recycling operation, which again casts doubt on both the system's overall singularity and its notable modernity. To be sure, we might wish to read SS interest in a 1940 Breslau University Ph.D. thesis by one Victor Scholz, morbidly entitled 'On the Possibilities of Recycling Gold from the Mouths of the Dead' as simply one further manifestation of a notably anal-retentive trait, which necessarily converted into the extraction of every last gram of gold, platinum, and other metal embedded in the jaws of those just gassed.[240] But the Nazi search for dental gold, while hardly less crude in its operation than the way officials, gendarmes, and auxiliaries burnt bodies during the *Aghet* to get at precious items secreted in body orifices, was also rather closer to Ottoman practice in its ulterior purpose.

For instance, Shalom Cholawsky reports a particularly furious row between Kube, whom we have already met, and his SS chief, Eduard Strauch, in July 1943, in which the ensuing insults back and forth actually revolved around the fact that Strauch had extracted gold teeth from Jews murdered on their joint Belorussian patch which he had then deposited with the SS in Berlin, not with Kube in Minsk.[241] Personal venality was something Himmler made a point of abhorring; he even talked sanctimoniously about the 'holiness of property',[242] underlining in doing so the very strange fantasy world he seemed to inhabit. Kube was hardly an isolated culprit in the eyes of one so supposedly incorruptible. The General Government was commonly referred to as the 'Gangster-Gau' while in the 'wild east' territories beyond there were administrators aplenty with kleptomaniac appetites every bit as voracious as that of a Dr Reshid.[243]

The SS, however, both as an institution and as a group of individuals, was equally self-serving. In Auschwitz opportunities for personal gain evolved so rapidly into a syndicate for corruption that in late 1943 Himmler felt impelled to carry out a special investigation, the result of which was that 700 staff from here and other camps were discharged or put under arrest. Hoess, though clearly implicated, escaped punishment by being elevated to a more senior position in the WVHA, returning to Auschwitz in time for the Hungarian Jewish *Aktion*.[244] It is clear that at the top of the 'system' there were exemptions from the standard rule. Himmler, after all, had demonstrated his largesse to the German settlers of Zhitomir and elsewhere with goods from the Auschwitz and Majdanek storerooms, while in July 1944 some 2,500 watches found their way from the WVHA hoard onto the wrists of Berlin residents who had suffered bomb damage. Attempting to ingratiate an increasingly restive and demoralized German population by way of filched Jewish valuables, nevertheless, was small beer when set against the systematic method by which dental gold and the wider proceeds of death camp appropriation ended up in a special SS account in the Finance Ministry—where the profits from sale of goods were used to offset loans to finance a plethora of SS economic enterprises.[245]

Looked at through this prism, and especially at the Nazi twilight, it was the overweening defence of the SS's own interest which stands out as one of the abiding features of the 'system'. We need to remember that Himmler's original intention for Auschwitz—as for Lublin—was as an *Interessengebiet*, a special SS-supervised zone geared towards the realization of Himmler's pet projects. In the Auschwitz case, a whole range of experimental agricultural and industrial programmes was centred on the construction of an entirely new set of facilities by the chemical giant IG Farben, whose remit was to produce synthetic rubber and liquid fuels in conditions of wartime petroleum scarcity. The expansion of the Auschwitz concentration camp was thus geared at the outset not to its extermination role but rather to providing labour for a critical facet of Germany's military-industrial complex and in order to build a model 'German town' (to replace the already existing Polish one), thereby ensuring that specialist IG Farben workers would settle in the area.[246] The SS, in other words, were only partially able to realize the sort of economic power wielded by their NKVD counterparts, given the ongoing autonomy and muscle of German corporate enterprises under Nazism. Yet by having a slave labour source at their command and increasingly in demand from the private sector, the SS ensured that they were well positioned to seize their own empire-building advantage.

To be sure, to suggest that the SS interest shifted radically towards hyper-exploitation of Jews for monetary gain at a time when the Auschwitz machinery of death was operating at full tilt sounds not just contradictory but crass. Yet, given overall labour scarcity on the one hand, and the—albeit dwindling—reservoir of remaining work-capable Jews in Auschwitz and satellite camps on the other, the value to the SS in hiring out their captive asset proved a significant factor in the ascendancy of the WVHA over the RHSA in the final years of the war.[247] Clearly, if this represented a new emphasis on productionist thinking over the straightforward exterminationist, it was both short-term and cynical in the extreme. Himmler had yet to waver from his commitment to fulfilling the special orders entrusted to him by Hitler. Rather, the final push to the intensification of Jewish (and other) labour—through a more forceful inveigling of Germany's corporates into the process as purchasers of this SS-appointed resource—highlights the manner in which the regime's commitment to genocide became caught up with the more pecuniary calculations of its chief agents.

This might be taken as reiteration of our point that Nazi genocide, elements of its doubtful modernist technique notwithstanding, was as mired in the peculiarities and frailties of human behaviour under stress as any other genocide. The one way in which the perpetrators perhaps excelled is a tribute not so much to the cleverness of their overall 'system' as to their basic cunning. The application of Zyklon B as standard killing agent in Auschwitz was essentially merely fortuitous (and we might wish to note in passing the irony of gas as a military application being first developed by a German-*Jewish* scientist, Fritz Haber, in the Great War and of his further post-war involvement in the development of prussic acid for pest control, leading to the formation of DEGESCH, the manufacturer of Zyklon B.)[248] The next best-known aspect of the Auschwitz system, the medical experiments, including those most infamously conducted on child Jewish and Roma twins by Josef Mengele, were in turn, crude, macabre, grotesque, and nearly always lethal.[249] But where the camp authorities showed genuine flair was in their efforts to deceive the victims as to their imminent fate. At Chelmo, arriving deportees were ushered in a friendly manner into what appeared to them to be a 'castle': in fact a country house at the end of which were the gas vans. Once in, no return. Further improvisation in the dissembling ploy involved the simple ruse of putting up a notice saying 'bath house', or 'shower room', where arrivals were required to enter into one of the Operation Reinhard gas chambers. At Auschwitz a van displaying the Red Cross emblem accompanied the victims to their final destination. The van was actually delivering the prussic acid.[250] When it came to the great *Erntefest* massacres the organizers went to elaborate lengths to conceal what was actually intended, the trenches prepared by Jewish prisoners being dug in a zigzag pattern to give 'credence to the claim that they were intended as protection against air raids'. On the day of the actual killing, the up to 18,000 prisoners were organized like an assembly line with female SS on bicycles and a spotter plane with two-way radio communication to keep track of the flow, while amplified music blaring out from two loudspeaker trucks sought to lull the Jews into a false sense of security.[251]

So, in the end, the SS became notably efficient in conveyer-belt killing processes, in the process assimilating themselves to much of their own euphemistic language with regard to what they were really engaged in. Some of the time their dissembly techniques also quietened the victims, though often panic set in, the result of which was chaotic scenes in and around the sites of death which the camp guards suffocated with terror and exterminatory violence.[252] Lying to their victims, and lying to themselves, could not however disguise one singular truth about Auschwitz. It had never been intended as a site of mass European Jewish extermination; it became so because of the failure of Hitler's war against the West, and, more immediately, against the Soviets. Having failed to deport Jews en masse beyond Europe, the Nazis' ideal site for expunging the Jewish problem was at Mogilev, still effectively off the map, indeed at the far eastern end of the rimlands. When it became clear in the face of Soviet military fightback that this would not be possible, the Nazis brought their unfinished rimlands business back into the arena of metropolitan Europe. Geographically Auschwitz was at the exact point where these political, economic, and ethnographic conditions—those of metropolis and of semi-periphery—met. 'A kind of central European Crewe' is one way Auschwitz has been described.[253] The explicit reference here, of course, is to its railway junction, which underpins how this 'ordinary' east Silesian town became the necropolis to which Jews from across the continent were conveyed, year on year, at Eichmann's directorial behest. But its symbolic significance is altogether more acute. Ever since the Middle Ages, Auschwitz had been at the boundaries not only between the Two Germanies of Austria and Prussia but also at the point where the emerging avant-garde, industrial-cum-capitalist West separated from the imperially-organized, agriculturally centred, and polyethnic world beyond. However, this did not prevent it from becoming the key interchange between these two worlds. In the nineteenth century, East Upper Silesia had been dubbed the *Dreikaiserecke*, 'the three Emperors' corner'—hence the importance of the railway lines that ran through Auschwitz between Berlin, Vienna, and St Petersburg.[254]

The Soviet liberation of the camp in January 1945 would bring an end to this singular geographical status, along with reprieve for some 6,000 sick but surviving inmates who had not been 'evacuated' westwards by the retreating Nazis. No consolation was on offer, however, for well over a million Jews who had perished there.[255] But other peoples, albeit in smaller numbers, had been killed there too. They included Roma.

THE ROMA: AN ADDITIONAL COMPLICATION?

Acknowledgement that, alongside Jews, Roma were also victims of Nazi genocide has been altogether slower in seeping into public consciousness. Indeed, the very terminology of genocide as appropriate to description of the Roma fate during the Second World War has been hotly disputed and contested in both legal and academic fora.[256] It is true that of an estimated 885,000 Roma living in Europe at the beginning of the war we have only a sketchy idea of how many were actually murdered. Most estimates put the figure in the 190,000 to 250,000 range—itself a staggering number. But there is the possibility that it could be as high as half a million, which would amount to a 70 per cent mortality.[257] A key aspect of the resistance to accepting even the lower range as prima facie evidence for genocide revolves around notions that for that phenomenon to occur a given set of ingredients or some preconceived, preferably intended trajectory towards destruction would be required. This argument, of itself, flies in the face of the accumulated evidence on the manner in which the Nazi Jewish genocide, or—as I would prefer—*genocides* occurred. This could signify that those sceptical researchers who are using Jewish destruction as their guide, or model, for the Roma case, might be doubly in error. Few would dispute that there are crossovers and similarities in the fate of the two peoples. The methodological issue really is whether we should treat Nazi policy and practice towards the Roma as an adjunct to that developed towards the Jews, or rather as something which (while it might at times have had much in common) was driven by largely discrete criteria.

For example, if we were to take Auschwitz as a key indicator of the Roma fate, in the expectation that this would follow the pattern of Jewish destruction, we could well end up confounded. Auschwitz was indeed a major though not the only destination of Roma deportations from primarily Central and Western Europe as well as from more local Roma communities in Poland. But transportation to Birkenau did not begin until early 1943 and none of the Roma who arrived there were immediately marched off to the gas chambers, as were the Jews who had not been selected for work. In fact, the Auschwitz Roma—so long as they remained in the camp—were not hyper-exploited, even though a previous Reich decree had sought to assimilate 'Gypsies' found guilty of crimes by the regular courts to the Jewish 'annihilation through work' condition.[258] Instead, the more than 20,000 Roma who between spring 1943 and August 1944 were inmates in Birkenau[259] were incarcerated in a family camp separate from all the others and in which men, women, children, and newborn babies were able to stay together as family units, without being shaved, or deprived of their clothes or other possessions they had brought with them.[260]

This already begins to sound disarmingly benign, as if the Nazi intention was only to detain the Roma, not harm them. Even the first two instances where Roma were gassed en masse—in fact over 2,700 of them in total—in March and then May 1943, could be read as misadventure, a consequence of the SS fears in particular of epidemic outbreak. In both instances the victims were suspected of being ill with typhoid fever. What this fails to take into account is the wretched conditions in the camp which produced or exacerbated already existing typhoid and a host of other highly contagious diseases. As a consequence the majority of the estimated 19,300 Roma who died at Auschwitz were victims not of the gas chambers but of illness and hunger.[261] Once again, reading the evidence thus would seem to divorce Roma death from Nazi responsibility. The manner in which healthy and ill Roma were crowded together in the confined space of the camp *anticipated* demographic collapse. This had happened before when 5,000 Austrian and German Roma had been deported in October and November 1941 into the Łódź ghetto. Confined to a tiny quarter from which Jews had been forced out, and with the windows of the buildings consciously smashed in by SS personnel during mid-winter, the occupants rapidly succumbed to typhus. No medical aid was forthcoming except that volunteered by Jewish doctors. The authorities however, had got their pretext. Bar a tiny handful sent for work, the Sinti, Kalderash, and other clans in the ghetto were among the first there to be dispatched to their deaths at Chełmno.[262] While one response in Birkenau was to follow this precedent, another tack adopted by Mengele and his team was to maximize the opportunity provided by the smorgasbord of disease to observe, cultivate, and experiment with cures. As a consequence, it was not just child twins who ended up on Mengele's slabs for dissection. The whole captive population was turned effectively into a guinea-pig colony to be experimented upon at will and dispensed with once surplus to requirements. No wonder that when room was needed for a further batch of incoming Hungarian Jews, in early August 1944, the remaining Roma population was liquidated without compunction.[263]

Even so, one can only be struck by the disjuncture between the Jewish and Roma experience in Auschwitz. The very fact that Hoess made no concerted effort to consciously split up or destroy the gypsy camp for well over a year after its foundation strongly suggests that there was no plan for its imminent eradication, or possibly that Nazi policymakers were so confused or at odds about what to do about the Roma that they were unable to arrive at a clear set of guidelines. Himmler, with overall responsibility for the matter, had issued what appeared to be a definitive order, in mid-December 1942, for the deportation of Roma from most of northern and Central Europe to Auschwitz.[264] If this was intended to offer coherence it was belied by Himmler's own repeated change of mind on the matter. Following the conventional wisdom, the Reichsführer-SS had previously assumed travelling Roma to represent a security threat, making them effectively 'spies', and thus secondary agents of the chief Jewish enemy—rather in the same way that suspect peasants during the Soviet collectivization drive were accused of being kulak 'hirelings' or 'choirboys'.[265] The initial consequence—at least on paper—had been a limited form of gypsy extermination, sedentary Bergitka Roma in Poland for instance, being less threatened than those who were itinerant. But then Himmler seems to have had doubts even about the nomadic Roma, his official diary note—interestingly following a meeting with Heydrich in late April 1942—stating 'No destruction of the gypsies'.[266]

So, how does one explain the ongoing lack of clarity? The very fact that there was no general deportation order until nearly a year after Wannsee suggests that the Roma question was not a wartime priority as was the Jewish case. Hitler's non-intervention on the issue also clearly relaxed the demand for urgency. The release of the Roma women and children from Semlin in early 1942, when their Jewish counterparts were all murdered, has never been adequately explained, but perhaps this too had something to do with Himmler's wider unease on the matter.[267] It was not just from this quarter, however, that there seemed to be an 'official' retreat from the exterminatory thrust. A draft OMi decree in July 1942 had proposed that all Roma—sedentary and itinerant, including *Mischlinge*—should be dealt with in the same way as Jews, an order which certainly reflected practice on the ground at this juncture. Yet when nearly a year later the decree was finally published it read as a complete volte face, exempting both categories from murder and instead proposing that Roma should be placed in special 'work and education' camps. Reaffirmed by a Rosenberg circular at the end of the year, this superficially sounded like Nazi policy which had not so much put off 'now' to 'later' as abandoned the mass murder of Roma—at least in the occupied eastern territories—altogether.[268]

Could it be that, in the course of attempting to think their way through to the point of mass murder, and considering what it was *exactly* that they found objectionable about this dispersed and clearly non-threatening set of communities, Nazi policymakers simply tied themselves up in knots? And could it even more bizarrely be that their attempt foundered in critical part because of their confused efforts to turn social and cultural prejudice into racial categories? Who were the really 'bad' gypsies: the ones who had settled down and intermixed with the wider population, perhaps spreading a perceived 'criminality' around them? Or the supposedly more 'racially pure' gypsies who wandered around but otherwise kept themselves firmly at arm's length from settled society? Among the first category there were Roma living as citizens in the Reich whose categorization as delinquents was manifestly false. How else could one account for the many thousands contributing to the war effort, often in the Wehrmacht, or armaments factories? Kripo officials attempted to circumvent this particular problem by defining such 'good' gypsies as 'socially adjusted', benevolently offering large numbers of them sterilization as an alternative to deportation.[269] But Himmler's ongoing interest in the historic origins of Aryan superiority took a further twist when, under the influence of scholars in Ahnenerbe he increasingly came to the conclusion, probably sometime in early 1942, that 'pure' Roma were among the descendants of the supposedly primordial Indo-Germanic master race. In which case, rendering them *Zukuntflos* would clearly be seriously in error. His solution, agreeing, interestingly, with Robert Ritter, though from a different perspective, was that the 'true' Sinti and Lalleri should not only be allowed to roam, but should even be provided with a special reservation for the purpose.[270]

Again we seem to be moving by degrees down a road which might suggest a conscious Nazi avoidance of genocide and in which Himmler himself, the man with the power of life and death over nations, was the chief Romani defender. To be sure, behind closed doors, there were intense discussions—in late 1942 in particular—about the Roma fate. Himmler's shift towards a supposedly more selective policy was ranged against Bormann, Goebbels, and the justice minister, Thierack, all of whom seemed to favour blanket deportation, followed by extermination. On one level, we might wish to interpret this split as yet another turf war fought within the Nazi elite and in which Bormann's rising star, close to Hitler, was a significant element—with the Roma themselves simply pawns in the game.[271]

But on two other scores such an interpretation would fail to get to the heart of the matter. First, the dispute about general deportation as opposed to Sinti and Lalleri freedom to roam referred only to the relatively limited number of Roma in the Reich. Focusing on the fate of these alone is thus a little like focusing on the German Jews who made up less than 2 per cent of the Jewish death toll in Nazi Europe.[272] And with the exception of cases such as the Bergitka, Himmler made no strident effort to protect Roma communities outside the Reich. On the contrary, for the most part he left the matter to his HSSPF emissaries on the ground—with utterly murderous consequences.

To be sure, this is where we enter onto terrain where our detailed knowledge of what happened to Roma, at particular times, and in particular places—in marked contrast, of course, to our knowledge of Jewish mass murder—becomes patchy and indistinct. In the French Unoccupied Zone, several hundred Roma suffered enormously from malnutrition and disease in a handful of camps—including the 'model' camp for travellers at Saliers. However, they were not deported to Auschwitz or other German killing grounds.[273] Yet the fate of the Saliers group stands out as the exception to the rule when put against the several thousand Roma incarcerated in occupied France and Belgium, large numbers of whom were deported under the terms of the Auschwitz decree. Here again, though, the issue of the fate of Roma in, or from, the west of Europe is in quantitative terms dwarfed by the picture in the rimlands. Henry Huttenbach singles out eastern Latvia, Belorussia, the Crimea, Serbia, and central Poland as the regions where the killing was most intense.[274] This clearly is not a blanket picture and the point may be that some Einsatzgruppen commanders, or security police chiefs, may have pursued their gypsy prey with more zeal than others.

This equally may tell us why some Roma communities, nomadic groups in particular, had better chances of survival than others, and almost always more than Jews. In the latter case the victims were sedentary and therefore much more vulnerable to being rounded up either for execution in situ or deportation to the gas chambers. Nomadic Roma were necessarily moving targets. To kill them, first you had catch them. Huttenbach cites elements of the Vestika and Xaladitka clans in both parts of Poland and western Russia avoiding this fate by melting into the forests.[275] Of course, many rimland Jews also escaped likewise into forest and swamps, especially where the opportunity for such action was greater, further to the east. But once there they needed open-air resilience and well-tuned environmental skills to match for individual or group survival. In such conditions it was almost certainly better to be a Rom than a Jew. Other cases suggest geopolitical fortune working in Roma favour. Albanian Roma in Kosovo, for instance, found themselves under the protection of the dominant Italian power, while after 1943 the situation here was too chaotic for the SS to mount concerted operations against them.[276]

However, none of this gets around the fact that where SD police chiefs sought to conduct anti-Roma operations they did so both systematically and with a vengeance. At the outset of Operation Barbarossa, Heydrich's 2 July order to the Einsatzgruppen did not specifically identify Roma on the list of those marked down for on-the-spot execution. Nevertheless, this did not prevent many commanders interpreting the order as including them.[277] Einsatzgruppe A in the Baltic arena seems as including to have operated on the clear assumption that Roma were active supporters of the partisans, spies, or covered by the blanket description of being subversive elements. Donald Kenrick and Gratton Puxon report a notably large massacre conducted by Einsatzgruppe B at Rodnya near Smolensk in which over a thousand Roma were killed. Ohlendorf's Einsatzgruppe D on entering Simferopol in the Crimea, towards the end of 1941 also lost no time in exterminating the large, settled Roma community there along with Krymchaks (a local Turkic-speaking 'Jewish' variant) and 'mainstream' Jews.[278]

Highlighting particular massacres such as these gives an impression of a staccato rather than concerted anti-Roma drive in the eastern territories. Kenrick and Puxon, however, offer an estimate of some 30,000 Roma killed in Nazi-occupied Soviet territories in the course of the war, equivalent perhaps to half of those living in the region.[279] More to the point—and here one can draw parallels with the Jewish case—the drive did not abate with the demise of Operation Barbarossa. On the contrary it seems to have been ratcheted up in the post-invasion phase. In the Ostland arena, Jeckeln spoke rather opaquely of the 'Gypsy question...being solved by the police in the exercise of its own jurisdiction'. Certainly, in the period from April 1942 to March 1943, nearly half of the estimated 3,800 Roma in Latvia were liquidated.[280] Elsewhere in this period, attempts to preserve the sedentary versus itinerant distinction were repeatedly lost in the intensified atmosphere of anxiety about partisans and the support roaming Romani bands were allegedly supplying to them. In the Ukraine, looking like a gypsy was enough to end up among the corpses in Babi Yar.[281] Neither the decree stating that gypsies ought to be kept for their own good in work and education camps, nor even a special scholarly mission under Himmler's auspices to study the Baltic Roma, proved any impediment to the destruction of, for instance (mostly in 1943), nearly all the thousand known Roma in Estonia. The death toll included the entirety of the ethnographically distinct ninety-strong Lajenge clan from the Tartu region.[282]

The genocide of small, discrete groups such as the Lajenge is significant. Roma did not and do not today generally operate as a single, monolithic entity—'a reflection of how they are seen by outsiders'[283]—so much as as a mosaic or network of diverse, dispersed, if ethnically and culturally related, peoples. While Jewish lobby groups, such as the grandly-entitled World Jewish Congress (WJC) attempted at the time to bring international attention to the fate of Polish Jews in Operation Reinhard, Polish Roma were also being sent to the gas chambers or shot in the open air, in repeated massacres. Yet there was no public Roma voice to alert President Roosevelt, or Prime Minister Churchill, to their plight. Nor, indeed, post-war, was there a wider societal urge towards recognition that what had happened to European Jews also happened—along a somewhat different route—to Roma. The discrepancy is note-worthy. Jewish academic study, followed by overt political efforts to build 'a monu-mental industry of remembrance'[284] around the Holocaust, were never matched by anything comparable from Roma quarters. How could there be when the Roma's socio-economic—and with it educational—profile, continues to remain so abject? With the *Porrajmos* a matter of intensely personal suffering, or shame, for the survivors, or even a basis for group memory suppression—'forgetting'—piecing together the specifics of Roma destruction across the rimlands and beyond became the work of a dedicated few, prepared to work at the margins of Holocaust studies and against the grain of most public interest, or support.

Yet it is in this general indifference to the Roma fate that we have our second clue as to why what we are dealing with is a very distinct genocide. The very man-ner in which the post-war German federal courts stonewalled restitution to Roma survivors for decades by claiming that the police in the Nazi era were simply responding to the gypsies' own 'asocial' behaviour speaks volumes about not just German but a much more general and ongoing European negativity towards them.[285] Prejudice in itself is a long way short of genocide, and even being consid-ered, as Gunter Grass has put it, 'the lowest of the low'[286] does not constitute an explanation as to why Roma should have been the target for extermination— except perhaps that in Nazi terms eliminating such a group, as in the case of the mentally and physically ill or challenged, has a certain *logical* ring to it. To be sure, as Steven Katz has opined, 'the Nazis were confused and uncertain about the status of Gypsies in essential ways, as compared to the self-assurance about the transcen-dental negative status of Jews'.[287] Yet actually, this is as irrelevant to the unfolding of the Roma killing as is the federal courts' post facto circumvention of its true causation.

The attempted destruction of the Roma occurred *in spite of* the Nazi's convo-luted effort to pin down their alleged racial deficiency, not because of it. When Bormann contested Himmler's belated endeavour to talk up a supposedly undi-luted Roma racial value he not only claimed Hitler would object to any change of policy but, much more tellingly, proposed that it 'would not be understood either by the population at large or the lower ranks of the party leadership'.[288] If Bormann was correct, then this would make popular antipathy towards the Roma much closer to what Goldhagen has described as a 'culturally shared cognitive model'. Except, of course, Goldhagen had in mind a grass-roots antipathy to the Jews, whereas what Bormann was implying was a widespread anti-gypsy sentiment which percolated far and wide into the Nazi party. In other words, to paraphrase Goldhagen, Germans hated gypsies but did not need racial science to desire their elimination. By this same reasoning, moreover, the rise of Hitler was not so much the cause of Roma genocide, as its opportunity.[289]

What is certainly striking about the timeline of Roma destruction is that there is no clear trajectory, nor by the same token, any tapering off of the killing as the war reached its end. Much of the killing indeed, not just at Auschwitz, seems to have *accelerated* towards the last months of the war. This included some 800 Roma murdered in early 1945 at Mauthausen, the harshest, most hyper-exploitative of the concentration camps within the Reich, while a February directive from the Justice Ministry to the Linz prison ordered the execution of all Gypsies 'when prisons near the front line were evacuated'.[290] Equally striking, however, is the knowledge that in the face of the continued round-up and deportations of German and Austrian Roma through to the summer of 1944, there appears to have been no noticeable communal disquiet or dissent. Provincial party officials supported by Kripo continued to interpret the Auschwitz decree liberally in order to ensure that their localities could be proclaimed 'Gypsy-free', just as Sipo and Order Police functionaries operating in the east continued to ignore directives which would have spared thousands of Roma from the accusation of partisan collaboration.[291]

In choosing to take initiatives in this way—in many of these instances even wilfully side-stepping instructions from the centre—were such officers of state responding to higher Nazi imperatives of 'applied biology', or actually to something entirely more deep-seated and visceral, emanating not so much from the German as from the wider European psyche? Bauman's modernity thesis, and in particular his 'weed-less garden' metaphor, offers a neat way of rendering Nazi behaviour a function of the former. But the repeated manner in which officers at the periphery blanket-charged gypsies as subversive, degenerate, criminal—and 'black'—suggests a psycho-sexual disgust and phobic loathing whose roots are to be found less in modernist racial science and much more in an atavistic and, one might add, ontological aversion to the 'other'. In this instance, the 'other' happened to be the nearest equivalent in most sedentary Europeans' eyes to the 'primitive savages' of the colonies. And again, one can only note that such grass-roots animosities, which have culturally bound so many *gadze* together, did not abate in post-1945 Europe. They simply lost their immediate genocidal edge. So, perhaps, Nazi modernism in its aspiration for a hygienically cleansed bio-politics did offer, after all, a pretext for a branch of the European family to do what many other Europeans always wanted to do to their backyard aborigines—before, and since. And, as we will note in the next chapter, under the Nazi umbrella, many others joined in the killing spree.

Certainly, it is ironic that no place could be found in this project for Himmler's romantic rendition of the authentic Roma as 'noble savages', nor for his imagined locale where they would freely roam. His grasp on the direction of project, indeed, seemed to falter in the final war years—when arguably other priorities, including the Jewish one, continued to be uppermost in his mind. To be sure, for genocide to take place still required a *framework* of state persecution, of which Himmler was an undoubted if not the sole architect. However, as Michael Zimmerman has adduced, the lack of an a priori programme to destroy the Roma did not preclude a result which *was* genocide.[292] All it needed was approximate guidelines for state functionaries and especially security police chiefs to act as its prime drivers. Nevertheless, it is difficult to imagine Roma genocide taking place outside of the wider, more all-encompassing context of Jewish genocide/s. But as the war unravelled, that Nazi project—though with no consolation, of course, for its continuing hundreds of thousands of victims—seemed to be heading towards entropy.

DENOUEMENT BY WAY OF GEOPOLITICS

What happens to a process of genocide when the perpetrators, previously seemingly unbounded in pursuit of their quarry, find themselves in military retreat, even threatened with political demise? In the case of Rwanda, the Hutu Power regime kept up its murderous assault on its ethnic and political enemies regardless. But, as we have noted, the whole sequence lasted only one hundred days, while the *génocidaire* leadership, along with vast numbers of its rank-and-file accomplices—undoubtedly aided by French covert support—was able to make its escape across the border into Zaire. Hitler and his entourage had no such let-out. At Casablanca, in early 1943, the Allies had committed themselves to Germany's unconditional surrender. The disaster at Stalingrad came hot on its heels. Sooner or later, defeat would become total, the regime extinguished, its leaders probably arraigned on crimes against humanity charges (amongst others), Germany perhaps even liquidated as a political concept.

Or was there a way out? Militarily, there appeared to be no satisfactory answer to this conundrum. Politically, however, there was one time-honoured precedent which offered the regime a glimmer of hope—if anybody, that is, was prepared to contemplate running with it. You sought to make terms with one side of the alliance ranged against you. In this case that meant splitting Western 'system' from Soviet antisystem, thus in all likelihood resetting the terms of the struggle, with Germany now a partner preferably of the winning side. By 1943 any chance of a strengthening and clearly vengeful Soviet Union being this partner was all but fantastical. Indeed, a quarter century on, the very notion of a reverse Peace of Brest-Litovsk with the 'Bolsheviks' sweeping aside the rimlands to take dominion over the German *Heimat* was arguably the very nightmare which kept the Wehrmacht intact and fighting. Most Germans thus did not need the Nazis to see that salvation could only come from the Western Allies. And, of course, this was precisely the impetus for those in the non-Nazi elite who joined the secret generals' plot in their 1944 attempt to assassinate Hitler, take the reins of power, and sue for peace with the West. Even with such men at the helm, however—had the 20 July plot succeeded—it is highly doubtful that London and Washington would have been deflected, at least not at this moment, from their wartime commitment to Stalin. So, how could the Western Allies conceivably have broken ranks with Moscow to make a deal with the Nazis?

Let us leave that problem to one side, for a moment, however, and concentrate on how Himmler, one key Nazi who *was* making the calculation, would have perceived the odds. Bulking large would have been the Jewish element of the equation.

As we have already stated, there was no actual Jewish dimension to the geopolitics of the Second World War and in Western Allied eyes the fact that they had to deal with it at all simply added a very unwelcome complication to their policy deliberations. To which we will shortly return. For Himmler, however, as for all true conspiracy believers, behind Churchill and Roosevelt was the world Jewish cabal. Thus, winning over the Western Allied governments would have to involve both somehow convincing them that whatever had happened to millions of European Jews in the course of the war had not involved any conscious programme of extermination and at the same time guaranteeing that those communities who were still alive would not be further threatened or harmed. In other words, it would entail a project of what we would today call Holocaust denial even as mass extermination was still proceeding.[293]

If this sounds as fantastical as the Nazis coming to terms with the Soviets, in 1943, or 1944, the point we have to bear in mind is that Himmler did make a number of secret, extraordinarily Byzantine, indeed utterly convoluted moves in the final years of the war not only to conceal the truth from the West, conceal but to use the 'Jewish card' as a route to doing business with the Allies. The project sounds doubly fantastical when we know that Himmler was duty-bound to Hitler no less, to pursue Jewish destruction to the bitter end, while there is nothing in his personal record to suggest a change of heart or mind with regard to his totally Judaeophobic world view. On the contrary, even as he 'pragmatically'—actually extremely clumsily as well as belatedly—attempted to 'trade' Jews, Himmler's public utterances are self-evident proof of his unrepentantly murderous malevolence towards them.[294]

Even so, one of the peculiarities of the situation was that Himmler's entirely unauthorized manoeuvres not only had to involve cloak and dagger tactics vis-à-vis the Allies, but also had to be disguised from a regime still committed, at least on paper, to a streamlined 'Final Solution'. This is not to say that others in the regime were not aware that what they had done to date might come back to haunt and even destroy them. There was after all, a *domestic* as well as foreign policy issue to consider. Explaining to future German generations, long after the Jews had been eradicated, that this had been done for their wellbeing as well as for the good of civilization was all very well from a position of assured and unassailable German power in the world. However, it might be much less easy to sell to a contemporary public which was increasingly restive at the prospect of looming defeat and with it of probable Allied retribution. Goebbels, at the onset of Operation Reinhard, in late March 1942, might have committed to his diary that 'no other government . . . and no other regime would have the strength for such a global solution of this question',[295] but little over a year later Bormann 'by order of the Führer', was issuing a circular to the entirety of the executive elite, including the RHSA and HSSPF, requiring their public silence with regard to 'any mention of a *future* total solution'.[296]

Clearly, by this time, the scale of the Jewish atrocity had seeped out far and wide into German public consciousness. Nor were the Propaganda Ministry's media outlets noticeably backward in intimating the outcome even if knowledge of the Jews' exact fate was supposedly under lock and key.[297] But could inadvertent disclosure of the whole truth lead to a public backlash, perhaps even to the sort of societal destabilization which the Nazis always related back to their 1918 'Jewish' incubus? Few 'ordinary' Germans were as prepared to openly defy Nazi policy *tout ensemble* as were the Munich White Rose group of students who paid for it with their lives. But when some 200 Gentile wives of Jewish husbands rounded up for deportation, began to spontaneously demonstrate outside the Berlin Jewish administrative offices in the Rosenstrasse where the Gestapo had incarcerated their spouses in late February 1943, a swelling crowd of demonstrators over the following week presented the regime with a singular problem. To now deport not just these men but the *Mischlinge* from these marriages to the east could lead to a wave of questions about the *wider* scope of the 'Final Solution'. We can read the release of the Rosenstrasse prisoners and the abandonment of deportation of many thousands of intermarried and part Jews from Germany as a notable victory for non-violent protest in the face of totalitarian power. But what is more likely to have been behind the regime backing down—with the proudly defiant Goebbels actually taking the key decision—was the fear that details of the extermination programme might now become general knowledge.[298] It is no surely no coincidence that later that summer Himmler gave secret orders to the SS to begin the process of erasing traces of *all* the killing grounds—with Paul Blobel, one of the early Einsatzgruppen mass murderers, put in charge of the operation.[299]

Blobel had in fact already been hard at work in the autumn of 1942, digging up no less than 100,000 corpses at Birkenau—from the period prior to the installation there of the dedicated crematorium—and incinerating them.[300] However, the notion that a relatively small squad—*Sonderaktion* 1005—was somehow capable of working its way round both the Balkans and 'Lands Between' disappearing the entirety of the physical evidence is bizarre to the point of being risible. More pointedly for Himmler, by the time Blobel began his efforts the Allies were already quite well informed as to the range, scale, and main methods of the 'Final Solution'.

Jodl, at the Nuremberg trials, may have described the undertaking as a 'masterpiece of concealment' but British decrypts of Order Police radio communications, which were not covered by Enigma—the advanced coding machine used by the German military and RHSA—meant that Whitehall's intelligence services were able to compile highly confidential reports of the open air mass killings of Jews in the course of Operation Barbarossa. They were read, amongst others, by Churchill.[301] Certainly, it took somewhat longer for a full—and coherent—picture to emerge of the all-encompassing nature of the death camp killings. There were, too, some critical mishaps on the way. One was a failure in August 1942 by the Swedish government to pass on to the Allies details of the gassing technique, as conveyed to one of their diplomats by Kurt Gerstein, a genuinely distressed SS officer, responsible for shipments of Zyklon B, to, amongst other users, the Auschwitz camp.[302] However, in the following months Allied intelligence was in receipt of various reports from Polish and Jewish as well as neutral (including Swedish) consular sources as to the existence of the gas chambers. Equally critically, in November, these varied sources were corroborated in person—to both British foreign secretary Anthony Eden and later Roosevelt—by Jan Karski, the Delegatura's official courier who himself claimed to have been smuggled in and out of Bełzec to view what was happening there.[303]

Karski's mission had direct and almost immediate consequences. The Polish government-in-exile did not sit on its accumulating evidence of Jewish destruction but instead compiled it into a full report which in turn, on 10 December 1942, became the basis for a direct *démarche* to the Allies. Would they, the Poles asked, find a way of bringing pressure to bear on the Germans so that the killing operation might be halted? Their petition came at a moment when a wider societal awareness—aided by increased media reportage of the European Jewish fate—was equally building up into a grass-roots clamour for something to be done. It was even mirrored in the Soviet Union. A press release in *Tass* declared that Germany had initiated 'a special plan for the complete extermination of the Jewish people'.[304] The joint Allied leadership felt impelled to respond. Seven days on from the Polish diplomatic move, they made a joint declaration outlining the destruction of the ghettos and the transportation of 'hundreds of thousands of entirely innocent men, women and children' to their deaths. With notable resonances of the Entente declaration on Armenia twenty-seven years earlier, they reaffirmed 'their solemn resolution to ensure that those responsible for these crimes shall not escape retribution'.[305]

Clearly then, for Himmler, the cat was out of the bag. Not only did the Allies know the terrible Nazi secret but they were now promising their own vengeance for what had been done. But was this not itself proof that the Allies were in thrall to the Jews? Into 1943, as the Allied blanket bombing raids on German cities became continuous and catastrophic, Goebbels went into propaganda overdrive to represent this 'terror bombing' as the work of the Jewish enemy, the outcome of which, ironically, was to reinforce a conviction at much of the German grass roots that if the Jews were responsible it must be in retaliation for *Kristallnacht*, or for whatever had been done to them 'in the east' since then. Goebbels' misinformation thus, was double-edged—inadvertently, or implicitly perhaps, accepting a case for Nazi atrocity but attempting to turn it into a basis for an even more desperate and fanatical German commitment to the failing Hitler cause.[306] By the same chop logic, this time from a Himmlerian perspective, could not Jewish conspiracy-inspired 'information' to the Allies be turned back on itself and proved to be disinformation, thus unlocking the door to the West's capitals? In which case, for Himmler, was the Allied declaration evidence not so much of danger but rather of an opportunity?

Before we dismiss this speculation as further evidence that to do so is to engage with the ludicrous as well as dangerously grotesque, let us remind ourselves of certain commonalities that such 'thinking with the Nazis' has with other more 'normative' elite calculations of this moment. For instance, paradoxical as it may be, the Polish *démarche* in December 1942, at least according to David Engel's reading, was itself predicated on an assumption of the existence of 'Jewish power' in Western capitals. Actually, there was nothing new in this view: successive Polish governments since the end of the Great War had obsessed about Jewish influence as a factor working *against* the Polish interest. In late 1942, however, they came to the entirely pragmatic conclusion that advertising the Jewish disaster then taking place primarily on Polish soil might work *for* Polish interests, in the sense that it might bring greater Western attention to bear on a wider Polish suffering which the government-in-exile deemed had been lost to view.[307] For a brief period, too, Jewish leaders were encouraged by the success of the Poles to believe that they might be able to change Allied policy, the Zionist David Ben-Gurion for instance proposing a slew of strategies to get the Nazis to terminate their killing programme, including the bombing of German cities in direct reprisal for the murder of the Jews.[308]

For a Goebbels, or a Himmler, knowledge of such responses it would have confirmed what they had *believed* all along: 'the West' really was in the hands of its Jewish master puppeteers.[309] This, in turn, would be to prove how wrong one can be. The Allies in December were responding to what they saw as humanitarian pressures emanating from various directions, including public opinion. The one thing they had no intention of offering was a declaration which would commit them to some change of geopolitical course. Indeed, appropriate public utterances aside, the point of their statement was to enable them to rapidly resume wartime 'business as usual'. Thus the only link which can be established between Allied Jewish policy, on the one hand, and Nazi Jewish policy, on the other, is the former's absolute repudiation of the latter's basic operating premise. The great tragedy for European Jewry is that its desiderata, in order to be saved, fell precisely between these two irreconcilable stools.[310]

Many volumes on the subject, of course, have gone to considerable lengths to demonstrate something more: that the Allies showed unconscionable indifference to Jewish suffering, a complete lack of imagination, or even downright anti-Semitism.[311] One can certainly chart a whole litany of straightforward 'realist' interests which put a spanner in the works of meaningful 'rescue'. Ongoing Jewish and other humanitarian efforts to have Washington and London commit to providing assistance to fleeing Jews, including the necessary travel documents and safe havens beyond the Nazi reach, foundered primarily because neither Great Power would countenance large numbers of Jewish refugees ending up in their metropolitan or, in the British case, imperial territories. This reasoning did not preclude small-scale actions, for instance to facilitate the passage to safety of groups of young children, as rescued or sometimes ransomed by Jewish efforts. But when it came to anything which impinged on raison d'état Washington and London went to considerable efforts to stonewall or circumvent any alternative strategy. As a result the much touted Bermuda conference of April 1943 in which State Department and Foreign Office met to discuss rescue plans was, as much as Evian five years earlier, a model of diplomatic spin and practical pointlessness.[312] Finally, when it seemed that there might be a genuine opening for mass rescue, in the summer of 1944—when the Regent Horthy offered to let the Hungarian Jews leave the country—the British response was not to dispute the genuineness of the offer but to charge that it was a German destabilization tactic, the aim of which was to flood Jews into the Middle East: in other words, to sabotage HMG's Palestine policy.[313]

If these narratives point to any number of Allied avoidance tactics, what perhaps they do not get to the heart of is the Allied fear of playing straight into the hands of the Nazis. That is, of seeming to conduct the war as if it really were 'a Jews' war' in which they, the Allies, were the Jews' proxies. The Nazis read the war as one between themselves and two systems, the West and the Soviet Union, both of which were supposedly Jewish-run and Jewish-controlled. The Soviet response was to simply refuse to acknowledge the inference, or that its Jews had in any way been singled out for annihilation. This came with its own notable contradiction in the form of the wartime Jewish Anti-Fascist Committee (JAC) which though conceived by rimland Jews and sympathizers, Moscow sponsored, not least in order to encourage Western support for the Soviet war effort.[314]

The Western Allies, from their own perspective, equally rejected the notion that any non-state, minority community had leverage on the conduct of the war. This did not discount some ambivalent 'recognition' of the singularity of Jewish suffering and hence some accepted leeway for humanitarian efforts. This support, however, came with firm caveats that such efforts could not be a burden on US or British coffers, nor involve the creation of additional administrative bureaux. The formation in February 1944 of the US War Refugees Board (WRB)—despite the lack of reference to Jews in its title—was in these terms an extraordinary departure, in significant part the consequence of the Roosevelt administration's new anxiety that its inaction since Bermuda would be exposed to public scrutiny by a growing and clamorous refugee lobby. Clearly, late in the war, the Western Allied line that the war against Germany was a matter of undiluted raison d'état and was not to be deflected by other agendas was beginning to become a little frayed, even if the WRB played only a minor role in the last-ditch US and other western Jewish efforts to save what was left of European Jewry.[315] However, the Western Allies remained adamant that no direct Jewish pressure would be allowed to interfere with the conduct of military policy. When it came to the issue of bombing the railway lines into Auschwitz, or the camp itself—something which was logistically conceivable from the summer of 1944, at the height of the Hungarian Jewish exterminations there—its Jewish proponents were met with a flat refusal from Allied military and political chiefs. The only Allied bombs which fell on Auschwitz-Birkenau were ironically those intended for the IG Farben Buna plant up the road at Monowitz—where large numbers of Jewish slave labourers also happened to work. The bombs had missed their target![316]

*

So, does this tell us that Himmler's subterranean Jewish policy, involving concealment of the 'Final Solution' on the one hand, seeking to trade some of the surviving Jews on the other—with both as a route to peace negotiations with the Western Allies—was a wasted effort? The simple answer has to be a resounding 'yes'. The more complex and with it controversial answer might be: 'not where those efforts could be shown to have purchase with regard to the Allies' *own* strategic interests'. Himmler would have known for instance that the West sided with the Soviet version of events at Katyn in order to preserve their friendship with Stalin, though doubtless he would have been heartened if he had equally known that they engaged in a high-level cover-up to blame the Germans for a war crime which was demonstrably not of their making. If Roosevelt and Churchill were prepared to lie in the interests of the Soviet alliance, the key question for Himmler would have been, would they be willing to do the same on the Nazis' behalf, should the West–Soviet alliance begin to fragment? In 1943, as the Allies still struggled for military mastery, there was little evidence of any such split taking place, though it is significant that Himmler's instructions for the expansion of Aktion 1005 did come in the wake of, and were almost certainly galvanized by the furore surrounding, Katyn.[317] In other words, Himmler was already looking to a cover-up of the mass graves of the Jewish dead as part of his insurance policy with the West.

It is also observable that in 1943 various limitations were placed on the immediate destruction of *some* Jewish communities. Between February and August, for instance, a halt was called to deportations from Terezin to Auschwitz, and thereafter when deportations resumed, instead of the deportees going straight to their deaths a special Czech-Jewish camp (akin to the Gypsy camp) was established at Birkenau. For a while too there was a hold on a cohort of Polish Jewish children being sent to the gas chambers, while convoluted—and ultimately abortive—efforts were made to exchange them for Nazis or Nazi sympathizers held by the British.[318] All this could be argued to be no more than a subterfuge, part of the Nazi game-plan to conceal the truth about the ongoing mass murder. In the following year there were even more pronounced efforts, including one to inveigle the Swiss and more specifically the International Committee of the Red Cross (ICRC)—practically a sub-category of the Helevetic polity—into endorsing assurances of the continued survival and wellbeing of the Jews in Terezin, and even a supposed yeshiva in Bratislava.[319] But there was also the curious case of the 5,000-strong community of Danish Jews, the majority of whom, in the autumn of 1943, appear to have been allowed to escape en masse across the channel between Copenhagen and neutral Sweden, practically under the noses of the German security police. The political situation in Denmark under German occupation was almost tolerable compared with most of the rest of Nazi-dominated Europe, but this moment happened to be one of local emergency in which a national uprising seemed imminent. Even so, Werner Best, Germany's pleni-potentiary in Copenhagen and leading SS light, turned a blind eye worthy of a Nelson to the Danish rescue operation, even as the decision to round up and deport the Jews was on the cusp of being implemented. And to add to the curiousness of the episode, while his police powers were transferred to a new HSSPF, Himmler neither notably reprimanded nor sacked Best for his dereliction.[320]

How much weight should one attach to the Danish affair? Bloxham specula-tively links it to Himmler's two speeches in Posen in subsequent days in which he stated that the task of Jewish destruction 'had been accomplished'.[321] Clearly, this sits uneasily with the ongoing trajectory of Jewish killing which continued una-bated almost to the very end of the war. The sparing (temporary or otherwise) of particular selected communities (whether the Danish community was intended as one of these or not) remained however a very calculated aspect of a Himmlerian proposition that they might add grist to his attempt to find an opening to the West. Certainly, the fact that Hitler at the end of 1942 had already endorsed his proposal that rich Jews might be ransomed, or those with foreign passports could be exchanged with the Allies for German POWs, gave Himmler the official alibi he needed to take the subterfuge further. A special 'star' camp had been created at Bergen-Belsen exactly for such purposes, even as the wider Jewish mass killing reached its zenith.[322] But it was not until the spring of 1944 that the Reichsführer-SS was presented with his signal opportunity to really run with his clandestine, if thoroughly misconceived, scheme.

By this time, the writing was on the wall for the Nazi regime. The Red Army was breaking through into the rimlands, the Western Allies gearing up for D-Day. Fascist Italy had already changed sides the previous year, even while the Wehrmacht attempted to keep a hold on the peninsula. All eyes by March 1944 were on Hungary, which Western intelligence agencies now anticipated would jump the Axis ship if the Allies would provide the necessary guarantees for its sovereign integrity. Clearly, Budapest was looking to Washington and London to pull its chestnuts out of the fire and so save Hungary from Soviet tutelage. But the prize for *all* the Allies was also great if Hungary did defect, its contiguity with the Reich and hence the realignment of the strategic picture in Central Europe if it did so leading surely to a radical shortening of the war. The Nazis had known for months that something was afoot and pre-empted it by taking over the country on 19 March—though without removing Horthy as its head, or his administration. Concomitant with invasion was the clear intention to eliminate Hungary's estimated three-quarters of a million Jews from the *strategic* equation. As we have already noted, part and parcel of this carefully planned operation was to utilize as many as possible of the able-bodied among them for hyper-exploitative purposes. When Horthy had conceded to Hitler in person, just prior to the takeover, that Germany might take 300,000 Jews for work in German war industries, on neither side was this intended as a euphemism for *immediate* extermination.[323] However, if this makes the Hungarian Jewish destruction in some sense distinct, nothing had fundamentally changed in terms of the Nazi analysis of the Jewish responsibility for the situation in which it now found itself. If, in 1941, at the time of their offensive thrust into Russia the argument had been that the Jews had to be eliminated because they were the Bolshevik vanguard who would direct the partisan attack in the rear, so now, with Germany on the defensive, the argument was practically identical. Edmund Veesenmayer, Hitler's Central European expert and the soon-to-be plenipotentiary in Budapest, said so very clearly, in late 1943, when in a memorandum to Ribbentrop he proposed that behind the Hungarian peace bid was the Jewish 'Enemy no. 1'. They would, said Veesenmayer, do everything in their power to sabotage 'the struggle for the defence of the Reich'.[324] Or turned on its geopolitical head, the refusal of the Horthy regime to play ball with Nazi *Judenpolitik* was proof-positive that it was seeking exit from the collapsing Nazi camp.[325]

For our discussion, however, the significance of the Hungarian events as they began to unfold towards Jewish destruction in the high spring and early summer of 1944 is twofold. First, Allied pressure on Horthy did not desist, but rather became more centrally focused on the issue of the Jewish deportations to Auschwitz. With the involvement of a range of diplomats from neutral countries, including the Vatican, but with the Western Allies clearly orchestrating the campaign, one might read this as further evidence that Washington and London had worked their way beyond their standard 'realist' script and were now essentially motivated by a concern to save Jewish lives. Certainly, by early summer, nobody in a senior position of responsibility in Whitehall, or the White House, could claim they did not know or understand what was at stake. Indeed, very precise details from Auschwitz on the imminent Hungarian *Aktion*—as provided by two escapees whose information reached the Allies via Switzerland—reinforced the Jewish lobby argument that time was of the essence. And, as a matter of fact, the pressure on Horthy did intensify towards the end of June, he himself interpreting the US bombing of Budapest railway station on 2 July as a direct act of 'Jewish revenge'. His response, soon after, was to suspend the deportations.[326]

Nevertheless, the degree to which the Western Allies were really motivated in their actions by the imminent danger to the Jews is at the least discussable. If they were so concerned, why did they not attempt to broadcast information about Auschwitz to the Hungarian Jewish masses faced with extinction and so fragment the deportations programme?[327] Instead their efforts were high-level, the focus essentially on Horthy and getting him to break with the Germans, which indeed he finally did attempt, though not until mid-October, and then entirely unsuccessfully. The irony is that the one person who most definitely would have read all these Allied moves as 'Jewish-inspired' was none other the Reichsführer-SS. This brings us to our second significant element: Himmler's clandestine counter-move.

What was Himmler playing at, in the spring and summer of 1944? He remained in principle loyal to Hitler but knew perfectly well that an internal crisis was brewing. Yehuda Bauer has persuasively demonstrated that this included his knowledge of the dissident generals' intended move against the Führer. Himmler's own relationship to this scheme, thinks Bauer, was of a 'wait and see' nature but with the clear intention that in the event of the scheme's success, he himself would intervene, the security apparatus, *not* the generals, taking over the reins of power. With key impediments (including Hitler) out of the way, he then could get on with the serious business of negotiating with the West.[328] Again, if we take into account both the hubris and the confabulated world view of the man, this is an entirely plausible proposition.

Bauer also offers evidence to suggest that discreet contacts with the US Office of Strategic Services (OSS)—the precursor of the CIA—had taken place during 1943, which would dovetail with Himmler's efforts to selectively trade or put off the death of some Jewish groups. The critical Nazi intermediary in these moves, moreover, was Walter Schellenberg, head of the espionage bureau *Ausland* (Department VI) of the RHSA but perhaps more significantly one of a new, younger 'realist' school within the SS prepared to 'think the unthinkable' in order to save the regime. This included, as and where necessary, handing over large numbers of surviving Jews to neutral third parties such as the Swiss, a project Schellenberg would particularly espouse a little later on, in the autumn of 1944.[329] Himmler could not do anything so bold without igniting Hitler's ire which would then have put him irrevocably in the traitors' camp. Hence, his sideways effort at the time of the Hungarian 'crisis' to make contact with leaders of Vaada, a Zionist rescue group within the Budapest Jewish community which was willing to consider negotiating with the SS in order to save Jewish lives. His unlikely conduit and emissary was none other than Eichmann. In April, he secretly put on the table to Vaada an offer to free 1 million Hungarian Jews (hence ostensibly in line with Hitler's 1942 concurrence with ransom packages) if Vaada in return could provide 10,000 Allied trucks to the Nazis. Where the Allies and their trucks really came into this equation must have seemed entirely opaque—while the proposed use of Joel Brand, one of the Vaada group, as go-between was all the more so, in that he had no standing with anybody of importance whatsoever bar (and this only at third or fourth hand) the Zionist leadership in Palestine. On the other hand, what Eichmann ostensibly was offering Brand was tantalizing: papers to travel to neutral Istanbul to negotiate with Allied representatives for the first thousand trucks, and on his return—with the assurance of their delivery—not only would 100,000 Jews be released but the same thereafter for every further batch of one thousand trucks. Eichmann even promised in one of these meetings to 'blow up' Auschwitz.

For Brand and his group here was the opportunity to save the Hungarian Jewish community. The problem was that as soon as the British got their hands on him in Aleppo, they realized the full extent of the ruse. The real player in the mission was not Brand at all but one Bandi Grosz, who at Department VI behest accompanied Brand to the Middle East. Grosz's actual role was to renew contact with the OSS—as well as British intelligence—and on the back of the faux trucks proposal cajole London and Washington into more serious if still secret meetings with the likes of Schellenberg, as a prequel to a separate peace. Instead, the British interned both Brand and Grosz, read their separate efforts as two sides of a Nazi ploy to sabotage and/or blackmail the Allies' war effort, and very publicly broadcast their rejection of the mission. As for Himmler, his cover was not blown. Grosz, after all was a low-grade Jewish spy formerly run by Canaris' increasingly untrustworthy intelligence agency, the Abwehr. And that agency had been dismantled on Hitler's orders in February 1944, damning Grosz thereby as an unreliable witness. As for the Hungarian Jews, for the time being at least, their extermination went on.[330]

In which case, one might legitimately ask, why expend effort charting what was to an all intents and purposes an ill-conceived and hopelessly misjudged farrago of a scheme which failed to bring the 'Final Solution' to an end? After all, it was not just Hungarian Jews who were being killed in the final countdown to *Götterdämmerung*. Italian Jews, more Slovakian Jews, Jews from the Greek islands as well as from Łódź in toto and Terezin in part, were still being shipped to Auschwitz in the autumn of 1944.[331] And the killing continued into the New Year, not least as the SS attempted to evacuate—mostly on foot—its Auschwitz and other Polish camp labour forces in the direction of the remaining concentration camps in the Reich. En route, in freezing conditions, and without adequate food, shelter, or support for the increasingly wretched and ill, prisoners, both Jewish and non-Jewish, perished in their tens of thousands. For the Jewish prisoners, however, the direct killing went on unabated. The several-hundred-mile marches round an imploding Reich were also for many of them death marches in which the accompanying SS guards took the opportunity, often with great zeal and blood-lust, to massacre their charges.[332] In this sense, nothing had fundamentally changed or slowed down the Nazi urge to kill Jews. Nor would Hitler have wanted it any other way. To the bitter end he remained consistent in his hatred and firm in his orders that the SS were to blow up all the camps and with them their Jewish prisoners on the point of surrender to the Allies.[333]

The fact that the end did not quite happen in this way, however, presents us with a different dilemma. That the process was curtailed and in the final paroxysms of the Reich not turned into a bloody liquidation of *all* the remaining Jews in the camps was chiefly on account of Himmler. Something of his efforts to put a spoke in the works of the very project of which he had been chief architect, thus, was of some ultimate consequence. So given the knowledge that some hundreds of thousands Jewish lives were saved as a result, does this mean that we might in retrospect find some small ounce of sympathy for this twentieth-century *génocidaire* par excellence?

The proposition, however, is misconceived. The issue is not simply one of Himmler the monster being also Himmler the man with feet of clay—in other words, a fearful human being, like others, who faced with punishment seeks to find some excuse by which he can prove himself innocent of wrong-doing. In a secret, unprecedented and entirely extraordinary night-time meeting with Norbert Masur, the Swedish and himself Jewish representative of the WJC, on the estate of Himmler's confidante, Felix Kersten, on 22 April 1945, Himmler offered an explanation of what had happened to European Jewry. In this account death through typhoid epidemic bulked large, the crematoria were the only way the SS could combat the disease spreading to themselves and, of course, a blameless Himmler claimed he was now being accused of cruelties whose roots were to be found in the Jewish-led 1918 uprisings which had affected both Germans and Jews alike.[334] This craven performance on its own should arrest any tendency we might have towards giving him the benefit of the doubt.

The very fact that he met with Masur, however, is of great significance. Indeed, it demonstrates an aspect of Himmler's *consistency* to the bitter end. In the upshot, for the Reichsführer-SS there were two forces that counted in the world: the Germans and the Jews. Their struggle was at its foundation racial but it was also clear, in the conditions of adversity that the former now found themselves, that the dialectic would have to be broken off for the time being—necessitating coming to peace terms with the 'enemy'. The WJC—or running a close second, the US Jewish aid organization 'the Joint'—from a Himmlerian perspective were as close as one got to the true centre of that enemy power. This rather suggests that Himmler, even at this eleventh hour, believed that interceding with 'the Jews' would somehow save not only his skin but that of the German nation.

This game-plan, we have already suggested, was the nub of Himmler's 'blood for trucks' grand design, a year earlier. When the Allies had refused to play ball, Himmler ought to have recognized the dead-end nature of his own reasoning. Instead, he persisted. And with that comes our paradox. Many thousands of Jews who would otherwise have been killed lived to tell their tale. To be sure, there was no further grand design. Yet under Himmler's aegis SD Department VI continued to seek undercover contacts with the 'Joint' and WJC. Whether it was via the Swedes, Swiss, or ICRC, what we have to remember is that behind all these cloak and dagger efforts was Himmler's unshaken conviction that negotiations with and about 'Jews' remained the best path towards his elusive goal of contact with London and Washington. Again, clandestine and horribly tortuous as Department VI's game was, the removal of prying Abwehr eyes (its operation having been taken over by the SD itself) made playing the Jewish card just that touch more conceivable. Also in-built into the strategy was the winding down—though not, as we have seen, the complete cessation—of the killing operations. The last transport to be exterminated at Auschwitz was from Terezin, on 30 October 1944. Thereafter, the SS began dismantling the crematoria. Two months earlier, Himmler intervened directly to halt the deportations from Hungary to the death camp as he was to do again at the end of November to call off what had become death marches from Budapest to the Austrian border.[335]

By this juncture much of the direct intervention to help Jews in the Hungarian capital was coming through the neutral consulates, including diplomats prepared to put themselves in the line of fire to provide actually quite legally dubious *Schutzpasse*—papers of protection for Jews threatened either by the SS on the ground, or the newly rabidly anti-Semitic Arrow Cross administration. Clearly, as power rapidly ebbed from the Nazis and their proxies, the Swedes, Swiss and other neutrals were able to play a critical role in their own right in favour of the genuinely humanitarian interest.[336] Even so, the Swedish, Swiss, Joint, WJC, and Vaada rescue efforts would not have been able to proceed without intermediaries on the SD side acting for the Reichsführer-SS.

Not that Himmler did not remain fearful that he would be exposed from within the apparatus as 'a traitor and saboteur of Führer orders'.[337] Eichmann—always a reluctant player in the Hungarian 'trucks for blood' scheme—in early December 1944 had to be ordered into line by Himmler himself. But there was also Eichmann's fellow-Austrian and close associate Ernst Kaltenbrunner, who had succeeded Heydrich as RHSA head and who refused to have anything to do with Himmler's plan to forestall the liquidation of the camps.[338] As the latter moved more hastily from the following January to arrange for the open release of selected Jewish groups, the internal split within SS ranks began to become serious, not least as Himmler's expressed orders forbidding the killing of any more Jews were repeatedly ignored by officers at the cutting-edge of the death marches.[339] And there was still Hitler to contend with. When it became public knowledge that Himmler had arranged for 1,200 Terezin inmates to be released to Switzerland in early February 1945—a further desperate ploy to open lines to the Western Allies—the Führer's subsequent rage had Himmler rapidly back-tracking on his previous intention to deliver the concentration camp populations safely to the ICRC.[340] Until the very last days of the regime he proved incapable of making a decisive break with Hitler on the latter's Jewish policy. When he finally did so, he was stripped of his offices by a Führer raging from his Berlin bunker at the world, the Jews—and a German people who had failed him. By then, too, despite his last-minute efforts to release Ravensbrück's women prisoners and ensure the peaceful transfer of Bergen-Belsen to the Allies, the options had long run out for Himmler. Cornered by the British in late May he bit on his own cyanide pill.[341]

We might read this final denouement as a struggle between a pragmatic Himmler and a diehard Hitler, or, down through the ranks of the SS and wider Nazi entourage, as between realists and exterminators. But this would be to vastly overdo the distinction. It was not pangs of conscience which had taken Himmler down his final 'softer' path, but the entirely naïve if not fantastic notion that there remained an alternative to Nazi self-destruction. One has to ask who then were the realists? But in seeing the looming certainty of defeat as bound up with what had happened to the European Jews, on the one hand, and the supposedly irresistible forces of world Jewry on the other, Himmler and his clique of negotiators chose to read the situation as a dialectic—albeit an entirely misconceived and false dialectic. In this, of course, they were no different from Hitler and all the other true believers, save in their singular insistence that if you told a pack of lies and covered up the 'Final Solution' tracks you could somehow not only get away with mass murder but even reshape geopolitical realities back in your own favour.

When the British and Americans entered Belsen and Buchenwald they saw with their own eyes the truth of the matter. It was, of course, in its own way a very distorted truth. The piles of bodies and the sight of an unfathomable assault on humanity were imbibed in the West for many decades thereafter as the essence of Nazi genocide. Actually what their soldiers had witnessed at this point was the terminus of genocide as well as something more indicative of the broader descent of defeated German state and society into breakdown, chaos—and decentralized violence.[342]

What ultimately could not be avoided—despite many of the best Allied efforts to do so at Nuremberg and far beyond—was the degree to which Nazi atrocity was bound up from beginning to end with a projective vision of Jewish power. For such a dispersed, minority people the Jews seemed to be imbued by the Nazis with the most phenomenal potency and resilience, even when the very heart of their physical and cultural existence had been blotted out by Himmler's men. That the Western Allies did not quite seem to understand, or perhaps more accurately, wish to understand the nature of the Nazi projection, is itself noteworthy. On one level, it conveniently let them off the hook from having to deal with a pathology which intruded to the core of European geopolitics. Yet on another, it ought not to have been so difficult to grasp. Anti-Semitism, or more accurately, Judaeophobia, remained a *cantus firmus* within swathes of wartime state and societal life far beyond Hitler's Germany. But then, perhaps, to have looked this phenomenon in the face might have required Western observers, then as now, to have considered how it was that *other* rimlands' genocides committed against Jews—and also Roma—emerged out of the war without being the direct product of the Nazis.

3

Other Europeans and the Destruction of the Jews

SETTING THE SCENE

Every society, in relation to the Jews, must work to destroy them—whether we will call this extermination, expulsion, or assimilation, does not change the essence of things. Both Judaeophiles and anti-Semites want to destroy the Jews as Jews, that is, as representatives of a separate society.

'Anti-Semitism and the Jewish Question',
Głos (editorial), October 1886[1]

For all the complex and tortured trajectory of the Nazi assault on the Jews, if we could draw a line there and agree that European Jewish destruction was driven, organized, and carried out, if not always by German anti-Semites then, at the very least, at German behest, the work of the historian would be so much easier. 'No Hitler, No Holocaust' should offer us a sound axiom.[2] Hitler led, the Germans followed. Or if we wanted to take the alternative Goldhagen line, that the Germans were already potential eliminators, Hitler instead provided the occasion for the realization of *their* deepest desires.

Alas, the matter by either standard or Goldhagen route is not so simply foreclosed. The Holocaust writ large may have required a hegemonic centre, provided by the Nazis. And *that* regime was domestically a product of German society. So far, so clear. But the scope of the Jewish killing was pan-European, embracing not just countries which came under direct Nazi tutelage and some where puppet regimes were installed, but others, again, which were technically autonomous sovereign states, even if partners to the Axis. One might wish to dispute how relevant this was: surely the point is that under their sway the Nazis could call the shots whenever and wherever they chose? Except that this is to ignore that Nazi absolute dominance was relatively short lived and, even during that period, so long as the war remained to be won, the German Foreign Office remained highly cautious about overstepping the mark. As for the Jewish question, the Nazis never *on their own* had the bureaucratic machinery, let alone manpower, to bring the 'Final Solution' *throughout* occupied Europe to completion in wartime conditions. Obversely, while partner states' leeway to defy Nazi diktat may always have been circumscribed, it was never so circumscribed as to render them utterly powerless.

At the heart of this chapter, thus, is a question: not so much to what degree did other Europeans, in their respective state or societal configurations, assist the Nazis in their exterminatory Jewish and Roma projects; but rather, especially where they retained state sovereignty—albeit in the context of ephemeral Nazi domination—did they consciously drive their own national anti-Jewish agendas towards the actuality of genocide? Or did they change course, away perhaps from the finality of eradication but not necessarily from the possibility of mass eruption? And where they did not eruct all of the Jews, did they seek to remove those of them in their midst whom state and society considered beyond redemption?

The menacing, not to say vitriolic statement from a Polish journal at the head of this chapter is included simply to remind us that animus towards the Jews was neither new, peculiar to the Germans, nor marginal. We have already stressed that in the wake of the Great War the tendency became bound up not only with 'New Europe' nation-building, but with a potentiality for violence the likes of which had not been seen since the mid-seventeenth-century Khmelnytsky massacres. Indeed, in the European rimlands arena, one might go one further step and agree with Joseph Rothschild that in the interwar period it was 'the only really potent international ideology', regardless of whether the polities and societies there were protégés of the Western alliance or of the revisionist camp.[3]

Might this help delimit complicity in actual Jewish suffering during the Holocaust to an eastern frame of reference? That would certainly be convenient, in that it would reinforce the sense of an historic split between the avant-garde nation-state polities in the West, with their more coherent civil societies, and those more nascent ones in Eastern and south-eastern Europe, where ethno-religious distinctions remained to the fore. Convenient but unfortunately inaccurate: the fact that Germany, with its strong sense of civil society, opted for Nazism would seem to put an immediate spoke in that wheel. The role of neighbouring France, in its post-1940 Vichy incarnation, would appear to undermine the supposition further still, through its willingness to collaborate with Nazi 'Final Solution' deportations as well as to initiate its own anti-Jewish measures. To be sure, that is not the full story. Vichy's responsibility in Jewish destruction went as far as assisting the Nazi removal of thousands of Jews from France, but not to the point of introducing its *own* killing machine. Perhaps that provides a place to begin this chapter: a differentiation between the various non-German state and societal responses to the Jews, and Jewish mass murder.

Helen Fein, in an early and at the time ground-breaking analysis of those differences, pointed to elements of resistance which were founded on the democratic underpinnings within societies and on well-grounded notions of a universe of obligation, which extended across religious and ethnic boundaries.[4] That might account for strong countervailing tendencies within French society against the Vichy programme, though, as Fein discovered, it also embraced societies in Eastern Europe with less obviously democratic credentials. Bulgaria, for instance, was one state which, through wider protest, forestalled *part of* the German deportation programme. The degree to which one might draw general conclusions from such disparate cases, however, is less easily discernible. Fascist Italy was notable in protecting not only its own Jews but also Jews in areas where its military held wartime sway; at least, that is, until

Mussolini's polity collapsed in 1943. Antonescu's Rumania, having commenced its own independent project of Jewish genocide in 1941, did a volte-face the following year and—quite duplicitously—attempted to portray itself as another Jewish 'protector'. Hungary's Jewish population remained largely intact until the German military takeover in 1944. All these countries were right-wing, authoritarian, and overtly fascist or para-fascist in their orientation. The Netherlands, by contrast, with its pronounced history of liberalism and tolerance, proved abject in its failure to defend its Jews. But then, the Netherlands was not just an occupied territory but one where for geostrategic reasons the occupation regime was notably severe. That would seem to take us back to our starting place, of German overall responsibility for the Holocaust. Independent states, perhaps even paradoxically those most Axis-inclined, were in a better position to safeguard their Jewish populations against the Nazis, if they so chose, while those who were subjugated were not. No wonder, then, that the Netherlands along with Greece and Poland lost over 80 per cent of their respective Jewish populations. Once the Nazis took over other 'friendly' states in their sphere of influence, Jewish chances of survival in them also radically diminished.

So far, then, we seem to have a picture of European involvement in Jewish extermination which is highly dichotomous. On the one hand, the overriding factor would seem to be German wartime control of a country combined with its determination to carry out the extermination policy there. Hence, one might argue—with various caveats—the exceptionality of the Danish case. On the other, we have multiple players with varying degrees of political autonomy whose behaviour towards their Jewish populations appeared to oscillate during the course of the war, with enthusiasm for the Nazi grand design necessarily receding as Nazi fortunes themselves spiralled downwards.

But even this assumption may be too simplistic. Was there an independent variable at work? By which I mean, to what extent were the autonomous state elites in the Nazi constellation making judgements about their own Jewish populations based not so much on the overall 'Jewish question' as presented by the Nazis, as according to their own understanding of the profile of those populations combined with economic and/or political forecasts as to the benefits that might accrue from eliminating all or some of them? Of course, the very nature of anti-Semitism always complicated any attempt to disaggregate internal Jews from their avowedly international dimension. And after 1917, the ready acceptance among so many European elites and demotic movements alike that Jews and Bolshevism were one and the same strongly played to the Nazi argument that what was at stake was not the defence of any single state but that of European civilization writ large. This wider anxiety certainly provided one pull factor towards the Nazi camp among right-wing elements, especially—though far from exclusively—in a rimlands where the Soviet threat was perceived as ever-present. This, in turn, carried with it a German assumption that they could look to satellite states, or for that matter vanquished societies, to support or even participate in their exterminatory project. Indeed, where local polities or populations took the matter into their hands, so much the better.

The problem for the Nazis, however, was that their new post-Versailles European anti-system was still predicated on the existence of *nation* states. And barring those states which had been swept aside by the Nazi reordering, the remainder were still highly protective of their sovereign rights and, for that matter, prerogatives with regard to their own minority, including Jewish, populations. This suggests, on the wartime issue of what to do with the Jews, the evolution of not simply a two-way but a three-way dynamic between each state and the Germans, and there again with regard to their respective Jewish population, which would also speak against uniformity of practice. Thus, French and Bulgarian ambivalence towards the German destruction process, at two ends of the continent, is the main point of discussion in the section after next. This is succeeded by a more geographically focused consideration of the Balkans, where a notable eagerness to do the Nazi bidding on the part of the Ustasha had, as its counterpoint, high-level military and civilian efforts by the Italians to resist this trajectory. If both tendencies proved vulnerable to overall shifts in the balance of Balkan power, the next section—which concentrates on those regions of the 'Lands Between' where the Nazis swept away recently imposed Soviet rule—begins by looking at a very specific genocidal 'moment' at the outset of Operation Barbarossa. Again, though, there is an element of comparison and contrast. If strong evidence might suggest the urge by elements of local populations in the Baltic and *kresy* regions, in the absence of their previously-existing states, to kill Jews, or put themselves at the disposal of the Nazis for the same purpose, how should we understand the apparent drag on such tendencies emanating from the Polish shadow state? Pre-war Polish animosity to the Jews in a country heading rapidly towards its own version of para-fascistic authoritarianism was on a par with other states in the rimlands. The fact that Poland as a state was dissolved in 1939 leads us to ask what might have happened if the Colonels, on their own account, had been able to pursue their anti-Jewish trajectory.

In our penultimate section, however, we can chart one case, that of Rumania, where despite subordination to the Axis, a rimland state carried out its own unequivocally independent genocide against Jews. To be sure, we can again hedge this with caveats about its timeline, extent, even its attempted reversal. One thing that seems to be becoming apparent from this exposition so far is the relative weakness of these rimlands polities compared not only with their more dominant neighbours but in relation to the wider geopolitical scene, and the manner in which this reality circumscribed their ability to do exactly as they might have pleased had they been stronger states. But, paradoxically, a *lack* of freedom of manoeuvre might also have worked to their advantage, or at least those elements among them with very specifically anti-Jewish agendas. In our final section, therefore, we will assess the actions of those Hungarians who used the occasion of the Nazi thraldom in 1944 to work hand in glove with Eichmann's team, even as this ostensibly went against the grain of official Magyar policy on the Jews.

But then, how at odds was the path pursued by the Hungarian Interior Ministry clique in the spring and early summer of 1944 with that of its predecessors or of the broader Sztójay administration of that moment? Perhaps before we can even consider the multiplicity of subordinate state (or non-state) responses to the Jews, across Europe, we need to return to that issue of an independent variable in national thinking. In other words, we need to offer a brief reconsideration not so much of European Gentile perceptions of Jews as of the differentiation *between* Jews which went with it.

TOLERABLE JEWS AND IRREDEEMABLE JEWS

Historically, the annoying thing about 'the Jews' was they could not be properly categorized. To describe them as a religious group was insufficient, inexact, or irrelevant. As far as religion was at all was concerned, it was the transgressive nature of their relationship to Jesus Christ, or rather the way it had become embedded in post-apostolic theology, that mattered for *most* Christian believers. A more scientific biblical exegesis, much of it paradoxically deriving from Germany, may have tentatively reached the point by the Second World War where it could acknowledge the fundamental Jewishness of Jesus, but this had little or no impact on the consciousness of most Europeans. Underpinning everything which said that the Jews were irredeemably 'other' was thus the legacy of nearly two thousand years of irreconcilability to the ubiquitous presence on Christian soil of those who had supposedly first rejected the Lord and then been responsible for his death. To ignore such charged emotional stimuli, especially in an Eastern Europe where religion really did still matter at all levels of communal, societal, and political interaction, would be to side-step what was foundational to anti-Semitism. But then this was part of a *longue durée* of mutually fraught Jewish-Gentile relations, whereas what was actually gaining ground in the years leading up to 1939 was the recrudescence— again very particularly but not exclusively in the rimlands—of a more virulent strain of the phenomenon. Or was it actually mutation? Put aside all the racialized discourse with its dubious assertions of a medical and scientific authority, it was the alleged responsibility for the Bolshevik revolutionary movement, and the unbending conviction which went with it that an atheistic Soviet Union was being run and organized in order to encompass Christian civilizational destruction that, once again, nailed the Jews as fomenters of an age-old subversion and destabilizing treachery. Except now, there was an eschatological timeline which demanded not passivity in the face of the oncoming catastrophe, but resolute vigilance and defiance. For those who read the world in binary terms, economic collapse, rapid social change, and political uncertainty were all simply signs of a master emplotment in which the Jews were the existential threat; they, the Europeans, their fearful victims.

Except that this was clearly not the only narrative on hand. The largely successful integration of Jews into the wider body politic had been one of the major products of modernity, at least as it developed in the nineteenth-century West. And fundamental to this process, paradoxically enough, had been nationalism. By redefining the Jews as not a separate corporate entity, the standard medieval formulation, but as a body of individuals, with legal entitlements and responsibilities on a par with all other citizens, liberal political philosophy created a formula for Jewish emancipation without reference to the whole fraught backdrop of religious objection. At least in theory. Certainly in the West, as we have seen, settled Jewish communities embraced their usually new-found secular status with vigorous enthusiasm. In France they redefined themselves as *israélites-français*, in Germany as *deutscher Staatsburger jüdischen Glaubens*, in Britain hardly less pompously as Englishmen or Britons of the Mosaic Persuasion. Believing themselves liberated from the legal constraints and social prejudices which had previously hemmed them in, proponents of this *Haskalah*—the 'Jewish enlightenment'—proposed that Jews were, like Christian denominations, practising their faith in a defined private sphere but otherwise fit for purpose to pursue public and occupational roles on a par with everyone else.[5] One consequence was an increasing plurality and complexity in Jewish modes of behaviour. Intermarriage, for instance, became more common, notably in the German world, where identification with the national culture was marked. While such assimilation did not lead to a complete unravelling of Jewish communities, a sense of the debt owed by the emancipated to their emancipators often expressed itself in an exaggerated sense of patriotic identification, or, as one Russian Jewish observer noted of the leadership of early twentieth-century Anglo-Jewry, in 'monstrous...expressions of loyalty'.[6]

Even so, one might propose that, with regard to an Eastern European context that included the great demographic bulk of Ashkenazi Jewry, the Western European formula for Jewish emancipation offered itself as a plausible model for emulation. If the old Judaeophobic poison had been lanced by giving the impression that Western Jews had been tamed and domesticated to Western national but civic norms—however misconceived the underlying premise—could one not at least argue that if it had worked in London, Paris, or Berlin, it would equally do so in Budapest, Bucharest, or Warsaw? Moreover, there was already evidence in favour of the proposition. As the Dual Monarchy embarked on an emancipatory path in the later 1860s, it was not just Austrian Jews, but metropolitan and urban Magyar ones too who began to fervently identify with the dominant national culture. And in return, it seemed they were welcomed as co-workers in processes of state-led national modernization. As the urge to national self-determination grew in the Russian and Ottoman empires, so too there were forerunners in the Jewish camp— usually highly wealthy or already well-acculturated groups and individuals—who were prepared to throw in their lot with emerging (if dominant) indigenous national movements. Significantly, elite Western Jews considered it their duty to offer their support for the creation of new nation states. When, in 1878, organizations such as the French Jewish *Alliance Israélite Universelle* came to Berlin to lobby the Great Powers about Balkan Jewry, it was not the sovereignty of the new post-Ottoman polities there to which they objected: they simply wanted the assurance, guaranteed by the Powers themselves, that Jews qua Jews would be granted the same secular rights and freedoms as other subjects; in other words, to be treated as equal nationals of their respective nation states.

The fact that they ran into a perfect storm, however, underscores the manner in which the Congress of Berlin represented a significant historical turning point for European Jewry, just as, in a not entirely dissimilar manner, it did for the Armenians. Russian foreign minister Alexander Gorchakov, for one, famously warned his fellow diplomats not to 'confuse the *israélites* of Berlin, Paris, London, or Vienna, to whom one would assuredly not withhold these rights, with the *juifs* of Serbia, Rumania and several Russian provinces who...were a veritable scourge to the indigenous population'.[7] Here, then, a clear distinction was being made between Eastern and Western Jewry. The latter were, according to Gorchakov, lacking in threat to the advanced polities and societies of which they were accepted as part. But his equal implication was that the demographic weight of the former, combined with their almost monotonal middleman profile in an environment which had a long way to catch up in terms of economic take-off, would result in suffocation of any movement towards an *indigenous*-led development. By further implication, most Jews could not be *indigènes*. Rather, they were outsiders, or even 'invaders' who had come from somewhere else—presumably the formerly Polish Pale of Settlement—whose presence in embryonic polities such as Serbia and Rumania was thereby disruptive of any 'natural' evolution.

Worryingly involved in such an analysis was not only an early but significant repudiation of rimlands Jewish aspirations to be included within any universalized set of state obligations, but also a shifting boundary as to where the rimlands began and ended. Jews in Vienna, according to Gorchakov, were on the right side of the boundary. Perhaps that boundary, for the time being at least, extended too to Habsburg Budapest, with Jews acknowledged there as 'insiders'. On the strict proviso, that is, that they acted in consort with a Magyar modernization drive against the putative urges of Slovak, Rumanian, and other subordinate national groups. Where that left traditional, orthodox Jews on the Hungarian side of the Dual Monarchy borders, who may have crossed at some stage from Galicia into Transylvania or Slovakia, or, by the same token, Jews in the Rumanian province of Moldavia, who included quite recent settlers from across the Carpathians, was another matter altogether. Certainly, when Bucharest leaders talked about emancipating Jews in 1878 and thereafter, it applied to a tiny, wealthy, and—more importantly—serviceable fraction of that community, or those who had proven their loyalty to Rumania through military participation in its struggles for independence.[8]

Even then, however, there was a further implication in Gorchakov's protest which blurred the distinction between acculturated (Western) and 'unreconstructed' (Eastern) Jews. By going out of their way to support the struggle for their co-religionists' emancipation in faraway countries, were not those in London or Paris interfering in business which was not theirs and also demonstrating that they always put their loyalty to fellow Jews before that to their own country? Looked at with clear sight, what groups like the *Alliance* were attempting was actually no different from more general public-supported efforts by the European Powers to come to the aid of their fellow Christians in the Balkans. What is telling about the anti-Semitic undercurrent from 1880s onwards, however, is the way the parallel Jewish effort fed a fundamental cognitive dissonance. Just as Armenian *dhimmi* were meant to know their place in a strictly defined and Islamic-sanctioned Ottoman pecking order, so uninvited Jewish 'interference' on their own account, in the conduct of international relations, confirmed—certainly for the likes of Gorchakov— that the world was being turned upside down. Indeed, some of the seeds of the *international* Jewish conspiracy motif emanate from this point—the *Alliance* in particular marked out by anti-Semites as the official front for world Jewry's demonic project of Christian enslavement.[9] There was a further unfortunate consequence. While elite Western Jewish organizations did not desist in their efforts to defend the rights of, or ameliorate the position of, their rimlands brethren, their more discrete post-1878 approach on these matters was increasingly paralleled by a domestic distancing between themselves and incoming waves of *Ostjuden*. In this sense, Gorchakov's differentiation between 'good' but numerically insignficant *israélites* and a 'bad'—by implication vast, unwashed, and hence unhygienic—mass of migrant *juifs* was to a considerable extent imbibed and internalized by Western, or Western-aspiring, Jewry.[10]

In the wake of the Great War these negative trends were simply exacerbated. The efforts of 'New Europe' regimes to cover up internal deficiencies by blaming Jews for anything and everything which went wrong became almost standard fare. Indeed, one might interpret this tendency as among the classic danger signals we have previously identified as *conditions* for state-led genocide associated with second wave, old/new, strong/weak polities.[11] Post-1919, these components were repeatedly evident in the manner in which political elites compensated for the actual fragility of their very novel states by exaggerating, even fetishizing, supposed heroic national pasts in order to both legitimize and bolster up ideals for a homogenized, ethnically-based present. If this was the aspired-to route to national 'strength', the constant fly in the ointment was a Jewish foreign body which could not only not be absorbed but whose ongoing presence further weakened the anticipated healthy prognosis. According to the 'New Europe' script, other Christian minority peoples might be assimilated into the social organism, even if by thoroughly coercive means. The Jewish presence, by contrast, was a cause for neurosis not simply by being there, but because of its connectedness to forces outside the country that were allegedly bent on disrupting the state's self-willed, developmentalist path.[12] Hence the assumptions about Judaeo-Bolshevism—and also about Jewish malevolence in its broadest, mythic sense. If New York and London Jews had sought to undermine national sovereignty by forcing the Minorities Treaties on the new states in 1919, it was this same cabal who had used the Sudeten business in 1938 to try to catapult Europe into war. Nor was it just the aggrieved nationalists in the east who claimed to recognize this hidden hand. The insistent pre-war rallying cry of the French rightist movement Action Française proclaimed, 'Behind Czechoslovakia it is the Jews who are pulling the strings.'[13]

If all this tells us a great deal about how highly insecure social formations took refuge in the utterly paranoid conviction that they were the victims of a *stateless* community (and hence little or nothing about the Jews themselves), two further complicating aspects need noting before we can consider some of the wartime consequences across Nazi-dominated Europe. The first is in the nature of Jewish response. Through to the Congress of Berlin, the standard *Haskalah* commentary on anti-Semitism had been to discount its persistence by pointing to the pace at which Jews were proactively embracing the forces of change. But it is also significant that when in the early 1880s anti-Jewish pogroms exploded on the Russian side of the 'Lands Between', some of the most fervent proponents of the assimilation route *there* began to despair that this in itself would suffice. Leo Pinsker sought to put his finger on the problem when he proposed that so long as the Jews remained a 'ghostlike apparition of a people without unity or organisation, without land or other bond of union, no longer alive, and yet moving about among the living', Gentile fear of the condition would *always* express itself in hatred.[14] In other words, for the new breed of Zionists, of whom Pinsker was a forerunner, the only antidote to the Judaeophobia of other nations was for the Jews to 'return' to being one themselves.

Henceforth, an increasingly intransigent Zionist position in the rimlands—and, thus, in considerable measure a mirror image of the nationalisms around it—rejected the notion of any possibility of compromise or middle ground between Jews and Gentiles until a compact territorial solution for the Jewish question had been found. But by pursuing this argument, mainstream Zionists, while claiming to speak for all Jews—as, in a sense, assimilationists before them had also done—were beating their own path towards discriminating between 'good' Jews—in their case those who saw themselves as national—and 'bad' ones, who were still mired in a redundant, even obscurantist past. Russian Zionists of the famous second wave immigration (*aliyah*) to Palestine in the early 1900s even described the Jewish rimlands environment which they were leaving behind as the *shmutzige shtetl* (filthy village), thus emphasizing a self-referential distinction between their vanguard, progressive selves and a Jewish diasporic majority who had yet to realize their own intrinsic worth.[15]

Here, then, was an internal Jewish paradox. Jewish nationalists in the years leading up to the Second World War evinced an ambivalence about their relationship to fellow, usually traditional, orthodox *yidn*, primarily of the former Pale of Settlement, similar to that of those equally 'progressive' Jews who were drawn to Marxism (sometimes with notable Zionist overlap and combination) or, again, to assimilationists—particularly, in the latter case, when it came to *Ostjude* immigrants. And this tendency, as we have already inferred, represented a form of conscious or sub-conscious mimesis of a broader European anxiety. One might add that it also happened to be entirely consistent with a more general, modernist urban horror—whether expressed in nationalist or internationalist terms—of what was perceived as the shambolic, disorganized, superstitious backwardness of the village-based polyglot rimlands. The difference in the progressive Jewish case was that the horror did not as a rule express itself through a racialized discourse. Modern Jews might look with a degree of distaste or even contempt on other, backwater Jews, but the separation was usually perceived as being reparable through cultural change.

To assume, however, that among Gentile detractors a racialized discourse was the standard route towards a reification of the Jews into one absolute monolithic entity might itself be to overstate the case. To be sure, racial science gave Nazism the pretext it required to represent *all* Jews in exactly such terms, thus making the rapacious, pernicious, disease-carrying stereotype of the *Ostjude* the archetype for the entire 'race'.[16] Yet, as we have seen in the previous chapter, this did not prevent a frisson of disquiet among middle-ranking officials when nicely spoken fellow-Germans were massacred on arrival in Riga in late 1941. Indeed, the very manner in which the architects of the 'Final Solution' separated out some of those Jews they perceived as echt Central Europeans to be sent to Terezin, or gave exemption from immediate deportation to the married partners and offspring of others, suggests that there may have been a subliminal sense in accordance with which cultural mores still operated even among true Nazi *génocidaires*.

Which brings us to the significance of our second complication, as opportunities for a wider non-German participation in the elimination of European Jewry expanded from 1941 onwards. Even at this late stage, the impact of the Western emancipationist ideal continued to have a residual bearing on the thought-processes of rimlands elites. There were some fascist groups, of course, such as the Iron Guard, or Arrow Cross, who embraced the Nazi racial tenets hook, line, and sinker. But most mainstream, usually right-wing, anti-Semites tended to operate on the more cultural premise. Jewry, as an entity, was something which had to be destroyed, just as *Głos* had proposed back in 1886. And in the best of all possible worlds that could be best achieved with regard to the majority by having them 'disappeared' to somewhere else. It was no coincidence that among the most enthusiastic supporters of Zionism were other rimlands nationalists who saw in the creation of a Jewish Palestine the answer to their most intractable problem. But those Jews—usually a distinct minority—who had become sufficiently well acculturated to national state norms and ideals might be 'disappeared' by gentler methods, and without the necessity of their *physical* removal.

Thus, if in the context of Nazi hegemony state elites saw a unique opportunity for the removal of their own perceived *Ostjuden*—the ones who not only would not or could not fit their top-down, monocultural criteria for inclusion within the body politic, but whose economic and/or political profile also allegedly threatened its very integrity—there remained alongside this a perhaps rather obstinate alternative script. This stated that those Jews who had been around for decades, better still centuries, who more or less looked like *us*, behaved like *us*, had imbibed *our* sense of values, and thus thought of themselves hardly as Jews at all but more as true, patriotic members of *our* (imagined) homogeneous community, ought to have whatever wealth they or their ancestors had taken from *us* returned to the national treasure, and certainly be made to do labour in the national cause, but they need not *necessarily* be eructed.

Rather suddenly the legacies of yesteryear came home to roost in a Europe of ostensibly independent states that was in practice subordinate to Nazi hegemony. If you were a Jew, where you had been born, where your parents had lived, the dates and papers proving where and when your or their naturalization had occurred became quite literally matters of life and death. Indeed, the incoming rules and regulations hardly served to foster a new-found sense of Jewish communal solidarity. On the contrary, even in crisis mode, their net effect was to reinforce all the boundaries and distinctions which, at Gentile bidding, Jews had been busily throwing up between themselves over the previous century.

COLLABORATIONIST STATES WITH
AMBIVALENT RECORDS

That nation states might enact legislation which separated some or all Jews from the rest of the population—implicitly or explicitly, thereby denying them citizenship rights—suggested not simply a repudiation of the democratic and liberal values which had accompanied the Western-led march towards modernity, but a conscious regression to policies more associated with the *ancien régime*. In medieval and early modern times polities had regularly shown their antipathy towards their Jewish (or Roma) inhabitants by kicking them out across territorial boundaries. Yet statelessness in the past had hardly existed as a concept, and Jews (or indeed Roma) who had been living in one sovereign entity might simply set up shop in another. In a Europe of nation states, by contrast, to lack citizenship—to be *apatride*—was to be no one, a literal non-'entity'. In the context of Nazi Europe it was to be deliverable into whatever black hole the Nazis had devised for the removal of such blanked-out persons.

This last sentence may be a necessary caution given that the leaderships of independent states who delivered Jews or Roma to the Nazis in the period 1941–4 may genuinely not have known, or claimed not to have known, that deportation eastwards meant extermination. But in a critical sense (even putting aside the fact that sooner or later the truth about the gas chambers did become known at state if not societal level) this is beside the point. When, in early July 1942, the newly reinstated Vichy French premier, Pierre Laval, informed Theodor Dannecker, the Gestapo head of Jewish Affairs in Paris, that stateless Jews in both Occupied and Unoccupied Zones of France 'will be turned over...for evacuation' and that as for Jewish children remaining in the former 'the matter does not interest me', he was effectively consigning both the children and their families to oblivion anyway.[17] That such a statement, moreover, could come from a *French* leader was little short of devastating.

Revolutionary France had been the forerunner and foundational stone upon which the whole Jewish emancipation process had spread throughout Western and Central Europe. Revolutionary diktat had swept away Judaic autonomy but granted to Jews within the ambit of the French polity equal citizenship rights. More precisely and importantly, this meant that to be or to become French was a matter of civic, not ethnic, qualification. Children born in France were automatically French citizens, regardless of their parentage. As for adults who sought asylum or permits as economic migrants and were granted rights of domicile, there was nothing to prevent them applying at some further stage for naturalization. The French version of nationalism thus appeared to be at marked variance with the way it was intrinsically understood to the east, in the 'New Europe'. It claimed to be colour-blind when it came to Jews, or any other ethnic or religious group. What it demanded was absolute loyalty to France and complete assimilation to French cultural, behavioural, and linguistic norms.[18]

In this supposedly liberal credo, however, lay the fatal flaw which gave Vichy the let-out by which to divest itself of the Jews it did *not* want. For the native, self-styled *israélites français* who saw the terms of the original emancipation decrees as proof of a symbiosis between French and Jewish interests, the possibility that even under the rightist administration which had made peace with Nazi Germany their own security might be in jeopardy seems to have taken some time to properly register. Perhaps this was assisted by a convenient historical amnesia regarding the repeated bouts of political hostility which greeted Jewish emancipation at its outset, not to say the sustained anti-Semitic climate around the Dreyfus affair of the 1890s. That said, it was much more difficult to ignore the rising tide of hate which swirled around them in the 1930s.

Some of the themes were familiar enough: accusations of financial corruption at 'honest' Frenchmen's expense, combined with wider charges that the Republic was in danger of succumbing to the interests of malevolent outside forces. The leftist-orientated Popular Front premiership of Léon Blum in 1936 was a particular incitement to those on the right who believed that the country was on the verge of a Jewish–Bolshevik takeover. But the proudly Jewish Blum was also the butt of repeated insinuations that the country was being manipulated in the interests of an 'Anglo-Saxon-Jewish conspiracy'.[19] Set against the background of the Depression and the darkening clouds of war, one can read the resurgence of the Jewish bogey as evidence of a society in deep disquiet as it failed to get to grips with economic and political crisis at home and what appeared to be its vertiginous decline on the international stage. Indeed, the acute and bitter sense held by significant sections of French society of being victimized at the hands of a tiny percentage of the population (no more than 330,000 out of 43 million)[20] reads much more akin to the sort of paranoia endemic to European rimlands elites of this period.

Where assimilated French Jewry—*autochtones*—had their own let-out came in the way that Gallic anti-Semitic ire tended to focus much less on them and much more on recent waves of Jewish immigrants from Eastern Europe. The congregation of tens of thousands of the latter in particular quarters of the major urban centres—the Pletzl of Paris being the most obvious—made their collective foreignness conspicuous in a period when hostility towards *métèques* (foreigners) was on the general rise. By the 1930s, the gentler attitudes in the wake of the Great War, when French governments had welcomed a major influx of labour from many countries to meet manpower shortages, had all but dissipated. It was the *juifs*—the *Ostjuden*—who bore the brunt of the renewed xenophobia. They were not just seen as different, but charged with being intrinsically threatening. The communists and radicals among them—and there were certainly some—were subversive fomenters of class conflict (French accusers conveniently forgetting that France had for a century and a half been home to highly radicalized working-class movements of all hues), while the intellectuals of the Pletzl were rootless cosmopolitans whose sole aim was to disintegrate traditional French life and values (again, as if one could imagine a France without home-spun dissidents).[21] As for the rest, whether working class, or professionals—and there were certainly increasing numbers of the latter as new waves of refugees fled Nazi Central Europe from the mid-1930s—they were clearly occupational competitors, *clandestins* (illegal immigrants), or, worst of all, an out-and-out security threat.[22]

It was the removal of these actually quite disparate and fragmented groups, in addition to the most recent Jewish incomers of all—those who had fled primarily from the Low Countries in the immediate context of war—which represented the nub of Vichy's Jewish agenda. That there was at the very least a putatively independent Vichy policy is important to emphasize. France had been unequivocally defeated by Hitler in the summer of 1940 and was forced to sue for terms. The result was the creation of two zones, the northern and western one occupied by the Germans, and a southern rump run from Vichy. However, French law and administration, at least in principle, applied in both. Moreover, though the Vichy regime, under Marshal Pétain, saw itself as extremely constrained and circumscribed by the Armistice, at least there had been one—the only case of its kind in Nazi-dominated Europe. Thus, the varying administrations which constituted the regime from 1940 to its demise on Allied liberation four years later were not simply puppets of the Germans, nor, despite the rightist orientation and in some cases clearly fascist inclinations of some ministers and personnel, a cipher for German orders. To be sure, during the course of the war, Vichy's weakness became increasingly exposed. Nazi demands for increased industrial and agricultural output as well as French labour service amplified a grass-roots opposition, which rapidly escalated into outright resistance—in effect an internal war *franco-français*, not seen since the days of the Revolution. Beleaguered or not, Vichy's raison d'être, as particularly exemplified by Laval, rested on the conviction that collaboration with the Nazi new order was the sine qua non whereby France would regain its full sovereign unity, integrity, and international (including colonial) freedom of action.[23]

As such, its Jewish policy can be treated as essentially dual track. In the first instance, it provided a bargaining counter with the Germans. As the latter wanted many things from Vichy, other than simply its Jews, going with the flow on the 'Jewish' demands and sometimes even expanding on them offered a way of deflecting attention from, or providing a quid pro quo in relation to other interests which Vichy sought to protect. One might in this sense propose that the regime qua regime was not in practice obsessed with the Jews, as was Hitler's entourage, but that it was prepared quite cynically to hand over Jews as part of its relatively limited negotiating toolkit. However, simultaneously Vichy was in haste to devise an independent Jewish policy of its own. Certainly, one can see elements in this of what Michael Marrus and Robert Paxton have described as a 'preemptive strategy'.[24] Aware that the Germans were bringing in their own ordinances aimed at registering Jews and their property in the Occupied Zone in anticipation of property confiscation and 'Aryanization', Vichy sought to rush through its own regulatory decrees, heralded by the *Statut des juifs*, issued on 3 October 1940, which now defined Jews as a racial rather than a religious community.

It is important to note that there was no initial German pressure on the regime to initiate its own discriminatory policy. True, this entailed a certain irony, as an anxiety that the French were making all the running helped precipitate the issuance of the German ordinances a week earlier. Browning has described this as 'a cycle of mutual intensification'.[25] To be sure, Vichy policy evinced strong elements of Nazi borrowing. The creation in both zones of a single coordinating body for French Jewry—the *Union général des israélites de France* (UGIF)—under the aegis of a General Commissariat on Jewish Affairs in March 1941 was an idea that its first head, Xavier Vallat, took directly from Dannecker.[26] Vichy, however, was not interested in mimesis for its own sake. On the contrary, the *Statut*, and the flurry of anti-Jewish legislation which followed, showed the regime to be extremely proactive on its own account.

Two policy goals stand out. The immediate one was to nail the Jews as responsible for the war, and hence France's humiliating defeat. This explains the exemplary removal of Jews without pension or compensation from a slew of administrative, military, and other state posts, and the sacking of teachers, perhaps a particularly keen example of raw scapegoating against those who had allegedly emasculated France through their 'demo-liberal hybridisation'.[27] More closely aligned to the emergence of a classic genocidal process were Vichy's efforts to expropriate Jewish business, property, and assets. Part of the aim here was clearly competitive: to get at Jewish wealth before the Germans did. But this purpose was also fully in keeping with a broader economic restructuring fundamental to Vichy's much vaunted 'national revolution'. Today, we remember the domestic policies of the regime primarily in terms of its attempted restoration of ultra-conservative and traditionally Catholic values, making its rightist, authoritarian complexion more closely akin to that of Franco's Spain rather than Hitler's Germany. But there was also a strongly technocratic, modernizing side to Vichy, the ultimate aim of which was to strengthen the country's long-term economic efficiency in the post-war world.[28] Eliminating 'Jewish influence in the national economy' thus not only carried with it opportunities for the seizure of assets which would accrue to a cash-strapped national exchequer but would enable it more closely to concentrate its industrial potential.[29] Here, then, were notions of freeing up a national economy dissimilar in principle neither from the Ittihadist agenda in 1915 nor, for that matter, from the slew of rimlands polities, twenty-five and more years later, who interpreted the uncompensated seizure of Jewish wealth not simply as a quick fiscal fix but as a route to genuine economic independence.

In practice, in France as elsewhere—even putting aside the vast over-expectations associated with the scale of Jewish wealth—recovering the proceeds from the official sale of expropriated properties and goods for the national exchequer proved entirely more cumbersome and leaky. The green light for Aryanization ensured that all manner of chancers took matters into their own hands to relieve usually the smallest and more vulnerable Jewish manufacturers and shopkeepers of their businesses at knock-down prices. Where assets, totalling by 1944 an estimated 5 billion francs, accrued to the French treasury, 'much of the proceeds were spent on the fees of lawyers and accountants'.[30]

Notwithstanding these problems of implementation, what was implicit in the expropriation project was an intended outcome in which the Jewish inhabitants of France would either be entirely subordinated and marginalized—or *removed*. For *israélites* this separation from the nation of which they had assumed themselves to be an intrinsic part was upsetting and hurtful enough, regardless of its implications in terms of unemployment and impending penury. But for recently naturalized, or yet to be naturalized, or stateless Jews, the potential consequences were entirely more frightful. The process of legal separation and expropriation makes little sense without the assumption that at least a substantial proportion of those affected would be removed from the body politic. Indeed, in this sense we are back with all such implicitly genocidal projects, whether Anglo-Cromwellian in Ireland, Jacksonian on the 1830s American eastern seaboard, or for that matter Ittihadist, with eructation of a community the prelude to the state-legitimized seizure and/or redistribution of its individual and collective resources.

But then, it is also clear that Vichy's Jewish agenda was not purely instrumental, at least not in a straightforward economic sense. If it had been, its foremost target would have been the longer established and entirely more affluent native element. Instead, at its heart was a drive to remove those perceived as culturally, politically, even biologically alien, or, as Vallat put it to the French chief rabbi referring to the recent 'invasion of our territory', the 'host of Jews having no ties with our civilisation'.[31] Given that it was the Germans who had actually invaded France, Vallat's assertion, not least given that he was a self-proclaimed patriot and no great lover of the Boche, would seem decidedly odd. Yet the degree to which the regime was in earnest is evident from the speed—within a month of the armistice—with which it established a commission to review all naturalizations since 1927 with the aim of revoking citizenship of those deemed 'undesirable'. Clearly, as the real invaders could not be accused of crimes against the people, substituting them with some bunch of foreigners would have to do. That this meant, above all, Jewish foreigners, is further evident from the decree, only a day after the *Statut des juifs*, requiring the internment of those living in the Unoccupied Zone in special camps, forced labour units, or in places where they could be placed under police controls. And if there was any doubt about Vichy's ultimate plans for them, these could be laid to rest when the then Ministry of the Interior, under Admiral Darlan, issued a circular to all prefects the following summer, spelling out that the interned Jews would not be 'allowed to integrate themselves into the national collectivity' and that everything needed to be done 'to achieve their departure from France'.[32]

The key question for Vichy was: how? The obvious answer was to ride the Nazi tiger. The Germans were already applying their own discriminatory practices in the Occupied Zone: it was easy enough to put the blame on them for any more draconian anti-Jewish measures which followed, especially if this involved deportations. But at the outset of the occupation, if anything the Germans wanted Jews expelled southwards into the Unoccupied Zone, while Vichy was in haste to have as many of the refugee Jews as possible eructed in the direction of Germany—a clash of purposes which as one commentator has put it 'was met with stupefaction and anger on the part of Nazi officials'.[33] Moreover, once armed resistance—including attacks on uniformed Germans—in the wake of Operation Barbarossa and then Pearl Harbor had begun, the Nazi security apparatus in Paris was in no mood to distinguish between Jews who were 'foreign' and Jews who were 'native'. The RHSA showed its hand on 12 December 1941—clearly a moment of heightened Nazi anxiety—when it rounded up over 700 Jewish notables, businessmen, and professionals, some of whom were executed, the remainder finding themselves included alongside earlier foreign Jewish suspects on the first thousand-strong transport to Auschwitz from France in late March 1942.[34] To reinforce the point, Dannecker had been drawing up his own mass deportation plan, which, even taking into account logistical difficulties, looked forward to the mass eructation of *all* Jews from France and the Low Countries.[35] Regardless of what Vichy might want in terms of Jewish policy, the balance of power seemed to be shifting inexorably towards that of the occupying power.

Yet, in practice, the matter was not so simple. Ultimate responsibility for the fate of France lay with the German military command in the Occupied Zone. Its great fear, however, was that to destabilize the policy of collaboration would be to undermine the occupation itself.[36] Even into 1942, when resistance was increasing, the Germans deployed fewer than 3,000 policemen of their own in occupied France, a figure to be compared with the 200,000 Germans in uniform required to fight the Partisans in Yugoslavia.[37] To avoid that sort of commitment, the Nazis were thrown back on French manpower and administrative capacity to carry through their coercive programmes. Or, to put it another way, if they wanted to deport Jews from France they needed the gendarmerie to round them up and keep them captive pending their removal from the main detention camp at Drancy. It was in this that Laval had his opening to negotiate terms more amenable to Vichy.

Dannecker, in June 1942, sought to speed up the deportation programme by demanding the round-up of 22,000 Jews from the Paris region and 10,000 more from the Unoccupied Zone. Implicitly it was a proposal which cut across any differentiation between those who were French citizens and those who were not. The Vichy negotiating team, fronted significantly by the young, newly appointed, and dynamic secretary-general of national police, René Bosquet, chose not to dispute the figures. Rather, Bosquet's chief concern was that the French police might be *seen* to be complicit in the round-ups. But on this point, when push came to shove, Bosquet actually relented: what was more important was that the French had control over *who* would be deported. And, indeed, on this score the Vichy people got exactly what they wanted. The round-ups did *not* include French citizens: though actually, as a consequence of the already noted Laval intervention in the negotiations, this involved one important caveat. Children born in France—in other words French citizens by automatic right—would be deported along with their 'foreign' parents. To be sure, children under the age of two along with their mothers, or mothers-to-be, were exempted from the order, as were a handful of other specified categories. But in general terms, a key Vichy desideratum had, at least on paper, all but been fulfilled: the removal of all Jews who had entered or been born in France after 1 January 1936.[38]

There was, of course, the rather unfortunate fact that the deal highlighted the abnegation of the regime's authority in its own autonomous zone, as well as the likelihood that the whole spectacle of what Vichy referred to as 'repatriation'—not least the removal of children—would be pilloried in the West. Laval attempted to pre-empt the bad press by writing to French embassies to explain that:

> This measure was taken out of concern for national health and hygiene and is free of any doctrinal consideration: it is merely intended to free our soil of the presence of immigrants who have slipped into our country in excessive numbers over the last few years.[39]

In addition, there was the further problem that the subsequent *rafles*—the big 16 July Paris round-up, in particular—upset lots of bystanders. There was no ghettoization in France—again, the Nazis had desisted from imposing that policy. As a result, when French policemen raided apartment blocks and dragged out families, bussing them in full public view to the Vel' d'Hiv' sports stadium and there incarcerated them without any adequate facilities for up to a week before shipping them off ultimately to what was (unknown to them or French society) extermination at Auschwitz, French public opinion was shocked and jolted.[40] What up to this point had been largely indifference to the fate of, or downright hostility towards Jewish refugees in particular, or the Jews in general, now turned for many towards sympathy. True, something of a shift had already begun the previous month, certainly in the Occupied Zone, when Germans had ordered all Jews there to wear the Star of David.[41] But the palpable involvement of the French authorities in the inhumane treatment of children and old people represented something closer to a rupture. As Julian Jackson has pithily put it, 'After 1789 it was the state that had protected Jews from the periodic anti-Semitic murmurings and violence of civil society; while under the Vichy regime, it was the populace that protected Jews from the state.'[42]

Arguably, the verdict is rather too concise. There remained plenty of Frenchmen who supported the deportation policy, had gained from it through the acquisition of Jewish goods and property, or who, as members of the volunteer fascist *Milice*—especially towards Vichy's end in 1944—cooperated wholeheartedly in the later German round-ups of Jews. Against this number, however, there were many others whose growing opposition to Vichy included efforts to come to the assistance of Jews, hide them, support escape routes across the Swiss and Spanish borders, and welcome fleeing Jewish survivors into the swelling ranks of the *maquis*. And there was, too, an important public face to this protest, not least that involving leading members of the Catholic hierarchy, some of whom broke ranks with the regime of which they were nominally and sometimes very overtly supportive to denounce its deportation policy.[43]

However, that still leaves something of an open question. Was the survival of the majority of the Jewish inhabitants of France under Nazism a result of widespread populist sabotage of Vichy policy, or was the regime's own ambivalence towards the Jews itself a contributory factor? By 1943, as Nazi demands for the mass removal of French Jewry to the east became unambiguous and repetitive, the Vichy response seemed to be heading in the opposite direction. For instance, having signed the draft of a law in June which would have abrogated the citizenship of some 16,600 foreign-born Jews naturalized since 1927, by August, Laval was informing RHSA officials who took it as the green light for another major round-up that no such law would be promulgated. Yet as Susan Zuccotti notes, 'Had Laval similarly resisted German demands the summer before, he could have saved thousands of foreign Jews with equal impunity'.[44]

But then Laval does not seem to have *wanted* to save foreign Jews. His unpublished post-Liberation memoirs, written when he was imprisoned and being tried as a traitor, speak of his efforts 'to save the majority of the *French* Jews', of which the June 1942 decision to dispense with the foreign elements was a necessary, indeed honourable, part.[45] Laval's further self-exculpation, that the decision had been to enhance the country's integrity and sovereignty, reinforces the point that Vichy's purpose all along was to maximize the opportunity which Nazi control presented to remove the *juifs* beyond the Pale, while claiming to protect the *israélites* within the fold. Indicative of this intention was a further major round-up initiated and conducted by the French police in February 1943, in which they grabbed over 1,500 unnaturalized Jews but avoided French citizens. The episode represented the nadir of Vichy's Jewish programme. All those taken were either elderly and sick people in old people's homes and hospitals or the very young in orphanages. The great irony is that the subsequent transports from Drancy included one thousand French citizens who had previously been detained for minor infractions of the German racial laws but whom the French police were now powerless to protect against Nazi diktat.[46] The Vichy attempt to channel the 'Final Solution' in France in favour of its own more limited ends was proving itself to be not simply feckless but also utterly feeble.

Even so, by late summer 1943, a policy shift was in motion. In September, Laval informed prefects that they were not to participate in the arrest of French Jews; though, rather more pointedly, neither were they to intervene when foreign ones were taken.[47] One might argue this was a case of having closed the stable doors after the horse had bolted. German troops and police had been operating with impunity in both French zones since late 1942. Moreover, having previously cooperated with the Gestapo, not least through the sharing of lists of Jewish households compiled by the gendarmerie, Vichy's ability to hold back *German* security round-ups was heavily compromised. In the early months of 1944, French police often even participated as the Gestapo attempted to arrest and deport *any* Jews it could lay its hands on, across the length and breadth of France. That the numbers who suffered this fate was in the thousands rather than tens of thousands can in large part be attributed to self-willed Jewish rescue efforts (more often than not initiated by radical immigrants) aligned with the dispersal networks run by the Resistance.

One might at this point wish to note as a subtext to this story the persistence of the historic internal Jewish divide. UGIF—supposedly both representing and with a duty of care for all French Jews, but run in practice by the old *israélite* elite—continued to largely operate within the confines of the law. As a consequence, it exposed to deportation thousands of the most vulnerable within the community—primarily stateless or yet to be naturalized Jews. In a late and tragic example, in July 1944, just three weeks before the liberation of Paris, it refused to intercede with the Germans to prevent the deportation of a convoy of children for fear that it might compromise its *own* existence.[48] Thus, establishment Jewry implicitly acquiesced in Vichy's discrimination between those worth saving and those who were dispensable with, to the point that some were prepared to rationalize to the effect that the removal of the latter would end state anti-Semitism and return France to the imagined status quo ante.[49]

This may sound unnecessarily harsh. The issue might more charitably be considered perhaps as one of cognitive failure, a case of grasping too slowly how under German duress the rules of the game had changed. Yet, in being party to the long-standing *French* differentiation between upstanding citizens and dubious foreigners, UGIF, perhaps unconsciously, played a small role in bolstering a Vichy agenda which was anything but honourable. And yet there remains in this verdict the obvious paradox: when Laval and fellow collaborationists in effect claimed after the war that 'without me, it would have been worse',[50] there remains a grain of truth in their protestation. The success of the Vel' d'Hiv' round-ups lay not only in the energetic zeal and organizational efficiency of Bosquet's men, but in the simple fact that the Ministry of Interior could deploy thousands of gendarmes for the task. Laval's foot-dragging the following year may have been born of utter cynicism—fear that to accede to RHSA demands would be to exacerbate the dwindling of Vichy's domestic support; a keen awareness that after Stalingrad the very notion of collaboration was rapidly becoming redundant—but without the administrative planning and manpower resources of the French state, the German security police were poorly positioned to enact round-ups of their own. Their military and civilian superiors were also hesitant to further rock the French boat. When they made an exception, in September 1943, giving the green light to a single SS unit to conduct its own round-up of an estimated 25–30,000 Jews taking shelter in the recently evacuated Italian zone around Nice, the *Aktion* stands out as one of the most overt examples of Nazi brutality in its pursuit of the 'Final Solution' in Western Europe, but one in which 'only' 1,800 Jews were actually caught.[51]

Is it these commissions and omissions of the Gallic state which ultimately offer the clearest guide to the statistics of Jewish destruction in France? Very possibly. It was recent Jewish refugees and immigrants who were the overwhelming majority on the seventy-odd convoys deported between March 1942 and August 1944. Indeed, of the estimated 77,000 Jews who were executed in the country or who died in the camps, 70 per cent were 'foreign'. As this component, however, represented only around 41 per cent of the total Franco-Jewish community in 1940, the imbalance between their fate and that of *autochtones* is striking. Transfer the French children of foreign parents and recently naturalized Jews who died to the foreign list, and one is in fact left with 6,500 *French* Jews who were murdered, or less than 9 per cent of the *israélite* total, compared with 45 per cent of the *juifs*.[52]

Yet that also leaves the equally startling statistic that three-quarters of the Jews in France—clearly mostly from the older, established community—survived the 'Final Solution', a figure that compares favourably with the considerably higher death-rates in Nazi-run Belgium and the Netherlands. The irony of ironies that this owed not a little to Vichy was clearly too much for a post-liberation France committed to the more preferable pretence that Laval and company were just a small clique of traitors and the vast majority of French men and women heroic resisters. Much better thus to simply blank out the whole messy business of what had specifically happened to France's Jews and instead return to a standard liberal narrative in which ethnic, religious, or other distinctions were irrelevant because everybody—that is everybody embraced within the civic inclusion zone—was the *same*. The immediate result was that the mostly foreign Jewish survivors of the camps who came home to reclaim property found their pleas for justice outweighed by the state's protection of incumbent tenants (a large phalanx of whom had enriched themselves at the deportees' expense), while any urges survivors may have had to tell their stories were met with a an almost blanket collective will to suppress or forget.[53] For several decades after the war, French commemoration or even comment on the specificity of Jewish suffering, let alone a French role in it, disappeared down a giant memory hole.[54]

*

Comparing French policy towards its Jews with that of wartime Slovakia at first sight would seem not entirely apposite. France was an avant-garde nation state with a long tradition of democracy and civil society. At least until 1940 it was also a respected great power on the international stage. Slovakia was none of these things. A rural province under the thumb of the Magyars, more recently a very subordinate partner in the Czech state, not only was most of the Slovak region a rural backwater but it had little in the way of a home-grown or long-standing political elite. Those who became so in 1938 on the break-up of Czechoslovakia owed their elevation to Berlin. Under its explicit 'protection', could one call the untried and untested Slovakia of President Tiso an independent state at all ? Certainly, when the Germans invaded Russia there was no question that Slovakia would join the tripartite pact and so do Hitler's bidding.

Yet while the Nazis made onerous demands on Slovakia, as they did on all their satellite states, their diplomatic interface with the regime in Bratislava was as of one sovereign entity to another. The initial proposal to remove the country's Jews, we may remember, came from the Slovaks, not the Germans. This very fact offers parallels with Vichy France, though the Tiso regime's apparent intent to make a clean sweep of *all* its Jews suggests something more comprehensive and extreme than anything its Pétainist counterparts ever contemplated. To be sure, Slovak anti-Semites may have mentally organized their own distinction between bad Jews and utterly execrable ones. Those living in eastern Slovakia, or the adjoining Subcarpathian Rus (Ruthenia)—with a historic background of religiosity which related them to a heavily Hasidic Galician milieu (from which many of them had originally migrated)—were more likely to fall into the latter category. Indeed, they had been the butt of a fledgling Slovak People's Party, to which Tiso was political heir, since the 1880s.[55] It is significant that in the confused period in late 1938, when embryonic Slovakia was forced to give ground to Hungarian control of Ruthenia, Tiso found a scapegoat in the Jews of the region and, in the interregnum before Budapest formally took over, made a point of preventing their entry into residual Slovakia, whether they were technically entitled to it or not.[56] However, if the strictly orthodox and other-worldly Hasids of the Subcarpathian region were a figurative world away from the 'progressive' Jews of central Slovakia—a significant segment of whom provided core professional and economic services to the wider community—this too was grounds for bitter resentment by the nationalists. Making up not much more than 4 per cent of the total Slovak population, the Jews as a whole were nevertheless viewed before 1919 as proxies for the Hungarians, and after that date as agents of Czech domination.[57] Twenty years on, the new regime had no compunction about expelling 100,000 Czechs from Slovak territory.[58] Why not do the same with the Jews?

It is true that as a general rule any diasporic minority in a plural state tends to align itself with the dominant nationality as a matter of self-protection. In the Slovak Jewish case, the collapse of rule from Prague and its supersession by that of Bratislava laid bare the redundancy of a historic Mercurian role in an Apollonian society. Slovak Jewry's distinct socio-economic and cultural profile within a broadly peasant sea had not been a cause for conflict so long as local nationalism had not intruded its own 'Slovakia for the Slovaks' agenda into the relationship. The fact that Slovak nationalism was relatively slow, weak, and ultimately dependent on a powerful—as it so happened Judaeophobic—patron to carry through into *nation*-state building, more or less ensured that the country's Jews would be a target for any forced-pace economic Slovakization programme. Eliminating them as perceived professional and economic competitors was already standard East European fare with or without the Nazi example as guide. Nazi ascendancy, combined with the collapse of the League of Nations, ensured that wholesale expropriation of Jewish businesses and property by individual states was par for the course. In the absence of any obvious developmental potential of their own, Slovak haste to lay hands on middleman assets offers a particularly pointed example of a state desperate to achieve a quick (if delusory) economic fix.

Was it inevitable that the corollary to this programme would be wholesale Jewish eruction? Not necessarily. We may remember that the original early 1942 Bratislava effort to have 20,000 Jewish workers sent for labour in Germany was to avoid having to accede to Nazi demands for *Slovak* labourers.[59] The upping of the ante to get the Germans to take the Jewish families too—and effectively do with them what they willed—came from Slovakia's much more overtly Nazi-leaning premier Vojtech Tuka, rather than from Tiso. Yet to have rejected the German response in 1942 would have been tantamount to looking a gift horse in the mouth. According to the deal, Bratislava could look forward to the removal of an increasingly destitute Jewish mass who otherwise threatened to become a burden on the state. More importantly, in return for a per capita fee for their transport to occupied Poland, the regime was guaranteed its right to take possession of all Jewish abandoned property and businesses.[60] A constitutional law giving post-agreement legitimacy to the deportation programme was accordingly passed through the Slovak parliament, with only one abstention, in May. The consequence of the arrangement was both stark and rapid. Between the spring and autumn, up to 58,000 Slovak Jews—between two-thirds and three-quarters of the community— were deported primarily to Auschwitz, with organization and implementation carried out by the indigenous paramilitaries of the Hlinka Guard or their Volksdeutsche equivalents. And at least something of the fate of the deportees seems to have been known to the regime from the very beginning, in part thanks to Bratislava's papal nuncio, Burzio, who warned that the programme condemned a large part of the

Jews 'to certain death'. However, this did not stop a quick turnover of thousands of confiscated businesses at knock-down prices, or the distribution of properties to the regime's friends.[61]

Yet once again, as with France, a regime intent on getting rid of its Jews as quickly as possible seems to have equivocated as regards completing the exercise. Deportations were halted in October. Should we read this as a belated case of cold feet, or even perhaps a realization that Slovakia could not properly function at the local level minus its Jewish doctors, pharmacists, and other professionals? The change in the fortunes of the war clearly may have played some role, though what is interesting in the Slovak case is how early the regime seemed to change its tune. Nor can the role of unusually proactive Jews themselves be discounted from the equation. The working group around Rabbi Weissmandel in Bratislava, having early on uncovered the truth about the deportations, devised its own stratagem to buy off Dieter Wisliceny and the other SS project managers in Slovakia with the ruse that they—the SS officers—were instead setting up Jewish work camps in the country. Weissmandel's group then famously stepped up its game with the Europa Plan to try and ransom the remnant of Europe's Jewry, inevitably involving it thereby in Himmler's own convoluted efforts to trade them for Western peace negotiations.[62]

However, something else seems to have been at play which speaks more about a power struggle for, almost literally, the soul of the regime. Described by Stanley Payne 'as a more backward and rightist, clerical version of Vichy',[63] the Slovak People's Party administration was united in its commitment to authoritarian rule but divided between the more overt Nazi-orientation of Tuka, supported by interior minister Alexander Mach, who headed the Hlinka Guard, and the more obviously Catholic and conservative faction around Tiso. It was the latter, however, which in so far as it could claim popular support, commanded the wider grass-roots following. And it was from this same source that the brakes on the deportation programme began to be applied. It was no coincidence that the change in policy paralleled Tiso's successful extension of his presidential authority over that of his premier. And when Tuka attempted to turn the tables the following spring by, among other things, attempting to bring the RHSA back into play to resume the deportations, the move was met with a condemnatory pastoral letter signed by the entirety of the Slovak episcopate and read in churches throughout the length and breadth of the country. Significantly, the Vatican's emissary seems to have played a critical behind-the-scenes role in orchestrating the protest. The fact that the Vatican was at this time cautiously proud of its manifestly Catholic, anti-Bolshevik Slovak—as well as Croat—protégés, yet also infamously lacking in any public statement of its own on the 'Final Solution', makes Burzio's involvement in fanning the opposition all the more striking.[64]

At least as striking, however, is the way Germans themselves backed off after the bishops' protest. A great bulwark of tradition in Central Europe had drawn its line in the sand, and Berlin had blinked. One might simply retort: too little, too late. The Slovak bishops had not spoken out against removing Jews from the body politic, nor the sequestration of their worldly goods. The country's Evangelical Church had at least protested when it had mattered, the previous year, though lacking the muscle of the Catholic hierarchy to halt the deportation process. In France, too, it was Protestants rather than Catholics, perhaps recognizing their shared affinity with Jews as an exposed minority, who were quicker to attempt to offer tangible assistance. Yet by publicly enunciating a basic detestation of cruel treatment of fellow human beings, the bishops in Slovakia, like their counterparts in France, had impacted on the policy of state. No more Jewish deportations at the behest of the Tiso regime were to occur. It may also be relevant at this point to note that while Roma were interned in labour camps and suffered accordingly, here, as in the Vichy Unoccupied Zone, the consequence was hunger and illness often leading to escalating mortality, but not deportation leading to mass extermination.[65]

Sadly, this was not the end of the story. A Slovak national uprising led largely by liberals and communists in August 1944 precipitated German military intervention, which in turn provided cover for the RHSA to resume the deportation programme. They were assisted by special squads of the Hlinka Guard, which may remind us of another general rule: that as state authority ebbs, the monopoly of violence fragments with it. Ironically, too, the Germans' ability to systematically run their prey to ground also faltered. But for the next two months they were still the dominant military and security power in Slovakia, the consequence of which was that more than a thousand Roma may have been massacred, while over 12,000 Jews are estimated to have been sent to Auschwitz and other camps.[66] Even so—as in France—the space opened up by the authoritarian state's own evasive action also provided opportunities for flight, resistance, and, for the lucky few, survival.

*

Bulgaria provides a final example for this section, which superficially, at least, would seem to break the mould. Today the country's wartime Jewish narrative is remembered—and generally celebrated—as one of 'rescue', not destruction. The fact that Bulgaria falls within one and arguably two of the zones we would constitute as rimlands—and thus with neighbours known for their virulent anti-Semitism—would seem to confirm its exceptionality. The further fact that Bulgaria was a satellite member of the Axis camp, having joined the Tripartite Pact in March 1941, but continued to pursue an independent foreign policy—a critical element of which was its decision *not* to declare war on the USSR—would seem to reinforce its profile as a polity whose behaviour and actions went against the standard 'collaborationist' grain. Through a mixture of state stonewalling and widespread elite but also demotic resistance, Sofia not only halted Jewish deportations from Bulgaria *integrale* but prevented the Germans from attempting to restart them. Indeed, the manner in which Orthodox Church, parliament—the Sobranje—and the wider public mobilized to non-violently thwart the programme, including a plan by leading clergy to lie down on the tracks in front of the deportation trains, is quite exemplary. And what had been forestalled once, in mid-March 1943, was repeated again in late May, when a ruse to remove Sofia's Jews to the countryside pending their eruction was swamped by crowds of protesters with the Metropolitan Stefan and members of the royal court prominent among them.[67]

By the same token, the relative lack of harassment or threat to Bulgaria's Roma during this period, both in the country itself and neighbouring occupied Macedonia and Thrace, is noteworthy—so much so that a post-war Roma mythology has developed of the good king Boris who protected them.[68]

But is this a case of remembering what we prefer to remember and airbrushing out those elements of the story which are less digestible? Certainly there were some structural reasons why Bulgarian anti-Semitism was less stark than, for instance, in neighbouring Rumania. Partly this was owing to the simple fact that though of long standing, the pre-war Jewish community, numbering hardly 50,000 and constituting less than 1 per cent of the total population, was predominantly urban and artisanal, and for the most part kept itself to itself in a society where the peasant masses were predominant and politically strong. Indeed, the very traditional nature of an essentially Sephardi community, which had been one of the historic millets under pre-independence Ottoman rule, gave to Bulgaria's Jewry the appearance of being thoroughly embedded in the country's life and history while not sufficiently integrated into the flow of its economic or political modernization to offer grounds for resentment or perception of tangible threat.[69] In fact, as so often in such cases, there was an element of amnesia here. Bulgaria's fraught and bloody drive to full independence in 1908 had been accompanied by bouts of intense, violent xenophobia against Greek, Armenian, and Jewish middlemen, as also against the Turkish or Muslim element of the population. The fact that it was often the other, more high profile, 'minorities' who bore the brunt of nationalistic hostility did not preclude occasions where Jews were the targets of economic accusations and pogroms.[70]

Paradoxically, however, the Bulgarian mythic self-perception as a country free from anti-Semitism[71] may have been a factor energizing the anti-deportation movement in the spring of 1943. The problem is that this is only one side of the story. As the country moved into the Nazi sphere, from February 1940, the new administration under Bogdan Filov took on a more fascistic complexion, one consequence of which was the forcible expulsion of foreign Jews fleeing from elsewhere in Nazi-occupied Europe but also from the Dobrudja. This region, 'regained' from Rumania as one of Germany's emergency 'awards' to its satellites in the wake of the Nazi–Soviet Pact, involved an exchange of populations, but one in which the region's Jewish inhabitants were treated as Rumanians.[72] These moves seemed to signal that if Bulgaria's metropolitan Jewry were 'protected', those at the periphery or beyond might expect pretty much the same treatment as France's foreign Jews. In fact, the Law for the Protection of the Nation, passed—albeit with some notable dissent—through parliament in autumn 1940, while relatively mild compared with other states' anti-Jewish legislation of this period, seemed to augur the exclusion of *all* Bulgaria's Jews from its universe of obligation. The fact, moreover, that a special Commissariat of Jewish Affairs was created under the auspices of the Interior Ministry in summer 1942, and with powers to issue decrees on Jewish questions—without reference to parliament—suggested that Sofia, notwithstanding its supposed history of Jewish toleration, was now moving not only fast on the Jewish question, in tandem with other collaborationist states, but also to Germany's tune.[73]

Indeed, it was a conscious leak from the Secretariat in early March 1943 of the imminence of deportations being then organized by its head, Alexander Belev, in coordination with none other than the RHSA's Theodor Dannecker, which sparked off the public protests.[74] The intensity of the opposition and the fact that it embraced a wide spectrum of Bulgaria's political and bureaucratic elite, alongside cultural and religious figures, cannot be gainsaid. Nor that this mobilization spoke powerfully to the existence of a plural, civic dimension to Bulgarian society, which not only exposed the political isolation of arch-anti-Semites of the Belev type, but which ultimately contributed to a radical anti-fascist shift in Sofia's wartime political orientation.

But, and it is a very big but, the protests came too late to stop the deportations of nearly 11,400 Jews: in other words, almost the entire Jewish communities of western Thrace and Macedonia.[75] For them there was no reprieve. Nor was any compassion shown by the Bulgarian gendarmes who rounded them up, terrorized them into handing over their valuables, and proceeded to pass the time with mock executions and the rape of teenage girls while they and their prisoners awaited barges to take them from the makeshift camps of their incarceration up the Danube to Vienna. Only then did the Bulgarian guards hand over their charges to the tender mercies of the Germans for the final leg of their journey to Treblinka. Perhaps one might speculate that no such humiliation and degradation would have been meted out to these hapless people at the hands of Bulgarians if western Thrace and Macedonia had been firmly encapsulated within Sofia's realm, as its leadership had sought in 1878 and later, during the Balkan wars. But then, as fully-fledged citizens of Bulgaria, the Jews of Sérres, Kavala, and Drama, and of Skopje, Bitola (Monastir), and Stip, might not have suffered this fate at all. Details of Belev's supposedly highly secret deportation plan began rapidly to leak out when his Commissariat secretary realized that in order to meet the 22,000 quota for the first consignment of deportees, some 8,500 specially selected 'undesirables' from the 'old' community—in other words, bona fide Bulgarian citizens—were to be included.[76] It was in response to the projected simultaneous round-up of *these* Jews in Sofia and other such cities, not those in the occupied territories, that the campaign of protest was mounted and escalated towards its ultimate success.

Which leaves us with something disturbing, if rather familiar, about the pattern of Jewish destruction under Bulgarian rule. While there were undoubtedly some figures, especially within the religious establishment, who called for a halt to *all* deportations, others at the heart of political power, not least the king himself, appear to have been quite ready to dispense with what was to them an extraneous Jewish element. Significantly, when the ageing Boris visited Berlin in April, he gave a clear hint to Ribbentrop that the Macedonian and Thracian Jews could be deported—knowing full well that they had already been removed. But in front of Hitler he refused to be cowed. The Jews of Bulgaria were to be dealt with as Sofia saw fit. They could be ghettoized, expelled from the cities to labour camps in the countryside, and there put to work in road construction. But these were matters of Bulgarian domestic concern of which the royal regime was the ultimate arbiter.[77] In putting down such a marker, Boris was spelling out another familiar message about the lengths to which states would go to defend their rights to sovereign, independent action. By the same token, he was effectively saying, just as Laval had done, that the fate of Jews who did not belong was of no concern or consequence.

One might perhaps add that the Jews of the 'new' territories were not so far away, either physically or mentally. During the Balkan wars, those in nearby Salonika had been consciously courted as part of Sofia's international campaign to confirm its rights to the region.[78] Was the willingness to see the back of Thracian and Macedonian Jews thus a subliminal form of revenge? Nearly all political leaders in rimlands Europe operated on the premise that 'the Jews' were powerful on the international stage, above all in the Western camp. Boris may have lacked the conspiracy-laden mindset of a Marshal Antonescu, in which everything which went badly for Rumania was a result of Jewish sabotage. But in the Bulgarian case was there also, however residually, a sense that the Jews of the lower Balkans *ought* to take a hit for their or their fathers' alleged failures to come to Sofia's assistance when, a generation earlier, it had really mattered?

For lack of evidence, the suggestion is entirely speculative, even while it remains consistent with a standard tendency to blame the Jews for what should have been a matter of reflecting on one's own national or international failings. The irony is that for the Jews of Bulgaria proper, the persistence of the international power motif may have been their salvation. Just as in Slovakia and France, demotic and/or elite protest and resistance in Bulgaria clearly made a significant contribution to residual Jewish survival. However, the real clincher was geopolitical calculation on the part of the incumbent state. And for Boris and his entourage in early 1943, that hinged, in the wake of Stalingrad, on the likely outcome of the war—a war in which the Jews by dint of their supposed influence on the Western camp were perceived to be a crucial factor. The regime's consequent moves towards self-extrication from the Nazi camp—attempting to steer clear of the twin pitfall of succumbing to the advancing Soviets—were thus directed, just as we have already seen in the case of Horthy's Hungary, towards winning the support and advocacy of London and Washington. In these terms, defying the Nazi diktat on the Jews simply became a necessary and also achievable objective.

For exactly these same geopolitical reasons, however, the attempted policy shift proved abortive. The Western Allies did not come rushing to Sofia's assistance, in part because they had only limited resources to do so, in much greater part because they had already conceded Bulgaria to the post-war Soviet sphere. Whatever the now democratic-leaning regime attempted to do to signal its intended secession from the Axis thus proved insufficient to win Allied approval. Yet critically, as the Red Army approached in the high summer of 1944, and a largely communist-sponsored Partisan movement prepared to overthrow the government, there was no military counter-move by the Nazis.[79] The true rimlands by then were beyond the arc of Germany's grasp. And, of course, there was no real Jewish factor in this shifting geopolitical landscape. But Sofia's perception of the Jews as a card to be played, combined with the abandonment of any Wehrmacht move to occupy the country—compare and contrast with Hungary—ensured that nearly all of the Jews of 'old' Bulgaria avoided the standard European Jewish fate.

THE BALKAN ARENA—EXTERMINATORS
AND PROTECTORS

The manner in which the Bulgarians collaborated in the deportation of the Jews of neighbouring Macedonian towns does not suggest that it might have been different in Salonika—had it, too, come under Sofia's control. But in the grand carve-up of Yugoslavia and Greece into zones of military occupation after the Nazi *Blitzkrieg* seizure of the Balkans, in April 1941, the Germans considered the port-city far too strategically important to award it to anybody but themselves. The decision sealed the fate of its estimated 49,000 remaining Jewish inhabitants. In mid-March 1943, they were assigned to transports to the General Government just as were the rest of Macedonian Jews. The noticeable differences were threefold. First, this operation was under the direct supervision of Wisliceny, like his RHSA colleague Dannecker demonstrating a set of specialist transferable skills in the matter. Second, the community was deported not by boat but by train from the port station built at the turn of the century by a Jewish financial magnate as the terminus of a railway network designed to link the Balkan semi-periphery with metropolitan Europe. Third, this was by far and away the most significant single Nazi liquidation of a post-Ottoman Jewish community stranded on the western side of the Aegean. It also happened to be one notable for its strides towards a very Western-orientated modernization.[80]

Had the occupying army in Salonika been the Italians, we might fairly speculate on a rather different turn of events. It would almost certainly have led to a delay in the timetable of destruction, which in turn could have provided scope for the dispersal, escape, or rescue of at least some of the city's Jews. That we might single out the Italians as the most likely protectors of Jewish communities in the Balkan theatre—and indeed elsewhere where Rome's occupying power prevailed—may at first sight seem a little odd. Mussolini's Italy, after all, was not a satellite of Nazi Germany but, uniquely, a co-equal belligerent in the European Axis camp. And as the only other self-created fascist state, it was hardly surprising that it should also be a sponsor of the Croat Ustasha under Ante Pavelić, a fascist movement which once in power in the so-called Independent State of Croatia (NDH), Italy hoped to manipulate in its own expansionist interest down the eastern Adriatic coast. What is immediately striking about the NDH, however, is that despite its fundamental weakness, and, as one commentator has put it, its 'preposterous incompetence',[81] this did not prevent it from launching its own utterly spectacular genocidal assault on the Jews and Roma under its control.

As we will see in the next chapter, this had little or nothing to do with its actual dependency on Berlin—or Rome—or its willingness to kowtow to the former's directives, despite the good marks it received from Heydrich at Wannsee for its self-initiated action.[82] In fact, the NDH's primary target was not its Jews but its Serbs. But this did not prevent the regime moving with speed from racial exclusion and economic expropriation of Jews within weeks of the state's founding to their outright extermination, in the wake of Operation Barbarossa. As a result, Zagreb became one of first cities in Europe to be violently rendered *judenfrei*. Round-ups followed throughout the country, including Bosnia. Brought to a complex of hast-ily thrown together camps centred on Jasenovac on the Sava, the Jews were quite literally butchered to death by the young bucks of the Black Legion militia, the shock-troops of the Ustasha movement. Of an estimated 36–40,000 Jews on NDH soil, some 23,000 ended their lives here, with another 7,000 murdered in the Ger-man camp system.[83] Some 26,000 Roma, little short of the entire community in the NDH, also perished in and around the Jasenovac complex, either in 1941 or, following a more pronounced series of round-ups, in early 1942.[84]

In fact, murdering Jews, Roma *and* Serbs together in hastily improvised Balkan massacres was a monopoly neither of the Wehrmacht nor of the Black Legions. Very much of their own volition, though surely following in the contours of Ger-man precedents from the previous year, commanders of the Hungarian *Honvédség* conducted a reprisal raid on Novi Sad and its hinterland in January 1942—in response to alleged Serb partisan action—in which some 4,000 civilians were summarily executed. Indeed, the manner in which mostly Jews and Roma in Novi Sad itself, the capital of the former Bačka (Vojvodina) region of Yugoslavia—now reincorporated in Hungary as the Délvidék—were marched in freezing condi-tions to the banks of the Danube, lined up en masse, and shot into the ice, may well have been intended as a dread signal from Budapest that Hungarian rule over non-Hungarians in the Balkans—and elsewhere in the newly 'restored' Magyar lands of the rimlands—would be every bit as ruthless as that of the NDH, other occupying powers, or, for that matter, as it had previously been in Hungarian-occupied Serbia during the Great War. Little consolation derives from the belated 1943 official Budapest investigation into the conduct of *Honvédség* officers held responsible for the massacre. The investigation was designed for Western con-sumption at a time when Horthy was trying to find an opening to the Western camp.[85] As we will see further on, Jews, Balkan or otherwise, had scant grounds for seeking protection from a Budapest source as the Nazi vice continued to close around them.

Which rather leads us to ask, where could Balkan Jews and Roma find safety? There was flight to the Partisan strongholds in the mountains, a highly perilous undertaking even for the able-bodied—and which, moreover, carried with it every likelihood that those who made the journey would eventually be killed in the mas-sive German-led counter-insurgency operations mounted against Tito's forces. In Croatia, for those who had survived thus far, there was a belated chink of light for those Jews who either converted to Catholicism or who married a Catholic partner in church. The NDH enacted racial laws on German lines but also proved itself to be thoroughly contradictory, not least when it found grounds for allowing honor-ary Aryan status to the Jewish or part-Jewish spouses of the Ustasha leadership, Pavelić included. Behind the efforts to save Jews through conversion was the lead-ing cleric in Zagreb, Archbishop Stepinac; behind him the Vatican.[86] A consider-able element of the Croat Catholic priesthood was deeply implicated where not direct perpetrators in the atrocities committed by the NDH. But the regime hardly wanted an open split with the Vatican, which, while not officially recognizing the beleaguered regime, offered a degree of tacit support.

However, even putting aside its ambivalence with regard to Croatia—and indeed Slovakia—the papacy had only limited powers of persuasion with which to deflect state drives to genocide. In practice, that left only one temporal power with the ability to do something to halt the 'Final Solution' in the Balkans: Italy. The fascist republic's seemingly good record when it came to Jews—and Roma—clearly offers something of an enigma. It can hardly be put down to the regime's innate Catholicism, even if Mussolini did bring to an end the festering conflict between church and state in the 1929 Concordat. And if an easy-going Catholicism was clearly part of the cultural mix which gave to the Italians a persistent profile abroad as a people more committed to *la dolce vita* than to hard-nosed, authoritarian-led nation-state building, a small dose of recollection of Mussolini-led atrocity may be necessary before we get too weak-kneed and sentimental about the country's humanitarian mythology.[87]

In *The Rise of the West* we noted the late 1920s counter-insurgency strategy of the Italian army under General Graziani in Cyrenaica, the consequence of which was the death of 60,000 of its inhabitants in concentration camps on the Marmarica plateau.[88] For good measure, Mussolini's strivings for imperial living-space led him a few years later to direct Graziani to indiscriminately bomb Ethiopia, use scorched earth tactics and mustard gas to bring about the country's subjugation, and have his blackshirts execute thousands of Ethiopian civilians, notably Coptic clerics.[89] Nor did the onset of hostilities in Europe lead to a mitigation of such colonial military practice. On the contrary, with the exception of the use of gas, all methods were deployed in Italy's Balkan sphere of operations, initially against the Greeks, then in Croatia, Montenegro, and Slovenia. In the latter case, the attempt to subjugate the Ljubljana region, involving hostage-taking and the mass internment of thousands of Slovene non-combatants—children included—on the island of Rab, proved so calamitous in terms of the loss of human life that even the Vatican complained.[90]

If these examples might suggest not so much a gulf between German and Italian methods of counter-insurgency but rather elements of similitude (which might in turn give us pause before we begin noting the differences), we might equally need to be reminded about Italian *domestic* persecution of its Jews. To be sure, the deportation of the peninsula's Jews to the death camps was entirely German-led—in the hands initially of the ubiquitous Dannecker. However, the deportation was only attempted when in September 1943 Italy's generals surrendered to the Allies, deposed Mussolini, but then suffered the ignominy of a Wehrmacht takeover of the centre and north of the country where the Anglo-American invasion had yet to penetrate. With Italy now turned into a war zone, and what was left of the fascist state (the Salò republic), struggling to reassert its control over and against the directives of the German occupiers, as well as Partisan resisters, the SS ability to conduct unrestrained round-ups of its own was held in partial check. That said, Salò fascists attempted their own ferocious round-ups of those Jews they could lay their hands on in the north, and even where this was intended as a policy distinct from the 'Final Solution' clearly offered the RHSA their captives on a plate to deport them when they got the chance. More keenly, Dannecker and his colleagues were able to expedite the removal of nearly 7,000 Jews from Italy, in large part on the basis of lists held by the Directorate-General for Demography and Race, founded specifically by Mussolini in 1938 as part of his efforts to enact legislation geared towards the separation of Jews from the Italian body politic.[91]

The anti-Jewish laws of 1938 have been generally viewed as part of the effort by Mussolini to more closely align Italy with Nazi Germany, the major geopolitical consequence of which was the 'Pact of Steel' the following year. In other words, the public exclusion and humiliation of the country's Jewry was considered the necessary price for an alliance intended to make Italy the political equal of the most powerful state in Europe. Whether or not Mussolini, at this point, bought into the Nazi racial ideology is a matter of some controversy.[92] What matters for this discussion is twofold. First, the sweeping nature of the legislation profoundly impacted on Italy's Jews, who found themselves not only excluded from public office and from the country's educational system but also often reduced to penury as their assets were frozen. More significantly, in addition to being delineated henceforth as 'inassimilable aliens', those Jews who had entered the country or acquired citizenship after 1919 were now subject to expulsion and/or placed in internment camps.[93] Second, and this is the *more* interesting point, the new policies went down very badly not only with the Italian public at large but in the fascist party itself: perhaps not surprisingly given that anything up to 10 per cent of the estimated 30,000 Jews in Italy were party members. The standard party line before 1938 was that 'the Jewish problem does not exist in Italy', a view which also happened to reflect general public sentiment. Italy, indeed, was rather unusual in continental Europe in its lack of anti-Semitism. The main explanation for this absence lies in the tiny percentage of Italians who were Jews (much less than 1 per cent) and, more broadly, the longevity of the community, or rather city and regional *communities*, which embedded them as part and parcel of the historic pre-unification mosaic, combined with the paucity of *Ostjuden* immigration into the peninsula.[94]

The issue of Jewish numbers relative to the larger population, allied to the degree of Jewish integration into the latter, clearly *is* significant in explaining to a degree the weakness of home-grown anti-Semitism in a limited number of countries. Italian parallels with Denmark and Finland both come to mind, the latter being another party, from 1941, to the Anti-Comintern Act, but one which steadfastly refused to hand over its 2,000 Jews to the Germans. As with the Italians, so with the Danes, Finns, and, perhaps with some added caveats, the Bulgarians, the Jews were not generally perceived as a bio-political threat to state or society, thereby marginalizing those Nazi-inclined elements who claimed the opposite. But what was more remarkable about the Italian wartime record is the manner in which this extended beyond domestic policy, or, more accurately, translated into a form of active yet highly practical *counter*-policy.

As we have already noted, a common tendency of European state administrations operating within the context of the 'Final Solution' was to draw a distinction between 'good' indigenous Jews and 'bad' foreign ones, the latter being the unfortunates who could be thrown to the Nazi lions. In the Italian case, however, the military commanders on the ground in the Balkans backed by diplomats and civil servants not only refused to hand over Jews in their zones of occupation to the Germans but often, even energetically, sought to offer refuge to Jews facing extermination in neighbouring ones. To be sure, there were some piquant as well as tragic ironies in some of these efforts. Those holding Italian nationality in Salonika were protected by the Italian consul there, while there were even attempts to extend Italian citizenship to Central European Jews stranded in Macedonia.[95] For the rest of Salonika's Jewry there was no such succour. Meanwhile, in the Ionian islands, where Rome sought to take control of their assets, lock, stock, and barrel, local Jews were expropriated 'in precisely the way so many other Europeans were doing'.[96] As for those who had survived the initial massacres in Croatia, commanders of the Italian Second Army there sought to keep the Ustasha at bay eventually by moving the survivors off the mainland to Rab, where incarcerated Slovenes had previously been so egregiously maltreated. The NDH significantly made no objection. So long as they could keep hold on the Jews' sequestered assets, they were content for the Italians to intern the Jews as they saw fit, even if this was technically on the Ustasha patch.[97] As for those among the Italian commanders who were prominent advocates of this Jewish rescue project, one name particularly stands out: General Mario Roatta, otherwise known as the most ruthless Italian advocate of reprisals and hostage-taking in the Balkan theatre.[98]

For all the strange contradictions in this situation, however, the fact remains that the Italian military were the nearest thing on offer to protection for what remained of the Jews in the Balkans. The situation was identical in the eight departments east of the Rhone which the Italians marched into when the Wehrmacht took over the French Unoccupied Zone. The Italian refusal to hand over Jews fleeing into the Rhone glacis, to either the Germans or Pétainists, soon became a subject of some considerable friction between the Axis partners, as well as with Vichy. Surviving Roma from Ustasha and German onslaughts in Slovenia and Croatia also found refuge with the Italian military, as did others further south in Italian-occupied Albania. Many of the former were able to cross directly into Italy, from where most were shipped to Sardinia. Here, they were not incarcerated but left to fend for themselves. Extreme hardship undoubtedly, but out of immediate harm's way.[99]

How do we account for this persistent Italian—*fascist*—obduracy in the face of Nazi diktat? In fact, when Mussolini received an official request from Ribbentrop in August 1942 for Italian assistance to complete the Jewish round-up in Croatia, the Duce scrawled the words *nulla osta*—'no objection'—on the memorandum.[100] The immediate answer to the question, thus, would seem to be that the senior and middle-level officers of the military and supporting civil hierarchy consciously sabotaged orders from the very top. If this was the case, it would seem to make the contrast between Italian behaviour and that of other comparable satellite elites all the more remarkable. Michael Mann's telling remark that 'modernity's evil has been more ideological and blood-spattered than bureaucratic and dispassionate'[101] would certainly seem to be applicable not just to German perpetrators but a range of *other* national administrators and military men eager to oil the wheels of Jewish elimination. In the case of Italy, however, Mann's insight would seem to operate in an altogether different direction. Its commanders and diplomats were neither bureaucratic nor dispassionate in the manner in which they used wile and subterfuge, mixed with heavy doses of wilful dilatoriness, to put spokes in those very same wheels. Jonathan Steinberg has represented these efforts as a form of conspiracy.[102] Certainly, the fact that Mussolini's occupation subordinates seemed to enter into this line of action as a collectivity gave them some power with which to take effective action, otherwise unavailable to individuals acting alone. In France, for instance, there were a handful of high-ranking military dissenters, such as the Grenoble commander General Robert de Saint-Vincent. He refused to use his troops to round up Jews for deportation in August 1942, but for his pains was summarily sacked.[103]

Could it be, however, that the group nature of the Italian response was informed not simply by philo-Semitism but by a streak of hard-headed calculation? One, moreover, in which senior officials were not so much working away from but rather 'towards' Il Duce?[104] Italy had taking a belated plunge into war on the German side for its own strategic, empire-building reasons. Once the tables began turning—actually much earlier for the relatively weak Italians than for their northern neighbour—the logic of the situation pointed towards trying to create as much distance as possible between themselves and their erstwhile Axis partner, not least so that come the Allied reckoning, Rome might sue for peace as an entirely *independent* player. Mussolini's diplomats and generals repeatedly spoke to him of Italy's prestige and honour when they strove to prevent the handing over of the Jews to the Germans. A particular crunch point came in February 1943, when Ribbentrop—in Italy to bolster the febrile alliance—unsuccessfully raised the issue in person. But speaking of one's prestige was simply another way of articulating a state's sovereign right to act in a way it saw fit, not proof of some overriding humanitarian concern.[105] When a Laval or an Antonescu spoke about removing the Jews, they also reached for the honour or prestige button to support their case. And did so, again, when—attempting to extricate themselves from the German grip—they changed tack.

The difference in the case of the Italians was that by mid-war they were not only quite openly playing their own 'Jewish' game—nowhere more so than in the Balkans—but in the process were threatening to provide an object lesson on how to do it to all the disgruntled Axis satellite states equally seeking insurance policies against an almost certain Allied victory. The Nazis understood this situation all too well. A thoroughly exasperated Ribbentrop exclaimed, 'Our efforts with regard to the governments of Croatia, Rumania, Bulgaria and Slovakia to deport the Jews resident in those countries have also encountered great difficulties…because of the attitude of the Italian government'.[106] The further irony, however, is that Rome's grace towards Jews in its Balkan sphere also happened to be part of a wider shift in its strategic *actions*, which at the very least one might consider problematic. For instance, the Italians' inability to bring the Serb insurgency to heel in their area of control, hence undermining the viability of their projected Adriatic annexations, drove them towards co-opting one element within it—the anti-communist Chetniks. The latter, however, were not only the deadly rivals of the Ustasha but also a thorn in the side of the Germans, still, supposedly, Italy's co-occupier in the region. But by handing over much of eastern Bosnia to a Chetnik puppet administration, the Italians also exposed the *Muslim* population of the area to systematic massacres perpetrated by the Chetniks, which were arguably on a par with those committed by the Ustasha against Jews, Roma, and Serbs.[107] Indeed, to add to the already mired complexity of this picture, not only did these massacres steer many Bosnian Muslims towards the *Germans*, who for their own broader, including geostrategic, reasons wanted them on side, but also provided grounds for the surviving—mostly Orthodox—Roma within the NDH to pass themselves off as part of the minority Muslim Roma community![108]

The long and short of this fraught Italian occupation scene was that being apparently nice to the Jews did not automatically translate into a universal benevolence. The part-parallel Bulgarian record also carries a similar deficit. Almost simultaneously with Sofia's efforts to derail the Jewish deportations, Bulgarian officials not only resumed their Great War terror against recalcitrant Greeks in Thrace and Macedonia but attempted once again to forcibly convert their native Muslim Pomak population to Orthodoxy. The project—ultimately reversed by the incoming communist regime—was embarked upon with unrestrained violence. Yet many of its most earnest and active supporters included those who had been vocal in their opposition to the Jewish deportations.[109]

To return to the Italians, it is true that in practice their own counter-insurgency operations never quite reached the levels of unrestrained mass murder as did those of their German counterparts. But then, to act as a restraining force in the Balkans the Italians had to be strong on the ground. When the Italian army, following its capitulation to the Allies in the autumn of 1943, surrendered to or fled from the Wehrmacht, its whole divide and rule edifice in the Balkans, as also in southeastern France, promptly collapsed. Among the casualties were its Chetnik protégés, many of whom were quickly rounded up by the Germans and in some instances executed,[110] as well as those Jews in and around Nice caught in the infamous SS razzia. As for the long-standing, nearly 2,000-strong Jewish population on Italian-occupied Rhodes, it was the last community in the region to be rounded up, alongside the Jews of neighbouring Cos, and deported to Auschwitz.[111] The Italian collapse, indeed, poses the question: how does a defeated national society behave towards an even more exposed—and possibly already hated—minority community when the organs of state and with it military defence are no longer there to protect any of its citizens?

NON-GERMAN PERPETRATORS IN THE NAZI-OCCUPIED RIMLANDS

One of the most striking features associated with the initiation of Operation Barbarossa was the manner in which Jewish communities in the immediate line of the Wehrmacht assault were *also* attacked and sometimes massacred by their Gentile neighbours, as if some latent hatred had been given permission to explode into open and unadulterated violence. Nearly all of the atrocities of this kind happened within days or weeks of the start of the offensive, either in the hiatus between the departure of the Russians and the arrival of the Germans, or soon after the latter had arrived. One particularly well-documented and much debated case is that of the small town of Jedwabne, in the Podlasie, where almost the entirety of the Jewish part of the community—not less than 340 men, women, and children—were put to death by elements from the Polish part on 10 July 1941, certainly under German eyes but without their direct participation.[112] Jedwabne, however, was far from an isolated incident. Elsewhere in the Podlasie and Volhynia at least twenty other small townlets were sites of 'indigenous' massacres, with most of the perpetrators Ukrainians rather than Poles.[113] A very similar sequence of anti-Jewish massacre occurred in eastern Galicia. The evidence suggests that these attacks were carried out with whatever—usually agricultural—implements were to hand. Boards spiked with nails, crowbars, pitchforks, and axes were the standard weapons, supplemented by fire, especially where the victims could be driven into barns and then set alight.

Even so, such attacks were not simply a matter—if indeed they can be defined at all—of an undifferentiated mass of peasant villagers running amok. Male volunteers were usually at the cutting-edge of the killings, often organized into paramilitary units, or as in Lithuania, further to the north, as self-styled 'partisans'. Here, rural attacks were eclipsed in scale by those which took place in towns and cities, especially Kovno (Kaunus). Again, one infamously grisly incident—the torture and then clubbing to death of some fifty Jews at the Lietukis garage on Vytautus Prospect on 25 June—was actually only one facet of four days and nights of killing in the city and its Sloboda suburb, in the course of which some 3,500 Kovno Jews perished. The first efforts of these 'white armbands', as the Lithuanian militias were also called, claimed an estimated 7–8,000 of their fellow Jewish countrymen.[114] In Latvia, a simultaneous spasm of atrocities was carried out by the so-called Aiszargi militia. The other Baltic state, Estonia, was arguably only spared because there were very few Jewish inhabitants to kill in the first place, and these were mostly able to flee east, given that the country was in the lee of the immediate German assault.

Further south, however, in military sectors where Hungarian or Rumanian troops were the Axis 'liberators', mostly nationalist Ukrainian militias and self-appointed vigilantes were responsible for the synchronous contours of anti-Jewish violence. The key difference to these grass-roots massacres in the case of the Bukovina, was that they also ran in parallel to massacres largely perpetrated by the Rumanian army, police, and the specially created Esalon Special (like the earlier CUP *Teşkilât-ı Mahsusa* a special operations security unit). Indeed—while there is some debate as to whether these massacres were consciously directed from Bucharest, or themselves a spasm reaction to a local panic—the Rumanian authorities in and around the city of Iaşi were undoubtedly responsible for the most spectacular anti-Jewish massacre *not* led by Germans in this embryonic Operation Barbarossa phase. The victim tally may have been as high as 15,000.[115] What was even more remarkable about this particular atrocity was that it was conducted on Moldovan soil, certainly close to the frontier with but not on territory which had been otherwise occupied by the Soviets as a consequence of the previous Nazi–Soviet trade-off. If it is this aspect, and the fact that the slaughter was at least in part organized by the apparatus of an incumbent state, which gives to the Iaşi episode a distinct singularity, it equally throws into sharper relief the violence instigated by non-state actors across the length and breadth of the 'Lands Between', where, in a trice, recently imposed Soviet rule had evaporated.

Should we read this sequence, then, not so much as organized massacre but rather as a chaotic pulse: an anarchic 'moment' of populist frenzy which, taking its cue from the Wehrmacht advance, as surely fizzled out when the contours of German rule solidified? That would seem to make the violence less identifiable as genocide and more like the 'pogroms' of the 1880s or early 1900s, where the (in that case) tsarist state eventually intervened to restore order. Except that, in the 1941 instance, there are clearly two rather important complicating factors. The first is that there were, especially in eastern Galicia, some more obviously systematic massacres which took place somewhat later—most notably the so-called 'Petliura days' in Lwów, in which Ukrainian militia clubbed to death some 2,000 Jews during a three-day orgy of killing at the end of July.[116] The second is that while German control in these regions was by then complete, and hundreds of security police and Wehrmacht men were witnesses to these killings, rarely did they intervene to halt them.

Might this imply that behind all these supposedly 'grass-roots' atrocities was the hidden, or not so hidden, hand of the SS? We know that Heydrich sought to incite rimlands rage against the Jews as part of his Operation Barbarossa remit, and that some of the Einsatzgruppen commanders, notably Dr Walter Stahlecker, the head of Einsatzgruppe A, were active proponents of the project. We also know that Stahlecker and his subordinate commander, Karl Jäger, strove to take credit for much of the 'pogrom' success in the Baltic region.[117] This, too, has led a number of historians to conclude that there was no widespread popular enthusiasm or even spontaneity in these events. The argument is in part confirmed by various security police reports, including from Stahlecker himself, that the attempts to foment pogroms required considerable Einsatzgruppen input, and in some cases completely misfired.[118]

However, while Einsatzgruppen incitement *failures* offer a convenient alibi for those who would seek to distance the various 'Lands Between' nations from the taint of genocide, there is simply too much evidence from this initial phase that points in the opposite direction. To be sure, Jedwabne-style massacres were uniform neither in their incidence nor in their trajectory. And they clearly metamorphosed over time into something in which the indigenous role *became* subordinate. An Einsatzgruppe round-up of the supposed Jewish 'leadership' of the townlet of Horokhov on 12 August, for instance—in other words, a good month or more after the initial spasm—had the Germans as the shooters but the corralling of the Jewish men and boys over fourteen undertaken not only by Ukrainian police but also by high school students, who 'outed' their fellow pupils.[119] Open eagerness to beat up and terrorize Jewish neighbours, even relish in the prospect of their murder, was thus still evident, even while the occasion to directly kill them on terms the Ukrainians saw fit had been diluted by subordination to German command—and method.

Wehrmacht anxiety at the nature of 'native' killing had first surfaced at Kremenets—the largest of the initial phase massacres in Volhynia, where 800 Jews had been bludgeoned to death. On this occasion, in fact, the rear army commander General von Roques *had* intervened to halt it. We might read this as another aspect of the latent tension between the SS and the military: clearly, some of the subsequent orders by field commanders (as we will see in the Rumanian zone in our next section), prohibiting soldiers from either participating in, or even observing, 'unlawful acts' were not just paradoxical but entirely bizarre in the light of the RHSA brief to encourage exactly such mass killing.[120] Yet the orders also point to a more general, if equally bizarre and misplaced, German notion that there was some intrinsic distinction between the 'correct' dispatch of the 'enemy' (women and children included) as supposedly conducted according to a civilized rule-book, and the type of 'savage' violence meted out by rimlands peoples themselves.

All these perceptions and projections aside, we are still left with the question: how are we to account for the phenomenon of indigenous anti-Jewish violence in these zones recently acquired and then exited by the Soviets? A simple answer could be that this is what one might expect of regions where society had been so pulverized not just by the Soviet onslaught but by two decades or more of violence, social engineering, and ethnic reordering. Going right back to autumn 1914, certainly in eastern Galicia, the retreat of Habsburg state power, in the face of the Russian offensive, had acted as a catalyst to communal disorder, mostly directed at Jews.[121] It was they again who bore the brunt of *local* mayhem when, in late 1938, the Subcarpathian Rus found itself, for that brief moment, subject to neither Czech, Slovak, nor Hungarian rule.[122] The collapse of Poland in September 1939 had seen a similar breakdown in the eastern *kresy*, though here with Poles often the main target of subaltern violence. All this points to what might happen anywhere in the sudden absence of stable state authority, with the ensuing vacuum creating 'danger for any minority surrounded by hostile neighbours'.[123] More tellingly, perhaps, it underscores the degree to which whatever sinews of cross-community solidarity had existed in the rimlands before the Great War, these had been shattered in the succeeding inter-war period as irrevocably as had the zone itself. The fact that in the 1941 sequence one kernel of perpetrators, certainly in the Ukrainian region, seem to have been former members of the locally recruited Soviet *militsiia* (police) implies not only an attempt to divert attention from their own Soviet-interregnum collaboration, but a willingness to go with the grass-roots flow of violence, whoever the victim group.[124]

However, is the notion of a political hiatus leading to some Hobbesian state of anarchy sufficient to explaining the scope and intensity of the specifically anti-Jewish attack? Roger Petersen identifies rage and resentment as particular ingredients. Which in turn poses the question of whether latent, if in other respects commonplace, anti-Semitic elements were waiting for an opportune moment to erupt; or whether there was some other, new, clinching factor? John-Paul Himka, again considering the specifics of the Ukraine, has valuably differentiated between long-term structural factors associated with Jewish religious difference and folk-cultural 'otherness,' as well as perceived middle-men exploitation, on the part of an historic Polish landowning *szlachta*, and more immediate—as he terms them, 'conjunctural'—factors, associated with recent events and memories.[125]

Through the pages of these two volumes, we have hardly been able to avoid the persistent and often entirely raw animus of *many* Europeans—certainly not only in the rimlands—against their Jewish neighbours. Yet in the context of the Holocaust it is extremely difficult to paint a *uniform* picture of Christian priesthood or laity either condoning the abandonment of the Jews or spearheading their murder. Where the Vatican abjectly failed to speak out, and Catholic clergymen in various countries, especially in Slovakia, Croatia, and, of course, Germany itself, took a more active role in their destruction, there is equally a record of papal nuncios in Hungary and Slovakia, and bishops in France as indeed also Slovakia—as we have seen—making their voices heard against the deportations, even where these efforts proved too little, too late. Parish priests, notably in Italy and France, were altogether more courageous, when they hid Jewish survivors. The mosaic of Catholic response was mirrored among the other denominations, with minority sects (themselves sometimes historically persecuted) often taking a proactive lead in favour of Jewish support and rescue.[126] The liberated Soviet lands proved in no way exceptional to this bricolage landscape. A Jewish eyewitness reported that when the killing began at Jedwabne and surrounding villages, the priests did nothing to halt matters when village leaders proclaimed 'that it was time to settle scores with those who had crucified Jesus Christ, those who had taken Christian blood for matzoh'.[127] Church services where Catholic or Orthodox priests greeted the murder of the Jews with prayers for their congregations' deliverance were certainly commonplace. Later on, in the summer of 1943, Bishop Hyborii, the head of the Ukrainian Orthodox Autocephalous Church, used the occasion of a funeral procession in Vinnitsa—for bodies recently exhumed from an earlier NKVD massacre—to reprise the story of Christ's suffering at the hands of the Jews.[128] Yet if this sounds all too familiarly atavistic, compare and contrast Bishop Hyborii with Lwów's Uniate Metropolitan Sheptyts'kyi, whom we previously encountered at the time of the Russian invasion of Galicia in 1914. Sheptyts'kyi may have been a key figure-head of Ukrainian nationalism, but that hardly prevented him from calling down divine punishment on all those who shed innocent blood, nor his active farming out of Jewish escapees for hiding to a network of monasteries, Seventh-Day Adventists, and ordinary peasant women.[129] Or consider further the humble Ukrainian peasant women who of their own volition, according to another significant Jewish eyewitness, blocked a column of Jews being deported from Rumanian Dorohoi by getting down on the road, beating their breasts, raising their fists, and screaming at the *pretor* in charge of the column, 'You Burzhui ['bourgeois'], how can you be so hard on human beings?' The *pretor* proved powerless against their protests, the result being that the deportees were saved—at least for that moment.[130]

But if this only serves to confirm the historic complexity of Jewish/non-Jewish relations in the rimlands, albeit as backdrop to their almost always pitiless unravelling in the course of the 'Final Solution', neither can we discount the raw immediacy of the conjunctural factors in the early summer of 1941. In the very days before Operation Barbarossa got under way, the NKVD had been conducting major eastward-bound deportations from the entirety of their conquered belt.[131] This was on top of the relentless round-ups of suspects and the merciless elimination of underground political cells which had continued to resist or had attempted to sabotage the cementing of Soviet rule in the 'Lands Between'. The forests of the Lomza area, which included Jedwabne, for instance, had been the site for a major NKVD military operation the previous summer to wipe out a potential Polish insurgency there, followed up by yet another action to remove local activists, just before 22 June 1941.[132] The majority of the peoples occupied by the Soviets may not have become so directly involved in these dynamics of violence. Nevertheless, where they remained committed to an independent pre-Soviet national existence— or, in the case of west Ukrainians, an imagined one—their embitterment at what had befallen them would have been compounded by disorientation, exhaustion, and bewilderment at the speed with which the communists swept aside both the human figures as well as the institutions of interwar authority. Moreover, even in the conditions of the chaotic Soviet retreat from 22 June onwards, the NKVD did everything in its power to ensure that there would be no return to that status quo ante. The thousands of 'socially dangerous' individuals incarcerated in jails in the region not yet removed to the east were swiftly liquidated, though one might add in a manner quite unlike the standard, clinically professional, and highly secret executions of which Katyn had been characteristic. On the contrary, these jail massacres were hastily organized, grotesquely vicious affairs, on some occasions using the most basic implements to hand to bludgeon, hack, and butcher their victims to death.[133] The often palpable relief and gratitude which local people demonstrated to the Wehrmacht on having been liberated from the Soviet yoke thus had as their corollary cries for revenge and retribution when the jails were opened up. Necessarily, these cries were ones which the SS were all too ready and willing to fan. That said, what is most significant is the way in which, in the absence of obvious Soviet authorities to attack, the full fury of grieving and enraged families and communities fell on the Jews.

It is now estimated that some 20–30,000 prisoners were murdered by the NKVD in eastern Galicia and the *kresy* alone.[134] And there is certainly a close correlation between some of these lurid jail discoveries and the immediately subsequent Jewish massacres. In Lwów, where up to 3,000 people had been murdered by the NKVD in the Brygidki prison, some of the first wild Jewish killings—before the more obviously organized 'Petliura days'—were directed against Jewish men who had been rounded up to clear out the bodies of the murdered. Similar events took place notably at the Zolochiv fortress and at Borysław, near Drohobycz.[135] Meanwhile, at Lutsk the SS used the NKVD murders there, along with the death of two handfuls of Wehrmacht soldiers in the struggle for the town, as a pretext for the mass execution of some 1–2,000 Jewish inhabitants.[136]

If either direct tit-for-tat reprisal or incitement in that direction by the Germans was the immediate cause—or at least spark—for some of the first wave pogroms, this still fails to account for the many which took place before the NKVD killings were discovered, or the Germans had even arrived to try to orchestrate a response.[137] More pointedly, none of this really explains why indigenous reprisal against unarmed, neighbouring Jewish civilians were deemed the right and proper way of replying to the atrocities committed by the Soviets. Most Jews, after all, had also been dislocated, pauperized, and forced to see their places of worship and houses of learning culturally vandalized by the incoming communists, just as had other rimlands communities. Jewish suffering equally included—especially for those with Zionist or Bundist leanings, or assumed 'bourgeois' wealth—incarceration and/or deportation to the east. If crowd anger vented itself on Jews in substitution for what they could not otherwise hit out at, could it be that a charge of some perceived *political* Jewish attachment to the communists—in other words, an entirely conjunctural condition—was linked, perhaps subconsciously, in the perpetrators' minds to some deeper, more historically embedded sense of their Jewish neighbours having mortally transgressed?

A way into this perpetrator mindset might be assisted by what we noted earlier in this chapter about cognitive dissonance. Jews in pre-modern Christian Europe, like Armenians in the Ottoman Empire, were sometimes (not always) tolerated—and hence were tolerable—where they stuck firmly to their subordinate socio-economic roles in the accepted scheme of things; and actually, in the case of the Jews, not just in *Christian* Europe. A notable, if entirely exceptional, example of an exterminatory Muslim crowd assault on a Jewish community occurred in Moorish Granada in 1066, when it was alleged that the community's leader, Joseph ibn Nagrehla, was abusing his role as vizier to the king. The very fact that a Jew might have such political power at all in this set-up was itself dissonant. That Joseph had inherited the position, in effect, from his father, who was considered at the time and in subsequent readings to be a 'wise' vizier, further underscores the point about a subordinate ethno-religious minority *not* overstepping the mark. Whether Joseph actually did so is for our purposes immaterial to the argument.

What matters is the idea that where such occasional figures exercised wider political authority this always had to be within strictly defined limits as determined by the sovereign power, and absolutely never for the *perceived* benefit of the minority interest.[138]

Fast-forward to our region in its post-1939 Soviet incarnation, and we find the allegation not just of broad Jewish acclamation of, but active participation in, the new communist-imposed regime widespread among the wider population, though perhaps most keenly of all from elements of the now deposed elite. Thus, looking back from September 1941, what General 'Grot' Rowecki, the head of the underground Armia Krajowa (AK) chose to recall from the moment of Soviet takeover in eastern Poland was not the swathes of the population, Ukrainian and Belorussian in particular, who had readily lent themselves to the new regime, but rather the Jews 'even before the retreat of the Polish units' who 'had displayed red flags and built triumphal arches to welcome the Bolshevik army'.[139] Jan Karski, also reporting the situation to the Polish government-in-exile but this time from early on in the Soviet occupation, in February 1940, interestingly used a very similar turn of phrase. Having claimed that the Jews had made the most of the communist takeover to advance their own economic position, among other things through the black market, loan-sharking, and pimping, he went on to note:

> The attitude of the Jews towards the Bolsheviks is regarded among the Polish popula-
> tion as quite positive. It is generally believed that the Jews betrayed Poland and the
> Poles, that they are basically communists, that they crossed over to the Bolsheviks with
> waving banners.[140]

So whatever other ethnic communities might have done, it was the Jews' alleged flaunting of their enthusiasm for the communists which was *the* unforgivably pro-fane act. And whether it was only some—in fact mostly young, many already leftist-inclined Jews—as opposed to the Jewish majority who were implicated in this tendency, this, again, from the formerly dominant elite perspective tainted each and every one. Might one not further speculate that behind the anger at what they had seen, or claimed to have seen, was a profoundly embedded, religiously-informed sense that *any* Jewish involvement in the ruling politics of state amounted to the shattering of a taboo? When Jews thereafter did indeed enter in considerable num-bers into the Soviet-run administrations of the 'Lands Between', it was thus not just seen as a betrayal of the loyalty *owed* by all Jews to their Christian masters, nor just 'the feeling of being politically dominated by a group that has no right to be in a superior position',[141] but rather a dread confirmation that by entirely diabolical means the world—*their* Christian world—had been turned upside down. Hence the particularly obsessive focus at the time, and as it later developed into a post-war myth, on those Jews who had been elevated into the senior ranks of local NKVD branches and, by a further twist of the mythic narrative, oft-repeated tales of their merciless brutality. The fact that one such story which did the rounds in western Volhynia, in the summer of 1941, was of a woman called Hanna Berenstein, who was purported to have been a particularly sadistic torturer of both men and women, underscores the enormity of the Jews' perceived trespass.[142] As with the so-called 'Gerwani' of the (failed) Indonesian communist coup of 1965, the fact that women were believed to be in the vanguard of the violent, sado-erotic supersession of what had legitimately come before, adds a lurid but gendered rationalization to the insist-ent cry—according to Karski and other witnesses—that Jewish treachery would, in some imminent 'day of reckoning', be repaid 'in blood'.[143]

The pulse of anti-Jewish violence in the rimlands during the summer of 1941 did not come out of nowhere, therefore. Describing it as the consequence either of latent anti-Semitism or that of spontaneous, localized, anarchic glee at the window of opportunity to fleece vulnerable neighbours presented by the German invasion, does not suffice to address its fundamental political motivations. Whether con-ducted by townspeople or rural folk, these were conscious revenge attacks against a part of the population which was not just deemed to have collaborated with the Soviets but was held to be directly responsible for the liquidation of national hopes and aspirations. In this sense, while the popular assault could not be followed through unilaterally or comprehensively as the region passed into German hands, it nevertheless represented a culmination of intense anti-Jewish passions, whose modern origins began with the advent of grass-roots nationalism in the rimlands on the one hand, and the all-encompassing *Żydokomuna* psychosis on the other. As one Lithuanian participant in the assaults later remembered, 'Almost no one among the people spoke of "Soviet power"; people spoke of "Jewish power".'[144]

*

It is surely no accident, therefore, that the Baltic states, Lithuania in particular, were at the epicentre not only of the initial 'Lands Between' assaults but of the provision thereafter of substantial numbers of local collaborators in the German 'Final Solution'. The Soviets' whirlwind destruction of Baltic independence had not gone unresisted. In fact, in Lithuania, the last of these states to succumb in June 1940, resistance had been extraordinarily intense, led by what was left of Lithuania's own secret police, the Saugumas, and, linked to them, the Lithuanian Activist Front (LAF), the more militant, but not overtly fascistic, of two organizations which sought to keep national hopes alive. The LAF pinned these hopes on Nazi support, giving whole-hearted assistance the following year to the Wehrmacht in the 'liberation' of Vilnius (Vilna) and Kaunus (Kovno), and for which in turn it seemed to be rewarded when Berlin acquiesced in the creation of a provisional government. Logically, this relationship should have cooled when the Germans resumed full control of the whole Ostland region in early August.[145] However, willingness among at least a section of the 'partisans' led by Algirdas Klimaitis to pursue Jewish extermination seems to have continued undiminished. Indeed, not only were *most* Lithuanian Jews dead by the end of 1941, considerably in advance of elsewhere in the Nazi-occupied east, but it has been suggested that something between half and two-thirds of the 254,000 murdered in the course of the war met their deaths at the hands of fellow Lithuanians. No wonder that early Einsatzgruppen reports were so complimentary about the unit they founded out of the 'partisans'—the Labour National Guard.[146] Thereafter, under German security police command, some twenty Lithuanian police battalions created from the Guard, or from additional volunteer cadres, were responsible not only for the hands-on liquidation of some 220 *shtetlach* in Lithuania itself, but many other massacres outside Lithuania where they were later deployed. One battalion, the Twelfth, became particularly notorious for the conspicuous zeal with which it carried out *Aktionen* in occupied Belorussia; to the point where a German administrator, in Sluzk, pleaded for their removal—for fear of further destabilizing relations with the remainder of the local population.[147] In Lithuania itself, not only was the largest single indigenous Jewish mass killing—at the Ninth Fort in Kovno on 29 October—coordinated by similar such units, even if the Germans did the actual shooting, but an 130-strong Saugumas-led Lithuanian security police force continued to assert its essential autonomy from German interference by rounding up and interrogating at will individual Jewish suspects in the infamous Lukiškės prison in Vilna.[148]

One might still counter that all these efforts, as well as being the work of a minority of pro-Nazi elements, were founded on an essentially opportunistic premise: namely that doing the German bidding would sooner or later be recipro-cated with the latter's restoration of Lithuanian independence. The weakness of this argument becomes transparent, however, when set against the broad nature of popular involvement in the killings—at least, that is, in the early months. Again, we might try to further explain Lithuanian eagerness to participate in Jewish mass murder as a particularly pronounced case of getting in its retaliation against an ethnically separate component of the population perceived as having gone over to the Soviet side. It is certainly true that many Jews were involved in the new Lithua-nian SSR. The Jewish profile in particular ministries, especially industry—where the newly appointed minister was himself Jewish—was high. And it was also the case that initially five of the twenty-one seats on the Central Committee were held by Jews. The ethnic composition of the leadership of Lithuania in 1940 thus has resonances in miniature of Bolshevik Russia immediately after the October revolu-tion. And it is certainly also true that in addition to economic planning and other bureaucratic posts, there were Jews who joined the ranks of the Komsomol, the army, and the NKVD. Indeed, often cited in nationalist, exculpatory accounts is the fact that Major Gladkov, the head of the security commissariat (NKGB) in Lithuania, was by birth Jewish.[149] The further fact that Gladkov was one of many NKVD operatives shipped in from Moscow to investigate and eliminate *all* sus-pected counter-revolutionaries, political and religious Jews *included*, is rarely men-tioned in these accounts.[150]

Which rather underscores the motivation behind the Lithuanian anti-Jewish drive. At stake was not what percentage of Jews wholeheartedly embraced or participated in the life of post-1940 Soviet Lithuania, when that, as a fraction of the total, was not and could not be sufficient to constitute any kind of Jewish takeover. Rather, the Jewish sin lay in *any* of their number participating in the political life of the coun-try without the dominant population's leave to do so. Paradoxically, this did not mean that Lithuania had been a particularly harsh environment for its Jews in the interwar years. If there had been a primary political enemy in this period it was the Poles, and it was they, rather than the Jews, who bore the brunt of popular animus when Kaunas finally wrested control of an otherwise mostly Polish Jewish Vilnius as a by-product of the Nazi–Soviet 1939 carve-up. Indeed, one might go further and say that it was the essentially benign nature of the Smetona regime with regard to its Jews which led right-wing nationalists to claim that Smetona had all along been in thrall to Jewish interests.[151] But here lay the rub. Despite the fact that Jews *actually* had been frozen out of Lithuanian politics for the previous eighteen years, when independent Lithuania spectacularly folded in the face of Red Army diktat in 1940, it was the classic 'outsiders operating from within syndrome' which took over as the standard explanatory narrative. Acclamation by some Lithuanian Jews of the Sovi-ets could only amplify this convenient explanation. And instead of looking into either the country's own failings as a polity or, perhaps more precisely, its inherent geopolitical weakness, its 'partisans' chose instead to read what had happened as an act of criminal fifth column betrayal or, by further comparison, a magnified and speeded up version of the German 'stab in the back'. No wonder, then, that when the LAF, on the coat-tails of their Nazi patrons, stormed back the following summer they saw this as their own 'redemptive', 'perpetrators' "never again" moment'. And one they chose to mark by issuing a proclamation declaring null and void 'the old rights of sanctuary' granted to Lithuanian Jewry by the great fourteenth-century leader Vytautus. Of course, that had been a long time before; which makes all the more striking the fact that the LAF chose to refer to this event as legitimation for their call to fellow Lithuanians to make a final 'reckoning' with the Jews.[152] The implication in this still 'deeply Catholic' country[153] was quite clear: the Jews had broken the terms of their asylum, had repaid historic Lithuania's kindness with treachery, had sought to overturn the dispensation of heaven in favour of a diabolical—Soviet—hell.

What was true of the Lithuanian situation carried through at least in part into neighbouring Latvia. To be sure, Stahlecker reported to Berlin that getting pogroms going here was more difficult than in Lithuania. The initial Latvian strike force—the so-called Arajs Kommando—numbered no more than 300 men. It was largely drawn from individuals with hard-right, more overtly pro-fascist, military, and anti-Bolshevik backgrounds, many on a personal level gagging for revenge against those perceived as having been responsible for the deaths or deportations of family members. Even so, of an estimated 85,000 non-combatants killed in the Einsatzgruppen first sweep, the unit's tally was believed to be 26,000, mostly Jews, but also significantly including many Roma and mentally ill people, as well as communists. And, in fact, the Arajs Kommando was quickly augmented by many other younger men, especially from the closed universities and from national student fraternities, ready and willing to be inducted into German-led Latvian auxiliary police battalions.[154]

As with Lithuania, hard-headed calculation about a restoration of sovereignty may have been an aspect of elite Latvian thought processes. Hitler was firmly set against such an eventuality, though Himmler, by contrast, increasingly came round (especially after Stalingrad) to accepting Latvians and Estonians as Germanic or neo-Germanic peoples, not least with recruitment in mind of some of their number into the depleted ranks of the Waffen SS.[155] Again, however, whether Latvian nationalists were able in 1941, or for that matter in 1944, to second-guess contingent Nazi policy-making in the Baltic does not really explain the commitment and often zeal with which the auxiliaries continued to do the Germans' dirty work, their cruelty on occasion provoking the same negative comment from civil administrators as had that of their Lithuanian counterparts.[156] In Latvia itself, the vast majority of the 66,000 Jews trapped in the country at the start of Operation Barbarossa were dead by the end of the year. And just as with Lithuanians at Kovno Ninth Fort, where annihilations had been the essential cogs in the wheels of German execution, so in the equivalent destruction of Riga's Jewry, in two great mass shootings at Rumbula, on 30 November and 8 December, it was Latvians who provided the auxiliary force.[157] Equally, in Estonia, the very small residual Jewish population—963 to be exact—which had not fled with the Soviets was rounded up and eliminated on an individual basis by the country's own quasi-independent security police force, itself closely linked to the Omakaitse, the home guard formation uniquely granted German authority in the occupied east to conduct self-defence and counter-insurgency operations on its own account.

Added to the fact that this gave Estonia the dubious distinction of being the first European 'country' to become completely *judenfrei* under Nazi rule, the self-willed nature of the Estonian Sipo's *génocidaire* activity is further emphasized by the murder of the country's indigenous Roma, including one notably pitiless execution of three score of women and infant children at the Jägala concentration camp in March 1943.[158]

What is notable in the Estonian case is the Jewish killing in the absence of a sufficient 'fifth column' to blame for the Soviet trauma. Similarly, while Latvia had a backdrop of interwar Jewish/non-Jewish relations, these lacked much by way of cultural interaction, or, for that matter, acute communal tension. To be sure, partial Jewish involvement in the communist administration, with the presence of another Jew—Semyon Shustin—as an imported Russian overseer of the Latvian NKVD,[159] just as in Lithuania, offered crude grounds for anti-Jewish mobilization once the German opportunity presented itself. Indeed, in the atmosphere of intense collective humiliation and 'loss of self-worth', as a consequence not just of the Soviet conquest but of their own inability to effectively resist it, one might read Latvian chauvinist scapegoating of a primary minority community as an almost predictable case of collective psychological compensation for the fresh but raw memory of national passivity in the face of a more powerful enemy.[160] Taking back the power which 'rightly' belonged to the nation through the substitution of a Jewish for a Russian bogey thus did not *necessarily* require some historical-cum-religious underpinning; nor indeed a Nazi-informed racialization of the communal target or targets. The killing of Roma as well as Jews might lend itself to the latter assumption.[161] But might we not equally read the ongoing elimination of both these communities by Baltic nationalists operating under a German screen rather as a case of cleaning the slate in the expectation that some time, in the not too distant future, their countries would not simply to be restored to themselves but restored as altogether stronger, more coherent, more fully homogenized entities?

*

Whether such anti-minority agendas could genuinely operate *without* a historical backdrop of real or imagined anxiety about biological pollution, cultural contamination, or political emasculation at the hands of such groups is at the least discussable. Estonian participation in Jewish mass murder leaves the door ajar on the possibility. But there is also the Ukrainian nationalist case to consider, not because the historical–religious baggage of anti-Semitism did not exist here—it very clearly did—but rather because Ukrainian hopes for some future national *self*-liberation have to be set against the extreme brevity of political independence in the recent past. To be sure, memories of post-Great War independence were kept alive on the once Habsburg, then Polish-controlled terrain of Galicia, and it was from here, within the confines of the General Government, that Nazi support for a localized Ukrainian administration fostered hopes among the ultra-nationalist OUN that further German advance into the Soviet Ukraine might be the basis for rekindling a much grander national dream. The OUN's fundamental misconception about German intentions in the region (*pace* Rosenberg's cautious but ultimately overruled support for the notion of a puppet—though not OUN—entity) proved critical to the manner in which the movement descended from early 1940 onwards into an intense and extremely violent internecine struggle between OUN-B (Bandera) and OUN-M (Melnyk) factions. While the consequences of these developments are entirely germane to our next chapter, what matters here is the manner in which revolutionary Ukrainian nationalism of the OUN ilk chose to typecast Jews as 'Muscovite stooges' and anticipate their removal from Ukrainian soil as a sine qua non for the creation of a revived Kiev-centred state.[162] In this light, Lwów (Lviv) and other east Galician massacres in which the OUN signature was evident in summer 1941 might suggest at least as much an attempt to fashion the demographic contours of a future polity as a taking of revenge for such alleged Jewish sins as being Soviet acolytes, NKVD agents, or for that matter historic allies of the Polish *szlachta*.[163] A further paradox lies in the fact that east Galicia had not been a particular arena for grass-roots Ukrainian anti-Jewish hostility until quite recently.[164] As with the Balts, so here too it was the palpable shift in nationalist thinking towards the most extreme methods for dealing with internal enemies—as amplified by the Soviet trauma—plus the cover provided by the Nazis' own exterminatory agenda which accounts for the self-willed genocidal efforts of groups such as the OUN.

None of this is to dispute that the main thrust of rimlands killing came from the Germans, or that where rimlands people were participants it was primarily as *their* subalterns: colonial subalterns at that. This might further suggest the need to carefully discriminate between those early killings where the political agendas of national actors was primary, and the much more standard pattern throughout the rest of the war whereby those who killed Jews, Roma, and others did so because they had volunteered for or perhaps been inducted into German-officered auxiliary *Hilfspolizei* units, Himmler-authorized para-military *Schutzmannshaft* battalions, or became labour and death camp guards trained by the SS in the Lublin-province town of Trawniki. The majority of an estimated 3–5,000 'Trawniki men' were Ukrainian, but there were significant numbers too of Balts, ethnic Germans, Poles, and Russians.[165] As for the *Schutzmänner*, the twenty-six original formations in existence by late 1941, with some 33,000 participants, had swelled to 75,000 by July 1942, and a staggering 300,000 by the end of that year.[166] Much larger numbers of local officials provided administrative support functions to the German police and civil authorities supervising these units, thus magnifying again the degree to which the 'Final Solution' in the east was dependent on indigenous collaboration.

However, it is less easy to infer that the great bulk of these rimlands collaborators were primarily motivated—as a majority of their forerunners may have been—by either national objectives or unadulterated anti-Semitism. The willingness to don a subaltern uniform may have been a good deal more (albeit tastelessly) banal. Most of the initial Trawniki cadres, for instance, were drawn as Soviet POWs from Wehrmacht camps, where their likely fate would otherwise have been death through starvation or gruelling forced labour.[167] Indeed, are the repeated reports of these individuals' extreme brutality in Treblinka, Sobibor, and elsewhere any wonder, when their most recent life-wrenching experience had been on the receiving end? One might go further and propose that given the degraded culture of the rimlands, with its extreme poverty, hunger, and often pitiless violence—especially under recent Soviet tutelage—the bar preventing German service inductees from enacting more of the same would hardly have been high. Conversely, the incentives to their participation, by the standards they knew, actually would have been rather great. Simply the opportunity for a steady wage, better rations, food perhaps to be offered or pilfered on behalf of family members, and—most tellingly of all—avoidance of the growing labour draft to the Reich would all be quite enough to have had droves of young men, and women, queuing up at the local enlistment offices. Rimlands life under the Nazis *was* social-Darwinian; perhaps all the more reason why one had to seize any short-term benefits that it could offer. A Polish journalist who witnessed the mass murder of Vilna Jewry at the nearby forest of Ponary throughout 1941 and 1942 noted, 'For the Germans 300 Jews are 300 enemies of humanity... for the Lithuanians they are 300 pairs of shoes, trousers, and the like.' Revealingly, he went on to note how those guarding the site started up a profitable trade in a range of items from the corpses, including silk stockings, furs, and gold extracted from victims' teeth; how they offered to shoot Jews to order when villagers asked for a particular size of clothes; but also how they violently fell out with each other over the proceeds.[168] In other words, the method whereby rimlands people extracted advantage from Jewish extermination was little different in kind from that applied by their Ottoman equivalents in response to the *Aghet*, or for that matter—with hardly more refinement (or concealment)—Germans in uniform abroad or as civilians at home.

One sober lesson to be reminded of here is that a wide range of ordinary people can be involved in genocide without imbibing the value-system of the elite perpetrators, or even necessarily having to rationalize, or justify to themselves or others, their participation. One notable eyewitness account confirms that the terrorization of Kievan Jews herded towards their mass death at Babi Yar in September 1941 was carried out by Ukrainian auxiliaries we now know to have been members of the Bukovinian battalion. Looked at in the broader context of genocidal violence, their behaviour may not have been all that exceptional: all we know from Dina Pronicheva's famous testimony is that they rained violent blows with clubs, sticks, and brass knuckles on the victims as they drove them through a gauntlet of policemen and vicious dogs towards the ravine, forcing the Jews to undress in the process and tearing away their children, who were thrown straight into the abyss.[169] What *exactly* was going on in the perpetrators' heads given the lack of their own frank testimony remains beyond our ken. We might surmise that finding themselves caught in a vice in their native province between Rumanians on the one hand and the incoming Soviets on the other, their newly found subservience to German diktat left them taking out their anger on the one group which could offer no resistance: the Jews. In this way we can perhaps speak of this and similar actions by rimlands policemen as the acting out of an ersatz power; and thus a form of subaltern genocide, even if at one remove.[170] The fact that Jews were always perceived as having hidden wealth could be read as giving to this genocide from below a certain class edge. The further fact that this inference tells us a great deal about the mindset of the terrorizers but nothing about the terrorized in no sense detracts from a common vox populi conviction that in fleecing what was on the person of Jews who were about to die anyway, or clearing out what had been their homes, the participants were taking 'back' what they had otherwise been denied.[171]

The legitimacy of such action, moreover, in part came through the authority vested in those at its cutting edge. One might cynically say: put a man (or woman) in uniform and give him a licence to do things which he would never otherwise contemplate, except in his most sado-erotic dreams, and he is bound to end up acting like a little Hitler.[172] What was at work in the German-occupied east, however, was not simply the criminal psychology of individual arousal but the collective framework, and more crucially colonial dimension, within which it operated. In fact, this did not require an eastern setting per se. In the Netherlands, the pro-Nazi Sybren Tulp, who also happened to be a former but senior Royal Dutch East Indies army officer, was in the summer of 1941 elevated by the occupying authorities to the post of chief constable of Amsterdam police, with direct remit to round up Jewish troublemakers and act as enforcer of the new German anti-Jewish regulations. Tulp's response to the challenge was to create a 300-strong battalion of ex-Dutch army men, which he could duly inculcate with his own colonial experience. His success in mobilizing the wider Amsterdam police to the job in hand was not actually wholly successful.[173] But might we not assume that had the Germans occupied Britain they would have found equally right-wing, authoritarian characters, including many drawn from imperial army and police backgrounds, who would have readily fallen in with the Nazi colonial method, including the racial segregation, incarceration, or indeed elimination of 'foreigners'?[174]

To be sure, this is speculation, as equally must be the question as to whether mere power for power's sake, without some additional personal or political compensation, could ever have been sufficient to sustain subaltern police formations in Hitler's empire. One might propose that the high degree of localized autonomy which Tulp's men derived from Nazi command afforded them the opportunity to act out macho, colonial fantasies of their own which necessarily had to be played out in entirely more circumscribed conditions among eastern auxiliaries, who knew their position to be on the lowest rung of the imperial hierarchy and whom their German overseers contemptuously referred to as 'askaris'. Again, to try to find a reason why so many diverse rimlands people were still prepared to do the Nazi bidding is to assume that there is a simple, or single, explanation. Belorussia as a region, for instance, was notable for its lack of historical anti-Jewish animus or 1941 summer pogroms, which most obviously links back to its weak national mobilization. Yet here, too, when push came to shove, locally formed police units proved perfectly capable of enacting the most extraordinary violence against Jewish fellow-citizens. As just one example, in November 1941, a recently enlisted unit of thirty men, mostly Belorussians but with Poles and Tatars among them, not only carried out their German officer's order to liquidate some 1,600 Jewish neighbours in their home town of Mir but, in a chaotic, frenzied, running massacre across the length and breadth of the town, behaved—according to one eyewitness—'as if they were at a wedding party'. Indeed, their considerable enthusiasm and relish for what they were doing was noted, including using bayonets against children or smashing their heads on tombstones, the Jewish cemetery being one of the main sites of this carnivalesque slaughter.[175]

Should we read such a narrative as going along with what was integral to the German project, the murderers extracting some added value in the form of sado-erotic gratification from the knowledge that they could do what they did with impunity? Or perhaps it was a prelude to throwing their weight around more generally on their own account, when their German officers were not looking or were out of sight? Because not all policemen's agendas were overtly political in the statist sense, it hardly rules out relationships of power between those who, through their uniform and instruments of violence, now had it at a grass-roots level, and those who accordingly had to bow to them in turn. In this sense the killing of Jews or Roma, either as a desirable supplement to their work or alternatively a highly unpalatable chore, was only the tip of the iceberg: what mattered were the opportunities, however ephemeral, for career advancement and/or venal gain which could come through the exercise of power; or, put more bluntly, for lawlessness, including rape, robbery, and the elimination of people one did not like—either directly or through ensuring that they were included in the forced labour draft—always dressed up, of course, as rough but ostensibly authorized justice.[176]

We need, too, to recall that from this perspective the behaviour of the Jewish police in the ghetto-run administrations also ran to type. This statement is indeed shocking in the light of what we know happened to these communities. Yet what we also know from diaries and other contemporary accounts of ghetto life—and death—is that in addition to the general breakdown of social cooperation and solidarity, and the ensuing descent into corruption and criminality among the more ruthless or simply hard-headed elements of these twilight communities, getting a Judenrat job in the police *appeared* equally to offer not only protection from 'deportation to the east' for oneself and possibly one's family, as well as the chance of better rations and shelter, but also the opportunity to lord it over other less fortunate folk. The result: it was the Jewish (rather than German or auxiliary), police who were noted for their cruelty and harshness, and recorded as ensuring that those at the bottom or on the margins of ghetto society, most especially foreign—often Central European—incomers (a notable inversion of the historic 'tolerable' versus 'irredeemable' Jewish profile), were the first to go on to the transports; and who were known as the policemen to whom, if one sought to be 'saved', one offered bribes or sexual favours.[177]

In this crude analysis, one might argue a crucial distinction is lacking between the Jewish police and other subaltern rimlands forces. The former were brought into existence by the Jewish councils as a way of *shielding* their communities from the worst. The fact that they failed, and that policemen who may or may not have joined these units to look after their own individual interest found themselves ultimately as expendable as any other ghetto Jew, can hardly detract from the principle at issue: namely the creation of as great a safety net around each Jewish enclave as was conceivably possible in the circumstances. But then, again—*pace* the Jewish reality of being one of absolute extremis—how different was the Judenrat reasoning from that of other subordinated ethnic communities in the 'Lands Between'?

Certainly, we might read the significant contribution of large numbers of ethnic Germans to the *Hilfspolizei* and *Schutzmannschaft* battalions, as well as local civil administration, as a matter of pure individual choice. However, viewed as the sum of its many parts, could one not equally consider such decision-making as tantamount to an effort to safeguard the lives and livelihoods of *all* rimlands Germans? To be sure, the very fact that the invitation to support the Nazi new order was coming from fellow Germans who looked to their racial kin as a first line of reliability in a sea of otherwise alien and hostile *Untermenschen* would have presented incentive enough—even if in practice ethnic Germans were invariably treated by their Reich-born superiors with contempt. But the simple fact that so many joined paramilitary units, including from historically quietist groups such as Baptists and Mennonites, more pointedly underscores, once again, the extreme vulnerability of these fragmented and often isolated communities, whose fortunes indeed had been in precipitous decline since at least the Great War. From this perspective, the chance to do the occupiers' bidding, as administrators or 'low-level perpetrators', might have been greeted less as the assurance of a firm place in the Nazi sun and more a last chance saloon in an already shattered 'Lands Between'.[178]

The ethnic German experience thus highlights a more general conundrum facing all those who became rimlands proxies to the 'Final Solution'. Was this the way to a place of greater safety, or did it simply tie oneself and one's community to a passing, unstable order in danger of being swept away with the return—and revenge—of the Soviets? By being privileged on dubious racial grounds, ethnic Germans found their way into senior NCO positions in the gendarmerie, and even security police apparatus, the Wehrmacht, and, later on, through mass compulsory conscription, into the Waffen-SS. By this route, towards the very end of the war, full Reich citizenship was granted to both those who served and their parents.[179] But what use was this if the price paid was to be part of the spiralling casualty list of German soldiery wiped out (more likely than not in some entirely foreign place) in the face of the relentless advance of the Red Army; or to be part of a mass evacuation westwards, the consequence of which was a *Deutsche frei* 'Lands Between'?

If the bottom-line purpose of participation in the Nazi project for relatively weak or 'squeezed' ethnic groups in the rimlands mosaic was thus not ideological per se, but to enhance a long-term autonomy and frame of reference within which to organize their *own* secured *nationalized* development, then clearly aligning themselves in this way was always going to be a high-risk strategy. More particularly, it came down to a matter of timing. As military occupiers operating at a distance from their own Central European base, yet having fallen far short of victory, the very Nazi mobilization of local auxiliary police and administrative personnel was an implicit recognition of some future quid pro quo. To be sure, the rather similar scenario which had presented itself to the German generals in the Great War, and to which they had responded by encouraging a calculated degree of national differentiation, had been ruled firmly out of court by Hitler. Yet in practice, more particularly once the fortunes of war from Stalingrad onwards pointed to the necessity of maximum rimlands involvement—that is, if the Red Army steamroller was still to be halted—the Nazi 'men on the spot' had little choice but to contemplate their own 'mobilization of ethnicity'. In 'White Russia', for instance, Kube's winks and nods at the Belorussian Self-Help Organization, *Samapomach*, implying that they might move beyond charitable soup kitchens (financed almost entirely from the proceeds of Jewish expropriations) towards becoming the embryo of an autonomous administration, were, in a sense, realized when in late June 1944, the recently created Belorussian Central Council staged a national congress in Minsk.[180]

The only problem was that not only was the council attempting to achieve this conjuring trick against the backdrop of a now prolonged Soviet partisan insurgency on their patch—Kube himself a prominent casualty from the previous autumn— but the entirely putative congress itself was conducted to the background tune of Red Army artillery. In other words, it was one thing for *Samapomach*, the Omakaitse, the LAF, the OUN, or whatever political-military guise such nationalist groups were operating under, to work towards that critical moment when the Germans might finally concede the principle of autonomy to them; but quite another to real-ize their ambition without the benefit of a Wehrmacht military screen. One thing that all of them had learnt, primarily through the police and paramilitary cadres that they had lent (or believed that they had lent) to the German interest, was that to secure their national terrain required the elimination of all other potential ethnic competitors. From this perspective, the participation of indigenous collaborators in the destruction of eastern Jewry became subsumed in an ultimately wider set of exterminatory imperatives for all the would-be national liberators. The most radi-cal—and spectacular—of these was the Ukrainian genocidal assault, from 1943, under the reformulated but now entirely *independent* guise of the UPA (Ukrainian Insurgent Army) against the Polish population of Volhynia and eastern Galicia: a subject to be more fully pursued in the next chapter. However, smaller scale exter-minations by the Belorussian auxiliary police of Poles on supposed Belorussian soil, similar AK counter-attacks against Belorussians *and* Ukrainians, as indeed the self-willed Omakaitse eradication of Estonian Roma,[181] equally exemplified the irrevo-cable collapse of any last vestige of inter-communal solidarity—and hence of some 'middle ground'—in the 'Lands Between'.

It is easy enough to lay the blame for these national radicalizations at the door of the Nazis; and it is equally difficult to see where else the nationalizing forces could have turned, given the geopolitical vice in which they found themselves from 1941. Yet it is also problematic, in the final analysis, to simply displace responsibility for the participation of indigenous auxiliary policemen in the destruction of Jewish, Roma, or other people on to the fascistic proclivities of the few or, failing that, the mindless brutality of individual psychopaths or, again, even if this was a significant factor, the desire to get even with alleged 'Muscovite-Jewish gangs'. Documents from the period emanating from OUN-M refer specifically to this last intent. And it was, in fact, through this same faction that the Bukovinan men at the cutting edge of the Babi Yar massacre were drawn.[182] In other words, while such low-tier *génocidaires* may not have been sophisticated political animals, neither was their behaviour simply Hobbesian. Their personal motives interacted with those of like-minded compatriots, feeding in turn into the world view of the OUN, as indeed all the other radical, pro-Nazi political movements who saw their goal as national liberation. Single-minded in their determination not to be returned to the Soviet yoke—the list of such freedom movements also included some Cossack and Caucasian groupings—they found themselves as a consequence not simply hitched to a Nazi power which for the most part treated them as at best useful fools, at worse as white 'niggers',[183]—but bound hand and foot to the Nazi method. The problem was that having thus committed themselves, they were in no position to extricate themselves once Hitler's eastern edifice began to crumble.

Thus, for a movement like OUN-M, the question by 1943 no longer simply regarded all the auxiliary police they had encouraged to enlist with the Germans; but rather what role they could play alongside other Ukrainian organizations, the Uniate Church included, in recruiting west Ukrainians into a new dedicated Waffen-SS division which they clearly perceived as a last-ditch defence of the homeland. Despite the fact that Nazi officialdom initially called the division 'Galicia', not 'Ukraine', and had no intention of using it only on Ukrainian home ground, the uptake—almost 100,000 volunteers—was successful beyond all expectation.[184] The 30,000 who eventually served significantly included large numbers of older men who had fought for the preservation of the Habsburg empire in the Great War. For their latest efforts, they were cut to pieces in the division's first encounter with the Red Army near Brody. After this mauling, Himmler became more supportive of the division's national character, agreeing to its designation as 'Ukrainian', in which capacity it became a major actor in atrocities committed in the course of the Nazi suppression of the Slovak uprising in late 1944.[185] Many of its participants were, of course, already old hands at mass murder, having learnt their trade against Jews and alleged partisans, as former members of SS-directed or other police formations. The irony for these Ukrainians, as for the Balts and others who had thrown in their political and military lot with the Germans, was that the tables would soon be turned, their engagement with Nazi mass murder boomeranging on their families and communities back home as the Soviet NKVD returned with a vengeance.

*

One rimlands national community would appear to stand outside the Nazi collaborative framework: the Poles. We might read this exceptionality as a consequence of Poland's particular two-sided destruction in September 1939. Already aligned to the Western Allies as flimsy guarantors of the country's independence in the face of the Nazi threat, Poland's actual elimination as a sovereign actor by both Nazis and Soviets ensured that its wartime government-in-exile had nowhere else to turn but to Western capitals. Even with the USSR in the Allied camp two years on—thus implicitly undermining the sustainability of Warsaw's pre-war territorial integrity—the London Poles remained as tied to the West for a return to the status quo ante as were their rimlands counterparts obversely dependent on German goodwill. One might say that the country's overall non-participation in the 'Final Solution' was thus a simple function of geopolitics. For any person or group to have supported *any* aspect of the Nazi programme within Poland—Jewish destruction included—consequently was tantamount to an act of national betrayal. Those who did so anyway, whether as collaborationist *policja granatowa* (dark 'blue' police) or on their own venal account, the so-called *szmalcownicy*—who blackmailed hiding Jews for money and then shopped them to the Germans—were liable in person, or in absentia, to the Delegatura's Directorate of Civil Resistance. That meant summary punishment by execution, or assassination. Strikingly, soon after the June 1942 liquidation of the Warsaw ghetto began, the blue police were withdrawn from participation, their places being taken by other Baltic and Ukrainian units.[186] On the more positive side of the coin, Żegota, an organization for assisting fleeing Jews (including by the provision of counterfeit documents to enable them to pass as Poles) was absorbed in the autumn of that year into the underground state's inner workings, with financial assistance from the government-in-exile. Gunnar Paulsson has estimated that, as a result, up to 28,000 Jews or, put another way, one in twelve of Warsaw's pre-war Jewish population, were able to go into hiding in the city, the largest single group of its kind in occupied Europe.[187] On top of that, as we have already noted in the previous chapter, the Poles were singular in their efforts to bring world attention to the Jewish fate at Nazi hands.

But such laudatory evidence can only leave us with the unsettling sense of some in-built contradiction. It is undoubtedly true that 'thousands of Poles...risked their lives to save the Jews'.[188] It is, however, equally the case that throughout the length and breadth of occupied Poland—in addition to extreme incidents such as Jedwabne—that there were hundreds, possibly thousands, of occasions, especially in villages and other rural localities, where Jews individually, in family or other groups, were tortured, raped, and often killed directly by Poles, or alternatively shopped by them to the German authorities. The immediate cause would appear to be that very standard one, the desire for Jewish loot, combined with the opportunity presented by the 'Final Solution' for villagers to make demands with menaces against very frightened and vulnerable people otherwise attempting to hide within their midst. This might suggest a pattern of *localized* violence grounded in the greed and envy of poor people but without wider socio-economic or political ramifications. But as Jan Gross has recently argued, this may be to too easily dismiss these assaults as the work of 'miscreants or "marginal" people', when the data from post-war trials makes very clear that that those leading these very often communal assaults were (just as at Jedwabne) the local elite: the mayors, police chiefs, and other respected leaders of village society. Add to this the perceptive commentary of Jerzy Braun, a contemporary Polish political observer, that the assaults were a concerted effort by 'young peasant sons and former urban proletarians, who once worked for the Jews' to clean out the Jewish middleman component from the towns and villages. Their aim, argues Braun, was to hold on to their gains at any cost.[189] His analysis, therefore, might suggest less a set of unconnected micro-events and more a discernible pattern of grass-roots economic nationalization by way of Jewish expropriation and murder.

If correct, this would also imply that anti-Jewish violence taking place on the ground in Poland was hardly distinguishable from elsewhere in the rimlands, bar the general absence of uniformed *indigènes*. Yet that still leaves a question mark as to the thinking and intentions of the Delegatura shadow state in Warsaw and, above them, the authorized guardians of Polish sovereignty: the London-based government-in-exile. For the latter, the importance of presenting a front of complete rectitude with regard to their Western patrons was a sine qua non. A critical early step in this direction was the formation of an administration in the wake of the country's defeat, with Beck and the disgraced authoritarian colonels repudiated and in their place a coalition of political groupings committed to the re-establishment of a liberal democratic order. Reassurance of the government's good intentions, not only for the benefit of London, Paris, and Washington but also for the nearly 10 per cent of the Polish population who were Jewish, would also have been garnered from its November 1940 declaration pledging that the Jews in a liberated Poland would have equality 'in duties as in rights' alongside other Polish citizens.[190]

Yet as David Engel has persuasively demonstrated, the *real* programme of the new General Sikorski-led administration hardly represented a break with Warsaw's fundamental interwar desideratum, namely mass Jewish emigration. To be sure, there may have been a critical distinction in the way the London Poles avoided or dissembled over the issue for the benefit of Western public opinion. But even when they seemed to go into conscious overdrive to evince support for the Jews, most obviously in autumn 1942 when they aligned themselves with Western Jewish leaders to alert the world to the 'Final Solution' on Polish soil, this was not only based on a very precise calculation designed to reinforce Allied commitment to the goal of Polish *national* liberation but was also itself rooted in the persistence—dating back to 1919 if not earlier—of the Jewish power motif. In short, in return for the government's good offices in helping to give credence and credibility to the truth of the 'Final Solution', the London Poles expected a Jewish quid pro quo in the form of the clout their leaders would bring to bear on the West's resolve to support the Poles against Soviet territorial demands, more particularly in order to safeguard the Riga Treaty frontier.[191]

What is noteworthy about the calculation is the way it presents us with a Polish version of the ubiquitous 'good Jew bad Jew' dichotomy. 'Good' Jews were those who by dint of their wealth or power could supposedly be mobilized on behalf of the Polish interest but who conveniently did not live in the country. An exception could also be made for those indigenous Jews who identified themselves first and foremost as Polish patriots—it was, after all, from this assimilated, largely Varsovian, minority that most wartime 'hidden Jews' were drawn. As for the rest, they continued to be perceived as an economic and political threat, as they always had been. Indeed, just as during the Polish–Soviet war of 1920–1, the threat was heightened under Nazi occupation by the conviction that, in the event of Red Army breakthrough, it would be preceded, supported, and made possible by the essentially Russophile tendencies of this 'enemy within'. Or, put another way, the charge of intrinsic Jewish disloyalty was not simply an aspect of *Żydokomuna*, but was part of a more deeply embedded Polish elite narrative which blamed the ongoing weakness of the country on Litwaks—immigrant Jews or their descendants from Russia at the turn of the century—who were not only 'foreigners' but allegedly pro-Muscovite foreigners to boot.[192]

This is not to propose that *all* Polish support for their Jewish neighbours was entirely cynical or devoid of empathy. The Warsaw underground leaflet from August 1942 which heralded the emergence of Żegota both called on fellow Poles to renounce silence in the face of German mass murder and urged 'our duty to condemn the crime'. Yet its author, Zofia Kossak, a profoundly Catholic nationalist, equally affirmed in the same leaflet, 'Our feelings for the Jews have not changed. We have not ceased to regard them as political, economic and ideological enemies of Poland.'[193] In other words, Kossak was speaking from a paradoxical position which was both humanitarian yet, in its implicit insistence that the Jewish question would ultimately have to be 'solved' in Poland, anti-Semitic. For pre-war political leaders such a solution had always been premised on 'peaceful and orderly' Jewish departure. And very similarly to the more overtly liberal Czech stance before and into the war, it gave itself benign credentials by proposing that this mass migration would come through its support of Zionism.[194]

The problem for the London Poles was that any wartime statements which seemed to be too readily accommodating to the Jews—for instance, by speaking of their 'common suffering' or even, as in August 1942, declaring that while Jews might wish to emigrate to Palestine as their national home, they were not obliged to do so[195]—were exactly of the kind which threatened to alienate their primary constituency back home. As early as February 1940 Karski, acting as courier for the Delegatura, had warned the exile government in person that the German anti-Jewish assault was *not* leading Poles to a greater sense of solidarity between the two peoples in the face of a common persecution but rather was 'creating something akin to a narrow bridge upon which the Germans and a large portion of the Polish society are finding agreement'. Indeed, Karski's analysis pointed to a concrete reason as to why many Poles might even be succumbing to 'moral pacification' in the face of German rule. The latter's anti-Jewish policies were enabling Poles to directly benefit economically. Three years on, Roman Knoll, head of the Foreign Affairs Commission at the Delegatura, more acerbically than Karski, reminded the London government not only how this process had worked its way through but also the consequences if the government ever tried to halt it:

> ...the position is such that the return of the Jews to their jobs and workshops is completely ruled out, even if the number of Jews were greatly reduced. The non-Jewish population has filled the place of the Jews of the towns and cities: in a large part of Poland this is a fundamental change, final in character. The return of masses of Jews would be experienced by the population not as a restitution but as an invasion against which they would defend themselves, even with physical means.[196]

What, of course, is shocking about Knoll's statement is that the vast majority of Polish Jews were by this time dead. True, they had mostly not died at the hands of Poles—there had been no official collaboration in Jewish extermination as there had been, for instance, in neighbouring Lithuania. Yet Knoll's memorandum says a great deal about the Polish national obsession of the moment. Even in conditions of worsening Nazi violence against themselves, many Poles were wringing their hands (just as equally many French would do after liberation) regarding the spectre of young Jewish survivors returning from the east, who would challenge the Polish gains, and perhaps, finally—in the worst of all possible nightmares—take over the country.[197] How would they achieve this fiendish stratagem? With and through the Soviets. Or, as one of the Warsaw ghetto uprising leaders, Yitzhak Cukierman, was informed by an AK liaison officer, 'We believe that the ghetto is no more than a base for Soviet Russia. A plan exists and [we] Poles know what it is.'[198]

Thus, with Jews—real or imagined—ready and willing to act as Stalin's Trojan horse, much of the Delegatura leadership in Warsaw had little time or patience with what it saw as the pussyfooting around the Jewish question that was emanating from London. Back in February 1940, Karski had attempted to alert the Sikorski people as to just how 'overwhelmingly harsh' and 'without pity' Polish domestic opinion was on the matter. Knoll, much more obviously speaking for that opinion, only a month later forwarded his view to London. It stated unequivocally that any post-war resolution of the issue would come down to a straightforward choice: 'Zionism or extermination'.[199] By 1943, of course, the need for the Poles to decide which Jewish exit strategy they would adopt had been relieved by Nazi agency. Yet many nationalist Poles remained unconvinced that the problem had gone away. By Zionism, Knoll had meant any territorial solution through which the Jews could be eructed. Indeed, he had had a specific territory in mind: the Black Sea area around Odessa, which duly delivered—presumably by magic—from Soviet to Polish hands, Warsaw would administer in favour of Jewish resettlement. Knoll was not alone in this aspiration. Faced with what it claimed would be a million Jewish survivors descending on Poland 'to deprive us of the fruit of victory'— thanks both to the Red Army and 'their (Jewish) influence in the West'—*Pobudka*, the underground mouthpiece of the ultra-nationalist, indeed falangist, National Radical Camp (ONR), proposed that southern Russia might be one place to which they could be sent. Apparently unsatisfied with what the Nazis had achieved on their behalf, the extreme grouping insisted, 'the Jewish problem in Poland must come to an end'.[200]

Neither Knoll nor the ONR, however, were the only political actors looking to the Odessa region for their zero-sum resolution of the 'Jewish problem'. Indeed, one did not have to be an out-and-out fascist to aspire to territory with which to remove one's unwanted Jews, or to bring one's own state apparatus to bear to accelerate an eliminationist process.

A STATE WHICH KILLED—RUMANIA

The irony of radical Polish imaginings about the north-western Black Sea region or, for that matter, the fact that this was also an area coveted by the OUN as part of their grand Ukrainian design, is that it was actually the epicentre of a fully fledged independent genocide by a third party: not the Germans, but the Rumanians. Granted, the Rumanian assault on its Jews and Roma was both geographically and chronologically limited. Not only was the more specific Rumanian Jewish annihilation of 1941 not pursued with the same steely determination as the

German 'Final Solution' into the latter part of the war, but the Antonescu regime, which had been responsible for the earlier mass murder, by this juncture was offering its credentials to the Allies as Jewish *protectors*. The supposed midway switch of policy notwithstanding, and putting to one side the efforts of a German (albeit reluctantly) created NDH, Rumania has the dubious distinction of being the only other pre-existing sovereign European state which, of its own volition, carried out a consciously *autonomous* physical elimination of Jews during the Second World War.

To be sure, the caveats implicit in this statement need additional clarification. The initial arena of the Rumanian genocide was congruent with the territory into which the Rumanian Third and Fourth Armies advanced eastwards as part of the southern flank of Operation Barbarossa (Army Group South), restoring thereby to Bucharest a Bessarabia and northern Bukovina ceded to the Soviets as a belated part of the Non-Aggression Pact carve-up the previous summer. The accusation of Jewish treachery and Soviet collaboration, including—according to the Rumanian security intelligence (SSI) reports—lurid tales of Jewish terror committed against retreating Rumanian soldiers, gendarmerie, and civilians in 1940,[201] was thus a proximate justification for state and vigilante vengeance the following summer, as it also was in the 'liberated' 'Lands Between' further north. That said, the killings perpetrated by the advancing Rumanians extended across the Dniester on to Soviet territory, where the Jewish citizenry were not and had never been Rumanian subjects. This transnational aspect, which places Rumania alongside Nazi Germany among a select handful of polities in the contemporary era who have committed genocide beyond their own state boundaries, is also noteworthy because the killings in and beyond Odessa represented an acute intensification of what the Rumanians had just before committed in the recovered provinces. Certainly, there was something very contingent about how these anti-Jewish atrocities began to spiral upwards in relation to the crisis of the wider military campaign. In this sense Rumanian behaviour mirrors in part the shifting contours of a synchronous German experience in occupied Russia. What one cannot lose sight of, however, is the degree to which the Antonescu regime had its own agenda. It was one which looked to the war as an opportunity for a much wider national 'purification', aimed at the removal—peacefully or otherwise—of practically *all* of its 5 million-plus non-Rumanian population.[202]

What is equally important to note about this programme is that it was *not* that of the Iron Guard, the indisputably fascist Rumanian movement which has become particularly remembered for its fanatical anti-Semitism. Certainly, from September 1940 until January 1941, in the wake of intense domestic crisis, the Iron Guard were coalition partners to Antonescu in what was called the National Legionary state. In fact, even then, the Iron Guardists were effectively excluded from the day-to-day business of the administration, which may explain their ill-fated attempt to physically seize power at the beginning of 1941. This was the occasion, too, on which the Legionaries went on their wildest and most dramatically violent rampage through the streets of Bucharest, leaving upwards of a thousand Jews butchered to death. The Legionary challenge to Antonescu, however, was put down by the army, though equally significantly with the assistance of German troops.[203]

In other words, Antonescu's programme did not have to derive from straight fascism to have its own brand of anti-Semitism, or virulent xenophobia. Indisputably of an ultra-right-wing, militarist, and authoritarian hue, the point about this self-styled regime of 'national and social restoration', and alongside that its determination to forge a Rumania without Jews or any other minority undesirables, was that it represented the fulfilment of aspirations from the normative mainstream of Rumanian political life and thought, not—as in the case of the Legionaries—from its margins.[204] An almost constant trope of Jewish economic, social—and indeed biological—takeover had suffused Rumanian political culture ever since the country's emergence as an autonomous post-Ottoman entity in the late 1850s. The attempt by the Great Powers at Berlin in 1878 to have the country's new rulers grant equal civil and political rights to the country's Jewish population as a condition for its sovereign recognition was greeted by opinion-formers and policy-makers alike as proof of *international* Jewry's malign and conspiratorial intent towards it. Mark you, there was in its rebuttal of the Great Power diktat the standard differentiation—Rumanian style—between Jews and Jews. A tiny handful who had served with the army, or were individually assessed—often after heated parliamentary debates—were granted citizenship.[205] After 1919, when Bucharest was finally forced to concede to the principle, a more crude distinction developed between Jews from the 'old' Regat territories and those who had become Rumanians as a result of the country's huge post-war territorial gains. Indeed, it was this sense of an authentic, uncontaminated Rumania being overrun by millions of foreign *jidani*—'yids'—by implication meaning Jews from the 'east', which was not only a very personal Antonescu obsession[206] but part of the background as to how and why the Rumanian state genocide emerged *where* it did.

To be sure, the overall Rumanian Jewish population, while nothing like the millions of Antonescu's fevered imagination, was sizeable. According to the 1930 census, it stood at nearly 757,000, making it the third largest in Europe.[207] More pointedly, Jewish demographics were strongest in Bessarabia and Bukovina, their contributions to the provincial populations being 11 per cent and 7.2 per cent respectively. Why should this have mattered? The answer is that in a traditional, plural—imperial—rimlands environment it would not have done, but that in one where elite statist prognostications were entirely geared towards modernization for and by way of the nation, the very existence of so many Jews (315,000 pre-war in the two provinces) represented a veritable stranglehold on development.[208] For such national planners, the Jewish concentration in major towns, particularly, in the case of Bessarabia and Bukovina, in the provincial capitals of Kishinev (Chişinău) and Czernowitz (Cernăuţi)—and more precisely in the commercial and professional sectors—simply added insult to injury. Nor was this just a matter of socio-economic or occupational statistics. Formerly Habsburg Czernowitz, for instance, far from being a hotbed of *Żydokomuna*, was distinctly cosmopolitan. Yet for the likes of Antonescu this too was anathema, conjuring up all the most egregious aspects of 'Jewish morality': free elections, public opinion, humanism, the League of Nations, indeed all the elements of the 'demo-liberal world' which nationalists saw as doing Rumania down, both at home and abroad.[209]

The direction of Rumanian travel on the Jewish question, even before the advent of the Legionary state, or Antonescu's absolute wresting of power, thus was unmistakable. Goga's 1938 efforts to make large swathes of Rumanian Jewry stateless had been stymied by Allied diplomatic pressure, but this had not prevented a new tranche of sweeping anti-Semitic legislation, on German racial lines, in August 1940—in other words, even while King Carol both attempted to keep hold of his throne and uphold a now precarious but traditional relationship with the Western Allies.[210] Of course, discrimination, persecution, even wholesale expropriation, while they may often be a prelude to it, are not the same as mass murder. Rumanian politicians, officials, and military men certainly salivated at the prospect of Madagascar as the ultimate destination for their Jews, just as did so many others from the 'Lands Between' in the run-up to war. But it takes something more to move into a conscious short-cutting of the exercise. In short, the Antonescu factor cannot be ignored.

Carol II's abdication in early September 1940, in favour of his son, came out of a crisis in which a second round of territorial losses to surrounding countries (precipitated by the Soviet demands on Bessarabia and northern Bukovina but under the ultimate adjudication of Nazi Germany) threatened the sovereign integrity and hence the ongoing viability of the kingdom. Bucharest's September moment of truth, thus, had something of the quality of Czechoslovakia 1938, Poland 1939, or, for that matter, Ottoman Turkey 1915 or 1919. The Turkish parallel is perhaps particularly important for the way its response to existential crisis was to take it out on the most hated communal scapegoat to hand. But that can hardly be divorced from issues of leadership. The rapid appearance of Antonescu at Rumanian centre-stage combines elements of both Enver and Kemal. The quintessential 'man on horseback', Antonescu became the hero of the September hour by sweeping away a discredited regime, confirming himself as self-styled 'Conducator' (Leader), with entirely unprecedented and dictatorial powers, and finally committing what remained of truncated Rumania politically and militarily to the German cause. There was a certain irony in this course of action, in the sense that far from shoring up the country's independence it simply subordinated it to the German embassy in Bucharest, ensuring that Rumania's all-important oil fields and other key infrastructure effectively came under Nazi control. A further consequence was that the country was overrun by Wehrmacht troops. Certainly, the argument can be made that this would have happened anyway, given that the Western allies were in no position to come to Bucharest's assistance. The more circumspect of old-style Rumanian politicians equally accepted this result, but considered short-term subjugation preferable to long-term disaster.[211] Antonescu's single-mindedness lay in his conviction that the only Rumanian future could be with Berlin. That was a position which supposed that Hitler would win his war, and hence the Nazi new order was here to stay.

Looked at through the prism of early summer 1941, however, one can see why the Antonescu gamble would have appealed to very many Rumanian patriots.

With France defeated, Britain in retreat, and the Soviet Union about to be consigned to the dustbin of history, the Marshal's personal commitment to Operation Barbarossa, through the provision of thirty Rumanian divisions to the campaign, was surely the best guarantee that, at any future peace conference the Nazis presided over, Hitler would show his gratitude by restoring to their rightful owner northern Transylvania and southern Dobrudja, relinquished respectively to Budapest and Sofia. Perhaps it would even lead to the conferring of new territorial gains, fulfilling thereby the gamut of nationalist aspirations for a Greater Rumania. In the interim, under the cover of Hitler's imperial aegis and in essential accord with the latter's own *Weltanschauung*, the Conducator might forge ahead with his own pet project for national purification. Such a project he knew, moreover, could begin with the Jews of the two 'liberated' provinces, by dint of the confidential information he had received from Hitler in person.

How much weight should we put on the special relationship between the Führer and the Conducator as a cause for Rumania's own war of extermination in the east? Hitler's unusual admiration for Antonescu—not something we otherwise associate with the former's behaviour towards other satellite heads of state, bar Mussolini— we know translated into one critical meeting, on 12 June 1941, in which Hitler apprised the Marshal of the emerging Nazi guidelines for the treatment of Soviet Jewry. Judging from other remarks Antonescu later made about surviving Jews being deported across the Urals, one can assume that the flurry of 'Jewish' orders which flowed from his prime minister's office over the next few preparatory weeks were geared towards bringing Rumania's anti-Jewish plans into line with the proposed German operation.[212] However, they equally represent a case of Antonescu taking full advantage of the opportunities which now presented themselves for a specifically Rumanian 'Final Solution'.

Again, looked at in terms of the personal profile of Antonescu, this would seem to underscore the actuality of Jewish mass murder as a consequence of a leader's own inner demons. For instance, it can be fairly surmised that an element of the mutual regard between the Marshal and Hitler was on account of their emotional affinity on all matters Jewish. Antonescu was a Judaeophobe through and through, behind which his physical detestation of specific individuals (not to say horror at close family Jewish ties) was an intense persecution complex in which international Jewry writ large was always the ubiquitous tormentor.[213]

Yet if in the summer of 1941 the Marshal led on this matter, his closest colleagues seemed only too willing to follow. Take, for instance, this part of a speech to the Council of Ministers by his prime minister and distant relative Mihai Antonescu, on 8 July, as the joint German–Rumanian military offensive began to gather momentum:

> There is no place here for saccharine and vaporous humanitarianism […] I do not know when, after how many centuries, the Rumanian nation will again enjoy this total freedom of action, with the possibility for ethnic purification and national revision. This is the hour when we are masters of our own territory. We must take advantage of it. I do not mind if history judges us barbarians. The Roman empire performed a series of barbarous acts against its contemporaries, and yet it was the greatest political

establishment. History will not offer us other moments of grace. If need be—use machine guns.[214]

In the heady excitement of the moment, the regime was clearly looking even beyond what might be done to the Jews to an altogether more wholesale 'cleansing' of minorities from Rumanian territory, and—with the most preposterous delusions of grandeur—as if it were heir to a great imperial actor. In practice, the immediate effort was limited to a hastily improvised set of military and police orders to eruct to the east the Jewish populations of the provinces that were currently being liberated. Even then, how exactly this was to be done was far from crystal clear. As with the CUP campaign against the Armenians of eastern Anatolia a quarter of a century earlier, the Rumanian official version a matter of apparently orderly deportation to a point of geographical remove where the Jews might conveniently disappear from view, while ostensibly remaining alive. Yet as with the CUP project, so here too wholesale disgorgement meant primarily residual communities of women, or those at the extreme ends of the age spectrum, on foot and possibly marching for a hundred or more kilometres to a frontier zone—in the Rumanian case, beyond the Dniester—where they could be cast off from state responsibility. In brief, given the precipitate nature of the exercise and the consequent lack of preparation or logistical support facilities—food, medicine, sanitation, or shelter included—it was bound (as with its historic Ottoman counterpart) to become a series of death marches, all the more so, in this instance, as its subjects were being propelled towards a military operation zone, not away from one.[215]

The Ottoman counterpart might further remind us that forced, compulsory mass movement of the young, old, sick, and lame cannot in itself suffice as explanation for the mass physical death of tens of thousands of people. In fact, we know from the post-war trials of many of the key actors that officers of both the Pretoriat, the police wing of army, and the hastily created gendarmerie legions tasked with restoring Rumanian civil authority in the provinces were issued with secret orders described as 'cleansing the ground'. If such terminology still sounds ambiguous and not necessarily Jew-specific in its intent, the verbal transmission of these orders down chains of command leaves much less room for doubt as to what was expected of these units. As a senior commander at one of the preparatory briefings jotted down in his instructions, 'all Jews without any exceptions and political suspects found within the radius of the respective posts to be shot'.[216]

Further evidence from the post-war trials suggests, moreover, that particularly zealous, including politically extremist, officers were tasked with spearheading this remit. Using the standard pretext of Jews having attacked Rumanian troops in the rear, the unfolding picture of military-style massacres through July and into August 1941 was in significant part the work of death squads[217]—though unlike the *çetes* responsible for comparable Balkan or Anatolian atrocities from earlier in the century, here wearing distinct military uniform. Was deportation, then, really a subterfuge for something more immediate, total, and preordained at regime level? All the evidence suggests that Bucharest's aim was indeed to 'cleanse' the countryside of Jews, but where the much larger numbers of town and city Jewry were concerned, to eliminate the allegedly dangerous elements among them—in other words their political and cultural elites—and deport the rest. The very ad hoc creation of the 160-strong Esalon Special, under the authority of the SSI—the secret police—on direct orders from the Marshal,[218] again suggests a Rumanian-style version of the Einsatzgruppen approach, but here geared towards the orchestrating of a massacre sequence on the one hand, and the eruction of (mostly town) survivors on the other. This pattern of authorized killing through top-down verbal instructions certainly seems to have worked most effectively in the Bessarabian countryside. The significance of such orders is also attested however in the more lacklustre performance of gendarmerie units in north Bukovina, where the senior officer on the ground had not been party to the 'cleansing' order briefing.[219]

Still, what is equally evident about the nature of this initial Rumanian assault is that it lacked the ability, the capacity, or the coherence to carry through a streamlined extermination in toto, while demonstrating its dependency on the Germans for the alternative programme of mass eruction. On the first count, the lack of sufficient specialist manpower resulted in the killing being thrown over on many occasions to ordinary soldiers. This had already happened in Iaşi where the troops of the Fourteenth Infantry Division had gone on an entirely uncontrolled killing spree. But to allow such free rein was to bring into play an entirely unpredictable variable: as one post-war indictment opaquely put it, participants became absorbed in 'inventing new ways of extermination for the satisfaction of their sadistic instincts'.[220] This emerging tendency was in fact compounded by the need to mobilize support from among the local 'liberated' Rumanian population to herd survivors of the executions on to the deportation marches. The involvement of male adolescents—'the Hotin boys' from the eponymous town in Bessarabia—as premilitary age guards, who then proceeded to gang-rape the women and girls under their charge, provides lurid insight into how an organizational programme at the limits of its logistical competence translated at the micro-level into an ever-widening maelstrom of bloody chaos.[221]

And as it did so it ran into increasing protest from, of all people, the Germans. How it could be that the Wehrmacht could complain of the 'disgusting excesses' perpetrated by people suffering from an 'eastern European concept of human life'—the particular verdict of General Wöhler, the Eleventh Army Chief of Staff—when their own Einsatzgruppen were demonstrably doing something very similar requires, perhaps, not a historian but a cultural psychologist's closer gaze. But what particularly seems to have upset nearby German commanders is not just the manner in which the Rumanians were indiscriminately torturing and killing women and children—Einsatzgruppe D at this stage had not got beyond male massacres—but were palpably *enjoying* it. The Germans clearly preferred massacre to be carried out decorously and on the clear, undisputed orders of those in charge.[222] To add to the obloquy, Einsatzgruppe D weighed in with their repeated objection to the Rumanians' 'lack of technical preparation', a not very subtle way of saying that their Balkan allies were not only incapable of organizing a proper massacre, but were also slovenly in clearing up after themselves. In other words, they were leaving the corpses unburied.[223]

The German slur on Rumanian competence, above all the implication that they were threatening the entire military operation through the potential spread of disease, dovetailed with a new contingency which threatened to throw the deportation programme into dramatic reverse. Antonescu's whole scheme was predicated on a military drive to the east, which would open vistas into which those Jews not already killed could be cast. Which, put bluntly, meant that if Operation Barbarossa failed to go to plan, or perhaps Berlin withdrew its support for the subordinate Rumanian agenda, all bets were off. But by high summer it was becoming quite unclear on both military and political grounds whether the Germans would allow the Rumanians to eject even the first tranche of Bessarabian and Bukovinan deportees (in other words, the survivors of the first massacres) across the Dniester. The Wehrmacht reinforced the point by either forcing those who had already crossed the river back onto the Rumanian side, or simply shooting them en masse. The Rumanians, however, had no plan B. There was no food and little or no shelter for the estimated 100,000 *misérables* who now found themselves forcibly encamped at or en route to the handful of riverine crossing points during the following weeks. And, not surprisingly, descriptions of the conditions in these makeshift camps repeatedly refer to their rapid descent into unmitigated squalor, the vermin-strewn bodies of the dead and dying amplifying further the German nightmare scenario of a typhus epidemic spreading from them.[224]

Antonescu was lucky that Hitler found him a way out of this impasse. In late July, the Führer had tentatively proffered to Rumania control of a slice of Soviet Ukrainian territory between the Dniester and the Dnieper. It is itself significant that Antonescu turned down the possibility of Rumanian rule extending to the latter boundary, citing lack of administrative resources. Thus while the *idea* of imperial acquisition in form of an extension of Rumanian colonization in this direction as compensation for the loss in particular of north Transylvania may have appealed to the leadership's vanity, Antonescu's request for a smaller territorial remit confirms what was already all too evident from the deportation programme: that Bucharest was actually a weak polity operating at the very limits of its logistical capabilities or efficacy. However, the firming up of a formal agreement, the Tighina Convention, a month later—conferring Rumanian administration of the area between the Dniester and the southern Bug, henceforth denoted as 'Transnistria'—at least got Antonescu off the hook of immediate dilemma of what to do with the deportees.[225] The ultimate aim was still to clear *these* Jews off the Rumanian horizon, indeed setting a precedent thereby for the wider movement of most if not all other Jews who remained Bucharest's subjects. In the interim, though, that is until Germany had vanquished the Soviets, Antonescu was settling for Transnistria as a *provisional* dumping ground for Jews or any other unwanted peoples, while equally providing Bucharest with a zone which could be milked and looted for all it was worth.

This exploitation agenda dovetailed with the supposed economic rationale for deportation—by way of expropriation of all Jewish assets. However practically wrong-headed and morally egregious this project actually was, the Rumanians now proceeded to squander even this opportunity through what Mark Mazower has described, more generally, as their 'unrivalled venality'.[226] The principled aim was to set up the river crossings as a customs border policed by officials of the Rumanian National Bank (BNR), who would require the Jews to deliver to them all the Rumanian currency and other valuables on their persons, for which they would supposedly receive a nominal exchange in roubles to enable them to continue their journey into Transnistria. By these means, Antonescu sought to garner a financial return from the deportation exercise which—just as the CUP had envisaged from their similar assault on Armenian pockets—would feed into the so-called National Centre for Rumanization. Legitimated in Bucharest's mental outlook as the restoration of assets to the nation filched by a parasitic and alien people-class, the recovered capital would be ploughed into an orderly programme of national development created by and for ethnically true Rumanians.[227] Or so read the technocrats' script. In practice, what Antonescu had initiated—from the very moment that the regime had declared open season on the Jews—was a rush for self-enrichment from the very highest participating officials, the BNR included, to the very lowest gendarmes or peasant onlookers. Antonescu's aim to have the inventory of Jewish abandoned properties made over to the BNR, for instance, was rapidly subverted as local administrators and police chiefs ensured that they received all the best pickings. A later effort to investigate these 'malpractices' itself descended into farce as the presiding investigator, the Bukovinan governor Calotescu, was—alongside his Bessarabian and Transnistrian counterparts—at the very time vying with the BNR and each other over exactly who would take the lion's share of these proceeds.[228] At the river crossings themselves, junior officers and subordinates alike were reduced to terrorizing Jews or shooting them outright to rob them of their remaining valuables, or to getting a fee from local peasants for the dead people's clothes. To add a note of singular grotesquery, the rivermen assigned to convey the Jews across the Dniester not only often stole whatever residual baggage they had, but then proceeded to hurl the unfortunates into the river, with the taunt that they wanted to see the miracle of the Red Sea re-enacted.[229]

The wider problem for Antonescu was not just that this meant that the state was *not* reaping the anticipated financial rewards. What was also evident was that far from the Jews being 'disappeared', they were simply being relocated to an outer zone of Rumanian hell. The regime's commitment to carry on regardless, however, is clear in the autumn decision both to remove the remainder of Bessarabian and north Bukovinian Jewry across the Dniester—in principle with more attention to administrative detail, in practice as shambolically as ever—and to include southern Bukovina and Dorohoi Jewry in the programme, signalling the widening of its scope to take in not previously Soviet-occupied areas.[230]

But just as the Germans had learnt from their larger landscape of eastern imperial conquest, removing tens of thousands of Jews to a place where there were already tens or hundreds of thousands of *other* Jews simply compounded the difficulty. It was in part as a result of this increasing gap between aspiration and reality that the Rumanians' own lurch towards a radicalization of the killing occurred. By December 1941, for instance, Antonescu's sheer desperation to be rid of Odessa

Jews at the heart of the Transnistrian community is evident in his outburst to ministers, 'Push them into the catacombs, push them in the Black Sea'[231]—suggesting not only a mental similitude between his inner self and the Dniester rivermen, but equally recalling the actual method by which the CUP on the Trazbon side of that sea had dealt with their 'problem' Armenians in 1915.

Antonescu had significantly added in the outburst, 'I do not want to know anything', the clearest documented indication that we have that he was looking to uniformed subordinates in the field to resolve the problem for him. Did Antonescu really imagine that Bucharest could wash its hands of genocide by devolving its implementation in this manner? What is clear is that the flawed nature of the military campaign acted as another contingent yet complicating factor, driving the Rumanians to ever greater anti-Jewish violence—though hardly in the process leaving Antonescu free of responsibility. The Rumanian political class, as we have suggested, were notably infantile in the way that they laid all political setbacks at a Jewish door. Setbacks, however, in the form of spiralling casualty figures at the front, were coming in thick and fast by the late summer, unrelieved by Rumanian efforts to meet the schedule for the taking of military objectives. Frustration mixed with anxieties about Soviet counter-attack may have played some role in the widening and deepening of Rumanian rather than Einsatzkommando city and town massacres, after, for instance, the capture of Kishinev.[232] What happened after the belated capture of Odessa in October, however, took massacre to a new level of atrocity—on a par with if not surpassing that of Babi Yar—and with the Rumanian military the primary hands-on protagonists.

As with the events in Kiev a month earlier, the trigger was a predictably familiar one. Having finally taken the all-important Black Sea metropolis, almost the entire headquarters staff of the Rumanian Tenth Army Division were blown sky high by a delayed action mine primed by the NKVD in what previously had been their own local command post. Orders for immediate reprisals came from the most senior surviving officer, General Trestioreanu. But these were upped by Antonescu himself who, Hitler-like, demanded 200 communists to be executed for every officer killed in the explosion and 100 for every enlisted man. Antonescu, explaining to himself that the bomb-blast was the work of Jews and that they were also the fifth column who would assist a feared Soviet amphibious assault, specified that 'one person from each Jewish family' was to be included in the retribution. With communist equalling 'kike', the Conducator was in effect goading his Fourth Army troops to take unlimited revenge on the 80,000 remaining Jews in Odessa who had not been able to flee with the retreating Soviets. Thus, in the absence of the more active and largely male Jewish element who had been able to get out, Antonescu chose to wreak Rumanian vengeance mostly on women, babies, and old people. In the succeeding four days from 22 to 25 October, army units supported by SSI and German SD attachments did so: in the city centre, along its suburban streets, and finally in the port area around Dalnik. Squeezing the victims into a confined square plus anti-tank ditches, barracks, and warehouses, they used every conceivable form of ordnance—machine guns, hand grenades, artillery, and a liberal supply of gasoline and kerosene to achieve their end. No fewer than 25,000 human beings, and perhaps as many as 40,000, from this once great cultural centre of European Jewish life, perished in the pyromania of the 'Odessa days'.[233]

Yet this was not the culmination of this particular sequence of killing. The Rumanians may have aspired to get rid of the entirety of 'Transnistrian' Jewry, if only to make way for their *own*. But logically this meant either murdering them *all* themselves or trying to eruct them beyond the Bug—that is, yet again into a German military zone further to the east, *beyond the rimlands*. In putting into motion the deportation of Bessarabian and Bukovinan Jewry in the first place, Antonescu had learnt the hard way the consequences of such initiatives—the only desirable escape from which was dependent now upon a complete German victory. But not only was the Conducator having to recognize by the early winter that there would be no convenient break-out which would facilitate his mythic 'Urals' goal; the very effort to remove on foot or by cattle car the remainder of Odessa and its hinterland's Jews was also bringing into play the one factor in the face of which even Hitler would be unable to rescue him: a typhus epidemic.

As a result, just as Rumanian efforts to eruct Jews from the two provinces across the Dniester had fallen foul of German public hygiene officials fulminating over the spread of disease, so in this repeat performance—now several hundred kilometres to the east—their comparable attempt to be shot of the Transnistrian Jewish remnant by ejecting them to the Golta district, at the far extremity of Rumanian control on the Bug, was met by even more dire warnings from the German *Gebietskommissar* across the river that the spread of typhus would not be tolerated.[234] On one level, nothing had changed. Conditions in the entirely makeshift holding camps on the Bug—in fact a handful of dilapidated *sovkhozy*—were as appalling as they had been on the Dniester, attesting to the Rumanians' ill-preparedness. The only difference now was that the 'solution' was going to have to come from them. The problem devolved upon the man on the spot, a gendarmerie lieutenant-colonel, Modest Isopescu. Undoubtedly, he took advice from Bucharest. But he also improvised with a frightening degree of resolution, setting about organizing with the assistance of the local Siguranţa (SSI) chief, Aristide Padure, the complete extermination of the estimated 70,000 to 80,000 Jews under his charge. The killings began just before Christmas, using scratch units of gendarmes, Ukrainian auxiliaries, and local Volksdeutsche. The task before them was immense, not least because temperatures in the area had dropped to −40 Centigrade. Even so, during the following two weeks, Isopescu's *génocidaires* dispatched between 40,000 and 50,000 inmates at the main Bogdanovca camp, using petrol, guns, and hand grenades. The killings were only halted for holiday celebrations, during which time Isopescu organized a sleigh ride round the site for Bucharest friends and relatives, and took photographs of what his men were accomplishing for select newspapers, while his men got themselves increasingly drunk as—in a separate section of the *sovkhoz*—they 'amused themselves' with girls whom they had saved from immediate execution.[235]

Isopescu was clearly no slouch. The mass liquidation of deportees was continued at the nearby Domanovca camp into the new year, with a third camp cordoned off to allow its inmates to starve to death. Isopescu, moreover, was vigilant in the creation of cremation pyres (a remnant of Jewish slave labour being kept alive for this task), ensuring that the tens of thousands of corpses were incinerated. By these means German 'public health' anxieties were also assuaged. Meanwhile, in the nearby Berezovca district, the last Odessa Jews who had not already perished en route were dispatched in similar fashion alongside others rounded up from nearby towns and villages.[236] The approximately 100,000 Jews murdered in the two districts, mostly in a few weeks straddling 1941 and early 1942, mark the apotheosis of Rumania's Jewish genocide.

*

Yet what followed offers a strange, twisted coda to this blood-strewn narrative. Into 1942, all the evidence points to Bucharest's intentions to evict more Rumanian Jews into Transnistria, both from the post-1918 territories and from the Regat. By late summer, leading Jewish intellectuals in the capital were panicking, believing such a general deportation to be imminent.[237] Their anxieties would seem to be corroborated by the then governor of Transnistria General Alexianu's sworn testimony at Antonescu's post-war trial, that once the eviction of Bukovinan and Bessarabian Jews was completed 'those from Moldavia and Wallachia would soon follow'.[238] While everybody was holding their breath, waiting for this to happen, the regime got on with evicting 25,000 Roma from *across* Rumania—some 12 per cent of Rumania's total Romani population into the province. The decree issued in May 1942 focused on itinerant Roma or 'sedentary' ones deemed 'a burden or dangerous to public order'. The order was a recipe for a confused and entirely arbitrary selection, not least as many Roma were *seasonally* itinerant. To add to the confusion, many of those deported should have been automatically exempted on account of having menfolk serving in the army.[239]

What the first Roma deportations certainly underscored was Bucharest's now all too evident policy to use Transnistria as a people dump. How literally this was meant in the Roma case is evident from their mortality figures: once there, at least half succumbed over the next two years, not as a general rule to executions, but to hunger and illness, as a consequence of being left to fend for themselves.[240] Jewish mortality in the province suggests an equally precipitous decline. When a Bucharest Jewish welfare representative was allowed to visit the ramshackle range of camps there, in the winter of 1942–3, they held an estimated 75,000 Jewish inhabitants, large numbers of them orphaned children. By the following November, the Ministry of Interior could confirm that under 51,000 were still alive.[241] Conditions in some of these camps were ghastly beyond belief. The open-cast mine at Tulcin, where thousands were worked to death, or Peciora, where the inmates were reduced through starvation to cannibalism, stand out in their hideousness. But, and it is a but, the very fact that a Bucharest Jewish relief organization was allowed access into the camps at all and could intermittently send to them clothes, food, tools, and medical supplies—from as early as March 1942—suggests a regime drawing back from rather than ratcheting up total extermination. Certainly, violent death for Transnistria's deportees remained a high probability but more likely at the hands of German security police—whose right to raid the camps for slave labour remained undisputed—than of Rumanian gendarmes.[242]

How then do we account for this change? Complaints about damage to the economy of the two liberated provinces, even in one notable case an attempt by Traian Popovici, the Gentile mayor of Czernowitz, to challenge the very moral basis of the deportation order, may have begun to have some limited impact on regime thinking.[243] One consequence of the pragmatic rather than the ethical objections, for instance, was that the late 1941 eviction orders began to differentiate between 'useful' and 'useless' Jews, the former category supposedly also including families of war veterans. The reprieve for these groups was certainly not intended to be anything other than temporary, and there is little indication either that Antonescu was swayed by the actually quite disastrous impact on Bessarabia and Bukovina that the removal of Jews, the closure of their businesses, or for that matter—minus Jewish doctors and pharmacists—the impact on the region's public health infrastructure, was bringing in its wake.[244] Even when Mihai Antonescu announced to the Council of Ministers on 13 October 1942 the decision to indefinitely suspend further Jewish (*and* Roma) deportations, it was clear that neither his view of the Jews nor the measures which he believed ought to be taken against them had changed one iota. The shift in policy, he claimed, was 'because of the international situation', and the damage current actions were having on the 'prestige' of the country.[245]

The statement carried intimations about the pressure building behind the scenes against a more general all-Rumania deportation programme. Galvanized into action by the leading (if usually among themselves fractious) Jewish figures in Bucharest, a veritable roll-call of political and religious dignitaries, plus the Queen Mother, papal nuncio, and Swiss ambassador for good measure, vigorously protested against the plan just as the Bulgarian elite would do some six months later when faced with a similar emergency. As then, so in this case, it is notable that collective, elite protest only really began when metropolitan Jewry were endangered, rather than their co-religionists at the national periphery or beyond. More decisive than internal objections appears to have been the protest note conveyed from US secretary of state Cordell Hull, which one month before the critical Council of Ministers meeting warned that if the deportations went ahead Rumanians in the USA could themselves face repressive measures. The note, indeed, came hot on the heels of more general declarations by both Roosevelt and Churchill threatening that such deportations would elicit 'punishments without precedent in history'.[246]

It might be argued that this was exactly the sort of message which was likely to have the likes of Antonescu confirmed in their verdict of international Jewish power once again at work. In which case, as they—like generations of Rumanian leaders before them—were fervent believers in it, it offered itself to the more adroit among Jewish leaders, such as the veteran Bucharest intermediary Wilhelm Filderman, as a potential trump card.[247] Thus the argument might go that should the tables be turned on the Nazis, and the Jews (on the back of the Allies) then stormed back to take their revenge, the only logical counter-move available to the Marshal was the application of the deportation brakes as a stepping stone towards an orderly retreat from the whole anti-Jewish policy. It is notable that Slovakia too began to pull back from its removal agenda around this same time, again suggesting another rather weak state beginning to interpret its own Judaeophobic instincts along rather different lines to a year earlier. What is notable is that both these states equally were working towards this crypto-pragmatic approach even before the decisive Stalingrad setback had materialized.

However, the mythic equation of Western Allies as either conduit or amplifier of Jewish power providing the basis for Bucharest's summer 1942 policy re-evaluation is only half the story. What is crucially absent from this account is Bucharest's own increasingly fraught relationship with its Nazi patrons, the Jewish sub-text of which reads not as 'Transnistria' but as 'Bełżec'. Here we seemingly revert to a more conventional Holocaust script, and one with the Jewish 'expert' in the Bucharest embassy, one Gustav Richter, the key agent striving to encompass a Rumanian Jewish exodus within *Germany's* comprehensively European-wide 'Final Solution'. Throughout the early part of 1942, this second, or perhaps dual track, extermination route appeared well on course. Richter had in place a Rumanian liaison team headed up by Radu Lecca (in effect Bucharest's equivalent of a Belev or Vallat), and on Richter's advice the self-governing Jewish community had been replaced by a government-appointed Judenrat-like body to do its bidding. Its first major task was to conduct a census, effectively providing the necessary information for wholesale deportation, not eastwards to Transnistria but northwards to the General Government.[248]

Richter seems to have assumed that he had Bucharest's green light for the trains to roll by early September. Where he, the RHSA, and German Foreign Office seem to have fatally miscalculated is in their assumption that Antonescu would be simply prepared to hand over the Jews as if they were no longer a *Rumanian* state issue. Or put another way, to have followed through with the implication that Bucharest was incapable of resolving its own internal 'minorities' problems was not just to challenge its integrity, and hence sovereignty, but to insult its very pride and dignity. These were not secondary matters in Antonescu's estimation. They came on top of an escalating mutual disenchantment between Berlin and Bucharest, the former's growing interference in the latter's internal affairs being met by an increasingly stubborn tendency on Bucharest's part to do things *its* way.[249] Thus while the regime may have agreed in principle to a general Jewish evacuation to the north, when Richter, without further consultation, in early August 1942, published an official press communiqué saying so, not only did this precipitate wider opposition but it may also have been received by the government itself as the affront legitimizing its own policy reorientation.[250]

This shift, however, as Sebastian Balta has recently argued, has to be understood in terms of Antonescu's changing assessment of Rumania's geopolitical fortunes. The assumption of a complete German victory—the basis upon which the regime had launched its assault on its eastern Jews in the first place—was no longer tenable. Indeed, after meeting Hitler again in October, Antonescu came to the conclusion that Germany had lost its war, and it was now incumbent on Bucharest to ensure that they did not do the same.[251] Repositioning Rumania so that it could present itself as a more independent player vis-à-vis the *Western* Allies, and in particular so that in any future peace conference—Antonescu's assumed scenario of how the war would end—it might still be able to negotiate for territories lost and gained, meant making the necessary gestures on the Jewish front. In this way, just as behind Hitler's back and somewhat later Himmler made the false assumption that the Jews were the key to a separate peace with the British and Americans, so Antonescu began his own tortuous unhitching of Bucharest from the 'Final Solution' and thereby from the Nazi fold. The tentative signs of such changed policy may indeed have appeared as early as late spring 1942, when the first transports of food and medicine were received in Transnistria.[252]

As with Himmler so with Antonescu: nothing had actually changed in terms of attitudes or, for that matter, ultimate intentions towards the Jews. To be sure, previous instructions to diplomats abroad effectively encouraging them to hand over Jews with Rumanian passports to the Germans were now replaced by orders granting such people entry visas back home. Transparently aimed at displaying Rumanian 'in-born kind-heartedness'—Mihau Antonescu's cynical words—to an Allied and neutral audience, the policy shift undoubtedly did, if belatedly, save Rumanian Jewish lives across Central and Western Europe.[253] Meanwhile, the much larger yet continually dwindling number of Bessarabian and Bukovinian Jews—and Roma—who had been left to survive as best they could in Transnistria were not allowed a similar right of return. Not until the Red Army was on the point of overrunning the province, in mid-March 1944, was this prohibition finally abandoned.[254]

Meanwhile, what gave the otherwise beleaguered Antonescu regime its distinctiveness was its attempt to forge its *own* Jewish agenda, regardless of German admonishments. Not that there was exactly anything new about it. In place of mass Jewish extermination, Bucharest now geared its efforts towards emigration, the primary destination of which was British Palestine.[255] A strange policy, one might think, given that not only were Britain and Rumania on opposite sides in the war but Palestine was out of bounds to all but the smallest number of Jewish immigrants. But then, part of the effort was to come into closer behind-the-scenes conversation with the British and Americans, and—as the Red Army got closer to enveloping and eliminating Rumanian forces—using this as a foil for negotiating a surrender to the Western Allies. Shades again of Himmler. Not that Antonescu and his clique could resist some shameless *chutzpah* in the process. One of the first overtures they made in late 1942—at the very height of the battle of Stalingrad—involved the offer to release the entire Transnistrian camp population in return for a down payment of some tens of millions of dollars.[256] Shades this time of the 1939 Schacht–Rublee negotiations, and similarly leading to an extraordinarily convoluted set of toings and froings between third parties, all leading more or less nowhere. What by late spring 1944 Bucharest had to show for its efforts was the emigration of some 3,000 Jewish orphans to Palestine,[257] and its much less gracious acquiescence in the return of the Jewish and Roma remnant from Transnistria. And, one has to add, the survival of some 375,000 primarily Regat Jews. All this proved too late to save either the Marshal or his regime, which fell not to the Soviets but to a crown-supported army coup in August 1944. Its leaders promptly ordered (just like their unloved Bulgarian counterparts) a political and military about-turn, joining the Rumanians to the Allied forces fighting Nazi Germany.

There is a significant little sequel to this saga. The posthumous Rumanian verdict 'on the Marshal, executed by the then communist-controlled administration in 1946, far from being one of execration, has steadily travelled in the opposite direction to a post-Cold War point where he is popularly hailed as 'the greatest Rumanian of the century'. As a national hero who stood up both to the Soviets and to all those at home and abroad who sought to imperil the country's path to a restored greatness, Antonescu is also now repeatedly credited with having saved Rumanian Jewry from the Nazis.[258] The fact that under his auspices the regime not only set out to asset-strip almost the entirety of that community and, once pauperized, to cast them into oblivion, has been suitably suffocated or sidelined in both Rumania's state and its societal consciousness. Only the turning of the military tide in 1942 ensured that Bucharest's self-willed genocide of some 350,000 Jews—at least 100,000 of them Ukrainian—plus some 20,000 Roma[259] did not become an even more all-encompassing act of mass murder, not just of Jews and Roma but of other minorities too.

HUNGARY: FROM COLLABORATIVE GENOCIDE TO LAST-DITCH AUTONOMOUS MASSACRE

One key driver in Rumania's late efforts to project its compassion for Jews to the world was in order to challenge negative comparisons then being made between itself and Hungary. In the midst of general war, the two countries, though supposedly on the same side, were in a state of acute territorial dispute over Transylvania, the northern half of which, as we have previously noted, had been 'returned' to Budapest in August 1940, and the southern half of which the Hungarians briefly, if disastrously, invaded in September 1944, just after the Rumanians defected to the Allies. Recent research has emphasized the degree to which the changing contours of Jewish policy in both capitals were a consequence not only of the relationship between themselves and Berlin but of a more regional competition with each other. Bucharest, for example, conveniently blamed the loss of northern Transylvania on the Magyarophile instincts of the region's Jews, one punishment for which was that any fleeing from there into the Regat were automatically deported to Transnistria.[260] On the other hand, Bucharest was enormously sensitive to the fact that up to spring 1943 not only did their own record of protecting Rumanian Jews elsewhere in Nazi Europe compare very unfavourably with that offered by the Hungarian consular service, but also that Budapest capitalized on this by bringing international attention to bear upon the anti-Jewish cruelty meted out by Antonescu's regime.[261]

The Magyar argument that they were the civilized nation, compared with their Latin neighbour, appears monstrous when set against the last great act of the Holocaust in 1944. As, indeed, set against the previous twenty years or more of growing Hungarian anti-Jewish discrimination. To be sure, the longer-term history of

Hungarian Jewish relations did not follow the same path as that of the Rumanians. The latter could claim no 'Golden Age' of interaction or symbiosis. The Hungarians justly could: the period of the Habsburg Dual Monarchy was one in which Jews had been positively encouraged by Budapest's ruling aristocratic elite to assimilate and help foster the country's path to modernization. Where Jews were well placed to participate in this project—primarily in the cities rather than the countryside—the results, in terms of their socio-economic, educational, and professional mobility, were often extraordinary.[262] The compact between state and community was further reinforced through a more general Jewish adherence to the Magyar language, which in areas such as Transylvania, where the credibility of a Hungarian majority was challenged by other 'national' groups, the Jewish alignment to the Hungarians often swung census data back in the latter's favour.[263]

However, while most Jews' fierce allegiance to Magyarism remained constant throughout the interwar years, nationalist opinion of, and behaviour towards, them turned decidedly sour. The experience of the Béla Kun regime in 1919 turned all Hungarian Jews by implication into Bolshevik subversives. Anti-Semitism, says István Deák, 'was the alpha and omega of the counter-revolutionary movement',[264] which brought Horthy to power as Regent. Jewish scapegoating for all Hungary's misfortunes was also especially intense among the tens of thousands of educated, middle-class Hungarians who fled those parts of the country ceded to surrounding states as a consequence of Trianon. It was Jews in the professions and universities— allegedly—who denied them jobs, blocked off their career prospects, and through their alien, liberal values (on top of their supposed Bolshevik inclinations) denied Hungarians their own authentic, organic path to salvation. Here, then, was an all too familiar picture of cognitive dissonance, Magyar-style, the erstwhile drivers of national development now accused of having not just overreached themselves but having done so in treasonable fashion, at the expense of the *true* nation.[265]

As war approached, and Budapest moved more firmly into the Axis camp, anti-Jewish animus was reflected in a series of laws aimed at restricting Jewish businesses and Jews' access to the professions, defining them as racial outsiders in the manner of Nazi legislation, and also requiring of male Jews compulsory forced labour service in military units. As in Rumania, as throughout nearly all Nazi-dominated Europe, so here in Hungary such legislation was indicative of more visceral desires to see the back of the Jews. Yet there is clearly also a striking anomaly in the Hungarian case, one which would even seem to contradict the general rule. Until the spring of 1944, the vast majority of an estimated 825,000 Jews on Hungarian soil at the onset of war (including many thousands of Jewish refugees from elsewhere in Europe)[266] were still alive, in contrast to the vast majority in the rest of Nazi-occupied or allied Europe, who by then were dead. The anomaly can fundamentally be put down to the regime's strenuous efforts to preserve Hungary's sovereign integrity and, from this position, once the runes on the likely outcome of the conflict were read and understood, to find some way towards a strategy of exit from the Axis. From this perspective, the repeated efforts of the government of Miklós Kállay to resist German demands for the Hungarian participation in the 'Final Solution' were part and parcel of a wider set of geopolitical calculations, the key audience for which was the Western Allies. In other words, if Jewish survival was a test of Hungary's ability to preserve both its independence and its manoeuvrability, any deterioration in that condition would be taken as evidence in Washington and London of Budapest's accession to the German will.[267] Which would seem to offer a straightforward explanation of how and why the extermination of Hungarian Jewry took place when and where it did. Hungarian efforts to beat a path to the Allies were stymied by the March 1944 German occupation of the country. A new collaborationist government under Döme Sztójay, though still technically account-able to Horthy, replaced that of Kállay. And Eichmann immediately set up shop in Budapest's Hotel Majestic, paving the way for mass deportations to Auschwitz.[268]

Was it then Eichmann's efficiency which explains what has been described as the 'smoothest administrative operation in Holocaust history'?[269] Such a verdict would both neatly and conveniently nail responsibility for Hungarian Jewish destruction to a German door. Eichmann's own musings on the matter, however, as recalled in the Jerusalem witness box, would seem to complicate the matter. Yes, he agreed, 'everything went like a dream'. But he continued, 'Hungary was the only country where we were not fast enough *for them*. They turned their Jews over to us like throwing out sour beer.'[270]

So how do we explain this discrepancy? If Horthy and the higher echelons of the state had sought to protect Hungarian Jewry up to 1944, surely we can at least absolve *them* of complicity in the matter? Yet there is clearly an ambiguity here. Administrations remained answerable to the Regent until his removal by the Ger-mans in October. So ultimate responsibility for the great swathe of Hungarian Jewish destruction by deportation in the May–early July window must at least technically rest with him. And while Horthy may not have been in the same league as an Antonescu, he certainly had form as an anti-Semite.[271] One question which might thus follow is: to what extent, if any, did the Horthy variant of anti-Semitism feed into the 1944 process of extermination?

One thing which is immediately noteworthy about Horthy's supposedly 'civi-lized' brand of anti-Semitism is how closely it mirrored Gorchakov's distinction—from three-quarters of a century earlier between acceptable, useful, 'acculturated' Jews and dubious, parasitic, 'eastern' ones. The conviction that Jews who had crossed from Galicia into northern Hungary in Habsburg times were not simply unassimilable into Magyar society but actually posed a mortal threat to its very existence was a Horthy prejudice that was shared by almost the entirety of the aristocratic ruling class.[272] Overlaying the prejudice, however, was a strong streak of pragmatism. To run Hungary's war economy needed Jewish money, industrial plant, technical know-how, and specialists to match—all of which Hungarian Jew-ish patriots, where they had these assets, were willing to give in ample measure. When the Kállay administration refused to comply with German directives for the implementation of the 'Final Solution' in Hungary, it was not, therefore, because it had gone soft on the Jews, or was proposing that that they were now all off limits. On the contrary, the very manner in which the wartime laws allowing for an eco-nomic sequestration of Jewish land and property tended to be selectively applied to the more traditional Jewish businesses in rural areas, above all in the territories recovered by Hungary since 1938, suggests a conscious design to discriminate between metropolitan Jewry and those on the rimlands periphery. While the former were recognized as worth preserving, if for reasons of utility alone, those who now made up somewhat short of half the Jewish population as a result of the incorporation of northern Transylvania, that part of Upper Slovakia now rechristened as the Felivdék, Carpatho-Rus, and finally the territories—renamed as the Délvidék—regained from Yugoslavia, were another matter altogether.[273]

This insidious distinction was thrown into further bold relief when Horthy was summoned to meet Hitler at Schloss Klessheim and account for Hungary's desertion from the Axis cause, just as the Führer was putting the seal on his secret plans to occupy the country. Horthy did not take the German demands lying down. However, he did agree to one in particular: namely to provide 300,000 Jewish workers for deployment in German war industries. Male Jews of military age from across the Hungarian Jewish community had already been conscripted into military labour units, sometimes with disastrous consequences. But not only was Horthy's consent to Hitler's demand the first occasion on which a Hungarian head of state had conceded authority to Germany over the fate of Jews *within* the country;[274] it was also, much more tellingly, in effect a green light to be shot of all the Jews that Horthy 'did not care for'. 'Galicians' and 'communists' might provide the Regent with convenient categories for differentiating between 'bad' and 'good' Hungarians, but what this boiled down to in effect was a view of Jewish worth which hardly extended beyond a tiny political and industrialist metropolitan elite.[275]

We seem to have arrived back on the same familiar ground we earlier encountered with Laval at one end of Europe, Antonescu or King Basil at the other. The fact that the so-called 'Galicians' were the sons and daughters of actually settled Transylvanian and sub-Carpathian Jews, who had demonstrated fervent loyalty to Habsburg Magyarism, counted for no more with Horthy than that evinced by 'foreign' Jews to democratic France did with Laval. In these as in other cases, there was—when push came to shove—a willingness, perhaps even an alacrity, to wash the state's hands of these supposedly 'bad' outsiders when the German opportunity presented itself. In Horthy's case, that meant giving a free hand to the Budapest bureaucrats who were willing to see to the nuts and bolts not just of signing over the labour element to the Germans, but of liquidating the rest. Horthy appears to have played no direct role in this process, the lack of either his signature or that of his Council of Ministers to the ensuing anti-Jewish measures clearly not affecting the outcome.

In the Regent's personal defence, it is sometimes suggested that his being increasingly prone to memory lapse—a symptom of old age and growing frailty—ensured that he was in no position to effectively intervene, one way or the other.[276] On the prosecution side, however, two factors stand out. The first relates to the actual schedule of deportations. Dividing up the country into six zones, the bureaucrat-cum-gendarmerie remit was to clear first Zone 1, Carpatho-Ruthenia, then Zone 2, northern Transylvania, then polishing off the three other primarily rural zones, until the mission was finally completed with the removal of the Budapest Jews in Zone 6.[277] One might argue, of course, that it was perfectly logical for the planners to work in this way from outer to inner, periphery to metropolis. And if one follows the German-led argument of military necessity, the more obviously eastern rimlands Zones 1 and 2, in spring 1944, were at their closest point only thirty miles from the encroaching front. Replace the names tsarist army with Red Army, eastern Anatolian Armenians with sub-Carpathian Jews, Turks with Hungarians, and one has a reconfiguration of the politico-geographical imperatives of that earlier deportation sequence. Except there is no evidence—even if one were to accept at face value the dubious Ittihad reasoning from 1915—of any incipient Jewish, Van-like uprising in the Carpathian passes. Indeed, if military security were the issue in 1944, then it would have been equally logical for the deportations to begin in Budapest, on the grounds that the largest Jewish concentration was there and—in their diabolical 'stabbers in the back' guise—it would be from there that the Jews would be most likely to attempt to overthrow the country's precarious adherence to the Axis. The question thus has to be asked: was it purely coincidental that the Jews Horthy cared for least were the same Jews carried off in the deportation sequence? And, following a second line of (imaginary) prosecuting counsel cross-examination, was it again purely coincidental that Horthy intervened on 7 July to call a halt to the deportations when the Jews he cared for most—the ones in Budapest—were themselves threatened with imminent destruction?

These are murky waters indeed, and not least because Horthy's transparent failure to countermand the deportation orders in the crucial May–June interregnum (whether for reasons of memory lapse or not) has also to be set against the one thing which finally did jolt him into action: the threat of Allied retaliation. The bombing raid on Budapest five days before his halt order offered the warning. Even then, the anti-Jewish operation continued for another two days, ensuring that all Hungarian Jews caught in the round-ups, barring, that is, those in the capital itself, were deported. At best, the circumstantial evidence would seem to point to Horthy's dispassion in the face of the destruction of the great bulk of Hungarian Jewry.

By contrast, there is no need for equivocation as to the anti-Jewish imaginings, if not consistently the actions, of Hungary's last pro-Axis government, that of Nyilas—the Arrow Cross. This overtly fascist party was in power in Hungary (in so far as one can speak of power in the context of a rapidly advancing Red Army) in the ebb of Horthy's bungled Axis decoupling effort in October. With the Regent deposed by the Germans and replaced by the Nyilas leader, Szálasi, the latter's short-lived regime can be described, by turns, as mad, bad and, in the person of the fantasist Szálasi, indubitably sad.[278] For certain, the regime made no distinction between 'good' Jews and the rest. Even in the last days of its imploding control over a besieged and bombarded Budapest, in the winter of 1944–5, its most fervent supporters—in fact, mostly 'teenagers and hoodlums'—went on repeated murderous rampages around what had become the two Jewish ghetto zones.[279] We remember, as we should, the obstacles thrown in the path of these killers by an ad hoc collection of very brave representatives from neutral state embassies, and also from the ICRC, as they increasingly attempted to coordinate efforts to find safe houses and fabricate ersatz red tape with which to protect the estimated 100,000 surviving

Jews still in the city.[280] But, ironically, part of the reason for their success was because the very weakness of the new regime. Its elevation to power was only by dint of the fact that Germans had run out of any other reliable partners in Budapest. And certainly the SD assessment of the Arrow Cross as too prone to pursue their own 'independent' agenda was rather borne out when Szálasi sought to block the SD's ongoing efforts to march the remainder of the Budapest Jews to the Austrian border to build anti-tank ditches there, preferring instead to redirect this still clearly expendable asset for the same forced labour but *within* Hungary.[281] In all probability, the Arrow Cross lacked a coherent blueprint for what it intended to do with the remaining Jews, which by this stage in the game should hardly surprise. Himmler, after all, of his own volition, had already sought to discontinue the deportations to Auschwitz.

However, whether Szálasi did or did not have an identifiable Jewish policy—over and beyond fleecing Jews of whatever money and valuables they had left—largely misses the essential point. Administratively inept, resource-starved and, in December, forced to evacuate the capital anyway, the fact was that the Nyilas's hold on power in Budapest had become so fragmented that in one famous incident the following month, on the cusp of the final Soviet assault, a Nyilas liaison officer joined with a local SS armoured division commander to forestall other Nyilas and German units intent on one final Jewish massacre.[282] It is not, then, that the Arrow Cross ought to be removed from the ranks of those who committed atrocities against the Jews, their final winter tally accounting for an estimated 7,000 deaths.[283] But by the same token to imagine that the movement was anything more than a grotesque coda to the Hungarian genocide would be to ignore the fact that the majority of the country's Jews had already been liquidated several months earlier. Just as focusing on the Iron Guard pogrom in 1941 in Bucharest obscures the main Rumanian genocidal action, so elevating the Nyilas role deflects attention from where it is really due.

Who then are our leading culprits? In the absence of Horthy and his immediate governing circle, we might expect the driving force behind a collaborative project with the Germans to come from other more willing ministers, or perhaps key if slightly subordinate elements within the Army General Staff, security apparatus, and Interior Ministry. This would be in line, for instance, with the manner in which Dadrian identifies the Armenian genocide as emerging through an inner party circle of protagonists, operating at one remove from 'normative' government but at the same time enlisting expert support and capacity. This line of reasoning would assume, crucially, not just genocidal intent but a sufficient body of intermediate actors committed to driving through practical implementation. It would also happen to place these in marked contrast to equivalent civil and military figures in the Italian-occupied zones up to late 1943, sufficient numbers of whom, as we have seen, joined together to sabotage (with or without Mussolini's consent) German diktat.

The comparison is especially relevant because of strong tendencies in Hungary to follow the Italian generals' lead out of the war. Developments within the Budapest War and Interior ministries, *Honvédség*, and local officialdom, *before* the

German occupation, indeed rather suggest an internal struggle for and against adherence to the 'Final Solution'. A concerted effort involving the military, the National Central Alien Control Office (KEOKH), gendarmerie, and security units to eruct 'stateless' Jews from the Carpatho-Ruthene region across the Galician border in the summer of 1941 proved precipitative to the Jeckeln-led massacres at Kamianets-Podilsky. The 'Galician' focus of Hungarian sensitivities should be noted, not least as local officials used the occasion as a pretext to deport not just refugees but Jews with indubitable Hungarian citizenship.[284] But while this reads superficially as rather similar to Bucharest's determination to use Operation Barbarossa as a cover under which to clear Jews out of its eastern provinces, the difference in the Hungarian case is in the high-level opposition the programme engendered. And not least from the then interior minister, Ferenc Keresztes-Fischer, who on news of what was happening across the border struggled—not entirely successfully—against elements in his own departments, as well as fellow ministers, to halt the deportations.[285]

The fact that after the German occupation Keresztes-Fischer ended up in a concentration camp may suggest, with hindsight, his isolation from colleagues. On the other hand, overtures to the Germans in 1942 to negotiate *further* deportations of 'alien' Jews appear to have been pursued in a decidedly surreptitious way, implying at the very least that this was not official policy. During this period, most of the running in this direction came from a senior general, József Heszlényi, who put himself in contact with a range of German Foreign Office, Wehrmacht, and OMi people, the conversations revolving around the removal of 100,000 or possibly even 300,000 unwanted Jews, either to Poland, Ukraine, or even Transnistria. One disturbing aspect of these *pourparlers* is that the numbers are the same as those which surfaced in the Hitler–Horthy exchanges two years later, alternatively suggesting that Heszlenyi's brief was to *appear* as an independent actor when, in actuality, he was pursuing genuine state objectives to remove the Jews of the newly incorporated territories. It is also significant that when the proposals arrived on Eichmann's desk he wanted none of them, arguing their lack of comprehensiveness.[286]

Either Heszlényi was conducting a government undercover stratagem, then, or operating on his own unauthorized account. The matter is not simply resolved, especially if we put the episode alongside the experience shortly before of the Novi Sad massacres, which appear to have been a case of *Honvédség* commanders, possibly backed by some officials in the War Ministry, carrying out an operation in defiance of the administration's wishes.[287] But to assume that the military were all for a policy of Jewish elimination would seem to be contradicted by their behaviour towards the estimated 150,000 male Jewish conscripts attached to the army in labour battalions. Conditions for these men were harsh and often lethal, unsurprisingly, given that the majority were operating on the Eastern Front with the Hungarian Second Army. This same army was overwhelmed and practically annihilated at the battle of Voronezh in January 1943. Thousands of other Jewish men, fatefully loaned to the Germans to work especially in Operation Todt mines in Belgrade, also perished, raising the Jewish army-related death toll to some 40,000.[288]

Yet there is a paradox. If the military had gone all out to lead a Hungarian Jewish genocide, they would have taken a leaf out of the CUP book and shot the entirety of this cohort out of hand, most likely as a prelude to the main German liquidation at Auschwitz. Yet this is exactly what did not happen. In the wake of Voronezh, War minister Vilmos Nagy sought on the one hand to increase Jewish numbers mobilized for the units (simply to make good an acute labour shortage), and on the other to protect them from excesses and atrocities, undoubtedly in some instances committed by *Honvédség* units. And further: the many young men who were called up for this service in the spring and summer of 1944 not only thereby escaped the deportations but were provided with a better if still slender possibility, ultimately through Soviet capture, of surviving the war.[289]

This highly gendered selection inevitably had one further disastrous consequence. Just as Red Army mobilizations of rimlands males in 1941 deprived the wider Jewish population of its potentially most protective element, so in Hungary 1944 the Jewish community was equally made vulnerable—and leaderless—in the face of what now befell it. But not by the Hungarian military. The movers and shakers of Budapest's collaborative genocide were primarily civilian officials, most particularly associated with the Interior Ministry.

To be sure, the elevation of the core *génocidaire* protagonists Andor Jaross to interior minister, and László Baky and László Endre to his side as secretaries of state, could not have been accomplished without the German invasion. Thereby ensconced in key executive positions, 'the deportation trio', as they later became known, were able to replace vast swathes of the central and regional civil service—including most city and town mayors and nearly all district governors—with individuals like themselves associated with pro-German, ultra-right parties, including the Hungarian National Socialists.[290] Indeed, it would be very convenient to label all these individuals as Nazi stooges. Without doubt, the cooperation between the central team and their German counterparts was extremely tight and synergic, as exemplified in the IV/4 unit under László Koltay, specifically created to synchronize the deportations with Eichmann's identically-titled outfit one floor down in the Majestic.[291] But the reason Jaross, Baky, and Endre were so zealous in fulfilling their remit to deliver the Jewish population (bar those already in Hungarian military units) to Eichmann was ultimately not a function of their thraldom to the Germans. They were acting in what they fervently believed to be the Hungarian interest, which would be realized through the complete elimination of *all* Jews from Magyar soil. Just as the Antonescu people in 1941 believed that their moment of opportunity had arrived, so Endre, here primus inter pares as Special Commissioner for Jewish Affairs, and with overall responsibility for the policing of the project, believed his moment of destiny had come.[292]

What is therefore immediately striking about the operation Endre and Baky put into effect from the first moment of the Sztójay administration's incumbency is on the one hand its degree of advance preparedness and on the other its extraordinary speed and efficiency. In contrast to the massively bungled Bucharest initiatives to clear their eastern provinces, the Budapest effort encapsulates almost to a T Bauman's understanding of genocidal modernity in action. Presented with the need for a legislative imprimatur for the interlinked aims of Jewish disenfranchisement, economic despoliation, and removal, Jaross was able to turn to Endre, who provided him with a thick file from his desk drawer to cover all the necessary draft laws.[293] In parallel, the Council of Ministers approved in secret a programme for the temporary ghettoization of to-be-deported communities, while again, Baky and Endre coordinated their efforts to create an extraordinary unit (XXI) of the Housing Department to hold the internees in the interim between their eviction and departure. Equally, they strove to synchronize their efforts with Eichmann's small team to meet German railway timetabling requirements. Indeed, the whole exercise of *actual* deportation had to be telescoped into a window of a few weeks, to fit in with the Wehrmacht's more pressing strategic needs.

If this all required precision planning, the results, statistically speaking, confirm that the Hungarian bureaucracy was more than up to the job. In this sense, the deportation exercise became *the* litmus test of the Hungarian state's professional credibility as a joined-up modern state apparatus. From 20 April, when the Interior Ministry reached its internal decision to activate wholesale deportation, it was a matter of a single week for instructions to the gendarmerie to be translated into the round-up of all Jews in Zone 1. The incarceration of Jews in Zone 2 followed on 3 May. Within seven days the astonishing figure of 98,000 people there were behind barbed wire. The trains began to roll from Zone 1 on 15 May, again ensuring that the sequencing between incarceration and removal by cattle-truck was fine-tuned. The entire procedure, moreover, was minutely detailed by the senior gendarmerie officer, Lieutenant-Colonel László Ferenczy, 'charged with oversight of the concentration and deportation process' as well as with liaison with the German security police. Again, it was almost as if statistics were being required to 'narrate success' not only at home but—where they mattered—abroad.[294] On 8 June, Ferenczy could report that 275,415 Jews from these zones had been transported in ninety-two trains, and consequently these areas were *judenfrei*. And in his final report on 9 July he could note with satisfaction that since the start date, 434,351 Jews in all had left the country, in 147 trains.[295]

If such raw data tells us that most of the estimated 565,000 Jews on Hungarian soil, or under Hungarian occupation, who, according to Randolph Braham, lost their lives during the Second World War perished as a direct consequence of this specific deportation sequence,[296] what it cannot convey is the merciless zealotry and sadistic enthusiasm with which Magyar officialdom got to work to have the deportees ready for their final departure. Or, for that matter, the enormous effort in man-hours, and personnel which the Ministry had to deploy, to complete the job on time: 20,000 gendarmes proved quite insufficient to the task, and whole swathes of professional people found themselves mobilized by their local prefects—in a way rather prefiguring Rwanda fifty years later—to help. We may recall the manner in which they fulfilled their remit in Munkács (Mukacevo), outlined towards the end of our previous volume's introduction.[297] The Parliamentary representative from this Ruthenian town noted how 'professors, teachers, public servants, are given short courses on how to carry out the *search* of the Jews in the ghetto, both as far as their persons and their homes are concerned. Next day these trainees in groups of three enter the ghetto and gather everything of value.'[298]

So, manifestly, the effort which went into the round-ups was about a great deal more than getting the Jews *out*. It was also fundamentally geared towards ensuring that absolutely everything which belonged to them stayed *in* Hungary. How seriously this project was pursued is evident from the way doctors, nurses, and midwives were also brought into the holding camps—the term ghetto gives too much solidity to communal buildings, disused factories, or brickyards hastily commandeered for the purpose—to extract any last piece of gold, jewellery, or coin secreted in orifices of males or females pregnant or otherwise. And witness accounts confirm that in all cases there was no hold on the torture meted out to the victims however young or old, vulnerable or frail, to achieve this object.[299]

Of course, what was going on here sounds viciously in keeping with what we have witnessed throughout this and the previous chapter. Hungarians, after all, were doing essentially the same thing as rimlands peoples and Europeans more generally when and where the opportunity presented itself: enriching themselves at the expense of a community who were about to get the chop—and conveniently so (for the most part) at second, German hand. But there is *a degree* of differentiation. The parallel Rumanian *state* effort to accrue to itself the primary proceeds of Jewish expropriated wealth collapsed at the first hurdle, through universal cupidity. By contrast, Hungarian bureaucracy's more rigorous control systems and arguably greater societal consensus as to what 'legitimately' belonged to the state, ensured that a significant proportion of an estimated 20 billion pengő (*c.* 4 billion dollars) of loot—according to contemporary US intelligence estimates—ended up in state coffers.[300]

So, could it be that the hands-on mobilization of the most nationally-minded yet civically conscious middle tier of Hungarian society as helpers in the expropriation process played a crucial role in its legitimization? The welter of government anti-Jewish decrees in spring 1944, perhaps above all the 16 April sequestration decree, which not only closed down Jewish businesses and concerns but stripped Jews of almost the entirety of their securities, savings, and personal possessions—in other words ensuring their overnight pauperization[301]—required, at the very least, some sort of public acceptance. To be sure, the process of government-directed economic noose-tightening had been going on for several years, regardless of the complexion of administrations. But spring 1944 suggests something more: that this really was the end of the road for the Jews. By linking the process of expropriation to deportation, involving pukka Hungarians in it for the sake of national rectitude, yet at the same time also finding a way for wider society to be direct economic beneficiaries, the Jaross team found their formula for popular acclamation. What the government really wanted was the serious wealth from Jewish businesses, property, and bank-holdings, plus 'the personal gold, jewellery and other transportable items of value'.[302] Even here, of course, there was seepage, as gendarmes and others in official positions on the ground pocketed what they could.[303] But this does not appear to have been anything as wide open as the Rumanian rake-off. Instead, a channel for demotic acquisitiveness was provided by allowing, even implicitly encouraging, the looting of what was left in abandoned Jewish households. This frenzied redistribution of Jewish assets not only directly advantaged swathes of the population, but in turn more firmly tied them to an otherwise failing regime.

This elite–demotic trade-off may also have been considered valid for another reason: it denied Jewish valuables to the Germans. Jaross himself intimated as much.[304] The Sztójay administration may have seen itself as tied to the Germans, but very quickly it found itself in fierce competition with the SS for the commanding heights of Jewish wealth, most especially the Manfred Weiss conglomerate of companies which included mining and armament manufacturers. The SS deal backed by menaces to take over the conglomerate's assets in return for safe passage of the companies' owners to Portugal directly overrode any Hungarian say in the matter.[305] Ensuring that the state held on to the remainder of Jewish 'treasure' for the long-term benefit of the nation would eventually involve a desperate and ultimately futile effort, in December 1944, to remove forty-two freight wagons of stolen Jewish goods—the so-called Gold Train—bound from Budapest to Austria; futile because much of the loot was filched en route by its Hungarian supposed custodians or impounded (where it was not directly pilfered) by victorious US troops.[306]

In the immediate term, however, direct seizure of Jewish financial assets plus the plunder and resale of Jewish properties was helping Budapest to absorb inflationary pressures and provide state finances with a stop-gap 'shot in the arm as war costs spiralled'.[307] Here are further grounds for speculating that Hungarian complicity in the deportation process went way beyond the Jaross-Endre-Baky clique. To be sure, we can identify a *political* distinction between them and the regime per se, as dramatically exemplified in early July when Baky attempted—unsuccessfully—to move gendarmerie units into the capital to defy Horthy's stand-down order on the deportations. The very fact that Horthy was not able to fully rid himself of the Sztójay people until late in August, and in the interim Eichmann, of his own initiative, continued to deport some inmates from camps only a stone's throw from the capital, may suggest how limited the Regent's power had in actuality become.[308] Yet if we were to look to the other *economic* side of the coin, there could be grounds for inferring that there was no real break between government policy before and after the July stand-off.

Indeed, the accelerated process of Jewish expropriation came *after* the official deportation halt with the public appointment, in late July, of Albert Turvölgyi as commissioner 'for the Solution of Questions Relating to the Jews' Material and Property Rights'. The very title speaks volumes as to Budapest's intentions. Provided with premises next door to the National Bank of Hungary in Szabadság Square, at the heart of the capital's financial district, the Commissariat became the hub for a massive countrywide operation involving no fewer than forty-two Financial Directorates. Each was tasked with managing the compulsory seizure, storage, and then transfer of Jewish valuables to government savings banks, or alternatively—where household goods were concerned—their direct resale to the public. There is no evidence that the wider public shunned this exercise in daylight robbery. On the contrary, the sales seem to have been 'immensely popular'.[309] Times were hard—and dangerous. A bargain purchase of some nice rugs, curtains, carpets, or a fur coat could only have been a welcome fillip, and a perfectly legal one at that. The driving force towards this one-off sanctioned redistribution of wealth may have been the men in the Interior Ministry. But once Baky and Endre had done their worst it was as if Hungary could get back to 'business as usual', using the Jewish proceeds to recoup something of the 'occupation costs' charged by the Germans, yet over and beyond that, imagining a time when the country rid of its 'parasitic' element could run its own economic affairs by and for itself.

As Ronald Zweig has persuasively argued, all this was built on a fantasy myth of fabulous Jewish wealth, by its nature vastly exaggerated but much more to the point only reproducible in the long-term national interest through the sustenance of the 'cultural attributes' which give rise to communal enterprise and entrepreneurship.[310] Cut that away by killing the Jews (at first or second hand) and you also eliminated your milk-cow. But then genocide was never based on such long-term integrated reasoning. In a social-Darwinian world, especially that of Second World War, Nazi-dominated Eastern Europe, the immediate logic was to take the quick fix short-cut to the money (regardless of whether it was or was not that tangible), and to hell with the consequences.

Actually, this was no more nor less than what had always been done by states who committed genocide. Recent work, especially by Martin Dean, has shown how intimately expropriation and murder went hand in hand during the Holocaust.[311] In the Hungarian case, once the commitment to the principle of the former had been made, the path to elimination may have been slippery, convoluted, and downright contingent on wider events and other players, while still maintaining its own internal logic. This in turn explains why, in the end, traditional sensibilities which made the distinction between nicely cultivated, professional Budapest Jews with veteran lapels and medals to prove it and poor, 'alien', 'Galician' ones counted for nothing. As it also may explain why *all* the Hungarian administrations of 1944, not just the palpably nastiest, were in some profound sense responsible for the outcome.

Hungarian behaviour, of course, when put alongside the anti-Jewish sentiments and actions of so many other supposedly civilized or not so civilized Europeans proved all too predictable. They, too, dreamt dreams of fabulous Jewish wealth, which, supposedly ill-gotten in its taking, would be returned to its rightful owners. They, too, were able to see a silver lining in German domination, in the opportunity it presented not just to despoil the 'kikes' but in so doing get even with them. To be sure, there were remarkable Europeans who went against this grain, rejected the method (even where they may have accepted the argument), and sometimes strove to resist, or to rescue their fellow human beings. That said, part of the reason these people were remarkable was because, statistically speaking, they were nearly always in the minority.

Here, then, was something very particular which distinguished the European Jewish genocides of 1941–5 from others of the moment, to be considered in the next chapter. Underlying their causation lay a deep, troubled, historical reservoir of unresolved feelings, animosities, and imaginings about or against the alleged killers of Christ. When it was all over, and the Nazi acolytes and fellow-travellers had been brought to trial, popular justice was seen to be done. In Hungary, the deportation trio were among the 146 individuals executed for war crimes and crimes against humanity. But no administration in immediate post-war Europe, not even in Soviet-run Hungary, dared to demand the return of homes, properties, and businesses to Jewish survivors.[312] Not just the Germans, not just the peoples of the rimlands, but Europeans everywhere—even where they had not directly murdered—took their genocidal revenge on the Jews, through relieving them of every worldly item they possessed. The Jews, like the Armenians before them, more often than not went naked into the abyss.

4

Wars of All against All

One clearly thorny question arises from any narrative of genocide which focuses only on Jews, or even Jews and Roma, in the context of the Second World War. The overall death toll among non-combatants vastly exceeded that of either group. In which case, is it really appropriate to discriminate between deaths through genocide and those of mass murder more generally? Would it not be more purposeful to begin with war as the overriding causative factor and from there chart how *its* escalation—or, if one prefers, cumulative radicalization—determined the scope, scale, and intensity of the ensuing sequence of atrocities? There have been some notable interventions in genocide studies which have veered in this direction. The late Eric Markusen, with David Kopf, for instance, compared Jewish/Roma extermination with the strategic bombing campaigns undertaken by all major parties but most particularly the British and Americans against German and Japanese cities, culminating in the atomic destruction of Hiroshima and Nagasaki. Markusen and Kopf's conclusion was that the death of hundreds of thousands of innocent and defenceless women and children in these campaigns might be deemed 'genocide in the course of war'.[1] Coming at the subject more recently and from a slightly different perspective, Martin Shaw has persuasively argued that while genocide is a distinctive form of war, it is, nevertheless, an extension of what he describes as *degenerate* war. In such cases, standard warfare against an 'organised armed enemy' becomes 'war against a largely unarmed civilian population',[2] closely mirroring thereby the Markusen-Kopf proposition.

These arguments are of particular relevance to a chapter whose primary subject is the wider range of European mass killings, particularly in the rimlands theatres of war between 1941 and 1945. Total war, as pursued by technologically advanced adversaries, brought with it the potential for the obliteration of populations. After the testing of the first atomic device at Alamogordo, New Mexico, on 16 July 1945, that potential became *omnicidal*. Yet in the context of the European war, the (non-nuclear) aerial bombardment of Western and Central European cities—the most obviously achievable method for the annihilation of what was and remain the most densely populated regions of the continent—was in per capita terms vastly exceeded by the scale of violent death perpetrated against rimlands peoples in the Balkans and 'Lands Between'. The fact that bombing was responsible for only a fraction of the fatalities in the 'East' and that considerably more can be attributed to relatively low-level technologies, the crudest of hand-held implements included, plus the use of systematic starvation, conjures up a ubiquity as well as intimacy to the nature of atrocity committed here, for which Shaw's term 'degenerate' seems particularly apt.

The key question to my mind, however, remains whether degenerate war or, as I might prefer, *degenerative* warfare, offers the most useful explanatory route towards genocide, or, indeed, is simply a synonym for the phenomenon. I offer the more adjectivally dynamic 'degenerative' because one way of approaching the issue might be to see if the unfolding, worsening, and by degree more 'totalist' pursuit of war by belligerents over time might bring in its wake a greater readiness to dispense with normative rules distinguishing surrendered POWs, or non-combatants, from active enemy participants, a consequence of which could well be genocidal outcomes. For instance, while there were some notable examples of SS- or Wehrmacht-perpetrated massacres against surrendered soldiers in the *Blitzkrieg* campaign against France and the Low Countries in summer 1940 (including, in many instances, French black colonial troops), the frequency of such killings—of not only disarmed soldiers but also civilians—increased significantly as the German military position in the West deteriorated, the massacres at Oradour and Malmédy in 1944 being particularly egregious.[3] But the very fact that they stand out is itself noteworthy. Hands-on massacre of this type, whether by German uniformed personnel or for that matter by their Western Allied adversaries, did happen but were *not* the norm in the campaigns of 1944–5. By contrast, in rimlands arenas such as Belorussia, where German military and police units were engaged in a constant and actually intensifying struggle with Soviet partisans from 1941 through to the former's expulsion in 1944, atrocity of this kind was practically par for the course.

By the same token, as both Western and Soviet allies pounded Germany towards military and infrastructural obliteration in the last four months of the European war, not only did the territory still held by the Nazis become literally a battlefield but distinctions between combatants and non-combatants correspondingly collapsed in what one historian has described as 'probably the greatest killing frenzy in the history of the modern world'.[4] Yet neither the British, nor for that matter the Germans, had set out from the start to reduce each other's cities to rubble: the intent to do so and the Anglo-American decision to make of it a strategic imperative was in significant part a consequence of the increasingly zero-sum nature of the *ensuing* struggle. Again, by contrast, from day one of the German invasion of Poland the war in the east was in every sense degenerate, involving both conscious efforts by the Luftwaffe to destroy Warsaw, later Belgrade, and then Soviet cities, and massacres of Polish POWs and civilians as a prelude to the much wider landscape of atrocity from 22 June 1941.

On one level, such distinctions simply confirm the qualitative as well as quantitative difference in the Nazi approach to war in the east, underpinned as it was by both racist ideology and dreams of a vast, murderous, colonial reordering. Yet, ironically, this still may not be sufficient to nail degenerate (or degenerative) war as either first cause or *the same thing* as genocide. This is not to suggest that in some instances the crossover may not be both possible and very palpable. In *The Meaning of Genocide* I attempted to consider genocide through the prism of war, delineating three types which might more clearly enable us to isolate genocide's incidence.[5] Let me briefly reprise the typology:

1. Type One: State war against other sovereign states.
2. Type Two: State war against other sovereign states or nations who are perceived to be 'illegitimate'.
3. Type Three: State war *within* the boundaries, or other territories, controlled by the sovereign state, against national or other groups who are perceived to be illegitimate.

In the case of the Second World War in Europe, there is for each type a correspondence with discrete actors. Type One, for instance, would have Nazi Germany pitted against the Western Allies. Type Two would have Germany pitted against Poland, Yugoslavia, arguably Greece, and most keenly the USSR. Type Three would encompass all the resistance struggles pitted against the Nazis, their allies, and proxies within the confines of German-occupied Europe, but most keenly the partisan insurgencies in the Balkans, Poland, and those mostly rimlands regions of the 1939 Soviet state overrun by the Wehrmacht. Using Shaw's entirely more vivid terminology, we could agree that each type either was 'degenerate' from the outset or moved into a degenerative condition as a consequence of the ensuing dialectics of violence; though, more exactly, through the stymieing of the respective self-identifying 'legitimate' states' efforts to bring the war to its successful, strategic, Clausewitzian conclusion. I emphasize this last point because it brings into play the mismatch between expectations founded in large part on assumptions of the military-technological superiority, organizational efficiency, and notions of better human worth (racially based or otherwise) of powerful sovereign state actors, and the reality of finding themselves in long-term struggles of attrition with enemies who were supposed to be incapable of putting up more than token physical opposition. The obdurate refusal of these enemies to 'know' when they were defeated, and determination instead, to fight on regardless—perhaps in the process killing many of the other side's soldiers, or civilians, or even sabotaging its plan of campaign—adds an important psycho-social variable to the degenerate condition, providing state actors with a faux-justification for acts of reprisal or retribution. Once that kicked in as a feature of war it was only too probable that a cycle of mutually intensifying resistance, retribution, and extended atrocity would ensue. In this sense, we can see a clear cross-reference between ingredients of both degenerate war *and* genocide.

Considering the range of atrocities committed during the Second World War, it is quite possible then to also infer that sequences of all three types of warfare contained within them elements or components we repeatedly associate with genocide. Take, for example, the Western Allied fire-storming aerial assaults, especially towards the very end of the war, on cities such as Dresden or, soon after, Tokyo. Though repeatedly bombed thereafter, the single attack on the Japanese capital on the night of 9–10 March, notwithstanding the final paroxysms of Hiroshima and Nagasaki, resulted in more deaths—at the very least 100,000—than any other single bombing raid of the war.[6] Yet while such instances may have been officially sanctioned on grounds of 'military necessity', the available records also suggest either quite open or, alternatively, subconscious desires among leading British and US decision-makers, Churchill included, to wreak vengeance on the Japanese and Germans in retaliation for atrocities they had previously committed against Allied civilians and POWs.[7] Such atrocities were, of course, committed by the German or Japanese state apparatuses of violence, not by their wider populations. The literal obliteration of Axis cities, and with them the incineration or asphyxiation of large swathes of their urban inhabitants, either by the RAF or USAF, thus return us to the possibility, implicit in Markusen and Kopf's position, of some wider genocidal intent.

It is at this point, however, that we run into the argument against the proposition. The case is unequivocal that the Second World War resulted in state-directed mass murder by *all* sides against non-combatants, arguably on an unprecedented scale, and with the additional charge that the Western Allies were also guilty of war crimes. But if we were to return to Lemkin's definition, and the terms within which this writer's studies have been formulated, what makes *genocide* different (not necessarily more egregious) from other forms of mass murder lies in the perpetrators' aim to so physically pulverize, suffocate, or emasculate the targeted group that it is incapable of functioning in a meaningful social or political sense *thereafter*. In the case of the Allied carpet bombing of German and Japanese cities, what then should have followed would have been more thoroughgoing programmes of violence, terror, and extermination in the wake of Axis defeat. Yet Allied efforts to feed a starving German post-war society (*pace* British prime minister Attlee's domestic unpopularity for bringing in a UK bread ration in order to do so) suggest quite the opposite; as equally do US occupation guidelines in Tokyo geared towards a peaceful and benevolent accommodation of Japanese society under the continuing auspices of the emperor.[8]

Compare and contrast these examples with some of the cases of state counterinsurgency—hence falling under a War Type Three rubric—which we have already adumbrated in the present volumes. The CUP assault on the Hakkâri Nestorians in 1915 was almost certainly also a case of genocide. Some of the Turkish republic's campaigns against specific Kurdish tribes in the same eastern Anatolian arena, culminating in the Dersim episode in 1937–8, deserve a similar appellation. Red Army warfare against communal groups, ethnic or otherwise, in some of the more intractable struggles of the late civil war—including for instance, the isolation and destruction of the Tambov insurrection in 1921—might equally be judged in these terms. The fact that communal destruction followed periods of intense, albeit asymmetric, warfare in which the insurgents also committed repeated and heinous atrocities, does not mitigate the final verdict. But then the critical factor distinguishing genocide from other forms of mass murder is not whether it is, or is not, a form of warfare (it almost necessarily has to be), the technological or organizational capacities involved, or even—in some cases—a *two*-sided viciousness to the struggle (hence with it the lack of moral restraint or limitations on the violence committed); but rather lies in the *shaping* of the ultimate outcome.

Whether intentional from the outset (in fact rare) or developing in this direction through contingent circumstances, genocide assumes a state-led social and political reordering of geographical space through the elimination of discrete communal groups, usually involving, too, the expropriation of their economic assets in whatever form these take—land, access to resources, direct monetary wealth. This brings us finally to the challenge of this chapter. In the context of this European war, we have already proposed that in the Western theatre the degeneration of warfare between Nazis and Allies did not carry through into any policy shift in favour of genocide.[9] The one obvious exception to this statement is the manner in which the 'Final Solution'—Eastern European focused as it was—*also* pertained to West European Jews, as, arguably, by the same or by a different route, it also pertained to West European Roma. Similarly, in the European centre-ground, while terrible things happened, including sequences of conscious obliterative violence against populations, these campaigns (again excepting the cases of Jews and Roma) did not carry over into the actuality of genocide. In Italy, for instance, where accelerating partisan warfare behind the German lines during 1944 intruded into the overall picture of Allied versus Nazi struggle, SS and Fascist reprisal against villages suspected of harbouring partisans led to civilian massacres in a summer and early autumn high-point entirely on a par with—and the scale of—Axis atrocity in Greece and the Balkans.[10] In the (Czech) Protectorate there were, of course, the two great massacres at Lidice and Ležaky in reprisal for the assassination of Heydrich. These were clearly instrumental in the sense that they were intended to convey a warning of what might befall the Czechs more generally. Nazi thinking, emanating from Hitler at the top, had clearly entertained the notion that the 'unassimilable' half of that population would at some point undergo deportation to reserves in Volhynia, or even Siberia. Hitler openly threatened the Czechs' aged President Hácha with its imminence, in the wake of Heydrich's assassination. Once the crisis had subsided, however, and the Czech population had proved suitably pliant to the German will, the danger of them becoming casualties of war, in the same way as their fellow Slavic Poles, Belorussians, and Ukrainians, rapidly receded.[11]

Would it have been different had a wider Czech resistance movement taken off in 1942? We cannot know this, nor whether such amplification of violence would have been because of, or in spite of, previous German genocidal intentions. Further east, as we have already suggested, the will to genocide was already much more implicit in the nature of German post-conquest planning. But the actual trajectory in this arena towards that end may have been less the result of attempted implementation of a paper exercise and than a consequence of entirely unforeseen shifts in the course of the war, both on the ground in the East, and as affected by the even larger 'global' struggle. Though again, this may have to come with the caveat that despite the spiralling dialectic of killing here—as in the Balkans—and under whichever warfare type, the term genocide may not actually be entirely appropriate as a label. But then, we may be forgetting something else: that the typologies we offered as possible routes towards encapsulating the phenomenon (or, for that matter, Shaw's also essentially state-centred explication) may not cover the entire spectrum

of possibilities. There emerged, after all, in both Balkan and 'Lands Between' arenas, a subset of internal ethnic struggles within the wider 1941–5 intra-state conflict which sit rather uncomfortably, even messily, outside the categories we have
proposed, but which might lead us in a more direct manner towards an understanding of the *goals* of genocide.

Where does this leave us? With an exploration of different levels of warfare as
they developed in the 'core' killing fields of the East, above all in the 'Lands
Between' and Balkan rimlands, and their relationship, or otherwise, to genocide.
In the first section of this chapter we briefly consider this through the great Nazi-
Soviet struggle—*the* classic case of War Type Two, and one which fundamentally
determined the course of the European war, and, to an overwhelming degree, the
post-war 'settlement' (or rather its 'Cold War' absence). Yet it is a struggle in which,
for all the atrocities committed, we find the term genocide only elusively applicable.

It is less elusive, perhaps, with regard to instances where German counter-
insurgency against partisans—(in other words, a War Type Three) spilled over
into a conscious effort to eradicate populations, either in a tightly defined urban
zone or across a much wider swathe of territory. Our next section, 'The war in the
rear', considers two somewhat contrasting but equally intense killing arenas. The
first is Belorussia. Here, Germany's effort to keep control of its military rear
involved it in an ever more desperate war with Soviet partisans, especially in 1942
and 1943, ensuring that whole swathes of the local population would be sucked
into the vortex. In Belorussia, more than anywhere else in the European war, the
likelihood of combatants and non-combatants alike being killed was at its greatest. But for the Gentile (as opposed to Jewish) victims, was this a consequence of a
German design for the long term, or simply bad luck at being in the wrong place
at the wrong time? A year later, and with corresponding Wehrmacht retreat westwards, the centre of the cauldron had shifted to Poland. Here was an arena where
national consciousness and with it the political stakes were altogether more
heightened, carrying the further potential that a partisan-style Polish challenge to
German rule might spark off some 'final' Hitlerite reckoning. In this second
instance, our main focus will be on the summer 1944 Warsaw uprising, where the
consequence was certainly genocidal in a localized sense. However, this episode is
offered as a pointer to another conscious project of state-directed destruction, yet
to be considered in these pages: urbicide.

The shifting politico-military scene—as Soviets advanced and Germans
retreated—added another complication for Poles, where they found themselves a
minority community in what historically had been the *kresy*. In this arena the Poles
were not in the rear but in the middle of struggles for power with other would-be
national contenders. Such conflict was hardly exclusive to the 'Lands Between'. In
our penultimate section we consider a veritable confusion of military-cum-political
actors in a dismantled Yugoslavia, more specifically centring on Bosnia-Herzegovina
where, we will argue, it was two subordinate players—ultra-nationalist Croats and
Serbs—who, while they may not have been responsible for the largest body-counts
in the fighting, were the ones truly committed to wiping out perceived communal
competitors.

In other words, it was in the interstices of the wider, multi-faceted 'war of all against all' in the north Balkans that a particular set of circumstances crystallized favouring political groupings who saw genocide as a tool towards what they perceived as their ultimate *national* redemption. Particularly noteworthy, however, is that while on the Croat side genocide was committed by an extremely weak state, on the Serb—Chetnik—side the perpetrators' actual sovereign power was non-existent. Here, then, we have an authentic *variant* of genocide, where a shadow state acts in lieu of, or more exactly in anticipation of, its actual accession. But if the Serb example is significant, a matching case of arguably even greater potency returns us in our final section to the Volhynian and eastern Galician countryside of the 'Lands Between'. Here, in 1943, the life and death nature of the struggle for military control became a matter not just of Red Army and partisans versus Germans, but of other indigenous forces, most especially the Ukrainian Insurgent Army (UPA), attempting to claim the territory—albeit against all the odds—for their own putative polity. To attain this, not only the Soviets but more particularly the region's Poles were perceived as standing in the way. The resulting genocide may have been in a limited geographical arena, and carried through with scarce supporting resources. However, its consequences in the ultimate resolution of the crisis of the semi-periphery would turn out to be long-lasting and profound, not least in the way the attempt would rebound on so many Ukrainians too.

A CLASH OF TITANS: THE SOVIET–GERMAN WAR AND ITS GENOCIDAL POTENTIAL

Putting aside the millions killed in combat, it was the millions more who were wantonly murdered defenceless, or in spite of surrender, which appears to give to the struggle between the forces of Hitler and Stalin a genocidal quality. It is to the racial ideology of the former, the contempt in particular for Slavic and 'Asiatic'—as well as Jewish—*Untermenschen*, that we tend most readily to attribute blame for this outcome. And it is easy enough to see why. From the very onset of Operation Barbarossa, the Wehrmacht's own statistics on Soviet POW mortality reveal just how wantonly the Germans cut off the chances of survival from their camp charges. It has been estimated that of a total of 5,160,000 Red Army men captured in the course of the war no fewer than 2,454,000 (and possibly as many as 3.3 million) perished.[12] Most of those who died, especially early on, were the victims of starvation, or more precisely the intentional refusal on the Wehrmacht's part to give *available* food to them.[13] The consequent rapid attrition took place despite a growing awareness of the Reich's own labour crisis.[14] But death was also meted out more summarily, again especially in the early phase of fighting, by direct—and repeated—massacre. Not only Jews and commissars were murdered in this way. The sheer numbers of surrendered prisoners may have been one paltry 'instrumental' justification for the peremptory dispatch of some. But the method of execution of nearly 5,000 of 8,000 POWs murdered in one such instance, at Berdichev's Krasnaia Gora (Red Mountain)—the victims' hands and feet tied, and skulls shattered by blunt instruments, as investigated post-war at four mass graves[15]—suggests that the SD and Wehrmacht units assigned to the task also took veritable pleasure in it.

The verdict would tally with what we know of how German soldiery were pumped up on Nazi propaganda which aroused their hatred against the 'inhuman', 'bestial', fanatical, and 'barbaric' subhumans they had been primed to destroy. An example as good as any is the fifty-page SS training officer magazine suitably entitled *Der Untermensch*. It also happened to be popular for months into the summer and autumn 1941 on news-stands back home, replete with photographs of supposedly devious and brutal Asiatic types.[16] Can we directly connect such officially promoted race-hate imagery with the manner in which in the early months of the war captured 'Mongol'-looking Red Army conscripts were lined up in droves and gunned down by their captors? They were not alone, of course. The German wilful denial of life to half or more of the Soviet men in uniform they captured speaks of a gendered mass murder[17] more characteristic rather of ancient empires than modern times.

But then a German will to eradicate Eastern subhumans hardly stopped at the men of fighting age. When Himmler delivered his infamous Posen speech in October 1943—mostly remembered for his utterances about the liquidation of Jews—he also made a point of saying, 'Whether 10,000 Russian women keel over from exhaustion in the construction of an anti tank ditch interests me only in so far as the ditch for Germany gets finished.'[18] The fate of Russians (or Czechs) was a matter of total indifference: these people's value only existing insofar as 'we need them as slaves for our culture'. Himmler's statement certainly tallies with everything we know about the way millions of women (and men) from the Soviet rimlands were terrorized and dragooned into hyper-exploitative labour in and for the Reich.[19] This process culminated in the drives by the German authorities to round up anybody left for the purpose in hastily improvised great 'treks', as the Wehrmacht fell back westwards across the Dnieper in autumn 1943.[20] Himmler's articulation of the fate of so many of those squandered in preceding and then succeeding efforts of this kind, however, suggests something other than simple *indifference*; or even a justification based on the 'higher' needs of a German war economy in extremis. Indeed, underpinning Himmler's statement can we not read the same racially-inspired sadistic impulses which had Hitler repeatedly demanding that Russian cities be bombed to smithereens, or the anticipation, by the likes of Agriculture Ministry planner Herbert Backe, of the 30 million 'superfluous' Slavs who would starve to death once Germany had conquered its Soviet enemy?[21]

The problem, with hindsight, as we will see in our next section, is that Nazi projections of *intentional* Slavic mass murder were swept radically off course once the exigencies of war intervened to force the Germans to revise their original grand designs. This did not mean that what then transpired lacked potential or actual genocidal components. Nevertheless, the very contingent nature of having to sustain an ongoing Eastern Front—and its huge rear—meant that any imagined wipe-out of *all* rimlands peoples and their equally imagined replacement by German or supposedly related Nordic settlers had inevitably to be put on hold for the war's duration. Indeed, after Stalingrad and the primary need to stave off total German defeat, the *central* (not only) thrust of Nazi policies towards its eastern *Untermenschen* could not but be geared towards their hyper-exploitation—albeit with their expendability taken into account—rather than straightforward physical elimination per se.

But if this was the case, can we not identify a strong degree of resemblance in, even identical, Soviet practice towards *German* soldiers and civilians ? Out of 3.1 million Wehrmacht men captured by or surrendered to the Red Army, perhaps as many as 1.1 million perished. A standard assumption might be that most of these deaths were a consequence of deplorable transit conditions or relentless hyper-exploitation, particularly in Soviet mines, rather than being caused by any con-sciously malign Soviet intent. Yet we also have the case of some 380,000 ethnic Germans deported for labour by the NKVD from the Soviet-liberated Balkans and 'Lands Between'—though also including East Prussia, Pomerania, and Silesia—towards the end of the war, of whom up to 100,000 may have died from similar causes.[22] But this would seem to conceal the much higher mortality rate among German soldiers and airmen captured by the Red Army early on in the conflict, including a staggering 90 per cent in 1941 and still 70 per cent in the wake of Stalingrad. Here again, the evidence points to large numbers summarily executed—often with gratuitous violence into the bargain—by their Soviet opposite numbers.[23] By the same token, in those parts of Germany that fell to the Soviets in early 1945, the initial weeks of occupation may have seen anything between 75,000 and 100,000 non-combatants killed by Russian troops.[24] And this atrocity statistic itself hides the much more systematic incidence of Red Army rape, of which possibly as many as 2 million German females (of all ages from small children to old women) were victims.[25]

What is immediately significant about the range and scale of these atrocities is that there was no official Soviet equivalent of Nazi race hatred. And there were also very clear orders from the highest level of the Soviet military command prohibiting the killing of POWs or, in the course of the Red Army advance into Germany, authorizing the shooting of uniformed looters and rapists.[26] This would seem to throw the onus for these atrocities on to the Red Army rank and file rather than the Soviet establishment. But something does not quite compute. The Red Army had no compunction about shooting its *own* soldiers, sometimes for very minor infractions. Indeed, during the course of the war it is estimated to have executed a staggering 157,000 of them—the equivalent of fifteen divisions—of which more in a moment.[27] But on the specific issue of responsibility for mass atrocities committed against German non-combatants we are still left with a gaping dis-crepancy between what Red Army commanders were uttering in official commu-niqués and what was happening on the ground. However, given that those committing the offences—in the case of the rapes a very substantial part of the advancing Soviet armies—would have been fully aware of the punishment they would have suffered for any crossing of the line, this can only mean that the Soviet High Command was condoning in practice what it was repudiating in public broadcast.

This was hardly unique. The 'Rape of Nanking', in December 1937, offers a classic example, in this case of the Japanese High Command—another notably draconian, disciplinarian entity with regard to its own troops—*deliberately* allowing,
even encouraging, its field and divisional commanders to pursue a campaign of
relentless terror, murder, and rape against the Chinese population of the surrendered Kuomingtang capital.[28] We may infer motives similar to those of the Japanese
in the Russian onslaught on both German POWs and non-combatants. Vengeance
for what they—the Germans—had done to Russia and Russians certainly enabled
the translation of elite intent into demotic will. On this score, we might further
infer that the appetite and culpability of the Stalinist political establishment for the
infliction of as much hurt as possible on German society was provided with a convenient alibi in the form of a narration of these events as the inevitable, hence
unstoppable, desire for revenge on the part of its common soldiery.[29] Yet mass rape,
looting, and murder by Red Army units did not only take place as the Soviets
headed towards Berlin. The evidence is now very clear that the Russian entry into
Budapest in January 1945 was accompanied by a similar sequence of atrocities;
as was the Russian campaign for the liberation of Poland, a country—unlike
Hungary—which was meant to be a wartime ally.[30] In short, while Stalin's regime
may not have been motivated by any overt racial ideology, its sub-contracted campaign of military rape and violence did constitute a project to punish *in advance*
not just Germany but any state-society which stood in its path of Eastern European
conquest. Thereby, it made clear to the conquered peoples that their embrace
within the communist fold was final and irrevocable, and that any thought of
resistance was pointless. Or, as Callum MacDonald has put it with regard to the
Rape of Nanking, the aim was to underline 'the powerlessness of the community
and the superiority of the conqueror'.[31]

The sequence of atrocities—Nazi and Soviet—and the rationale behind them,
therefore, suggests something *more* than degenerate war. 'The difficult truth', affirm
Mark Edele and Michael Geyer, 'is that the escalation of violence during Operation Barbarossa was followed by much worse between 1942 and 1944—and again
in 1944/5.'[32] Yet for all the escalation, radicalization, and barbarization in the conduct of war itself, and the inevitable suffering inflicted on civilians which went
with it, an easy fit with something we might call genocide remains elusive. Returning to the Soviet component of these wartime atrocities, perhaps another complicating factor also needs to be taken into account. The British and Americans turned
a very definite blind eye to what the Russians were doing on their long march to
the Nazi capital. One could argue that they were hardly in a position to do otherwise when they were committing enough atrocities of their own by way of aerial
bombing, though one might add that their military-political elites did not see anything questionable in their own behaviour—at least not until quite late in the
bombing campaign. More significantly, because they were united with the USSR in
their joint project to arrive at the unconditional surrender of both Nazi Germany
and imperial Japan, any questioning of Soviet military behaviour in the months
leading up to total Nazi defeat would have been considered not just a breach of
diplomatic protocol but a direct threat to the integrity of the alliance.

However, behind Western Allied silence was a calculus which directly involved people's lives, more precisely Soviet lives *for* British, imperial, and US ones. From 1942 onwards, Stalin had been very publicly calling for a (Western) Second Front to relieve the burden on the Red Army struggle with the Wehrmacht. In the upshot, the true Second Front campaign beginning with the Normandy landings in June 1944 came after the major battles fought by the Red Army had decided the course of the war. Implicit recognition of the debt the USA and Britain owed to the Soviet state for the human losses it had suffered, while a substantial part of their own military forces had been conserved—that is, until such time as Western commanders considered them *ready* for the fray—translated into Western acquiescence in a variety of Russian actions, including, as we have already seen, the atrocities at Katyn. But this also extended at the end of the war to handing over not only large numbers of renegade Russian troops, Cossacks in particular, who had sided with the Germans,[33] but also, in Saxony and Bohemia, Wehrmacht soldiers who had surrendered not to the Russians but the Americans.[34] And this on top of their silence about the forcible deportation of non-combatants from Germany, Hungary, and elsewhere in Eastern Europe, for Gulag-style labour in the USSR.[35]

How far down the road Washington and London were in fact willing to go in aligning themselves with a Russian project of specifically German subjugation remains a moot point. In 1944, the USA on its own account drew up the Morgenthau Plan—named after the then treasury secretary—which envisaged the partition, demilitarization, and deindustrialization of a defeated Germany. High-level US and British critics were quick to point out that the programme was tantamount to wholesale starvation of Germany's urban population, while Goebbels' propaganda ministry, having caught on to Allied discussions on the subject, made hay with the story that Roosevelt and Churchill had bought into a 'Jewish murder plan', which almost certainly contributed to ordinary Germans' resolve to keep on fighting.[36] The fact that a proper implementation of the Plan could well have spelt levels of starvation in Germany, resembling that which the Nazis had envisaged in Russia had they been able to implement Generalplan Ost, clearly carries its own peculiar irony, not least as it would have offered a more thoroughgoing project of extermination—through the denial of food—than the Soviets achieved in 1945 through killing and mass rape. There is a further irony in that while the main elements of the Morgenthau Plan itself were quickly shelved, one of the factors which eventually led to US and British action to begin feeding the Germans in earnest and from there to move to the Marshall Recovery Plan, was anxiety that the German population in the Western Allied zones of occupation would see communism, under Soviet auspices, as the more endurable option.[37]

The preservation of lives, in the first instance the lives of servicemen of specifically British and US nationality, and latterly those of West Germans, was thus paid for by the Western Allies in sweeping territorial concessions to the Soviets; in effect amounting to the dismantling of the whole rimlands zone in Eastern Europe (of which more in our concluding chapter) and the long-term, onerous price of which was the Cold War. The price necessarily included a human cost, again largely at second hand, in the form of the German POWs and civilians forced into Soviet labour service, whom the West did not intercede for, and whose survivors did not return home in many cases until the mid-1950s; and, as we have already noted, the many thousands of Cossacks and other Soviet nationals who were forcibly handed over to the NKVD, and whose fate was either summary execution or a more gruelling and awful path to likely death in the Gulag system. All this above and beyond the huge programme of national deportations at war's end.

This brings us to one final aspect of Soviet degeneracy where the parallels are to be found most keenly with the Nazis, not the Western Allies. The destruction or incarceration of those who fought on the German side—who might arguably be described as traitors—was extended to whole swathes of Soviet men captured by or surrendered to the Germans, plus large numbers, including hundreds of thousands of women, forcibly deported to the Reich for labour service. In addition, more than half the 157,000 death sentences handed down by military tribunals which we noted earlier were for soldiers who had *escaped* from German POW camps or had fought their way out of encirclement, particularly in the early stages of the war.[38] Tsarist Russia had an almost unequalled military tradition of squandering its manpower in futile and ill-conceived military assaults. In this sense, the Stalinist mode was simply a reiteration of the most grotesque of old practices. But in this so-called 'Great Patriotic War', those who been spared execution for supposed military dereliction were, invariably, simply reassigned to NKVD-controlled 'penal battalions', otherwise made up of Gulag or other camp inmates, and thrown into impossible, pointless, and often consciously suicidal attacks on Wehrmacht lines.[39] On top of this heinous practice, to then often wilfully pack off into penal servitude first the families of these men, and then at war's end a substantial part of the over 5 million NKVD-screened returnees from German POW and labour camps,[40] speaks of a regime utterly incapable of valuing its *own* people save as a statistical-cum-geopolitical pool of fatalities to parade before and shame its Western Allies.

In the initial stages of the war—when Germany was winning—Hitler's true, comparable contempt for his own people was masked by projections of victory which would not simply preserve but revitalize the Aryan at the expense of the allegedly racially worthless. The violence and murder done to the latter would be consistently pursued to the bitter end—witness the ongoing killing of Jewish camp survivors as they were marched back into the Reich in early 1945. But by that point, Jewish deaths were being dwarfed by German: indeed, in the last nine and half months of war German military and civilian casualties rocketed to 4.8 million, a figure 2 million greater than the country's wartime losses for the whole period up to July 1944.[41] This human disaster was to a great extent a direct consequence of the Führer's resolve that the whole country would go down with him, as the flames engulfed the National Socialist edifice. There would be no retreat, no surrender, only scorched earth and capital punishment for those who disobeyed orders—including more than 15,000 death sentences carried out in the final months against Wehrmacht soldiery. Many thousands more ordinary Germans were also summarily shot or hanged at the hands of the SS or police.[42] Whether or not Hitler at the end was specifically responsible for orders to flood the S-bahn tunnels under Berlin, where tens of thousands of civilians were sheltering from the Soviet assault, his overall culpability for unnecessary *German* loss and suffering is unquestionable.[43] Like Stalin's Russia, thus, Hitler's Germany was a democidal regime, even if in its case the statistical tally of fatalities points much more to those killed outside its national territorial range, in other words, non-Germans, rather than those within. However, if this confirms an R.J. Rummel form of verdict on the proclivity of 'totalitarian' states towards mega-murder,[44] it does not in itself offer prima facie grounds for accepting the totality of German and Soviet deaths as a matter of genocide. Perhaps we need to approach some of the same sequence of events through a different entry-point.

THE WAR IN THE REAR

Viewed through the prism of Nazi intentions at the onset of Operation Barbarossa, we can discern a clear and thoroughgoing genocidal agenda. Hitler's grand vision was of an entire territorial and population reordering to the west of a burnt border zone—a *Brandstreifen*—stretching from Bakuto in the south through Stalingrad and Moscow to Leningrad in the north.[45] All unwanted peoples in this post-Soviet, German imperium would either be eradicated (by starvation or otherwise) or deported across the border strip to the east. The great towns and cities of European Russia would be literally razed and obliterated. A residual, entirely subservient Slavic agricultural population would continue to produce food for the benefit of the Reich, but in due course they too would be largely superseded by a stream of German-cum-Nordic settlers who, over succeeding generations, were expected to bring the Aryan overlord population to 100 million.[46] In addition to the General-plan Ost spatial and infrastructural reorganization of this vast region in favour of its ultimate Germanization, racial screening of the colonized population would ensure that there would be no possibility of 'fecund' Ukrainians or other Slavs winning a long-term demographic struggle with the colonizers. Where elements of the subject population were deemed racially of 'value', their assimilation could be countenanced. Children of 'good blood' could be more directly incorporated into the Teutonic fold through German foster-parents. For the rest, from summer 1942, forced sterilization or abortion of foetuses (even into the fifth or sixth month of pregnancy) was Hitler's preferred method of population control.[47]

Such projections unequivocally accord with Lemkin's descriptive contours of genocide and his assessment, equally developed in *Axis Rule*, of what Nazi empire-building would look like. Certainly, *on paper*, the Generalplan Ost blueprint envis-aged a social and demographic engineering so great and relentless as to put the scale of any Stalinist equivalent, even in its most radical, implicitly exterminatory, collectivization-cum-famine phase, in the shade. Yet *in practice*, the Nazis could not deliver on their genocidal projections, at least not in the form envisaged. At bottom, this was simply a consequence of military failure. Without the defeat of the USSR, any German project to systematically reduce its indigenous population remained as stillborn as did its other grand design, to remove Europe's non-Soviet Jews to Madagascar, without the defeat of Britain. In other words, just as in the latter case so in the former, the intended genocidal path became transformed through entirely unanticipated contingencies into something quite different.

Actually, even this assessment may be too generous to the clarity of Nazi pre-invasion plans. Speaking of Poland in 1939, Jan Gross has rather provocatively posed the possibility that 'the Nazis were not cold-blooded enough to contemplate and openly elaborate a theory of empire based on genocide'.[48] Such sensibilities, if they existed, clearly do not compute with the manner in which the Wehrmacht liquidated Soviet POWs two years later. However, there is surely a case to be made for how the Nazis failed to do their sums properly with regard to the deleterious consequences to *themselves* of a very rapid decimation of the Soviet population. The failing is rather graphically captured in this extract from a senior, on-the-spot, Wehrmacht logistics officer, in early December 1941:

> If we shoot dead all the Jews, allow the POWs to die, deliver up the large part of the population of all the major towns to death by starvation, also lose part of the rural population through hunger during the coming year; the question still remains: who shall be left to do anything of economic value?[49]

The critique is all the more telling because by this time it was clear there was not going to be any immediate or even distant vanquishing of the Soviets, and that sustaining the German military struggle against them would be dependent, above all, on providing the Wehrmacht with food and hence an accompanying local labour force to supply it. As a result, we are confronted with the peculiar situation of some of the most hard-line, even genocidal practitioners in Wehrmacht and OMi ranks becoming among the most vociferous proponents of food relief to starving—primarily Ukrainian—peasants and workers. Among this unlikely crew of crypto-doves, for instance, was General von Reichenau, whom we have previously met as a leading mass murderer of Soviet Jews, POWs, and 'partisans'. His position, thus, in pressing for German-sponsored land reform, or even some level of local political autonomy—as equally supported in OMi by Rosenberg and Kube—had little or nothing to do with softening sentiments towards subaltern Slavs. Instead, it was impelled by pragmatic considerations, rather in keeping with how 'productionists' supported the survival of Polish-Jewish ghetto inhabitants against their 'attritionist' critics.[50]

This parallel Jewish experience, however, hardly offers comfort. The technical skills of a Jewish remnant in the Soviet rimlands, as also in Poland—as we know—offered no more than a temporary reprieve. And if there were those of the ilk of Kube who would willingly have continued with the arrangement, they were overruled by an SS apparatus which took its orders ultimately from Hitler. By the same token, we might infer that Nazi high policy in principle did not deviate from its anticipation of a similar end for Ukrainians, Russians, and other rimlands *Untermenschen*. After the open extermination of Soviet Jewry, there was certainly widespread anticipation among much of the rest of the population that they would be next in line.[51] If the general brutality of German behaviour seemed to confirm this verdict, even so the Nazi need for an ongoing labour supply, and not just of slave labour which might be used today and dispensed with tomorrow, seemed to offer a rather different outlook. The complication, even contradiction, moreover, seemed to go one stage further when, as we have already seen, the German authorities began widening the scope of those who could be inducted into the gendarmerie, other auxiliary units, or into the local administration of the occupied territories. From the Nazi perspective, to have begun arming elements of the local population over and beyond ethnic Germans, or the supposedly more 'racially' acceptable Estonians and Latvians, could only have been entered into with the greatest of reluctance, not to say psychological resistance. Yet there was a straightforward issue of necessity at stake. Behind the military front there were literally millions of hectares which the Germans could not control or administer on their own: the same arena in which fully-fledged partisan warfare had the genuine potential to unravel German rule for good. It is within this essentially—at least in the long term—untenable situation of occupation but not victory, a desire to throttle the indigenous population yet at the same time the need to utilize it as an auxiliary military or labour resource, that there emerged in place of the predetermined policy of population reduction a much more *reactive*, on-the-hoof set of exterminatory German occupation responses.

It has been suggested that as many as a million Soviet citizens in Nazi-controlled Russia became active collaborators with the occupation regime.[52] That in itself suggests that a more coherent German policy reformulation in support of the aspirations of rimlands peoples—even if still under German tutelage—could have brought on board a great many more, and in so doing helped shore up Berlin's ability and capacity to hold on to some or all of its 1941 and even 1942 territorial gains. Such a radical policy shift would be supported by quite standard counter-insurgency thinking as developed by post-war Western colonial and neo-colonial strategists. Their development in particular of the notion of 'hearts and minds' puts considerable emphasis on suffocating the spread of any incipient insurgency by isolating the insurgents from the majority population. But ipso facto such a result can only be achieved by offering incentives to the majority (sometimes involving in a literal sense buying them) to come on side. Or at least so the theorizing goes.[53]

Putting aside whether or not such thinking is generally efficacious, it certainly requires a huge leap of imagination to envisage a *Nazi* undertaking in this direction, especially in their Eastern imperium. That said, there remain some unsettling paradoxes. For one, Rosenberg's preferred 'soft' route to the preservation of German Eastern hegemony through a satellite system of quasi-autonomous national rimlands entities, plus the sweeping away of Soviet collectivized agriculture, not only suggested a degree of continuity with a Ludendorff-type model from the post-Brest-Litovsk period but was also the obvious counterpoint to any 'hearts and minds' military strategy: as Alexander Dallin has put it, a 'simplified recipe for the immunisation of the East'.[54] Second, everything from our previous chapter would point to there being no good reason why the near total genocide of the Jews in the arena would have stood as a block to local national movements giving their full, or at least qualified, support to the Nazis; provided, of course, that they could be assured of the latter's good intentions towards *them*.[55] Third, there is Stalin's reading of what was happening in the rimlands in the absence of Soviet rule. We will return to this in the next chapter, but suffice it to say that his personal expectation that a substantial proportion of the rimlands peoples *would* treacherously defect to the Nazi alternative was at complete variance with the official Moscow line of their eagerness for a happy, fraternal, and inevitable reunification with the victorious USSR. Perhaps the significant thing about Stalin was that there was always a half-truth to fuel the paranoia. And one which—in theory at least—might have been exploited by the Nazis in favour of their own self-preservation. Eventually, even Himmler grasped the nettle. But that was too little too late, and by then, anyway, the damage was irrevocable.

That damage came above all from two directions. It arose first as a consequence of the standard Nazi dictum—entirely in accord with traditional Wilhelmine military practice—that any form of people-based resistance would be met with lethal collective retribution. Given the racialized nature of Nazi self-understanding, the colonial underpinnings of their eastern undertaking, the irrelevance of Hague and Geneva-style limitations, and the fundamental zero-sum aspect of the struggle, it was inevitable that once straightforward military victory had eluded them, Wehrmacht behaviour in the rear would rapidly lurch towards more extreme responses—regardless of whether the ethnographic zone in question was a potentially 'friendly' one or not.

But the German direction of travel was also greatly exacerbated by the nature of Soviet and more specifically Stalin's input on the matter. As we have suggested in terms of a paradox, Stalin was *not* enthused by the idea of partisan warfare. Almost as a mirror image of Nazi thinking, for him to have unreservedly supported a Soviet armed insurrection at several degrees remove from Moscow's control—especially in the shatter-zone arena familiar to him from the civil war period—would have been tantamount to offering a hostage to fortune—especially should such an insurrection have developed its own independent momentum or perhaps even Makhno-like agenda. The previous Red Army schools created exactly with the invasion scenario in mind had all been dismantled along with their instructors and cadres during the purges. As a consequence, despite Stalin's initial call soon after Operation Barbarossa for Soviet citizens to rise up behind enemy lines, the partisan movement's initial bark was altogether greater than its bite. It was largely made up of party personnel, or Red Army units marooned behind the front line. And, until mid-1942, there was nothing anywhere close to a centralized command structure. Perhaps more significantly, from our perspective, the movement began as largely Russian or Belorussian, and hence lacked any significant rimlands components.[56]

No matter that it was not until that point that the partisan struggle really began to take off. Stalin's great success a year earlier was in conjuring up the illusion of a genuine 'people's war', to which nightmare Hitler responded by playing straight into the Soviet dictator's hands. Claiming that 'this partisan war . . . gives us the opportunity to exterminate anyone who looks askance at us'—an uncanny resemblance in itself with the Kaiser's 1900 utterances against Chinese Boxer insurrectionists[57]—the continuing stream of ever more apocalyptically shrill orders from Hitler, or the Army High Command, to the point where a December 1942 directive specifically forbade commanders on the ground the option *not* to kill women and children, ensured that many rimlands communities which in 1941 had been handing over partisans to the occupation authorities by 1943 were responding just as Stalin wanted them to.[58] Thus, initially conjured up as a phantom war, primarily in the minds of the two dictators, the partisan struggle had by then turned into a self-fulfilling prophecy of gargantuan proportions. And moreover, one in which the mutual escalation of conflict provided classic conditions for a dialectic of violence whose primary mass victims were those caught in the middle.

*

Nowhere better illustrates the results than what happened in Belorussia in the course of 1941–4. Here a War Type Three reached its absolute nadir. Indeed, the scale of German mass murder, over and beyond battlefield killing, was greater in this region than anywhere else in the entire European war theatre, accounting for between 1.6 and 1.7 million fatalities. Clearly this of itself needs some extrapolation. Christian Gerlach, arguably the leading specialist on the conflict, has broken down the numbers as follows. 700,000 Soviet POWs mostly murdered or starved to death in the wake of Operation Barbarossa. On top of that almost the entirety of the region's Jews, some half a million people, the last remnants of whom were liquidated by German security forces in the summer and autumn of 1943. In addition, 320,000 'other' people done to death as 'partisans', of whom the vast majority were Belorussian peasants—in other words 'ordinary' men, women, and children. These figures do not include those killed by authentic Soviet partisans, of which more below.[59] And there were also the several hundred thousand more Belorussian men killed in action as Red Army soldiers. Add on top of this the entirety of German or Soviet forced deportations either to the east or west between 1939 and 1945, and one ends up with Snyder's staggering verdict of half the 10.6 million pre-war population of the region 'killed or moved' in the course of the war.[60]

If, however, we were to concentrate simply on the partisan war, the figures would remain bewildering enough. One single German battle group tasked with defeating the partisans ended up with a tally of over 34,000 in the period between November 1942 through to March 1943 alone, or, put another way, an average of some 200, nearly all *civilian*, deaths every day of the campaign.[61] The very concentration of 'specialist' troops in this Army Group Centre rear area is telling. We may remember the particular role of HSSPF Bach-Zelewski as Himmler's right-hand man in the escalation of the Jewish mass murder under the pretext of partisan warfare in this same area, more specifically around the Pripet marshes, in late July 1941. It was Bach, at his own suggestion, who was reassigned by Himmler as inspector plenipotentiary of the so-called *Bandenkämpfverbände* ('Band-fighting Units'), in late summer 1942, with one might add some 15,000 German and nearly 240,000 *Schutzmänner* at his disposal for the pursuit of the counter-insurgency campaign. Jeckeln, that other notorious *génocidaire*, also figured prominently in this new range of operations, as commander of the first major 'sweep' with responsibility for the murder of over 18,000 people between late August and late September.[62]

The obvious question, though, is why here? Why was Belorussia the very epicentre of the partisan war? The answer in critical part purely a matter of geography. In the southern third of the republic, contiguous with the Ukraine, is Polesie, with its huge area of Pripet swamp, impassable to mechanized transport. As a result not only did the region provide thick cover and a line of retreat for guerrilla fighters; it also happened to offer the obvious corridor for their infiltration on foot, as they might head westwards from the Russian heartland into the *kresy* and rimlands 'proper'. The corridor's strategic importance thus might be compared with the Ho Chi Minh trail straddling Vietnam and Cambodia, in a later war, which a generation of US counter-insurgency strategists sought to obliterate by ever-widening blanket bombing—with inevitably catastrophic consequences for the peoples (and eco-systems) of that Indo-China border area. As with both US and North Vietnamese strategists, however, their German and Russian counterparts from some quarter of a century earlier recognized that *their* war hinged on the course of this emerging front behind the Front. Indeed, when Hitler spoke in October 1942 of 'the struggle against the partisans' as 'a life-and-death struggle in which one side or the other must be exterminated', he for once might have been speaking something close to the truth.[63]

In this, of course, there is a further supreme irony. As we know, the Soviet ethnic community on to whom the Nazis projected the entire responsibility for any would-be insurgency was the Jews. And to be sure, there were perhaps as many as 50,000 Belorussian Jews who fled from the ghettos to the forests, where they might have become if not the kernel then at least a *part of* a resistance effort.[64] Indeed, there was one Jewish partisan formation, the several hundred strong Bielski brigade which in recent times has become little short of revered. Yet Bielski's first priority was rescuing Jews—women and children included—and then keeping them alive, rather than fighting Nazis per se. Moreover, his unit was very unusual, first for its autonomy, second for its survival—most fleeing Jews were caught and killed by the Germans—and third because it still managed to cooperate with official Soviet partisan units.[65] Here we encounter another aspect of the irony: Soviet partisans, certainly initially, were very suspicious of unarmed, untrained Jewish escapees and of their intrinsic worth to the partisan cause, underlining thereby the gaping void between Hitler's fantasy of Jewish partisan threat and the reality on the ground. Very often, indeed, *real* partisans simply killed Jews.[66]

But then, it was not only Jews of whom Soviet commissars were wary. Belorussians, too, as and where they were inducted into the ranks, were to begin with accepted—just as were Jews—on grounds not of their ethnic background but of their party loyalty and hence reliability in the Soviet cause. Belorussian nationality, in any case, had always been considered by the Bolsheviks as little more than a convenient sophistry for dividing up a chunk of the western rimlands into a republic. With the partisan movement thus, initially, a largely extraneous Moscow import, with indeed many of the trainers and cadres parachuted into occupied territory, it was quite conceivable that any subsequent Soviet strategy to develop a grass-roots insurgency in this area, as elsewhere, might have remained stillborn. What ultimately gave the impetus was less the eventual shift of Soviet emphasis towards creating an authentic mass people's movement than the fundamental inability of the Germans to win rimlands 'hearts and minds'. If there were Wehrmacht intelligence officers who recognized the urgency of the task,[67] the more general, not to say obdurate, German failure at the very least to find ways and means of enabling the protection of the local population from the partisans, and treatment of the latter's attacks instead as evidence of the intrinsic culpability of all, ensured precisely the self-fulfilling aspects of the Nazi incubus. This, of course, combined with the other key factor which drove rimlands youth, both male and female, en masse into partisan ranks: the ever more draconian measures to press them into labour service bound for the Reich.[68]

This did not mean that partisan commissars on the ground stood idly by. At the very onset of Operation Barbarossa, Belorussian communist party directives had used bloodcurdling language to incite the populace to attack Wehrmacht targets[69]—again, almost as a mirror image of the Nazi projection. But the partisan leadership's more targeted aim appears to have been to quite consciously provoke the Germans towards an escalation of their reprisal policy against the indigenous population. One route towards this goal was *not* by attacking large German formations but focusing instead on murdering either small, isolated Wehrmacht units, or more particularly supposed *local* collaborators *and* their families. Alexander Prusin, for instance, notes than in the area around Slonim between April and November 1942, of the 1,024 persons partisans killed, only 112 were Germans, a substantially larger number low-level administrators and policemen, while the vast majority were teachers, writers, and 'members of educational, cultural and professional organisations that had worked for the Germans'.[70] By sewing terror thus, amongst people who were Soviet citizens, the partisans knew that they could thereby ensure German retaliation, and so make clear to the population at large that nobody would remain safe behind a wall of German bayonets—with the added bonus of the elimination of a budding native, non-communist national elite who, on Red Army liberation, might have become the focus for renewed resistance to the reimposition of Stalinist conformity.

If, then, the partisans were themselves responsible for the murder of many tens of thousands of people on Belorussian soil over and beyond the official figure of 17,431 killed as 'traitors',[71] the Germans inadvertently served the Soviet cause by a blanket retribution against *anybody* suspected of being just that. This included Belorussian nationalists; in other words, the very people best placed to at least attempt to assist bringing the population 'on side'. In spring 1942, for instance, some of their leaders were executed for daring to publicly criticize the Germans for burning down villages. By September the following year, when a German administrative office in Minsk was blown up by partisans, the SD administered 'justice' by arbitrarily rounding up and shooting 300 people in two adjacent streets—including not just women and children but many individuals known to be anti-communist, German sympathizers.[72]

In the scale of German atrocities, this represented hardly more than another minor incident. But it might go some way to explaining why so many Belorussians who might have stuck with the Germans went over to the partisans. The numbers included over 12,000 *Schutzmänner* and policemen who defected in the wake of Stalingrad.[73] The rise of the resistance movement in Belorussia was certainly meteoric. A force which was estimated to number 57,000 in January 1943 had swelled to nearly double that number by September.[74] Whether or not numbers ever reached the figure of 283,000 active combatants claimed by the commander of the Belorussian partisan brigade, it is clear that of some half million partisans operating for the Soviet cause in the occupied regions by the time of liberation, a very substantial number were doing so in the Belorussian sector.[75]

Such numbers would further suggest the success of Stalin's 'people's war', or put another way a mobilization which fused popular and party will or, to continue the Vietnamese analogy, communism and nationalism. But there is a harsher way of viewing this outcome—and its consequence. Physically able Belorussians who joined the insurgents did so because there was nowhere else to go. Or alternatively, they continued to vigorously fight as German stooges, for pretty much the same reason. The choice, in other words, was between getting aboard an accelerating train or trying to stop it in its tracks. But for the majority peasant population—in other words, those too old, young, sick, or disabled to move, and most obviously women in the absence of their menfolk as heads of households and often, in addition, mothers, possibly pregnant mothers, with children: they were the *tracks*. And to be there presented about as much room for manoeuvre as it had to their forbears in the struggles between Reds, Whites, nationalists, foreign interventionists, and free-booting warlords during the civil war period. In 1942 and 1943, to be sure, at the height of the struggle, the situation was more clear cut. There were the Soviet partisans who might appear in your village at any time. They would make speeches, demands, and accusations. They would administer rough justice to those deemed collaborators. Where they took it into their heads that the whole village had been complicit, they might kill everyone.[76] Of course, they might be people you identified as like you: speaking your language, including people you might recognize, possibly even from the village itself. By contrast, you were likely to live in complete fear of the Germans. But then if word got out that the partisans had been in your neck of the woods, and they—the Germans—sent out somebody at the crack of dawn to dispense some seriously rough justice against *you* for *their* crime, it might well be meted out by local administrators and policemen who, far from being foreign, were equally people you identified as like you: who spoke your language, and included people you might recognize, possibly even from the village itself.

In other words, if this is to denote mass killing as a consequence of War Type Three, the grass-roots communal aspect of the dialectic would appear to be less the result of any wildly popular acclamation for the insurgency, more a case of an essentially sedentary population being caught, or more exactly squeezed in the middle of Nazi state versus partisan conflict. Inbuilt in this situation was an element of civil war, but with the overwhelming majority of the casualties neither actual partisans, nor Germans, but 'ordinary' people. In this sense, Shaw's degenerate war thesis is entirely apposite. We might also want to add that the German SS-cum-military response was markedly like earlier German and wider European colonial practice in the way it held whole communities responsible for the armed resistance within their midst. That, with the one important caveat that behind the partisans' struggle was an immensely—and indeed increasingly—powerful Soviet imperial juggernaut, not the sort of patron the Herero or Nama might have been able to look to, in an earlier instance of unadulterated German colonial genocide.

Paradoxically, the awareness of an encroaching Red Army almost definitely contributed to the desperation and hence escalation of Nazi violence in the rear. Having eschewed the possibility of winning over the occupied population, an inversion of the Maoist dictum as to the insurgent fish swimming in a people's sea became an almost inevitable consequence of the German effort to prevent a complete military destabilization of front *and* rear. To starve the fish, the sea had to be drained. Ipso facto, the extremities to which the Germans went to accomplish this forlorn task contained their own inner logic. Riding out from their garrisons to eradicate pockets here, there, and everywhere of reported partisan attacks became an almost relentless but futile enterprise. Pinning responsibility for the attacks on the Jews was transparently useless by the end of 1942, when practically all of them had long been exterminated or incarcerated in slave-labour camps. And moving in force into the rural hinterland itself provided all the warning needed for the partisans themselves to melt back into the forest and swamp. That left the villagers upon whom to wreak retribution.

Eyewitness testimonies of German methods provide an all too vivid account of the results. In the Brest region, on 22 and 23 September 1942, three villages centring on Zabloitse were encircled one by one by Order Police Battalion 310, the menfolk forced to dig the graves, then the entire communities, primarily women and their children—bar a small element spared on grounds of their alleged 'reliability'—were massacred in the subsequent hours of daylight in a manner not so different from the better known Battalion 101 mass murders of Polish Jews of the Lublin district.[77] With one critical difference. In the Jewish killings, the villages and their non-Jewish inhabitants remained. In these antipartisan 'actions', the peasants' livestock was removed, the surrounding farmland torched, and the villages, as well as surrounding *khutors* (hamlets) and farmsteads, all burnt to the ground.

Hundreds died in each of the Brest killings. However, the scale of these mass murders was dwarfed by an almost simultaneous Volhynian Polesie massacre at the village of Kortelisy, near Ratne. There had already been executions of alleged partisans' relatives here in the summer. But this time not only the entire village but also peasants from surrounding villages were ordered to convene in Kortelisy's central square on 23 September. Here they found themselves effectively 'kettled' by Schuma squads, while the local district commissioner announced to them that, with the exception of a handful of village elders plus local police auxiliaries and their families, everyone was to be shot by the German Order Police company on hand for their involvement in partisan resistance. In fact, they were dispatched by a range of means. Of the 2,875 people killed that day, large numbers were women drowned in a pond, while others were bayoneted, or shot by pistol or sub-machine gun. Some villagers actually did escape or managed to hide. However, the death toll among these alleged partisan helpers included a staggering 1,624 children.[78]

On its own, alongside Oradour and Lidice, Kortelisy should stand as one of the great German-perpetrated, non-Jewish, civilian massacre atrocities of the Second World War. Yet not only is it almost unknown in the West, it also happens to be just an opening shot in a sequence of German counter-insurgency 'band-fighting' operations which obliterated 900 Belorussian villages and turned much of the former republic and surrounding areas into 'desertified' *tote Zonen*—'dead zones'. Yet this quite conscious German designation on its own suggests the degree to which any supposed military strategy of partisan containment had become almost an irrelevance by 1943. Operation after operation throughout the early spring, with ever more unlikely or discordant codenames—Easter Bunny, Gypsy Baron, Cottbus, the final one supposedly to 'clear' a huge area north of Minsk—all failed to defeat the insurgency, and had to find efficacy instead in daily kill quotas, as if to prove that the anti-partisan war was being won. The obvious and rather disturbing parallel is with the US 'body counts' from Vietnam and other post-1945 counter-insurgency campaigns,[79] which in turn might be to give the erroneous impression that a range of such modern operations were equally egregious.

That said, the parallels cannot be so easily elided. Creating what amounts to free-fire zones in which land and forest are scorched to remove cover, crops cleared or destroyed, and the livestock extracted has been standard military practice to sap a people's will to resist since time immemorial. So have raids, sometimes referred to as 'butcher and bolt',[80] where the aim is to enter an otherwise insurgent-controlled zone, eliminate the popular base of the insurgency, and then withdraw, in effect conceding that the zone in question is not recoverable to the recognized authority. If this was a major aspect of the USA's failing campaign in South Vietnam, it took on an even more violent ferocity in German-occupied Belorussia, where a 'special' Waffen-SS *Jagdkommando* unit, under Dr Oskar Dirlewanger, was at the forefront of a variety of military and paramilitary formations let loose for the purpose. The unit had already made its notorious mark back in 1940 on account of the manner in which it had combined alcohol-fuelled mayhem with the poisoning, torture, and murder of Jews and Roma in one of the camps it ran in Globocnik's Lublin hell. Perhaps this should not surprise when one discovers that the Dirlewanger brigade was unusual both for its specific intake of jail- or insane asylum-released criminals, paedophiles, psychopaths, rapists, and sadists included, and its later willingness to accommodate Slavic, including Russian, fighters, many with similar personal histories. We can clearly make some comparison here with the operatives of the *Teşkilât-ı Mahsusa* and similar *çetes*. The Dirlewanger men certainly also had their own penchant for pyromania: regularly herding their victims into large barns, setting fire to them, and then machine-gunning anybody who tried to escape. During their Belorussian tour of duty they are estimated to have been responsible for the deaths of at least 30,000 unarmed men, women, and children.[81]

Another variation on a more contemporary theme was the limited German attempt to subcontract a whole district to a native protégé, in effect a local warlord. The notion of strategic hamlets where insurgents would come face to face with armed and well-supported opponents from among the local population was to prove yet another unproductive counter-insurgency doctrine promulgated by the USA in Vietnam. Under Nazi aegis, the nearest equivalent was provided by Bronislav Kaminsky, a half-ethnic-German, half-Polish, anti-communist collaborator who had originally persuaded his immediate Wehrmacht command to provide a form of local autonomy in the Central Russian region to which he had been previously exiled by the Soviet authorities, in return for the creation of an indigenous 'band-fighting' unit. The result was on the one hand the so-called Russian National Liberation Army (RONA), on the other the so-called Republic of Lokot, both of which, as Mark Mazower has noted, the clearly psychopathic Kaminsky lorded it over with his 'own Kurtz-like penchant for violence'.[82]

Inevitably, the Lokot experiment, the most significant non-military part of which was the abolition of collectivized farms, did not last, not least as the Kaminsky brigade became more and more taken up with anti-partisan operations. But the fact that Kaminsky had 10,000 men under his personal command and a similar tally (mostly non-combatants) they had slaughtered, ensured Himmler's ongoing critical support, at least for the time being. It was this which enabled Kaminsky to reform his brigade first in eastern and then in western Belorussia, after the near-disastrous collapse of the German central Russian front from summer 1943. There were to be no more experiments of the Lokot type. Instead, in early 1944, the brigade was attached alongside Dirlewanger's—with whom it was already sharing compositional characteristics—to a much larger anti-partisan formation. Significantly, both of these most obviously blood-crazed units played significant roles in the last phase of Nazi mass murder in the Belorussian arena.[83]

There is moreover a final twist to this trajectory. If anti-partisan warfare at least in principle had previously operated on the basis of the need to kill actual or potential male insurgents, the necessity by now was to spare such young adults and their female contemporaries, and deliver them *alive* for slave labour in the Reich.[84] In other words, by this juncture, the Nazis had long given up on controlling Belorussia, the Ukraine, or indeed anywhere much in the rimlands. The whole focus instead had become simply one of labour and resource extraction on the one hand, denying that resource to the returning Soviets on the other. Another parallel might be noted, this time with the shift from 1941 to 1942 in the contours of gendered Jewish extermination. As with the Jews, so now a year or more on, it was the Slavic old, young, women, and children who were expendable, not because they presented a threat per se, but simply because they had no value as moveable bodies. Thousands paid for it with their lives.

Does this suggest that the nature and course of German anti-partisan warfare in the occupied East was ultimately determined less by ideology than by situational circumstances? The inference is particularly bewildering, as by implication it might imply that other states (whatever their avowedly democratic or liberal credentials), finding themselves equally ground down in a War Type Three, might respond in similar fashion. The obvious retort might be that responsibility therefore lies with the state in question not to get itself into the situation in the first place. To which again, one might reply, yes, but supposing for instance a popular insurgency had developed in a defeated Germany as Nazi die-hards urged: how might the victorious Allies have been forced to respond then? That question is mercifully counterfactual. No such insurgency *properly* materialized.[85]

But that might still leave the parallel with Vietnam. The USA and its allies consciously sought a confrontation here—the assumption being that they would militarily win. When this went horribly wrong, they not only found themselves in a conflict from which they were unable to extricate themselves in an orderly way, but in one in which the only military response could be increasing levels of violence against the insurgent-supporting, or at least sheltering, population. Clearly the Americans were not Nazis, and clearly they did not enter into repeated campaigns where *the aim* was to liquidate whole communities of this kind as the latter did in Belorussia, and in large parts of the Ukraine too. But the results of the US assault on Vietnam and by extension Indo-China more generally became so horrendous that the charge of genocide was very openly brought against them by several NGOs as well as public intellectuals.[86]

Paradoxically, however, if such charges fall down in the US case because no evidence can be adduced of a policy-making decision or decisions to exterminate the Vietnamese (whether in whole or in part), the same might also be true of the Germans in their anti-partisan struggles in the east. While genocide became Nazi policy against the Jews, regardless of whether there was a pre-existing blueprint or not, the mass murder of Belorussians as it developed especially in 1942 and 1943 was motivated by no rhyme or reason other than the effort to suffocate the growing success and territorial encroachment of the Soviet partisan movement. Resisting taking this sequence as an example of genocide certainly involves a rather fine distinction, even to the point of pedantry. And it certainly offers no consolation to the hundreds of thousands of Belorussians and Ukrainians murdered. But then, perhaps it is also a sombre reminder that hell on earth does not require the appellation 'genocide' to be so. There again, because this sequence of German rear-area warfighting did not proceed from strategic action to policy implementation, does this mean that other examples where the term might seem more apt, are also precluded?

*

Perhaps we need to reprise the situation in Nazi-controlled Poland, and how different it was, at least until quite late in the day, from that in occupied Belorussia. Bar isolated acts, there was no *widespread* evidence of partisan insurgency in the General Government—bar the Warsaw uprising in the Jewish ghetto—until 1943. This was not because of lack of will or preparation. The whole Polish societal effort was geared towards the moment when the underground AK might strike the blow which would deliver their country back to them—that is, before the anticipated arrival of the Red Army. Unlike the Belorussians, therefore, the Poles needed no outside goad to resist. The intensity of Polish patriotism indeed was not only in marked contrast to the lukewarm nationalism of their immediate neighbours due east, but was an ongoing incitement in itself to the German occupiers. So long as Poles saw themselves as Poles, there was German intent towards their 'denationalization'. This, as

we have noted, from a Lemkinian perspective already implied a form of genocide—with or without actual physical annihilation. But as Germans and Poles were
already locked into a dialectical struggle, it was inevitable that almost any act of
resistance would be treated by the authorities as a pretext for mass killing: witness,
as we already have, the AB-*Aktion* and its summer 1940 aftermath.

The emotional impact on the Polish intelligentsia of these events was sufficiently
intense, and so clearly pointed towards their complete destruction that considerations of a *sauve qui peut* nature began to infiltrate some elite thinking. Archbishop
Adamski in Silesia, for instance, ordered both clergy and people to register on the
German Volkeslist as a way of avoiding the fate of the hundreds of priests in Silesia
and Pomerania who had already been sent to concentration camps and murdered.[87]
At least 2 million Poles in the annexed territories actually sought the status, even
while this made their menfolk liable for Wehrmacht service. In a trice, it had become
better to be a Pomeranian, a Masurian, a Kashubian, than a Pole.[88] Or even to
accept, as in one exceptional case of collaboration in the Podhale mountain region
bordering with Slovakia, an appointment as 'Führer' over Goral mountain-dwellers
now designated, under Himmler's auspices, as a species of sub-German exotica.[89]

If this reminds us that, as further east—as also in western Europe—there were
Poles too who ducked, weaved, and even sometimes were prepared to throw in
their lot with the Germans, for the majority, opposition to Nazi rule, most especially in the General Government, was not only consistently 'national' but also
fuelled by a deep underlying fear that what awaited them was most certainly physical destruction. It was the visibility of the Jewish fate which by late 1942 was the
thing most tangibly driving them towards this conclusion. 'Grot' Rowecki, for
instance, in preparing a new set of AK orders in early November, tried to hold on
to the idea that the primary German objective was Polish absorption, though his
very next sentence read, 'Attempts to exterminate the resistant segments of our
nation by the methods applied against the Jews, however, cannot be ruled out'.
Seventeen days later, in a public declaration, the government-in-exile was articulating this position in altogether more apocalyptic terms, claiming not only that what
'today is taking place in relation to the Jews will tomorrow affect those that remain'
but equally stating that German activities amounted to 'an attempt to destroy the
Polish nation and wipe out any trace of its existence'.[90]

Was this just attention grabbing on the part of a Polish government aware of its
diminishing purchase with London and Washington, or was this *cri de coeur* actually
grounded in a sense of some imminent German foreclosure on the Polish nation? Up
to late 1942, there is plenty of evidence to confirm that Polish society, even without
the complete, though almost entirely *separate* liquidation of its Jews, was being relentlessly pulverized through hunger, forced labour to the Reich, and incarceration in
Majdanek, Auschwitz, and a host of other camps. We have already inferred the contrast with the Czech situation, where in spite of the iron grip of Nazi occupation, talk
of mass deportations from there had largely receded by the end of 1942. Indeed,
German dependency on Czech industrial workers for the war effort ensured something approaching normality for the Gentile population of the Protectorate—if anything in the final years of the war can be described as such. Meanwhile, Nazi leaders

continued to utter exterminatory vituperations against eastern Slavs. In 1944, Hans Frank for instance, envisaged a post-war world in which 'the Poles and Ukrainians and their like may be chopped into small pieces'.[91]

But while wish-fulfilment of this type may tell us a lot about mindsets, it does not necessarily offer us the most accurate guide to practical, even Nazi practical politics in the final two years of Nazi rule in Poland. Frank, in fact, was among those in the ruling establishment who sought to make concessions to the Poles, even on matters of political autonomy, just as had the German occupying authorities in Warsaw a world war earlier. So too, interestingly, speaking for elements of the security apparatus, did Bach-Zelewski, who urged that something needed to be done to win the AK over for the purposes of a common anti-Bolshevik crusade. After the Katyn revelations and the subsequent breakdown in official Polish–Soviet relations, the inference may not have been so utterly absurd. And indeed a small entourage of Polish political and religious leaders during 1943, a captured 'Grot' included, were courted accordingly.[92]

Is the subsequent failure of these overtures then tantamount to blaming the victims? There was little in the way of positive Polish response, bar from the Endek radical right, to the General Government blandishments, 'Grot' for the AK 'mainstream' paying with his life for his refusal to cooperate. And it is not difficult to see why. There had already been more than three years of undiluted violence and emasculation for which Frank and his like were responsible. While 'Grot' himself may not have been quite convinced that 'methods applied against the Jews' would also come to be applied against the Poles, he did claim in his November 1942 orders that he had made contingency plans of last resort for such a situation. And in this lies one element critical to what transpired subsequently. Whatever some of the Nazi crypto-doves in the General Government were thinking, or claiming, as to a more benevolent policy shift—and one has to add that their efforts were quite extraordinary in their cack-handedness, one-dimensionality, and cynicism—for most Poles little or nothing could budge them from a conviction that what the Germans actually intended was their obliteration. They were indeed brought to this conclusion, said the Wehrmacht commander in the General Government no less, on two counts: one, the raids—the *Fangaktionen*—to impress them into Reich labour work; two, the mass murder of the Jews, in which the Poles saw 'an atrocious picture of their own destiny'.[93]

Looking at the situation not with hindsight but from the time and place itself, who could fault this assessment? The Polish population in the *kresy* was already being sucked into the *Bandenkreig* in mid-1942, and AK efforts to defend them provided pretext for the SD murder of over 1,000 members of their intelligentsia in the area around Slonim and Baranovichi.[94] Both in the Polesie and Volhynia, the Polish minority position was complicated by Belorussian and Ukrainian national agendas, as we will see in the final section of this chapter. However, further to the west, around Zamość, in Lublin district, the German–Polish showdown was much more clear cut, as well as dramatic. What the Poles saw here, beginning in November 1942, was a concerted effort by Globocnik, still the SS regional supremo, to empty the entire locality of all its 100,000 and more inhabitants and repopulate the district with half as many German settlers. To appreciate exactly how the Poles would have understood this unfolding project we need first to remember that Globocnik's rule had made of the Lublin region the original epicentre of Polish-Jewish destruction. As for its country-wide extension, November 1942 was still in the midst of Operation Reinhard, again with results, in terms of Jewish depopulation and destruction, all too visible to the victims' Polish neighbours. The radical methods by which Globocnik's units cleared 116 villages in the first five-month phase of the parallel Zamość campaign—with the terminus for large numbers of the deportees either Majdanek or Auschwitz—could not but have aroused the fear that this was no more than a trial-run for a wider Polish Reinhard.[95]

Supposing, instead, the Polish underground had been able to lay their hands on Himmler's Generalplan Ost blueprint, would their fears have been assuaged? Hardly. The Lublin area, they would have discovered, was intended as one of the core islands of initial eastward-directed German colonization linked by key communication corridors (such as DG IV) to other hubs of emerging settlement, Himmler's own Ukrainian Hegewald complex included, the final destination of which was either the northern march of Ingermanland or Ingria (with Leningrad as its furthermost northern edge), or its southern Gotenland equivalent along the southern Dnieper, with the Crimea as *its* local heartland. Had the plan been realized, all rimlands ethnographic complexities in their 'Lands Between' manifestation would have been airbrushed out of existence through a *Raumordnung*—a spatial ordering or rather reordering—under Reichsführer-SS tutelage.[96] The earnestness of these plans is not in doubt; nor Himmler's constant meddling in the scheme, which, when first presented to him by Konrad Meyer's team, he rebuffed as insufficiently ambitious. The result was that even as the tide of war turned decisively against the Germans, and Hitler called a stop to all non-war-related projects, Himmler was still playing with his flagship—if now 'paper'—project. One smaller community which paid the price, for instance, were the 65,000 Finnish-related Ingrians peacefully 'returned' (*sic*) in late 1943 and early 1944 from their authentic homeland to Axis-aligned Finland, on grounds that Ingria, one day, would become an outpost of the Reich.[97]

If, then, retrospective analysis might reflect upon Zamość as both part of something entirely more grandiose, more specifically Himmlerian, yet by the same token less Polish-focused than the Poles themselves would have anticipated, what the latter could quite correctly see before their eyes was the escalating violence of the SS. Yet it is ironically in the grass-roots resistance of the Lublin communities to this violence that we can also see the roots of a more overtly genocidal development. What Globocnik's method sparked off was a form of localized partisan fight-back not specifically mandated by AK design, but explicable as defensive if spontaneous counter-violence. Polish peasants fled to the forests, but also took their revenge where they could for massacres kith and kin in the course of the deportations by hitting 'soft' German targets, especially incoming settlers. The SS in response not only carried out mass reprisals, but also attempted to both accelerate and widen the scope of the programme, adding a further 170-odd villages in the Lublin area to the evacuation orders and, in a second more intense summer

1943 campaign, striving to meet Himmler's goal to make Lublin district 40 per cent German by 1944.[98] In this they spectacularly failed. They could not persuade anything more than 10,000 'Germans', nearly all Volksdeutsche, to settle in the region—which is hardly surprising given how unsafe the district had become. Meanwhile, the alternative method of screening the local population itself in order to 'recover' the supposedly Germanizable among them failed to produce the required results. This, again, was not very surprising, given that Erhard Wetzel, one of the Nazi party's own leading racial demographers, had already disputed Himmler's exuberant forecasts of the extent of 'valuable' material among Slavic populations, the Poles in particular.[99] On the ground in Lublin, SS units resolved that problem by more direct means. They carted off discarded children from the screening programme to Auschwitz, where at least some of them were murdered with phenol injections. They confined others, both old and young, to special villages where they were starved to death. As for the fit but racially 'undesirable' remainder, they were largely deported to the Altreich as slave labourers.[100]

The complete breakdown in 'law and order' in the Lublin area as a consequence of the resettlement actions widened some of the already existing internal Nazi fault lines. One consequence was that Globocnik was reassigned to anti-partisan warfare in the Trieste area. But this could not halt the spreading of a now authentic and very active grass-roots resistance movement from its Zamość epicentre. Increased German anxiety was registered in mid-June with the declaration that the entirety of the General Government was now a *Bandenkämpgebiete*—a region threatened by bandits. Himmler also strove to stamp out incipient insurrection in colonial style, bringing in Franz Kutschera, a notably ruthless SS general, to prevent the revolt from reaching the capital. Attacks on Germans in Warsaw were met by street round-ups and mass in situ executions. The AK, recognizing the nature of German response, nevertheless responded the following February by assassinating Kutschera. A dialectic of violence was now well in train. The Germans executed 300 people for the assassination, mostly on the site of the by then razed ghetto. Between October 1943 and July 1944, 8,000 people were executed in Warsaw alone.[101]

If all this is indicative enough of a War Type Three conflict escalating out of control, there is still arguably a gap between an almost *unlimited* German retaliation against a subject Polish nation and a conscious effort to exterminate them, at least in the terms anticipated by its leadership in late 1942. However, that gap was arguably spanned twenty months later, in the high summer of 1944. It is significant that the shift was precipitated on the one hand by a crisis in the Nazi military as well as political situation, and on the other by the imminence for the Poles of their *other* worst nightmare: 'liberation' at the hands of the Soviets. On the first count, in the midst of Wehrmacht retreat on all fronts, the Nazis had been rocked on 20 July by the failed army bomb plot against Hitler, the lead protagonist of which, Claus von Stauffenberg, ironically had also been the architect of efforts to integrate Eastern manpower into the Wehrmacht.[102] Whether the attempt on his life made a badly shaken Führer even more psychologically prone than before towards extermination of the Reich's 'enemies' is unknowable. What we do know is that when the AK leadership made its decision soon after to seize the moment and launch an all-out uprising in Warsaw, Hitler responded in apocalyptic tones, prophesying that the Polish capital would be wiped off the face of the earth. Himmler answered him in echoing terms, promising not only the erasure of the city but a resolution of the age-old historical problem of the Poles 'for our children and all those who will come after us'.[103]

The Poles most certainly would have known from the Jewish, as from their own, experience that this is what they should expect. The burnt out ruins of the ghetto remained as an ever-present witness. Indeed, the manner in which the authorities brought Polish insurgents for execution there was as pointed a warning as imaginable against the Poles ever daring to attempt the same as the Jews. That the AK resolved upon this arguably suicidal course of action, however, was as much a consequence of the Red Army advance to the banks of the Vistula as the apparently fading fortunes of their German adversary. On 23 July, Moscow had announced the formation of a Polish Committee for National Liberation in Lublin, in effect setting up the spectre of a legitimate and openly communist alternative administration to the Delegatura's underground one. And Stalin simultaneously demonstrated exactly what he thought about Operation Tempest—the AK's effort to assert control in the cities and towns further east where the Wehrmacht was on the point of departure—by ordering entering Red Army and NKVD units to summarily disarm and deport their fighters. The failure of the AK operation, plus equally disturbing reports of the summary execution of AK officers and of the forcible reassignment of some of their men into the Soviet-controlled Berling army, were as good guides as any to the likely outcome of the uprising in Warsaw.[104]

Perhaps this can only underscore that, from a Polish perspective, this seemed a situation *like* that of the Warsaw Jewish underground in 1943. Of course, it was not: there was no predetermined assurance of mass annihilation, as there was in the Jewish case, except through the Poles taking up arms against the Germans. And, moreover, while the Warsaw Jewish fighters had nothing to look forward to bar the manner of their deaths, weapons in hand, for the AK the point of the uprising was, even in the face of death, to restore the independence of a sovereign entity. Underresourced, if not under-manned and with the chances of success incredibly slim, nevertheless, there was a strategic purposefulness to their effort. If the AK could deliver a knock-out blow against the Wehrmacht in Warsaw, the whole German position, just as in 1918, might rapidly unravel.[105] Meanwhile, faced with the AK in control of their own city, Stalin would have had little choice but concede authority to them. Or, put differently again, instead of being caught as in 1939 between the Nazi hammer and Soviet anvil, the Poles through their own collective heroism might end the war where it began, reversing the whole calamitous course of events since that moment.

That this was fantasy became all too clear within days of the beginning of the uprising on 1 August. Despite the early insurgent capture of central districts and western suburbs of the city, a German counter-attack under the direction of Bach-Zelewski was rapidly put in train, with both the Kaminsky and Dirlewanger's Brigades key SS components of the operation. Himmler's orders were explicitly not to spare anyone, combatant or non-combatant. Both Kaminsky and

Dirlewanger responded with unadulterated bloodlust. Having entered into Ochota district on 4 August, the former's men went on a week-long killing spree. The epicentre of their subsequent mass murders was in or around the Radium Institute, the cancer hospital founded by Marie Curie, and the 'Zieleniak', a former local vegetable market which became the site of a temporary holding camp. However, it would be more precise to say that the whole district became a murder zone, as Kaminsky's men cleared cellars with hand grenades, and set fire to entire streets and housing blocs regardless of whether there were people within. The killing was both indiscriminate and thoroughly sadistic, patients and staff in the Institute, women, children, and the elderly in the streets or in the 'Zieleniak' being set on fire or machine-gunned to death. Gang rape, nurses and nuns included, followed by murder, was an endemic aspect of these atrocities. But equally significant was the way the killers turned the fear of massacre into a vehicle for unrelenting round-the-clock robbery, taking valuables from the bodies of the dead, extorting the same with menaces from those still alive, and, where houses and apartments had been abandoned, searching with passionate zeal for alcohol and jewellery before, requited or not, they set the buildings alight.[106]

In a week of drunken frenzy, the brigade murdered some 10,000 of Ochota's inhabitants. Yet what happened in this one suburb can hardly be viewed in isolation. In fact, what Kaminsky's Brigade committed here was far surpassed in terms of numbers of fatalities by what SS units, primarily Dirlewanger's men, committed in the Wola district along the central line of the German advance down Górczewska and Wolska streets. On 5 August alone, they killed at least 10,000 if not 15,000 people, almost all of them women, old people, and children, rounded up house by house, and shot in the open air. What happened in Wola thereby represents the largest single massacre in modern Polish history.[107]

Putting aside any debate about normative codes of 'civilized' or 'just' war, was there some *military* logic to these killings? One could argue that the massacre of ordinary people, women and children included, in a concentrated space could serve a narrowly utilitarian purpose by terrifying either the insurgents themselves or the population at large into surrender. It was not, after all, even in the case of Warsaw, a given that everybody in the city would be an enthusiastic supporter of the revolt, even if the AK could count on substantial popular backing. Break the will to fight early on, or by turning the populace at large against the threat to themselves posed by the insurgency, and the reasoning might have been that initial mass terror could save the Germans from what they would themselves have most feared: a protracted and costly house to house struggle for control of the city, sapping into the bargain their own limited resources and energies. In fact, however, what the events of 5 August and subsequent days seemed to suggest was that as far as Warsaw's population was concerned the opposite was true. With nowhere else to turn for protection, survivors from the massacres fled into Warsaw's central districts, where the AK still had control, spreading with them graphic details of the atrocities they had witnessed. As a consequence, as Mazower explains, 'the insurgency assumed a new character: a defence of the city's inhabitants against massacre and terror'.[108]

But even to accept at face value the argument that there was some instrumental logic to the perpetrators' actions seems to be at striking variance with what was actually taking place on the ground. In the early evening of 5 August, Bach had given his first order that there was to be no more killing of women and children. Repeated again a week later, the order certainly had significance in that it appeared to be countermanding Himmler. Yet the new instructions seem to have altered little in practice, at least not initially. True, Kaminsky himself, still in the early weeks of the Warsaw operation, was ordered to Łódź, where he was tried for misconduct and shot by the Gestapo. His Brigade, too, was disbanded, reassigned to other units, and latterly largely liquidated in an AK revenge attack. But Kaminsky's demise had nothing to do with the Ochota atrocities per se, and appears rather to have been a consequence of a turf war between Himmler, his erstwhile patron, and the Bormann–Kaltenbrünner grouping, Bach stepping into the breach and using Kaminsky's serial misappropriations of his victims' watches and jewellery in the course of the action as a pretext for his execution. But if this would seem to tally with Himmler's distaste for individuals helping themselves to things which ought to have gone to the Reich (*sic*), in the circumstances this hardly constituted a hanging offence, given that other more senior officers, including Heinz Reinefarth, the Warthegau SSPF and overall SS commander in the Warsaw operation, were also amply rewarding themselves.[109]

Much more tellingly, almost as if in defiance of Bach's 5 August order, Dirlewanger's Brigade doubled the number of people it murdered during the following night and through the next day. Those killed included more than 1,300 patients and staff from two district hospitals. And whatever Kaminsky's thugs dreamt up in terms of gratuitous torture and capricious, sexualized violence in the course of the Ochota slaughter, Dirlewanger's equally mad crew matched. There were so many dead piled high in the streets, factories, and courtyards of Wola—itself adjacent to the burnt-out ghetto—that survivors were forcibly put to work burning the bodies in cellars, or on communal pyres, one of which was in a playground. Nor was this early sequence the end of the indiscriminate slaughter of Warsaw's civilian population. From early on, German tanks advanced using lines of women as human shields. The practice became standard until the very end of the battle on 2 October, when the AK finally capitulated. Part of the reason the fighting became ever more intense, even as the AK position became less and less tenable, was because captured insurgents, including the wounded, continued to be shot out of hand. Only Bach's personal initiative brought the fighting to an end when he responded to Western Allied recognition of the AK as part of a sovereign Poland's army, according them—women and men—the rights of POW status under the terms of the Geneva Convention.[110]

Bach-Zelewski's role is certainly intriguing. This undoubted *génocidaire*, in the context of Warsaw, attempted to put the brakes on mass murder, both by striving to restore military discipline to units who were clearly off the leash and out of control, and at the same time by setting up a holding camp outside the city at Pruszków, which became a place of sanctuary rather than extermination for thousands of Varsovian survivors. This in itself reads as something of a paradox; redoubled in

that Bach's efforts clearly failed to halt the trajectory of mass murder and destruction which was Himmler's, and above him Hitler's, absolute intention. While AK
combatants suffered 15,000 dead (getting on for half their number, though not all
directly from the fighting) with German military casualties possibly even greater,
no fewer than 150,000 civilians, heavily skewed towards woman and children,
were the overwhelming bulk of those killed. A significant proportion of these,
perhaps as many as 65,000, were victims of the first phase of the German operation, between 4 and 7 August, when Dirlewanger and Kaminsky's men were
entirely on the loose.[111] But the death toll after that point suggests that Bach, if he
was attempting to act as force for restraint, was insufficient to the task.

By late summer 1944, there were other things on the minds of leading Nazis
which may offer clues to their inconsistent behaviour. For instance, even Himmler
saw value in allowing surviving Warsaw insurgents their lives, again crudely miscal-
culating that the AK might at last be absorbed into his belated vision of some pan-
European, Waffen-SS fight against the communists.[112] Then there was the related
issue of how Nazi Germany might extricate itself from war with the West, which
would seem to explain, at least in part, Bach's largely unilateral efforts to signal a
German willingness to play by Geneva and Hague rules. But on the matter of the
sparing of the city qua city, Bach was completely overruled by Himmler. Here there
can be no equivocation as to responsibility. Having ensured that the city was pounded
with heavy weaponry and aerial bombardment in order to crush the uprising, in its
aftermath Himmler gave the green light for two further acts. The first was the
wholesale expropriation of all moveable items which had not been looted so far by
the city's SS conquerors. Delegations from German municipalities were specifically
allowed in to make inventories and remove what they could. Post-war Polish assessments indeed claim that as many as 33,000 railway wagons left Warsaw bound for
Germany, piled high with furniture, personal belongings, and factory equipment.
It was on the back of this free-for-all that Reinefarth, Greiser, and others were able
to make their own personal 'killings'.[113] In this sense alone, we can see the continuation of a process of total economic asset-stripping, which began in Warsaw with
the Jews.

The second act, too, can be related back to Jewish destruction, in the way that
Himmler had ordered the razing of the ghetto after the suffocation of *its* uprising.
What had been done there was now to be visited on the entire city, house by
house, block by block, street by street. Hitler as we have seen, fantasized about the
death and destruction of the great Russian and Ukrainian cities, yet never was
able to see his annihilatory vision translated into actuality. Once, within days of
the AK surrender, the last inhabitants of Warsaw had been forcibly evacuated—an
extraordinary event in itself—Himmler, with great purpose, set about the Polish
capital's systematic demolition. For the next two months, specialist squads of SS
and army engineers, equipped with flame-throwers and dynamite, brought down
homes, factories, schools, shops, municipal offices, palaces, museums, and monuments, all as if to prove that the Polish nation could be extinguished through a
literal deconstruction. The very last library was torched the day before the Red
Army entered on to the flattened site of Warsaw in January 1945.[114] In itself, this

act would fall firmly within Lemkin's original definition of genocide as composed of two inter-related elements of cultural vandalism *and* barbarism. Here was a clear intent to destroy the basic foundations of Polish society; devoid, moreover, at this late juncture in the war, of strategic purpose. But looked at through a broader historical prism can we confirm that the destruction of Warsaw constituted genocide?

If our obvious immediate precedent is again the destruction of *Jewish* Warsaw there is one obvious distinction to be made. While there were survivors of the Jewish uprising who went on to fight—and often die in its Polish successor—at the surrender of the latter, perhaps thanks in part to Bach, the Germans stopped short of all-out physical annihilation—though actually not all the Jews caught at the end of the ghetto uprising had been *immediately* killed: those not shot on the spot or dispatched to Treblinka ended up in Majdanek, where they may have had a few more weeks or months of piteous existence as slave labourers. Polish survivors from 1944, by comparison, were deported as slave labourers to the Reich or—in violation of the terms of surrender—to concentration camps. This was a horrendous fate but not necessarily a terminal one. The distinction, fine as it may be, is borne out in Snyder's commentary that while 90 per cent of Jewish Varsovians perished during the Second World War, the albeit still appalling figure for their Gentile counterparts was 30 per cent.[115]

Yet the Himmlerian manner in which the Nazis used the occasion of the uprising to encompass the wholesale spatial dismantling of a city whose pre-war population had stood at some 1.3 million might at the very least impel us to consider the 1944 German assault as a *variant* of genocide. The notion of urbicide has been the subject of much recent exploration,[116] and not just in the wake of some recent, very physical assaults on the people as well as material foundations of major urban centres, from Beirut to Sarajevo, Gaza to Aleppo. Of course, one might equally say that there is nothing new under the sun here. Carthage-style obliterations of cities and the mass murder, deportation, and/or enslavement of their inhabitants were a persistent 'maximalist' feature of the ancient world, and more recent world empires. In more modern times, the general assumption has been that such urban obliteration would come through aerial, especially nuclear, bombing or missile attack, and thus be accomplished in a matter of hours, or even minutes. Set against this proposition, the very idea that a city quarter or a whole metropolitan zone might be 'cleansed' of its people or infrastructure and/or the raison d'être upon which those people depend for lives and livelihoods—concrete slab by concrete slab—would seem to present us with something much closer to the wellsprings of genocide. It might not even require the actual physical destruction of the built environment: witness the mass evacuation of Phnom Penh in 1976, to which we will return in a further study. That there is now a whole military industry around the Pentagon-devised notion of MOUT (Military Operations in Urbanized Terrain) is testament to how much state security planners have become obsessed with the supposed threat to 'civilization' coming from urban insurgency in city environments.[117] We have already seen the human consequences of such thinking in the Russian battle for Grozny in 1994–5 and the US battle, a decade later, in Fallujah. As an example of building-to-building *military* combat the most obvious Second World War archetype is Stalingrad. But as the mother of all recent or potential *urbicides*, it is to Warsaw, 1944, that we would have to turn. This may also be the point at which degenerate war, in the way that Shaw describes it, intersects with the notion of genocide.

THE WAR IN THE MIDDLE (I): THE 1941–5 STRUGGLE FOR THE YUGOSLAV SUCCESSION

There is, of course, something critically missing from the above exposition of the final days of Warsaw: the geopolitical dimension. The Poles acted as they did at a distance from their clearly hamstrung Anglo-American sponsors. So they were thrown back on their own societal resources to synchronize their bid for liberation just before the entry of the Red Army. Once that bid had failed, all Stalin had to do was precisely nothing. He could have his armies sit on the other side of the Vistula and watch Hitler take his revenge on the capital, thereby paving the way for his own triumph. Instead of 1939, when he took only half, Stalin would now bring Moscow's own long-standing Polish 'problem' to an end by taking all. Naturally, he was far too deft to do absolutely nothing. Once it was clear that the Warsaw uprising was defeated, he made some nods at military (including his own Lublin-sponsored Polish army) action, while refusing to recognize the AK as anything other than a bunch of reactionary criminal adventurers or even pro-Nazi collaborators.[118] And the West, dependent on Soviet airfields to refuel but repeatedly denied that facility by Stalin, could do nothing further to help turn the tide in the insurgents' favour.

The Warsaw catastrophe was a stark reminder as to the vulnerability of national or communal military mobilizations against force majeure, especially where they could not count on some firm outside alternative force, or forces, to shift the odds back towards themselves. Either way, taking up arms against a German-led Axis was to practically incite retribution on a mass scale. And without the knowledge that at some point the geopolitical equation might shift not simply against the Axis but towards potential liberators, who might also be long-term partners in one's own societal reconstruction, the human sacrifice entailed became, arguably, quite senseless.

In the Balkans, our other Second World War-torn rimlands zone, such geopolitical calculations were by necessity intense. The very geography of the peninsula determined that it could be invaded by land—its mountainous terrain proving no obstacle to its rapid overrunning by the Wehrmacht in spring 1941—while equally it could be invaded by sea. When the Allies had made the attempt in the course of the 1914–18 conflict, the result had not been very successful. Nevertheless, the episode of the 'gardeners of Salonika' offered a salutary reminder to Hitler that Germany's strategic advantage could be rapidly overturned by an attack from the Aegean; hence the alacrity with which he resorted to *Blitzkrieg* against Yugoslavia and Greece in spring 1941. The same was true of Wehrmacht efforts thereafter to quash insurgencies which might have offered the basis for attacks in the rear, should the British, in particular, have resumed the effort.

The consequences of these anti-partisan operations were comparable with those in occupied Russia. In Greece, including Crete (the last Greek island from which the British had been ejected in 1941), the Germans destroyed over 1,000 villages and were responsible for tens of thousands of non-combatant deaths. When the Allied attack was at its most anticipated, in the wake of Rome's capitulation in late 1943, the Wehrmacht resorted to massacring thousands of their erstwhile Italian brothers in arms on the Ionian islands too.[119] In terms of fatalities, however, much worse were the combined effects of German requisitioning and the British blockade of the eastern Mediterranean, the consequent inflation and breakdown of food supply creating conditions, particularly in the first winter of occupation, in which some quarter of a million poor Greeks perished from hunger, especially in the major cities and on the islands. The numbers inevitably including great swathes of babies and children. The situation also bore comparison with the last great Hellenic calamity following the flight of refugees from Asia Minor in 1922–3. As then, so in this case, a significant proportion of those who bore the brunt of starvation in the 'black winter' of 1941–2 were Greeks from Thrace and Macedonia who had been eructed by the once-again incumbent Bulgarians.[120]

The Greek tragedy further complicates a landscape of mass murder in which genocide was only part. Axis counter-insurgency operations in Yugoslavia, primarily directed against Tito's Partisans, were even more intense, extensive, and relentless than those in Greece, with the range of these operations by early summer 1942 extending almost into the foothills of the Reich itself in Upper Carniola and Lower Styria. What happened to those caught within these operations might also be considered as part of a range. For instance, while suspected Slovenian partisans might be shot out of hand, their orphaned children might be assigned to Himmler's Lebensborn programme on grounds of their 'racial value' and thereby taken for adoption by German families.[121] For Lemkin, both elements of the equation would constitute genocide. But take another example: the great Axis offensive in the Mount Kozara region of the Bosanska Krajina in the summer of 1942, one of the largest counter-insurgency operations of the war. Marko Attila Hoare, noting that more than 24,000 Serbs were killed in the operation or its aftermath, 12,000 of them children, while another 68,000 were deported as slave labour to concentration camps either in the NDH or Reich, concludes that this was 'perhaps the most systematic genocide practised against the Serbs of NDH during the war'.[122] Tomislav Dulić reviewing the same episode, however, takes a somewhat different tack, differentiating between Wehrmacht goals in the operation and Ustasha ones. Both parties were agreed that the main purpose of the operation, as Hoare also notes, was to empty the region of a population deemed to collectively threaten a vital railroad link between Zagreb and Sarajevo, as well as access to the important Ljubija iron ore mine. But while the German aim was essentially strategic, allowing for at least some of the Serb peasants to eventually return to the region, Dulić sees Ustasha efforts to eliminate most of those who fell into their hands—including the majority of the infants and small children, who were incarcerated in camps where they were wantonly allowed to die through 'dehydration, diphtheria, famine, disease or murder'—as quite consciously genocidal in character.[123] The fact that the two main perpetrators of the killing started from different positions as to its purpose is hardly of consolation, indeed is quite irrelevant, to those who died. And the fact remains that it was the hegemonic partner, the Germans, who were responsible for *most* of the killing in the Balkans' counter-insurgency campaigns. That said, in terms of determining which elements of mass murder most obviously read as genocide, Dulić's differentiation is an important one. Ustasha killing was a matter not of short-term strategy but of long-term cleansing. In other words, it was programmatic in a way that the Nazi killing (bar that of Jews and Roma) was not.

This does not mean, of course, that Ustasha genocidal goals can be separated from the larger context of war in the Balkans. What the German overthrow of the post-1919 Western order—in shorthand, Belgrade—created was an otherwise undreamed-of opportunity for the realization of a new set of 'satellite' nation states over the body of the region's remaining ethnographic diversity. Even then, the notion that somehow the Ustasha, or other such ultra-nationalist groups, were the natural or inevitable heirs to this new Nazi dispensation cannot be warranted. The key paradox, indeed, is that the Ustasha's coming to power highlighted the degree to which Berlin's firm grip on the region was itself highly contingent, inconclusive, and beset from the very start by fears of its own overthrow.

The speed and apparent ease with which the Wehrmacht subjugated Yugoslavia in spring 1941 certainly can be read as evidence of that country's ongoing instability and acute internal tensions. There had been the Sporazum, the agreement arrived at in August 1939, by which Belgrade conceded something of the long-term Croat national demands for autonomy. But that had only been achieved by blocking out from the agreement all the country's other national or ethnic groups—including the Slovenes, who been part of the original tripartite Yugoslav conception. If the Sporazum thus confirmed the central fault lines of the Yugoslav power-play, Zagreb versus Belgrade, the very manner in which nine districts of Bosnia-Herzegovina were unilaterally added into the newly autonomous Croat Banovina simply exacerbated both Muslim and Serb fears in Bosnia that they were being sacrificed to some bigger political calculation.[124] Indeed, the fact that an ethnically and religiously mixed Bosnia-Herzegovina, soon after, was to become the very epicentre of genocidal struggles between Ustasha and Chetniks identifies it as the Balkan equivalent in miniature of the 'Lands Between', and the very fulcrum of competing national ambitions to do away with Balkan ethnic plurality for good. The entirely perverse question thus arises whether a successful German reordering of this rimlands arena, and with it a Nazi version of ethnic hierarchy, might have alternatively shut down, or at least suffocated, the region's internal ethnographic arguments, perhaps by the same sort of murderous method as the Nazis envisaged and attempted for Poland.

In the wake of Belgrade's capitulation, Hitler strove to do away with Yugoslavia as an entity, suppressing its Serbian centre, and dishing out its various provinces to Italian, Hungarian, and Bulgarian partners, or, in the case of Slovenia, directly sharing out the proceeds between the Reich and Rome. However, the notion of a strong, ruthlessly cruel German imperium in the Balkans, dictating to its peoples whether they might live or die, was immediately complicated by the small matter of imperial overstretch. With most of its troops committed from the summer of 1941 to the Eastern Front, Germany had to turn, at least in part, to its militarily unreliable partner, Italy, to maintain order in large swathes of Yugoslavia and Greece, and to other more local parties willing to act as Axis supporters or clients. In the context of the wider struggle for the survival of Hitler's empire, in which as we have already noted the Balkan theatre was likely to be hotly contested, this was in itself a recipe not for closing down but rather opening up pre-existing ethnic fissures. It was also one which ensured that in place of a single military narrative of struggle between Axis and Allies, conflict was bound to be many-sided, fought as much by local actors attempting to resolve their own immediate territorial and political quarrels as by the big international players, and with shifts in who was on the side of whom an almost inevitable corollary to a constantly changing balance of forces. In short, in the case of Yugoslavia, this was 'a story of many wars piled one on top of the other',[125] while in Bosnia-Herzegovina, the heartland of the 'national' struggle, it quickly degenerated into a 'war of all against all'. It is specifically in this latter context that we might identify genocidal agendas, actors, and outcomes.

*

First cause for the ensuing atrocities still rests with Hitler, through his fateful decision to appoint the Ustasha leader, Pavelić, as head of an 'independent' Croatia. Fateful on two accounts. The first was because this was not what was initially intended at all. Hitler's initial idea was to hand over Croatia to Hungary alongside other regions of Yugoslavia such as the Backa (Délvidék), thus returning practically all of what had been pre-1919 Habsburg territories in the region to Budapest's control. When Horthy turned this down, the Nazis' next port of call was Vlatko Maček, the leader of the majority Croat Peasants Party, with the invitation to form an administration in both Croatia proper and Bosnia-Herzegovina. What was actually being offered was a puppet state under German and Italian condominium, and with *their* occupation forces dividing up the country into respective spheres of influence. It was only when Maček also declined that Hitler, at Mussolini's prompting, turned to the Duce's (as well as Horthy's) sometime protégé, Pavelić, to govern the NDH.[126]

The second cause for the ensuing atrocities was that Pavelić's movement, as well as being entirely marginal to the Croatian political scene, was known as a dangerous terrorist entity. Given the Ustasha's ultra-right, fascist orientation, in itself this would hardly have been a deterrent to Nazi approval. But then the Nazis were also intrinsically wary of having fissile elements in charge of their client states (witness their critical, late 1940 support for Antonescu against the Iron Guard). There was, moreover, one particular reason why the Ustasha were recognized as a destabilizing force: their ethnic agenda. Again, this may read as odd given that when it came to Jewish—and Roma—destruction, the NDH administration did exactly what was required of it by the Germans. But demographically speaking,

Jews and Roma were only a tiny, marginal element of the population. What mattered to the Ustasha was the rest of the equation. Only 3.3 million of a total of 6.5 million inhabitants were Croats, while some 2 million or more—around 30 per cent—were Serbs. That left three-quarters of a million Muslims, and another 150,000 Germans to make up most the rest of a highly heterogeneous and often very intermixed ethnic mosaic.[127]

It was Ustasha intentions towards the Serbs which rang alarm bells with some of the Germans on the spot. Their senior military plenipotentiary, Edmund Glaise von Horstenau, a once-Habsburg staff officer and with views of the world to match, warned Berlin that the regime was seeking 'to govern a *Völkerstaat* (a state of ethnic groups) like a homogeneous nation state'. Glaise described the results as a 'Croatian revolution', adding for good measure 'that it was by far the harshest and most brutal of all the different revolutions that I have been through at more or less close hand since 1918'.[128] His horror at the Ustasha's 'utterly inhumane treatment of the Serbs' once again confronts us with the sheer schizophrenia of serving German officers ready and willing to condemn the bestiality of 'uncivilized' peoples, yet apparently quite incapable of seeing the beam in their own eye, let alone the responsibility for the chaos that whole regions of Europe were being plunged into as a direct consequence of their actions. Even so, there is evidence to suggest that Wehrmacht officers really were shocked to the bone by the 'wild' enthusiasm with which local Ustasha units set about their work of ethnic cleansing, even on occasion disarming offending units.[129]

On the other side of the equation, Hitler himself in meetings with both Pavelić, in June, and his war minister Kvaternik, in July, seems to have actively encouraged a policy of what he called 'national intolerance' as the appropriate route to the long-term *stabilization* of the Croat state. This view was also staunchly supported by the highly undiplomatic and probably incompetent ex-stormtrooper Siegfried Kasche, who had been appointed by Ribbentrop as Berlin's chief political representative in Zagreb. Hitler undoubtedly had his own reasons for supporting the general thrust of the NDH's anti-Serb policy. On 4 June, the Pavelić regime had agreed a 'resettlement' package in Berlin whereby the NDH would find room for 170,000 Slovenes who were to be deported from Germany's newly annexed Balkan territory. The Germans wanted the deportations concluded by October. The quid pro quo was that the Croats would be allowed to deport an equivalent number of Serbs from the NDH to the neighbouring rump of Serbia. Given the time frame involved, the onus was on Pavelić to carry out his own deportation programme with celerity. Pavelić's meeting with Hitler at Berchtesgaden two days later needs to be viewed in this context. Pavelić may well have interpreted Hitler's commentary as a green light for his Black Legions to do their worst.[130]

A further external goad in this direction would have been Mussolini's annexation of the northern Dalmatian coastline in mid-May, depriving the NDH not only of territory which had previously been included within it but of key ports, such as Split, to boot. The Italian diktat, coming supposedly from a fascist patron, plus Hitler's refusal to challenge it, underscores the complete dependency of the Ustasha regime on Berlin and Rome, not to say the shallowness of Pavelić's self-promoted elevation to *Poglavnik*—the leader of the Croat nation. Was it this fundamental weakness which drove him to prove his mettle by showing what he could *really* do on the matter of the Serb deportations?[131] The results certainly confirmed to the disgusted commanders of the Italian Second Army that the Ustasha were not the partners they wanted in the Balkans, Rome's orientation thereafter veering towards none other than the NDH's Chetnik adversaries. The desire to be shot of the NDH would also be consistently voiced by those in the German camp, such as Glaise, who insisted that Ustasha behaviour was leading to a *destabilization* of the region, and who urged that that the regime should be superseded by direct Wehrmacht rule. Significantly, while others, including of all people Heydrich, joined the chorus of protest at Ustasha methods—perhaps as much as anything to get back at Ribbentrop's efforts through Kasche to keep the SS at one remove in the Balkans—the Führer's commitment to the regime, while it might be budged, could not be broken.[132]

None of this, however, explains why Ustasha animus towards the Serbs was so virulent, nor how this translated into the actuality of genocide. Ustasha ideology might be described as akin to the 'blood and soil' variety at the core of Ben Kiernan's historical overview of genocide.[133] Indeed, notwithstanding the temporal, spatial, and cultural distance between themselves and the Khmer Rouge—the focus of Kiernan's major corpus of study—the Ustasha *do* evince elements in common. Like the former, while looking forward to a revolutionary overthrow of the incumbent order, *ustasvo* also harked back to a distant past, where *their* people had been simple, peasant sons of an authentic, autochthonous nation, but one also recognized (through the existence of a medieval Croat kingdom) as powerful actors on the international stage. Bulwarks of civilization, in the Croat case the proud bearers of the title *Antemurale Christianitatis* in the Latin West's struggle against Byzantium and the Ottomans, it was Croat adherence to the communal virtues of the *zadruga*, the peasant family commune, which ensured the purity of the nation, and thus the necessary strength with which to fend off the alien values of the 'oriental' east.[134] Here, then, was an utterly primordial, mythologized reading of Croat identity, even though that reading was actually a very modern product of nineteenth-century romantic nationalism. More precisely, however, the origins of *ustasvo* lay in a particular strain of nationalist thought which rejected the notion of a south Slav brotherhood, most obviously with the already independent Serbs across the Habsburg border, and which claimed instead that the Croats had always been a de jure independent nation. Under the 'Party of Right', from the 1860s onwards, this position was developed as an argument for freedom both from Hungarian and Habsburg dominance and also from Serb interference in the historic territory of 'Great Croatia'. And it was under Pavelić's leadership, at the end of the Great War, that this same political party—the forerunner to the Ustasha—rejected in toto any possibility of a Croat relationship, federal or otherwise, with Belgrade.[135]

But what had a mythic past got to do with hostility against the Serbs in the present? The two groups were actually remarkably similar in terms of language and culture down to the fierce familial solidarity of the *zadruga* system. And while feuds and vendettas may have raged between one commune and another in earlier times, these were exactly that: communal conflicts, not ethnic ones, nor evidence of some deep-seated, intractable antagonism. The 'Rightist' forerunners of the Usta-sha, more specifically their founding father, Ante Starčević, got round the *lack* of a specifically Serb–Croat narrative of conflict not so much by rejecting the similarity of the two groups tout court but rather by making claims about the degeneracy of the Serbs, especially those who were incomers onto Croat soil. The argument thus went that the Serbs might be distant cousins, even at some stage in the very distant past part of the same *Gothic* race—the conceit Rightists embroidered into existence as proof of their Western rather than Eastern (Slavic) credentials. What they were objecting to about the 'cousins', therefore, was not really racial or biological, cer-tainly not in the same way as the NDH would cite to damn Jews and Roma. Rather, the Serb sin was in considerable part a matter of rimlands geography. The Serbs were the folk who, living on the 'other' side of the Sava and Drava (Danube) rivers, which had been the historic European east–west boundary since Roman times, were irremediably tainted by their centuries of both subservience to and imitation of Oriental practices and thinking.[136]

Interestingly, this was rather like the Khmer Rouge rendition of what was wrong with the Khmer Krom, the ethnically Cambodian people from lower down the Mekong who, long outside the medieval Khmer 'empire' of Angkor, had become 'like' the surrounding but decidedly foreign Vietnamese of the region. The return of some Khmer Krom to Cambodia *integrale*, in the death-throes of South Vietnam, became for the incipient, beleaguered as well as utterly paranoid Pol Pot regime their worst nightmare of political and cultural contamination imaginable—and this on the very cusp of the regime's intended revolutionary cleansing of all the country's bad apples.[137] Where there was a difference from the Ustasha was that the so similar, yet so allegedly different, Serb bad apples had been migrating into 'great Croatia'—in fact fleeing across the river borders from Ottoman rule—for at least the last three centuries. Much worse, they had been given considerable rights and freedoms by the Habsburgs, amounting to a form of special status, in return for the defence of the military frontier—the Krajina—against Ottoman incursion.[138] That special status had actually been revoked in 1881. Even so, with the demise of Dual Monarchy rule, Serbs were bad not just on account of having brought with them the alleged unruliness and savagery of the uncivilized Balkans but equally so for being an independent element in the heart of Croat territory, and one, said its ultra-nationalists, that was really Belgrade's fifth column.

Here, then, was a classic, ready-made explanation for why a nation which *ought* to have been strong and independent was weak and forlorn. In the circumstances, it became debatable whether there was any point attempting to deal with the Serb 'settlers' anthropophagically: '*devouring* them and then metabolically transforming them into a tissue indistinguishable from one's own'. Perhaps the only effective solution was anthropoemic: *vomiting* these strangers out and 'banishing them from the limits of the orderly world'.[139] How convenient that the Nazis had provided the framework for exactly such a project. Except that in 1941 the numbers did not add up: the deportation exercise allowed for the removal of some 170,000 Serbs but, as we have noted, there were something in the region of 2 million of them on the territory of the NDH.

The disparity raises a standard conundrum associated with the inception of genocide: did the Ustasha set out to kill as many Serbs as they could, or were there structural reasons, or possibly other contingent factors, by which they 'ended up' going down this path? It is important to remember that the Ustasha, which in the early 1930s consisted of no more than about 2,000 supporters in Croatia, and perhaps a similar number in Western émigré circles,[140] was an already heavily brutalized, violence-addicted political movement. Not unlike some latter-day radicalized groups, such as ETA or the IRA, they saw what they were doing as a liberation struggle versus a repressive, colonial power. In the wake of the Radić assassination in 1928, and clearly deteriorating relations between Croats and the government in Belgrade, Pavelić's supporters had moved towards direct armed confrontation with it. An attempt in 1932 to incite a peasant-based rebellion in the Lika region, from which Pavelić himself hailed, proved abortive, except in the sense that a more intensive clamp-down by Belgrade served to underline the Ustasha point about state repression. The further involvement of subcontracted Chetniks to assist in the government pacification of Lika also played neatly to Ustasha utterances about Croatia being policed, run, and taken over by Serbs.[141] Now Pavelić from exile, mainly in Italy, would promote the idea that Croatia was in mortal danger, the very term Ustasha—meaning 'to stand up' or 'rebel'[142]—expressing that beleaguered quality we might equally associate with another infamous name, the Rwandan Interahamwe, or 'those who stand together'.

However, Ustasha pre-war terrorism hardly represented the authentic voice of most Croats. The movement's previous incarnation as the Party of Right had never polled more than 2 per cent of their vote.[143] It was in the extremely poor, entirely disadvantaged, but ethnically mixed mountain regions such as Kordun, Lika, and western Herzegovina that the Ustasha message had most grass-roots resonance. It is certainly noteworthy that it was from exactly these areas that a significant proportion of Ustasha's leading lights came, paralleling thereby several other examples in this study where a sense of emerging *national* threat to individual or group identity from the perceived 'other' precipitated a turn to radical or even extreme political action.[144] But if this is simply to restate that what one claims one is not—in this case Serb—is always fundamental to any form of ultra-national identity, it still leaves open the question as to how and why what was meant to be a programme of partial Serb deportation, in the spring and summer of 1941, ended up primarily as one of mass extermination.

One possible tack might be to suggest that it was the very weakness and isolation of the Ustasha in power which precipitated them into genocide. Untried in office—the core of the party was a few hundred returnees from exile—and with little or no administrative experience, the attempt to set up a range of agencies which would carry through the registration of deportees and the nationalization of their personal assets (not to mention finding provision for Slovene incomers and Croat returnees) foundered under the weight of shambolic bureaucracy and the regime's 'awe-inspiring venality'.[145] It might be added that the regime was vastly under-resourced in just about everything. Thrown back on the often very young militants from his immediate inner circle to get things moving, and this set against a backdrop of very remote and poorly connected regions at the best of times but in the present circumstances with whole districts, especially in Bosnia-Herzegovina, rapidly falling outside NDH control, might one not argue that it was Pavelić's delegation of authority to these zealots which explains the slide into massacre? The youthful profile of key *génocidaires* in the Ustasha militia, state security, and in the camps is certainly very telling. Practically the oldest and most senior among them, Eugen 'Dido' Kvarternik, the head of Ustasha internal security service (as well as son of the minister of war) was only thirty-one in 1941; Dinko Sakic, one of several incumbents as head of Jasenovac at that time, a mere twenty. Many of the most notoriously vicious guards there were in their early teens.[146] This, again, would seem to signal comparison with Hutu Power Rwanda and Democratic (*sic*) Kampuchea, the latter in particular a case where young hot-head commanders in faraway zones often forced the pace without direct authorization from the 'centre'. Comparable results in the wartime NDH had not only the Germans and Italians railing against 'unorganized' killings. Pavelić, too, as early as June 1941, threatened to court-martial anyone committing violence against the persons or property of any NDH citizen or subject, adding a few days later that resettlement was the job of 'certain ministries and their offices' and had 'to be done within a system'.[147]

Taking Pavelić's comments at face value, one might conclude that the central leadership of the NDH was either too feeble or too incompetent to prevent what its own second-tier party cadres were enacting in the field, or was literally overwhelmed by the scale and limited time frame of the resettlement programme it had set in train. Yet there would seem to be some inbuilt contradictions or at the very least tensions in this reading. For one thing, the regime qua regime seemed to know exactly what it was doing and, for that matter, in a rather efficient manner when it came to the destruction of the Jews and Roma.[148] There may not have been any predetermined NDH blueprint for *wholesale* Serb destruction. However, the speed with which its interior minister, Andrija Artuković, one of the older and more experienced members of the Ustasha clique, set up a special Office for Public Order and Security with powers to have anybody tried for high treason who was found to have offended 'against the honour and vital interests of the Croat nation...whether in deed or...mere intent' suggests the regime had some pretty fertile ideas about with whom it wished to settle scores.[149] Thus while the party-state constructed racial laws providing for its non-Aryans to be 'legally' dispatched to the Jasenovac camps, its kangaroo courts were equally up and running almost from day one to expedite the removal there of other dangerous elements in the population. This speaks, in the first instance, of a quite conscious elitocide. The murder of some 38 per cent of Orthodox priests by the end of 1941 is one key indicator. Most of the rest were deported. Similar fates befell teachers, professionals, wealthy peasants, and the like.[150] But if this underscores an Ustasha aim to eliminate the leadership strata of Serb society within its territorial boundaries, what of the rest of the Serbs whom they killed? The number of serving Serb priests in the NDH amounted to a few hundred. The total number of wartime Serb fatalities there may have reached several hundred thousand.[151]

One statement often cited as evidence of this wider genocidal intent is allegedly by Mile Budak, the education minister, who is said to have publicly proclaimed at a conference at Gospić, in late June 1941, that a third of Serbs would be deported, a third converted, and a third killed. In fact, the source, or its attribution to Budak, cannot be corroborated.[152] Putting that aside, however, there appear to be plenty of other confirmed speeches in which high-level officers of state vied with each other to offer the most tasteless utterances. Viktor Gutić, for instance, the NDH commissioner entrusted with the task of 'liquidating' the Vrbaska Banovina, in other words what had been the Yugoslav administrative framework for Western Bosnia, proclaimed in a meeting in Banja Luka in late May that 'all undesirable elements will be exterminated so that no trace will remain'. He went on to complain, in a manner worthy of a Reshid, that in his travels around towns in his region, such as Prijedor, that he had *not* seen Serbs hanging from the street lights or trees. Nevertheless, he found himself consoled by the knowledge that 'if by some mishap, Yugoslavia were reintegrated, at least we shall have reduced the statistical numbers [of Serbs] in favour of the Croats'.[153] Gutić was unequivocal that he had received orders from the highest authorities to cleanse Bosanska Krajina, and that his role was to encompass 'the economic destruction' and 'complete annihilation' of its 'undesired elements'.[154] Arguably even more inflammatory—and chilling—were the words of Juriev, the head of the religious department in the Ministry of Justice and Religion who, as reported by inhabitants in the town of Staza, made a speech in which he said:

> It is no longer considered a sin to kill a child of seven if he interferes with Ustasha law and order. Although I wear the robes of a priest I am often obliged to resort to the machine gun, and the minute anyone is against the state, or the Ustasha who are in power I make good use of it right down to the cradle.[155]

Was this just boastful rhetoric at its most insanely hubristic or actually commentary on what was already being put into effect? The speed with which the massacres began within days of the Ustasha takeover hardly suggests that this was something the regime was bounced into as a response to unanticipated events. Before the loss of Dalmatia, or Pavelić's meeting with Hitler, the belt of state-initiated violence was spreading with rapidity from an initial epicentre in Bjelovar district, east of Zagreb, to embrace Lika, Kordun, Banija, large tracts of north-west Bosnia (Bosanska Krajina), and eastern Herzegovina—all regions where Serbs were heavily intermixed with Croats.[156] To be sure, Ustasha ability to develop a unified assault on all these districts at once was limited. Moreover, as news spread of the massacres it precipitated localized Serb resistance, which slowed down the progress of the NDH militias. As a result areas of western Bosnia such as Bihać and Sanski Most were not taken and 'cleansed' until June. Some of the largest mass atrocities followed in the high summer months. These included places which became sites of repeated massacre. The valley at Velebit, where the abortive 1932 Ustasha uprising had occurred, became an arena in which up to 18,000 chained prisoners were brought in convoys for summary dispatch. The village of Glina in the Banija was the venue for no fewer than five massacres throughout the course of 1941, the nearly 2,400 people who were killed here including over 400 women and children.[157] Most of these episodes of extreme violence took places in rural locales, and though the composite term 'ethnic cleansing' was not used at this time, as it would be to describe events in the same region nearly fifty years later, the Ustasha sequence of either partial or total community liquidations strongly suggests a desire to 'cleanse' or 'purge' the territory of its Serb peasant inhabitants.

A further aspect which underscores the purposeful motivations of the perpetrators, its gruesome morbidity notwithstanding, relates to the topography of violence. Closely following the contours of the Ottoman destruction of the Armenians, here, too, the perpetrators went often to great efforts to utilize the landscape as a tool with which to inflict maximum humiliation, degradation, and pain in the process of killing their victims.

Much of mountain Croatia and Bosnia is *karst*, and consequently vertiginous in nature. Its gorges, grottoes, cliffs, crevices, and rocky hilltops now became part of a ritualized methodology in the literal ejection of the Ustasha's collective quarry.[158] Croatian Bishop Misić of Mostar, for instance, reported to Archbishop Stepinac in Zagreb in November, that some months earlier a trainload of young women, girls, and little children had been deposited at the station at Surmanci from where they had been taken up into the mountains, then thrown alive from the precipices into the ravines below.[159] The rivers, too, served similar symbolic purpose. The Sava and Drina, historic boundaries between east and west, were favourite sites at which thousands of victims had their throats slit before being tossed into the waters. Downstream from Jasenovac on the Sava, but also along the Neretva, near Metković in Herzegovina, body parts began to clog up the flow in such quantity—just as in the fluvial aspects of Rwanda's genocide half a century later—that they raised alarmed medical concern about the risk to public health.[160]

Comparison with Rwanda here is also evident in the extraordinary levels of sadistic enjoyment involved in the killing. Butcher's knives, pocket knives, hooks, hammers, mallets, and axes were all employed to gouge out eyes, mutilate women's breasts, and generally hack people to death. At the Jasenovac complex in western Slavonia, however, run under the supervision of Unit II of the Ustasha Security Service (the UNS), these tendencies reached unprecedented heights of frightful, pornographic luridness. Jasenovac, though much smaller than Auschwitz, was likewise situated close to a major railway junction and made up of several camps, whose official purpose was 'collection and holding'. It was not a place specifically created for Serb destruction but rather for the screening and removing of anybody who was an enemy of state. As a consequence, a whole range of people—Jews, Roma, and increasingly Croat, plus Bosnian Muslim, dissidents—were brought to the complex, alongside Serbs.[161] Many were immediately liquidated, but others were meant to be 'only' detained for a period up to three years and—as in the Nazi camps—put to hyper-exploitative labour. On one level, one might argue that the slide into chaotic killing was a consequence of lack of planning, limited capacity, and an inability to cope when numbers overwhelmed the complex's poor organization. Death from illness as a consequence of the fetid conditions, or through starvation, was also a high probability.

The various commanders of the operation, which lasted until March 1945, turned the issue of excess inmate numbers into an opportunity for nothing less than sport. Chief among them, Vjekoslav 'Maks' Luburić, a close confidante of Pavelić and prime mover in the creation of the camp system, distributed gold and silver medals to the most efficient assassins, boasting that more were killed here 'than the Ottoman empire was able to do during its occupation of Europe', and encouraging Stakhanovite-style competitions between guards as to who could kill the most people using the curved knife, the *graviso*. One Petar Brzica, a Franciscan scholarship student, is reputed to have won this competition on 29 August 1942, with 1,360 murders from a single night of throat-slitting.[162] Another commandant, in this case a defrocked Franciscan friar, Miroslav Filipović, according to one survivor 'favoured a mystical approach to the killings', personally dispatching prisoners himself before holding Holy Mass, in which he would 'preach about love for one's neighbour'.[163]

The sheer weirdness of what took place in Jasenovac, over and beyond the fact that this was an unadulterated, alcohol-fuelled slaughterhouse where as many as 80,000 or 85,000 men, women, and children were put to death,[164] suggests that its organizers in the process had 'lost it'; that is, lost even any sense of the purpose of the killing. This could provide a rather convenient route towards that real blame for the Ustasha genocide lies essentially with a small gang of fanatics and their lumpen henchmen, who were far removed from mainstream Croat society but who had taken over the apparatus of state, such as it was, against the grain of popular sentiment. It is certainly true that when the country-wide massacres began, many local administrative officials plus gendarmerie, military, and Domobran (Home Guard) officers filed damning reports protesting against the militia actions and claiming that the majority of the local Croat population were equally bewildered and aghast at what was happening in their midst. In practically all these cases, such officials also claimed that they had been powerless to prevent the killings.[165] But there is something which is problematic here: the general acquiescence in the face of the atrocities. One could put this down to sheer fear of the regime; yet such an assumption would seem to ignore that when Pavelić returned to Zagreb with his entourage in April 1941, they were met by deliriously enthusiastic crowds, while Maček for the Croat Peasant Party majority (albeit at German request) publicly called on his supporters, including the many people who were in bureaucratic and Domobran roles, to stay in their posts and obey government instructions. One critical result was that at a moment when Pavelić lacked insufficient cadres to fill almost any administrative function he was able to count on those of the HPSS to keep the country afloat—just—as well as being able to absorb many of the latter's local defence units in the now Ustasha-controlled Domobran.[166]

One might wish to blame Maček at this point for a signal error of political judgement. But supposing wider societal passivity was evidence of some tacit approval for aspects of the Ustasha programme, if not necessarily for their methods? Given that most Croats took their lead from the Catholic Church, the regime's commitment to outlaw—Franco-style—drunkenness, vagrancy, prostitution, and gambling, to 'clean up' private life, visit the death penalty on abortionists, and generally unite the nation by getting them into church seems at the very least to have won clerical endorsement, not least from Archbishop Stepinac.[167] His denunciation of the regime's killings might have made a decisive difference. Though the archbishop, along with a Vatican emissary, were clearly aware of and troubled by reports they received of Jewish and gentile suffering, leading to private representations to Pavelić on the matter, no *public* denunciation was ever uttered by Stepinac, or any other member of the Croat Catholic hierarchy. Perhaps a further clue to this ambivalence can be found in Stepinac's views, expressed as late as 1944, that it was the Croats themselves who were suffering wartime cruelty greater than any other nation, and that responsibility for the real evil which had befallen the country lay not at the door of the Ustasha but with 'the Serbs, the Chetniks and the Communists'.[168]

By such reasoning one might condone the obvious brutality of the regime as a necessary evil for difficult times, or even as the *only* way to defend a society whose very survival as a 'living organism' was perceived as being in danger of its. As Jonathan Steinberg has put it, 'nationalism in the Balkans was hardly a secular category; to be Croatian was to be a Catholic'.[169] And the people who were riding in to defend that threatened dual identity were none other than the revolutionary vanguard of the nation: the Ustasha. Far from being ill-educated, Pavelić and his leading acolytes included lawyers, doctors and other professionals, which ipso facto made them hardly 'outsiders' at all. Nevertheless, what is particularly striking is the number of Franciscan or Jesuit priests and seminarists among them. They included Dr Ivo Guberina, who combined headship of the Catholic Action organization with that of Pavelić's personal bodyguard, and close to half of the commandants of the twenty-one state-run concentration camps[170] The leading Zagreb, clearly pro-Ustasha, newspaper *Nedelja* put its finger on the pulse when it described the movement as a crusader organization. It went on to celebrate its accession to power by proclaiming 'Glory be to God, our gratitude to Adolf Hitler, and infinite loyalty to our Poglavnik, Ante Pavelić' for what between them they had done 'to disperse our oppressors and enable us to create an Independent State of Croatia'.[171]

It was the way this religious dimension strongly infused Ustasha ideology which gave to *this* genocide its special quality. Actually, the intermixing of national and religious components was not unique to this movement alone. The Rumanian Iron Guard, in its previous, sometimes better known incarnation as the Legion of the Archangel Michael, was so suffused with mystical hocus-pocus that it declared Rumanian Orthodoxy 'consubstantial with the national community'. It even declared that the regeneration of Rumania would lead to the salvation of its people's souls, living and dead.[172] The Legion in power would undoubtedly have carried through its own genocidal programme, though as with the Antonescu regime who did enact it, the primary and sustained target would have been Rumania's Jews. Clearly, Eastern European anti-Semitism was rooted in religious prejudice. But what gave the Ustasha *its* religious edge was more the sense of some deep-seated, historic struggle between Catholicism and Orthodoxy for control of the Croat border region. The former was under threat as never before from the forces of Orthodoxy as now combined and bolstered by the 'Belgrade' state. Or so thought the Ustasha. And Serbs living in Croatia were both Orthodox and adherents of that state. It was as if a variant of the Counter-Reformation was having to be played out all over again, with Franciscan priests, defrocked or otherwise, donning warrior garb over their monks' habits to become the self-proclaimed shock-troops of the struggle to oust the schismatics for once and for all.

The results of this sort of thinking are evident in the most significant of the massacres at Glina. In August 1941, several thousand Serb villagers are reported to have been brought here by truck on the pretext that their lives were to be spared through conversion to Catholicism. Instead, after having spent some of the night in a makeshift camp, several hundred were then driven into the village's Orthodox church where they were killed with axes and knives. Then the church itself was razed. The brother superior of the local Franciscan monastery at Cutnica actively encouraged his monks to participate in the massacre.[173] Thus was sacred soil cleansed through an act of conscious, premeditated profanity. Or, from a Serb Chetnik perspective, the martyrdom of a people proclaimed.

We must be wary of assuming that the Catholic Church qua church in Croatia was party to these events or any of the killings. It also had more pragmatic grounds for objecting to the manner in which certificates 'recommending' actual conversion from Orthodoxy to Catholicism were processed through local authorities in liaison with the Ministry of Justice and Religion rather than more directly through itself. Senior figures within the Vatican establishment were even less enthused by the sudden surge of conversions, Cardinal Maglione even giving the Croatian ambassador to Italy a good dressing down for what he called 'propaganda by violence'.[174] The rush to conversions, however, does tell us something about how Catholicism came into play to offer a paradoxical escape route for the Ustasha from having to carry through Serb mass murder to its optimal conclusion.

It is estimated that the regime murdered 180,000 Serbs in the first four months of NDH existence. By then Pavelić was being heavily lent on by the Italians and Germans to rein in the killing. An indicator that these efforts failed is evident in the final Serb death toll, which was almost double that initial figure, as also the fact that key *génocidaires*, in particular the Kvaterniks, father and son, were not relieved of their posts until late 1942. Pavelić himself seems to have made entirely contradictory statements for and against Serb annihilation, depending on when and to whom he was speaking.[175] That said, and as we have already seen, there was no *racial* impediment to an anthropophagic Serb incorporation into the Croat 'nation'. Rather, the issue was a national-political one, in considerable part represented by an Orthodox Church's perceived poaching of Catholic souls, thereby acting as outrider for Great Serb domination.[176] Hence the alternative solution to extermination: 'disappear' the Orthodox Church in the NDH, deny citizen rights to those who still adhered to this now obscurely entitled 'Greek religion of the Oriental faith', and thereby 'persuade' its rank and file congregations to accept the true universal faith, enabling them in the process to become good *Croats*. The very manner in which Serbs were now designated 'Pravoslavs' underscored their ambiguous status within the Ustasha universe of obligation. This veiled threat to submit, or else, meant that 1942 consequently became an 'assembly line' year for mass conversion, with the police always on hand at such 'events' to guard against thoughts of backsliding or the possibility of public disorder. Estimates of conversion range between 200,000 and 350,000.[177] It was also in 1942, however, that the regime moved to create an autocephalous Croat Orthodox Church, albeit in supposed communion with Rome. It was as good a way as any of acknowledging that the NDH's scheme of Serb denationalization could not be achieved by either direct destruction or mass assimilation, in the face of escalating Chetnik and Partisan resistance. Even so, accommodation through conversion continued to deny the Catholic embrace to any Serb priest, teacher, trader, artisan, or rich peasant, 'except in cases where personal integrity can be proved': in other words, to anybody who might represent part of an *active* Serb intelligentsia.[178] Serb elitocide thus remained an ongoing NDH objective, while 'on the ground Ustasha militia continued to conduct a blanket policy of reprisal'.[179]

The last statement should remind us that having made the project of Serb cleansing its fundamental raison d'être, the Ustasha precipitated a dialectic of communal violence. As a consequence, any question as to whether things might have been different had they opted 'only' for forced assimilation, or whether Serbs might have acquiesced in this lesser evil, becomes academic. What we can say is that state violence made for communal insurrection, and that this rapidly spread beyond the immediate districts where the Ustasha attempted to massacre or deport Serbs to parts of the NDH such as eastern Bosnia, where Serbs were the majority and Croats a minority, or non-existent. Describing this movement as Chetnik or Partisan at one level, however, rather misses the point. As Hoare makes clear, the insurrection began as something essentially defensive and demotic. It was determined not by politics or ideology, but first of all by a sheer grass-roots will to survive, involving flight to the hills, and second by a desire for revenge against those who had wiped out families, clans, and villages. The movement's spontaneous combustion, indeed, ensured that both communists and Chetniks were essentially caught on the hop and had to join it, not the other way round.[180] This also meant that initial distinctions in Bosnia-Herzegovina between insurgents who wore the badge of the Partisans and those wearing that of the Chetniks were nominal; the distinction insofar as it existed at all more a matter of local loyalties and commanders. Early on, it even appeared as if the two movements might develop a joint Bosnian command. However, by the end of 1941, this pragmatic arrangement had broken down so completely that the Partisan–Chetnik war became the most intense of the internecine conflicts within wartime Yugoslavia, alongside the Partisan–Ustasha struggle. The details of the breakdown in this relationship are outside our immediate ambit, but they relate to the political orientation and evolving principles of the core leadership of both Chetniks and Partisans. These aspects are relevant here inasmuch as they may help to explain each movement's respective proclivities towards mass murder and/or genocide.

*

In so far as we can speak of a coherent political-military entity, 'Chetniks' is really shorthand for those Serbs who coalesced around Colonel Dragoljub 'Draza'

Mihailović in his refusal to capitulate to Axis rule from April 1941, and who gave their loyalty to the royal Yugoslav government-in-exile in London. Mihailović's designation of his forces as the Yugoslav Army in the Homeland (JVUO) thus offers on paper a sort of Serbian version of the AK, with Delegatura functions thrown in for good measure. Against this one has to be reminded of three things. First, unlike in Poland, internal divisions within the JVUO were legion from the start. Second, if we can speak of a Serb shadow government, in the same breath we have to affirm the existence of genuine if residual Serb polity under the collaborationist Nedić regime in Belgrade, and with its own Wehrmacht sponsored, 34,000-strong, armed forces. Finally, when Mihailović was enunciating the cause of status quo ante Yugoslavia, he was actually proclaiming the cause of Greater Serbia, meaning that there were no obvious grounds for adherence to the Chetniks by any of the country's disparate national or ethno-religious communities, apart from Serbs. Throughout the war, moreover, Mihailović was beset by one overriding strategic problem which helped to underline his movement's fundamental weakness: was he going to openly challenge Axis rule, or was he going to play a waiting game in the expectation that, with its power waning, the Yugoslav plum would eventually fall into his lap? The latter was clearly his own (if not necessarily all his commanders') pragmatic preference. But effectively doing nothing made him appear hardly less quisling than Nedić. Indeed, Nedić, by protecting Serbian autonomy and—after the mass Wehrmacht reprisals at Kragujevac and Kraljevo in October 1941—Serbian lives, was arguably offering a more clear-sighted strategy for Serb 'biological' survival, whereas Mihailović's mixed messages and increasing gravitation into first the Italian, then (in more convoluted fashion) the German orbit provided additional grounds for the shift of British Balkan strategy away from JVOU and towards Tito.[181]

Eventual open Whitehall support for the Partisans was predicated on the latters' willingness to take on Axis forces; and clearly not their political complexion. In itself, Partisan belligerence was an invitation for more Kragujevacs and Kraljevos on a countrywide scale, which was exactly Tito's ruthless calculation. By demonstrating that this was a war of life and death, the aim was to incite the population to general insurrection. By such means, the Yugoslav Communist Party (KPJ) sought to give its assistance to what it saw as the main battle being waged by its Soviet patron on the Eastern Front: a case of internationalist goals taking precedence over national ones.[182] Nevertheless, by leading an ever-widening national liberation struggle, Tito was also calculating that this would be the route by which the KPJ would take power in Belgrade. The slogan of 'Brotherhood and Unity' became an essential element in the Partisan toolkit through which all Yugoslav peoples were encouraged to work together for a federal, non-sectarian future.

There were good tactical reasons for adopting this tack. The largely proletarian base of the pre-war KPJ had been limited to a small industrial sector. By offering itself as a People's Liberation Movement in 'the anti-fascist struggle', the Partisan leadership was seeking to transcend its narrow class-based image yet at the same time projecting the idea of an entirely new version of Yugoslavia in which all the south Slav nationalities, Bosnian Muslims and Macedonians included, would be equally recognized. Curiously, with the half-Croat, half-Slovene, ex-Habsburg army NCO Josip Broz—Tito—at the helm, this suggested aspects of an earlier Austro-Marxist, Dual Monarchy-focused argument for consociationalism, as much as for the initial Bolshevik experiment in national pluralism.[183] The paradox is that what was being presented as a way of transcending national conflict was the very thing which ensured an even more intense struggle with Yugoslavia's competing national forces. It was, after all, quite a feat to have both Ustasha and Chetniks lining up behind Italians and Germans—themselves usually at loggerheads—in order to liquidate any possibility of a Partisan-controlled 'liberated' zone. This also meant that if one's personal ambition was to survive the war in Yugoslavia, joining the Partisans or, as in the case of most Jews and Roma, seeking their protection, was, alternatively, a fairly sure recipe for its extinction.

However, for Serbs on the ground, more particularly those in Bosnia who had been provoked into rebellion through the Ustasha massacres, avoiding death may not have been the only or prime reason for being swayed away from the Partisan camp and back towards the Chetniks. In November 1941, the Mountain Staff of the Bosnian Chetnik detachments issued a proclamation in which they claimed that the rebellion had been launched for 'the holy Cross and golden freedom, for the King and fatherland, for the Serb nation and the Serb Orthodox faith'. Whether precisely true or not, what is immediately striking is how much this statement seemed to contain elements of an Ustasha mirror image. Here too was the sense of a whole nation under mortal threat; of an indissoluble link between the fate of that nation and its religion; and of an appeal to its true peasant sons to rise up and retake what was rightly theirs. But the proclamation went on to make an accusation. Who was trying to hijack this authentic struggle for the Serb nation? The atheistic communists. And how was this becoming manifest? Through the way in which communists were intruding non-Serbs into not just the rank and file but the command structure of 'our fighting peasant companies' (this still at a time when Partisans and Chetniks were supposedly united). And who, moreover, were these non-Serbs? 'Jews, Turks (Muslims), and Croats' who were bound to dilute and contaminate the 'pure Serb struggle'.[184]

One might argue that a grass-roots Bosnian Serb desire for vengeance was being hijacked here by an overtly chauvinist Chetnik agenda. Or again, more problematically, perhaps this chauvinist message actually *had cultural resonance* with many Serbs, whether they supported Chetniks, Partisans, or neither. What is clear is that Chetnik—and much initial Partisan—counter-violence was not directed for the most part at the Ustasha or Croats per se, as one might expect, but at *Muslims*, including in regions such as eastern Bosnia where there had been few Ustasha atrocities. Serb hatred of Muslims seems to have been widespread. Even Milovan Djilas, the Partisan's leading theoretician, claimed that in his own native Montenegro and in the neighbouring Sanjak, 'the hatred between Muslims and Orthodox ... is primeval, attested by rebellions and invasions, epics and visions'.[185] Djilas's comments would seem to make this animus primordial to Serb identity, in the same way as the Ustasha would claim for Croat identity vis-à-vis Serbs. If so, it operated in the absence of any obvious Muslim *political* threat.

Since the Ottoman retreat from the Balkans, definitively confirmed by the creation of Yugoslavia, the region's Muslims were in effect a number of discrete minority communities primarily in Bosnia-Herzegovina, the Sanjak, and Kosovo. It is certainly true that this situation fostered an incipient effort to create a nation-wide Muslim political and communal consciousness. This had nothing to do with religion per se—if anything the community was in advance of both Serbs and Croats in its Westernizing, urbanizing, and secularizing tendencies. Instead, it represented an awareness that in the context of what was in practice a multi-ethnic modern state, specifically Muslim interests needed both protecting and developing. This tentatively emerging identity hardly meant that all Yugoslav Muslims behaved or voted as a monolithic bloc, though given Serb dominance in terms of parliament, administration, and resource-allocation, Muslim deputies were more likely to tactically line up with their Croat than their Serbian counterparts.[186]

During the war, this picture became much more complicated. Bosnian Muslim involvement as German proxies, leading to the creation of the Waffen SS 'Handzar' Division, though often cited, did not come until late in the war and could be seen as a result of *their* 'back to the wall' fears, *after* the range of Serb atrocities committed against *them*. To be sure, the Division also committed anti-Serb atrocities in eastern Bosnia, for which responsibility lay with the German command's 'anti-Partisan' directives, even if these atrocities were interpreted locally as proof of Muslim hatred against Serbs. In fact, the exquisite Muslim dilemma was that they were caught between the devil and the deep blue sea.[187] Pavelić had sought to co-opt Muslims into his administration as a way of deflecting any possibility that the third largest ethnic community in the NDH might line up with the second— the Serbs—against Zagreb. This also conveniently involved a neat Ustasha piece of sophistry to the effect that Muslims were really the pure 'flowers' of the Croat nation, thereby denying them a separate national identity but confirming, in Chetnik eyes, Muslim perfidy and treacherousness against the Serb cause. In the context of the first great pulse of Ustasha genocide in spring and summer 1941, there were certainly influential Muslims, especially in parts of Herzegovina where there were few Croats, who were prepared to encourage and incite grass-roots anti-Serb violence and property seizures. Creating a localized advantage against Serb domination translated into some Muslim participation in the Black Legions. On the other hand, as early as August, members of the Bosnian *ulema* were not only publicly protesting against NDH broken promises to Muslims as a community but also against Ustasha atrocities and forced conversions being perpetrated against their Serb neighbours. As a result, the information on Muslim involvement and opinion in this early violence is conflicting. The frequent reference to the sight of the Muslim fez in anti-Serb attacks may well have been a conscious Ustasha subterfuge by which to deflect blame onto Muslim 'delinquents'. Yet *ulema* condemnation of Muslims who resorted to extortion and violence suggests genuine alarm—and disgust—at the degree to which communal elements were climbing onto the Ustasha bandwagon.[188]

What was to be done? To declare common cause with the Partisans was not particularly clever given the uncertainty of wider communal backing and the frequency with which Axis forces sought to liquidate Partisan enclaves. Having truck with an openly atheistic organization hardly inspired Muslim confidence. Moreover, whatever their High Command was saying, on the ground in Bosnia Partisan behaviour towards Muslims was often indistinguishable from that of Chetniks. Was the best approach for Muslims, therefore, to take a chance on the Partisans anyway, concentrating on self-defence where it was possible; or align themselves with the unequivocally strongest player (at least for the moment) in the region? At least the Germans were the nearest thing on hand to the Habsburgs, to whom up to the time of the Great War the Muslims of Bosnia-Herzegovina had always been able to look for protection. The very fragmentation of Muslim responses a world war later is evidence that this assurance no longer applied. Indeed, the Axis division of the Balkans into spheres of influence ensured that the Wehrmacht could offer no guarantee of Muslim safety in the face of Chetnik attack.

It is noteworthy—and as we have seen highly ironic given their strong association with the protection of Jews in the region—that the most widespread sequence of anti-Muslim massacres took place when the Italian Second Army handed over its positions to the Chetniks in south-east Bosnia and Herzegovina, in the high summer and late autumn of 1941, or, again, when tactical Chetnik advances or retreats occurred in essentially the same area, in the winter of 1941–2, the summer of 1942, and early 1943. The massacre sequence reads alarmingly like a roll-call from the Bosnian conflict fifty years later. The towns and local villages around Goražde, Foča, Višegrad, Žepa, and Srebrenica were all sites of what the chief Chetnik ideologue, Stevan Moljević, described as *čišćenje*, 'cleansing', in some cases, such as Foča, on repeated occasions.[189] In all cases, the desire to inflict cruel death without reference to age or gender distinctions was as standard here as it was on the Ustasha side. The mass liquidation of Muslims was also carried out regardless of whether local communities had, or had not, been involved in anti-Serb violence. For instance, at Kulen Vakuf, further west in the Bosanska Krajina, a major massacre was enacted in September 1941, in spite of the fact that most of the Muslim inhabitants had roundly refused to join in the earlier Ustasha killing of local Serbs. When the village was 'liberated', however, the Serb insurgents, supported by local peasants, went on a three-day killing spree, including the hacking to death in a meadow of hundreds of women and children using knives and farm implements. As many as 1,350 people in total were exterminated. What is also notable about the Kulen Vakuf massacre, and the subsequent razing of the village, is first that its perpetrators were nominally members of a Partisan detachment, and second that Ustasha Home Guard prisoners captured in the fighting were subsequently released. The mass killing here, in other words, was not simply reprisal, but involved the conscious liquidation of the Muslim community.[190]

Was there, then, some systematic Chetnik plan of genocide against Muslims? The fact that at Kulen Vakuf it was a Partisan unit which had been responsible for the massacre suggests something rather more localized than that, the decision of a commander acting on his own volition, perhaps even in response to demotic pressures from his rank and file. Indeed, it raises a wider question as to whether genocide can ever emerge as the totality of separate, individual actions *from below* or perhaps, once began, whether copy-cat massacres can develop a momentum of their own. Even had it wanted to, it is difficult to imagine how the JVUO, from its extremely tenuous parastate position and almost complete dependence on the Italians, could have marshalled sufficient resources to carry through a sustained anti-Muslim assault. The infrastructure of concentration camps, even the appallingly organized ones the NDH possessed, was out of the question. Moreover, the highly contingent and reactive nature of the JVUO's existence, and with it the necessity of devolving orders to regional commanders, meant that while in one sector units might be exterminating Muslims, in another they might be cooperating with them against Ustasha, or even Partisans.

This sort of tactical pragmatism was hardly peculiar to the Chetniks. By mid-1942, as the Partisan movement began to make serious inroads into NDH territory, the Ustasha were also prepared to enter into a set of arrangements with Bosnian Chetnik commanders, whereby the latter's authority was recognized in areas where they were already in control. This amounted, as Hoare has pithily put it, not just to 'the establishment of a Serb parastate within the framework of the Croatian state' but a 'model of multinational coexistence...organised on parallel, nationally exclusive lines'.[191] This rather suggests that when an ideologically driven movement is faced with extinction it will go to monstrous lengths, even to the point of sharing power with its bitterest enemy, in order to survive. If the deal underscored Ustasha feebleness, the belated early 1944 JVUO abandonment of its Great Serb stance in favour of a federalized Serb-Croat-Slovene polity (a return, by a roundabout route, to the original 1919 'Yugoslav' conception) may suggest how desperate and untenable its position had become.[192] Yet the Partisans, at one of their lower ebbs, behaved not unsimilarly. Just as their leadership were prepared to turn a blind eye to massacres of Muslims by Bosnian Serb units who may have come over from, or might otherwise have joined, the Chetniks, so in spring 1942, Tito was even prepared to consider collaboration with 'progressive' elements in the otherwise utterly 'fascistoid' NDH, so that the Partisans might concentrate on the 'main danger' to themselves at that moment: coming from the Chetnik bands and Nedićites.[193]

The almost bewildering alacrity with which all Balkan parties were prepared to make and break deals with one another certainly tells us something about the pitiless nature of 'war of all against all'. But it might also in a strange way explain why projects for the complete extermination of communal enemies could not be pursued *à outrance*. At least not *immediately*. So long as no single party had dominance, each had to bend its position to what was achievable in the short term, or defer (in the case of Ustasha and Chetniks) to German or possibly Italian patrons. When Nedić, for instance, drew up a memorandum for the future ethnographic make-up of an enlarged Serb state which would include Bosnia-Herzegovina—and which it was hoped would be the prequel to an NDH relinquishing of several east Bosnian districts to Belgrade—the proposal envisaged the expulsion of all Croats but implied the assimilation of remaining Muslims. On the latter score, there is no evidence that this is what Nedić actually wanted. However, as it was written for a German audience and the Muslims were *their* clients, long-term projections were better concealed. With the staunchly pro-NDH Kasche still Berlin's main man in Zagreb, the implied shift to favour Belgrade at the expense of the NDH was stonewalled anyway.[194] But the point of noting the episode is that it might suggest that tactical considerations may have put limits on strategic ambitions—including full-scale genocide.

There are certainly grounds for assuming that the JVUO clique, had they had a wider freedom of action, would have sought to eruct the entirety of the Muslim population from a projected Greater Serbia. A fragment from Mihailović's diary in spring 1942 reads, 'The Muslim population has through its behaviour arrived at the situation where our people no longer wish to have them in our midst. It is necessary already now to prepare their exodus to Turkey or anywhere else outside our borders.'[195] Key figures whom Mihailović could count on to offer more precise policy recommendations for such sentiments included the politician Dragiša Vasić, and the Bosnian Serb lawyer from the Krajina Stevan Moljević; both alongside Vasa Cubrilović, whom we have previously encountered; who had been prominent pre-war spokesmen of the Serbian Cultural Club, which effectively advocated the jettisoning of Yugoslavia in favour of a territorially expanded but homogenized Serbia. Moljević is particularly remembered for his wartime articulation of such a project, suitably entitled 'Homogeneous Serbia'. This 'radical optimal solution to the Serb national question' envisaged what amounted to an imperial Serb state, including all of Bosnia-Herzegovina, Dalmatia, and much of Croatia. Any Croats on this territory would be 'exchanged' to a rump Croatia, which would be self-governing but linked, along with (an expanded) Slovenia, to Serbia. Thus, while Croats would be firmly subordinated to a hegemonic Belgrade, they would have a place within a reformulated 'federal' constellation. Moljević, however, envisaged no such place for Muslims. For them, *čišćenje* meant deportation to Turkey or Albania.[196]

Two things ought to be of note from Moljević's tract, as also through its *cultural* linkage to Mihailović's diary entry. First, as with *ustasvo* thinking, here, too, there is an implicit notion that the ongoing debility of the nation must lie with its historically grounded contamination by some foreign idea or body. Whereas in *ustasvo* that damage lay in the Serbs who came across the river borders from the Ottoman empire bringing their impure or debased 'oriental' ideas with them, in *cetnistvo* it was not so much the Croats who were the fundamental peril, but the indigenous population who had abased themselves to Islam. In both instances, therefore, race per se was not at the root of evil, but rather prolonged contact with an alien religion and hence thought-system. But the specifically Serb national question which followed related to the apostate Muslim population, in other words Serbo-Croat speaking communities indistinguishable in physical appearance from other Balkan peoples. Were they recoverable for the nation? Or, to put it in religious terms, could they be returned to a 'pure' state through 'water' (i.e. baptism—as neighbouring Bulgarians had attempted with their Pomaks), or was their sin so heinous, not to say intractable, that the only way to save not them but the national body itself was through 'blood' (massacre)? For the best part of a century Serbian ultra-nationalists, as indeed south Slav nationalists more generally, had taken their cue for an answer to this question by way of an influential epic poem, *Gorski Vijenac*, 'the Mountain Wreath', written by the Montenegrin Orthodox prince-bishop Njegoš. At the core of its 1846 narrative is a mythic showdown between Orthodox Montenegrins and Slavonic apostates, in which the massacre-strewn resolution to their struggle is the burning down of the dwellings of 'our home-grown faithless devils' so that 'no trace' of them is left.[197]

The mythic message, then, is clear: there could be no compromise with Muslims, home-grown or otherwise. Even so, something remained ambiguous in the way the likes of Moljević or Mihailović chose to interpret it. Was their aim the root and branch removal of the Muslims at some future date, perhaps through some notional peace settlement-related 'transfer' or 'exchange'; or was the cleansing Moljević spoke of a cipher for a more immediate Montenegrin-style settling of accounts? Vasić, responding to his colleague's memorandum in early May 1942, believed the dilemma could be resolved after the war, when, just as in the aftermath of the last one, other countries would be too busy with their own problems to care about whether an unwanted population was being annihilated somewhere else. Vasić's conclusion: 'if we are wise, this question of cleansing or resettling and exchanging of populations will not be that difficult'.[198]

Here, then, is the second point of note about the Moljević tract. While its recommendations were clearly incendiary, there is no firm evidence that Chetnik exterminatory violence against Muslims was their *direct* consequence. Such grounds for doubt would also be in keeping with the very weak and fragmented nature of Mihailović's command structure itself militating against any systematic programme of genocide. Dulić offers a telling, practical example of this Chetnik handicap. An Ustasha goal in any communal assault might be to murder the leading members and perhaps remove the rest to a holding camp, while at the same time attempting to ensure that the victims' houses remained intact for Slovene incomers or Croat 'returnees'. By contrast, the Chetniks lacked any of the infrastructure or operational framework which gave such discriminatory planning point or plausibility. As a result, their attacks were much more likely to be 'premodern' and brigand-like in their method, killing everybody they could lay their hands on, destroying everything—houses included—and fleeing as rapidly as possible, burdened down by all the possessions from the attack that they been able to pillage.[199]

The apparent discrepancy between Chetnik and Ustasha methodology in killing, however, is not sufficient to dismiss the former as outside the bounds of genocide. On the contrary, what makes Chetnik genocidal violence so compelling is that it was achieved with even less coordination than the Ustasha could muster, almost as if its commanders *knew* what was expected of them. Mihailović implied as much in his post-war Titoist show-trial, when he spoke of his men revenging themselves—allegedly for Muslim attacks—and the Drina, as a result, becoming 'a river of blood'. We have already noted the symbolic significance of the river. For those who saw in Bosnia the potential for a cross-communal harmony and unity, its bridges expressed exactly that aspiration. For ultra-nationalists of Chetnik or Ustasha type, it was this same ideal which was anathema. When the Chetniks brought thousands of Muslims to the bridges to slit their throats and then toss them into the river, this was not, thus, just a matter of vicious killing. It was a public demonstration that any notion of coexistence between Serbs, Croats, and Muslims was an abomination which they, the perpetrators, were obliterating for now and for ever.[200] The passion with which Chetniks entered into this task was something they shared with the Ustasha. It was also reflected in the Muslim death toll, with estimates of 75,000 killed in Bosnia alone, the majority of these at the hands of Chetniks, the largest proportion from direct massacres in the south-eastern corner of the country. This would translate into a proportionate loss of 8.1 per cent, a higher figure than for Yugoslav Serbs overall, though one might add that the percentage Serb loss *within* the NDH was considerably greater.[201]

To be sure, statistical analyses of the ethnic losses suggest that throughout Yugoslavia and across the wider Balkan theatre, communities were sucked into varying degrees of murderous, internecine strife with one another. Writing in 1944, Lemkin, for instance, was particularly concerned as to the fate of Serbs currently under Bulgarian rule in the Macedonian region and renewed Albanian attacks on Serbs in Kosovo, which he characterized as genocide.[202] Everywhere, indeed, where debatable political boundaries had been drawn across ethnographic realities, whether in the Great War or earlier, the renewed instability and uncertain tenure of Axis rule proved too great an incentive for aggrieved national groups to resist redrawing them once again.

That Bosnia-Herzegovina, however, became the centre stage for altogether more sweeping and murderously genocidal violence than elsewhere was not simply circumstantial, or a facet of violence begetting more violence. The Ustasha assault on Serbs, the Chetnik one on Muslims, were consistent with long-term— if, nevertheless, very modern—programmes for the homogenization of perceived national space, and with both parties staking their respective prospects for communal salvation on the removal and/or elimination of most, if not all, members of the 'other' group seen as representing the existential threat. If Axis rule unleashed the latent conditions for these mass murders, it also, paradoxically, prevented them being brought to an 'optimal' conclusion. The Ustasha remained in power to the bitter end in Zagreb in May 1945, their murders undiminished, albeit with their proclivity towards wholesale Serb destruction heavily curtailed by the Germans. Mihailović's ability to act as he might have liked was hobbled from the very outset by the lack of any firm territorial base and his dependence on Italian patronage. With the Italian surrender, the JVUO was as good as finished as a military force, as was its ability to exterminate its communal and political enemies. This left the Partisans, with Stalin (at least for now) their main sponsor and the might of the Red Army as insurance, to take control of all Yugoslavia and impose their communist version of national reconciliation, while meting out quite spectacular summary justice to fascist collaborators. All this, in short, underscored that projects of genocide in the Balkan rimlands could not be carried through without favourable geopolitical circumstances. But that raises a further question: can genocide ever be attempted, let alone accomplished, by non-state actors in complete defiance of such realities?

THE WAR IN THE MIDDLE (2): THE UKRAINIAN–POLISH WAR

The attacks followed a pattern. During the prelude, there were Orthodox priests who blessed axes, pitchforks, and knives in the church. The first bad omen to the Poles might be when Ukrainian acquaintances stopped talking to them, although Ukrainians who lived close to the targeted communities were often kept in the dark about the assault plan. In 'mixed' villages such a plan involved painting crosses on Polish homes. Flares were common attack signals, and the clothing of some attackers might suggest that they were German soldiers or Soviet partisans. One ruse was that they came to coordinate the fight against the Germans. Often there were three waves of attackers. First, there was a walking crowd of SB officers, UPA members, and ordinary villagers. Then there were UPA members on horseback. Finally there was a ring of male and female villagers, who looted property and strip-searched the dead. Indeed, among the killers were also ordinary Ukrainian villagers of various ages and of both sexes. If attackers doubted a potential victim's ethnicity, they demanded that he or she recite the Lord's Prayer in Ukrainian. As for Polish children, some were let go, or were taken along as servants. The attackers dynamited the Roman Catholic churches. No more than a few days after the massacre, the attackers ordered Ukrainians from nearby villages to bury the bodies.[203]

Thus Karel Berkhoff describes the growing wave of anti-Polish atrocities which began in western Volhynia in February 1943. Other more explicit accounts make it abundantly clear that the violence meted out was every bit as lurid and grotesque as what was still taking place a rimland away, in Bosnia. Tales of the axemen who led the attacks were legion, as were tales of the manner in which villagers deployed their sickles and pitchforks to mutilate, disembowel, decapitate, and generally hack their victims to death. The involvement of slow torture as prelude to killing brings Rwanda to mind, as does its mercilessness. Ukrainians with Polish wives and children had no choice but to kill them, or suffer death themselves. Those who spoke out against the violence, including priests and bishops from the Autonomist Orthodox Church, were likely to be murdered too.[204]

As Berkhoff's information equally makes clear, while the attacks may have been frenzied they were far from mindless. On the contrary, these were highly organized, centralized, and coordinated liquidations as prepared and directed by the Sluzhba Bezpeky (SB) security arm of the UPA. And what begun as a series of probing attacks in the Sarny and Kostopil districts of Rivne province in February and March was extended outwards beyond the historic Austrian–Russian boundary on the Zbruch, to involve mass destructions of Polish villages in both western Volhynia and eastern Galicia: as far south as Tarnopol, as far west as Lviv (Lwów). Three great pulses of violence ensued, in the spring, the high summer—with an estimated 167 attacks on 11 and 12 July alone—and a further major one at the very end of the year. By then perhaps as many as 50,000 Poles had been massacred in some 900 localities. Another 350,000 had fled. As a result, in some areas of this western Ukrainian country, the Polish population completely disappeared.[205]

This was clearly the UPA intention—which might make their actions one of extreme ethnic cleansing. But then the primary modus operandi by which the UPA sought to clear the Polish population was mass killing, which would equally render their efforts as genocide. To be sure, it was a genocide committed in a relatively small (and remote) area; and against the Polish casualty figures one would also to have to count an estimated 10,000 Ukrainians murdered by Poles in retaliation.[206] The mutual element of the killing would thereby suggest that if this was genocide it was also, by the same token, a form of internecine—or civil—war. But then there were strong elements of that too in the genocides committed by the Ustasha and Chetniks. What was fundamentally different in the UPA case was the lack of an outside sponsor. The Ustasha had a state—of sorts—and the nominal support of Berlin. The Chetniks were closer to the UPA in being no more than a shadow state. But, at the very least, the JVUO were the representatives on the ground of a recognized sovereign entity. The UPA had no such official standing or patronage. Their achievement of statehood had to be accomplished by force of will, together with whatever human and other resources they could muster. Fundamental weaknesses on this score plus the lack of a machinery of state to carry through their agenda in a systematic way would have many scholars debating as to whether such an entity had the capacity to commit a sustained, systematic, ethnically focused mass murder.[207] The extraordinary paradox of the UPA programme is that the extermination of the Poles was conceived not as an act of state, but as its midwife. By targeting an area of mixed Polish and Ukrainian population, and through genocide making it wholly Ukrainian, the UPA sought to create the territorial framework upon which a sovereign and independent Ukraine would be a fait accompli, albeit in the UPA's own utterly totalitarian image.

What is equally extraordinary about this UPA—actually OUN-B—ambition is the degree which it flew completely in the face of geopolitical reasoning. One can see that its key protagonists—the most radical elements in an already radicalized movement—predicated their action on that key element of high-risk calculation common to all would-be national liberators in the German occupied rimlands: namely, how to bring maximum force to bear in order to bring territory under their control at the critical hiatus between Nazi evacuation and Soviet occupation. The OUN were not alone in recognizing that the calculation had to take into account other would-be national competitors who might equally claim the same territory as theirs. The attention of underground Lithuanian groups, too, was much exercised by anticipation of a struggle with the AK over the fate of Vilna and its hinterland, as that moment of truth drew near. Yet such a struggle was likely to sap Lithuanian energies in the face of a much more powerful and invidious Soviet threat. That hardly prevented a major break-out of violence between scratch

Lithuanian and Polish forces in spring 1944, which rapidly descended into attacks on each other's villages. However, there appear to have been brakes on this inter-group violence, perhaps, in part, the result of more moderate Lithuanians recognizing that in the absence of a German umbrella the only way to keep the Soviets at bay was to come to some arrangement with the Poles.[208] As things turned out, it made no difference to the Lithuanians' fate. With the Germans gone and the Poles smashed, their remaining insurgents had to fight it out on their own against the Red Army and NKVD.

Perhaps, then, the radical OUN-B analysis that the only way to stop the Soviets in their tracks was to have a chunk of territory firmly in their hands *before* the Germans left was not so far-fetched after all. But did that require the complete elimination of the region's Poles? The decision to go for this maximalist route can be traced to the secret third conference of the Bandera faction, held near Lviv in mid-February 1943. With Stepan Bandera himself incarcerated by the Nazis in Sachsenhausen, and the Nazis themselves reeling from Stalingrad, it was the new, young leadership of the movement in Bandera's absence, men of the ilk of Mykola Lebed and Roman Shukhevych, who now forced the pace towards the ethnic cleansing project. Both were graduates of the German security police school in Zakopane, hence both had form as participants in the 'Final Solution'. The conference decision also coincided with a major defection of some 6,000 serving Ukrainian *Schutzmänner*, in both Volhynia and the General Government, along with their equipment. This was not simply fortuitous.[209] The OUN-B had been stockpiling weapons at the German police academy at Rivne and inducting its Ukrainian trainees—otherwise there to study the arts of Nazi mass murder—into its own ranks for some time. The cutting edge of what was to become the UPA's strike force would be the very same men who had learnt their trade in the destruction of eastern Jewry.[210]

But where did the decision on *Polish* destruction come into the equation? The destruction of the Jews, in which OUN members had been German proxies, meant that one critical demographic element in their calculation had already been eliminated. Strategically speaking that left three others: the Germans, Soviets, and Poles. The issue of the OUN relationship with the Germans is sufficiently convoluted, fraught, yet significant to this story to require us to say a little more below. It was surely the renewed arrival of the Soviets in western Ukraine which ought to have given the party its greatest cause for concern. There had already been a devastating Soviet strike, led by the renowned partisan leader Sydir Kovpak, deep into German-occupied Ukraine in late 1942. Kovpak followed this up in August the following year with a raid which cut through into Galicia in the direction of the Carpathians, exposing the utter feebleness of German defences in the 'Lands Between'.[211] If this was a warning of what the OUN could expect with even greater consequence, their chosen 1943 preparation was at the expense of their third, and weakest, rival—the Poles.

Thus, one could read this as a very cold-blooded, entirely social-Darwinian calculation, encapsulated in the UPA slogan 'a strip of free Ukraine for every dead Pole'.[212] Moreover, pre-war, the OUN had hardly been significant as an organization in western Volhynia—where this project was intended to be put into effect. The OUN heartlands were in eastern Galicia. The fact that the Poles were already thin on the ground in the former region, perhaps no more than 400,000 people (or 16 per cent of the total population) and spread thinly across its 30,000 square kilometres, would have underscored an entirely cynical OUN view that without them the Ukrainian case for the national self-determination of western Volhynia—for instance, at some future international peace conference— would have been all the stronger.[213] Before such an imagined audience, OUN leaders might have added that Polish counter-claims based on pre-1939 sovereignty were laid bare by their continuing refusal to countenance anything beyond political, civil, and cultural rights for the majority population.[214] The very inability of Warsaw to recognize Ukrainian claims to autonomy, or even an acknowledgement that it was guilty of a historic wrong in trampling over these rights in the recent past, would certainly have reinforced a hardened wartime OUN argument that the Poles ought to be paid back in kind. But then, killing Poles en masse to make the point would seem to suggest something more than a purely clinical assessment of the situation. Scratch the OUN world view a little deeper, and we might arrive at the wellsprings of latent tendencies markedly consistent with a potential for genocide.

*

We may remember that the origins of the OUN were bound up less with the failure to create a large Kiev-centred Ukraine on former tsarist-controlled soil in the wake of the Russian revolution and more with the immediate demise of the Western Ukrainian National Republic (ZUNR) at the end of the Great War, on what had been Habsburg Galician territory. However, for Ukrainian ultra-nationalists the two events were linked by a common disastrous thread. In the case of Kiev, the domination of 'the soft democratic Central Rada' had denied the regime the necessary survival instincts it might have learnt had it turned more rapidly and unequivocally to the Directory's hardman, Petliura. ZUNR's failure was even more abject, and could be summed up in the manner in which, having taking power in Lviv on 1 November 1918, it then threw its chance away by not imprisoning the city's Polish intelligentsia, thereby giving the latter a free hand to organize the rebellion which ousted the Republic two weeks later.[215] Here, then, were grounds for a classic 'perpetrators' "never again" syndrome' in which hatred of what the Poles had done was matched by an awareness that Ukrainians, through their own lack of ruthlessness, had allowed it to happen.

It was exactly out of the frustration of the 1918–19 failure and the desperate alienation that followed that the OUN was spawned. Some parallels with the Ustasha are immediately evident. OUN supporters read Polish control of (formerly Habsburg) Galicia in a very similar manner to the way the Pavelić people viewed Serb dominion over (formerly Habsburg) Croatia. In both cases, what took place thereafter was read as both colonization and national oppression, regardless of whether Belgrade or Warsaw attempted to carry through their own centralizing policies in a more liberal or accommodating manner. In this sense, the OUN became yet another fascist-leaning, ultra-nationalist movement which, repudiating the possibility of compromise with the 'colonizing power', sought instead to work for its revolutionary overthrow. In practice, again like the Ustasha, this involved the metamorphosing of an already marginal radical movement (the Party of Right in the Croat case, the Ukrainian Military Organization, UVO, in the latter), into a more overtly terrorist one. Both, in fact, took this new path in 1929, a year malodorous with political and economic turmoil and foreboding across the continent. In both instances, too, the lurch towards violence, sabotage, and assassination was in large part a consequence of the influx of younger, especially student, types into movement ranks, whose sense of hope for the future had been dashed on all fronts, and whose response was the sort of revolutionary vanguardist strategy which began in the Russian arena with the nineteenth-century anti-tsarist Narodnaya Volya.[216] Young west Ukrainians' disillusionment would have been all the keener into the early 1930s as the potential for freedom across the Soviet border was stifled, suffocated, and then utterly snuffed out in waves of Stalinist terror, collectivization, and exterminatory famine. OUN cadres, again rather like their Ustasha equivalents, took refuge in racialized explanations for both Ukraine's historic thwarting and ultimate resurgence. The veteran socialist-turned-integral nationalist Dmytro Dontsov told them that their economic displacement was caused by the minorities on *their* soil. Ukrainians could not afford to balk even at their physical eradication.[217] The country's anguish could only be resolved, declared another of their theoreticians, Maksym Orlyk, when the entirety 'of *moskali* [Russians], Jews, Poles, Madiars [Hungarians], Tatars and others' had been swept out and a 'pure' Ukraine committed to the mobilization and development of 'all its biological strength' had filled up 'the entire ethnographic space'.[218] It was legitimate, too, stated the OUN's 'Ten Commandments' (shades here of another infamously inflammatory document of the same title which fed into Rwanda's 1994 genocide) to take everything from these foreigners 'to expand the strength, riches and size of the Ukrainian state'.[219]

The OUN sense of injury clearly embraced a range of alleged enemies over and beyond the Poles. Indeed, the OUN's proposed solution, by way of a national liberation to the shores of the Black Sea, made Ustasha ambitions seem almost puny by comparison, even if it underscored that, like their Croatian counterparts, the OUN people would need a heavy-duty outside sponsor if their imaginings were ever to be translated into the realm of political reality. Just as the Ustasha gravitated towards the Italians for moral and material sustenance, so the OUN leadership in exile was more than ready to render itself serviceable to German designs, in return for Berlin's support. To be sure, this hardly resolved the OUN's immediate conflict with the Polish state before a liberated Galicia could even contemplate its further role as Ukrainian Piedmont. Thus, at one level, the Polish–Ukrainian conflict of the 1930s continued to follow similar contours to that of the Serb–Croat struggle, and became one in which an increasing number of (especially) young people were drawn into OUN ranks by the almost inevitable dialectic of state versus terrorist violence. Even so, the majority of Ukrainians remained steadfastly on the sidelines.[220] Thus, one significant dissimilarity between OUN and Ustasha is that in the former case, while there clearly were shades of a historic, cultural, as well as geographic divide between Polish Catholicism and Ukrainian Orthodoxy in its various permutations, as there were Ukrainian clerics willing to lend their moral support to OUN actions,[221] the dominant Uniate position—as represented most forcefully by our old friend Metropolitan Sheptyts'kyi—while supportive of Ukrainian statehood (and an army to match), was entirely unambiguous in its condemnation and detestation of OUN terror. On this score, Sheptyts'kyi remained entirely consistent until his death in November 1944.[222]

Where the OUN trajectory diverged decisively from that of the Ustasha was in relation not to its primary Polish enemy, but to its supposed German friend. Despite, as we have seen, Berlin's great reluctance in the matter, the NDH became a client-state within the Axis system in 1941. OUN exiles in Berlin had good reason to assume that a German thrust to the east would reward them similarly. In 1918, Austro-German occupation of the region had led to the installation of an albeit puppet regime under the hetman, Pavlo Skoropadsky. In turn, this had been the launching pad for the more truly independent, if short-lived, Ukrainian republic. The OUN's not unreasonable calculation was that if they demonstrated willingness to do Berlin's bidding in its Polish campaign, this time they would reap the benefit. The Soviet drive into western Volhynia and eastern Galicia in September 1939 rather spoiled that estimation. More keenly, where German policy on matters Ukrainian was really going might already have been gleaned from the way Berlin ignored calls for assistance from 'the Republic of Carpatho-Ukraine' declared by Ukrainian nationalists as Czechoslovakia was dismembered, only to be wound up twenty-four hours later as the Hungarians marched into the region.[223]

Two and three-quarter years later, the OUN were still prepared to back the German horse, two 600-strong units of OUN men (one of them in the Great War uniform of the Ukrainian Sich, which had fought for an independent state under Habsburg command) taking to the field, this time under the auspices of the Abwehr. The units' value to the latter in rousing fellow-Ukrainians to support the Wehrmacht advance, incite anti-Jewish pogroms, and eliminate 'enemies' on the ground, members of the Polish intelligentsia included, was undoubted. Canaris was a strong supporter of their cause, as was Rosenberg.[224] But as we have seen, there were no prospects for an OUN equivalent of a semi-independent Croatia under Hitler. At a strictly regional level, within the Galician areas of the General Government, German support for Ukrainians to participate in the administration, plus support for their schools, culture, and cooperative movement, signalled a clear intent to advance the interests of a specially appointed Ukrainian Central Committee at the expense of Poles—and, of course, Jews.[225] But if this policy continued in the expanded district of Galicia after Operation Barbarossa, it did not extend into the rest of Axis-occupied territories which the OUN deemed 'Ukrainian'. The Rumanians were the recipients of the newly conquered lands across the Dniester. And what the Antonescu regime chose to do closer to home in the northern Bukovina, including a project to clear out the significant, increasingly OUN-supportive Ukrainian minority there, was not something Berlin was going to turn into an

international incident. As things transpired, Bucharest never got beyond the planning stage.[226] But any vestiges of hope that the OUN might be able to wrest some
level of autonomy in the territory Berlin designated as Reichskommissariat Ukraine
were rapidly dashed by brutal German diktat.

In fact, both competing factions of the OUN had laid out careful plans to
take over local and regional administrations in the wake of the Wehrmacht
advance. OUN-B's big moment came in Lviv on 30 June 1941, when they publicly declared the restoration of an independent Ukraine. That of OUN-M came
a few months later when they appointed a mayor and city administration in
Kiev, as they had already done in many other provincial centres. While on the
latter score there was a short hiatus in which Germans and Ukrainians appeared
to cooperate, within weeks the experiment was over and most of the OUN protagonists had been either sent to concentration camps or executed out of hand—
many of their bodies ending up, ironically, in Babi Yar.[227] The same fate had
already been visited on the Banderites, as many as four-fifths of whose leadership were killed by the Germans in 1941–2, while their organization was
declared an enemy of the Reich. The Nazi message that the Ukrainians were no
more than *Untermenschen* and would be treated accordingly could not have
been more unequivocal. As for the Abwehr-sponsored military units, attempted
mutinies were swiftly put down and the men effectively impressed into police
battalions, whose first port of call was to assist in eliminating Jewish 'partisans'
(*sic*) in Belorussia.[228]

OUN had staked its whole enterprise on a war which, with German backing,
would bring it to the goal which had eluded Ukrainian nationalists twenty or more
years earlier. Yet by the end of 1941, that goal was as distant as ever, if not more so,
one key consequence being that an already deeply fractious divide between the two
wings of the movement reached the point where remaining cadres began gunning
each other down almost wherever they encountered one other. The outcome of this
internal bloodletting was in part determined by who proved the less pitiless in the
assassination stakes. But the Melnykites were also arguably more handicapped by
their insistence that, despite what had happened, there remained no choice but to
hold on limpet-like to the Germans. For the Banderites, by contrast, what had
always been a pragmatic relationship was now sundered, demanding that the
movement strike out on its own entirely independent course. One might read this
full crystallization of the OUN-B position as further evidence of its political imma-
turity. What had always marked off the Banderites from the supporters of Andrii
Melnyk was a generational gap, which also carried with it the absence of a strong
attachment to the Habsburg military experience, a memory which would again
eventually cause so many OUN-M followers to gravitate into the ranks of the SS
'Galicia' formation.[229] But what use was there in dying for the Germans if there was
no tangible quid pro quo?

The problem for the rump Banderite leadership, therefore, lay not in the potential popularity of their unilateralist intentions, but in how they could conceive of
any such programme without it looking like anything other than national suicide.
Perhaps that was half their point. The situation was already so extreme in 1942 and

into 1943 that going for broke became in the circumstances *more* logical. By then, it was not just the Germans who represented imminent danger. The potential for some sort of Polish–Soviet rapprochement, and hence collaboration—this in the period before the Katyn discoveries—would inevitably involve a further block on Ukrainian aspirations;[230] and this time, perhaps, not just for a generation but for the foreseeable future. Here were further grounds for seeing the OUN-B decision for action, in February 1943, as a response to imminent crisis. With the movement with its back to the wall, the likes of Lebed and Shukhevych had to determine on getting in their retaliation *before* 'the others' could achieve overwhelming dominance in the Ukraine. The onus upon them thus involved the *immediate* securing of *a* territory, which might then act as a power base for future expansion.

There is one final, actually fortuitous, element in this mix which helps further explain the OUN-B direction of travel, and so returns us to the matter of genocide. On the margins of western Volhynia and Polesie there was already a quasi-independent enclave which had the potential to serve as the Banderites' projected *foco*.[231] Since the summer of 1941, the Germans had subcontracted control of first the Sarny district and then further east around Olevsk to a local warlord, 'Taras Bulba' Borovets, whose initial credentials with the Germans—rather like Kaminsky—were his military flair in having extinguished Soviet resistance in the area. What began as a force of around a thousand men known as the Polissian Sich became the basis for what Borovets soon thereafter called the Ukrainian Insurgent Army (UPA). Initially, this was quite separate from either OUN faction, though it clearly making its own waves late in 1941 in the cleansing of Jews, Poles, and partisans from its zone of operation. Early in late 1941, or early 1942, there seems to have been a falling-out between Borovets and his German patrons, one aspect of which may have been Borovets's objection to the latters' economic over-exploitation and labour demands on his patch. By degrees, a reformulated UPA became an anti-German force, though one which was sufficiently powerful to have both SIPO and neighbouring pro-Soviet partisans coming to provisional arrangements recognizing its local authority.[232] Was it this autonomous track record, above all, which determined that Borovets's force, organizational title, and territory was not so much fused as forcibly appropriated by the Banderites? What is clear is that it was with this OUN-B co-option of the Borovets formation that, as Prusin puts it, 'the Polish-Ukrainian conflict *mutated* into the most bloody civil war fought in the borderlands'.[233]

One aspect of the ensuing bloodletting was the number of Ukrainians caught up in it and killed by the OUN-UPA. These included many loyal to Borovets—who attempted to form his own parallel organization. He himself escaped the ensuing slaughter. The OUN-B had never taken kindly to criticism. Once established in its west Volhynian forest and hill fastnesses, the elimination of dissenters practically became the corollary to what one of the new breed of UPA strongmen, Dmytro Kliachkivsky ('Klym Savur'), described as the creation of a 'single war camp'. On one level, this was about the mobilization of manpower and food reserves, a sort of Ukrainian 'war communism', in part to further consolidate as well as expand the UPA's independent zone.[234] It was Kliachkivsky as prime conceiver of the UPA military structure and commander of UPA sector north who, as high summer approached, gave the orders for the 'total physical liquidation' of all Poles aged between sixteen and sixty. But the directive also seems to have been closely intermeshed with UPA awareness that a full-scale military confrontation with the Red Army was imminent. The Soviets were at this moment breaking out from the Kursk salient. Thus, as the attacks on previously unharmed Polish settlements gathered momentum in south-west districts of the region in mid-July and accelerated around Liuboml towards the end of August, war and genocide became part of the UPA's *same* putative state emergency.[235] It was as an act of self-defence, the UPA would argue, that the Polish fifth column had to be eliminated. But August was also a month in which the SB resorted to extensive purges of people whether or not nominally within their own ranks. These included surviving Jews—tailors, shoemakers, doctors, and others—whom the UPA had pragmatically enlisted previously as ancillary support, as also various 'national' sub-units of Georgians, Uzbeks, and the like, who as POWs or Schuma deserters had been impressed into UPA formations.[236] All these elements were now considered actual or potential NKVD agents and were eliminated accordingly. But so too were large numbers of Ukrainians, both local to the area and also large numbers who had helped swell UPA ranks from the former Soviet Ukraine. Evidence is sketchy, but in summer 1943, it appears there may have been an internal UPA crisis involving an eastern Ukrainian challenge to the 'core' Galician leadership, who then reasserted their authority with lethal force. When it came to terror, the SB were well-organized; they even had a concentration camp close to the UPA headquarters at Velky Stydyn, near Kostopil.[237] But for all its security apparatus and military rigour, this was also a fundamentally weak regime, operating at the limit of its possibilities, and with an increasingly restive, not to say terrified, population under its totalitarian control. Under pressure from all sides, with no obvious way out of the project to which it had committed itself, nor allies to come to its assistance, it is little wonder that the UPA's increasing siege mentality and its ever more violent responses bears notable similarity to the paranoia of the Khmer Rouge.

As a result, UPA declarations, soon after the purges, of a more democratic and socialist orientation, including promises that all ethnic groups would have equal political and civil rights in a future Ukrainian state,[238] could only have come across—in particular to the remaining Poles in the vicinity—as tantamount to a sick joke. Indeed, the intensity of the UPA onslaught against them achieved something which by any other account would have been unimaginable: their flight into the arms of the Germans. At a time when the AK was supposed to be preparing for Operation Tempest, not only were Volhynian Poles joining German police units—usually those that Ukrainians had left to join the UPA—as the quickest route to weapons and retaliation, but the London government-in-exile found itself drawn into the conflict by mandating the formation of a special AK Volhynian Infantry Division, tasked in the first instance with combating the UPA threat.[239] Rather as in the Serb–Croat conflict, by early 1944 every party in the Polish-Ukrainian struggle seemed ready and willing to change places and line up with their own worst enemy, whether for necessary temporary advantage or to

take vengeance upon those they held collectively responsible for their own immediate suffering. AK self-defence units on the ground ignored strictures from London about harming civilians to cleanse Ukrainians from districts where Poles were
ethnically stronger or more closely matched. In mid-March, for instance, they
burnt down fourteen Ukrainian villages in the Chełm region, murdering 1,500
villagers in the process, 70 per cent of whom were reported to be women and
children.[240] AK actions of this type were sometimes assisted by residual groups of
Jewish fighters as well as Soviet partisans. The Wehrmacht might support such
efforts or strike against them. Ethnic German *Selbschutz*, also faced with their own
communal liquidation, had little compunction in also massacring Ukrainians.[241]
Meanwhile, the UPA, under pressure from the Soviet advance, extended its anti-
Polish onslaught onto eastern Galician soil, paradoxically also intensifying thereby
its struggle with the Wehrmacht. This, however, did not prevent the Ukrainians in
the SS 'Galicia' division linking up with UPA units in February to commit a major
anti-Polish atrocity at the village of Huta Peniacka in Tarnopol province.[242] While
the wider UPA effort was clearly running out of steam (indeed, in the summer of
1944 it was forced to resume a tactical alliance once again with the Germans in the
face of the 'common' Soviet threat), the impact of its programme on the Poles of
the western Volhynia was unmistakable: mass flight in the direction of the General
Government.

How then should we assess the efforts of the UPA in a history of genocide?
Today, a standard nationalist Ukrainian response, a little like that of many contemporary Croat responses to their Ustasha past, is most likely to be one which emphasizes the heroic aspects of the struggle for liberation and independence. In the
specifically UPA case, one could add for good measure the sacrifice of fighters who
fought and often were executed not only by the Soviets (the Croat equivalent being
Tito's forces) but also by Germans. It is absolutely true that the UPA struggle was
one waged against quite impossible odds, underscoring what latter-day sympathizers with that struggle might read as martyrdom.[243] And, in the final upshot, it was
not Germans and Poles lined up together to snuff out the Ukrainian national
movement, but Poles and Soviets—again a seemingly unlikely combination—
signing an agreement in September 1944 for the exchange of both Poles and
Ukrainians into each other's territory. Indeed, it was Soviet and Polish republic
military forces who cooperated thereafter to ensure the speedy 'voluntary' removal
of the third, Ukrainian party from Polish soil.[244] Squeezed into this vice and suffering on top of unmitigated Soviet horror, and three years of Nazi hell, is it not right
and proper to remind ourselves that at the heart of the genocidal violence inflicted
in these years, Ukrainians were more victims than victimizers?

The problem with staying with attention fixed on this grand landscape of catastrophe is that it avoids the particular. In the recent past, this may have been a case
of simply—though perhaps rather charitably—not having sufficient archival evidence at hand, or from other sources, to construct a detailed picture of Polish–
Ukrainian interactions in 1943 and 1944.[245] Recent scholarship would suggest this
that might have been the case in the past, such a position is no longer tenable in
the present. The UPA did not fall into a prolonged episode of systematic mass

murder by misadventure. They consciously chose to plough this furrow as their route to the creation of a homogeneous Ukraine. To be sure, they needed the occasion and pretext, the latter in part provided through reports of AK attacks on Ukrainian collaborators, confabulated into the much more lurid but propagandistically valuable narrative of a Polish intent to exterminate the west Ukrainian population in entirety.[246] Equally, the UPA learnt from others, about not only the practice but also the possibilities which went with genocide. It is difficult to conceive of the UPA destruction of the Volhynian and Galician Poles without the prequel of Nazi destruction of the Volhynian and Galician Jews—in which, of course, Ukrainian nationalists were excellent students when it came to imbibing the preparation, techniques, and system of organized mass murder. Before that, they also learnt, at first or second hand, the instrumental value of terror—and atrocity—as meted out by the NKVD. Soviets and Nazis, thus, had much to answer for. Yet the UPA in its previous OUN or UVO incarnations had already spent two decades plotting the violent nationalization of Ukrainian space without either Russians or Germans as classroom tutors. Even after the shatter-zone events of 1914–21, even after the creation of a hubristic, pumped-up Poland, the region's ongoing cultural and ethnic heterogeneity should have offered the clearest sign that turning western Ukraine into the crucible of a one-dimensional Ukrainian polity was neither plausible nor acceptable.

The irony is that it was not Bandera and his followers who were yesterday's men, but those like the saintly Sheptyts'kyi who clung on to the possibility of ethnic coexistence, even in the context of an imagined, independent Ukraine.[247] That said, what is so frightening about Banderite thinking in early 1943 is the way it embarked *knowingly* on a zero-sum game. Theirs was an altogether high-risk strategy, but one predicated on the calculation that winner takes all. And in a convoluted manner, just as the goal the Ustasha strove towards through genocide in 1941 was realized some fifty years later, so separately the UPA's equivalent, in 1943, also bore fruit at the end of the twentieth century. In the interim, though, the major beneficiary of cleansing of the Poles was not the UPA, but Stalin.[248] He had thoroughly imbibed the nationalist lesson from the Polish–Ukrainian conflict, and as a consequence of the Soviet reconquest of the rimlands now returned with a commitment to conclude the unmixing of its populations. That unmixing, however, would be in the geopolitical interests not of the redundant Versailles system, but of the victorious anti-system, turned superpower.

PART TWO

POST-WAR 'PACIFICATIONS'

5

Stalinist Reordering: Russian Peace

SETTING THE SCENE

Out of the jaws of catastrophe the USSR emerged triumphant. In the end it was Berlin, not Moscow, which was pulverized into submission. And in that same end it was not a victorious Hitler commanding the 'Heartland' but a Stalin commanding Eastern Europe. If Soviet communism was Nazism's 'messianic twin' then truly it was also its nemesis.[1]

Explanation for this dramatic turning of the tables was not something the Kremlin was likely to set time aside to ponder upon. History, after all, was already pre-set on a course towards the inevitable victory of socialism. If there had been miraculous deliverance in the face of the Germans it was because people and party had made it so, even if God had also seemingly been deployed through the medium of an Orthodox holy synod to hastily bless the people's colossal sacrifice. Stalin's own hand in projecting the Soviet fight-back as that of a Great Patriotic War, a war in which defence of the homeland was a matter, above all, of defending Russia and *Russianness*, was clearly manifest. The irony of a provincial Georgian, even inadvertently, having made himself into the country's Atatürk was not something of which to be ashamed. The patriotic mobilization of *nas narod* simply demonstrated the special role of Russia as harbinger of what 'the unalterable laws of history' had always guaranteed. That, of course, combined with Stalin's prescience in not only having driven through a crash-course in industrialization but in founding much of it on a specially created Urals–Siberian metallurgical base to which factories in more vulnerable western Russian or rimlands areas could be relocated in the event of any (temporary) military setback. Thus could the Soviet regime justly claim, at the end of the Second World War, to have firmly consolidated both its domestic and foreign position in readiness for its ultimate challenge: the defeat and, with it, supersession of the 'degenerate' Western system, ushering in the final millennial phase of the historical dialectic. Not simply was Russia in 1945 victorious; with its control of both heartland and extended European rimlands, it had become a superpower.

Yet how much had Stalin or his entourage really forgotten (or chosen to bury) the inconvenient truth from the war's early days? Put aside Stalin's own extraordinary refusal to countenance—in the face of repeated intelligence evidence—the possibility of Nazi invasion, even when it had commenced, the scale of the military rout in the hours, days, and weeks following the opening of Operation Barbarossa pointed towards an apparatus of state almost paralytically incapable of giving coherent orders and, equally significantly, a Red Army rank and file of which huge elements were unwilling to be led or to fight.[2] Among conscripted troops especially, though far from exclusively, from the recently annexed rimlands there were constant reports of men who fought their way towards Wehrmacht lines *in order to surrender*, and of the killing of officers and commissars who stood in their way.[3] Beyond the immediate front, the NKVD reported that peasants in particular were anticipating an end to rule by 'Bolsheviks and Jews' with something approaching equanimity. Certainly, as Wehrmacht units advanced into the Baltic and Ukraine, they were greeted with the traditional welcome of bread and salt. But the speed with which Soviet rule in these regions seemed to unravel—in fact, a speed greater than that which had accompanied the great tsarist military retreat of 1915—suggested not simply an absence of love for, or loyalty to communism but, more exactly, a desire to be rid of it for good, even if it that meant, for the time being, foreign, German, tutelage.[4] One telling indicator is the lack of popular resistance to the Wehrmacht capture of Kiev in September, and the outrage expressed by large numbers of Kievans at the NKVD's efforts to blow the city centre sky high by delayed-action mines after they had left. Another is the widespread looting of government stores as a way of taking back what the people insisted was rightfully theirs.[5] Certainly, on the military front, stiffening Red Army resistance had by this juncture denied Hitler his timetable of Soviet collapse within three months of the commencement of campaign. But the Wehrmacht's continuing advance to a point where, by late 1942, they had reached both the northern Caucasus and the vast, nomad inhabited steppes between the Don and Volga, suggested the degree to which the Soviet hold on most of the Russian core was balanced out by German control in much of the USSR's western and south-western rimlands. To be sure, the Wehrmacht breakthrough to the Caucasus and Kalmyk steppes was short lived. But, as we have already seen, where the Nazis were able to impose their authority, they were also able to enlist men for their own military formations. Estimates of exactly how many Soviet citizens donned German uniform range between 650,000 and 1 million people.[6] The majority of these 'traitors', whether they joined from POW camps as Red Army deserters or of their own direct volition, were from non-Russian rimlands populations.

The baldness of this statement needs tempering with the recollection that the majority of rimlands conscripts mobilized for service in the Red Army fought and died in vast numbers alongside Russians and peoples of other Soviet nationalities; just as in reverse it is probable that if more ethnic Russians instead of rimlands peoples had come under German sway, *they* could have been the dominant element in the Nazis' military and paramilitary subaltern units. The kernel of an anti-Soviet *Russian* army, in fact, existed through the person of the captured Red Army general Andrei Vlasov. But given that Hitler refused to countenance any such *Untermensch* entity, Vlasov's *overtly* Russian nationalist alternative to communism, while backed notably by Himmler, was never put to the test, except as a belated footnote to the final days of an imploding Nazi empire.[7]

This chapter's interest, however, is not in the variegated elements of actual or potential German-sponsored, anti-Soviet wartime opposition per se, but rather in the Stalinist regime's ongoing *perception* of it. As the Red Army strove to 'liberate' all the territories held by the USSR from 1939–40, so the Kremlin became increasingly fixated on *particular* rimlands communities whose wartime conduct was charged as being one of collective betrayal. This blanket ascription of guilt is noteworthy on several counts. In the first instance, the so-called 'Punished Peoples'—the meat of our first section—were not suspect on account of inhabiting territories forcibly incorporated into the USSR as a result of the Ribbentrop-Molotov carve-up. The six peoples—Karachai, Kalmyks, Chechens, Ingush, Balkars, and Crimean Tatars—deported en masse mostly to Soviet Central Asia between November 1943 and May 1944 were all bona fide recognized nationalities under Soviet law, with 'autonomous' territories and administrative-political structures to match. In other words, they were as much part of the pre-1939 Soviet national fabric as any other recognized ethnic entity operating within the *korenizatsiia* structure. Moreover, their 'Asiatic' background and geographical position, primarily in the Black Sea and Caucasus border regions, meant they were not immediate or obvious candidates for German attention or grooming as collaborators. Yet while in the western rimlands collaboration by parts of the Baltic and Ukrainian populations was certainly ongoing and continuous for the duration of the occupation, a much more marginal and/or ephemeral engagement with the Germans from elements of these six groups determined a Soviet payback in the form of comprehensive deportation of *all* their number. The *qualitative* distinction between this set of 'total' deportations and the more partial ones for other communities extended, however, to the complete erasure of the 'Punished Peoples' as recognized *national* entities. Not only did this involve a foreclosure on their political-administrative status; it also involved 'toponymic repression' of all evidence of their prior relationship to their homelands, including excision of all Soviet references—as for instance in the *Great Soviet Encyclopaedia*—to their indigeneity.[8]

Of course, one might argue that from a rigorous Marxist standpoint national culture was essentially an anachronistic relic anyway and, therefore, under Soviet auspices it could be no more than a 'historically transient phenomenon' en route to a centralized-state-led 'transition to socialism'.[9] In which case not only did the USSR have no particular responsibility to preserve the national existence of obscure borderland peoples, but consciously facilitating their anthropophagic assimilation into the socialist embrace might actually enable their rapid ascent from primitiveness to the joyous ranks of *Homo sovieticus*. But putting aside the cynicism of such reasoning, let alone that through a Lemkinian prism any such coordinated attempt to disintegrate the essential foundations of national groups could be defined as genocide (whether or not it involved their mass killing), the very manner in which the Kremlin chose to punish these discrete communities as population aggregates exposed a glaring contradiction in its own Marxist logic.

Up to this point, the Soviet anti-system had always proclaimed an aversion to any implication that it might operate some 'zoological' (by implication Nazi) distinction between one human group and another. Where people committed crimes against state and society, of course, they had to be punished. But Soviet law was still built on the notion that human beings, while they might behave as 'class' enemies, were usually still redeemable through re-education, and, even after Gulag correction, might still be returned to the light as well as challenge of Soviet life. As we saw in Volume One of this study, there had been crisis moments from very early on in the Bolshevik period when the supposed principle had been close to being jettisoned. This had occurred most notably when Don Cossacks had been almost slated for comprehensive destruction on account of their *Cossackdom*. But while, thereafter, class-based formulae such as de-kulakization became a cover for the excision of whole communities as alleged socially dangerous 'enemies', while again—as during the mass operations of the Great Terror—accusations of sabotage or spying for foreign powers became the pretext for entirely more targeted and lethal assaults on ethnic groups, the regime continued to hold to the official line against any overt racial or ethnic hierarchism. Indeed, in a sense it continued to do so even after the deportation of the 'Punished Peoples' by offering opaque and very belated information on the fate of some—if not all—of these communities. To have gone the whole hog on the matter would have been in effect to acknowledge that within the Marxist-Leninist universe there existed national communities not only with an intrinsic *biological* kink, but which as a result were the USSR's 'eternal' enemies.

In fact the regime, by choosing to punish these peoples en bloc, was tying itself in ideological knots. If the human trajectory was set on a course in which Soviet communism was bound to win, then it surely followed that the removal of evil people was 'not merely an act of defence but the execution of the will of history'.[10] But if that was so, how could it be that it had taken the war to uncover the whole truth about Chechen, Crimean Tatar, and the others' malevolence? Or was it rather that their wickedness had been so carefully hidden in preparation for the moment when they would attempt to strike that the indomitable USSR had somehow failed to spot a conspiracy in progress? Again, this either showed the Soviet security apparatus in a rather poor light or, alternatively, made the regime's paranoia seem more like its Nazi equivalent.

However one approached the matter, the very fact that the Politburo had chosen to make entire national communities culpable for the alleged actions of some of their number implicitly if not explicitly created a distinction between ideal type Soviet *ethnies* who were 'good', virtuous, even heroic, others who were irremediably 'bad' and hence dangerous, and presumably a further range who were somewhere in between. Moreover, this was not some one-off decision from on high. It marked a clear tendency towards ascribing to different nationalities a fixed, unalterable set of primordial and 'virtually racialized' characteristics.[11] It is surely significant that this shifting landscape of Soviet attitudes towards nationality was paralleled by its evolving thinking on the relationship between *Russians* and the rest.

Lenin had been vociferous in his criticism of 'the Great Russian chauvinism' of the tsarist era when it came to non-Russian nationalities within the empire. A first test for the incipient Bolshevik regime in the civil war period had come when the possibility of border nations going their own way was countered by Stalin's insistence, as then commissar of nationalities, that for them to do so would be to lay the proletarian revolution open to the forces of imperialist reaction.[12] The early Leninist-Stalinist balm proffered to truculent local revolutionaries had been by way of a promise of cultural indigenization linked to an accelerated developmental programme aimed at raising the weaker groups out of 'backwardness' and thus toward a socio-economic equalization with the more advanced nations. If this concept of a genuinely fraternal Soviet federal union was real enough during most of the 1920s, the implicit inference from the civil war period that what really mattered, when push came to shove, was the Russian heartland became self-evident in the mid-1930s. This was the time when Andrei Zhdanov propounded the theory of 'the lesser evil'. What was so telling about this proposition was that the incorporation of nations such as Ukraine or Georgia into the *tsarist* empire was effectively justified by its Soviet successor on grounds that having lost their geopolitical viability it made more cultural and religious sense for such nations to be absorbed into imperial Russia rather than other neighbouring states—whether Ottoman, Persian, or Polish.[13] In effect, behind regime theoretician Zhdanov, Stalin was proposing that what was both good *and* necessary for the tsars (as indeed for the imperially subjugated peoples) was equally good and necessary for the USSR. Or, put another way, for all the tortuous ideological convolutions aimed at making it seem Marxist-Leninist, Stalinist policy towards hardly less than half of the Soviet population who were non-Russian had firmly returned to the same 'nationalist thought patterns', and hence anxieties and phobias, fundamental to Russian *derzhava*—'Great Power'—rule.[14] If the immediate pretext for the excision of the six nations, therefore, was the specifically German drive to Russia's far south-western rimlands, this had little or nothing to do with any specific wrongdoing on the nations' part, and everything to do with Stalin's resurrection of the tsarist empire's imperatives and fears about its border regions.

An obvious paradox presents itself. While tsarist ministers repeatedly wrung their hands about the dangers from especially Muslim, but not only Muslim, peoples of the Caucasian and steppeland rim, and discussed sometimes ad nauseam the removal or even extirpation of particularly troublesome 'tribes', they more often than not prevaricated on implementation, or scaled back their original deportation projections to the point where humanitarian catastrophe did not ensue. The serious exception was the mass Circassian eruction of 1864 in the extended aftermath of the Crimean debacle.[15] Even during the Great War, however, the Romanov polity seemed to lack the organization, capacity, or will to put into effect far-reaching border deportations, including that of Muslim groups from the Russian–Turkish frontier zone, at that time under consideration.[16] One thus might argue that what Stalin, behind the façade of Soviet-Marxist orthodoxy, accomplished a world war and its aftermath later represented a *genuine* realization of tsarist imperial objectives.

The achievement certainly owed everything to one particular tsarist legacy: the conquest and consolidation of Central Asia under Russian rule, as finally completed in the late nineteenth century. Without the great, sparsely populated expanses of Kazakhstan and Uzbekistan in particular, Stalin would have been hard pushed to find an extensive space into which to dispatch his 'Punished Peoples', on top of all the kulaks and western rimlands deportees already dumped east or north of the Urals before the onset of war. On the other hand, another irony of high-Stalinism, as a result of its (among Russians actually very popular) push towards the primary interests of the Russian nation as true bedrock of the Soviet system, was that the regime could largely dispense with former tsarist ambivalence as to the ulterior purpose of that bias. Tsarism, in its imperial reach, had always sought to temper brutal conquest with the co-option of local ethnic and religious elites, ensuring a degree of at least cultural and linguistic continuity with what had come before. By contrast, by the time of Stalin's successors, almost all that was left of the 'affirmative action' Soviet experiment in *korenizatsiia* was a set of entrenched, almost entirely self-perpetuating and corrupt republican leaderships, most especially in Central Asia, who otherwise ran things according to Moscow's diktat. As for the rest of the national republics and oblasts, already bereft of anything resembling independent elites as a result of the earlier Stalinist purges, they would henceforth have no choice but to carry through the regime's bidding and to march in increasingly standardized formation to a *Russian* tune.[17]

Looked at in this retrospective fashion, the fate of less than 900,000 members of the six 'Punished Peoples' might be seen as little more than a footnote to this wider project of social engineering.[18] Yet even treating this episode as at the most extreme end of agendas aimed at diminishing or suffocating the entire non-Russian ethnographic landscape obscures the fact that many other nationalities qua nationalities also suffered extreme, exterminatory violence as a consequence of Stalin's ongoing and post-war geopolitical and security intentions. Our second section offers a brief overview of the wider range of deportations in the mid- to late 1940s—and, in some instances, through to Stalin's death in 1953. The leading Russian demographic analyst of the deportation process, N.F. Bugai, adumbrates a total of fifty-eight Soviet communities deported in whole or in part on ethnic or national grounds. This amounted to some 3 to 3.5 million people. Indeed, in the early 1950s, the vast majority of 'special settlers' removed to places usually thousands of miles from their homelands were from such ethnic groups.[19]

An apologist for what Stalin undertook in this period might argue that deportation, even forced mass deportation, is not the same thing as extermination. One might extend the apologia further by proposing that while the USSR was removing its universe of obligation temporarily, or even in perpetuity (as in the case of the 'Punished Peoples'), from specific nationalities, the same did not apply to the individuals who up to that point had been members of these nationalities. This would read almost identically to the US dictum on the enforced nineteenth-century sedentarization of the surviving native American tribes, 'Kill the Indian, save the man'.[20] In our final chapter, we will return to the exclusion of both forced assimilation and deportation from the rubric of the 1948 Genocide Convention to which Soviet drafters—though hardly as sole culprits—were party. Regardless of the Convention, it is perfectly logical to argue that the Soviet path to genocide, even with the tangible crystallization of the ethnic factor, remained sui generis. Set against the axiom of 'socialism in one country', the USSR might continue to claim that its anthropophagic solution to troublesome minorities was entirely legitimate and involved no intent to physically extirpate anybody. The principle simply hid the practice of a militarily enforced internal exile, dispersal, and enforced re-settlement far away, in usually entirely inhospitable surroundings: the very process of which, as we will see, without adequate state assistance, threatened whole peoples with mass death.

The emphasis on deportation, however, even putting aside these potentially or actually lethal consequences, also obscures the massive level of direct, ongoing mass killing by the security agencies in the wake of the Soviet reconquest of its border regions. These operations were most intense and long-lasting in the western Ukraine and Baltic, reminding us that the resistance to Stalinist incorporation, which had begun in 1939 and 1940, reached its bitterest paroxysm *after* the postwar re-establishment of Soviet authority. The result was a partisan struggle—this time with elements of the national movements pitted against the Soviet rather than Nazi military and security apparatus—every bit as merciless as what had come before in these same rimlands under German occupation.

To be sure, this was counter-insurgency, War Type Three, with more mass deportations as its corollary, rather than genocide per se. But there was certainly a new geopolitical context to this crescendo of state versus community violence. Having turned the entire region of Eastern Europe into his personal sphere of influence, and with the West either unable or unwilling to directly challenge the new communist puppet regimes there, Stalin's ability to 'resettle' national groups in the interests of Soviet/Russian stability and peace now extended beyond his western borders. With those borders now moreover moved several hundred kilometres further west, national groups like Poles stranded on the soil of Ukrainian and Belorussian SSRs could be legitimately evacuated en bloc to a sovereign Polish state; not least given Warsaw's territorial compensation for losses to the USSR by those acquired from a defeated Germany. Thus, Stalin set in motion the conditions for a general population homogenization which had been the elusive desire of the 'New Europe' national leaderships a half century earlier. By this method, the multi-ethnicity of the rimlands and hence the whole problem of national, ethnic, and religious minorities—the very starting point for Lemkin's concern—could be cancelled out for good. Here, then, was a further paradox. Despite the fervent detestation of communism by the vast majority of its populations, Stalin was providing a green light and model for how Eastern Europe could be *nationally* transformed. One immediate consequence was popular support for Warsaw's participation in joint Polish–Soviet security campaigns not just to extirpate or remove the residual pockets of the UPA on Polish soil, but to disperse any minority group, such as the Lemkos, tainted by the inference that they, too, might be 'Ukrainian'. In microcosm, thereby, the Lemko episode became a signpost for the much wider 'unmixing of populations' in the 'Lands Between' which mark the culmination of this European rimlands sequence of genocide and its lesser variants.

But if on the spectrum of genocide these post-war transfers and ethnic cleansings might be deemed sub-'optimal', there is one final coda to the specifically Stalinist assault on Soviet nationalities which at the very least deserves our curious attention. In the final section of this chapter, therefore, we return to the Europeans' phantasmagoric idée fixe—the Jewish 'danger'—but this time in high-Stalinist guise. What had been building up over a period of years from 1948, or earlier, with accusations against 'Jewish nationalists', 'Zionists', and 'cosmopolitans', both in the USSR and East European satellite states, exploded on to the front page of *Pravda* in early 1953, with the charge that there was a Doctors' Plot to poison or otherwise kill Soviet leaders. Allegedly linked to US intelligence and to the most senior levels of the Soviet security apparatus, whom they had also supposedly turned, the plotters were openly portrayed through classic anti-Semitic stereotypes worthy of *Der Stürmer*.[21] All that was lacking was a *direct* charge involving the uncovering of an international Jewish conspiracy.

Was this the final unhinging of Stalin's paranoid, delusional mind in his dotage? Further evidence that the *vozhd* shared with the Führer the darkest nightmares of Jewish takeover? Or was this rather a dying Stalin behaving more like his Romanov predecessors who feared the Jews, who endorsed the *Protocols* for 'proving' Jewish cosmic malevolence, and whose most earnest desire was the wholesale clearing out of these vermin from across the length and breadth of Mother Russia? Rumours were rife at the time of Stalin's death in February that was there to be not only a show trial of the plotters, but the mass deportation of Jews to the east, perhaps even mass shootings. There is no way of telling whether this would have happened had Stalin lived. The evidence is fragmentary and elusive. Set in terms of the broader crisis of the semi-periphery, one can only note that just as Hitler, threatened with war against the liberal system in 1939, blamed world Jewry and promised exterminatory retaliation against them, so the *vozhd* in 1953, threatened at this arguably most dangerous time in the Cold War with direct, possibly even nuclear, confrontation with the USA, equally conjured up a Jewish enemy more deadly and potent than the myriads of enemies whom he had struck down in the course of his quarter century reign of terror.

THE DEPORTATION OF THE 'PUNISHED PEOPLES' AND THE FEAR OF RUSSIA'S PAST

When is a genocide not a genocide? An entirely unsatisfactory answer to this oxy-moronic riddle might be: when it is enacted by a regime which dresses it up as something else. The question then becomes: does the removal of the six 'Punished Peoples' fall into this category? Norman Naimark has responded by proposing that the Soviet intent was not to destroy these people as people but to disappear them as *nations* 'through assimilation, and detachment from their homelands'.[22] A more recent, closer analysis by Alexander Statiev has sought to further distance Stalinist practice from any exterminatory impulse by emphasizing both the lack of geno-cidal intent and the conscious effort to absorb the excised national groups among host populations. Beria, for instance, notes Statiev, envisaged that small groups of special settlers would be 'dispersed among collective farms with Russian, Kazakh, Uzbek, and Kirghiz populations', where the settlers' children, taught in Russian, would consequently forget their native culture.[23] This sounds intriguingly, even disarmingly, close to the preliminary CUP plan from 1910 to shift non-Turkish populations around Ottoman Anatolia and its hinterland in the quest for their ultimate incorporation into a pacified Turkified mass.[24] As with the CUP scheme in its initial form, so in the case of the Stalinist 1943–4 deportation project: while the social engineering aim was overt, an intention to actually exterminate whole communal groups remained absent. Statiev underscores this aspect in relation to the Soviet programme by noting the disbursements the deportees were entitled to, in part for the loss of assets and property as a consequence of their exile, in part to provide them with the wherewithal, including fresh livestock, to start again as farmers in their new locations. He does not deny massive mortality among deportees. Instead, he implies that this amounted to a form of collateral damage as a result of poor planning, administrative snarl-ups, the inability or unwillingness of distant republics to ensure the wellbeing of the incomers, and wartime resource scarcity.[25]

However, in a critical sense these explanations beg a more fundamental question: why should any group of people *need* to be deported en masse in the first place? In the CUP instance, whatever we make of their reasoning, the realization of deportation orders related to an immediate wartime emergency in which Armenians particularly were singled out as a security threat. For the Karachai and the groups who followed them, the public justification was essentially the same but backdated, in the sense that collective treasonable activity had already supposedly taken place, which implied, in turn, that their subsequent removal and with it national disintegration would prevent further recidivism. In neither case do such justifications for draconian action sit easily with contemporary or later assertions that CUP and Soviet regimes respectively continued to undertake an ongoing duty of care towards the deportees in their individual capacities. To be sure, what makes the fate of the 'Punished Peoples' different to the Armenian example is the lack of outright physical annihilation as accompaniment to deportation. Yet on another level, the very fashion in which the Kremlin sought to implement the removal of the six nations, and thereafter obliterate them from the past, present, and future existence of the USSR, directly confronts scholarly considerations which have sought to find some trace of benignity in Stalin's grand design.

As we have already noted, the regime's political goal was the administrative excision of the six nations and their respective republics, with the exception of the joint Kabardine-Balkar ASSR which simply became a single Kabardine SSR.[26] The disappearance of these units off the political map—with their territories divvied up between neighbouring republics—was paralleled by comprehensive rewrites of Soviet official history which either belittled, negated, or simply airbrushed out of existence these groups' prior reality as members of the Soviet polity of nations. The 1944 *Great Soviet Encyclopaedia*, for instance, contained no citation of the Chechens at all, except by obscure reference to the danger of muridism as a movement fostered by English agents: an absence all the more marked by comparison with the *Encyclopaedia*'s entry twenty-four years earlier when the Chechen's national hero, Shamil, had been extolled as a scourge of tsarism.[27] Again, the only *Encyclopaedia* reference to the Crimean Tatars in the further 1953 edition was limited to the charge that this supposedly warlike and predatory people were responsible in the thirteenth century for tearing away the Crimea from what had belonged to Russia since time immemorial and making it part of the lands of the Golden Horde.[28]

The implication that these peoples—if anybody remembered their existence at all—deserved 'unpeopling' for heinous crimes committed against historical rather than contemporary Russia may actually provide the most telling clue as to the real causes for their deportation. By contrast, what stands out at the moment of their mass eruction is the regime's conscious effort to both hide their 'disappearance' from public view and make it irrevocable. The deportation sequence itself was enacted under the cover of complete state secrecy. Wider public awareness of what had happened only came more than two years later, in June 1946, with a terse *Izvestiya* announcement of a Russian Soviet Federative Socialist Republic (RSFSR) Praesidium decree that the Chechens, Ingush, and Crimean Tatars had been 'resettled' in other regions of the USSR, where they had been 'given land together with the necessary government assistance to set themselves up'. This was a consequence, stated the *Izvestiya* communiqué, either of their direct support for the German struggle against the Red Army—including 'against the Soviet authority in the rear'—or, in the case of the bulk of these populations, of their failure to take counter-action against 'the traitors to the fatherland'.[29] No mention was made of the three other national communities who had been deported at the same time, while the brief reference to 'resettlement' in other unspecified parts of the USSR offered about as much reassurance as to their respective fates as one emanating from a Talât, or Himmler, on Armenian or Jewish deportations to the 'east'. Meanwhile, the manner in which all traces of these peoples' cultures and connections to place—religious buildings, monuments, cemeteries, sacred artefacts, archives, communal chronicles (*teptary*)—not to mention the minutiae of domestic life—ornaments, furnishings, tableware—were equally ransacked, wrecked, ploughed into the ground, or set ablaze should leave no doubt as to the descriptive terminology Lemkin would have deployed had he known at the time the full facts.[30]

Indeed, the comprehensive and final nature of the six peoples' punishment would create legal, logistical, and political difficulties years later when Stalin's successors would little by little attempt to row back on the original deportation decrees. Rescinding the restrictions on movement imposed on the survivors and their subsequent family groups was one thing; allowing them the right of return to their original homelands, compensation for their losses, or the restoration of their political autonomy was quite another. On the matter of the Chechens and Ingush, in 1956, Nicolai Dudorov, the then minister of internal affairs (MVD), warned that any attempt at their return from Central Asia 'would inevitably lead to a whole range of undesirable consequences'. Perhaps Dudorov had in mind that any effort by these peoples to take matters into their own hands by returning to their former homes without leave to do so would be violently resisted by Russians, Ukrainians, and others who had taken their place; as happened in subsequent years.[31] Similar efforts at self-repatriation by Crimean Tatars backed up by their own remarkable grass-roots campaign to have the authorities overturn the ban were met by repeated Soviet stonewalling, further expulsions of returnees, and persistent harassment of Tatar activists. Even the issue of rehabilitation of their good name proved fraught, the 1967 decree in effect rescinding the earlier charge of collective German collaboration only being officially issued in Tashkent and the Central Asian republics.[32] Not until the premiership of Boris Yeltsin, at the very end of the Soviet era, was there a concerted Russian governmental effort to apologize to all the deported peoples in full public view. His 1991 Law on the Rehabilitation of Repressed Peoples listed 'forced deportation, the abolition of national-state formations, the redrawing of national-territorial borders and the establishment of regimes of terror and violence in special settlement camps' as elements of state policies amounting to 'slander and genocide'.[33] Ironically, even this pungent statement and subsequent decrees aimed at national-cultural restitution and compensation have failed to bring closure to the original Soviet sin, certainly at least insofar as the Chechens and Crimean Tartars are concerned.

That said, the long-drawn-out suffering and brutalization of these communities in the three-quarters of a century following deportation concerns us here primarily only as regards the degree to which it sheds light on whether what was quite obviously a programme of denationalization was also tantamount to genocide. For Lemkin, any coordinated action aimed at a 'targeted...destruction' of a people on 'the basis of ethnicity' would be so by definition.[34] That the appellation is appropriate would also seem to be confirmed by the 1991 Russian law, even with its rather jejune reference to *both* the defamation ('slander') of the repressed peoples and their actual destruction. But then, the very fact that at this moment, on the cusp of Soviet collapse, there were large numbers of survivors of the event and of their descendants to protest at their suffering might suggest that there had either been no *thoroughgoing* programme of physical annihilation back in 1943–4 or, alternatively, that it had fallen short of intentions. In which case, Yeltsin's official utterance regarding genocide might tell us more about the crisis state of Russian domestic politics in 1991 than about what actually had happened during the deportation sequence and its aftermath almost half a century earlier.

Looked at through an essentially one-dimensional demographic lens what we can say in the baldest terms about these events comes in two parts. In the first, the actual process of resettlement led to huge mortality among the deportee populations. While early studies before the demise of the USSR inferred mortality rates as high as two-fifths—Aleksandr Nekrich, in the late 1970s, for instance, proposed at the extreme end a mortality rate of 46 per cent among 194,000 Crimean Tatar deportees[35]—the subsequently lower figures provided by researchers with full access to the Soviet archives still confirm an incredibly bleak picture. Bugai's analysis, for example, estimates that 19.6 per cent of the Crimean exiles and 17.4 per cent of the Kalmyks perished, while these numbers were exceeded by losses among the north Caucasian deportees of 23.7 per cent of their number. Put in different quantitative terms, this last figure would read as a 349 per cent average annual mortality as set against a 1.7 per cent Soviet baseline rate from 1927 to 1931.

Of, then, some 264,000 deaths among ethnic deportees up to 1 July 1948, according to official NKVD-MVD figures, the vast majority came from the six punished nations.[36]

The second part of the quantitative equation, however, reads more positively. While in the first two to three years of resettlement deaths vastly exceeded births for all six peoples (and the other deported ethnic groups), there was a gradual recovery, indicating better or improved conditions in the special settlements. This was reflected in firm evidence, by 1949–50, that births were exceeding deaths.[37] Thus though what had been done had seemed to have the potential to accelerate to entire population group collapse, this had been averted, one might assume by each group's collective will to live but also, at the very least, by the absence of further state action which might have impeded that determination. The only problem with this statistics-centred approach is that it tends to deepen the discrepancy between those who argue that there was a Soviet state intention to exterminate these peoples all along, and those who argue that this cannot be the case, by reference to the flattening out of the mortality figures followed by the more healthy demographic upturn thereafter.

There is, however, a different way of addressing the matter which might return us to what we considered in Volume One with regard to the famine sequence of 1932–4. Here we noted that the genocidal nature of regime behaviour was not evident through direct physical extermination of entire groups (of which the Nazis were clearly the practitioners par excellence) but through a callous omission to provide them with necessary, or sufficient, means to survive in the face of *known* adversity, or, alternatively, through conscious strategies aimed at blocking them off from being able to look after themselves. If this verdict on the relationship between the famine and genocide were transposed to the deportation sequence, what would matter would be less the negligence or incompetence of Uzbek, Kazakh, or other receiving authorities to provide incomers with the accommodation, food, and resources for survival that they had been ordered by relevant Soviet ministries to provide, and rather more the *expectation*, on the regime's part, that these requirements would—for a number of contingent reasons, most obviously general wartime scarcity—*not* be available or forthcoming. In other words, just as during the famine, the Stalin clique anticipated that their actions, even where they were wrapped up in dubious humanitarian foil, would have the effect of mass death, whether or not they used additional military or police force to directly kill people. Indeed, they did not need to, once the *initial*, military side of the deportation operation had been successfully realized. In fact, all they had to do was precisely nothing, as the consequences of their prior, lethal, decision-making were devolved on to somebody else's shoulders. One might add that according to this line of thinking there was no particular requirement to kill *all* Karachai, Kalmyks, or whoever. Only rarely is total obliteration the desideratum of genocidal practitioners. The more usual aim is to so thoroughly emasculate the group in question that its ability for reproductive recovery as a self-identifying group is negated. And, thus (so the genocidal reasoning would go), the hegemonic state and/or society might look forward to a 'safe' future in which the supposed political, societal, cultural, or 'biological' threat to itself has been nullified. In these terms, while it is a moot point whether Stalin's achievement was particularly long-lasting or efficacious (the bitter Russo–Chechen conflict since the mid-1990s is one key indicator suggesting otherwise), the archival evidence at hand would strongly suggest that the aim, through deportation and ongoing hardship in some distant clime, was to both disrupt and overwhelm the communal existence of the groups in question to the point where *as groups* they would simply collapse in on themselves.

This also explains why the provision of accommodation, work, or sufficient food to sustain the deportees in their places of exile was an entirely secondary, not to say marginal, consideration compared with the main NKVD thrust: their campaign geared towards the surgical removal of the six peoples and dismantling of their republics. Indeed, the manpower, logistics, transport, and broader range of resources which were marshalled and brought to bear by the Soviet security apparatus to encompass these mass eruptions was nothing short of sensational. And this, we may remember, at a time when the USSR needed every last ounce of these same reserves to bring the war with the Nazi enemy at last to its definitive conclusion. It has been estimated that 40,200 rail-trucks were required for the Ingush-Chechen operation code-named *Chechevitsa* ('Lentils') alone. Or, put another way, 180 complete trains.[38] One near-parallel event which invites comparison is the Eichmann-coordinated removal of Hungarian Jewry to Auschwitz. The Serov-coordinated equivalent in Russia's Black Sea, south-western littoral, however, was altogether more complex. It involved six sequential campaigns, not one, run to an even tighter set of schedules than that envisaged by the RHSA Budapest team, yet involving a range of distant destinations in Central Asia to which the entrained deportees were to be dispatched mostly in the dead of winter. But arrival of the deportees at these termini was itself predicated on the assumption that they could be screened, registered, rounded up en masse, and with such celerity that it would pre-empt the onset of otherwise inevitable disorder, or worse—given these were supposed to be seriously dangerous populations—insurgency. It is significant that almost every leading NKVD figure was drafted into the project's organization and planning, with apparatus head Beria for a time taking personal control of *Chechevitsa*, while his Politburo rival Voroshilov was mandated with overall supervisory command of the Crimean operation.[39]

As the key responsible agency, the NKVD was clearly on its mettle. Every possible contingency which might derail the project had to be considered and prepared for. Serov's meticulous pre-planning for *Chechevitsa* underscores the fact. Preparations began some five months before zero-hour at dawn on 23 February 1944. Serov's high level tactical team included Chekists covertly planted in the Chechen capital, Grozny. Their task was not simply to carry out an exact registration of the population but equally to make detailed surveys of the region's entire physical geography, so that escape by all potential mountain, ravine, and forest trails could be intercepted. Another very particular headache was how the NKVD might intrude vast numbers of special troops into the region without inviting local suspicion. Thus, as with similar SS campaigns, disinformation became a critical element of the NKVD plan, in this instance through developing the story that these were 'Red Army units assigned to tactical training in mountainous conditions'. Further deception was employed on 22 February itself—this being conveniently Red Army day, and so an occasion to gather large numbers of the populace in public places ostensibly for celebrations. In practice, it was to isolate, kettle, and neutralize them. Finally, very much in line with another SS technique of divide and rule (and terrorize), the republic's leadership was informed of the impending operation just a few days before but given the opportunity to collaborate in its swift completion. This carried the promise that they and their families would be provided with a special train echelon to Alma Ata and permitted to take 1½ tons of household goods with them, compared with the 500 kilograms per family allotted to most of the rest of the population.[40] One can only imagine what would have happened to the republic's Council of People's Commissars had they refused.

Their cooperation clearly played a crucial role in the smooth timetabling of the Chechen deportation, with Beria reporting to Stalin on an almost daily basis as to how well it was going.[41] The NKVD head had good reason to be pleased with himself. Chechen resistance to Russian control had been ongoing for well over a century. Even repeated Soviet efforts at brutal pacification had failed to prevent renewed and often very tenacious insurrection from some of its mountain *auls*, right up to the 1940s. Yet in the space of little more than a week, Beria's men had made a clean sweep of not far short of 480,000 Chechens and Ingush from both the republic's lowlands *and* highlands. Their efforts were not unrewarded. All the leading organizers of *Chechevitsa*, alongside Serov, received the Order of Suvorov, 1st Class, a military award normally reserved for outstanding planning and generalship. These included a whole slate of senior Chekists, deputy people's commissar Bogdan Kobulov, and Victor Abakumov, head of the recently formed SMERSH, the military counter-intelligence wing whose supposed goal was to ferret out internal espionage plots, foremost among them.[42]

If all this confirmed the NKVD as the truly efficient cutting edge of Soviet high modernism, none of their deportation success would have been possible without an overwhelming concentration of military personnel, hardware, and, hence, lethal force. The sheer naked terror of the programme is evident right at the beginning with the Karachai round-up in early November 1943. An estimated 63,000 members of the community were slated for removal (in fact there were another 6,000 on top of that who were actually deported). But for this purpose over 53,000 NKVD men were deployed. Put more precisely, given the high proportion of children among the deportees, this meant there were more than two armed Chekists for every adult. Or again, remembering that most of the able Karachai men were away in the Red Army, force majeure was primarily applied against women (old, young, and pregnant), old men, or those invalided out of the army. If one has any doubt, moreover, about how the deportation was enforced in practice, recent research confirms that the round-up operation was conducted in the middle of the night, with pregnant women and wounded soldiers dragged from hospitals, and the entire 69,000-strong cohort then holed up for three days in whatever requisitioned buildings such as sanatoria and laundry houses could be made available. They were then forced at bayonet point on to Studebaker trucks to the railheads, where they were packed on to cattle trucks, sometimes ninety to a car.[43] The Studebakers add piquant irony, given that these were part of US *matériel* lend-leased to Stalin to help defeat the Nazis. More sobering is the information that Karachai who attempted to resist or flee were summarily shot, as were those who strayed more than five metres from the deportation trains whenever they halted.[44]

The Karachai operation set the tone for the rest. Over 93,000 Kalmyks were swept out of their ASSR in December in train echelons of 2,000 to 5,000 heading for Siberia or Kazakhstan. Their departure was followed by the much larger number of Chechens and Ingush—nearly half a million people—in late February, the over 44,000 Balkars the following month, and the 183,000 Crimean Tatars in May.[45] We can only imagine what it must have felt like for the victims to be faced with the full might of an NKVD *military* apparatus, whose 'normal' function was to halt and execute retreating Red Army units. A whole panoply of border, interior, railway, and convoy troops, including a 'Special Purpose' division trained specifically for deportation work, were on hand to enforce the Presidium writ. Their corps d'élite comprised infantry, cavalry, aircraft, and, reportedly, in the case of *Chechevitsa*, a whole tank army.[46] There was no question then of this being a purely policing operation. There were no dvoikas or troikas, as there had been during the *Ezhovshchina*, to assess who was guilty and who innocent. Every last member of the six 'Punished Peoples', babes in arms included, was guilty by dint of ethnicity. The menfolk serving far away in Red Army units—many decorated war heroes, partisans, and often party cadres—found themselves demobilized and sent on (though sometimes a considerable time later) under NKVD supervision to the special resettlement camps, thereby swelling the overall numbers of deportees. Members of the six peoples living outside their national republics also found themselves rounded up and sent east. Only women who had married out to other nationalities could avoid the communal fate. Those who had married in could only do so by filing for divorce.[47]

Otherwise, enforcement of deportation was absolute. 'No one was to be left behind.'[48] The case of the handful of fishing and salt-panning villages on the eastern Crimean coastal spit known as the Arabat grimly illustrates the point. A genuine NKVD oversight in the Tatar round-up meant that that these outlying villages were initially left unmolested. When the error was brought to the attention of Kobulov, two months later (even more perversely, at a 'victory' banquet to toast the operation's success) his furious response was not to organize another train echelon to Uzbekistan, but to order the villages' *immediate* physical elimination. In haste, to placate their superior, the method of dispatch chosen by Kobulov's Crimean subordinates bore uncanny resemblance to that employed on the other side of the Black Sea against Armenians a world war earlier. Loaded on to an old boat in Genicsek port, the 'undeported' were put out into the Sea of Azov, where the boat was sunk by opening the kingston (ballast tank valve). Those not drowned were finished off by machine-gun fire. The majority on board were women and children.[49]

The Arabat incident, however, was not the only occasion confirming the primary 'cleansing' goal of the NKVD remit. In addition to those gunned down during the Red Army day celebrations in Grozny—euphemistically alluded to in

Beria's report to Stalin—recent reconsideration of a 1956 inquiry into what happened when NKVD units attempted to clear the mountainous and very poorly connected Galangozhsk region of Chechnya has revealed a wholesale massacre. Having decided that getting all the villagers from the *aul* at Khaibakh and from surrounding *khutory* to the nearest railhead was unfeasible, given the required timetable and the depth of snow, the commanding officer, Colonel General Gvishi-ani, ordered a drastic solution. In the case of Khaibakh itself this involved driving its remaining inhabitants—nearly all old people, sick, and children who were deemed unable to make the forty-eight-hour trudge on foot to the railhead (horses and oxen having already been confiscated)—into the collective farm stable. It was then doused with gasoline and set alight. The stable was then raked with automatic gunfire to prevent further escape. Accounts vary as to how many died: it may have been as many as 700.[50] But though this was the largest of the killings in Galangozhsk, it was also far from unique. Alexander Yakovlev reports that in 'Mekhasti, the biggest rural Soviet in the region, all the inhabitants of thirty-two of its thirty-four hamlets were massacred'.[51] Where the journey on foot over the mountains was attempted, there was no mercy for those who fell behind. They, too, were shot or bludgeoned to death. What happened in Galangozhsk in Febru-ary 1942 was thus comparable to anything CUP cadres could have devised in their efforts to rid Anatolia of its Armenians, or indeed any Nazi police battalion under its instructions to cleanse another rimlands zone of its Jews and 'partisans'. For his pains, Gvishiani received the Order of Suvorov, 2nd Class.[52]

To be sure, a much larger number among the six slated populations were not gunned down on the spot but entrained to the east. The efficiency of Serov and his planners suffocating the possibility of effective resistance on the one hand, and the marginality of outlying and remote areas where the project's breakdown led to exterminatory violence on the other, thereby subverts any *overt* parallel between this mass eruction and Nazi or Ottoman sequences where mass death was intrinsic to the design. The general availability of rail transport and careful preparation to get deportees on to it meant that there were *relatively* few death marches in the Soviet events. A modicum of advanced administrative planning also meant that there were the barest bones of a framework allowing for *some* of the deported population to survive in their resettlement camps. However, one can only wonder what consolation this was to all those—bar the mere handful able to escape the dragnet—who ended up on the cattle-cars to Central Asia.

What almost definitely would have been treated by the NKVD as superior, best practice in the techniques of deportation—Beria claimed to Stalin that the troops committed 'no excesses at all'[53]—would have seemed as a terrifying, brutal, and ongoing life-threatening nightmare to those on the receiving end. Survivor testi-monies from Crimean Tatar sources repeatedly report that deportees were given sometimes as little as five minutes to pack their bags in preparation for the journey. Winter travel for most of the deportees, without adequate warm clothing and food, certainly sounds like a recipe for illness and death in itself. But the Crimean witnesses suggests that the *spring-time* weather in which they were deported offered little protection either. To be sure, official NKVD figures suggest that many fewer

Crimean Tatars died in transit to the relatively clement Ferghana valley, for instance, than Kalmyks deported in the dead of winter and in the direction of Siberia: 0.1 per cent compared with 1.7 per cent.[54] But then, could it be that the NKVD consciously or otherwise misreported the mortality figures, or simply could not convey the reality of these death-dealing journeys? Naimark's own conservative extrapolations from Soviet state records suggest that some 10,000 Chechen and Ingush *alone* died from disease, hunger, and cold in the process of deportation, compared with the 2,500 from all six nations as reported by the security apparatus. Naimark also observes that other reports by health officials included hardly-veiled complaints to leading Politburo figures against the NKVD's refusal to allow what were meant to be scheduled stops for food and medical care.[55] This would again tally with not just the Chechen experience of deportation but that of the Crimean Tatars in which, contra the NKVD figures, *thousands* died of thirst. One deportee from the peninsula, Ayshe Seytmuratova, later recalled that people spoke of the sealed railway trucks as 'crematoria on wheels'. Lacking fresh air, people simply suffocated to death. Only in Kazakhstan did the railway guards toss the corpses out from the trains, though without further ado as to burial.[56] Many people, she added, 'went insane'.

There are issues here which statistical survey or even empirical study cannot hope to address, including the fact that traditionally gender-segregated family- and clan-based Muslim and Lamaist groups would have been *particularly* traumatized by being closed in together and forced to defecate in full public view of one other. One might argue that this was the least of their worries given that the thoroughly unsanitary conditions in the box cars provided the perfect environment for the spread of typhus. Lack of food, for days or weeks on end, would equally have led to slow, agonizing deaths. Robert Conquest reports instances of whole trains abandoned as a consequence.[57] But for the survivors who made it to their destinations, or those Red Army men who arrived later, only to find family members dead or mentally scarred beyond belief, it is an open question whether ongoing physical suffering including disease or, alternatively, psychic collapse was the main factor leading to *spiralling* death tolls in the weeks, months, and years that followed. Another Crimean Tatar witness, Yusif Suleymenov, in a sense only skims the surface in his 1969 recollection that:

> They took us and unloaded us in Urta-Aul like cattle for slaughter. Nobody paid any attention to us. We were hungry, dirty and ill. People became ever more ill, and started to swell from hunger and began to die in families. I want to say that from our village, where there were 206 people, a hundred died. I myself buried eighteen. Out of seven households of my relatives not one remained.[58]

The deportees' sense of alienation and despair as a result of what had been inflicted upon them also has to be weighed against the resentment against them from the mostly collective farm communities among whom they were thrown. The Crimean Tatars particularly found themselves the butt of xenophobic antipathies among many Uzbeks, not least as the latter feared the incomers—mostly, of course, old people, women, and children—might take scarce food resources away from themselves. Material and emotional support from earlier, more settled deportees, including kulaks and political prisoners, certainly sometimes offered a 'rescue' lifeline to the new arrivals. The threat from the locals also, with time, tended to diminish as they encountered the first invalided and demobilized Red Army men arriving to join their families, while also discovering that the rather secular Crimean Tatars were nevertheless fellow Muslims.[59]

One might choose to read such information as an uplifting story of human solidarity set against the omniscient and omnipresent power of the state. A century earlier, and an ocean and continent apart, the so-called five 'civilized' nations, and many other Native American peoples besides, had found themselves forcibly ejected into the vastly overcrowded reservations across the Mississippi—overcrowded, that is, in terms of the human populations that this already heavily degraded environment could itself support. Yet, despite vast losses, they had managed to pull through, cheek by jowl with the deep interior's natives. By the same token, ingenuity, resilience, and common cause enabled large numbers of *our* latter-day six peoples also to survive. The problem is that the building of that common cause took time, patience, and empathy: conditions which, in the initial weeks and months of ongoing war and severe food shortages, were hardly abundant. Many local receiving authorities, as well as anticipating the day when the deportees would be returned en bloc to whence they had come, also took advantage of the situation by taking food relief intended for the deportees and redistributing it to the collective farms. They also often ignored requests to provide accommodation for the incomers (sometimes for the simple reason that there wasn't any available at the collective farms to which they were mostly sent). A similar requirement that the new arrivals be provided with livestock for their sustenance was also circumvented through the provision of *young* livestock to them. These animals would have been useful in the long term but in immediate circumstances were useless, given the deportees' need to provide milk for their often many and famished children. Putting aside assumptions about the special settlers' agricultural adaptation to their new environments—many Crimean Tatars were urbanized, most Kalmyks were nomads—short-term survival thus converged on the provision of a daily food ration. Set by Moscow at 200 grams of bread, less even than besieged Leningraders received in the worst winter of 1942 and in which, as a result, hundreds of thousands of the latter had died, it should be no surprise that even where this meagre ration was distributed to the deportees it did not prevent their perishing in great swathes.[60]

Certainly, one might wish to note various contributory factors to this tragedy for which it would be more difficult to *directly* blame Moscow. The obvious absence, especially early on, of able-bodied men in what were (mostly) intensely patriarchal societies meant that the ability of the deported womenfolk to articulate their urgent needs, let alone to be listened to, given the equally intensely patriarchal nature of the reception communities, is very likely to have handicapped the deportees' chances even further. Culturally, the notion of begging was considered shameful among the north Caucasians. This, too, impacted on survival prospects among these groups, though it did not prevent additional friction when deportees resorted to petty pilfering from indigenous neighbours, and hence to wider accusations of collective criminality.[61] But what all this really tells us is that having set the murderous process in train, the Kremlin then simply washed its hands of it. The regime knew what the results would be of its decision for deportation. Its culpability for the genocidal outcomes cannot simply be displaced on to secondary actors, let alone the victims.

*

However, if this is the case, it can only underscore the need for answers to two interlinked questions: why *these* deportations in the first place; and why these particular groups? In fact, as we will further describe below they were not alone. Several more small national groups were deported from the Black Sea littoral in toto, or in part, soon afterwards. The distinction of the six groups lies in their being singled out as a series of 'bandit nations' whose members were officially accused of having committed treasonable wartime acts in support of the 'German fascist aggressors', and who as a consequence were punished by banishment to other parts of the USSR.[62] Any search for an explanation ought obviously to begin therefore with examination of the veracity of the Soviet claim.

The first thing that is immediately evident is that the Karachai deportation was not the first of its wartime kind. In September 1941, nearly 439,000 Soviet Germans were compulsorily evacuated, mostly from the Volga German ASSR but also from the contiguous Saratov and Stalingrad Oblasts. Much larger cohorts of urban or dispersed Germans—there were still even after the 1939–40 'transfers' of rimlands Volksdeutsche to the Reich an estimated 1.5 million ethnic Germans in the USSR—were also immediately, or soon after, caught up in this process.[63] The main territorial deportations, however, followed very similar contours to those both before and after. They were NKVD-organized, with Serov as always at the helm, involved long cattle truck journeys to designated work camps and special settlements in Central Asia and the east. They also produced similarly disastrous outcomes. Official figures of over 60,600 deaths in the special settlements in fact mask a vastly more catastrophic rate of attrition, one notable extrapolation putting the figure as high as 200,000 to 300,000 for the period 1941–44, or somewhere between 14 and 21 per cent of the ethnic German population.[64] One reason for the high mortality, also involving one notable difference between this and the 1943–4 deportations, is that nearly all the able-bodied adults, both male and female (including those withdrawn from the Red Army), were drafted into a new 'labour army' where, toiling under hyper-exploitative Gulag-type conditions in lumber camps, railway construction, and industrial plant building, their numbers rapidly plummeted. In some instances, this was practically on a par with death rates in Nazi slave labour camps. A further knock-on effect was the high mortality among children as a result of being left untended and uncared for in the special settlements.[65]

If this would seem to confirm that the impact of the German Volga and related deportations was every bit as genocidal as that visited on the 'Punished Peoples', what is less obvious is the element of calculated malice aforethought that was evident later on. It might be tempting, for instance, to read the ethnic German deportation as a useful short-cut towards the enslavement of a quite sizeable bloc of the population for the purposes of a new 'war communism'. By grouping the Germans alongside other Soviet citizens, whose background as Finns, Rumanians, Hungarians, or even Italians supposedly put them into the same camp as the Axis enemy, the regime gave to itself a pretext for both detaining these people as a precautionary principle and utilizing their manpower, practically for nothing, for often the most hazardous and onerous war-work. The logic of such action, after all, was not a million miles away from a US government which rounded up over 100,000 of its ethnic Japanese citizens or subjects and interned them en bloc in camps in the Californian desert.[66] Meanwhile, the British government interned a large chunk of its Italian and German 'aliens' aged sixteen to sixty (the latter, of course, mostly Jews), and saw fit to deport sizeable numbers of these to camps in Canada or Australia, in one case, as a result of a U-boat sinking of a transport ship, the *Arandora Star*, with thoroughly calamitous consequences.[67] These US and British internment programmes, of course, lacked the hyper-exploitative, killer element of the Soviet case. But the basic nation-state-at-war principle was the same: interdict aggregate ethnic populations on the grounds that their number might *include* potential fifth columnists, or saboteurs, and remove them to somewhere as far as possible away from places where they might be of direct assistance to the enemy, which would seem to make of the Soviet decision about the ethnic Germans, at least in the first instance, as less a case of conscious vindictiveness and more one of preventative 'security'. After all, large numbers of (though not quite all) Ingermanland Finns from around Leningrad were 'administratively' resettled or mobilized for NKVD labour units at around the same time as the ethnic Germans,[68] which given the Wehrmacht and Finnish military push on Leningrad seems to make some precautionary sense. And looking back a few years, the wholesale deportation of the Korean population from the Soviet Far East, at a time of heightened anxiety about a Japanese invasion and Tokyo's feared use of the Koreans as fifth columnist proxies, offers the obvious non-genocidal parallel, as well as a precedent, for the Presidium order of 28 August 1941 on Volga German resettlement.[69]

However, there would seem to be a much darker side to the order, not least given its clear enunciation not of preventative but '*punitive* measures against the entire German population of the Volga region', not to say its additional rationale to 'prevent mass bloodshed'.[70] The self-justification was predicated on the claim that there were thousands of agents and spies among the region's ethnic Germans primed to go into action on the side of the invaders. Yet such a claim stands in marked, not to say perplexing, contrast to the situation earlier in the month when the creation of local defence units in the republic and the Volga Germans' enthusiastic support of a regional defence foundation were being regularly touted by Moscow as counter-propaganda to Nazi blandishments to Soviet Volksdeutsche to support their side. The Volga republic, indeed, stands out as a rather exemplary Soviet national community, and one which as a result had remained relatively intact and unscarred during the waves of state repression throughout the late 1920s and 1930s, even during the worst moments of the *Ezhovshchina* 'German operation'.[71] The Kremlin charge of some alleged collective betrayal thus came out of the blue. Assessing *its* change of mind, however, can only be speculative. What we know is that Beria and Molotov had made a clandestine visit to the republic at the end of July, and this is reported to have been followed by the KGB staging of a German landing there with 'airborne troops', rather in the way that the Nazi organized their Polish fake attack on the German border town of Gleiwitz as the pretext for Operation Case White.[72] Cross-reference this with the very first Soviet High Command allegations that ethnic Germans had fired on its troops withdrawing across the Dniester (though one might add very far away from the Volga ASSR), and we have our first strong, if not corroborated, indication that what was going on here was the opening shots of a concerted effort to either scapegoat the ethnic Germans, socially engineer the community off the Soviet map, or both.

Of course, it would have been entirely consistent with Stalin's tenacious instinct for survival to attempt to deflect blame for the regime's ongoing and monumental military failure onto some alleged enemy within. It was indeed one of the elements of elective affinity he shared with Hitler. We may remember that the Führer's entourage received the news of the deportation as a direct provocation, which in turn fed Hitler's own enraged determination to deport Jews eastwards from the German Reich. The irony is that the 28 August decree, even with its official publication in the Volga republic's newspapers, may have sat uneasily with the *Soviet* regime—at least initially. Certainly, in spite of the winding up of the long-settled Volga ASSR and 'transferring' of its population eastwards, with all the inevitable deaths from dehydration and sickness which that entailed, there were other aspects of the programme which lack the harsh ruthlessness that was visited on the Karachai and the others. Being compensation certificates for the loss of property and assets in advance, and being allowed to prepare for the arduous journey and to take small amounts of food and domestic and agricultural equipment with them all mitigated the very worst consequences of being dumped in Siberia or Kazakhstan which deportation augured for the Germans. On the other hand, being able to bring in the harvest before they left, depart in relatively good order, and then being assigned very primitive accommodation on arrival was hardly compensation for what the community would have to physically and emotionally endure thereafter.[73] But perhaps what is most important, in the broader trajectory of wartime Stalinist violence, about the eruction of altogether some 800,000 Germans in autumn 1941[74] is not the 'softly-softly' manner of their removal—especially when put alongside the implicit violence of labour army press-ganging—but the fact that the regime had found for itself, albeit by rather ad hoc means, a strategic purposefulness in the charge of ethnic collaboration.

What clearly made it so serviceable was the ease with which the charge could be made to stick. Did elements of the Soviet Volksdeutsche who found themselves under German occupation aid and abet the occupiers? Yes, of course they did. Did elements of the six punished nations subsequently do the same? The answer, again, is affirmative. Though the German occupations of the national republics in question was sometimes very brief—sixty-five days for instance among the Balkars, and in the case of Chechen-Ingushetia practically non-existent, the Wehrmacht only for a moment capturing a smidgeon of this territory—one can certainly identify lesser or greater degrees of collaboration or attempted collaboration among parts of each population. Among the Karachai and Balkars, the Germans fostered national committees and encouraged them to look forward to a time when the *kolkhozy* would be dissolved.[75] The same type of cajoling also took place in the Crimea, but this time with talk of the revival of the *Milli Firka*-led autonomous Tatar government, as had operated after the revolution. The Germans even allowed the return to Simferopol of the exiled former Cabinet member Ahmed Ozenbashly, to prove the point. Crimean Tatars certainly served in local German-organized village defence brigades, or, usually through the POW route, in *Hilfspolizei* units.[76] With the Kalmyks, the overtly militarized aspects of collaboration were even more marked. This included the creation of a dedicated cavalry corps and a not insignificant role in anti-partisan warfare during the period of the German retreat. During the Warsaw Uprising, Poles often referred to all SS auxiliary units as 'Kalmuks', even while, as we have seen, most such units were drawn from Ukrainians and Belorussians. In return for Kalmyk participation, however, the Germans encouraged a locally run intelligentsia-led administration to reignite interest in both the Lamaism and nomadism stifled under Soviet rule.[77]

The real question, however, is not whether parts of each of these communities collaborated with the Germans or were able to wrest advantage from that collaboration. Rather, it is whether they were unique in doing so. After all, it was not only specific Caucasian nationalities whom Hitler considered 'reliable' in terms of German-sponsored military formations, but Muslims more generally.[78] Possibly as many as 35,000 to 40,000 Volga Tatars participated in such formations. Yet their whole communities were not deported as a result, as were their Crimean cousins.[79] Nor were the Turkomans, Kirghiz, Kazakhs, or, for that matter, Uzbeks, despite the fact that large numbers of Soviet POWs from these ethnic backgrounds also served in German uniform.[80] There is, of course, the famous Khrushchev quip about the Ukrainians from his 'secret' speech to the Twentieth Party Congress in 1956, when he began to reveal to the comrades something of the truth about who had been deported at the end of the war. The Ukrainians had avoided that fate, he said, 'because there were too many of them and there was no place to which to deport them'. The comment was apparently received with 'great laughter and animation'.[81] Clearly, one did not have to have been a Muslim, or a Buddhist, to have been a collaborator. Good honest Belorussians had served with Kaminsky, good honest Russians with Vlasov. Perhaps one could even wryly add to Khrushchev's witticism that if Stalin had had a magic wand he would have vanished the whole lot, and directed a Soviet society with no nationalities in it whatsoever.

But instead of making light of the matter, let us instead go back to those who *were* actually deported. The Stalinist argument that *these* communities were removed because of the treasonable criminality of large numbers of them, and the passivity in its face of the rest, simply does not wash. At least *not sufficiently*. There were Chechens who acted as anti-Red Army saboteurs, or even 'fifth columnists' in the sense that the recently formed inter-agency secret police unit GUBB (Main

Directorate for the Struggle against Banditry) adopted in pronouncing its internal verdict.[82] Indeed, on the cusp of the abortive Wehrmacht advance into the republic, there were some quite dramatic insurgent attacks on Soviet forces, not least against the Grozny military school, with the loss of 200 cadets, as they attempted to evacuate towards the Chechen mountains. But for every Chechen or Ingush who made common cause with the Germans, there were many *more* Chechens and Ingush, in fact two divisions-worth, ready and willing to lay down their lives for the Soviet cause. What is both poignant and ironic about their *voluntary* participation on the Soviet side is that, without proper rations or weapons provided by the High Command and without any air or artillery support, one of these divisions heroically but suicidally bore the brunt, in early August 1942, of the German assault across the Don towards Stalingrad. For their pains, the whole Chechen-Ingush population was duly blamed for the front's collapse.[83]

Perhaps what this most keenly reminds us is not just that the Soviet state in its wartime inventory of heroic versus treasonable acts was extraordinarily selective in what it chose to remember and what it chose to forget, but that this selectivity carried distinct ethnic markers. All of the six 'Punished Peoples', the Kalmyks included, could point to high levels of participation in both Soviet partisan units and regular Red Army formations, with consequent massive losses plus clutches of military medals and honours.[84] On the other side of the equation, those that endured months or years of Nazi occupation, as especially was the case with Crimean Tatars, were soon disillusioned with German promises, as the usual range of indiscriminate anti-partisan atrocities and round-ups for forced labour kicked in.[85] The Soviet regime, however, chose consciously to ignore this mixed picture in favour of a verdict of collective criminality.

This prompts the question of whether there was something intrinsic to these particular communities which raised Kremlin hackles and, if so, whether this was something which they held in common. The immediate answer to this second question can only be a 'not exactly'. True, five out of six communities were Muslim, the Kalmyks the odd man out by dint of their Lamaism. But scores of Soviet ethnicities were Muslim, and others Buddhist, thereby failing ethnic separateness as explanation at the first hurdle. Nor were these six peoples socio-economically or in a broader sense culturally all of a piece. There were some passing comparisons, notwithstanding notable linguistic distinctions, between the Mountaineer north Caucasian groups. However, *these* communities shared little or no common occupational traits either with the actually rather Westernized, increasingly urbanized and certainly secularized Crimean Tatars, or, at the other end of the spectrum, with the Kalmyks. Indeed, despite Soviet efforts at sedentarization and, for a time, rather successful *korenizatsiia*-informed educational modernization, the Kalmyks had been unhinged (through collectivization) from an historic nomadism for hardly more than a decade.

If, then, there is a template at all, it would seem to be made up of two broadly interlinked sets of factors. One is a background of ongoing ethnic opposition to Soviet rule. The other is geography, which would squarely bring us back to the geopolitics of the rimlands. Together these variables were amplified by the circumstances of war and German occupation. Paradoxically, however, what occupation and its possibilities threw into relief were those much deeper, *Russian*, fears of encirclement which clearly predated the Soviet era, sometimes by centuries.

*

Pre-war opposition to Soviet hegemony, even where dampened for a time by *korenizatsiia*, came from many ethnic quarters, but with Central Asia and the Caucasus as notably recidivist epicentres.[86] The attempt to suffocate these tendencies in the *North* Caucasus by embracing all its Christian *and* Muslim peoples inside a single RSFSR had clearly not succeeded, at least not if the July 1937 operation to clear the region of 14,000 'anti-Soviet elements' is anything to go by. The NKVD sweep had been geared, among other things, towards a complete erasure of Muslim religious opposition,[87] which itself might suggest that some of the ethnic elements of the republic such as the mostly Christian North Ossetians were considered by the authorities as less disruptive than others. The near-simultaneous dismantling of the all-purpose republic in favour of smaller, supposedly more acquiescent, ASSRs and autonomous oblasts, however, does not seem to have extinguished opposition from all quarters. The Chechens and some of the other neighbouring mountain peoples—Ingush, Karachai, and Balkars—stand out for their obdurate refusal to cave in to Soviet diktat: hence the appellation of 'bandit nations'. The Chechens, in particular, would seem to offer an object lesson in how a relatively small and remote population group might continue to represent a particularly enervating thorn in Moscow's side.

The Chechen refusal to comply with either tsarist or Soviet conceptions of order and progress was embedded in their identity as Nakh, Noxche, or sometimes, as aligned with the Ingush, as Vainakh—'our people'. This was as good a way as any of demarcating themselves from all other groups, as was the persistence of their possibly 8,000-year-old autochthonous—hence non-Turkic and non-Indo-European—language.[88] If this particularly marked self-conscious ethnic identity was one aspect of Chechen difference, the thing which had most fascinated the outside interest of nineteenth-century romantics of the Pushkin or Lermontov ilk was the openly egalitarian nature of the village *aul*. In effect, the 125 clans which constituted Chechen society represented a form of communism avant la lettre. Chechnya had never gone through a feudal 'stage'; its people had not suffered class antagonisms. But where there were disputes—usually of an honour-bound, blood-feuding variety—these were settled with the knife.[89] In short, Chechnya as an idea was equally both an inspiration and an affront to Marxists, while its 'arrogant' and 'hot-blooded' menfolk, even in the Gulag, were, said Alexander Solzhenitsyn, individuals nobody, even from the apparatus, dared to cross.[90]

There was one other ingredient, however, which both reinforced Chechen identity and ensured their irrepressible will to resist, and so, obversely, had Soviet policymakers and opinion-formers foaming at the mouth. As late as 1947, a major scholarly conference denounced Caucasian muridism as 'an ultra-reactionary current of militant Islam'. One leading—interestingly Armenian—conference participant complained that Chechen notions of freedom were the 'freedom of

backwardness, of downtroddenness, of darkness, of Asiatic primitiveness'.[91] Muridism's heyday in the Caucasus had in fact been in the early to mid-nineteenth
century when the sufi Naqshbandi and Qadirya brotherhoods had laid the foundations for a militant, highly disciplined, yet mystical opposition to tsarist takeover. Transcending ethnic divisions, the sufi *tariqat* had linked together Chechens,
Daghestanis, Circassians (Cherkessy), and many other mountain peoples in this
common cause. To be sure, the insurgency had been suffocated or pulverized
through the final military defeat of Shamil and the genocidal obliteration of the
Circassians.[92] Yet, especially in Chechnya, through the influence of the *tariqat*, the
sufi path had lived on into Soviet times, not to say been the basis of repeated resistance all the way from the *ghazawat*—the holy war of 1921—through to a new call
for rebellion initiated in the Galangozhsk district in early 1940. It is surely no
coincidence that Soviet 1944 punishment against the Chechens took the form
here of direct, retributive atrocity. Nor that the regime saw fit to remind readers of
Groznenskaia Pravda—as the rebellion spread after the onset of Operation Barbarossa—that 20,000 party personnel or Red Army men had been killed in the
region since the establishment of Soviet rule. The reminder was accompanied by an
accusation of contemporary German complicity. Yet the rebellion had begun at a
time when the Soviets were in effective alliance with the Germans themselves.
Indeed, the 1940 insurrectionists made hay with the occasion of the Ribbetrop–
Molotov Pact by making a ringing declaration in which they promised that the
Caucasus would become a second Finland in the struggle against the yoke of Red
imperialism, and that their example would 'be followed by other oppressed
nations'.[93]

Here, then, was the Chechens' original sin: *not* collaborating with the Germans,
but challenging Soviet authority *of their own volition*. Of course, most Chechens
were not party to the insurrection, which made all the more galling the fact that it
was younger, communist-educated intelligentsia, not old-style murids, who were
at its helm. But, of course, the Kremlin's phobia was never simply about the threat
of a localized good example knocking over the Soviet apple cart. It was about outside states using the occasion to spread the disorder through their 'agents and
spies', and thus using it as pretext for their own military-led takeover bids. During
the *Antonovshchina*, it had been the possibility of a link-up between the Tambov
rebels and the Poles which sent shivers through the Kremlin. And we may remember the efforts the regime went to obliterate this potential Vendée as thoroughly as
had the Jacobins when faced with their own archetypal rebellion. In 1940, the
reignition of the Chechen call to arms fed into precisely the same Soviet idée fixe,
but this time with the Poles only as bit-players. It was the *Ingiliz*—the British—
who were supposedly the real hidden hand behind the mountain insurrection, just
as nearly a century before, in the aftermath of the Crimean War, tsarist state officials had convinced themselves that distant London's manipulation of Caucasian
unrest had the potential to unravel Russia's relatively recent hold on the entire
Black Sea littoral.[94]

If we look at some of the other deported nations, very similar causative neuroses
manifest themselves. Back at the Twelfth Party Congress in 1923, Stalin had

intoned, 'All we have to do is make one small mistake in relation to the small ter-
ritory of the Kalmyks, who have ties with Tibet and China, and that will affect our
work in a far worse way than mistakes in regard to the Ukraine'.[95] From his then
vantage point, Stalin might have been thinking of just a few years earlier in 1918.
At that time, when he had been trying to hold together the civil war Tsaritsyn
Front, the Kalmyks had been a potentially destabilizing factor. Their leader, Prince
Tundutov, had requested Ludendorff to send German troops to their assistance.
Ludendorff had not come to their rescue, but he had run for a while with the
notion of an independent Tatar republic in the Crimea. Why here? In part as an
adjunct to that German imperial dream—the one equally pursued by Hitler—to
create German colonies in the peninsula; but equally the idea was to dominate the
whole Black Sea arena by way of the Crimean ports. Except Ludendorff, recognizing German overstretch, proposed to hand over the Russian Black Sea Fleet to
Germany's Ottoman ally. And from that *Turkic* perspective the obvious local clients for such a scheme were none other than the Crimean Tatars.[96]

Ludendorff's scheme was stillborn, but that still left the Crimean Tatars as a
potentially capricious quantity within the Soviet firmament. What gave them an
edge, in a way quite different from the Chechens, related to the rapidity of their
self-motivated Islamic yet *national* modernization. Jadidism, the movement for a
wider *pan*-Islamic educational, linguistic, and cultural reform in keeping with the
modern world, had begun in the 1880s—in the Crimea.[97] Political self-awareness
of the possibilities of a Muslim national movement across Russia had come quickly
in its wake. The Bolsheviks had been perfectly happy to foster such radical Muslim
tendencies when these were aimed at the imperialist powers outside Russia's own
borders. The possibility of such secessionist movements taking hold on *Russian*
soil, however, was an altogether different matter. At the 1921 Party Congress, Stalin
reiterated the issue by stating that it could only result in 'imperial bondage for the
border regions and a weakening of the revolutionary might of Russia'.[98]

The original sin of the Crimean Tatars, therefore, lay not so much in being specifically German pawns or, for that matter, White Russian ones, though the fact
that Wrangel's last bastion had been on the Crimea would have served as yet
another accusation to throw in Tatar faces. Rather it was the ability and potential
of a movement such as *Milli Firqa* to lead all Muslim Russians, or perhaps if not
all of them then a large part of their Russian Turkic-speaking number, towards a
separate, alternative path of progress—and worse, without reference to the Soviet
model at all. In the early 1920s, the Leninist strategy in the face of this apparent
threat was to try to co-opt the movement and let it develop its own autonomous
republic under relatively benign Soviet sponsorship. When this proved all too successful, the regime's response was violent in the extreme. That the Tatars might in
turn have looked to a German enemy as a way of restoring the status quo ante
certainly seems to have fed a further bout of pre-emptive NKVD violence very
similar to that which we have already noted in the western rimlands, as the Soviets
beat a retreat from the peninsula in late autumn 1941. It may actually have been
the Kremlin intention to deport the Crimean Tatars en masse to Kazakhstan there
and then, only the speed of the Soviet rout denying them this possibility.[99]

Yet what is equally interesting about Soviet wartime behaviour towards this by now distinctly minority element of the Crimean population is how much it seemed to hark back to a time when it was not the Germans, nor even the British, who threatened to disrupt Russian control of its Black Sea region, but the *Ottomans*. Surely the notion that Crimean Tatar political ambitions lay in the development of some pan-Turanic confederation, under Istanbul's aegis, was sheer moonshine? Hitler, for one, ruled out of court any notion of a common Turkestani nationality from any Nazi occupation agenda.[100] More importantly, the late Atatürk's previous eschewal of any such goals in Turkish foreign policy should have unequivocally put paid to the spectre. This is why Soviet paranoia could only have fed on the news that the German Foreign Office (GFO) in late 1941, and again in spring 1942, was busily cooking up a series of exchanges and meetings with known pan-Turkic-leaning officers in Ankara, the main purpose of which seems to have been directed towards a rekindling of the German-Turkish alliance of 1914–18. Given the Wehrmacht capture of the entire Crimean peninsula in late spring 1942 and its subsequent march on the Caucasus, it was quite plausible that Ankara could have been tempted to 'do a Mussolini' and throw in its lot with the Nazis at that moment when German liberation of historically Ottoman-connected lands appeared imminent. At this point, too, the GFO seemed to be willing not only to entertain a stronger Ankara involvement plus ideas originally drafted by Rosenberg for a Black Sea confederation of 'peoples', but to widely broadcast the supposed involvement in these plans of both Crimean Tatar and North Caucasus émigré groups.[101]

As various commentators have noted, the GFO démarche, at root, was another poorly executed example of its efforts to muscle in on power games in which other Nazi state agencies were making all the running. Alexander Dallin even refers to its attempt to get up a conference on these issues as 'farcical'.[102] By the same token Ankara, no sooner than it had reignited the embers of pan-Turanism, rapidly put them out again.[103] Soviet assumptions that a phalanx of Muslim or other communities were primed to rise up in support of the Germans or Turks at their first signal may thereby tell us a good deal more about NKVD security neuroses and arguably Stalin's paranoid imagination than it does about the strength or purposes of southern rimlands opponents.

Though perhaps, again, the notion that Stalin was consumed by his own projective fear of these peoples may be somehow missing the point. There, was, after all, nothing particularly knee-jerk about the project to deport them. There appears to have been a Politburo discussion of the subject as early as February 1943. From around this same time, entire army units comprised from the six nations were dissolved and ominously converted into labour battalions.[104] Certainly, concrete deportation plans do not appear to have become operationalized until the autumn. Even so, what was then put into effect was a highly clinical, organized, and calculated exercise in the expulsion of peoples from their homelands and with the intention that this would be for all time. This might further suggest that the German invasion (and its subsequent defeat) simply offered an opportunity to settle scores with these peoples, not just for their allegedly troublesome behaviour under the Soviets, but as historic enemies of Russian *derzhava*.

Truly, there had been a time when all six nations, in their different but sometimes quite linked ways, had challenged the very power of Muscovy. A Crimean
Khanate, itself a successor to the great Mongol Golden Horde which had dominated Russia throughout much of the Middle Ages, had continued to take tribute
and slaves from the Russian lands well into the sixteenth century. As late as 1571,
it had even burnt Moscow to the ground. Later, as an autonomous polity, only
nominally under Ottoman suzerainty, it had repeatedly stymied the Muscovite
advance to the Black Sea all the way to the 1780s.[105] Balkars and Karachai, though
like the Tatars Turkic-speaking, had been closely aligned and enmeshed with Circassian resistance to the subsequent tsarist efforts to subdue the north-west Caucasus, for which the Circassian tribes had suffered their genocidal removal in the
mid-1860s. Not only were all these groups, encompassing the Chechens and
Ingush, too, part of that North Caucasian barrier which continued to frustrate the
Russian advance towards both Persia and Central Asia, but their ability to stand
firm suggests much less outside manipulation and much more how internally
cohesive and autonomous these 'primitive' peoples really were.[106] One might say
exactly the same of the Kalmyks, whose antecedents had been yet another strand
of the terrifyingly powerful Golden Horde, yet who, in the face of both Russian
and Chinese pressure in the eighteenth and nineteenth centuries, had seen their
ancestral lands eaten away, their nomadic societies depleted, starved, and
pulverized.[107]

Can one speak of what Stalin did to these peoples in 1943 or 1944 as the unfinished business of tsarism? Was the reason that other contiguous communities such
as the Ossetians and Kabardians were spared that they had collaborated in earlier
centuries in the Russian advance, or even defended the regime's all-important
Georgian Military Highway over the Caucasus?[108] It was absolutely true, given that
the North Caucasus was contiguous with the three main sources of Soviet oil and
gas (in Georgia, Azerbaijan, and across the Caspian), that this made it into a vital
strategic zone.[109] And never more so than in the context of total war. But one could
hardly claim that this made any of its inhabitants, in a collective sense, into a geopolitical threat to Moscow. In political-military terms *those* collectivities were mere
shadows of their former selves. Yet was it exactly this: that they *represented* a past
when Russia had not been all powerful, up to and including its western and southern borders, which demanded a final, clean sweep of them? One can only add that
implementation followed a classically ancient yet thoroughly imperial form:
sorgun—mass people removal—albeit with all the accoutrements and resources of
the modern security state to ensure its total and final outcome.

CONSOLIDATING *RUSSIA'S* RIMLANDS

Not that we can draw a line under the deportations to May 1944 and conclude
that Stalin's appetite for a social remodelling of the rimlands had been sated. On
the contrary, the fate of the 'Punished Peoples' proved to be a prelude to a further
clearing out of a whole range of peoples, first from the Soviet–Turkish border zone,

then from further afield in the Black Sea area, and finally the 'Lands Between' Baltic and Ukrainian arenas. What is striking about the first two of these three subsets of additional socially engineered misery and death is that there was no further Politburo attempt to explain them away as just Soviet response to local subversion, or German collaboration. The Wehrmacht had never made it to the Turkish frontier region. As for the Meskhetians, the 77,000-strong and largest of the deported communities in these parts, most commentators would agree with Alan Fisher's verdict that they 'were nothing to do with anything'.[110] Indeed, as a group they had previously been considered by the Soviets as too heterogeneous as well as politically underdeveloped to merit even their own autonomous oblast. As one consequence, when they were erected to Uzbekistan and Kazakhstan, in mid-November 1944, there was no state announcement of the fact nor changes to official maps or encyclopaedias as there had been, for instance, with the Chechens and Crimean Tatars. Not until twenty-four years later was there any government acknowledgement of this grand disappearing act, and then only because Meskhetian survivors, like the Crimean Tatars before them, had begun to protest.[111]

What, then, was *their* sin? By cross-reference with some of the other smaller groups deported in this same cohort the answer would appear to revolve around the fact that they were a historically Turkicized and/or Islamicized fraction of the Georgian borderland population. This would seem to throw some of the blame for their fate onto the specific prejudices of Beria as a Georgian towards local non-Mingrelian minorities: rather, that is, than assuming some wider grand design. It is certainly true that there was an idiosyncratic quality as to who was caught up in the November dragnet. Alongside Turkic-speaking Turkmen, Karakapakh, and Kurds there were also Adzhars, a Muslim but otherwise Georgian-speaking community, less than 1,000 equally Islamicized but Armenian dialect-speaking Hemshin or Khemshili, and what amounted to two railway cars-worth of local Poshas (gypsies).[112] Adzhars, it was true, had some form as resisters to Russian rule, whether tsarist or Soviet. They had risen up most recently in the late 1920s, and before that, as we saw in the previous volume, played a small role in Enver's Great War efforts to carry the Pan-Turanic cause onto Russian soil.[113] But so had many Laz, a community—with the exception of some embroiled by misadventure—who were spared the 1944 deportations.[114] If the onus, moreover, was supposed to be on trans-Caucasian communities who had shown some inclination towards supporting the Germans, Beria might just as easily have picked on the (Christian) Armenians. Georgians as a rule didn't like them either, and given that there was some evidence that Rosenberg had wanted to inveigle hard-line Dashnaks into a German-sponsored Armenian National Council and, in late 1941, even authorized the formation of a Wehrmacht battalion recruited from Soviet-Armenian POWs, there were sufficient grounds—at least by flimsy Stalinist standards—for action against them too.[115]

In practice, however, the deportations of the actual targeted groups had little or nothing to do either with the Germans, or for that matter Georgian sensitivities, even if the actual November operation was a joint Georgian and Soviet NKVD affair.[116] The issue was propelled rather by Russian imperial geopolitics going back more than a century. Back in 1829, under the terms of the Treaty of Adrianople, a militarily mauled Ottomania had conceded to its tsarist adversary recognition of suzerainty over Georgia, but also in the process ceded further border districts, the majority of whose *indigènes* remained religiously and culturally Ottoman. These included the Meskhetians, their historic Georgian origins notwithstanding. By any serious political reckoning, such Ottoman origins hardly amounted to treachery against Moscow or the threat of pro-Turkish sabotage. Yet the matter of these people's loyalty or otherwise came to the fore once more in 1915 when the tsarist Council of Ministers initially gave the green light for and then back-pedalled on their eruction. The last word on the matter, however, came when Beria charged the Meskhetians with serving 'Turkish intelligence agencies' and 'implanting bandit groups'. On this occasion, however, in November 1944, it led to their definitive excision.[117]

All this could be construed as just wretchedly bad luck for the Meskhetians and the others, given Stalin's determination in the high summer of 1944 to pronounce pay-back time on the Turks for their brief, hastily-renounced peccadillo with the Germans. With the war going famously in his favour and with the Red Army swinging into Bulgaria, the *vozhd* found himself in pole position to exert maximum pressure on Ankara. In keeping with the wider project of grand imperial restoration of the lands lost during Great War and revolution, Stalin clearly had his sights on regaining all the lost border Caucasian districts including Kars and Ardahan, a project which ironically also had Armenians at home and abroad in a state of feverish anticipation.[118] In practice they had nothing to cheer, as Stalin drew back from direct military or political confrontation with the Turks. This did not lead, however, to a reprieve for the Georgian border peoples. In a three-day period in mid-November, up to 116,000 of them were eructed in twenty-five train loads towards Central Asia. Officially, they would lose 14.6 per cent of their number in the process of transit and resettlement. In fact, unofficial sources suggest perhaps as many as a third of them died. This should hardly surprise. The at least three-week journey was in the midst of winter, and the Central Asian authorities had pleaded with Moscow that they were already suffering overload from previous deportations. A typhoid epidemic then rapidly kicked in on the deportees' arrival in Uzbekistan, further proving with lethal effect the inadequacy of the reception centres.[119]

However, there was nothing essentially fortuitous or contingent about these people's destruction. Just as with the 'Punished Peoples', so here, too, the aim was to ensure that the Meskhetian and others' entire cohort—including serving soldiers, Komsomol cadres, and party officials—would all be swept out from their homelands for good, and their land and jobs taken by other supposedly more reliable Caucasian peoples. The fact that this whole exercise in people replantation often proved just as miserable and sometimes disastrous for the incomers was also largely immaterial for the Stalinist state.[120] What mattered was the long-term consolidation of the borderlands under firm *Russian* control, a consideration so serious and strategic that, long after Stalin was gone, the Soviet authorities—despite having conceded the fact of deportation—continued, point blank, to refuse the Meskhetians their actual return.[121]

Equally significant in such operations is what constituted a borderland in Soviet eyes in the first place. Even before the Meskhetian banishment had begun, the recently liberated Crimea, for instance, was effectively designated a border zone, despite being far from any actual frontier, from which whole swathes of population were duly removed. We may remember that the Crimea suffered particularly horribly under German occupation from late 1941 to April/May 1944, with 92,000 people or something in the region of 10 per cent of its entire population murdered by Nazi executioners.[122] One reason for the intensity of the violence in this period was that the Crimea was a major theatre of Soviet partisan operations, in which large numbers of Crimeans were themselves participants. However, this clearly carried no weight with the NKVD. Indeed, hardly had the peninsula been recaptured but Beria authorized multiple ethnic cleansings of ethnic Bulgarians, Greeks, Armenians, and Rumanians, plus practically anybody else deemed 'foreign' or having a foreign passport.[123] This on top of the complete excision of the Crimean Tatars.

The Bulgarian eruction, by some highly tendentious chop-logic, may have been justified by reference to the role of some Bulgarians assisting and abetting the German occupiers, even though Sofia itself, while a party to the Axis, made a particular point of not participating in the invasion of the Soviet Union. But if finding cause for the blackening of the ethnic Bulgarians is problematic enough, the Soviet expulsions expert Pavel Polian is at a complete loss to explain the assault on the Greeks. Greece, after all, had suffered German invasion just before Operation Barbarossa, and, thereafter, was a major arena of communist, pro-Soviet partisan action. This hardly made all Black Sea Greeks—the vast majority of whom had no obvious connection with the Hellenic state—enthusiastic Stalinists. But, even from spring 1942, Beria's response to the threat of further Wehrmacht advance into the Caucasus and far reaches of the Crimea was to go completely the other way and tarnish them all as 'anti-Soviet, alien, and suspicious elements', deporting swathes of them east accordingly. The pressure on these coastline Greeks was kept up in spring 1944, when they constituted by far the largest single group (bar the 'Punished Peoples') of the estimated 66,000 additional people banished from the Crimea and Caucasus.[124] More dispersed communities from the Kuban and southern Russia followed. And then, in mid-June 1949, there was one final grand sweep almost on a par with the NKVD 'national' operations from 1943–4. All remaining Greeks—at least 40,000 in total—inhabiting the northern Black Sea littoral as far as Abkhazia, close to the Turkish border, were rounded up by special troops in a single night, with two hours to pack, and sent in sealed trains, that is in the usual execrable, death-dealing conditions, to Kazakhstan.[125]

Did their transgression thus emanate from the same source as so many of the other southern rimlands peoples: from a remote historical connectedness to Ottomania? It was certainly true that a large number of Pontic Greeks had fled into the Soviet Caucasus and Crimea in the period of Greco–Turkish violence and atrocity of the early 1920s, joining in the process longer settled Hellenic communities of similar provenance. By these routes the majority of Soviet Greeks could be traced by origin—or indeed passport—to the southern Turkish shores of the Black Sea.

But to be blackened by Moscow on the grounds of having been the *victims* of someone else's violence would seem both harsh and thoroughly illogical. Unless, of course, Stalin's real reason for embracing the Greeks in his list of rimlands enemies was on a different account. The Greeks, like the Jews, like so many Armenians, were not only commerce-orientated but commerce-orientated by way of diasporic, family connections to a wider world beyond the stultified confines of the USSR. In other words, by dint of this expansive cognitive map they could not be so easily taken in, or emotionally bludgeoned, by what comrade Stalin said or demanded. They were, indeed, like their historic middle-men competitors, true cosmopolitans.[126] Grounds enough in the menacingly intensifying climate of Cold War and Soviet paranoia to be cast out from the temperate climes of the Black Sea and expelled into the frozen wastes of Siberia, or the unforgiving deserts of Central Asia.

But this post-war round of deportations was far from being simply a Greek tragedy. According to Nekrich, an estimated 80,000 Georgian Muslims, previously spared from the Meskhetian operation, were banished to Kazakhstan in 1947.[127] But it was in the Baltic zone and along the western Ukrainian rimlands that the deportation project really reached its climax in the period 1947 to 1949. Operation Vesna ('Spring') carried off over 49,000 men, women, and children from the Lithuanian cities of Kaunus and Vilnius in March 1948. The same 'eternal' exile to the east was awarded to another nearly 95,000 'bourgeois nationalists' and their families the following March, this time from across the Baltic republics. The operation's code name was equally surreal: Priboy, 'the wash of the waves'. The deportees would have noted, however, that this was intended as no sentimental reverie, 76,000 MGB (formerly NKVD) special troops and party operatives being deployed against them. Similar operations had already removed 75,000 OUN suspects from western Ukraine by late 1947, on top of an estimated 100,000 from three years earlier. Further south, a Moldavian operation in July 1949 carried off in thirty train loads another 35,000 to 40,000 family members suitably blackened as kulaks or fascists in the direction of the Soviet Far East. In all, some 380,000 to 400,000 people were thus eructed in these post-war operations.[128]

Of course, the pacification of the Soviet countryside and the accompanying deportations of kulaks in the early 1930s had been an altogether grander, more all-encompassing affair. But then the context had been different. The destruction of an autonomous peasant society had been designed to pave the way for the internal social and economic reorganization of the USSR as a command economy. The deportations of the post-war period were essentially about the reconquest of the former *tsarist* rimlands, albeit under Soviet auspices. The project had got properly under way in the late 1930s, more particularly in the wake of the Ribbentrop–Molotov Pact. But after the war it was resumed with lethal force against all those national groups, or, more exactly, their respective elites, as they stood, or were assumed to stand, in the way of a final, belated consolidation of Russian *derzhava* to its borders.

*

Through the prism of reconquest we can begin to see the broader exterminatory implications of Stalin's rimlands programme. Deportations alone suggest an ugly determination to be rid of whole swathes of unwanted peoples, but perhaps rather like Hitler's aborted plans for the mass 'evacuation' of European Jewry, falling short of explicit orders for their actual physical annihilation. However, in the drive to restore the lost frontiers of 1941–4, the Soviet regime found itself opposed by *some* indigenous national forces whose will to resist was just as determined as anything which had confronted the advancing colonial powers at the fin de siècle. In contrast, thus, with the situation in the Meskhetian homeland, where continuous Soviet wartime control ensured that the community's removal was an unopposed fait accompli, in other instances where the loss of that wartime control had provided a seedbed for the emergence or, as in the Baltic republics, re-emergence of an independent politics, Moscow was confronted on its return with a genuine dialectic of violence. Or put another way, just as German encroachment onto authentically Russian soil had fuelled a partisan opposition which the Wehrmacht could only defeat, or failing that stymie by brutal counter-insurgency, so similarly the Soviet attempt to reconquer the Baltic and west Ukraine could only be achieved by militarily crushing their national movements.

Was *this* tantamount to genocide? Our previous chapter review of the German–partisan struggle as centred on Belorussia in 1942–3 certainly implied that one could end up with a vast proportion of the population dead as a consequence, even in the absence of any considered German occupation strategy to eliminate them through counter-insurgency. The Soviets clearly did plan in advance for the *removal* of whole peoples. But these projects related to relatively small to medium-sized groups and were predicated on NKVD strategies which, in preventing or deterring resistance, were also designed—mostly—to *avoid* direct mass murder. Where the strategies misfired, wholesale killing could result, the Arabat incident in the Crimea being one obvious example. But where the NKVD apparatus was really thrown off balance was in circumstances where a significant part of the population of a newly 'liberated' territory was already mobilized and organized to resist the reimposition of Soviet order. This was doubly so where that population was too large to be deported en masse. In such circumstances, Moscow was confronted with a War Type Three as open-ended as anything which had dogged the Germans.

The immediate apparatus response to the threat of such protracted armed struggle was pre-emptive overkill. An early indication of what might be in store for resisting communities was presented in early 1943 in the Uchkulan district of the Karachai ASSR, soon after the German withdrawal from it. Here, an incipient anti-Soviet insurgency—the so-called Balyk army—was met by Serov with the aerial bombardment and flattening of ten villages. Some of the survivors of these massacres were sent for forced labour, but all those who could not undertake the seventy or 100-kilometre forced march to the transit points at Nalchik or Kislovodsk were shot on the spot. These, according to one account, included children, wounded war veterans, and the elderly, as well as local communist party officials.

The account also claims that all those sent for labour perished.[129] More generally, Karachai Red Army conscripts often already in labour battalions were demobilized, then either shot or redeployed for forced labour, very much repeating the male Armenian experience from a world war earlier.

What is striking in the Karachai instance is how military pulverization of this allegedly traitorous population preceded their en masse deportation by many months, the latter policy arguably developing as a fail-safe extension of the former. A similar sequence can be seen in the Soviet liberation of the Crimea in late spring 1944, both partisans and Red Army going on a two-week killing spree against Tatars in Simferopol and its hinterland, presumably both to exact revenge for their alleged treachery and to eradicate any ongoing Tatar opposition to Soviet rule.[130] But if this demonstration of Soviet military power was essentially against a phantom enemy, thereby obscuring the Kremlin's ulterior goal of ethnic reorganization of the Crimea and a broader southern frontier belt, any notion that force majeure could deliver the liberated western frontier zone in like manner was rapidly confounded by the presence there of genuinely tenacious resistance movements.

The continuation of a Baltic underground into the early 1950s, described in one study as 'the most long-lived and heroic guerrilla struggle in post-war Europe',[131] seems to have forced the NKVD to ratchet up its counter-insurgency tactics. Faced with repeated lethal attacks on not just Soviet functionaries but local collaborators and their families, the apparatus deployed both vast numbers of NKGB troops on the ground and, just like the Germans before them, native units with a remit to penetrate and then help liquidate the enemy. With these Soviet-led destruction battalions facing off against the self-proclaimed national forces, the result was guerrilla warfare in many respects as vicious and internecine as in the years of the German *Bandenkämpfung*, albeit with no attempt on Abakumov's part to repeat the scorched earth and dead zones method previously employed by Bach-Zelewski. The most important difference between the two events, however, was that without superior outside force to come to their assistance, the insurgents' struggle (unlike that of the Soviet partisans) was doomed.[132] Even so, in the period 1947–8—that is, after two years in which counter-insurgency sweeps had been at their most intense—an estimated 25,000 people were killed in further such operations in Lithuania alone, suggesting in other words that the resistance was far from defeated.[133] From this perspective, the sheer scale of the 1948 and 1949 Baltic deportations—far in excess of the earlier ones from 1941—might equally suggest not so much a long-considered blueprint for the mass excision of 'bourgeois-nationalists' as a contingent attempt to clear out all 'bandit' elements and their extended families as a path towards some ultimate pacification. Nicolas Werth, for one, thinks that in addition to perhaps as many as 250,000 Baltic people deported to special settlements between 1944 and 1953 another 150,000, or something around 5 per cent of the adult population, ended up in the Gulag in this period.[134]

Such savage subjugation of recalcitrant border peoples and even the mass attrition which went with it, however, is arguably not the same thing as wholesale extermination.[135] In the longer term the Kremlin would seek to suffocate the Baltic peoples and their independent aspirations by flooding the region—especially Estonia and Latvia—with Russian incomers,[136] even if this strategy is interpretable as a form of genocide by *other* means. However, in the Ukraine, more precisely in its western Volhynian and eastern Galician parts, the Soviet reconquest was at least as violent as in the Baltic, if not more so, but with, arguably, much more far-reaching ramifications for the ultimate homogenization and hence elimination of the western rimlands qua rimlands. Certainly, the sheer intensity of the struggle between returning Soviets and the UPA-OUN is reflected in some of the statistics from the Soviet Ministry of Interior and other government agencies. Operating significantly from across the remote border country between the Ukraine, Poland, and Czechoslovakia, the Ukrainian underground mounted more than 14,400 'terrorist raids' between July 1944 and March 1953.[137] In response, the NKVD claimed a tally of 103,000 'bandits' killed already by January 1946. Many of these deaths would have been in some of the initial pitched battles in which the UPA attempted to defend its 'liberated' territory. Over 10,600 were killed in initial military contact between February and May 1944, Another 11,000 died in a single NKVD drive between 10 January and 23 February the following year. These first full-scale encounters seem to have been as intense and pitiless as anything from the annals of Soviet counter-insurgency dating back to the *Antonovshchina*: no prisoners taken, the distinction between combatants and non-combatants largely ignored.[138]

However, the UPA-OUN underground did not simply collapse as a result of the overwhelming military odds thrown against them. Nor, despite the acute asymmetry of the struggle, were casualties confined solely to the insurgent side. In the first period of conflict to December 1946, the UPA killed 12,000 Soviet functionaries and alleged collaborators.[139] Just as they had struck with genocidal terror against the Poles in 1943, so thereafter they struck back at anybody, Ukrainians included, Ukrainians indeed especially, who aligned themselves with the authorities. The result was that Ukrainian on Ukrainian violence became—like the *franco–français* struggle in the Vendée of the 1790s, or that between Kurdish *peshmerga* and Kurdish *jahsh* in the late twentieth-century contest for Iraqi Kurdistan—the most bitter and unrelenting aspect of the Soviet-insurgent dialectic. Increasing local resort to the destruction battalions as the most secure way to defend oneself and one's family from UPA ravages was matched by the large numbers of educated youth, intelligentsia, and even factory and mine workers, from as far away as the Donetz, fleeing to the insurgency.[140] The ongoing resilience of the underground and its adaptation to classic guerrilla struggle, the survival of its last authentic leader, Shukhevych, until cornered and gunned down in 1950, perhaps, above all, a residual peasant adherence to the movement fuelled by the Soviet drive to implement both dekulakization and collectivization, underscored the limits to which a 'final solution' to the insurgency could be enacted against the entirety of the west Ukrainian population.

To be sure, parallels with the original French pacification of the Vendée *are* pertinent. Military tribunals and 'special jurisdictions' gave the NKVD something akin to carte blanche to eliminate not just OUN suspects but their extended families and communities with impunity. Staged trials of activists also gave the regime

the opportunity to portray them as Nazi stooges and hirelings, and hence a 'violation of the natural order'.[141] The charge of being in league with foreign enemies
could then be extended to the Uniate Church, the attempt to emasculate it in the
wake of Sheptyts'kyi's death evident in the round-up of some 1,800 of its clergy (of
whom 200 are known to have been executed) followed by an NKVD-supervised
(and not entirely successful) effort to force the remaining Uniate priesthood to
break with Rome and submit to absorption into the *Russian* Orthodox Church.[142]
Meanwhile, the attempt to dragoon the wider peasant population was enacted
through compulsory collectivization, with the 1930s enforcer Kaganovich no less
at the helm, and with the same threat of starvation as before hanging over those
who demurred. And just to add a raw piquancy to the threat, large numbers of
people from east Ukraine descended on the western countryside in 1946, famine
once again stalking the collectivized countryside as it did in the pre-war Soviet
Union. Nor was the influx of outsiders just a coincidental by-product of these
events. Soviet policy, just as Jacobin policy with regard to the Vendée, consciously
strove to reconfigure the underlying demographic as well as political structure of
western Volhynia and eastern Galicia as an appropriate response to the insurgency.
Swamped by Russians or Russified Ukrainians in party, administrative, manage-
rial, and perhaps most importantly of all, educational posts—a trajectory actually
at variance with the Baltic republics where Moscow sought to bring on native communist elites—surviving OUN supporters had no opportunity to contest the new
dispensation, at least not in situ.[143] The most active were packed off to the Gulag
in their tens of thousands where, alongside their Baltic counterparts, they constituted a major post-war element of those denoted as 'particularly dangerous' or 'war
criminals' ripe for incarceration in special regime camps, *lagpunkts*, in the furthest
extremes of the Soviet Arctic. Here their ongoing political protests and 'insubordi-
nation' spilled over into a range of strikes, revolts, and break-outs which rocked the
camp system mostly after Stalin's death, albeit too far away to affect the situation
back home.[144] As for their wives and children, these constituted the majority of
over 182,000 west Ukrainians deported mostly to Central Asia between 1944 and
1952, the largest contingent of which—nearly 78,000—were rounded up at gun-
point in a single twenty-four-hour operation on 20–1 October 1947.[145]

One might argue, thus, that the mass deportations from the western Ukraine,
depriving the OUN of its core indigenous following, were Stalin's *necessary* action
by which to prevent a more terrible descent into even more mass murder; and
equally, of course, to contain the spread of the *Ounovtsy* disease. Isolate the cancer
and then surgically remove it was doubtless also Jacobin reasoning in 1793–4.
The whole truth of Stalin's bloody triumph in the formerly Polish Ukraine, however, is more paradoxical. Stalin won by making the vast majority of *Soviet* Ukrainians believe that this was their victory too, and he did so by effectively stealing
OUN's *nationalist* clothes; or, perhaps more cunningly still, by taking a leaf out
of his own mythic Great Patriotic War narrative as primarily meant for Russians
and applying it equally to the Ukrainians.[146] They, too, were *nas narod*, and to
prove it Stalin gave them a sensational victory present. The Ukrainian SSR's borders
were now moved radically westwards to encompass not only all of the majority

Ukrainian-speaking tsarist territories lost after the Great War, but as far as formerly Czech-controlled Transcarpathia, which had never been part of the Romanov empire. Also included in the new Ukraine were once Habsburg, then Rumanian Bukovinian lands centring on Chernivitsi (Cernowitz), plus nearly all of Habsburg, then Polish eastern Galicia.[147] Of course, taking Lwów and its hinterland had been a cherished tsarist war aim in 1914, just as had been the intent to forcibly convert Sheptyts'kyi's Greek Catholic flock to Orthodoxy. But if Stalin's carry-through was still fundamentally for Moscow's benefit, the conjuring trick lay in the way it also pumped up Ukrainian *national* self-esteem. To be sure, 'official propaganda in western Ukraine endlessly reiterated that the reunification and progressive development of Ukrainian lands were only possible within the "brotherly family" of the Soviet people'.[148] But Lwów, almost completely shorn of its Polish and Jewish communities, was henceforth indisputably the (west) Ukrainian cultural capital of Lviv, while its children and those of all the 'reunited' provinces were equally destined to imbibe their sense of place within the fraternal constellation through Ukrainian as well as Russian textbooks.

With the Ukrainian SSR the largest single beneficiary of Second World War territorial changes, and with the transfer of the Crimea from Russian SFSR control in 1954 a seriously significant additional prize, OUN dreams for a great, unified Ukraine had been more or less fulfilled: in effect, for the first time, and by none other than their arch-enemy, Stalin. But nationally-minded Ukrainians could also look to the *vozhd* for the achievement of that other great OUN aspiration: national homogeneity. It was not just that the 'reunited' peoples of post-war Ukraine were being encouraged to think of themselves as no longer Galician, Rusyn, or Bukovinan but as part of a single authentic nation. Rather, what mattered was the route by which this ethnographic reality was, again thanks to comrade Stalin, being made manifest: through the removal of all those extraneous elements who would otherwise have spoilt the imagined picture of joyful Ukrainian community.[149]

While the ethnic cleansing of large numbers of Rumanians and Moldavians from what had become the south-eastern oblasts of the extended SSR was part of this homogenization drive, its major component was actually the result of an internationally-recognized agreement between a now communist-controlled Warsaw and Moscow, as initially drafted in September 1944 and then officially confirmed the following January. A sort of northern Lausanne, albeit with 'voluntary' in place of 'compulsory' cleverly if entirely meretriciously written into its terms of reference, the agreement provided for the 'repatriation' of 1.5 million Poles from newly annexed Soviet territories, in exchange for half a million Ukrainians from a radically territorially reshaped Poland.[150] As with previous internationally-agreed projects for the 'unmixing of peoples' across national boundaries, the project could be read as a legitimate method of two-way population 'transfer' without recourse to genocide. From this perspective, the USSR might, if it so chose, claim that its project had achieved another key OUN objective by socialist, non-violent means. It also incidentally signalled that for Moscow, Poles, as well as remaining Jews from the historic *kresy*, were no longer considered assimilable as good citizens of the USSR—as had been attempted in 1939—but were better eructed westwards.

By the same token, for the Ukrainians themselves, the message from on high, mediated through then Ukrainian party secretary Khrushchev, was equally transparent: be very grateful for what the USSR has achieved for your nation through removing the Polish colonists and landlords.[151]

In practice, as repeatedly was the case in modern exchanges of population, the agreement was a recipe for further inhumanity and atrocity.[152] The immediate pretext for further violence was the post-1945 attempt by the UPA, after its Red Army mauling, to relocate its centre of operations to the fastness of the Bieszczady mountains south-west of Lublin—an area which, though largely Ukrainian-speaking, remained within *Polish* borders. This in turn put pressure on the now communist-dominated authorities in Warsaw to coordinate with the Soviet security and military apparatus in cross-border operations aimed at the destruction of the remaining insurgency. Soviet rather than Polish interests in the matter were exemplified in the fact that key officers on the Polish General Staff supervising the anti-UPA campaign included Red Army men in Polish uniform.[153]

But the Poles themselves hardly needed encouragement to participate. Within two of the three infantry battalions they deployed were significant numbers from Volhynia intent on exacting revenge for earlier UPA atrocities. However, the primary method of these units was mostly one not of direct encounter with their guerrilla adversaries but rather of softening up the base Ukrainian population in the region with a view not simply to depriving the UPA of possible sustenance from them but more precisely to arriving at that population's wholesale flight or coerced removal. What softening up might entail in practice is exemplified in the single attack on the Subcarpathian village of Zawadka Morochowska (Zavadka Morokhivs'ka) close to the Slovakian border, towards the end of January 1946. Led by one Colonel Stanisław Pluto, a Red Army officer in Polish uniform but himself of Polish background, his unit appears to have run amok using their bayonets to mutilate and/or disembowel fifty-six villagers, nearly all women, old people, and children before they proceeded to burn them alive. The attack was far from unique, says Snyder, but typical of dozens of such massacres.[154]

Of course, we could choose to read these attacks clinically as part of a strategy to provoke the UPA to break cover, even retaliate against Polish villages, thereby reinforcing the justification for the widest possible cleansing of Ukrainians. It is certainly the case that the Ukrainian partisans were drawn into efforts to block the deportations which began in earnest in the summer of 1945, their successful attacks on bridges and other communication hubs largely forcing the Polish military out of the local countryside and acting as a rallying point around which more general Ukrainian resistance to 'repatriation' might coalesce. This in turn led to an accelerated Polish effort to clear out the Ukrainian presence once and for all. In the three months between April and June 1946, the specially tasked Operation Group Rzeszów was responsible for some quarter of a million Ukrainian 'repatriations' across the border, the main bulk of the over 482,000 Ukrainians deported eastwards by the Polish authorities up to this time.[155]

Yet there were still people speaking a form of Ukrainian who had yet to feel the full brunt of Warsaw's wider social engineering goals. Up to this point, the Lemkos had mostly escaped forcible deportations. We encountered them in our previous volume as a classic example of a rimlands community steadfast in its commitment to an identity founded upon not national allegiance but habitus. Though perhaps amounting to a third of the Polish population definable as 'Ukrainian' at the end of the war, these transhumant pastoralists of the Subcarpathian Beskidy range primarily 'saw themselves as members of the Russian family of nations in the inclusive and pluralistic sense of the term'.[156] Actually, this meant that considerable numbers—perhaps as many as 90,000—did voluntarily migrate to the Soviet Ukraine at war's end, believing that they might be able integrate themselves into *kolkhoz* life. Rapid disenchantment with this reality ensured that many Lemko migrants attempted to return to the Beskidy soon after.[157] Relatively few Lemkos, however, were prepared to throw in their lot with the UPA, when the latter infiltrated into the region. Rather like the Meskhetians, their crime appears to have been one of straddling a mental as well as geographical space, which upset the neat tidiness of the nation state and its boundaries; of which, especially in immediate post-war circumstances, the Polish communist leadership was keen to demonstrate to fellow Poles its credentials as the best guarantor.

The broader *Polish* context to the final assault on the Lemkos is in part very significant here. The new Soviet-imposed and supervised Polish Workers Party (PPR) regime left societal aspirations for a genuine independence high and dry. Western Allied acquiescence in the face of Stalinist diktat, including their confirmation of Soviet sovereignty in the eastern Polish territories previously engorged in 1939, underlined the degree to which they had abandoned the legitimate London-based government-in-waiting. The onset of the Cold War did not alter the palpable isolation of Poland from the possibility of outside Western help, even while grass-roots Polish opposition to the new order remained passionate. Indeed, there were in 1946 units of the otherwise disbanded AK still fighting in the lost *kresy*, as there were on actual Polish soil, pretty much in the same manner as the UPA and Baltic resistance movements. And these Polish resisters equally tied down large numbers of both Soviet and Polish government forces even while driving the country towards the abyss of civil war.[158] But what could have amounted to an ongoing brutal stand-off between PPR and people was to a degree alleviated by the former's growing presentation of itself as the latter's true defenders.

One aspect which gave breathing space for the new regime, paradoxical as it was, was the sweeping land reform which finally gave to the Polish peasantry something which had eluded them under more conservative interwar governments.[159] Another was the overt appeal to an ethnically-based nationalism. One important signal of this novel line in Polish communist thinking came in May 1945 when, speaking of the country's German inhabitants, Władysław Gomułka, the PPR general secretary, publicly pronounced, 'We have to throw them out, since all countries are built on national, not multinational principles.'[160] To be sure, the statement was not directly pitched in this first instance against the rapidly diminishing numbers of Ukrainians. What Gomułka was actually referring to was the genuinely significant millions of German citizens (over and above the Volksdeutsche) who were now marooned in Poland. This was a direct consequence of the anticipated western territorial award offered by the Allies, at the February 1945 Yalta Conference, in compensation for the lost eastern territories. When the award was finalized at the succeeding Potsdam Conference that summer, these Western Territories, extending to the Oder-Neisse line, went deep into what had formerly been undisputedly German heartland, though they constituted some 32.4 per cent of what was now post-war Poland.[161] In so doing, they provided plentiful room for 'repatriated' *Zabuzanie* Poles (those historically living east of the Bug)—but necessarily at the expense of incumbent (or returning) Germans. There was further irony, of course, in the fact that this also represented a searing retributive retort to what had been Nazi settlement policy for western Poland. But Gomułka's intervention also offered an additional fillip for the winding up of Poland's historic stake in the rimlands. It was as if, by drawing a line under Piłsudski's multi-ethnic 'eastern' vision, the PPR had plumped instead for the long-standing Endek goal of people-homogeneity, even in a territorially reshaped Poland much of which was now on *German* soil.

To be sure, this unexpected PPR embrace of the integral nation looks entirely less remarkable when put alongside Stalin's determination to create a big, homogeneous Ukraine. Or, for that matter, the way in which Polish-speaking Volhynians, a community historically rather indifferent to rimlands difference, became among the most vociferous of Polish nationalists when displaced to the new Western Territories.[162] In a critical sense, what was thus happening in Poland—as equally in the Ukraine—was a case of state and society coming together to put an end to the very notion of rimlands. And who did Poles ultimately have to thank for this newfound sense of national unity and coherence? Comrade Stalin. As equally for guaranteeing their new western border with Germany. Who paid the price? Not just the millions of deported Germans, of whom more in our final chapter, but entirely inoffensive minority groups like the Lemkos.

The pretext for Warsaw's final drive against them *in their supposed capacity as Ukrainians* was the alleged UPA ambush and murder of the controversial general and then deputy defence minister Karol Świerczewski in the Bieszczady foothills in late March 1947. By this juncture the Soviets' direct interest in Polish counter-insurgency operations had receded, now that the 'exchange of populations' had been largely completed and the UPA resistance—insofar as it represented a cross-border threat—for the most part bloodily pacified. So while Soviet security and military placements (of the ilk of Świerczewski) still played an important role in the subsequent *Akcja Wisła*—Operation Vistula—as indeed did Czech forces, this was a project fundamentally designed and executed by the Warsaw, not Moscow or Prague authorities. And, indeed, the very fact that it used as its codename Poland's great river running through the centre of the country towards near Danzig on the Baltic—rather than the eastern fluvial boundaries of the San, Bug, or Zbruch—was a quite conscious statement of the operation's purpose. Described by its leading architect, and former Piłsudskian, General Mossor as aiming to 'resolve the Ukrainian problem in Poland once and for all', the actual operational orders involved not a Lemko deportation from the Beskidy eastwards across the international border into Ukraine (which would have been disallowed by Stalin anyway), but instead north-westwards to the 'recovered' territories. Here these 'Ukrainians', their identity documents marked with a 'U', were to be broken up as communities and resettled 'with the widest possible dispersion', nowhere in excess of two to three families per area.[163]

What this then sounds like is a further variation on first the CUP, then Soviet theme of internal deportation of problematic ethnic communities as the necessary prelude to their anthropophagic disintegration, which, in the longer term, the project to a degree achieved.[164] More immediately, however, the Operation Vistula violence meted out to the Lemkos during the spring and summer of 1947 was every bit as vicious as in the previous Soviet-led anti-UPA operations. This displayed all the usual aspects of the standard counter-insurgency formula; close military–security cooperation in the surveillance and then encirclement of villages, the shooting of those who attempted to resist, military convoys to ensure no escape, the isolation and removal to camps of those deemed most intractable. Nearly 4,000 were sent to the former Auschwitz-Birkenau sub-camp at Jaworzno. Among these unfortunates inevitably were large numbers of women and children. Many died through typhus epidemics, abuse, and general mistreatment. In addition, children and old people in particular perished on the transports. No fewer than 175 individuals were executed directly as UPA collaborators. The total death toll stands at perhaps close to 600. Statistically speaking, out of 140,000 deportees encompassed in the operation's dragnet the mortality may appear relatively small, seemingly confirming that while draconian, its ultimate intent was not genocidal. Even so, Snyder describes it as 'the most massive exercise of terror by the Polish communist regime during the entirety of its existence'.[165] The paradox lies in the fact that it was also the antechamber to renewed Polish nation-building, just as getting rid of the *kresy*'s Poles was antechamber to Ukrainian nation-building.

This is the point at which we come full circle. Operation Vistula may have been a Polish project, but it could not have taken place nor continued on its particular trajectory without Stalin's crystallized route-map for the expurgation of a heterogeneous 'Lands Between'. Five or ten years earlier, the supposedly difficult ethnic elements in this western rimlands mix were 'sorted' by deporting them *eastwards* to the most distant, remote, and usually inhospitable places in the old tsarist empire. That route actually intensified, as we have seen, for great swathes of rimlands 'minority' peoples in the period 1945–50. But for the Poles it was to be different. There was no Stalinist diktat to extend population exchanges to other now communist-dominated East European countries where mixed populations, as for instance in Transylvania, still existed. The decision to remove the *Zabuzanie* Poles *westwards* thus was a special case. It was not just a matter of being shot of a whole population group by evicting them to some other (non-Soviet) state, though we might note the counterpoint of Hitler's entirely unsuccessful 1939 attempt to dump eastern Jewry on the USSR. Stalin's 'genius' in his Polish and by extension Ukrainian solutions was that making these peoples apparent *national* masters in their own vastly strengthened homogeneous houses disarmed them entirely when it came to the small matter of their independent politics. In so doing, he bolstered *Russian* geopolitical control way into Central Europe just as the Cold War was 'hotting up'.

THE JEWS: RUSSIA'S LAST COMMUNAL ENEMY?

The heightened atmosphere of fearful anticipation which marks the beginnings of the new Soviet confrontation with the West, more specifically the USA, poses a problem question for this analysis. Are those communities which were henceforth accused, terrorized, and perhaps deported by the MGB, on grounds of their alleged espionage for or connivance with the Americans, part and parcel of a successor story to the crisis of the semi-periphery, the crisis of the rimlands? Or are they actually part of those crises' unfinished business? It is alarming as well as intriguing to find in Bugai's list of deported groups towards the very end of the Stalin years Soviet communities of Assyrians and Jehovah's Witnesses, as if to remind us that however small and politically insignificant an awkward religious sect or ethnic fragment might be, Stalinist Russia could behave towards it just as an Ittihadist Turkey or Nazi Germany might have done.[166] But then there is one group whose absence from the list of Soviet deportees would surely single out Soviet behaviour as entirely distinct from at least Nazi obsessions about its mortal enemies.

During all the years of Stalin's rule, never once had there been an *official* denunciation or attack on Jews qua Jews. People who were Jewish, of course, had been increasingly harassed, purged, vanished to the Gulag, or executed in great numbers, irrevocably changing as a result the very complexion not just of Soviet intellectual life but of its government administration, economic, foreign policy, security, and military arms in particular. To be sure, there were moments when this diffused, apparently colour-blind assault showed potential for crystallizing into something overtly anti-Semitic. The Russian Jewish investigative journalist Arkady Vaksberg, for instance, has identified 3 May 1939, the day that Maxim Litvinov was removed as Soviet foreign minister and his Commissariat surrounded by NKVD troops, as one such moment. Litvinov was Jewish, as were swathes of Soviet diplomats and ambassadors, large numbers of whom (though not Litvinov himself) were now summarily sacked and driven off to the Lubyanka.[167] Vaksberg argues that this was the prologue to a new run of show trials aimed at unmasking yet another elite conspiracy in league with a foreign power. This time, however, demonstrating that the enemy within were clearly internationally-connected Jews, says Vaksberg, was a critical part of Stalin's game-plan for making up to Hitler.

In itself, this does not prove any particular Stalin animus over and above a pragmatic readiness to dispense with *any* group of people who stood in the way of his single-minded agendas. This would be consistent, too, with the constant postponement, then abandonment, of the projected show trials and, indeed, after Hitler had invaded Russia, his formation of a specifically Jewish Antifascist Committee (JAC) whose purpose was to promote the wartime Soviet cause to the West. Equally, behind the public visage, it is difficult to pin down Stalin's exact feelings about Jewish people. There is no doubt that Stalin told and encouraged crass Jewish jokes within his immediate entourage. But mockery of Georgians (like himself) or Armenians in this close circle was also par for the course. Indeed, when it came to the wrath of the great leader, anybody, whatever their ethnic credentials, Russian or otherwise, could be the butt of his acerbic put-downs, which more often than not also foretold the unfortunate individual's impending eclipse, not to say physical liquidation. However, the implication that Stalin was no more anti-Semitic than he was anti-Muslim or anti-Polish (a particular pet-hate) should correctly leave us unsatisfied. A welter of anecdotal evidence, not least from his troubled daughter, Svetlana Alliluyeva, would suggest that his phobias about Jews went much deeper; that the show trials of so many leading Jewish-born Bolsheviks in the 1930s, were implicitly anti-Jewish; that, above all, the figure of Trotsky lurked on in the shadows as a Judas-type incubus, even after 1940 when he had been bloodily dispatched with an ice-pick by a Stalinist agent in far-away Mexico.[168] But on a public or semi-public level, at least until quite late in the day, Stalin had a shrewd riposte to any insinuation of some inner anti-Jewish animus. Was it not the case that when popular anti-Semitic diatribes were voiced, he was the first to denounce them? Was it equally not so that when people who happened to be Jewish were exposed as 'enemies of the people', one could always point to some other 'Jewish' person whom Stalin had just awarded or acclaimed for their services to Soviet society? And Stalin was also known for having Jewish friends, not least Kaganovich. The fact that the man was a crude, uneducated, cringing sycophant, and, even by Soviet standards, one of the unloveliest human beings in the entire Stalinist constellation, was beside the point.[169] How could the *vozhd* be an anti-Semite when everyone knew that Kaganovich was his great mate? Or that there were known to be plenty of other Jews in critical state and security functions way into the 1940s? Or, again, that those who cared for leading Politburo members were doctors with Jewish names? For that matter, what of social relationships within the tight confines of his inner circle, which included many Jewish wives, not least those of Molotov and Voroshilov?[170]

All this information was packaged into a very definite official facade of what has been described as 'anti-anti-Semitism'.[171] This demands that one ask why it was so radically overturned in the final years of Stalin's reign—to the point where at the very twilight of his life the 'Jewish' threat clearly came to the very centre stage of his moral and mental universe. There is, for sure, the possibility that it was the darkening clouds of Cold War which precipitated the shift. Stalinist chop-logic might reason thus: that post-war Soviet Jews were showing signs of a turn towards chauvinist nationalism; that this aligned them with foreign Zionist interests, which also made them susceptible to CIA designs to use them as spies and saboteurs from within the USSR. As (alleged) concrete evidence of these tendencies, the secret trial and guilty verdicts delivered against thirteen out of fourteen JAC members in summer 1952, followed by their execution, was simply proof of some broader Jewish maleficence. The JAC trial, indeed, was one of some seventy analogous trials across the length and breadth of the country.[172]

Does this get us to the explanatory heart of the late-Stalinist anti-Jewish campaign? Very far from it. But it is worth pursuing for a lap, if only because its basic charge of a Jewish national separation inimical to Soviet interests evinces elements in common with the justification for the punishment and deportation of other *national* communities. The JAC, as we have noted, was founded in August 1941 at

Stalin's behest. It was not his original idea, but that of two Polish Bundist leaders, Victor Alter and Henryk Ehrlich, who at the time of the collapse of Poland had been trying to get up the idea of a world association of leading Jewish cultural and scientific figures who would help rally the fight against Hitler—only to find themselves the guests of the NKVD. Stalin, at this point, clearly had no use at all for an independent, let alone high-profile, international Jewish body which was proposing to wage war on his friend Hitler. As for the idea of a Jewish nation, his views, dating back to 1913 when Lenin had entrusted him with the task of enunciating a social-democratic position on nationality, were essentially negative: a 'paper nation', yes, but one without any tangible basis in reality. The always pragmatic and, in summer 1941, vastly beleaguered great leader, however, was hardly going to look askance at the possibilities which Alter and Ehrlich's scheme now seemed to proffer. 'World Jewry' and, through them America, could be mobilized not for the general but the specific struggle of the USSR. A committee was duly got up, almost all of whom were 'Jewish by name only': communist party stalwarts, unknown in the West but with a small core of Soviet Yiddish writers, and with a chair—the great Yiddish actor and director Solomon Mikhoels—who was the one figure with a modicum of celebrity status in the wider Jewish diaspora. Notable by their absence, however, were the Bundist leaders: Stalin having no further use for them, the NKVD dispatched them soon after.[173]

If all this so far suggests a rather lacklustre entity firmly under Moscow's thumb, the energy with which the JAC, Mikhoels in particular, went about its efforts, a propaganda trip to the West included, defied all expectations. Riding high on their acclamation in the USA and elsewhere, it is with hindsight hardly surprising that the JAC's *own* sense of role and purpose began to expand over and beyond its official remit, and not least as it began to get to grips with the extent of the Holocaust on Soviet soil. One consequence was that a team under the writers Ilya Ehrenburg, then Vasily Grossman, set about compiling a record of the mass Jewish killings—*The Black Book of Soviet Jewry*—which Mikhoels then petitioned Stalin's propaganda chief, Andrei Zhdanov, to clear for publication. Detailing the specificity of Jewish destruction, however, did not compute with the contours of Stalin's Great Patriotic (primarily Russian) War narrative, and became in itself a black mark against the *Black Book's* compilers, and the committee more generally. *The Black Book* never saw the light of day in the USSR.[174]

However, more heinous still in Kremlin eyes was the manner in which the JAC began to respond to grass-roots Jewish pleas for help, especially from either direct survivors of the killings—particularly from the rimlands zone where the vast majority of Soviet Jews had been exterminated—or returnees, especially from Central Asia, whose repeated experience was of local hostility, more particularly against their efforts to find new jobs and old homes. In fact, these tensions were not relayed only through the JAC. Following a series of anti-Jewish riots in Kiev, both in the wake of German withdrawal in spring 1944 and then more seriously in the summer of 1945, a group of Jewish war veterans attempted to use contacts with *Pravda* to petition Beria and Stalin directly about the extent of the hostility. Stalin, of course, was *meant* to be against anti-Semitism, which, after all—according to correct 'Soviet-think'—was nothing more than a crude tool of reactionaries and counter-revolutionaries. But here was a novel situation in which Soviet Jews were not only openly expressing their *singular* suffering, but pitted against 'ordinary' Russians and Ukrainians. These very often included local party bosses, who—as elsewhere in post-Holocaust Europe—were seeing 'kikes' as a challenge to their new (Jew-free) social and economic order.[175] We will come back to how Stalin interpreted these social tensions a little further on; as we will also need to consider a little more how they impacted on the Soviet Jewish majority who had escaped the killings and, up to this time, had largely been seeking what amounted to a self-willed anthropophagic absorption into *Russian* life.[176] What matters here, though, is how the JAC response to the post-war crisis of Soviet Jewish identity became the basis for the Kremlin's indictment against it as a vehicle of independent Jewish nationalism.

The nub of the accusation centred on a collective letter from the JAC leadership to Molotov and other senior Politburo members in late February 1944. It proposed the creation of 'a Jewish Soviet socialist republic' in the Crimea and a government commission to scope and develop its implementation. There was, in fact, already a Jewish autonomous region, in faraway Birobidzhan, in eastern Siberia. It had never passed muster as a place where Jews who felt seriously about maintaining and developing a Yiddish culture were going to seriously migrate to in droves.[177] The Crimea, by contrast, had already been the site of numerous Soviet-sponsored Jewish collective farms in the 1920s—themselves a conscious Jewish communist riposte to the blandishments of kibbutz-style socialist Zionism. More to the point, the Crimea, in terms of geography, climate, and general potential, was exactly the sort of benign environment (in utter contrast to Birobidzhan) in which both resettling what remained of the shattered Jewish communities of the rimlands and revitalizing their cultural life was a plausible proposition. This is clearly what Mikhoels and his committee had in mind. Could it be, too, that through the senior party placements on the JAC (including, inevitably, one very senior NKVD minder), Mikhoels had some forewarning of the Crimean 'space' which was soon likely to become available when the peninsula was liberated and the Crimean Tatars eructed? In which case, the very notion of a Jewish territorialization there may have had initial encouragement from the highest reaches of the regime. Certainly, the letter to Molotov's office was originally addressed to Stalin.[178] That speculation aside, and again reaching for the longer view, the JAC *démarche*, for all its undoubted good intentions on the one hand and indifference to the fate of the Tatars on the other can only be seen as spectacularly mistimed. Indeed, the letter offered firm confirmation that the group were innocents abroad, yet playing with fire.

We have already seen that the Crimea was a subject of acute geopolitical sensitivity to the Kremlin, the result of which was that ultimately it was not only its Tatar inhabitants who were expelled from it but also, among others, Greeks and Bulgarians. We may recall too that these expulsions, far from being a single one-off affair, intensified as fears of direct conflict with the Americans grew. The fact that an Anglo-French force had actually landed on the peninsula nearly a century earlier clearly acted as one potent reminder of how the West might conceivably use the Crimea again as a theatre of operations. Three years after the JAC memorandum, the enunciation of the Truman Doctrine and the closing embrace of Turkey within the emerging US global security system upped the ante on how the Americans, perhaps operating from across the Caucasus, might seek to subvert Russia from a Crimean foothold. The charge-sheet in the JAC interrogations, that the real purpose of creating a Jewish 'bourgeois democratic' republic in the Crimea was to offer exactly that, thus speaks volumes as to the length and breadth of Stalin's paranoid imaginings in his final years. Western defensive moves on the USSR's southern littoral had been transformed into utterly offensive ones. And a 'cabal' of Soviet Jews, supposedly piqued by their failure to achieve national—even secessionist—objectives, had become outriders for a renewed Western imperial interventionism.[179]

What makes these confabulations all the more extraordinary, the JAC's naivety on the Crimean issue notwithstanding, is that the Jewish card had not only been part of Stalin's response to wartime emergency, but part of his ongoing post-war foreign policy portfolio to combat US 'encirclement'. The JAC's wartime networking with leading Jews in the USA had thus been encouraged by the Committee's Kremlin minders as a way of bringing US Jewish money to the Soviet fighting effort. That part of the anti-JAC indictment which focused on its contact with the powerful US Jewish charity the Joint—significantly a frequent bogey at the heart of Hitler's conspiracy-filled world view—was because Stalin had desired that contact; and, to the extent that the JAC was accused of links with Zionists and Zionism, could also be put down to the fact that on his US visit Mikhoels had been encouraged to appeal to Jewish national sentiments.[180] Later, at a time when the MGB had already for two years been busily preparing its dossier of charges against the JAC, its nationalizing tendencies included, Stalin was giving his overt support to the creation of the state of Israel. It ought not to have escaped his notice that the JAC's Crimean scheme was not to separate from but to find a way by which to more fully embed Russian Jewry as a self-respecting communal entity *within* the Soviet family of nations. To that extent, the JAC's basic orientation was anti- or, at the very least, non-Zionist.

The developing campaign against the Committee, which broke into open view with its official November 1948 liquidation, thus tells us very little about its actual nationalizing tendencies. It was Stalin, not they, who was making all the running on that score, even if we might surmise that his ephemeral pro-Zionist stance had little or nothing to do with sympathy for the cause but everything to do with weakening British rule in Palestine. Soviet efforts, over and beyond voting for the creation of Israel by the UN partition plan for Palestine, in November 1947, included logistical support for Zionist boats operating from Bulgaria and Rumania as they attempted to break the British sea blockade of illegal immigrants, plus, after the declaration of the State the following May, a green light for the delivery to it of Czech arms, which arguably proved decisive in Israel's first victory over its Arab neighbours.[181] But logically, if Stalin was so enthusiastic about Zionism, then that ought to have carried over into encouraging, or at least giving the opportunity to, Soviet Jews to emigrate to Israel, a notion which never seems to have been remotely contemplated. By contrast, there is certainly some tantalizing anecdotal evidence to suggest a shift in Russian Jewish opinion around this time in favour of Zionism. The arrival of the first Israeli ambassador in Moscow, the Russian-born Golda Meir, in September was greeted with something akin to messianic expectations by its Jewish inhabitants, especially when she soon after attended services at the central Choral Synagogue during Jewish New Year. Some 10,000 Jewish Muscovites were there to greet her, the largest single civil gathering in the capital for twenty years.[182] Even the regime's leading Jewish wives appeared to have been swept up in the euphoria, the warm exchanges in particular between Meir and Molotov's wife, Polina Zhemchuzhina, a leading old Bolshevik in her own right, arguably the final goad to Stalin's decision to have the latter expelled from the party and incarcerated in a labour camp. Thereafter, Zhemchuzhina's previous good relations with the JAC, especially with the late Mikhoels, became central to the MGB's efforts to prove a high-level Jewish nationalist plot to take over the Crimea on America's behalf.[183]

Mikhoels, of course, was not there to be further implicated in this increasingly murky and far-fetched witch-hunt. He had already been eliminated by the MGB in a carefully prepared traffic accident, out of the way in Minsk, the previous January.[184] His absence, however, does raise a question: supposing he *had* been in Moscow to greet Meir, would he have actually given his powerful voice to the new, non-Soviet act of Jewish nation-building? We cannot ever know, nor indeed whether Mikhoels' affirmation could have bolstered Russian Jewry in any mobilization around Zionism. The rising crescendo of state-wide sackings from office and security-led terrorization of Jews, from late 1948 onwards, suffocated what had always been only the faintest of possibilities. Even thus, while nationalism and Zionism remained the main cover story of the charge-sheet against the JAC, we have more or less exhausted any exploration which might suggest that Stalin was motivated by Jewish nationalism as the *primary* cause of his growing anti-Jewish hostility; or, for that matter, that this same national sentiment had become the main motivating force within Russian Jewry. To be sure, if the latter had been the case, it might well have had significant ramifications for the regime, but only when set against the main Soviet-Jewish social and cultural trajectory since the time of the revolution. In order, therefore, to get to the heart of the matter, we need to retrace our steps somewhat.

Evidence of grass-roots Russian Jewish support for Zionism can be traced to 1917 when, before the Bolsheviks took power, a preliminary Russo-Jewish Congress had delivered a majority of votes for it rather than for socialist or other parties.[185] But that had been when most Russian Jews were still domiciled in the Pale of Settlement. The majority of Jews who were still living in that area in 1939–40, that is, who had not otherwise fallen under Nazi occupation, only became citizens of the Soviet Union at this point. In these parts, a religiously traditional, culturally Yiddish, economically marginal existence continued throughout the interwar years as the dominant Ashkenazi way of life. To an extent, this was also true in the western republics of the USSR (also formerly part of the Pale) where a sizeable yet demographically ageing percentage of Jews clung on to remnants of the old life against the rough winds of Soviet change. Yet here we run up against the overwhelming consequences of genocide. It was exactly in this 'Lands Between' rimlands zone, whether on the western or eastern side of the pre-1939 Soviet border, that Jews were most likely to have been predisposed to some form of nationalizing tendency: Zionist, Bundist, or otherwise. The same Jews, that is, who were to be the vast majority of the 2.6 million mass-murdered by the Nazis, or their accomplices, on Soviet soil.[186]

In other words, the Soviet Jews who by reified association with the JAC were the butt of Stalin's post-war animus could not have been of a rimlands variety, because these were nearly all dead. Stalin's target instead was those who had either migrated from the time of the revolution to the major urban or metropolitan areas, most obviously Leningrad and Moscow, or their descendants. Though perhaps no greater in number than those killed in the rimlands, their demographic profile clearly made them both the mainstream and (at least on paper) future potential for continued Soviet Jewish life.[187] Simply from a geographic standpoint, any Stalin campaign against them could only be a heartland, not a rimlands, matter. But it was made doubly, indeed crucially, so for another reason. Under the tsars, the possibilities of a Jewish *sliianie* ('merging') with the Russian or Slavic ethnic majority had been looked upon with nothing less than unadulterated horror. As a consequence, Jewry's pre-revolution legal status as *inorodtsy*, the term most usually applied to the 'uncivilized' nomad or mountain peoples of Central Asia and the Caucasus, underscored the degree to which they were considered to be at several stages removed from the possibilities of assimilation.[188]

The revolution reversed this position entirely. Not only did Lenin encourage Jews to fill the administrative functions largely vacated by Russians (or Germans), but he publicly acknowledged Bolshevism's debt to them in its time of need.[189] Embraced thus by the revolutionary state, large numbers of Jews responded in kind, rushing headlong into the ranks of Soviet officialdom, and in the process dispensing rapidly with the linguistic, socio-economic, and cultural baggage which had previously most clearly identified them as distinct. How rapidly so many of them came to the heart of the Soviet state is reflected in some key occupational statistics. Jews represented less than 2 per cent of the overall population. Yet in 1937, before the full effects of the *Ezhovshchina* began to be felt, while they made up only 5.7 per cent of the *party* and only a marginal element in its Soviet Central Committee, they were the major ethnic element in senior *government* posts, greatly in excess of other comparable minorities, such as the Georgians and Letts—not to say Russians. More telling still, they constituted the primary ethnic component in the apparatus of Soviet state survival. We have already noted their almost exclusive position within the foreign affairs elite. But in the NKVD, while not quite so absolute, forty-two out of 111 top Chekists identified themselves as Jewish. In fact, within key directorates such as labour camps and resettlement (including deportations), and in some of the most sensitive security areas such as counter-intelligence and foreign intelligence, the Jewish preponderance was overwhelming.[190]

Of course, what is immediately striking about this profile is the degree to which it seems to confirm not only the pre-revolutionary Russian incubus but the more pervasive European fear of some ultimate Jewish state and societal takeover. Hitler's personal anxieties about Jews may have been thoroughly pathological in nature but articulated politically as a *Verjudung* (Judaization) scenario accomplished through communist agency. This was the same worst nightmare of Europe-wide believers in *Żydokomuna*. For such believers, the fact that the majority of Soviet heartland Jews were neither Chekists nor government officials would also have been immaterial. Indeed, a further statistical analysis of the Jewish occupational range over and beyond direct government, to include senior academic, intellectual, scientific, and technocratic positions, would have simply reinforced the anti-Semites' canard that Soviet-style *sliianie* had simply delivered the state into Jewish hands.

Right through the 1920s and arguably through the 1930s, it was precisely the universalist, colour-blind persona of the USSR which ensured Jewish immunity from such imprecations, a position which at least officially held even during the worst period of 'Trotskyist under the bed' fears. This certainly makes it more difficult to pinpoint exactly when the overtly anti-Jewish campaign did begin. Vaksberg notes that Jews in institutional scientific and artistic positions were already being sacked in great numbers from summer 1942 onwards—thereby undercutting the plausibility of the Jewish nationalism charge, given that this was not to officially surface for another six years.[191] On the other hand, getting rid of Jews from senior office would be consistent with Stalin's agenda to project the war effort as *Russian*, with bona fide Ivans at the helm of all high-profile patriotic institutes and organizations. We can still ask the question whether the Jewish firings were a matter of misplaced expediency, or whether Stalin really was beginning to fear 'insider' Jews on exactly the same grounds as classic anti-Semites. Or, to ask it another way, was the emerging new line method, or madness?

The argument for the latter derives from various sources, suggesting that after the first of several strokes in 1947, the ageing Stalin became even more paranoid and delusional than previously. His proneness to mood-swings and readiness to depart from standard protocol to openly denounce alleged enemies—Jews included—became famously pronounced in what for many present was his quite astonishing semi-public speech to the Central Committee Praesidium in December 1952.[192] Thereafter, it was a short step to going for the jugular with the embryonic Doctors' Plot, ordered at the great leader's direct behest into the public arena, through *Pravda*, the following month. Here seemed to be direct evidence that Stalin had created his own full-blown Soviet version of an international Jewish conspiracy. The 'doctor-murderers' were intent on poisoning and killing him off along with the rest of the Politburo. They, in turn, were in cahoots with the 'international Jewish bourgeois-nationalist' Joint. And the latter, of course, were working for British and US intelligence to encompass the 'terrorist' destruction of the USSR. This entire phantasmagoria would seem to reduce the Judaeophobic space between the *vozhd* and the late Nazi dictator to a smidgeon.[193]

Yet there clearly *was* a difference. Stalin's paranoia by the late 1940s was encompassing a whole range of people near and far, including members of his own family as well as most, if not all, his immediate *political* entourage, none of whom, bar Kaganovich, was Jewish. Where the issue of Jewishness pervaded the picture was not, however, in the accusation of treacherous Jewish nationalism per se but in the much more all-encompassing charge of 'rootless cosmopolitanism'. To be sure, the accusation of Zionism seemed to confirm that at least some Jews were working in their own separate interests, just as nationalist Chechens or Crimean Tatars were, and that this made them potential tools of foreign powers. The alleged JAC narrative fell more or less into this category. But the national or national-Zionist storyline was always rather insipid when set against what Stalin was actually trying to express about the all-pervasive Jewish infiltration of Soviet, more precisely Russian, life. Hence, we might note the 'creeping barrage' nature of the attack. The onset of the shift against Zionism was heralded in *Pravda* in September 1948, followed soon after by the suppression and arrest of the JAC people. The new focus, however, was on flushing out 'cosmopolitans', signalled with a flurry of *Pravda* articles from January the following year.[194]

If this was madness, there was clearly method in it. The USSR may have become by late 1948 a very powerful state, vastly so compared with its perilous position even a few years earlier. Given its reach on the global stage, to even speak of it hereafter, as we have previously done, in terms of anti-system might itself be inapt. The Soviet-led communist bloc was now an unequivocal competitor with the West; yet, by the same token, the USSR was not just threatened and vulnerable in its international position. Yes, there was the possibility of war with the West over Berlin—or later Korea—and with it nuclear obliteration at the hands of a USA which, until the first Soviet bomb in August 1949, had a monopoly in the field. And there was, too, the danger of Moscow's hegemonic position being challenged by other national communists. An imminent Chinese communist victory against the Kuomintang was yet to presage Mao's break with Moscow. But, closer at hand, an independent Titoist line in Yugoslavia posed the possibility of a genuine communist alternative to Stalin, a situation to which he reacted violently with a series of Eastern Bloc party purges, most ruthlessly in Hungary.[195] These potential threats from within the wider (anti-)system, however, also highlighted Stalin's weakness at home. Could his regime still be toppled or disintegrated from within? Might there be 'a stab in the back'? If so, from where would that stab come?

Here, once again, we might wish to note how the underlying structural weakness of the Soviet state, or at least Stalin's fear of losing control of it, seemed to have its outlet in an inference almost identical to Hitler's: that overthrow would come through the Jews. The notion is potent not least because in the Soviet case Jews really were part of the political fabric. Imagining them as a monolithic threat is certainly fantastical; but then, Stalin's conjuring up of their supposed malice by way of their cosmopolitanism has something more akin to the Spanish Inquisition about it than Hitler's crude racism. The implication, indeed, is that just as crypto-Jewish *conversos* supposedly wheeded their way into the early modern Iberian states to spread their 'Jewish' infection around them, so 'Jews who claimed to be Russians in order to appear Soviet' equally turned 'every Russian in high position' into 'a potential Jew'.[196] The inference that it was 'cosmopolitans without a fatherland' or 'persons without identity' who were the carriers of this disease, moreover, was all the more insidious because it did not ever need to articulate the word 'Jew' at all. Instead, everybody knew the score through the basic semiotics.

That said, if this still suggested method, there was something very high risk about it. By inferring that the Jewish threat was working its tentacles into the very highest reaches of government, Stalin was effectively going over *its* head in what amounted to a direct appeal to the *Russian people* to save the day—a sort of Maoist cultural revolution avant la lettre. But if this sort of demotic call to arms was compelling as a notion, it was also highly fissile—and thus dangerous. After all, when US senator Joe McCarthy made almost mirror-image charges—at the core of which was his famous June 1951 speech claiming to have uncovered 'a conspiracy on a scale so immense as to dwarf any previous such venture in the history of man'—and with a very similar 'Jewish' sub-text regarding Jews' presence in government, the media, and Hollywood, it was entirely unclear where the assault would end and who ultimately would be encompassed within it.[197] The very fact that the McCarthyite campaign emerged at an identical moment to Stalin's 'Doctors' Plot' narrative, had as its backdrop equally existential fears of nuclear obliteration, plus an evil cast of fifth columnists and spies to boot, suggests too how the world's leading supposedly liberal democracy could fall prey to the same psychopathological tendencies as *both* Hitler and Stalin. Returning to the latter, however, the fact that the great leader seemed to be seriously ready to bid for populist passions in a state otherwise known for its top-down, meticulously calibrated, police controlled, and usually highly secretive determination of 'enemies', perhaps suggests how desperate he had become. And, perhaps, also in need of a story to justify to the Soviet masses why it was necessary to have one last clearing out not just of 'real 'Jews' but by extension contenders for his throne who had become *like* Jews— not least Beria, Molotov, and Mikoyan—none of whom, interestingly, while they may have been complicit in it, actually believed one iota of the Doctors' Plot.[198]

But where was all this leading? Stalin's fabrications and McCarthy's allegations were both geared towards the mobilization of mass hysteria as a way to justify a major state clampdown against alleged internal enemies. But as far as Jews specifically were concerned, the Soviet leader's aim appears at this point to have become altogether more far-reaching—and consciously lethal. This is why he *needed* something like the Doctors' Plot as his casus belli in the first place. The attempt to get up the JAC case in such a way that it could be broadcast to the nation and the world as a show trial had already collapsed in on itself, the result being that the defendants were tried in camera and then done away with off-scene. The prosecution evidence the MGB had attempted to bring together had simply been too flimsy. One consequence was that its now head, Abakumov, was himself accused and then executed for both protecting and being involved with the 'Zionists'.[199] Zionism henceforth, too, became just another catch-all term for malign, alien, internationalist tendencies, usually but not exclusively on the part of Jews. In that sense, it also became on a par with or—however contradictorily—equivalent to cosmopolitanism. The only problem with the latter terminology was that it was simply too abstract *on its own* to incite direct popular violence.

Enter the idea of a conspiracy involving 'a band of beasts in human form' prowling the corridors of the Kremlin.[200] This was certainly as good as any script for a science fiction horror film: behind the benign visage of the regime's most trusted and leading physicians a clique of 'doctor-wreckers' lurking, who would stop at nothing to murder the great leader. *Pravda*'s infamous (Stalin himself-edited) editorial on 13 January 1953 announced 'Evil Spies and Murderers Masked as Medical Professors'. In case anybody was in doubt as to who was being accused, the satirical *Crocodil* magazine followed with a clearly *Der Stürmer*-like illustration of a white-coated figure with a loathsome physiognomy revealed behind a kindly academic mask.[201] To arrive at this sensational revelation, however, Stalin had had to turn to a new crew from the MGB ranks to concoct an appropriately fantastical narrative. The Ezhov-like instrument at the centre of this investigation was one Mikhail Riumin. His fall from grace was as rapid as his rise, but not before he had 'discovered' information that the Kremlin's doctors—nearly all of whom happened to be Jewish—had not only killed Stalin's erstwhile heir apparent, Zhdanov, but were working with JAC 'nationalist' conspirators plus senior echelons of the MGB, including Abakumov, the latter for good measure also being accused of killing one of the doctors, in order to conceal the wider plot.[202]

At this point we might note one piquant little irony. The number of top-rank Jewish medical professors among those doubling as Stalin and his clique's carers— the press made an unusual point of publishing a list of Jewish-sounding names— should not in any sense surprise.[203] Jews had had a high profile as physicians for centuries: it entirely tallied with the Talmudic injunction of *pikuah nefesh*—to *save* life. Whether these particular highly assimilated Soviet individuals saw themselves as behaving according to Jewish tradition is another matter. What we can say with certainty is that once inside the Lubyanka their MGB accusers made sure that any such injunction was turned on its head: the round-the-clock beatings and torture of these sometimes themselves aged and in some instances ailing doctors were designed to fast track them towards the confessions they would be required to utter in what was now anticipated as an imminent show trial. And though, in fact, not all the doctors rounded up *were* Jewish, Riumin's team made no bones about impugning the Jewish credentials of those who were. For instance, Colonel Vladimir Komarov, even after his own arrest in February 1953, appealed directly to Stalin 'to give me the opportunity to use all my inborn hatred of our enemies to take revenge on them for their villainies, for the damage they have done to the state'.[204] That Komarov meant none other than Jews when he spoke thus is confirmed, moreover, by what he had previously said to Solomon Lozovsky, one of the JAC defendants:

> Jews are low, dirty people, all Jews are lousy bastards, all opposition to the party consists of Jews. Jews all over the Soviet Union are conducting an anti-Soviet whispering campaign. Jews want to annihilate all Russians.[205]

That Chekists would have employed any manner of verbal taunts and racial abuse to get what they wanted from *all* accused people, whatever their origins, can hardly surprise. What is astonishing here, however, is the manner in which Komarov was given full rein to act in an overtly anti-Semitic way by the highest state authority. We know this to be true because it was Komarov who, having been so crucial to the JAC trial, also took the lead role in the Prague investigations which led to the so-called Slánský trial, in November 1952. In this farrago, the general secretary of the Czech communist party, Rudolf Slánský, and thirteen other leading cadres were brought to trial on charges of treason and espionage and either executed or given terms of life imprisonment. The eleven executed were all Jewish. It was no coincidence. The outing of prominent Jewish communists in the Eastern Bloc as 'traitors' was not in itself novel. With an initial Jewish conspicuousness in most of the Stalin-imposed regimes of Eastern Europe otherwise notable for their lack of popular support, throwing the most 'internationalist' (cosmopolitan) or, more crudely put, 'alien' figures to the lions was one cheap, diversionary tactic for damp-ening demotic resentment or even finding some ephemeral grounds for grass-roots acclamation. But before Slánský, the anti-Semitic scapegoating had been implicit rather than explicit. Indeed, given that the usual charge was one of Titoist devia-tionism, other more popular 'national' communist personalities also fell foul of these witch-hunts, Gomułka in Poland, though not tried or executed, being one obvious casualty.[206]

What was entirely different about the Slánský trial was that it was the *Jewishness* of the defendants which was particularly paraded as the source of their evilness, the thing which predisposed them to do wicked things against the state. To be sure, it was done behind the cover of the defendants' supposed connivance with Zionism, the new, big, Soviet bogey: even though Komarov was never quite able to work up a storyline in which both Tel Aviv and Washington were in equal measure behind Slánský and company's crimes. Nor, for that matter, was the colonel able to make a link to the Doctors' Plot, again in spite of the Slánský affair clearly being intended as a dry run for the latter's public broadcast. All that aside, what Czech society was being asked to imbibe and affirm, in the words of the leading Prague daily *Rude Pravo*, was that no Czech could have committed these crimes, 'only cynical Zion-ists, without a fatherland' who 'had sold out to the dollar', yet who were at the same time guided, by among other things, 'racial chauvinism'.[207]

Retrospective views such as that of Tony Judt condemn the trial as a 'criminal masquerade, judicial murder as public theatre'.[208] That is clearly the case. But just as with the intended Doctors' trial, the whole point of the exercise appears to have been to whip up through the press an unadulterated Judaeophobia whose antici-pated catharsis, preferably in the form of direct communal assault on Jews, in turn would provide a pretext for the state to intervene in order to put things to rights.

We can only speculate in the absence of precise documentary evidence what exactly Stalin's game-plan was, or from where (if anywhere) it was derived, as he moved towards inciting this full-blown scenario on Soviet soil. The obvious Nazi precedent was *Kristallnacht*. But given that this had not been an unalloyed success story for that regime, Stalin is more likely to have wanted to create as much dis-tance as possible between the 'justified' rage of the Slavic masses and a government whose institutional good name lay in resolving the cause of the disruption so that the country could be rapidly restored to order. More plausible, then, as model was Russia's own recent tsarist experience. The spate of apparently locally-inspired pogroms in the wake of the assassination of Alexander II in 1881 certainly pro-vided the then regime with its pretext for the May Laws, which both blamed the

Jews for the disturbances *and* sought to deny them movement, most particularly in the direction of the Russian heartland. After the dramatic events of 1905, a repeat sequence of pogroms orchestrated by the ultra-nationalist Black Hundreds, apparently without direct government support, had justified a further wave of draconian clamp-downs, including, once again, severe restrictions on Jewish movement.[209] In both instances, the state line was disingenuous yet clever: the first priority being to immunize the people from the object of their fear and loathing; the second, to do so in such a way that the Jews themselves were 'protected' from the people's righteous anger.

The unfolding Stalin sequence from early 1953 closely followed these contours. Indeed, preparations included the production of a million copies of an MVD-published pamphlet entitled 'Why Jews must be resettled from the industrial regions of the country'.[210] In parallel, a letter was concocted (and then re-concocted), supposedly coming from a galaxy of leading Soviet Jews themselves. Many out of fear were certainly prepared to put their names to this travesty. In it they denounced their 'reactionary' brethren, which necessarily included the wretched doctors, but adding for good measure all those 'bourgeois nationalists' who had thrown in their lot with Zionism and US Jewish 'millionaires'. However, the letter then went on to beseech Stalin on behalf of 'the great Russian nation' to allow the 'progressive' remainder—Jews, after all, the letter acknowledged, had always had all their rights guaranteed by the Soviet constitution—to be removed to a place of greater safety. Here, then, was the crux of Stalin's subterfuge. The tolerable Jews, aghast by the irredeemable malice of so many of their own kind, were getting down on their hands and knees to ask him to exact summary punishment against the evildoers, yet also to intervene, the great merciful tsar that he was, to save the remnant. No nasty insinuation, therefore, that deporting the Jews en masse was anything like what Hitler had intended. Instead, the mass 'evacuation' to Birobidzhan and elsewhere in Siberia was to take place because the Russian Jews had requested it themselves. Only here could these survivors, tainted by their contact with the 'bad' Jews, be 're-educated', so that perhaps one day in the distant future the 'good' ones might return to full Soviet life.[211] Meanwhile, throughout February, convoys of freight cars were shunted on to the reserve tracks round Moscow, lists of those of Jewish extraction prepared, the Gulag authorities given orders for a new mass influx of prisoners, and thousands of barracks hastily hammered together for those to be resettled in Birobidzhan.[212]

The only element missing from the scenario so far was the *Russian* people. 'Beat the Jews and save Russia' had been a constant popular refrain from tsarist times. But could it also be that Stalin was reminded of how it could be purposefully inserted into *his* storyline by reference to what had happened in the immediate aftermath of the war, not so much in Russia and the Ukraine but elsewhere in Eastern Europe? Grass-roots violence against Jewish survivors did not diminish in the wake of the Nazi retreat. It has been estimated that more Jews were killed in Poland, Hungary, and Czechoslovakia in the eighteen months after the war than in the ten years before it. In Poland, notwithstanding the endemic bloodshed of this period, Jews were clearly particular targets of repeated demotic vengeance, borne out in a death toll of 150 in the first four months of 1945 and 1,200 by April 1946.[213] The pogrom at Kielce, in July of that year, especially stands out, not only because it was the worst of its kind—the forty-two Jewish deaths included whole families—but because several thousand Polish people participated, including soldiers and militiamen.[214] Even more striking is what sparked off the mass disturbance: a rumour that a Polish child had been kidnapped by the Kielce Jews in preparation for a ritual murder. It was exactly this sort of lurid, blood-curdling fantasy which fitted Stalin's programmatic plot to a T. The Polish authorities' efforts to pass death sentences against some of the perpetrators had the effect of inciting popular anger even more.[215] And whether Stalin had noted the fact or not, a similar incident in the Slovak town of Topol'čany, a year before Kielce, would have been exactly the sort of story which could have been used as supporting disinformation with which to fan the flames of the Slánský allegations.[216]

Once out in the Soviet press, the Doctors' Plot certainly seems to have got the rumour-mill going as intended. Letters started pouring into papers resonating and amplifying the charge of life-threatening activities supposedly conducted by Jewish doctors and health-workers throughout the Soviet Union, but also spreading a much wider diatribe against all Jews as untrustworthy, disloyal, and villainous. Some of these vox pop utterances appear to have gone off on a different tangent: for instance asserting that the Jews were like Chechen and Crimean Tatar fifth columnists and that they, too, might attack Russia from the rear.[217] But for Stalin it mattered little what the accusation was, so long as the anti-Semitic fire could be sufficiently stoked in readiness for the show trial of the Doctors, in March. According to Vaksberg the mise-en-scène had been even more minutely prepared:

> Naturally all would receive the death sentence. The execution would take place on Red Square, where dozens of scaffolds would be set up. The furious crowd would tear the victims away from their guards and lynch them, despite the soldiers' heroic efforts to control the mob. Immediately thereafter, pogroms would begin throughout the country.[218]

But before all could be put in motion something unexpected happened. Stalin died. And it could not have been the Jewish doctors who had killed him: those still alive were languishing in MGB cells.

*

The death of the great leader on 5 March 1953, most probably by natural causes,[219] presents us with an interesting historical dilemma. With Stalin's death, his ruling circle brought the case against the Doctors rapidly to a close. The hand of Beria is especially evident in the MVD public announcement just a month later that the whole thing had been a fabrication. That said, it did the newly reinstated head of an again powerfully combined MGB and MVD (state security *and* internal affairs) little good: his Central Committee colleagues had him arrested in July on the entirely trumped-up charge of being a British spy. Behind that was their fear that Beria was rather too openly attempting to wrest the succession from the collective 'them' for his singular self.[220] Doubtless few from among the great Russian masses would have shed a tear when he was executed the following December. As for public opinion about the Doctors' Plot, one noteworthy piece of information is that some 35 per cent of letter writers to *Pravda* refused to accept the new government line. Yes, they insisted, there had been a plot![221]

Even so, the unfolding scenario was stopped in its tracks: no show trial, no pogroms, no mass deportation. The Jewish fate in the USSR was not to be that of the Kalmyks, Chechens, or many other peoples. It is estimated that some fifty Jews were executed as a consequence of the Plot, out of 500 actual arrests.[222] Clearly terror and violence, but no actual genocide. But one might want to go further and say that the whole thing does not add up anyway: 'no instructions or directives sanctioning or preparing for such a deportation have ever been found'; as for the very idea of a show trial and mass deportation, 'these would have been out of keeping with Stalin's behaviour in the post-war period'.[223] A rather strange comment, one might consider, given all we know about the great range of post-war ethnic deportations. As for the absence of documentary proof of Stalin's intent, one might want to tersely reply that there is no similar Hitler order (at least not one which has come to light) for European Jewish destruction. To be sure, Stalin was not Hitler, and we have ourselves wavered between reading the former's anti-Jewish campaign, even as he became more unhinged, as one primarily propelled by instrumental reasoning as opposed to being driven by the sort of inner demons we might rather associate with Hitler. Even then, perhaps, the very notion that Stalin might have stepped outside his own comfort zone to begin moves towards a much less predictable set of outcomes is, perhaps inadvertently, what is most tantalizing about the doubting commentary. Our argument indeed rests on the plausibility of Stalin's extraordinary break with his normal practice—that is, in appealing to and inciting the crowd—*precisely* because of the nature of his confabulated Jewish enemy. However, one cannot but concede one crucial point. Show trial, pogroms, deportations may have been imminent. But in the absence of detailed documentary corroboration one way or the other, the case for what might have happened is necessarily counterfactual.[224] But then the question arises, should we leave it there? Are we looking at a not particularly consequential might-have-been or, instead, the culmination of an anti-Semitic sequence whose ramifications are not simply Russian, but return us to the bigger picture of semi-periphery crisis?

One thing we can say for certain about the events of 1948–53 is that while Stalin may not have succeeded in 'disappearing' Soviet Jewry off the heartland map, he more or less achieved a complete erasure of Jewish 'life', certainly in the public sphere. Across the length and breadth of the USSR, Yiddish newspapers, schools, theatres, cultural and academic institutes, and libraries were all shut down. What was precious to Jews in a religious sense, torah scrolls, prayer books, and the like, were literally slung out on the rubbish heap; their custodians, including rabbis and other community leaders, the most obvious candidates to be accused of Zionism and sent away to the Gulag, or worse.[225] If this was not the full-frontal 'barbarism' of Lemkin's original exposition, it was certainly full-frontal 'vandalism'. Moreover, this was in addition to the wider campaign to eliminate

Jews from public life and position, and a new wave of arrests and executions from 1950 on similar charges, percolating to all sectors of Soviet institutional, intellectual, and industrial life.[226] On top of that, we ought not to forget the first three 'open season' months of the Doctors' Plot, during which the community was in almost perpetual fear of the noose dangling over its collective neck.[227]

Miraculous the reprieve may have been. But what is equally significant is that Stalin's death did not lead to conditions for a Jewish re-entry into Soviet life. The doctors may have been released, the sentence against the JAC people repealed—in secret—but until Gorbachev's *perestroika* there was no posthumous rehabilitation, nor, for that matter, for the wider community. In truth, Soviet Jewry had entered a no man's land. They had not been deported en masse as almost definitely intended. Yet continuing to live *as Jews*, while assuming societal acceptance, educational prospects, social and professional mobility, clearly did not compute. Much better to hunker down, dissemble background, integrate through sex and marriage with 'ordinary' Slavic neighbours, and, as a people, thus 'disappear'. After all, Stalin, early on, had said there was no genuine Jewish nation, while mainstream Marxist reasoning all along had insisted that the only path to a resolution of the Jewish 'question' was the anthropophagic one.[228]

Except, from the *Russian* perspective, was this not exactly the problem? The Jews had already infiltrated society. After Stalin, the ones who continued to insist on being Jewish, proclaimed they were Zionists, and demanded they should be allowed to emigrate to Israel, were in a sense easy to deal with, at least internally. You could let them go, or alternatively isolate them, perhaps by incarcerating them in jail or psychiatric hospitals, or sending them into internal exile, as the difficult, un-Soviet, almost definitely traitorous 'refuseniks' that they supposedly were. State anti-Zionism continued not just as a function of Soviet foreign policy towards the Middle East but as a useful safety-valve for diverting grass-roots resentments against a well-recognized scapegoat.[229] Zionism's equation with fascism became standard. Fraternal, communist Poland in another crisis year for the Bloc—1968—went even further, claiming a renewed international conspiracy against the integrity of *Polish* state and nation, the specific and concerted accusations against Jews (past and present) leading to two-thirds of the country's remaining 30,000 being forced to emigrate.[230] What was so blatantly obvious about *these* Jews, however, was how utterly assimilated and committed to a communist future nearly all of them were. Once again, it was not Jewish nationalism which was the *real* danger, but supposedly Jews disguised or masquerading as ordinary citizens, taking over the functions of state, industry, media, academia, and culture, for their own nefarious, malevolent, and destructive purposes. Are we not back with the Okhrana's case for the *Protocols*? And was this not exactly the sort of conspiracy motif which exploded on to the Russian stage in the wake of *perestroika*, this time promoted not so much by old-style Stalinists but by a range of noisy, overtly nationalist groups, like Pamyat, convinced that all the bad things which had happened to the country as a result of Bolshevism were the fault of the Jews?[231]

Whatever his path to this same destination, in the end Stalin was clearly as in thrall to the *Protocols* motif as was Hitler. He may have gone about his response in a more cunning and calculated way, but even in proposing to disappear the Jews by deportation we may note, once again, the similitude between his and Hitler's *original* calculus. What Stalin had which Hitler craved for but lacked were the opportunities provided by geography. They were the same ones that Halford Mackinder had identified as key to global, geopolitical advantage. What 'the Heartland', or more precisely its most remote and distant margins, gave to Stalin was the ability to be rid of all, or at least nearly all, his perceived problem *ethnies*, the Jews included. Yet perhaps what is more shocking than any inference about Stalin's anti-Semitic convergence with Hitler is the former's recognition and indeed confidence that he too could count on a groundswell of popular acclamation.[232] By contrast, what stands out about post-revolutionary Russian Jewry itself, or more exactly those who migrated from the rimlands to the great urban centres, is the warmth and, in retrospect, naivety of their embrace of every aspect of Soviet life. In this tendency, their behaviour, of course, was very akin to late-Wilhelmine and then Weimar German Jews, many of whose Yiddish-speaking forbears also came from the historic Polish Pale of Settlement. If Berlin, Leningrad, and Moscow were thus at the centre of this avant-garde assimilative urge, we would surely also have to add Vienna and Budapest as further examples of metropolises which, at the fin de siècle, and into the first decades of the twentieth century, provided the very model for how Jews, dispensing with their religious, social, and geographical origins, might pursue their love affairs with the idea of taking on a new and very different identity. It was certainly here, in the capitals to east and west of the 'Lands Between', that this striving for Jewish tolerability, and with it immersion into German, Russian, or Hungarian renewal, was at its most hot-house intense. And it was in each of these same capitals, one by one, that the Jewish effort to become part of the national whole was most rudely and unequivocally rejected.

The guts of the old Jewish Ashkenazi world were wrenched out in Hitler's Holocaust, in the rimlands. But the ideological struggle for and against the possibility of Jewish integration began and ended in the metropolitan heartlands. In Russia's case, the verdict was delivered by Stalin himself. In effect, it stated that the presence of Jews was inimical to the health and wellbeing of Russian, even Russian communist society. It would be another near-on forty years, after the end of the USSR, when the transmission of the verdict would finally take full effect, albeit, paradoxically, with a now highly Sovietized and intermarried Russian Jewry taking the matter into their own hands through self-sought emigration to Israel, the USA, or wherever else might have them.[233] In historical terms, however, if we are looking for the moment when the fundamental Jewish aspect of the semi-periphery's crisis came to a close, that moment was not with Hitler's demise, but eight years later, with Stalin's last and, on this occasion, mercifully aborted deportation of this same troublesome people.

6

An Expurgated Rimlands

SETTING THE SCENE

All the proposals for large scale 'transfers' of population which are being so freely canvassed as a panacea for international problems...spring from the same kind of political philosophy as that of the Nazis—namely that anything can be accomplished by grandiose and violent means.[1]

Leonard Woolf, *The International Post-War Settlement* (1944)

We started this war with great motives and high ideals. We published the Atlantic Charter and then spat on it, stomped on it and burnt it, as it were, at the stake, and now nothing is left of it.[2]

John Rhys Davies (Labour), speech to House of Commons, 1 March 1945

Attempting to determine when a historical sequence of events begins and ends—what historians call periodization—is usually a fraught and contested business. Proposing that a sequence of genocides belongs to one period and a further sequence to another is thus problematic enough. But then, supposing that some scholars may not recognize some of the sequence as genocide at all? For many Holocaust scholars, the Nazi destruction of European Jewry is the only event which truly merits the term for this and perhaps any other period. To suggest that in its immediate aftermath, there were other 'events' to which the term might also apply—even though the scale of killing and death was considerably smaller—might seem to almost wilfully blur and confuse the Holocaust's full horror. Then to throw in for good measure that a significant proportion of the post-Holocaust victims were not only ethnic Germans but that their fate was part and parcel of the *same* rimlands crisis as that which befell the Jews can only add insult to injury. It conjures up the possibility of a moral equivalence. It could even be interpreted as a slur on the memory of those who perished at the hands of the Nazis. To paraphrase Tony Judt, what they did to 'us' and what we did to 'them' should be understood in different compartments and with a different 'moral vocabulary'.[3]

This concluding chapter recognizes that the terrain is fraught. But in terms of seeing and understanding the historical pattern of modern genocide it cannot flinch from avoiding the aspects which might upset, irritate, or embarrass. We have already proposed that the specifically Jewish element of catastrophe did not quite finish with the Allied destruction of Hitler's empire, but had a further strange

Soviet coda, only relieved by Stalin's death in 1953. The termination of the wider sequence of genocidal violence in eastern, eastern-central, and south-east Europe largely predated this by several years. By 1947–8 a great wave of people-expulsions, particularly but not exclusively of Germans, had been concluded. These developments coincided with the firm consolidation of Soviet hegemony in these same regions either by direct territorial acquisition (or, as in the case of Poland, by additional territorial adjustment), or by the immediate or more staged takeover of the body politic. These two factors, national homogenization on the one hand, and the Soviet uniformization of society on the other, taken together heralded not a repositioning of the European rimlands further to the west but their complete or almost complete expurgation. That the result was not absolute is evident in the recrudescence of a very similar form of expulsion-focused violence as a consequence of the break-up of Yugoslavia in the early 1990s. It is noteworthy that this very powerful aftershock took place in a rimlands arena where back in the mid-1940s, despite going communist, neither the imposition of Soviet control nor the suppression of all but one national identity took place. But this exception to the general rule is also instructive in terms of reading back to ourselves the genocidal nature of what took place in the main expulsion sequence, nearly five decades earlier—a matter we will pursue in a moment.

Ironically, if we take the cut-off date for the main sequence to be 1948, it leaves one further item of import hanging unsettlingly in the air. Is the UN Convention on Genocide (UNC), as adopted by the General Assembly in December that year—but itself the result of a two-year-long, and often tortuous, drafting process—something which we should understand, in part or in whole, as a response to the violence which was taking place in the rimlands then and there? Or if not, what does that tell us about the future prospects for dealing with genocide through the Convention? But then, if the UNC drafters intentionally sought to divorce themselves from immediate realities, perhaps that would simply reinforce a case for arguing that the UNC was the child, perhaps the not very happy child, of a new international determination to treat forcible deportation as outside the purview of genocide. In which case its formulators had either learnt nothing from European rimlands events ranging back over the last several decades, or had consciously decided that forcible deportation *ought to be* excluded from the list of genocidal crimes to be prevented and punished in the post-war world.[4] Which, in turn, would simply deepen the conundrum: should a historical reading of the UNC be situated within a period about to end, or one about to begin? Or, perhaps even more alarmingly, is the *historical* legacy of Lemkin's big idea—as opposed, perhaps, to its international juridical or possibly social scientific one—not particularly germane to understanding the genocidal trajectory either before or beyond 1948?

However, rather than being utterly dismissive of the UNC omission, let us briefly survey the post-war European scene of devastation, and more particularly the displaced millions within it as seen by contemporary observers—and indeed many others since then. Thus, one way of limiting a charge of genocide *through expulsion* against particular ethnic or religious groups at this juncture would be to embrace these groups within a different ambit: that of refugees. Was not the continent as a whole 'choked' with them, as a conscious or contingent consequence of the Nazi reordering? On the eve of D-Day, Allied military planners estimated that they might be having to take responsibility for over 11 million displaced people in Central and Western Europe, even leaving aside uprooted Germans. A year later, the Soviets claimed 14 million such people in their zones of control. The total figure may have been more like 30 million.[5] More pointedly, as Michael Marrus graphically illustrates, all sorts of people were among these *misérables*: 'Nazi collaborators and resistance sympathisers, hardened criminals and teenage innocents, entire family groups, clusters of political dissidents, shell-shocked wanderers, ex-Storm Troopers on the run, communists, concentration camp guards, farm labourers, citizens of destroyed countries, and gangs of marauders'.[6]

Their experiences were all very different and their proposed directions of travel at war's end equally multifarious. But in the chaos of Europe, an Allied screening of them according to specific, let alone appropriate, categories was not always so simple, while getting them home by a direct route was almost impossible, as Primo Levi's famous post-Auschwitz tale of his return to Turin by way of a circuitous train trip *eastwards* into the Ukraine attests.[7] The problem with this sort of approach is that by throwing everything—and everybody—into a single, if fraught, picture of what one might call 'picking up the pieces from a world in ruins', it removes from the equation the very intentional, state-directed, large-scale projects of the time geared towards the one-way, no return ticket, compulsory, and by whatever means, mass eruction of *specific* populations. Even inadvertently, quite current and otherwise very good studies can too easily appear to subscribe to the looser, less damning interpretation. For instance, we read in one recent analysis:

> People moved all over Europe either to return home, because the Nazis had transported them to another part of Europe, or, in the case of Germans in Eastern Europe, to escape vengeful regimes, which wanted to cleanse their territories of anyone associated with the regime which had decimated their countries.[8]

Read more closely, and one becomes aware that this statement is referring to some of the interpretations from the 1940s rather than those of the present. Even so, and read in isolation, one might be forgiven for assuming that people becoming displaced was a function solely of Nazism. Or that where violence occurred, it was quid pro quo retribution for what the Nazis had done, rather than being motivated by any other agenda. The problem here is twofold. First, retribution is a regular, indeed standard, ingredient in genocide. On its own it may be insufficient as sole driver towards a state's systematic destruction of communal groups. And it is certainly true that how such emotions are shared collectively and are worked through into a practical and sustained project of mass murder remains an area where more research is needed. We have certainly proposed, through the notion of a 'perpetrators' "never again" syndrome', one causative trigger whereby memories of some traumatic moment in the past in which communal actors allegedly slurred or challenged the integrity or pride of the nation state have resurfaced at some further crisis moment to both reignite and legitimize a violent state assault on the entirety of that tainted community.[9] Even leaving aside the Nazis, it would be impossible to imagine, for example, the CUP attack on the Armenians or the

Antonescu regime's on Bessarabian and Bukovinan Jewry in the absence of retributive urges. And these cases are particularly relevant here because each retributive
impulse was merged with state goals aimed at *ethnically cleansing* state territory of
these particular communities. Though as a consequence, therefore, there were
Armenian or Rumanian Jewish survivors from the process who became refugees,
nobody who has seriously studied either process of removal would simply describe
the main bulk of victims solely in these terms. Similarly, looking at the European
post-war mass removals—and this takes us more sharply to our second point—
those affected were neither displaced, uprooted, nor simply in flight from their
countries of origin. To be sure, they may have been 'in fear of being persecuted for
reasons of race, religion, nationality membership of a particular social group or
political opinion', the standard post-war UN prescript for establishing refugee
status.[10] But this definition fails to convey the essence of their departure. These
communities were violently and viciously vomited out. The German term *Vertrie-
bene* ('expellees') may be somewhat inelegant, but at least it captures the forcible
nature of the eviction—and not just of ethnic Germans—from homeland and
habitus.

Where the argument for comparability between post-war expellees and evicted
Armenians or Rumanian rimlands Jews weakens is in the *scale* of their respective
suffering. In the latter instances, most of those eructed were directly killed or perished as a consequence; in the former, *most* survived. Perhaps one might continue
the distinction by proposing that the majority of the expellees were not in any
sense slated for extermination, though one might add that there is huge doubt as
to whether the *expellers* cared one jot as to whether they actually lived or died: an
assertion which is reflected in the expellees' death toll. A total figure from *all* the
immediate post-war eructions, otherwise officially designated as 'exchanges' or
'transfers' (whether Soviet-sponsored or at the behest of individual polities), in
Eastern Europe and the Balkans is difficult to confirm. Figures of over 2 million or
even 2.5 million dead alone out of up to 15 million German expellees may well be
overestimates, even though these continue to be standard assumptions, especially
in Germany.[11] A recent overview by Mark Kramer posits that out of 1.5 million
total deaths, 1.4 million of these were German, with the rest largely made up of
Poles, Ukrainians, and Hungarians, the latter particularly from the Titoist evic-
tions from the Vojvodina.[12] But even if we were to go with the most cautious
contemporary research, in which German civilian deaths have been estimated in
the range of 500,000 to 600,000, and most of these in the context of the final
stages of Red Army advance into Germany *integrale*, the numbers (especially as a
percentage of total expellees), *in any other period*, would still be recognized as vast.[13]
Estimates of civilian deaths during the 1990s Yugoslav ethnic cleansing (when the
term became standard), while quite horrendous, remain nowhere near as high as
those for the earlier episode. Yet what happened later, in Bosnia in particular, was
regularly treated, both politically and juridically, as at the very least an antechamber to genocide, some of the post-event International Court of Justice (ICJ) trials
at the Hague seeking to indict leading as well as lower-level perpetrators for that
specific crime.[14]

If the ICJ ultimately failed to deliver a verdict on Serbian *state* responsibility for what happened in 1990s Bosnia as genocide,[15] nevertheless, the very fact that the issue was forensically examined at the highest levels of international law can only underline the discrepancy between the common usage of the term in this case and a continuing cultural or political resistance to it for the post-1945 sequence. This tendency becomes all the more perplexing when one begins to fill in the picture of what happened to the targeted communities in *both* cases. Thus, recent studies of Yugoslav ethnic cleansing (incidentally, not the only 1990s rimlands zone in which this took place: parts of the former-Soviet Caucasus present equally horrendous parallels) confirm conscious state policy and/or more localized efforts to isolate and threaten targeted individuals and communities; to make life and livelihood untenable for them in the places where they were living; and to intimidate or terrify those same people towards direct flight or, failing that, towards some form of compulsory, organized removal. The whole panoply of what followed will be familiar reading. This included the role of paramilitaries as the cutting edge of efforts to soften up the targeted group, along with the incarceration and often hyper-exploitative abuse of the able-bodied in concentration or labour camps. Gender-specific assaults, most obviously developed through mass rape to sap the community's physical and emotional wellbeing and sense of integrity, were standard. Finally, there was genocidal-style atrocity in the form of repeated murder or massacre committed again by local militias or state security forces (acting either overtly or covertly), to ensure a clean sweep of the districts and regions in which the wholesale eruction of the targeted element was intended.[16]

Yet these ingredients were all there, and arguably even more rigorously and terribly in the mid-1940s sequence. In Poland and Czechoslovakia, for instance, the actual deportation of ethnic Germans was preceded by an entire grill-work of state discrimination on the one hand, direct physical intimidation on the other. Again, we would recognize these aspects as standard fare in the isolation and immiseration of Jews in Nazi Europe before extermination. But at the end of the war, it was not Jews but Germans in Poland and Czechoslovakia who were deprived of citizenship rights on grounds of their 'collective responsibility' for the sins committed by the Nazis and, hence, were cast out beyond the universe of societal obligation, the loss of jobs, salaries, licences to work, and pensions all following. Properties were expropriated, radios, bicycles, telephones, and cars taken away, the use of public transport, even speaking German in public, banned. For this there was, of course, Nazi precedent, as there was for the now compulsory requirement to wear special armbands identifying the wearer as German. But the Czechs and Poles did not flinch from utilizing these techniques to achieve their anthropoemic goals. If the state provided the legal framework, and municipal authorities the bureaucratic enforcement, it was the people on the ground, soldiers, state security, and ordinary policemen, though also self-appointed communal vigilantes and neighbours aplenty who acted on the assumption of state authority, or of their own volition, to mete out summary punishment, pillage, and murder. Through them, able-bodied 'Germans' were identified, arrested, locked up, and removed for heavy labour, ensuring that the vulnerable remainder were interned, beaten up, robbed of their belongings, thoroughly demoralized, and often sexually assaulted in preparation for their ultimate removal.[17]

Of course, one might propose that there is a missing element here. There may have been an initial sequence of 'wild' expulsions in which all sorts of terrible things were done, massacres and death marches included; there may have been, too, slave labour camps in situ or far away in the USSR; but there were no reception centres which were actually extermination facilities. Quite so. The reason so many of the expellees survived was because they were—especially, ironically, if they were German—received and, as far as possible, cared for in those parts of occupied Germany, especially the US and British zones, where Herculean efforts were made to feed, shelter, and immunize them from disease. In other words, efforts were made to keep people alive. Mark you, the starved, sick, and near-death condition of vast multitudes of these incomers—disproportionately made up of women accompanying the very young, old, and already infirm—was so terrible that at key receiving points such as the Stettiner and Lehrter railway stations in Berlin, Allied observers repeatedly made comparison between what they saw and what they had seen in, or read about liberated Belsen, Buchenwald, or Dachau.[18]

There is also something else to consider before we too readily emphasize the saving grace, compassion, and, behind them, liberal values of the Western Allies. The Soviets may have been the new, big, hegemonic power in Eastern Europe giving the imprimatur for the deportation trains to once again roll, this time *westwards*. But the US and British, certainly in a geopolitical sense, were also complicit in and co-responsible for determining that the nation states of the now old 'New Europe' should this time round be allowed to relieve themselves of some, if not all, of their problematic ethnic populations. It may indeed have been Germans whom London and Washington had uppermost in their minds. However, having given the green light at Yalta, then Potsdam, for their removal, the Western Allies also (at least initially), turned a blind eye, or at the very least refused to censure, the much wider range of atrocity-laden actions by both Soviet and Eastern European polities which bring our great rimlands phase of genocide to a close.

In a recent assessment of how current researchers have been rethinking the Armenian genocide, Uğur Ümit Üngör has proposed that the 'genocidal process can metaphorically be imagined as a three-tier Matryoshka doll', made up of interlinked micro, meso, and macro tiers.[19] Having considered in outline the scope, scale, and range of the rimlands extirpation in our next section, the following one proposes—again briefly—to summarize the actions of the front-line perpetrators: the micro level; as well as something of the thinking of elite national opinion formers and policymakers: the meso level. Üngör's insistence on a bigger picture, which includes 'the international context and the structure of geopolitical power relations', however, is particularly germane to this chapter. Without considering something of the close interplay not just between the Soviets and main national actors but equally between the Western Allies, those same actors and Soviets, a macro level explanation for how our larger sequence concluded would again be incomplete. If this is effectively our middle section, our two further ones have final things to say about this immediate post-war period, while also looking ahead to the terrain

An Expurgated Rimlands 367

beyond 1948. A penultimate section, therefore, attempts to consider what light, if any, a reinforced international commitment to the concept of the nation state (a commitment sealed through acceptance of violent ethnic removals) throws on the founding of the UNC. As implied earlier, this terse, historical commentary will consider the Convention only in so far as it might reveal its shaping—or lack of it—through the then contemporary or historically recent genocide scene. Attempting to assess the UNC's place within the context of post-colonial nation-statehood and the Cold War must await a further volume, of which our last section is harbinger. It seeks to summarize the end of the crisis of the rimlands and hence of the semi-periphery. However, it also adumbrates the emergence of a new international framework which, while clearly in key respects different from the eurocentric one of 1912–53, marks the beginnings of a further, indeed more universally toxic, phase in modernity's drive for terrestrial dominance.

WHAT HAPPENED: THE SCOPE, SCALE, AND RANGE OF EXPULSION AND MASS MURDER

Genocidal violence and deportations swept through a great arc of Eastern Europe and the Balkans as both a direct and an indirect consequence of the final Red Army victory over Hitler. In so doing, the epicentre of violence was pushed way to the west or north of the traditional contested rimlands zones, impacting, above all, on German populations. The main bulk of these were Reichsdeutsche, in other words citizens on territories which had been part of pre-1939 Germany. They made up most, though far from all, of the 9 million who fled or were expelled from what was now a reconstituted Poland as far as the Oder-Neisse line. But almost 3 million expellees were from Czechoslovakia, and many hundreds of thousands more from Yugoslavia, Rumania, and Hungary.[20] Together, thus, these various German subgroups, both Reichsdeutsche and Volksdeutsche, constituted what in historical terms had been the most loyal eastern hinterland, including post-Ottoman frontier communities of the two Germanys, both Habsburg and Hohenzollern. Now they were the prime victims of the final and irrevocable shattering of the vision of a unified Eastern German empire as represented by Hitler.

Yet their torment, some of which was very visible to Western observers, particularly in the Czech lands, obscures to a significant degree the equally if not more horrendous violence which accompanied the wider ethnographic recasting during this sequence, especially in the Balkans. Moving into this southern, more authentically rimlands, arena, to be sure, it is not always easy to ascertain whether the main driver to mass murder was ethnicity, class, or an unholy mixture of the two. The range of peoples caught up in these struggles was certainly variegated. That might also suggest that proposing any wider rimlands pattern, linking the Eastern European and Balkan trajectories with the near-parallel Soviet eructions of entire, definably ethnic peoples, cannot be a very exact one. On the other hand, one tendency which continued to link them all was the forcible Soviet deportation of many Volksdeutsche, and others, *eastwards*. Some of this flow was not of whole communities (the remainder of whom simultaneously or soon after were most usually deported westwards) but only the able-bodied, for immediate hyper-exploitative purposes. In spite of the horrendous death-toll of this programme, one might arguably dispute this aspect being precisely genocidal. Yet within the eastward flow there *also* figured the 'repatriation' of entire communities, who were effectively slated for destruction. The fate of some 30,000 Russian Cossacks, whose menfolk had fought with the Wehrmacht, stands out, not least as at war's end they were among over 2 million Soviet citizens who fetched up under Western Allied military jurisdiction but whom Stalin insisted should be handed over forthwith to the Soviet authorities.[21] Right from the beginning, therefore, there was distinction or tension between deportations and sometimes off-the-scene mass atrocities which served Soviet interests, with or without the support of the Western Allies, and those which were organized and directed by 'New Europe' elites, communist or otherwise, in line with their own social engineering agendas—again with or without the support of the Western Allies.

Finally, however, we should not forget one final movement, confirming that the expurgation of the rimlands involved the resolution or near-resolution of the legacy of not two but three empires, the third being the Ottomans; a direction of travel which was aimed primarily at getting still unwanted Balkan people associated with the Ottoman past removed in a south-eastern direction towards Anatolia itself. The other side of this coin was more Turkish action geared towards removing or suppressing 'minority' peoples who did not fit Ankara's conception of a monocultural unity and identity, involving a set of actions for which the term genocide may or may not be appropriate; and, indeed, within a time frame at slight variance with our main chronological contours. Taken together, however, what is remarkable about this end-of-war and immediate post-war sequence is the rapidity with which our entire three-part rimlands arena was *largely*, finally, cleansed of its multiethnic character, and thus the determination with which all participant nation states used the opportunity to achieve this outcome.

*

To develop this plot a little more fully, let us begin with the actions of our fundamental Soviet driver. Ethnic Germans, technically Soviet citizens or not, as well as other collaborating communities, had been in almost continuous, fearful retreat alongside the Wehrmacht, ever since the major Soviet advance began in late 1943. Those unlucky enough to be caught by the Red Army were dispatched without compunction. A 600-person column of women and children from around Himmler's Hegewald complex, for instance, met this fate in mid-November of that year. Those Volksdeutsche from these treks who made it to the still VOMi-controlled camps in the Warthegau, by early 1945 were simply rounded up by the arriving Soviets and placed in sealed freight trains, bound for special settlements, hard labour, and very probable death in the Trans-Urals region.[22] Yet this was only a foretaste of Soviet vengeance once the Red Army had burst into East Prussia. A Red Army massacre of possibly seventy or more villagers (as well as French and Belgian POWs) at Nemmersdorf, in October 1944, accompanied by mass rape and cruel tortures of those killed, was duly reported and closely investigated when the village was for a time recaptured by the Wehrmacht. Though almost certainly magnified for propaganda effect by Goebbels, Nemmersdorf nevertheless set the tone for both what the Germans feared of the Red Army and what the latter actually did as its advance continued through East Prussia, Pomerania, and Silesia towards Berlin.[23] The main consequence was mass civilian flight, which was very probably Stalin's exact intention, not least in order to help pave the way for a Polish takeover of Reich territory as far as the Oder-Neisse.

By the end of the war perhaps as many as 6 million Germans had fled or had been evacuated from what the Poles would subsequently refer to as the 'recovered' (*sic*) territories.[24] This movement, then, was technically distinct from either expulsion or deportation, in that despite the conscious Soviet goad it was enacted by the Germans themselves, albeit propelled by their overwhelming panic at what would happen to them if they stayed. Yet, to prove the case of being caught between a rock and a hard place, flight was also exceedingly perilous, with masses of refugees on the open road exposed to Red Army air, sea, or ground attack. In the last few months of the war, as Germany approached its 8 May *Stunde Null* (zero hour), the scale of death, both military and civilian, reached catastrophic levels. To the east of the Oder-Neisse river alone, perhaps as many as 75,000 to 100,000 German civilians were massacred by Soviet troops.[25] Efforts to mount seaborne evacuations from the East Prussian Hela peninsula were extraordinary, even superhumanly, heroic—over 1.5 million non-combatants and 700,000 soldiers were actually transported by boat to places of relative safety. Yet, at the same time, they led to huge loss of life, epitomized by the Russian torpedoing of the *Wilhelm Gustloff*, with nearly 9,000 out of 10,000 people on board perishing. Such dangers were compounded by US and British aerial attacks, some 200,000 Silesian refugees bearing the full brunt of the fire-bombing of Dresden two weeks later.[26] The fact that from a Holocaust perspective we remember the mass exodus from east to west in this period as a matter of forcible, pitiless death marches from Auschwitz and other camps, in the direction of those still within a diminishing Reich, simply confirms that victimhood in these last months of Nazism had become utterly, totally, bewilderingly confused as well as all-embracing.

To add to the complexity of the situation, not all Germans, for whatever reason, did in fact flee. A recent survey cites a figure of 3.6 million who attempted to stay put, though what is more significant about this figure is that the number was heavily skewed towards the very young, and very old women. The Russians eroded the survivability of this impoverished residue all the more—that is, over and beyond mass rape—by literally press-ganging those they could take among the able-bodied, mostly men, for labour deep inside the USSR. They added to this tally from among the estimated 1.25 million east Germans who, unknowing of the danger, attempted to return to their homes at war's end.[27] At first sight, one might treat this human levy as very much like the Nazi wartime drive for *Ostarbeiter*, in other words a particularly nasty violation of human rights, albeit one entirely propelled by the USSR's serious labour shortfall brought on by Nazi invasion. The Western Allies in principle, moreover, accepted its legitimacy, treating it as an aspect of 'reparations in kind'—in other words, compensation for Soviet war losses—alongside the surviving industrial plant which was hastily dismantled and dispatched to the USSR without Western demur.[28] Simply filching civilian Germans, however, had a dubious ring about it, and, as we now know from Soviet archives, was a particular matter of anxiety to Himmler when, through the offices of the ICRC in February 1945, he attempted to get the British and Americans to put pressure on the USSR to halt it. It is a matter of some rich, dreadful irony that his Soviet counterpart, Beria, got round Western misgivings about the operation by claiming that many of the Germans 'arrested' were 'caught in the act of committing terrorist or subversive acts' or 'agents and official personnel of the enemy intelligence and counter-intelligence services', the sort of charge list which reads rather like a Himmler justification for dispatching *Soviet* citizens, Jews in particular.[29] The distinction, of course, is crucial. The large swathes of particularly East Prussians and Upper Silesians who were deported were not directly liquidated. On the other hand, the physical and mental condition of many of these people, as acknowledged by Beria himself, was already so poor that those who did end up working in Soviet mines, construction, and heavy industry died like flies. The number may not be as high as the 45 per cent proposed by Maurice de Zayas, based on German Red Cross information which estimates that 874,000 German civilians were abducted to the USSR, a figure more than three times greater than the total number of '*Westarbeiter*' stated in Soviet records. Even so, Polian's always more cautious estimates, at least in percentage terms, are not so very different from those of de Zayas: 38.9 per cent of Reichsdeutsche 'arrestees' died: some 66,500 people.[30]

If this is to acidly reiterate that the Soviet use and abuse of slave labour was hopelessly inefficient, not to say a very poor return on the expenditure absorbed into the Gulag system, it also underlines the fact that the Soviet drive to subjugate, pulverize, and destroy a broader ethnic German vitality in Eastern Europe was only secondarily about labour needs. At the root of the much wider dragnet designed to clear out Volksdeutsche from the now Soviet-dominated half of the continent was a standard Chekist 'security' bias, which in turn explains why *in themselves* the removal operations were actually extremely efficient and well planned. The usual ingredients were evident. Serov was key planner. There was close coordination with SMERSH. There was an upgrade of the administrative Directorate for the Affairs of POWs *and* Internees (UPVI to GUPVI) in preparation for the new prisoner influx. And, of course, there was meticulous timetabling and internal ordering for the state by state 'mobilizations' (*sic*) of target groups—all conveniently to be accomplished under the cover of ongoing war, with the usual, vast complement of special NKVD troops deployed to each operation.[31] In this way, all the last major subsets of rimlands Germandom, from the Donauschwaben (Danube Swabians) of Yugoslavia and Hungary to the Siebenbürger (Transylvanian) Saxons of Rumania, were denuded of their most active surviving components, practically ensuring the unsustainability of the remainder of these communities in situ.

But then, it was not just ethnic Germans on whom the NKVD wished to lay its hands. Large numbers of Bukovinan and Bessarabian Rumanians as well as ethnic Germans fled en masse into Rumania *integrale* as the Red Army began to 'liberate' this territory in summer 1944. With the Rumanians switching from Axis to Allies in August, Bucharest had no choice but to cooperate with the Soviets' forcible repatriation of some 56,000 of these people over the following month; their destination not home but labour camps deep in the Soviet interior. The manhunt not surprisingly extended to other groups, notably Balts and Hungarians who had fled with the Germans in the direction of the Reich. In Budapest, certainly, Arrow Cross collaboration with the Nazis was paid back in kind by the Soviets with mass deportations from the city of up to 100,000 people. Local quotas for forced labour service in Hungary were meant to be first and foremost of ethnic Germans; yet it is significant that in annexed Transcarpathia, and in adjacent north-eastern Hungary, able-bodied Magyars were systematically rounded up village by village, as one study notes, 'not only to increase the number of forced labourers in the USSR but also to "pacify" a given region and to change its ethnic composition'. The number of deportees, both ethnic German and Hungarian, from Transcarpathia and its hinterland is put at 50,000.[32]

*

The Czech Moravian capital of Brno, or Brünn as it was known to the Germans in this mixed city, had played host in 1899 to a highly significant Austro-Marxist conference, one where their Social Democrat Party committed itself to the mutual equality of all self-identifying national peoples within the empire. Forty-six years later, on 30–31 May to be exact, Brno gave its verdict on such high-minded ideals. Having interned practically the entirety of its 30,000 Germans more than two weeks earlier, and subjected them to abuse, rape, robbery, and murder, almost all of those who had not already been sent to concentration camps elsewhere in the country were forced out of the city by its National Committee and marched to the Austrian border. The event became a veritable death march, 1,700 of the 20,000 mostly women and children on it perishing through direct violence, illness, and starvation. On arrival at the border, neither would the Austrian guards let them enter nor the Czechs allow them back. In the no man's land where the survivors were forcibly encamped, typhus began to rage.[33] When something similar had happened on the German–Polish border at Zbąszyń—the place where effectively 'stateless' Jewish refugees had found themselves caught between two unyielding states seven years earlier—the event had equally caused international consternation. But what particularly raised Western eyebrows in 1945 was that it was Czechs, not Nazis, who were behaving in this pitiless and brutal way: the very same Czechs whose exiled wartime leadership had used every occasion to remind the Western world what a civilized and humane people they were.[34]

Yet Brno was no one-off event, and what it portended put Soviet efforts at the forcible removal of Germans practically in the shade. From the moment when national rebellion had broken out in Prague on 4 May, in the very last days of Nazi rule, a 'pogrom atmosphere' had prevailed.[35] In the great city itself, pent-up fury was unleashed in a tidal wave of anti-German mob justice, rather reminiscent of what had befallen Jews in Kaunas, Lwów, and elsewhere in the interregnum between the collapse of Soviet rimlands rule in June 1941 and the arrival of the Wehrmacht. Except if the Czech violence was a spasm, it was a very prolonged one indeed. Part of what kept it going was rumours or reports of ongoing Nazi terrorism or sabotage—so-called 'Werewolf' activity. A series of unexplained explosions in munitions warehouses in the Sudeten town of Ústi nad Lebem (Aussig) at the end of July sparked off one particularly notorious incident, in which a Czech rampage through the town centre led to women and children being thrown off the bridge into the Elbe and then shot at. All told, those who died in the massacre were numbered in at least hundreds, though some reports put the figure as high as 2,700.[36]

It was not only the very explicit violence which shocked Western observers. Incarceration of perhaps 150,000 Germans in scores of squalid, cramped holding camps across the country led quickly to a charge in the British press of 'Czech Belsens'. Many of these had previously been Nazi camps, most poignantly of all Terezin. But the treatment meted out to the imprisoned Germans, with guards and others intruding repeatedly to molest, rob, and generally terrorize inmates, on top of the more persistent killers—conscious denial of food or medical attention plus rapidly deteriorating sanitation—aroused a measure of Western sympathy for Germans at a time when it was in notable short supply.[37] To be sure, such public bewilderment, if not outrage, in response to the newspaper reports from Czechoslovakia were in part the consequence of having very little or no awareness of the much wider scope of atrocities concurrently being committed all across Central and Eastern Europe. That said, one might add for good measure than even some of the most hardened Soviet observers seem to have been moved by what they saw. Even Serov, from the Soviet zone in Germany, reported to Beria on great numbers of Sudeten Germans who were committing suicide *after* they had crossed the border. There were also reports of whole family groups who, refusing to budge, had dressed up in their Sunday best, placed all their dearest religious and family mementoes around them, and then killed themselves 'by hanging or poison'. And, to cap it all, there were repeated stories of German women and children turning to Russian soldiers to protect them from the Czechs, the persistent danger of being raped by the Red Army men notwithstanding.[38]

However, what all these narratives of violence mask is the underpinning purpose. The Czechs, in the early summer of 1945, were as hell bent on removing their territorial concentrations of ethnic Germans as were the Poles. In the former case, that meant above all dislodging and then expelling the Sudetens, the main bulk of the estimated 3.5 million Volksdeutsche—including refugees from further east—then in the country.[39] Up to this point, with the Red Army operation centred further north, there had been no voluntary mass flight of Germans from Czechoslovakia westwards. Instead, from mid-May, the Czech method was to apply coercion and terror to get them to move accordingly. However, these 'wild expulsions', as they became known—with the Sudetenland the epicentre of the effort—were also effectively predetermined by another critical factor: time. The great post-war conference of the Allies to agree major outstanding territorial and linked issues arising from the European war was scheduled for mid-July. The Allies may have already agreed in principle to what the Czechs described as *odsun*: 'transfer'. To be sure, the very terminology was dubious: ethnic Germans were as much part and parcel of Czechoslovakia's ethnographic landscape as any other 'autochthonous' community. But by 1945, such niceties had become a political irrelevance. The Czechs had their agenda, and the assumed key to ensuring there would be no

Allied backsliding on the matter was to get as many expellees as possible across the German and Austrian borders, thereby establishing indisputable facts on the ground which the Big Three presumably would then accept as a fait accompli. The whole emphasis, thus, was on rapidity of process, and for that purpose a no-holds-barred set of actions while the window of opportunity remained open. The results in terms of numbers speak for themselves. Perhaps as many as if not more than 800,000 Germans were expelled from Czechoslovakia into the Allied zones of control from the end of war to the beginning of Potsdam. From Poland in the same period, where the immediate emphasis was on clearing the border zone and ensuring displaced Germans west of the Oder did not attempt to return, the number was perhaps half that.[40]

Nevertheless, the point is this: if we wish to pinpoint a period when Czech and Polish violence was at its most overtly genocidal, it was in these summer months *before* the Allies confirmed that expulsion would become standard and compulsory, and that they themselves, through the Allied Control Council (ACC), would oversee the entire operation in a 'humane and orderly manner'.[41] Thereafter, one might argue, the expellers had a vested interest in ensuring that the 'transfers' were done by the book. Actually, this hides a multitude of factors on the ground which ensured that being displaced from one's home, then transferred with minimal food or care by rail or boat to an alien place, alongside tens of thousands of others, was no less traumatic or potentially life-threatening than when an Eichmann or, for that matter, a Serov had been in charge. The inferred comparison, on one level, is indisputably erroneous. Neither *génocidaire* would have accepted any responsibility for the wellbeing or, for that matter, survival of their cargo. Yet after Potsdam, the logistical implications for the Allies in ensuring the movement of *millions* of Germans as allocated to their respective zones, without the whole thing converting from genocidal potentiality into humanitarian catastrophe, were simply mind-boggling. That this did not lead to absolute catastrophe, we can read as a tribute to the Allies' military-bureaucratic organization: this in spite of huge resource deficiencies, not least in rolling stock, and abominable winter conditions, both in 1945–6 and even more so in 1946–7; plus continuing degrees of Polish or Czech non-compliance or obstruction of the ACC terms of reference which were supposed to make for orderly and safe exit.

Alternatively, we might read the deportations in rather more sober terms. The very process of mass expulsion was bound, against the best, even Herculean, organizers' efforts, to come unstuck. The Allies were in no position to oversee the methods used for the ongoing eviction from hearth and home of the expellees, the usual expropriations of monies and valuables, not to say violations of persons which went with that. Nor were they in a position to ease a host of contingent circumstances for those waiting for transit. At one remove, they could not, for instance, provide shelter against often appalling weather, the result of which was that illness, hunger, and sheer cold combined to lethal effect. Needless to say, within a population group already physically and emotionally weakened through war, starvation, and stress, the very young, old, and sick—the latter actually technically prohibited from boarding the transports for fear of the infection they would spread—were the

ones who suffered most, or died. As always, in such cases, it is difficult to determine the degree to which it was direct physical violence or camp conditions which
led to spiralling mortality figures. We may note that transit conditions became
only relatively tolerable after spring 1946, that there were further crisis moments
thereafter, as the ACC resisted further Polish or Czech violations of the agreement,
and that finally, most importantly, the majority of the *Vetriebene* survived rather
than perished. The obverse side of the story, however, remains stark. While figures
of 272,000 deaths from the Czech lands alone, equating to 8 per cent of the ethnic
German population, appear with hindsight to be gross overestimates, revisionist
figures still speak of 30,000 or 40,000 Czech German dead within the wider category of 600,000 Germans (primarily from Czechoslovakia and Poland) who died
in the course of flight and expulsion.[42]

*

The largest single population movements, and the ones closest to Western observ-
ance, the Czech and Polish expulsions, are far from the whole story, however. Nor,
particularly when we start moving further south and into the Balkans, was it simply
a question of ethnic Germans on the receiving end. It was certainly true that the end
of the war marked complete and irrevocable rupture for Donauschwaben communities, such as those of the Banat, which had been a particularly notable example of
a regionally-based German society and culture for hundreds of years. Divided up
between Rumania, Yugoslavia, and Hungary as a consequence of Trianon, the
Banat's classic rimlands multiculturalism had been under threat for a quarter of a
century. In 1945, with ethnic German involvement in Nazi occupations the pretext,
Rumania and Yugoslavia moved towards their own anti-German cleansing agendas
over and beyond the deportations meted out by the Soviets. However, it was not
just Volksdeutsche, able-bodied and dependent alike, who found themselves
assigned to labour camps, very often just vacated by the SS or Ustasha, as a consequence. In these two countries, as indeed in Czechoslovakia, incoming administrations were especially eager to expunge Hungarians too from their territories. Given
that Budapest had been an Axis power, and one which had committed its own range
of atrocities during the war, it followed that ordinary local Hungarians would be
subject to retribution and expulsion just as much as ordinary local Germans. In
Yugoslavia, for instance, more especially in the Vojvodina province of the old
Banat, the number of Hungarians interned and massacred in camps and outside—
estimated at some 15,000 to 20,000—may have exceeded ethnic Germans killed in
the same period.[43] Paradoxically, a very similar sequence of extreme violence against
Hungarians—as well as Germans—by Rumanian paramilitaries in northern Transylvania (to which Bucharest clearly gave the green light as soon as it switched sides
in favour of the Allies in August 1944) only came to a shuddering halt when the
Soviets stepped in to order the just-returned Rumanian administration out of the
province. It came too late, however, to prevent the mass flight, as Bucharest clearly
intended, of most of the Hungarian population of the region. The return of many
of the fleeing Magyars and their resilience in northern Transylvania to the present
day is in critical part the legacy of Soviet interference in the matter. By the same

token, US and British objections at Potsdam to the mass Czech deportation of some 200,000 Hungarians from Slovakia stymied Prague's long-range intentions for a Magyar-free polity. Instead, Prague was forced to negotiate directly with Budapest for a Slovak–Hungarian exchange of populations, but with the actual consequence that most Hungarians in Slovakia remained where they were.[44]

Clearly, the wider geopolitical interests of the big powers could act as a brake on atrocities which might otherwise have taken place in post-war Eastern Europe. Yet this consideration could also work the other way. A desire not to alienate the new regimes, especially where that might lead to complications for, or between, the Allies themselves, or simply an assessment of atrocity reports which concluded that there was no direct threat to their own interests, equally meant that there were multiple instances where the Allies turned a blind eye to extreme violence. The Tito regime literally got away with mass murder on both counts. If Germans and Hungarians, in that order, were the main ethnic targets of its reordering, potential groups three and four on Belgrade's list were the Italians of the Istrian peninsula and the Albanians of Kosovo.

To be sure, in the Italian case the narrative is a complicated and contested one. Under Mussolini's rule, it had been the majority Slovenes and Croats of the region, 'redeemed' from the defeated Habsburg empire after 1918 as Venezia Giulia, who were the subject of cultural and economic repression. In the context of the Second World War, the Yugoslav Partisan struggle against fascism, as it extended into the peninsula, included a mounting range of attacks on believed collaborators, in which the *foibe*—the local karst ravines, grottoes, and caverns—figured prominently as killing or dumping grounds, just as they had done for Ustasha attacks on Serbs further south. But if the wartime Partisan attacks were mostly on Italians in their capacity as fascist officials, *carabinieri*, or fellow-travellers, and, moreover, need to be seen in the context of the Italian incarceration of Slovenes on Rab, or by way of the more infamous Nazi Risiera di San Sabba camp in Trieste, the immediate post-war Yugoslav drive to take control of Istria up to and including Trieste vastly sharpened the specifically *ethnic* stakes of the game. With resolution of the future territorial determination of Istria temporarily on hold through a de facto division between Anglo-Americans (zone A around Trieste) and Yugoslavs (zone B), the latter began ratcheting up the pressure on Italians in their zone to leave. The *foibe* became a renewed part of the strategy. Several thousand Italians, though not the 20,000 often cited in Italian studies, paid with their lives. Certainly, the issue as to whether Tito wanted all Italians out, or only those who were political and economic 'enemies of the people', is part of the contested history—the communist regime at the time actually accusing Italian nationalists and the Church of fomenting panic when Italian mass flight began. The upshot was an almost wholesale Italian exodus from the Yugoslav side, 250,000 to 350,000 people all told, which was brought to a head in 1954 with the formal international award of zone B to Belgrade—but without any *actual* Yugoslav resort to direct ethnic cleansing or deportation.[45]

The fate of a fourth 'enemy' community, clearly scheduled in some of Tito's advisers' minds as ripe for wholesale removal, again underscores communist Yugoslavia's forging of its own, in some respects rather 'atypical', path of state-building violence. Many Albanians had aligned themselves with the Italians in the course of the war, and when the latter departed from the Balkans in 1943, there had been a belated, rather half-hearted German attempt to raise a volunteer Albanian SS division, including men from technically Yugoslav Kosovo. One consequence was that even some Albanian Partisan commanders were fearful of what Belgrade imposition would lead to at the war's end, an open insurrection in the Drenica valley—a notable centre of Kosovar nationalism—being met by the regime with the destruction of forty-four villages and many thousands killed.[46] The one thing the Partisans were not squeamish about was the ongoing use of instrumental violence to impose communist writ. Yet what followed in some ways can only surprise. While ongoing Kosovar resistance was ruthlessly stamped out, Yugoslav Albanians as a whole were not collectively held responsible. Instead, Kosovo was offered a high degree of provincial autonomy (again, paradoxically, alongside Vojvodina), albeit minus the full self-governing status of the six nations which now constituted the federal republic.[47]

Compare and contrast Belgrade's ostensible post-war encouragement of Albanian cultural difference with what happened to the remaining Albanian Chams still living across the border, in the Epirus region of north-western Greece. Here, too, the wartime situation had been complicated, not least as most Chams, utterly stifled under interwar rule from Athens, had sided with the pro-Albanian Italian occupiers. But some had supported the Greek communist-led National Liberation Front and Peoples Army (EAM-ELAS), which—like Tito's Partisans in Yugoslavia—had liberated much of Greece by the end of the war. The problem for the Chams, as indeed for the remaining Slavophones and Vlachs in Greek Macedonia, was that while their acclamation of the communists was quite logical—the latter, after all, were the only political grouping sympathetic to cultural autonomy for minority groups—the EAM-ELAS position began disintegrating as the British entered the post-German evacuation fray, to restore the pre-war Greek monarchy. In the Epirus region, they turned to the right-wing EDES resistance movement, in spite of the fact that its leader, Colonel Zervas, had struck a tactical alliance with the Germans in the last stages of their occupation and, as a passionate Venizelist, could hardly be described as pro-royalist. In short, one might argue that there were notably contingent factors at work in the two great anti-Cham village massacres perpetrated in June 1944 and in March 1945 by Zervas's men. Certainly, without explicit British support, the previously very weak EDES would have been in no position to carry fire and sword to the Cham districts, precipitating the mass flight of practically all the 15,000 to 20,000-strong community across the border into Albania.[48]

But is it sufficient to simply pass off these events as a very extreme case of retribution carried out by an essentially rogue element? Once again, we might turn to a 'what if' scenario, in which the Greek communists had not made a series of strategic blunders, and in spite of British and then US involvement had come out as the victors in the ensuing civil war. Such circumstances would have changed not only the fortunes of the diverse communities of the Greek north, but also very possibly the political complexion of the whole Balkan arena. If, that is, we can accept the implausible notion that the Western Allies would have deferred to such an outcome. Accepting what did happen, however, returns us to something very depressingly familiar yet consistent with broader rimlands trajectories. Not only did tens of thousands of Slavophone Macedonians and Vlachs, men, women, and children, flee, along with other communist fellow-travellers, to Yugoslavia and beyond, before or in the wake of the destruction of the last Greek communist resistance in late summer 1949, just south of the Albanian border; but also in the process long-term tendencies within the Hellenic polity towards enforced homogenization were reaffirmed. Just as post-Turkish expulsion Pontic and Anatolian Greeks, owing their lives to the notion of a unitary Greek state, were used and abused by nationalist politicians to help socially engineer ethnic and linguistic plurality out of existence in Macedonia and its environs, so post-war, once again, they became the demographic tools in the consolidation of that process.[49]

In these terms, Greek denunciation of Slavophone Macedonians as 'Sudetens of the Balkans' was really no different from Bulgarian vituperation against Muslim Pomaks, or for that matter Rumanian objections to Bulgarian-speaking Dobrudjans.[50] Everywhere in the Balkans, in the interwar period, Yugoslavia included, expunging the Ottoman legacy had entailed clearing out human diversity in favour of modern, streamlined national similitude. Further wartime rectification of borders—in itself the ongoing legacy of nation-state cupidity and grievance from the time of the Balkan wars—carried with it more explicit attempts to remove unwanted populations. As late as 1944, even as the Nazi position in the region was imploding, Rumania, Hungary, and Bulgaria were still using Berlin's good offices to carry through 'exchanges', Sofia alone since 1940 clearing out hundreds of thousands of Greeks, Serbs, and Rumanians—and also Roma—in its efforts to return southern Dobrudja, western Frakia, and eastern Macedonia to what it considered the Bulgarian fold.[51] But post-war communist Bulgaria was in essence no different, proving the point in 1950 with the deportation to Turkey of over 150,000 Bulgarian Turks and Pomaks, nearly all from the northern-eastern Varna region.[52]

Was this genocide? No. Or at least no more, one might argue, than were parallel Turkish efforts under the wartime radar screen to pressurize the remaining Greeks and Armenians of Istanbul to clear off. These had included the 1942 levy of a property tax, the *Varlık Vergisi*, which in its intentionally specific application was designed to throttle non-Muslim businesses. Those who failed to pay were, in the words of one commentator, 'shipped off to a labour camp in Aşkale, in eastern Anatolia, which, for a middle-class Istanbuli, was the Turkish equivalent of Siberia'.[53] However, it would take another dozen years for the Ankara regime to achieve the result it wanted, tensions over Cyprus in 1955 providing the pretext for a covertly government organized two-day mass rampage through Istanbul's Greek, Armenian, and Jewish districts (with shades, perhaps, of Stalin's imagined but never implemented anti-Jewish Moscow pogrom), which left thirty-seven Greeks dead, hundreds raped, thousands injured, but crucially precipitated the mass exodus of most of the over 100,000 Greeks still living in the old capital.[54] The event has been described as the Turkish equivalent of *Kristall-nacht*.[55] Justifiably so? Clinically standing back from the Istanbul pogrom yet pausing with regard to the German comparison, one might again say, 'no genocide'. But viewing it as a component within a long-term pattern of rimlands nation-state building—with genocide as its ultimate expression—one would surely and most decidedly say 'yes'.

Does this add up, then, to a comprehensive picture of some final, post-war rimlands expurgation? Somewhere in this blasted landscape, one might need to be reminded, one fundamental facet had yet in 1945 to be resolved: the fate of the Jewish survivors of the Holocaust. On top of those clinging on to life after the death marches in the displaced persons (DP) camps in British- and American-controlled Germany—a subject itself which invited some seriously negative commentary when the state of the camps was investigated by President Truman's special emissary, Earl Harrison—there were also those residual fragments in Eastern Europe who, having witnessed first hand neighbours' reactions to their continued existence, not least through the prism of Kielce, of their own volition became part and parcel of the great migration westwards towards those very same DP camps. As a result, Jewish 'refugee' numbers in the Allied zones in central Europe went from a few tens of thousands to something close to a quarter of a million by 1948. Their impact, indeed, so exercised the British Foreign Office that, in spring 1946, it even solicited Moscow as to whether some, or all, could be settled in Birobidzhan![56] Even had the Soviets agreed to this singularly odd request, it is unlikely that it would have shifted survivor opinion, or indeed Jewish opinion more generally, as to where the survivors should actually go. By the most convoluted route, therefore, the specifically Jewish, hence primarily 'Lands Between', aspect of the rimlands crisis appeared to be being brought to an apparent head though a self-propelled demand for national self-determination in a once authentically Ottoman province, albeit one beyond our genocidal rimlands. What stood in the way of this nationalizing goal, at least until 1948, was the post-Ottoman imperial power in charge of that province: Britain. Another imperial power, Russia, equally stood in the way of the return to Poland of the perhaps quarter of a million Poles who had been incarcerated in Soviet Central Asia in 1940 and 1941 but who had been unable to leave with Anders's army the following year.[57] Refused Polish passports and deemed to be citizens of the USSR, their fate may also remind us that if post-war resolution to the rimlands crisis was supposed to be about a political consolidation of ethnic communities within their given national boundaries, the misery and violence that ensued was a matter of what was visited on not just those forcibly eructed from what they had understood to be hearth and home, but also others who were actually denied finding a new one.

Yet there is one final collectivity of victims who need to be added to the litany, in part because they do not fit our generalizing national prescription, in further part because their fate really was catastrophic. As we implied, Tito's Yugoslavia at the war's end seemed to be travelling in a direction somewhat at odds with the rest of communist Eastern Europe. The regime had used massive violence against specific ethnic communities yet still proclaimed its commitment to a multicultural political settlement. And this, perhaps, had been exemplified in what may well have been an about-turn on Tito's part in his attempt to accommodate rather than continue the struggle with the Kosovars. But no such mercy was shown to those who had fought with the Chetniks, Ustasha, or other indigenous paramilitary formations, who, however nominally, had come under the Axis umbrella. In early May 1945, a great hotchpotch of these defeated units accompanied by their families, to the tune of tens of thousands, crossed or attempted to cross over the Austrian border, in the Ustasha case with many of their leaders, Pavelić included, with a view to surrendering to British forces who had taken up a position close to the village of Bleiburg. The British, after some initial prevarication, refused to take their surrender, and instead sought to repatriate all those 'Yugoslavs' in their charge to Partisan forces on the other side of the Slovenian frontier. The result was a series of massacres conducted by the Partisans over a period of days, either on the spot, and thus in earshot of the British, or after several days marching deeper into Slovenia, where large numbers were gunned down near the town of Maribor. The numbers of those involved are hotly contested. Mark Biondich cites 'judicious estimates' of 70,000 killed; it may have been more.[58] It is certainly true that many thousands of Ustasha, including Pavelić himself, made a successful run for it between the British and Partisan lines, and thereby escaped into Austria. It is also the case that not all those who were marched off by the Partisans were killed en route, the survivors ending up in camps dispersed throughout Yugoslavia. However, many tens of thousands of those who died either in the chaotic first killings, or later on around Maribor and Tezna, included huge numbers of women and children.

The killings between Bleiburg and Maribor thus represent the largest single incidence of mass murder in the European aftermath of the Second World War. The only comparable event in Europe since then is the infamous (male only) Srebrenica massacre in the Bosnian war in 1995. Yet the numbers murdered in the 1945 event may have been ten times greater than those at Srebrenica, and thus are more comparable in terms of scale with some of the Nazi massacres of Jews on Soviet soil in the high summer of 1941. The key difference, of course, is that large numbers of the Bleiburg victims were not innocents, but guilty of a range of genocidal atrocities stretching back to that year. Yet among those massacred were also large numbers of very recently mobilized young men in the Croat and Slovenian Home Guards, who would have had little opportunity, even had they so desired, to participate in such atrocities. And then there were also all the others not in uniform, including the women and children. There is one further paradox. It would be politically and indeed juridically difficult to pin a label of genocide on the Partisan action. Those killed, whether guilty or non-guilty of atrocities, included Croats, Slovenes, Bosniaks, and Serbs. But each of these communities was the recipient of nation status within Tito's federal constellation. Bleiburg was thus both a retribution and a reckoning; but—unlike the targeted post-war violence against Germans, Hungarians, and Italians in Yugoslavia—not an attack on the ethnic integrity per se of any of *these* peoples.

THE VIEW FROM THE NATIONAL PROTAGONISTS: PLAYERS ON THE GROUND, MAKERS OF POLICY

At one level, we should not be surprised by the nature or even the scale of retribution, partisan or otherwise, at the war's end. Reading the runes from within the US legation in Prague, back in May 1939, George Kennan predicted, 'If the tide ever turns, Czech retaliation will be fearful to contemplate.' And that was long before the full force of Nazi horror had even begun. Six years on and throughout the continent, west as well as east, ordinary people took out their anger at what the Nazis had done to them in a great wave of rough justice.[59] And where they could not vent it on Nazi officials or soldiers, ordinary Germans would do, alongside anybody who was deemed to have collaborated with the persecutors. There were no sensibilities or polite courtesies in these outbursts of *épuration sauvage*. Woe betide any woman accused—justly or unjustly—of having consorted with the 'enemy'. But being publicly shaved and humiliated, beaten up, and most likely socially ostracized for years to come was, however ugly, outbid in terms of sheer scale by some very specific instances of popular fury. These included the atrocities in Prague and its Bohemian hinterland which accompanied the Czech uprising on 4–9 May 1945. From the captured radio station in the capital, insurgents broadcast calls to 'kill Germans wherever you meet them'. It is unknown how many hundreds of civilians were lynched in the following days in the capital alone, but reports speak of villages burnt to the ground, Germans 'hung by their heels, from trees, doused in petrol and set on fire', and of Czech partisans, helped by civilians and nurses, aiding Soviet troops to break into places of either internment or refuge to publicly rape the sheltering German women.[60]

Throughout this study, we have implicitly or explicitly recited the lengths to which angry, vengeful people, men, women, and children too, will go to take out their personal hurt or sense of national humiliation on those they hold either directly or by association to be responsible. Dreaming up demeaning tasks, such as getting their often urbane victims to scrub the streets or public latrines with their bare hands, can be read almost as standard fare. But going further and having them endure unbearable torture is also familiar behaviour, as those who either seize the opportunity or are enabled to do so explore different techniques and invent games by which to sustain the victim's pain and degradation. Once we are into this dark territory, the power of the uniform is likely to amplify the possibilities, while command structures which, among other things, are supposed to keep violations in check, may—where officers are equally disposed in this direction—simply give added authority and impunity to them.[61]

What we thus know from the behaviour of those with the hands-on power in this sequence is how much it conformed to any other in this, or any, human epoch. For slow torture use water. From the former Nazi Zgoda concentration camp, near Świętochłowice in Silesia, taken over by the NKVD before being passed on to its Polish equivalent, a British observer reported that 'prisoners who are not starved or whipped to death are made to stand night after night up to their necks, until they perish'.[62] On the whipping, the observer may have had in mind the manner in which the clearly Jewish camp commandant, 'Salomon Morel, was known to strut about the grounds routinely pistol-whipping the inmates'. The Jewish background of Morel in itself offers no explanation for either his sadism or his ineptness in letting a typhus epidemic get out of control, to kill up to 1,850 of the 6,000 estimated mostly ordinary Silesians incarcerated in the camp during the course of 1945.[63] But the confession of his Polish counterpart at the Łambinowice camp, Czesław Gęborski, may give more inkling of the way wounds to mind and body can not only fester but can also turn into a septic reservoir. Indicted by the Polish authorities in 1959 for wanton brutality, Gęborski stated at his trial that all he was doing was exacting revenge for what had been done to him during the war. In one particular incident, in October 1945, he had his guards shoot down prisoners trying to escape from a fire that had engulfed one of the barrack blocks.[64]

For faster torture use fire. Lavishly used kerosene or gasoline is a standard item in the modern revenger's kit. Of the Prague pogrom sequence, Alfred de Zayas notes that 'German soldiers were disarmed, tied to stakes, then set on fire as living torches'.[65] The aptly named Revolutionary Guards were the retributive zealots of this type of vigilante action, which rapidly extended from the Protectorate into the Sudetenland. As such, an armband was often enough to make an erstwhile Czech worker or student into a feared and potentially lethal enforcer; and to make competing authorities, exemplified by the local national committees who were simultaneously attempting to create some orderly police presence in both metropolis and borderlands alike, back off or remain on the sidelines.[66] Indeed, in conditions in which it was unclear where exactly political and juridical authority resided, it was perfectly possible for the 'national will' to be enacted by whoever on the spot had a monopoly of violence. Such a man was Lieutenant Karol Pazúr, a Czech Defence Intelligence Service officer, who, on 18 June, was in charge of a military transport in eastern Moravia when its path crossed that of a train full of evacuated German civilians attempting to return home to Slovakia. In all, 265 people from that train, men, women, and children, were seized and, on Pazúr and another officer's orders, stripped of their clothes and belongings; then, after a mass grave had been dug, executed. Clearly, on this occasion, the 'elaborate spectacles of public humiliation' were dispensed with in favour of summary justice.[67]

But did this mean that extreme violence of this kind, here or for that matter perpetrated by another set of 'Partisans' on the Austro-Slovene border, was symptomatic of fuzzy chains of command or, perhaps, marked a hiatus which a centralized and de jure state authority had yet to fill? A Tito or a Beneš would have gone to inordinate lengths to distance himself from any suggestion that *he* was responsible for indiscriminate massacres. It may have been convenient thus to argue that the kind of atrocities perpetrated by lower military echelons technically under their purview were actually those of freebooters acting as a law unto themselves, in defiance of orders, or because of generally chaotic conditions beyond state control. Yet political elites, certainly throughout Eastern Europe, were of a single mind that there *had to be* retribution. Indeed, the very extensive run of heavily reported state trials both of German criminals and indigenous collaborators, and from very senior figures to relatively small fry, were designed to demonstrate to a public both at home and abroad *who* the genuinely guilty parties were and why their exemplary punishment was deserved. The key difference between this sort of justice and that performed by ordinary citizens, whether in state uniform or not, was in its official, formal, state organized enactment. Just as the Allied International Military Tribunal (IMT), which opened its proceedings in Nuremberg in November 1945, sanctioned the death sentences which it passed on senior Nazis through its understanding of itself as an internationally, legally constituted body, so national courts gave to themselves the same aura of juridical authority. And, one might add, with the same fundamental prescript: that the trials, in the words of one IMT formulator, were necessary to 'document and dramatise for contemporary consumption and for history the means and methods employed by the leading Nazis in their plans to dominate the world and to wage an aggressive war'.[68]

But, actually, that was not all. Allied statements at Potsdam reaffirmed that this war guilt pervaded and penetrated *German* society at large, and that as such *its people* were collectively responsible for the punishment they would now have to endure.[69] But did this offer justification, even legitimization, for the retributive peoples as well as the states of Eastern Europe to do exactly as they pleased? Was there, indeed, any real distinction between when ordinary people used menaces to clear out the occupants of neighbours' homes and when newly constituted or reconstituted political authorities used police, militia, or army in order to clear out these same peoples, in droves, from the country? We have seen in ample measure how ordinary Europeans took the assault on the Jews provided by Nazi overlordship as a green light to filch, rob, and generally despoil those who were in their reach, a tendency which reached its nadir when the latter (like Armenians and other Ottoman people before them) were undergoing the process of actual physical expulsion. And, as we have equally noted, the wartime seizure in this way of Jewish property, goods, and businesses was either reaffirmed or simply continued after the war, though potentially now under an entirely different alibi. As one perceptive Polish commentator in 1945 put it, 'For the Germans are left the guilt of the crime, for us the keys and the till'.[70] But the further difference now was that evicted Germans were receiving this same merciless treatment in equal measure, and there was further evidence to suggest that it was exactly those who donned the ephemeral uniform of Revolutionary Guards and the like who made the most of the opportunity. One consequence was that Germans deported from Czechoslovakia to the US-occupied zone in Germany, well after ACC arrangements allowed each to bring with them 25 kilograms of luggage plus up to 1,000 Reichsmarks, were instead arriving starved and wretched, often with nothing more than the clothes they stood up in. What the Revolutionary Guards had not taken, the Czech border guards certainly had.[71]

A US embargo on further transports in May 1946 sought to put a stop to these violations by insisting that expellees were accompanied by both cash and luggage,[72] but arguably without resolving the underlying issue. Blaming such behaviour on the vindictiveness or venality of ordinary people as they sought to fleece those being expelled was one thing—as one recent historian has put it, the Czech and Polish campaigns against Germans were 'at their core...struggles for home and property'.[73] But suppose this sort of popular response in practice simply acted as a smokescreen for more fundamental and long-lasting *elite* agendas? After all, it was easy enough for national leaders to keep prodding the populace with reminders of what the Germans had done to 'us'. Polish army directives in June 1945 specifically referred to German treatment of 'our children, wives or elderly people'.[74] But behind this particular order was Warsaw's rather frantic efforts to get as many Germans as possible off Polish soil at this point before the Potsdam summit had unequivocally ruled on the matter. In other words, the actions of Polish soldiery encouraging Germans to 'voluntarily' quit the country, while they may tell us something about widespread vengeful urges at the micro level, ought to focus our attention more keenly on how ideologically driven meso-level planners sought to mobilize such urges as one way of accelerating national 'cleansing' before Allied (that is, macro) disapproval or censure stymied or completely capsized it.

*

The key question, thus, for the newly incumbent Eastern European regimes, was not whether homogenization through ethnic cleansing was a good thing, but the more pragmatic one of how, or perhaps how much of, this could be achieved without wrecking a country's international standing. Proclaiming that expulsion was suitable punishment for those who had transgressed during the war might take a regime so far towards its goal. Proclaiming an ongoing national emergency might possibly take it one step further. Bucharest had begun interning ethnic Germans and Hungarians in Transylvania and the Banat almost as soon as the country had switched to the Allied side. Its argument was that those so interned continued to pose 'a hazard to the order of the state'.[75] But the result was tension with the Soviets, who particularly did not want the Rumanians having a free hand in northern Transylvania.

Even so, Bucharest had already achieved much of the Hungarian flight from the region that it had intended, through the massacres committed by its paramilitary units. Similar thinking geared towards changing the ethnographic landscape of the country, before the big powers might object, may also have propelled Tito's Anti-Fascist Council of the People's Liberation of Yugoslavia (AVNOJ), as soon as it took power in late 1944. A memorandum prepared for Tito at this time proposed that 'the solution of minority issues by population transfers' ought to be carried out by 'the military forces...in a planned and merciless way while the fighting still goes on'. The author of this document was our old friend Vaso Cubrilović, a name one might consider rather surprising given his long-time credentials as a Serb nationalist and Tito's as an ostensibly colour-blind communist. All the more so when one learns that Tito appointed Cubrilović the following year as minister in charge of population transfers and agriculture.[76]

But then, part of Tito's juggling act was to take majority nationalist sentiment with him on Yugoslavia's clearly radical new path. A desire for revenge against those held responsible for Serb suffering in particular—and not just for the huge human losses of the Second World War but for the world war before that—certainly translated into widespread popular support for the removal of ethnic Germans and Hungarians, as well as Albanians. The hostility of these three largest 'minority' groups to Yugoslavia, said Cubrilović, determined the automatic forfeiting of their citizens' rights. However, his insinuation could equally be read as a more diluted, more Yugoslav-tailored version of Moljević's wartime Chetnik plan for a greater Serb state minus *all* its non-Serb inhabitants. The emphasis of the Cubrilović programme was on the bolstering of a south-Slav entity with all, or at least most, of the non-Slav elements removed. But there again, like Moljević, the bottom line remained the cleansing from the country of communities which did not fit a long-time, politically determined prescript, and with an acceptance that extreme violence would be the method, under conditions of war and instability, which would enable its most complete achievement.

One irony of Cubrilović's proposal is that it sought to give some legitimacy to what otherwise would have been outside standard 'international legal norms' by invoking the recently enunciated Soviet model of Polish–Ukrainian exchange and with an added nod towards 'brotherly Soviet' endorsement in the request that they 'will help us solve the minority question in the way they have done and are doing'.[77] Doing things the Soviet way in late 1944 and early 1945 certainly seemed to be something at which AVNOJ excelled. Belgrade's own security apparatus, suitably entitled the Department for the Protection of the People (OZNa), was in every way as terrifying, bureaucratically meticulous, and all-pervading as its NKVD equivalent. It was OZNa, above all, which was responsible for the internment and mass execution of thousands of the hated 'Svabi'—ethnic Germans—as well as Magyars, especially in the Vojvodina, the epicentre of Yugoslavia's post-war ethnic struggle. The fact that OZNa (unlike the multinational army) was an almost exclusively Serb organization, its operations conducted under the iron fist of the interior minister, Aleksandar Ranković, may offer some explanation as to the mercilessness of the Vojvodina sweeps. Yet OZNa's victims were far from being only those targeted on national grounds. Indeed, former Nazi and Ustasha camps the length and breadth of the country filled up with so many hundreds and thousands of suspects from all backgrounds and walks of life that the penal system began to buckle under the strain. Meanwhile, the relentlessness with which OZNa pursued, locked up, and/or liquidated family members of Chetnik and Ustasha bands who had fled into the mountains seemed to confirm that the regime's aim was one of achieving mass ideological conformity as much as (an albeit federalized) ethnic unity à la Cubrilović.[78]

The extreme violence of Yugoslavia's immediate post-war trajectory, therefore, while it evinced aspects of the homogenization agendas central to other East European regimes, was also in some ways more akin to post-1917 Russian Bolshevik efforts to stamp out all and any perceived counter-revolutionary resistance. Indeed, a further Titoist paradox is that its security apparatus became so good at enforcing the regime's writ that it helped exacerbate Stalinist apprehensions that the country's rise to communism would be enacted quite independently of Moscow's hegemonic counsel. But then, Yugoslavia was unusual in having largely self-liberated itself from Axis rule and hence not being in political thrall to either Moscow, Washington, or London. The same was not true of the still transitional regimes in Czechoslovakia and Poland. In both cases, the position of the traditional nationalist leaderships, both at home and in London exile, hardened in the course of the war towards expulsion of *all* Germans on grounds of their collective responsibility. Yet at Soviet prompting, both the PPR in Poland and Czech communist leadership effectively adopted this same position, in the latter instance in spite of having significant number of ethnic Germans among its cadres.[79] Having created an unusual unanimity of purpose between parties otherwise at daggers drawn, the question of arriving at final solutions of ethnic questions boiled down both pre- and post-Potsdam to the degree to which these countries' elites could conceivably engage wider Allied support—both political and practical—for the realization of ethnic cleansing.

The question was a critical one, not least when set against the situation in 1939, again in 1940, when the Nazis had realized that no foreign power would either willingly accept or be forced to take the Jews that it wanted to eruct from its burgeoning empire. The post-war conjuncture which favoured Poland and Czechoslovakia's expulsion projects *not* going down the mass murder route, therefore, was in the most fundamental sense founded on the fact that an utterly defeated Germany had no say in the matter. And behind that, of course, that a victorious USSR in its own geopolitical interests was in a position to dictate the future shape of Eastern Europe to its Western allies. Whatever qualms, for instance, the latter might have held about the repositioning of Poland as a territorial entity greatly to the west of its former boundaries, they stifled them in deference to Stalin's wishes. Which, in effect, also meant that Moscow, Washington, and London would act together to ensure that the Germans eructed from Poland would be received into the Allied zones of occupation.

However, if these Great Power arrangements, in their very principle, should have acted as a safety net against a new wave of genocides, did they ensure that the possibility had been ruled out altogether, or that the role of the Poles themselves had been reduced to one of inconsequentiality? Not quite. As we have already seen, Polish, like Czech, anxieties pre-Potsdam, that the Allies might change their minds or put limits on the ethnic German deportations, precipitated a sequence of wild expulsions and with them the worst of the home-grown violence. But another issue which equally threatened to derail the more orderly departure of remaining Germans westwards was the sheer scale of Warsaw and Prague's respective projects. In Poland, covert Delegatura planning for the anticipated takeover of East Prussia, western Pomerania, and the Opole region in Silesia had actually been proceeding apace during the Nazi occupation. The Delegatura's Bureau of New Territories had even undertaken the training of several thousand people who would be charged with administering the region.[80] But putting aside the disruption to this programme precipitated by the ensconcing of the PPR-led government in Warsaw, the very fact that the Soviet plan to extend Poland to Oder-Neisse added many millions more Germans to the inventory of those required to leave threatened, in doing so, to put an almost impossible strain on authorities already struggling with resource scarcity and a wrecked communications infrastructure, not to say the chaos of near civil war.

In an uncanny, if upside-down, resonance of the Nazi resettlement plans for the Warthegau back in 1939–40, the Polish resettlement project for the now designated 'recovered' territories turned on quickly bringing into them enough compatriots—that is, primarily from an eastern Poland now absorbed into the USSR—to take up the homes and farms vacated by the departing Germans. The recent Soviet-sponsored Ukrainian–Polish 'exchange' (with some resonances of the 1939–40, one-way 'return' of 'Lands Between' Volksdeutsche) made for the partial demographic plausibility of project. But as always the devil was in the detail. Allocating residences for the incoming *kresy* Poles—putting aside their willingness or not (just as with the eastern Volksdeutsche before them) to be so resettled—could not be undertaken overnight. Which, in turn, posed further practical questions, such as who in conditions of extreme food shortages would bring in the essential harvest in these western regions. The hiatus confronted the Polish authorities with the necessity of keeping whatever able-bodied Germans they could muster back from deportation.[81]

The intention was clearly provisional, not least as it flew in the face of the deeper intention to liquidate the German presence from the 'recovered' territories as quickly and irrevocably as possible. But in so doing, it also threw up further dark parallels with the recent past. One of these was the emerging discrepancy between those who were now deemed economically productive and hence worth holding on to, and the vast majority of remaining German elderly, women, and children whose status had become in all too familiar language that of 'useless mouths'. ACC provisions clearly stated that expellees should be 'transferred' where possible in family groups, including able-bodied members. Yet there is abundant evidence that as the deportation process developed, even under ACC supervision, Polish authorities 'began loading the inmates of lunatic asylums, hospitals, orphanages and old people's homes' onto transports. If this tendency, as Matthew Frank infers, was 'the thin end of the wedge', nevertheless, less than 18 per cent of those arriving in the British zone by June 1946 were adult males and only 60 per cent of these fit for work.[82] So where were all the men? A majority, of course, were in Allied POW or Soviet labour camps. But if we take one western province, that of Olsztyn (Allenstein), as an example, most of the remainder had been assigned to large country estates or to specially designated 'ghettoes' where, wearing an 'N' (*Niemiec*: German) on their clothing, they were put to hard labour.[83] We may remember how Heydrich's infamous September 1939 *Schnellbrief* had been an interim holding measure to concentrate Polish Jews in major urban hubs, pending their wholesale deportation eastwards. Does knowledge of Polish provisional measures pending a Polish-German deportation westwards retrospectively soften our view of Heydrich's aims, or harden our view of Polish ones? The proper answer is neither. The Polish authorities in 1945 were responding to their mostly self-created emergency scenario, as Heydrich six years earlier was responding to a Nazi one. To the extent there is a similarity it lies in the discrepancy between the ultimate aim, in both cases, of comprehensive and rapid deportation, and contingent, practical issues curtailing it.

Poland in 1945 was far from the exception in this latter respect. Czechoslovakia, against its own better judgement and according to its own declaration on the matter in October 1946, had 'retained' over 300,000 Germans in 'essential industries'.[84] In now Soviet Lithuania, Polish-speaking peasants who otherwise ought to have been allowed transfer to Poland under the provisions of the eastern borderland 'exchanges' found their exit administratively sabotaged. It was the more urban, hence more nationally-minded, Poles that Vilnius wanted rid of. The peasants, by contrast, were too economically valuable where they were.[85] As for Poland itself, perhaps the most telling expression of the impracticalities of carte blanche deportation, yet again with close reminders of the recent Nazi occupation experience, was the manner in which peoples now designated as 'autochthons' in the western provinces, who had previously been allowed to classify themselves as Germans on the *Volksliste*, were encouraged after 1945 to 'verify' themselves as Poles. Why? Not because the people in question were identifiable one way or the other as either Poles or Germans. The linguistic and cultural identity of Masurians, Warmians, Silesians, and Kashubians, as in so many rimlands cases, was decidedly regional or local. Instead, their reclassification as authentic *indigènes* arose—regardless of whether they spoke Polish or not—from the simple (if arguably faulty) assessment that minus their German inhabitants and with insufficient eastern Poles to replace them, these regions would lack a self-sustaining, economically productive population.[86]

None of this deterred truly nationalist politicians of the ilk of the former government-in-exile leader Stanisław Mikołajczyk from demanding a clean sweep of all Germans, regardless of whether they had been pro-Nazi or otherwise; nor of Polish elites more generally seeking to erase German culture in its totality from the 'recovered' territories, a policy consciously broadcast as de-Germanization (*Odniemczanie*). But then, one might argue that Polish nationalism, especially of the Endek strain, had always had a hard, ideologically based animus towards Germans on class as well as ethnic grounds, as it did to all alleged 'alien' influences.[87]

Which makes our final port of call in this brief consideration of elite national thinking all the more telling, given *its* interwar credentials as the one remaining beacon of 'New Europe' multicultural tolerance. That, after all, had been Masaryk's great hope for a consciously hybrid Czechoslovakia. The position on such matters of his successor, Edvard Beneš—who returned to Prague once again as incumbent President in 1945—had by then metamorphosed into one as utterly uncompromising as that of Mikołajczyk. Even so, in the West there were hopes that the Czech leader would go about these things in a different way. True, he was in coalition with the communists, and also was eager to elicit Stalin's goodwill in support of his *odsun* ('transfer') policy. Yet Beneš retained considerable cachet with Washington and London, not only as a genuine democrat but as a supposedly trustworthy politician who would consult with *them* as to his proposals. Indeed, as head of the government-in-exile he had done exactly that, lobbying the British leadership in particular, almost incessantly from 1941, to support *odsun*, as well as openly publicizing the idea, soon after, through the prestigious British journal *Foreign Affairs*. Moreover, already during the war London and Washington had not only seemingly conceded that the principle gave to the transfer concept an aura of respectability, but also encouraged Beneš in the conviction that what he was doing was by the book.[88]

Beneš reinforced this case for legal and administrative rectitude by way of a raft of constitutional decrees on 'minority' matters issued in the six months immediately after Czech liberation. Retroactive Provisional National Assembly ratification came the following year.[89] When challenged by British officials and journalists on what was actually taking place on the ground in the Sudetenland in early summer 1945, Beneš insisted that such incidents were isolated, the result of grassroots 'high feeling', and entirely at odds with the government view that the German question would 'be solved in agreement with the Soviet Union, Great Britain, and the United States'. He even went so far as to claim that he had 'appealed to the people to be considerate, cautious and calm', and to deny that Prague had undertaken, or would undertake any expulsions without Allied authority. In short, Beneš' entire presentation of himself was as the voice of authentic Czech moderation.[90]

But something was clearly out of synch. The anti-German rhetoric of senior Czech politicians, even clerics, in the wake of liberation was little short of bloodcurdling.[91] The fact that Beneš himself did not openly use this sort of language led one British journalist to surmise that there was a split in the Prague administration, and that the more radical tendency was coming from its communist part. Yet it was Beneš, not the communists, who had been making all the running towards the idea of carte blanche expulsions during the war. Indeed, Czech communist commitment to minority rights and opposition to the notion that *odsun* would also include the very large number of German, including Sudeten, anti-fascists was only overturned in favour of the more incendiary line when it became clear that Beneš had Stalin's full backing.[92] As for the constitutional decrees which the Czech President initiated, these were as all-embracing and draconian as anything legally enacted by the Nazi state. The decrees withdrew all state rights and protection from Germans, on the basis of the 'unreliability' of persons of that nationality. This premise in turn provided justification for the confiscation of all ethnic Germans' property and assets preparatory to the 'uncompromising liquidation' of the entire community. However, the decrees were not limited to Germans. Hungarians were equally embraced within their terms, and on the same pretext that their punishment was a consequence of collective war guilt.[93]

One might instantly recognize in these enactments the removal of targeted groups from a universe of obligation, and, with it, a declaration of state intent which scholars have repeatedly warned of as carrying a potential for genocide.[94] The safety valve, one might posit, in this instance lay in Beneš' awareness that cooperation with the Allies would facilitate his expulsion agenda, combined with a fear that overstepping the mark might actually subvert or entirely sabotage it. But the situation, most particularly in the uncertain months before Potsdam, was finely poised. Beneš may have officially bowed to Allied demands to suspend the wild expulsions, but that hardly prevented him playing his own double-game by issuing secret directives through the Defence Ministry for their continuation, the aim clearly being to ratchet up pressure on the Big Three to formalize *odsun*.[95] The other side of this story is that Beneš largely failed to get his way on a unilateral 'transfer' of some 200,000 Magyars across the Slovak border into Hungary (as an intended first tranche in the complete exit of a Magyar community three times that size), the conspicuous absence of reference to Hungarian 'transfer' in the Potsdam declaration stymieing the regime's recently proclaimed intent to create a solely Slavic state.[96] Even then, it is notable how Beneš then resorted to classic CUP-style measures as the next best thing, over 41,000 ethnic Hungarians being internally deported from southern Slovakia, in 1946 and 1947, to a Sudeten region just cleansed of its ethnic Germans.[97]

In the upshot, this alternative—anthropophagic—project failed, as did the attempted 're-Slovakization' (*sic*) of tens of thousands of Magyars in Slovakia itself. Did it run out of steam? Or did it simply become clear to Prague that the formal route of exchanging Slovaks for Hungarians, as signalled by the bilateral agreement with Budapest in late February 1946, was not going to deliver the aspired-for Slavic purity? Whatever the reason, the restoration of Hungarian citizenship rights and, with them, the rights of Magyars to identify as such within Czechoslovakia (as indeed for those stranded in the Sudetenland to return 'home') are suggestive of the limits of such programmes, short of genocide.[98]

Yet the overall picture of Czech-initiated 'cleansing' speaks to much darker realities about post-1945 East European policymaking mindsets. More than any other polity, it was the Czechs who sought to carry through a comprehensive and thorough de-Germanization, as rapidly as possible and regardless of the economic and political consequences. That meant, among other things, bringing Slovak or even Bulgarian labourers into the Sudetenland to ensure the gathering of the 1946 harvest, rather than relying on held-back Germans to do it, as it also meant jettisoning retributive trials of thousands of Volksdeutsche 'collaborators' on the premise that it was more important to be shot of them across the western border, while the going was good, than to keep them in internment camps pending their eventual prosecution for war crimes.[99] Even so, Beneš, in prioritizing *odsun* as the state's most essential task, was neither some rabid right-wing nationalist, nor a closet Stalinist, but a highly experienced, internationally acknowledged statesman, operating squarely in the liberal mainstream. That said, when Beneš demanded a Czechoslovakia free of Germans and Hungarians, he not only spoke for the entire Czech political spectrum but represented a much wider, popular desire to see all place-names, monuments, buildings, cultural, and physical landmarks either erased of their 'alien,' imperial connections or simply blotted out from the landscape.[100]

As Lemkin wrote, 'Genocide has two phases: one, destruction of the national pattern of the oppressed group, the other, the imposition of the national pattern of the oppressor.'[101] Yet here was the irony. Not only, in 1945, was it the Czechs—and their eastern neighbours—rather than the Germans who were doing what Lemkin himself had most feared as a consequence of the 1919 'New Europe'; but in nation-state terms this was not atrocity at all, let alone genocide, but the realization of *normalizing* goals which had been first thwarted, again not by the Germans; but by the victorious Western Allies at Versailles.

THE MACRO PICTURE: THE GEOPOLITICS
OF THE EXPULSIONS

Does this simply reinforce the fundamental shift in the post-war geopolitical land-scape? Or, put more crudely, was the reason why violent homogenization of East-ern European states could proceed apace that the new big player on the block was the USSR? In their own 'security' interest, the Soviets wanted the ethnic Germans, if not necessarily all other minorities, expunged from the arena. And they were quite prepared to insist on German removal even where a subject state was reluc-tant, or resistant, on the matter. Many Budapest politicians, for instance, worried that to accept a carte blanche Volksdeutsche excision from Hungary would be to open the floodgates to neighbouring countries to claim that Hungarians, on grounds of their own wartime collective responsibility, should equally be removed from theirs. Stalinist propaganda towards the end of the war had not only taken on an openly Russian but more precisely pan-Slavic tone—even if clumsily dressed up as 'Leninist new Slavism'. The flight or enforced deportation westwards, by 1948, of over 200,000 of the around half a million ethnic Germans in Hungary could be seen first and foremost as a consequence of direct Soviet pressure on Budapest to carry through the Kremlin's immediate political agenda.[102] But it might equally be read as part of a conclusive reversal of the victory of the 'Two Germanies' (of which 'Hungary' at that moment had been a constituent part) over Russia and its Slavic protégés in 1918. A world war on, however, what was perhaps most significant about Moscow's neo-imperial extension to the west was that it was achieved under the paradoxical guise of Russian championship of the Versailles order.[103] And, one might add, a very maximalist version of it, in which Slavic Poland, Czechoslovakia, and Yugoslavia were not only restored as states but were so without being encum-bered by safeguards protecting their minority populations.

It was those Western Allied-imposed safeguards—the Minority Treaties—which were now being buried; which might read as yet a further example of the liberal system's acquiescence in Soviet diktat as the necessary price to pay for the USSR's overwhelming contribution—and sacrifice—for Hitler's defeat. After all, there had been Western suffocation of the truth about Katyn, as there had been the whole litany of shameless retreat over Poland; the forcible handing over of the Cossacks; even the manner in which, at Yalta, Churchill had accepted without further demur Stalin's quip that there was no need to worry about moving 5 million Reichsdeut-sche from the additional territory to be handed over to Warsaw, as they had all fled anyway in fear of the Red Army.[104]

Yet was all this a matter of Western cravenness? Superficially, the answer might seem to be yes. In August 1941, even before the USA had entered the war, Roo-sevelt and Churchill had made a joint statement of Anglo-American intentions for a post-conflict international order. This Atlantic Charter, as it became known, among other things looked forward to a world in which self-government was restored to those deprived of it; where territorial changes or aggrandizement would not be made against the wishes of self-governing people; and in which, in one particularly ringing phrase, all nations would be afforded 'the means of dwelling within their own boundaries and in which all the men in all the lands may live out their lives in freedom from fear and want'.[105]

Here, then, was what in many respects was a more keenly internationalist restatement of Wilsonian self-determination, implicitly heralding, even if this was not Churchill's actual intention, Western decolonization. To be sure, the charter was essentially a wartime propaganda tool and never intended as a detailed recipe for future world governance, even if its further references to global cooperation also heralded the founding of the United Nations. Nevertheless, what is most memorable about it in the light of Teheran, Yalta, and Potsdam is the apparent overturning of its core principles, just as John Rhys Davies charged in his House of Commons speech quoted at the head of this chapter. Yet perhaps what is more telling still is in what the charter failed to say in the first place. Liberationist African and African American voices quickly picked up on the absence of any explicit mention of colonized peoples.[106] But closer to home, what is equally pertinent is the lack of reference to any people-entity other than sovereign nations. That, after all, had been the exact point of the Minorities Treaties within the context of a multi-ethnic rimlands: to protect the physical integrity and cultural identity of all the communal aggregates otherwise too small, or too weak, to protect themselves: *not* from outside powers but from the newly dominant domestic national forces.

However, the omission of any mention of such safeguards, either in the Atlantic Charter or in other major Western declarations of the war or immediate post-war period, was not due to febrile oversight. Oliver Harvey, a high-ranking figure in the British Foreign Office put the matter confidentially but acerbicly soon after the Atlantic Charter declaration, when having pronounced the Minorities Treaties a 'curse' he proposed that at the next opportunity to resolve the question minorities should have to 'opt between exchange and absorption, having no special privileges'. By special privileges, Harvey meant cultural, linguistic, or other rights of any ethnic or religious group over and above what pertained to a polity's population *as a whole*. More tellingly, the solution to such minority groups, he proposed, was through *exchange*, whether of Germans or Jews, in order 'to produce compact national units'.[107]

In a nutshell, Harvey had encapsulated where British and more generally Western demographic thinking was going on Central and Eastern Europe, regardless of the Soviet factor. The 'problem' was not nation states, but those who were extraneous to them. The prime example, however, was not so much the ubiquitous rimlands Jews of 1919 (even without comprehensive figures to confirm the fact, their massive depletion at Nazi hands a quarter of a century on was self-evident) but rather the ubiquitous ethnic Germans, whose shared culpability for the Nazi crimes of war, through their ongoing presence, allegedly threatened the peace. The principle of collective responsibility having been accepted, the further one enshrined in the Atlantic Charter, of people dwelling within their own boundaries, could only become congruent with the former through endorsing ethnic German transfer; in other words, their expulsion. Or as Churchill put it, in October 1943, attempting to square the circle just before the Moscow conference of foreign ministers, 'We have no desire to keep any branch of the

European family of nations in a condition of subjection or restriction, *except* as may be required by the general needs and safety of the world'.[108] But did these two elements, the abandonment of minority rights and the notion of collective responsibility, translate into an unequivocal Western acceptance, even a promotion, of people-deportations? Here the answer has to be slightly more convoluted. To be sure, Churchill's much-quoted House of Commons speech on the subject of specifically German expulsion, on 15 December 1944, would seem to firmly nail the case for the prosecution. In it he stated:

> Expulsion is the method, which as far as we have been able to see, will be the most satisfactory and lasting...There will be no mixture of populations to cause endless trouble...A clean sweep will be made. I am not alarmed by the disentanglement of population, nor am I alarmed by these large transferences, which are more possible in modern conditions than they ever were before.

Churchill went on to cite the Greco–Turkish transfer as both precedent and model of good practice, leading him to conclude that in the German case, 'I cannot see any doubt whatever that the Great Powers, if they can agree, can effect the transference of population'.[109] Taken together with not unsimilar speeches by Roosevelt and other Allied figures, the Churchill statement would thus seem to give credence to a generalized historical wisdom that the Western Allies approved the expulsion method. However, as Matthew Frank has demonstrated, there appears to have been, at least among British policymakers, a key distinction between support for the *principle* and enthusiasm for the *practice*.[110] Previously, advocates of the former, such as Mackinder as far back as Versailles, had been few and far between. After Lausanne, there had been growing acceptance that compulsory 'population transfer'—with that selected euphemism to the fore—might be 'a rational and progressive choice of "last resort" where intractable minority problems were concerned'. But the issue thrown over to various Whitehall think tanks from 1940 continued to provoke considerable anxiety among the gathered experts as to whether such large-scale movement could be accomplished in an orderly and regulated way 'involving a minimum of human suffering or economic disruption'.[111]

Tellingly, one of the most trenchant critics of the whole idea was C.A. Macartney, who, we may remember from Volume One of this study, as former League of Nations Secretary, was consistently opposed to standard nation-state 'solutions' to national minority problems. Yet even Macartney, presented now with the necessity of offering an opinion before this particular expert committee, proffered that while compulsion was 'barbarous' there might be circumstances where population transfer might be a 'desperate remedy'. More tellingly still, when he continued to object to further consideration of expulsion schemes, he was effectively overruled by none other than Arnold Toynbee, the committee's director, whom we may equally remember through his personal witness of the Greco-Turkish experience, not to say through his analysis of the Great War Armenian events, had full cognisance of what compulsory deportation actually entailed.[112]

Perhaps it was Toynbee's awareness of having the Americans potentially on side to practically implement an orderly 'reshuffling of populations' which made him retract his own previous misgivings. Back in 1923, he had posited that the 'time, capital, organisation and good offices of a neutral power' might be the medium through which hundreds of thousands of Greeks and Armenians could be furnished with the possibilities provided by 'inter-migration and re-plantation'.[113] The USA had not been party to Lausanne. Yet it is interesting to note the manner in which Roosevelt grasped the nettle during the Second World War, setting up his own high-level, actually top-secret, think tank, the so-called 'M-Project' (M for Migration), whose remit was to consider the mass migration of anything between 10 and 20 million extraneous Europeans. Typically American in its 'can-do' thinking, the M-Project's vast array of wartime studies was predicated on the supposition that all manner of surplus populations—Roosevelt's thinking was especially driven by the Jewish 'refugees' on the one hand, concern as to a more general demographic crisis on the other—could be settled *somewhere*, even if that meant in practice depositing them in very obscure corners of the globe. As if Nazi Madagascar-like colonization could actually be achieved in a benign and liberal manner by a genuinely global power deploying maximum expertise, planning, and resources to the problem, and carrying it through by way of a UN-administered International Settlement Authority (ISA).[114]

In the upshot, Roosevelt's death spelt the demise of the M-Project. But even supposing he had lived long enough to provide the necessary impetus to the formation of an actual ISA, it is difficult to gauge how it could have ameliorated the immediately devastating impact of the expulsions of Germans to which the USA, like Britain, was party. As the British experts had intimated, it was the sheer scale of the Potsdam-endorsed of Germans transfer—some 8 or 9 million human beings, as opposed to the earlier estimates of some 2 to 3 million—which, by high summer 1945, was already threatening to turn it into a 'refugee melt-down'.[115] Even those like Harvey who had originally extolled the expulsion principle, with the alibi 'that we have Hitler's authority for mass deportation', were having serious doubts. What if a vastly extended population transfer actually mobilized long-term German revanchism? And what if it was carried out so brutally, as another FO official opined, that it caused 'a strong movement of public sympathy for Germany'?[116]

In fact, this is exactly what happened as news of 'Czech Belsens' and the deteriorating situation at the Berlin railway stations developed over the summer. Public alarm in Britain turned to anger, and to increasingly urgent calls to stop the 'mass expulsions' before they turned into 'mass exterminations'.[117] British liberal opinion, indeed, began to mobilize around a 'Save Europe Now' (SEN) campaign initiated by the radical British Jewish publisher Victor Gollancz. *His* moral credentials were unimpeachable. Gollancz had been among the most vocal and active critics of Munich and the Molotov–Ribbentrop Pact. Even more outspokenly, he had been among the small handful of Britons who had brought attention to the singularity of the Jewish plight under the Nazis and had sought, through grass-roots campaigning, to spur the Allies towards remedial action.[118] Now, SEN highlighted the undeniable fact that if millions of Germans were expelled in a great sea of destitute humanity, vast numbers of them would die from starvation, neglect, and disease.

The Allies at Potsdam had taken upon themselves a duty of care to prevent this outcome, through the provision of food and shelter at the receiving end of the process. And they had also intoned that removal and transit itself, that is as primarily conducted by the national expelling authorities, had to be orderly *and* humane. But set against these strictures they had also agreed to implement the transfers rapidly. It was somewhere in this gap between the responsibilities the ACC had obliged itself to fulfil, and the unspecified yet urgent timetable specified for completion of the task, that there lay the threat of a colossal humanitarian disaster. When the Nazis had attempted mass deportations of Poles and Jews from the Warthegau back in 1939–40, they had avowed no duty of care but had had to radically slow down or even curtail transports when they recognized that the receiving authorities in the General Government could not, or would not, receive any more. Five years on, the Allied Zones of Control were actually even more devastated than had been the General Government. Yet the Allied zonal administrations were being asked to take in numbers of expellees far in excess of anything the Nazis (or for that matter even the Soviets) had earlier set in motion. Indeed, as Gerhard Weinberg has put it, this was 'the largest single migration of people in a short period of which we know'.[119] The logical response was to do what SEN was demanding: repudiate the transfer policy, and insist that would-be expellees instead be readmitted into their own home polities and societies.

But herein lay the rub, and with it an exquisite dilemma for the *Western* Allies. The expeller states were no more going to relent as to their determined agenda to get rid of their ethnic Germans than they were going to welcome back with open arms the Jewish survivors whom they had encouraged to flee. Which posed a further, fateful question. What would the Czechs, the Poles, and the rest do if the Allies point blank refused to accept more expellees? The answer was already staring London and Washington in the face. The expelling states had abundantly demonstrated that they were quite capable of acting as they had *learnt* from the Nazis, in the early summer of 1945. Denied an outlet for those earmarked for removal, and doubly denied the Allied assurance that they would take them, Prague and Warsaw's anti-German violence was bound not only to escalate but also to take on an entirely unpredictable quality. In short, the Western Allies were caught between a rock and a hard place. By late 1945, many leading British politicians were in sympathy with, if not covertly giving encouragement to, the SEN campaign.[120] But to have done a volte-face and to have gone back on Potsdam would not only have been to radically destabilize the already rocky alliance with Stalin but also to have completely disrupted, if not utterly destroyed, the relationships with the relevant meso-players, most particularly the Czechs and Poles, who, after all, were certainly Britain's immediate reason for having gone to war.

In these circumstances, was it really more humanitarian to repudiate the transfer programme or to attempt to make the best of a bad job? Or, perhaps, as a more serious alternative, to put energy, resources, and manpower into making it work? In the Allied shift towards this more robust and energetic response, we may note one final irony. Everything deportation-related that we have observed thus far in this study has suggested heavy inputs of military-style operational planning, combined with clear command structures, and efficient bureaucratic systems, not to say carefully calibrated resource allocations, to produce the necessary result. Or put another way, successful deportations could be construed as a practical exercise in modernity, while their failure would imply its insufficiency. In either case, however, deportations in the modern world have nearly always acted as companion, cover, or prelude to genocide. By marked contrast, the Allied participation in the German deportations evinces advanced modernity being deployed in the interests of genocide *avoidance*. Indeed, on this occasion it was precisely large-scale resource deployments, a truly massive public hygiene and sanitation campaign to prevent the spread of typhus—including, yet more ironically, the unsparing use of the new, Allied-developed, and supposedly miracle insecticide DDT—combined with what Marrus has described as the soldier's 'bureaucratic zeal for classification' which ensured that millions of lives were not discarded but saved.[121]

Meticulous railway timetabling helped facilitate the destruction of Europe's Jews. Here, in a largely unsung parallel narrative, it ensured the belated safe evacuation of most of Europe's far-flung Germans. The British-coordinated Operation Swallow, for instance, may have been inaptly named, but its daily transports by boat and rail from transit hubs at Stettin and Kohlfurt, over a six month period in 1946, ensured the evacuation from Poland into the British zone of some 1 million people, without serious loss of life. At its height in July, 9,000 deportees a day were being securely moved in this way. This did not mean that Allied tensions with the expellers ceased. The ongoing failure to provide basic rations and the cramming of expellees into unheated box wagons by the Poles is a reminder both of how close to the edge of breakdown Operation Swallow itself came, and why the British, on more than one occasion, suspended it.[122] But once out from the expelling states, the life-chances of survivors were likely to improve rather than plummet. And that was fundamentally because of the efforts of US, British, and also Soviet military authorities, the coordination between them, and the supporting, if less happily coordinated, role of the newly founded civilian United Nations Relief and Rehabilitation Administration (UNRRA).[123] And all this, one might add, on behalf of Germans, in 1945 undoubtedly the most collectively unloved people in Europe.

However, before we get too carried away with Anglo-American liberalism, goodwill and benevolence, it may be well to be reminded of these powers' accompanying geopolitical calculations. Independently, both Washington and London made hard-headed assessments of the overall situation and responded accordingly, though not always in complete accord. Whitehall, for instance, was always much more sanguine about the economic implications of Europe being divided into Western and Soviet spheres of influence than was the White House. Yet neither power simply caved in to Soviet or, for that matter, lesser state pressure when their own fundamental interests were at stake. The result might be the turning of a blind eye to the consequences of Cossack and other repatriations to the USSR. Or, for that matter, coming to an uneasy arrangement with the Yugoslavs over Trieste and its Istrian hinterland—thought at the time by military planners to be a potential flash-point for East-West confrontation—in spite of the toxicity that represented for its ethnic Italian population.[124] But when the British or Americans were confronted with something they considered a proposal too far, they stonewalled it. Beneš' urgings for a complete Hungarian eruction from Slovakia was one example. As for the Soviets, when, during 1946, the British and Americans began to view Stalin's tightening grip on Eastern Europe as a direct threat to themselves, they not only started questioning the admissibility of the Oder-Neisse line but also began raising the drawbridge on their continued involvement in the expulsions agenda.[125]

But by then, of course, most of the deportations had already taken place, and with full British and American compliance. Neither party had participated in the procedure out of duress. To be sure, they had set down a whole series of practical markers to ensure that the flow of expellees was manageable and regulated. Yet, at the same time, not only had 'they joined the Soviet Union in lending international legitimacy to coercive population transfers on a scale unprecedented in peacetime' but in the process they had confirmed the expulsion sequence as a result of 'an international consensus of victors and victims'.[126]

This consensus has even been described as 'one of the last acts of unity on the part of the wartime Grand Alliance'.[127] That the USA, in particular, with its strong rhetorical voice on human rights and its non-participation in the Lausanne accords, should have given its imprimatur to the expulsions, suggests just how much reasons of state underpinned such a policy shift. That said, those reasons are not enigmatic.

To be sure, there might be little to choose between German and Russian domination of Eastern Europe: 'the chastisement of scorpions as compared with the whips of Russia', as Mackinder had put it in 1919.[128] But firm Soviet control of the region—ostensibly, too, as ally of the West—removed the whole issue of provisionality and uncertainty which had pervaded the Versailles settlement. Even more of a plus, that stability involved bringing the Eastern European states under Soviet authority. Again, in 1919, Mackinder had proposed the creation of a stable group of new Slav states as a *second* best to Russian domination. The Soviet–East European linkage created in 1945—expurgating in the process the whole notion of territorial rimlands—in effect doubly met the Mackinder prescription. It created stability. It is certainly true that once the Western Allies recognized that this stability came in the form of a communist political straightjacket, they did not like it one iota. Yet despite all the later Cold War talk of communist 'roll-back', a predictable, Soviet-controlled Eastern European glacis was implicitly accepted as politically preferable to what had been seen as an almost anarchic zone of irredentist troublemaking in the interwar years. Too far away to be properly amenable to control by the West, as summed up in Neville Chamberlain's much-cited Munich Crisis comment about Czechoslovakia as a 'far away country of which we know nothing', was it actually not more convenient for London and Washington to simply wash their hands of the lands behind the 'Iron Curtain', as Churchill in March 1946 now delineated Europe to the east of a Stettin-Trieste line?[129] The bottom line was that the 'cartographic carnival launched at Yalta' made geopolitical sense.[130] After all, it allowed the West to get on with securing and protecting its political-cum-economic interests in the imperial or neo-imperial periphery, where its monopolies of violence were assumed to be unanswerable. True, this made Mackinder's 'Heartland' analysis out of date.

A British Cabinet sub-committee in 1944 listed only one area in Eastern Europe in which Soviet interests potentially collided with Britain's own, and that was through contiguity with the Mediterranean basin.[131] That determined that if Stalin had intervened to oppose British intervention in Greece, in that or following years, a further World War could have broken out there. But Stalin did not intervene. As a consequence, while the Iron Curtain may have presented itself as the fault line along which East-West confrontation might have exploded into nuclear war at any time, the very fact of its almost glacially frozen and hence *largely* predictable permanence over the next forty-five years meant that Britain, and even more the USA, could dispense with anxieties about the European semi-periphery, or its expurgated rimlands, and so, finally, resume their struggles for *global* dominance.[132]

Once we accept the trade-off elements of the Potsdam settlement between liberal system and Soviet anti-system, its corollary, by way of the excision of Eastern Europe's historic multi-ethnicity, falls starkly into place. As ex-US President Hoover—otherwise, as we may remember, the man charged with American relief efforts geared towards keeping post-Great War Europeans alive—succinctly put it, 'moving people is hard' but less hard 'than the constant suffering of minorities and the constant recurrence of war'.[133] Minorities, in other words, particularly made for political instability. But one might argue they made also for something else which was near-anathema to the modern policymaker: a lack of clarity. Shifting minorities where possible into 'compact national units' ultimately made for a 'tidier' postwar Europe with 'fewer loose ends'.[134] No wonder so many scholars who have written about this culminating moment in the forcible violent, homogenization of the European rimlands have found it difficult to distance themselves from the Panglossian view that in the upshot everything is for the best in this best of all possible worlds.[135]

LEMKINIAN CONSEQUENCES

However, if Western support for this grand scheme of ethnic cleansing was founded on raison d'état (and given post hoc licence by commentators unable to imagine state political organization around any other master concept than that of the nation state), what does this tell about the contemporaneous making of the Genocide Convention? As we have already suggested, many of the political as well juridical problems which beset its drafting and which 'made the document virtually inert from the very start',[136] would seem to have had very little to do with 'real time' genocidal events. This might in itself suggest that an historical examination of the Convention and its value, or not, in relation to a growing global incidence of genocide *after 1948* is something best reserved for a further volume. Having said that, the glaring discrepancy between this major, new, even paradigmatic instrument of UN-sponsored international law, and its apparent lack of any insight drawn from the sequence of European state violence against national groups in the period almost *simultaneous* to that in which it was being drafted, surely demands *some* comment.

After all, for scholars of genocide, international recognition of the need for a convention, as promoted through Lemkin's insistent one-man advocacy, has been universally applauded as perhaps the great breakthrough event in the struggle to create a world in which communal groups would be free from fear or persecution.[137] 'Genocide is the denial of the right of existence of entire human groups' reads the first line of the resolution adopted by the UN General Assembly in December 1946. And, going on to affirm that genocide is 'contrary to moral law and to the spirit and aims of the United Nations', one can agree with Dirk Moses that this is 'pure Lemkin'.[138] What is less easy to discern, however, is what the essentially Western Allied founders of the UN were responding to as grounds for running with Lemkin's big idea. The obvious answer is the Holocaust. Some commentators, historians included, have taken it as a given that the convention was a recognition and response to the Nazi genocide of the Jews.[139] And, to be sure, Lemkin's concept had already been deployed in the IMT trials as an aspect of their Crimes against Humanity category of indictments. But the degree to which this IMT–Jewish genocide relationship was the foundation stone for the Convention is more debatable. On the one hand, the very fact that 'deliberate and systematic genocide' had been charged and 'particular…national, racial or religious groups…Jews, Poles and Gypsies' named, gives weight to an international recognition which began with 'a crime…undreamt of in history'.[140] It is also true that *later on* in 1947, in the solely US-supervised so-called RuSHA trial of Nazi officials associated with the reordering of Europe on racial lines, convictions on grounds of genocide were recorded, as they were too of individuals like Hoess and Greiser, in separate Polish state trials.[141] On the other hand, however, in the initial, major Nuremberg trial, not only was no one convicted of genocide, leading Moses to consider that the term 'was deployed as a rhetorical flourish' but, more importantly, key US and British IMT planners actually went to considerable lengths to de-emphasize the racial, more precisely Jewish, aspects of the trial presentations.[142] One result was that Lemkin himself was distraught at the outcome, and even more so because the final IMT judgement very precisely excluded from its jurisdiction crimes committed in times of peace, in other words, in this instance, before 1 September 1939.[143]

In fact, the impetus towards the Convention in a critical sense came from efforts to *overthrow* the IMT war-orientated time frame. And those efforts significantly came from outside the Great Powers—more precisely from Indian, Cuban, and Panamanian delegates present at the first UN General Assembly in New York. Thus, we might read the trajectory leading from Assembly resolution to convention adoption as a form of Third World prising open of the juridical monopoly on such matters as held up to this moment by the Allied hegemons.[144] And with the shift towards a wider, more durable remit, to include times of peace as well as war, and drafters for the proposed document drawn from among many UN countries, and with Lemkin initially one of them, the possibilities of arriving at an outcome more in keeping with his own intention to create a legal formula aimed at securing the cultural as well as physical underpinnings of group existence, ran high. Putting aside, however, the radical paring down of the document through successive draftings, which, among other things, left the convention bereft of what Lemkin saw as its cultural essence—more on which below—what is equally striking is its drafters' refusal (whether Allied or otherwise) to accommodate into its wording the one thing which then and there was demonstrable either of the will to genocide, or actual genocidal practice.

The term 'deportation' had actually been included as one of many atrocities cited as Crimes against Humanity in the summer 1945 charter establishing the IMT.[145] At first sight this makes its subsequent exclusion from drafts of the Genocide Convention all the more extraordinary. Only by placing the omission in a wider political context do we arrive at sober explanation. First of all, the impetus towards large-scale denazification of German and indeed other European societies was, by 1947, already rapidly declining, as the growing confrontation between East and West threw up new military and political imperatives. Or, put more bluntly, punishing swathes of individuals as perpetrators of or collaborators in Nazi crimes, while possibly appropriate on paper, when set against the exigencies of the emerging Cold War was increasingly perceived by Allied and state elites as disruptive of social cohesion and national integrity and, therefore, much better swept under the carpet. As a result, it was perfectly plausible in the early 1950s, say, for an Israeli diplomat to be greeted at the West German Foreign Ministry by a former SS officer, or, indeed, to have gone to a guest lecture in a prestigious government-sponsored institute given by a leading Nazi racial hygienist.[146] By extension, not only was there no statist retreat or apologia for the expulsion process, but its underpinnings, founded on the collective responsibility of whole communal groups, effectively became a fixed pillar of the post-war European order.[147] On this basis alone, any remaining pretence of minorities' safeguards became defunct; as did any residual notion in the former rimlands regions that coercive assimilation might provide an alternative route towards the resolution of minority (as opposed to majority) 'problems'. Even the forcible eruction of groups such as the Lemkos from one part of Poland to another were only implemented because there was nowhere outside the country to which to eject them. Viewed in Baumanesque terms, therefore, the European triumph of the anthropoemic over the anthropophagic was pretty well absolute by the time the convention drafters were getting down to their work.

But where did this leave Lemkin's good intentions? A fear of political instability as a consequence of the 'New Europe' denial of citizen rights to heterogeneous elements of the population had been critical to the Minorities Treaties of 1919. The formulators of the Treaties, then, had seen their creation as unwelcome but, in the circumstances, *necessary*.[148] For good measure, they deemed abhorrent the violent knock-on effects of doing nothing, including the sort of mass flights or direct vomiting out of whole communities which had accompanied the previous great round of nation-state building during the Balkan wars. A quarter of a century on from Versailles, a fundamental acceptance across the spectrum of UN participant states of exactly such ethnic cleansing suggests that elite opinion on the issue had not so much progressed towards Lemkin but actually regressed, with the most obvious evidence for this being the absence of the very words 'deportation' or 'expulsion' from the Convention text.

A slightly more charitable view, perhaps, might be to suggest that the convention drafters recognized that there was a great big elephant in their deliberating room, but felt constrained from admitting the fact in deference to the makers of Potsdam. We know, for instance, that US government comments on the draft convention actually registered alarm that the proposed definition of genocide 'might be extended to embrace forced transfers of minority groups such as have already been carried out by members of the United Nations'.[149] But as if to assuage in advance any possibility that they might provoke a scandal, comments from the Secretariat's draft of the convention make clear that 'Mass displacement of populations from one region to another...do *not* constitute genocide'. True, there was a caveat in the recognition that such population displacement could '*become* genocide if...attended by such circumstances as to lead to the death of the whole or part of the displaced population'. William Schabas, noting the further reference to people 'driven from their homes, and forced to travel long distances in a country where they were exposed to starvation, heat, thirst, cold and epidemics', takes this to be an 'unspoken reference' to what happened to the Armenians in 1915.[150] Leaving aside, however, that nobody in 1947 was charging Ankara—a fully paid-up member of the UN—with genocide, the further inference is also crystal clear: the starvation, heat, thirst, cold, and epidemic which had been visited on the recent millions of expellees and deportees could equally not constitute genocide because these 'displacements' had been conducted by other fully paid-up members of the UN.

Thus, being charitable to the convention drafters is not appropriate. Faced with one open *démarche* by a state delegate, that of Syria (though bizarrely, given what it was itself doing at the time, backed by Yugoslavia), to introduce displacement—but not deportation—as a belated amendment into the definition of genocide, the other General Assembly delegates, led by the USA, Britain, and the USSR, ganged up to resoundingly defeat the proposal.[151] And as if to confirm that the legal experts were in one accord with the policymakers, when four years on from the Convention, in 1952, the issue resurfaced at a meeting of the prestigious Institut de Droit International, rapporteur Giorgio Balladore Pallieri seems to have spoken for the gathering when he stated 'that there was nothing in international law to oppose the legitimacy of population transfers and that they were even, in certain circumstances, *desirable*'.[152]

Yet if Pallieri sounds like someone speaking 'with the logic of an ethnic cleanser'—Schabas's words—the fact is that Pallieri was simply regurgitating the standard progressive wisdom of the age. This, after all, was the language of the M-Project, and one, one might add, particularly championed by the demographer Eugene Kulischer and the migration expert Joseph Schechtman, who shared Lemkin's East European Jewish refugee background—and anxieties—but who had come to conclusions on the way towards resolving minority issues entirely at odds with those of the international lawyer. Kulischer's more measured work considered the problem at heart to be one of European overpopulation leading to war. Durable peace could only in turn be restored, he thought, by regulated migration of the surplus to the 'underdeveloped' world. His major 1948 study *Europe on the Move*, Mazower proposes, 'could be read as a distillation of the basic M-project outlook'.[153] However, Schechtman, whom we might arguably read as Lemkin's true nemesis, had two years earlier produced an equally important study on the same theme: *European Population Transfers*. His analysis was more tightly structured around state-organized transfers and 'exchanges', during and immediately after the Second World War. Yet rather than deploring such compulsory movements, instead Schechtman repudiated Minority Rights as an obstacle to world peace, more or less sidelined international law as the way of protecting such groups, and proposed that the post-war situation actually lent itself to *more* radical transfer programmes both within and beyond Europe, in order to finally put an end to minorities by making them part of territorially compact majorities.[154]

In juxtaposing these two individuals with Lemkin, Mazower has not only queried whether the latter really did most keenly represent the then liberal zeitgeist, but in so doing has also probably gone further than any other serious commentator in questioning whether the Convention—alongside the Universal Declaration on Human Rights—was actually anything more than a promissory note 'that the UN's founders never intended to be cashed'.[155] Rather, however, than attempting to squeeze some smidgeon of solace from this debacle, Mazower has followed through the logic of his argument. The whole thrust of the new UN order was towards strengthening *national* sovereignty. In these terms, the Convention, therefore, was no more than 'a last genuflection to a *past* in which international law had been accorded more weight than could be allowed in the late 1940s'.[156] What had previously existed by way of the Minorities Treaties, to be sure, may have always been a poor sop for real action to protect endangered groups, but at least they had contained some notion of a guaranteed League supervision. The comparable Convention clause, by comparison, was almost risible in that it proposed that persons charged with genocide should in the first instance 'be tried by a competent tribunal of the State in the territory of which the Act was committed'.[157] Even worse, from Lemkin's perspective, the 'very soul of the Convention' expressed in his terminology of 'cultural genocide' was consciously dropped from the final document.[158]

*

However, if we are looking for a genuine test of Mazower's negative verdict, we need look no further than the actual reaction not so much to the Convention but in spite of it, from Lemkin's own ethno-religious community. While Lemkin avowed that his struggle for international safeguards against the threat of genocide was always for all people, in all places, and in all times, it is not too far-fetched to argue that the wellsprings of his understanding of, and sensitivity to, the cultural distinctiveness of groups on the one hand, and their communal vulnerability in the face of nation-statism on the other, was derived from his own personal Jewish experience. In a critical sense, this whole study has turned on the Jewish situation within the context of the broader rimlands crisis. And long before the Holocaust it was not just Lemkin who understood that the potential for Jewish destruction in *this* arena was as much wrapped up with the fate of Ashkenazi religion and culture as with that of its mostly Yiddish-speaking people. That is why Jewish interlocutors, at Paris, whatever their 'assimilationist' or 'Zionist' leanings, placed so much

emphasis on cultural and linguistic safeguards in their efforts to win minority safeguards. And it was the potential loss of these 'cultural and other contributions' to
humanity at large which Lemkin equally propounded in his contribution to the
1946 General Assembly resolution on genocide.[159]

Lemkin was thus operating at least at one level within a particular vein of Jewish
political thinking which continued to see value in the idea of diaspora Jews living
'together with' and 'alongside', not 'against', other ethnic communities.[160] Such
thinking was diametrically opposite to another vein, however, of which Schechtman was an arch-representative. That in itself should not surprise. Schechtman was
a revisionist Zionist, a close adherent of Vladimir Jabotinsky, and so of an immediate pre-war analysis which concluded that the Minorities system was dead, and
immediate, wholesale (albeit 'voluntary') evacuation of European Jewry—certainly
that of the rimlands—to a sovereign Eretz Israel was imperative. Jabotinsky, very
much in the language of a Cubrilović, had put the matter bluntly in 1939: 'If it is
possible to transfer the Baltic people [meaning ethnic Germans to the Reich] it is
also possible to move the Palestinian Arabs.'[161]

If this represented Zionist thinking of the time in its most radical form, what
matters for this discussion, however, is the manner in which the transfer model it
carried not only infiltrated the Zionist mainstream both simultaneously and in
succeeding years but also led to a more general Jewish realignment, if not around
the concept of transfer itself then certainly around the notion that the Jewish state
was the *only* guarantee preventing future Jewish victimhood. On the former score,
we may note the following assessment written by David Ben-Gurion in October
1941:

> In the present war the idea of transferring a population is gaining more sympathy as a
> practical and the most secure means of solving the dangerous and painful problem of
> national minorities. The war has already brought the resettlement of many peoples in
> Eastern and Southern Europe, and in the plans for post-war settlements the idea of a
> large-scale population transfer in Central, Eastern and Southern Europe increasingly
> occupies a respectable place.[162]

We may note that Ben-Gurion was at the time the acknowledged leader of the
Yishuv—the Jewish community in mandate Palestine—a socialist, and the man
who in 1948 would become Israel's first prime minister and leading statesman. We
may equally note that Ben-Gurion, in 1941, was directly picking up on the arguments then being heavily propounded by Beneš. In other words, if transfer was
good and respectable for the Czechs vis-à-vis the Sudeten Germans, it could equally
be good and respectable for the Jews vis-à-vis the Arabs. And if Ben-Gurion did
not state this implication directly, Chaim Weizmann, the renowned head of the
Jewish Agency for Palestine and future President of Israel, had already done so a
few months earlier in a personal conversation in which he had also presciently
noted that 'after this war the whole problem of exchange of populations will not be
such a taboo subject as it has before. It is going on now, and probably will become
part and parcel of the future settlement.'[163] To be sure, these statements were private and confidential. Britain was still very much in power in Palestine, and at that

time a relatively weak Zionist leadership felt constrained, or even ambiguous, about openly espousing an expulsion agenda. As for the consequences of a Zionist implementation of such an agenda, as it actually impacted on the indigenous Arab population of Palestine in the form of the *Nakba* (catastrophe) of 1947–8, that, as a set of events taking place outside our rimlands arena and, in part, as an episode of decolonization in some ways more akin to the Partition of India, we reserve the right to consider not here but in a further volume.

Insofar as these developments relate to the *European* 'transfer' sequence, however, what is striking is twofold. First, on Ben-Gurion's initiative, the leadership of the would-be Jewish state in Palestine mobilized its emissaries in Europe in a programme of what one might call 'do it yourself' transfer. Whereas Prague geared itself from the end of war towards getting all ethnic Germans *out* of Czech lands— preferably with the concurrence of Britain and the other Allies—in Tel-Aviv's case, its so-called *Bricha* ('escape') project centred round efforts to get hundreds of thousands of European Jewish Holocaust survivors *into* Palestine, both in defiance of the Mandatory power and in the teeth of Arab opposition. While in statistical terms this illegal migration movement was arguably not *that* efficacious—perhaps 30,000 refugees in old, hired, leaky boats actually running the British naval blockade of Palestine waters—*Bricha*'s wider purpose, to deliver a Western upsurge in support of the creation of a Jewish state, was phenomenally successful.[164] Second, in this way, the idea of Jewish refuge not only became firmly associated with statehood—especially with a US public—but also brought the vast majority of Jews world-wide into their own close, emotionally dependent relationship with, for, and behind Zionism.[165] Or put another way, Jews now looked to *their* state as guarantor that 'never again' would there be a Holocaust. Or, to return us to the subject of the Convention, while the vast majority henceforth would happily offer praiseworthy words for Lemkin's law, the practical choice between putting their trust in it, *on their own behalf*, as against having a strong national polity committed to sovereign action in the world on its own, *Jewish*, account, was crystal clear.

Yet in this widespread Jewish acclamation for Zionism we can surely read a further, searing paradox. We have seen how, considered through a Judaeophobic prism, a central charge against the Jews was that they stood aside from and were, indeed, entirely alien to the indigenous *nations* of Europe. During the Great War, and more especially Russian Revolution, a crude analysis of how this anti-national presence allegedly threatened the nations embedded itself in the notion of *Żydokomuna*. But in these pages we have never discounted the centrality of the Jewish contribution to radical, socialist, and more especially Marxist thought, or its visible, proactive aspect in the form of Jewish participation in revolutionary movements, both in Russia or elsewhere. To be sure, this participation was always representative of a minority Jewish tendency, particularly evident among its intelligentsia. But equally evident in that tendency was what one might call a Jewish universalism: a desire to treat (and to be treated by) all human beings as genuinely equal, regardless, of colour, creed, or background.[166]

Within Russia and the Eastern Bloc, primarily thanks to Stalin, any last vestiges of this universalism—negatively rebranded as 'rootless cosmopolitanism'—was suffocated out of existence. Indeed, 1948 was a key year in the take-off of the Soviet anti-Jewish campaign, in spite of Moscow's initial, again highly paradoxical, support for the Jewish state. But it was not only under communism that most Jews abandoned universalist idealism in favour of longings for Zion. Throughout the diaspora, deeply held assumptions about a continued Jewish life and security outside Israel began to falter, with that specific vein of Jewish cultural autonomism held by Lemkin and once large numbers of rimlands Bundists and the like all but extinguished. Because of the dialectics of Arab–Jewish conflict in Palestine, the scramble for the national life raft in 1948 was at its most intense and urgent in surrounding Arab and Muslim countries, where Jewish expulsions or flight, succeeding the Arab precedent from Israel, began to resemble the ethnic 'exchanges' from eastern Europe.[167] In the liberal West, the situation was more complex, a generalized Jewish support for Zionism, however, *not* translating into mass *aliyah*—emigration—in Israel's direction. There were even Jews in the West who continued to contest the national imperative, this minority position actually becoming more distinctively vocal in direct relation to Israel's intensifying coercion of, and violence towards, its Arab Palestinian population, particularly in the decades following Israel's post-1967 occupation of the so-called West Bank and Gaza strip. Some of this oppositional discourse was and continues to be framed in the language of human rights.[168] But, for all the wider utterances of Palestinian genocide, the notable absence of Lemkinian-style arguments espousing the UN Convention as the best tool for *prevention*—whether among Palestinians themselves, dissident Jews, or whoever—speaks for itself. For most post-*Nakba* Palestinians, as for most post-Holocaust Jews, the guarantee of security continued and continues to lie in their *own* nation state. And in the majority Jewish case, certainly, that brings with it forms of collective psychological denial as to the extent and scale of the violence perpetrated by theirs, or the more simple apologia that all is justifiable in a world which had abandoned their forbears to genocide.[169]

But there is one further clue as to why the Convention in 1948, and beyond, had little practical relevance specifically for traumatized rimlands survivors, Jewish or otherwise, or those in turn impacted upon by their displacement. It offered no sense of their historic relationship to what in all probability was, or at least had been, a cherished *local* habitus. The Convention's reference to their existence as 'national, ethnic, racial or religious groups' was all well and good, but read as if entirely abstracted out from any recognition that the traditional social, economic, and very possibly spiritual existence of a community was enmeshed with and likely to have been built upon the assurance of a stable, time-honoured space, even one *shared* with other peoples, not to mention other creatures. The omission of deportation as an act of genocide in the Convention's text is indicative of this abstractization. But perhaps what is more disturbing is how the omission simply reflects a modernism lacking not only empathy with, but simple cognition of, a world destroyed. In the 'realist' post-war order, where sovereign, territorialized and homogenized societies were both what constituted the polity of nations and what counted in international relations, Lemkin's efforts were certainly 'distinctive', but also utterly 'quixotic',[170] and, alas—certainly at the moment of the

Convention's adoption—with no practical purchase whatsoever on the conduct of nation states.

A NEW DIRECTION OF TRAVEL?

In a sentence which conjures up the deep, underlying, historical *and* geographical significance of the new post-war ordering, Andzej Paczkowski reminds us how it was 'from beyond the Wieprz, the Narew, the Vistula, the Pilica and the Warta rivers' that some 2.7 million Poles came to resettle the lands to the west, forcibly taken over from Germany.[171] In these events, it was not a matter of the 'Lands Between' becoming the 'Lands Beyond'. Instead, it was the closing down of the rimlands forever. And as we have seen repeatedly in these pages, the rivers themselves were not just the incidental boundaries of these great human changes; more often than not, they were actual sites in which the mass murder of people was enacted. The Bug, Dniester, Sava, Drina, Euphrates, and Tigris, and a whole host of other rivers too: their ravines, alluvial plains, fast-flowing stretches, and key bridging points were aspects of a geography of death in which the symbolic, sometimes highly ritualized, performance and spectacle of people-extirpation took place.

But in all this there was something more than the genocidal trashing of a landscape. In the state-sanctioned extirpation of the rimlands there was a conscious consigning to the dustbin of history of the rich ethnographic possibilities inherent within them. Possibilities whose regional and local markers, often as not, had been provided through rivers or, for that matter, mountain watersheds. It was as if one's sense of personal and communal relationship to an environment, more specifically of emotional connection to hearth and home, brook and meadow, place of worship, and family graveyard, had by state warrant and, above that, by international diktat been declared null and void, not to say utterly illegitimate. No longer could one be allowed to be simply *tutejszy*: a human being from some localized 'here'.[172] Nor, as Wielkopolanians and Pomerarians attempted to do when their landscape was swamped from 1945—ironically by those very same self-identifying *tutejszy*— unfurl the banner of regionalism in their defence of place.[173] The greater irony in all this was that it was these very same rimlands country folk, the sedentary and the perambulating passers through, the *shtetl* dwellers and transhumant pastoralists, who, while holding on tenaciously to the peculiarity of their sometimes obscure and (by the standards of modernity) entirely outworn social, religious, and folkloric practices were also, at the same time, the ones who were traditionally the *most* indifferent to difference; the very people who accepted that others lived among them, recognized the ties of interdependence and the value, often even where eschewing direct friendship, of neighbourly relations.[174]

And so it was, too, in the great towns and even cities of the rimlands. While the winds of modernity were the very factor which made the ethnic divisions sharper and more tense, fin-de-siècle Lemberg, Cernowitz, Vilna, or, for that matter, Constantinople, Smyrna, and Salonika, under their diverse, communally-ascribed names, were living proof that people of different religions, languages, and cultures were perfectly capable of living together. The very suppression of these names and of the multiple designations which represented their polyglot glory were, more than often not, however, the vandalistic sequel to the more directly barbaric practice. Where vast proportions of their urban populations were not either directly killed, or dispersed, to concentration or labour camps, their most obvious fate was to be cleared out to some entirely alien country of which they knew little or nothing. To be sure, it was the most radical post-imperial protagonists who proved the most powerfully energetic and murderous drivers of such rimlands fury. That said, one might equally debate whether it was less Nazi or CUP dreams of colonial conquest and settlement or, for that matter, Soviet communist ones of worldwide revolution, and more their perceived back-to-the-wall efforts at some 'great' *national* revival and consolidation, which proved to be at the root of their respective longings. What is entirely clear is that our rimlands sequence which began in the Ottoman Balkans in 1912–13 and culminated in the very heartlands of Central Europe in 1945–8, was an undiluted victory for the nation-state cause. Again, without the USSR to foster that cause, the manner in which great German imperial cities such as Breslau and Danzig were translated into Polish Wrocław and Gdansk would not have been conceivable. Yet when the Soviets themselves, having obliterated the equally culturally resplendent, former East Prussian, once Teutonic Knights' capital of Königsberg, mercilessly ethnically cleansed its remaining German population, and then absorbed it as Kaliningrad into the *Russian* federation, was this not, too, as strong a signifier as any of Slavic national revenge enacted over and beyond geo-strategic interest?[175]

The almost complete repopulation of cities such as these, as of those even more obviously polyethnic ones further to the now Ukrainian, Belarusian, and Lithuanian east, with incomers who had no historic or emotional connection with what had come before, determined a complete foreclosure on ancient habits of live-and-let-live. How could it have been otherwise? Without knowledge or memory or (hence) empathy with this very different past, the descendants of these settlers, whether in town or country alike—and constricted and constrained as they also were by communist education and the social regimentation of communist life— could only look askance on the now outside voices who talked of murdered communities, lost homes, and, sometimes, the desire for return.[176] As Krystyna Kersten notes of post-war Poland:

> Weakening of the social fabric was combined with the narrowing of national communities and the rise of xenophobia. Mistrust towards foreigners became a permanent fixture on the Polish stage, as did the conviction that everything foreign represented a lethal threat. Polish society acquired a sort of national unity that abolished the previous social, cultural and religious diversity.[177]

Which is what the demographic planners and policymakers wanted. In this respect, post-1946 Poland had aspects in common with a post-1923 Turkey. The Kemalists, too, as the Ittihadists before them, had envisaged a national society in which the intrinsic communal diversity of all the country's displaced people could be put to one side in favour of a state-determined assimilating present and cohered, unitary future. In this aspiration, the very nature of the previous decade (or decades) of catastrophe, in which traditional 'place' became 'no place', favoured the social engineers. Having already eructed or murdered most of the Armenians and Greeks, the anthropophagic path was reserved for all the (mostly) Muslims who remained, with the Turkish national curriculum the key to the developmental trajectory.[178] And herein lay exactly the parallel path trod by Poland's post-war elite. With the Germans evicted west, the Ukrainians east, and the Jews mostly dead, the project rested on turning all those lukewarm Poles from the *kresy* into proper nationalists, and getting their Silesian and Mazurian equivalents—the ones who so recently had pragmatically opted for the Volksliste—to be properly 'verified' as Poles, rather than just pretending to be so. As Aleksander Zawadzki, the first governor of Opole Silesia pithily put it, 'We won't allow any covering over German meat with Polish gravy. We must tell us ourselves firmly that in Opole region the exclusive and only rulers are the Poles.'[179]

The Nazis would have called it *Gleichschaltung*. Perhaps 'lowest common denominator nationalism' will do as a less lofty alternative. But looked at through the nationalizing prism, the key to success would seem to have been first turning a population upside down and inside out, thereby casting out or directly eliminating (or having eliminated for one) the elements the state did not want, and thus enabling it to fit the human residue into the prescribed template. After all, at least post-war Poland could *begin* with a population which was more or less subscribing to the national designation. Before the war, it had only constituted three-fifths. Czechoslovakia, by contrast, had seen much less internal displacement among its dominant nations but was undoubtedly doing well in the homogenizing stakes just by expelling its ethnic Germans. In 1930, they had represented 29 per cent of Bohemia and Moravia's population. By 1950, they constituted a mere 1.8 per cent.[180] However, if one wanted to consider really striking post-war national success stories, then perhaps the most obvious place to turn would be to the two most ubiquitous communities of the rimlands, certainly of the 'Lands Between'.

To speak of Jews and ethnic Germans in these terms sounds crass given their immediate pasts of extermination or violent expulsion. Yet the fact is that the two post-war Germanies on the one hand, Israel on the other, offer as good models as any for how to reformulate cohesive national polities out of the broken shards. In the western German Federal Republic most particularly, where thanks to US and British reception efforts 28 per cent of the population, even in 1960, were expellees, the post-war 'economic miracle' was in considerable part made possible on the back of the plentifully cheap but skilled labour provided by the expellees: an alternative economic route, if one likes, to what a Hitler or Himmler, a few years earlier, might have described as 'Reich strengthening'.[181] As for Israel, the overwhelmingly majority Jewish element of its post-independence population was either made up of displaced rimlands Europeans or dislocated Middle Eastern ones—a melange of very diverse refugee peoples if ever there was one but supposedly forged into a single entity through an entirely top-down, dirigiste programme of cultural integration, social engineering, spatial dispersal, and both military and educational inculcation of the state's national civic values.[182] Just as *Stunde Null* was the disaster catalyzing the social, demographic, and economic reorganization upon which Germany's rise to re-eminence in renewed Europe was founded, so the entirely new Jewish state's drive to its own technocratic and military power was shaped and legitimated through the crucible of the Holocaust and the further life and death struggle of the 1948 War of Independence.

At which point, reading into this narrative a case of unmitigated 'success' becomes rather dependent on one's point of view. Orest Subtelny's argument, for instance, speaking of the mass post-war Ukrainian–Polish exchange as 'the necessary precondition for the development of a mutually beneficial relationship between them'—adding for good measure that 'good fences make for good neighbours'[183]— apart from its dubious assertion in its own context, could only be applied to the case of Israel and its neighbours if one was suffering from a surfeit of sardonic irony. But then the cynic is faced with a question: how would *you* have made it better? We are back with Pangloss and the problem of imagining alternative, non-genocidal paths in place of the ones with which we have been concretely presented.

Is it thus naive, or even out of order, to ask: could it have been different? Supposing there had been no Balkan Wars, no assassinations at Sarajevo, or even then, if the warring powers of Europe had managed to settle for peace before the Central Powers had to sue for it, tragically too late for the Armenians, but saving the Turks from the humiliation of Sèvres, the Germans from Versailles (and thus Hitler)— even sparing Russia from revolution? As I write this, I am struck by more than simply the argument's counterfactuality, but its almost ludicrous implausibility. If not exactly through these specific events, surely the inbuilt structural tensions would have worked through some way, somewhere, and in the process confirmed the underlying toxicity within the European ménage? What matters, therefore, is not where and when the touchpaper was lit, but that the whole edifice was already primed to explode. That would make war in general, our specific sequence of wars in particular, the great accelerator, perhaps even, once begun, the central driving force for genocide. But to simply blame war itself for genocide, divorced from an underlying causative mechanism, would be to fail to get to the heart of the matter. After all, there were opportunities in the relatively peaceful years of the mid-1920s not only for reflection on communal relationships within states but even, albeit very ephemerally, as they affected relationships between states. This is why we spent a chapter in Volume One of this study exploring whether there were still paths by which Europeans, especially but not exclusively rimlands Europeans, might overcome their refusal to see in communal social, cultural, as well as political difference anything other than intractability and threat. And what did we get instead in this supposed peaceful intermission? Mass Turkish onslaught on its Kurds.

So does this bring us back either to deep, underlying aspects of hostility between different groups of peoples, or perhaps, to speak more historically, to some *learnt* tendency to hate? The centrality to this study of the Nazi genocide/s of the Jews presents hatred, as translated into an ideology of race, as the one most often repeated master concept explaining the urge to genocide. Yet convenient as it might be simply to confirm this conventional wisdom, it actually tells us both so much and so little about the causes of the phenomenon. Of course, nineteenth-century racial and hereditary theories, as most dramatically adopted by the Nazis as the very basis of their social system, became the raison d'être for a whole raft of policies geared towards subordinating and segregating not only Jews but also Roma and actually a whole swathe of supposedly *echt* Germans, on the grounds that they posed a threat to the biological health of the nation. One of the paradoxes of this situation is that programmes of sterilization were generally not applied to the former but to the latter two groups in very great numbers. However, assuming Jewry's alleged intrinsic inferiority, or even biological contamination of German blood, as pretext for extermination is wholly more difficult to fathom, let alone square with the evolving, contingent circumstances in which it took place. The same would also be true of other cases of genocide where race undoubtedly was a prominent and potent factor, as for instance in mid-1970s Cambodia and 1994 Rwanda. But in both these instances it is difficult to imagine race operating independently of other variables. That said, turned on its head, it *is* perfectly possible to envisage the persistence of racial prejudices in the absence of genocide. Consider, for instance, the manner in which Roma have continued to be not only the butt of widespread, European grass-roots antipathies through to the present day, but also the specific focus of ongoing 'criminal' research in the German Federal Republic well into the 1970s; and, to boot, using the same Ritter archives and involving some of the very same racial 'experts' who had advised the Nazi Interior Ministry.[184] Or, for that matter, consider the sometimes virulently phobic, anti-Jewish statements which continued to be articulated by the German and East European public, including religious figures, *after* the Holocaust.[185]

The persistence of specifically anti-Jewish hatred might lend itself to the further argument that what is at stake is not racial hostility writ large but an entirely sui generis condition of anti-Semitism. Clearly, the approach here has been to distance ourselves from any notion that genocide was peculiarly enacted against the Jews, even while at the same time iterating that anti-Jewish hatred was very real, much more generally European than anything specifically German, not to mention producing, in tandem with *other factors*, a people-destruction in a class of its own. Indeed, the Holocaust is all the more problematic not only because of its scale but also because its origins extend way back beyond the emergence of the modern nation state to a world in which contested religious world-systems, even paradoxically initially closely related ones, really did matter. That is part of the reason why we have generally favoured the term Judaeophobia over anti-Semitism, not least as it conjures up supernatural, even cosmic powers ascribed to the Jews, which were at the root of Christian theological and, by extension, popular fantasies and anxieties. What has been particularly relevant to our discussion in this study, however, is the manner in which this medieval Judaeophobic mindset was not simply re-seeded in the churned up soil of modernity but became entangled at the fatal 1914–18 juncture of pan-European crisis with competing views of international relations. Or, to put it in its starkest form, Jews were mass-murdered a world war later *not* because they were a specific ethno-religious group but because they were *seen* as *the* global political constellation which had to be overcome if international relations were to be re-set on their proper course: the gospel according to Hitler, of course, and one which at its core regurgitated the notion of an international Jewish conspiracy as if it were unimpeachable fact. All the more reason, one might argue, not to dismiss this deranged, paranoid Nazi view of the world as an irrelevance but to actually seek to understand its genocidal implications. The fact that contemporaneously, nearly all Jews, and nearly all liberal Western commentators, could not conceive of what Hitler, large numbers of Germans, or, for that matter, many other especially rimlands European collaborators were going on about, simply makes the dichotomy between the Nazi will to mass murder and Jewish individual and communal powerlessness in its face all the more jarring. Nevertheless, the Nazis killed Jews in the context of war because they viewed them as the ultimate security threat: the ultimate obstacle to the defeat both of liberal system *and* Soviet anti-system.[186]

But, in stating it thus, our argument about Nazi motivational drives actually goes some way to closing the gap between the aetiology of this genocide and most (if not necessarily all) the other genocides we have surveyed in this study. It is, perhaps, valuable at this point to register a German poll conducted by the USA in its zone of control in November 1946. In response to the question 'Do you consider that the extermination of Jews and Poles and non-Aryans was *necessary* for the *security* of *Germany*?', 37 per cent of respondents said 'yes'. But it is not so much the large numbers in agreement which might most surprise, as the telling phraseology of the question.[187] Interestingly, the *génocidaire* that most scholars of the subject would readily reach for as arch-exponent of the security paradigm would not be Hitler but Stalin. Yet he did so, time and time again, without directly drawing on race; in fact, officially refuting its admissibility when seeking a casus belli for his multiple attacks on Soviet and non-Soviet communities and peoples. As the unlovely expression goes, 'there are more ways than one of skinning a cat'.

However, Stalin was not averse to reference to nations. The whole communist relationship to the 'national question' we have seen to be an extraordinarily convoluted one. Nevertheless, the Soviet anti-system, not least thanks to Stalin's own early role as commissar for nationalities, accepted the nation as an authentic actor on the world stage and, within the Soviet constellation, as an appropriate framework for development. It is equally true that, doctrinally, the USSR evinced serious ambiguities about the historic role of Russian chauvinism in particular, and looked forward to a day when the whole panoply of Soviet national units could be dispensed with as part of the debris of communism's victorious struggle over capitalism. But in the interim the party accepted the nation's normative function, as indeed the very notion of nation states (republics) operating within—even while, perhaps, seeking to bring down—an international system of such nation states. Moreover, Stalin's own increasingly *rossiyskiy*, if less overtly *russkii*-informed world view ensured that security meant the defence of Russia as much as that of Soviet communism.[188] The consequences are self-evident, in the elimination of border peoples, even where that meant the folding up of *their* national republics. Clearly, some nations were more equal than others.

Which makes Stalin's championship of the pre-existing nation-state units of Eastern Europe at the end of the Second World War, and, with that, support for the ethnic cleansing of their *own* most unwanted national 'minorities', all the more revealing. After all, if we went back to the war's beginning and took Poland as an obvious case study, it rather looked as if Stalin entirely concurred with Nazi ideologue Rosenberg's view that 'twenty years of independence have shown that absolute sovereignty of small peoples wedged between two great states is unthinkable'. The inference is reinforced when we note that Molotov, in June 1940, told the Lithuanian leadership 'that in the present state of international politics, small nations are a complete anomaly'.[189] By the time of Soviet 'liberation', some 'New Europe' leaders may have been expecting exactly the same fate.[190] Thus, even discounting the sort of pulverization the Poles had suffered in the two years of the Soviet–Nazi accord, an equally plausible post-1945 scenario could have been a Soviet version of what the German High Command had contemplated on both sides of the old Russian border in the wake of Brest-Litovsk: namely, conscious emasculation of the then would-be national states by territorial readjustment, combined with greater support for the national minority elements within them. And given the clear insufficiency of cadres from the national majorities in most of these would-be communist party-led state apparatuses in 1945, it made some considerable sense to favour the national minorities (Jews included) from whom the communists could often draw greater support. The communists were nothing if not pragmatic: problems of party recruitment in Rumania and Hungary, for instance, leading them at the war's end to encourage Iron Guard and Arrow Cross fascists to migrate en masse into their own ranks.[191] But Stalin himself did not simply pick and mix when it came to the national question. On the contrary, his unequivocal endorsement of the 'New Europe' formula was as clear a statement as imaginable that the USSR in 1945 was accepting the basic political building blocks which the liberal system had inscribed for the region back in 1919. What Potsdam also demonstrated was that, just as the two anti-systems had previously colluded in a people-reordering of that same arena with all the genocidal potential which went with it, so this time round, the surviving anti-system, in collaboration with the hegemonic system, was also perfectly capable of its own lethal reordering act. To be sure, liberal system terms and conditions demanded that *this* sequence had to demonstrate peacefulness and restraint. But, at the same time, one could hardly gainsay that what the Potsdam parties were in the broadest sense seeking was a final stabilization of the region. In practice, that could only mean violent erasure of its multicultural—hence rimlands—aspects. Through this radical reaffirmation of the nation-state formula, the crisis of the semi-periphery, heralded by the shattering of the European empires in the period 1912–21, was finally brought to resolution.

*

In no sense, of course, had the expurgation of the rimlands brought the global struggle for dominance to a peaceful conclusion. It was perceived communal security threats *within* European states which had been stilled, not those between the emerging blocs of such states. True, the Jewish case was a reminder that a non-state actor could still be conjured up into a phantasmagoric threat encompassing both categories. In the heightened projection of the early Cold War period, the unleashing of such a potential still remained a possibility in spite of Hitler's best efforts to kill all Jews.[192]

But then the Jewish question had a new *normative* nation-state locus: for and against Israel. Here was a small facet of an emerging post-war global reality: the shift away from Europe. The rimlands had been shut down and, until partially reawakened at the end of the Cold War, there would be no more European or near-European genocides until the early 1990s. And until then, too, no more European war. To be sure, for the majority peoples of Europe or those now forcibly absorbed into them, the price itself was high, most particularly for those who now found themselves in what Judt has aptly called the communist 'prison-yard'.[193] Behind this Iron Curtain, dissent was a state crime, incarceration in prison or labour camp, even execution, the most extreme penalties on a spectrum of intimidating state security practices designed to enforce tight, blanket social control.[194] Though such practices were hardly exclusive to the eastern half of the continent: in Francoist Spain, long into the post-war era, tens of thousands of republicans from the civil war period were still incarcerated in labour camps as seeming proof that the Western hegemons were ready and willing to turn a blind eye to a hard European authoritarianism—not to say a regime whose existence had been predicated on Axis support—providing it covertly offered its airspace to the USA.[195] But the fact is that on both sides of the Iron Curtain, having completed their geopolitical trade-offs, what were now deemed the leaders of the 'Free World' as well as their communist adversaries, left it to their European nation-state minions—so long as they operated within agreed, respective system boundaries—to set their own state-orientated developmental goals. The result may have been very different societal complexions in East and West. One notable facet was that while Eastern Europe became much more homogenized, Western Europe, in its insatiable drive for cheap, industrial labour, became—certainly in its urban centres—much more multi-cultural. This, in turn, sparked off an entirely new range of ethnic and religious tensions than that which had marked rimlands heterogeneity before 1945. That said, for most ordinary post-war Europeans, from whatever background and for most of the time, it was making a living and seeking to fulfil consumer aspirations within the highly structured, fiercely competitive, albeit cooperatively tailored economic environment—as exemplified in the West by the growth and evolution of the European Economic Community (later European Union)—which became their central focus and raison d'être.

In a strange way, therefore, while post-war Europeans, particularly Western ones, would later embrace the 'memory' of the Holocaust, tangible, contemporaneous realities of war and genocide became strangely distant from their quotidian experience or understanding—even while waves of mass murder were perpetrated in abundance elsewhere. For, indeed, the struggle for global dominance had hardly abated. Goebbels, towards the end of the war, had correctly predicted that the struggle between Germans and Allies would be quickly succeeded by another one between Allies and Soviets, though he got it wrong when he thought this would quickly explode into all-out war which the Soviets would then win.[196] But then, for any astute commentator, Russia and the West as Allies had never been more than a blip, a case of having been of necessity thrown together by Hitler's menace, thereby masking the true long-term contest between them.[197]

What was truly different about the post-war situation, however, was the canvas upon which this contest was now being prepared. Europe might still be symbolically the epicentre of struggle, but to all intents and purposes Mackinder's 'Heartland' thesis was rendered redundant in the face of an emerging bipolar competition more sub-Saharan, Middle Eastern, Indian subcontinental, and merging into eastern Pacific in its range, than anything obviously Eurasian. This hardly prevented either side from shamelessly ransacking the Nazi imperial toolkit of genocidal violence in their respective bids for technological and military advantage. At the end of the war, US, British, and Soviet intelligence units feverishly worked their way through all available Nazi documentation they could independently lay their hands on, including from the camps, for information on how far Germany had got in its nuclear, chemical, and biological warfare programmes.[198] The Soviets dismantled the V-2 rocket sites, the rockets themselves largely built by concentration camp slave labour—and took them home along with their engineers. Meanwhile, the USA still managed to pocket chief rocketeer Wernher von Braun and some of his core team.[199] The CIA also added to their eventual tally a bevy of SS spy-masters and 'intelligence gatherers', and for good measure some other 'expert' rimlands practitioners, one of whom was the leading UPA *génocidaire* Mykola Lebed.[200]

One could continue with this particular theme, enumerating all the Nazi and collaborationist leaders who seemed to slip through Western intelligence fingers as they made their escapes by 'ratlines' to safe South American or other destinations.[201] Or, for that matter, focus on how some of the emerging Cold War military applications were first used in some of the last acts of rimlands mega-violence. Napalm B, for instance, was deployed in 1949 at US behest by Greek government troops in the final attacks on ELAS positions on the Albanian border, as one might expect with suitably devastating effect.[202] But as always in such cases, to focus on the minutiae, however ugly and gruesome, is to risk missing the bigger picture. And that, in the aftermath of Allied victory, was all about neither rimlands, nor semi-periphery, but colonial periphery.

With the creation of a United Nations, whatever Britain and other European colonial powers had anticipated, the stage was set for a major shift towards decolonization on the one hand, and the emergence of new nation states on the other. There had been a mere fifty-one such entities within the UN in 1945. Two decades later, there were 117. By the end of the century there were 189.[203] Yet the very creation of polities within this already prescribed and predetermined formulation meant that each and every one would have to go through the same processes of cultural homogenization, economic alignment to the international marketplace (or its Soviet command economy equivalent), and political consolidation, in effect according to the diktats of the hegemonic supervisors of the system. Of course, this was no more nor less than what was expected of, and enthusiastically accepted by, rimlands national political elites as they took on the mantle of independent, sovereign statehood in the wake of Romanov, Habsburg, and Ottoman imperial collapse. As with them, then, so now with the periphery national elites, the onus would be on transforming with celerity societally complex, disparate, polyglot communities of peoples into polities which were sufficiently coherent and unitary to withstand the onerous demands of global interdependence. The alternative would be to fall behind, or indeed, as the empires had themselves earlier feared as the rough winds of Western-led modernization swept over them, to enter into new forms of neo-colonial subservience.

It was ironic, in one sense, that the successor generation of former rimlands state actors were buttressed from the worst vicissitudes of these social-Darwinian ground-rules by none other than the Cold War. The unwillingness of either US or Russian hegemons to destabilize the Potsdam settlement ensured for all Europe a sort of protectionist zone in which their leaderships, by democratic mandate or not, might pursue radical developmental goals if they so wished, or for that matter relatively sluggish paths towards economic change, yet with the guarantee that there would be no existential threat to the fact of their *statehoods*. To be sure, there were moments when European states, particularly East European ones, were gripped by crisis—and violence. But these moments, 1956, 1968, and 1981, were when particular states had seemed as if they might break with the diktats of their system leader, or put another way, with the terms of the Cold War 'arrangement'. And, indeed, from below. Until the political crisis of Yugoslavia on the cusp of the 1990s (and that state itself a sort of exception to the 'arrangement' rule), when not only did it unravel but this lead to short-cut crisis management by competing, fissiparous elites within it, the possibilities of genocide in post-war Europe remained remote.

In the post-war *periphery*, by contrast, the situation was entirely distinct. The very fact of having to cohere at speed in the vortex of rapidly accelerating global economic change represented for an emerging phalanx of post-colonial states a crisis from the very start. Add to that, that their urges to nationhood—whether coherently organized or not—were played out against the backdrop and volatility of the bipolar struggle in which the new nation, or would-be nation, itself might represent contested superpower terrain, and the threat of acute destabilization, or even fragmentation, could only be amplified. Finally, throw in a legacy of Western racism, misrepresentation, and ongoing hegemonic control,[204] and we have suffi-cient reasons already for anticipating that the export of the Western national for-mula to the 'Third World' would bring with it the export of genocide. Events during the two years of the drafting of the Genocide Convention, in India, Pales-tine, Madagascar, and the Dutch East Indies, were no more than portents of things to come.

Major Incidents of Genocide and Sub-Genocidal Violence: Rimlands and Near-Regions, 1912–53

The list of incidents below—most of which are discussed in *The Crisis of Genocide*—all involved aspects of mass exterminatory violence or a response to its threat. On a spectrum of genocide, I have emboldened cases which, *in my view*, fall squarely within that rubric. The caveat of partial genocide, usually meaning that the assault was geographically limited or not ultimately brought by the perpetrators to completion, might be cross-referenced with the UN Genocide Convention formula of acts of group destruction 'in whole or part'. The list is not intended as an authoritative statement but rather as a shorthand guide to the repeat incidence of genocidal events, primarily in the rimlands. The list does not include incidents outside a specific Eurasian range.

BALKAN WARS

1912–12 Balkan peninsula, Macedonia including parts of Albania, mass ethnic cleansing of Muslims, Albanians, Bulgarians, Greeks, Serbs by respective parties (first contemporary 'war of all against all')

1913 Balkan peninsula, Macedonia/eastern Rhodope, forced conversions by Serbs of 'Bulgars' and of Pomaks by Bulgarians

1913 Balkan peninsula, Luma district, Dibra region, Serb-Montenegrin destruction of Albanian villages, **partial genocide**

1913 eastern Thrace, Rodosto-Malgara area, CUP extermination of Bulgarians, **partial genocide**

1914 western Anatolia, Turkish deportations and ethnic cleansing of Aegean Greeks

1914 Balkan peninsula (Macedonia), projected Bulgar-Greek-Turk 'exchanges' of population

FIRST WORLD WAR (THE GREAT WAR)

1914 Franco-German borderlands, localized German military massacres of Belgian and French civilians in war zone

1914–15 Russian western and south-western border regions, mass Russian military deportations and atrocities against Germans, Jews, and Transcaucasian Muslim communities

1915 Serbia and Albania, Central Power and Albanian massacres of Serbs, including mass flight (and death) of part of Serb population to Aegean coast

1915–16, eastern Anatolia and Syrian desert, CUP extermination of Ottoman Armenians (the *Aghet*), **genocide**

1915–16 eastern Anatolia, CUP attempted destruction and flight of Hakkâri Nestorians (Assyrians), localized destruction of other Syriac communities (*Sayfo*), **genocide**

1916 Turkestan (Central Asia), Semirechye region, military and settlers' assaults on rebelling Kazakh, Dungan, and Kirghiz nomads, including their flight into China, **partial genocide**

1916–17 eastern Anatolia, mass CUP forcible resettlement of Kurdish, including Dersim tribes, in direction of central and western Anatolia

1917–19 eastern Anatolia and Transcaucasia, 'war of all against all', involving Turks, Kurds, Armenians, and Azeris

FIRST WORLD WAR AFTERMATH

1919 Thrace, Greek-Bulgarian 'voluntary' population exchange

1919 Croatia, violent Serb repression of peasant insurrection

1919 Kosovo (Pec region), violent Serb repression of Albanian insurrection

1919 Hungary, 'White Terror'

1919 Baltic region, Freikorps 'White Terror'

1919 southern Russia, Don region, extending into Kuban region, Bolshevik attempted 'Decossackization'

1919–20 Polish-Soviet borderlands, Polish localized military massacres against Jews

1919–20 Ukraine and southern Russia, widespread Petliurist and 'White' military massacres against Jews, **partial genocide**

1920 Crimea mass Bolshevik killings of 'White' Wrangelists

1919–20 eastern Anatolia and Cilicia (Marash and Mersin districts), continuing Armenian versus Kurdish and Turkish conflict, including mutual ethnic cleansing

1920–1 north Caucasus, Bolshevik suppression of Chechen insurrection (*Ghazawat*)

1921 north Caucasus, Terek region, localized Cossack deportations by Bolsheviks

1921 southern Russia, Bolshevik destruction of Tambov insurrection (*Antonovshchina*, 'a Russian Vendée')

1921–3 eastern Thrace, western Anatolia, Black Sea (Pontus) region, Greek and Turk mutual massacres during Turkish War of Independence, culminating in mass ethnic cleansing of Anatolian Greek communities, **partial genocide**

INTERWAR PERIOD

1920–5 Soviet central Asia, Semirechye region and Ferghana valley, Bolshevik suppression of Basmachi revolt, including massacres and man-made famine

1925 eastern Anatolia, suppression of Kurdish Shaik Said revolt ('a Turkish Vendée')

1925–6 north Caucasus, renewed Soviet military suppression of Chechen autonomists

1927 Crimea, Soviet purge of Ibrahimovists begins

1930 eastern Anatolia, Mardin-Agri regions, Turkish suppression of Hoybun (Kurdish-Armenian uprising)

1930–2 USSR, including borderlands, dekulakization and collectivization of peasantry, **partial genocide**

1932–3 Ukraine, Don, Kuban, Kazakhstan, Volga, north Caucasus, Soviet regime-induced 'terror-famine' (*Holodomor* in Ukraine), **partial genocide/s**
1933 northern Iraq, Mosul region, aborted Iraqi military destruction of Assyrians ('Assyrian affair')
1935–6 Soviet western (including Baltic) and Caucasian borderlands, frontier deportations of Poles, Germans, Ingerians, Finns, and Kurds
1937 Soviet far east, Korean deportations to Kazakhstan and elsewhere
1937–8 USSR, including borderlands, NKVD (*Ezhovshchina*) mass operations
1937–8 Soviet borderlands, specific NKVD 'national operations' geared especially towards alleged Polish, German, Baltic, and Greek 'anti-Soviet' elements
1937–8 eastern Anatolia, Turkish military destruction of Dersim Kurds, **genocide**
1938 Kosovo, Serbs plan for 'voluntary' transfer of ethnic Albanians to Turkey
1938 Germany and Nazi-occupied Austria, amplification of attack on Jews, culminating in *Kristallnacht*

SECOND WORLD WAR

1939 Poland, localized 'ethnic' massacres in course of Nazi (and Soviet) invasions
1939 Polish western borderlands, Nazi massacres, including gas extermination killings of Roma, Jewish, Polish, and German disabled or psychiatric patients
1939–40 Soviet borderlands, mass Nazi evacuations of Volksdeutsche (ethnic Germans)
1939–40 Polish western borderlands, Nazi mass ethnic cleansing of Poles, Jews, and Roma (cross-reference with ethnic German 'evacuations' above)
1939–41 central Poland (General Government), deportations to ghettos, leading to mass death of Jews and Roma from western Poland and central Europe (including Nisko project), plus Nazi murders of Polish elite elements in AB and subsequent *Aktionen*
1939–40 Carpatho-Rus, Slovakia, southern Dobrudja, and northern Transylvania, radical 'exchanges' of Bulgarians, Rumanians, Hungarians, Czechs, and Jews begins, following Nazi-sponsored border rectifications
1940 western USSR, Soviet extermination of majority of Polish army officers and other elite elements held in camps (Katyn massacres)
1940–1 Soviet borderlands, mass NKVD deportations of elements of Polish, Baltic, eastern Galician, and Moldavian peoples to east
1941 Rumania, Bucharest, Iron Guard massacre of Jews, during attempted coup
1941 Soviet borderlands (including Crimea), NKVD massacres of borderland prison populations in response to Nazi invasion (Operation Barbarossa)
1941 Soviet borderlands, especially Baltic and western Ukraine, 'revenge' massacres against Jews by communal and local 'national' borderland police/military, under cover of Operation Barbarossa
1941 Soviet borderlands, Baltic to southern Russia, Operation Barbarossa first wave of SS and Wehrmacht mass exterminations of Soviet Jews (and Roma), **genocide**
1941 Soviet borderlands, Operation Barbarossa, mass Wehrmacht murder of Soviet POWs by starvation
1941 Rumanian borderlands including 'Transnistria', Antonescu regime deportation and or destruction of Bessarabian, north Bukovinan, and south Ukrainian Jews (and Roma), **genocide**
1941 Volga region, Russia, NKVD deportation of Volga Germans to Kazakhstan and east
1941–2 Croatia (NDH) including Bosnia-Herzegovina, Ustasha extermination of Jews and Roma, and deportation or direct massacre of Serbs, **genocide/s**

1941–2, Slovenia, Nazi deportation of part of Slovene population from annexed region into Croatia

1941–42 Nazi-controlled Serbia, Nazi massacres of Serbs, and extermination of Serbian Jews and male Roma, **genocide**

1941–2 Nazi-occupied Ukraine and Greece, facilitation of famine conditions leading to mass death in major cities

1941–2 Nazi-occupied Poland and Soviet borderlands, SS-directed mass deportation, and first exterminations of central European Jews, **genocide**

1941–2 Nazi-occupied Soviet borderlands, SS-directed second exterminatory wave against Soviet Jewry, **genocide**

1942 Hungarian-occupied Serbia (Délvidék), Hungarian military massacres of Serbs and Jews

1942 Czech lands, Nazi-perpetrated Lidice and Ležacky massacres

1942–3 General Government, SS-directed destruction of Polish Jewry (Operation Reinhard), and both local and deported Roma, **genocide**

1942–3, General Government, Zamość district, SS-directed mass ethnic cleansing of Poles

1942–4, General Government and Auschwitz, 'Final Solution' deportations of Jews from entire European continent to death camps, **genocide**

1942–4 Bosnia, Croatia, Serbia, Kosovo, Montenegro, Macedonia, Partisan-Chetnik-Ustasha et al., 'wars of all against all', plus Axis operations against Partisans

1942–4 Nazi-occupied Soviet borderlands, centring on Belorussian Pripet region, repeated anti-partisan sweeps leading to creation of 'dead zones'

1943–4 Nazi-occupied Soviet borderlands, western Volhynia, centring on Rivne-Sarny-Kostopol triangle, Ukrainian Insurgent Army (UPA) extermination of Poles, mass Polish flight, and beginning of local 'war of all against all', **genocide**

1943–4 Soviet Caucasus, Crimea, and southern Russia, NKVD deportation of specific Muslim ethnic peoples and Buddhist Kalmyks (the 'Punished Peoples'), **partial genocide**

1944 General Government, suppression of Polish national uprising in Warsaw, including systematic revenge massacres and destruction of city, 'urbicide' and **partial genocide**

1944 Auschwitz, destruction of Hungarian Jews, **genocide**

1944 Auschwitz, highpoint of Central European Roma destruction (*Porrajmos*), **genocide**

1944–5 Soviet-liberated western Volhynia and eastern Galicia, 'war of all against all', includes mutual Ukrainian-Polish ethnic cleansings, **partial genocide**

1944 Hungary, Budapest, Arrow Cross massacres of Jews

1944 Soviet Georgia and Transcaucasia, further NKVD deportations of small, indigenous communities including Adzhars, Khemsils, Meshketians, Georgian Kurds, and Poshas (Roma), **partial genocide**

1944–5 entire 'Lands Between', Volksdeutsche flight to west as Nazi new order in East crumbles, accompanied by major Red Army massacres and mass rape

1945 German eastern borderlands and Germany, SS-supervised death marches of Jews and others from eastern camps into Germany, **partial genocide**

POST-WAR

1944–5 Yugoslavia, Vojvodina, Titoist ethnic cleansing of majority Hungarian and ethic German populations

1944–54 Yugoslavia, Istria, Titoist massacres, and ethnic cleansing, or flight, of Italian population

1944–6 Greek Macedonia, Greek 'national' (EDES) ethnic cleansing of Albanian Chams and much of remaining Slavophone and Vlach populations

1945 Croatia, Slovenia, and Austrian borderlands, Titoist 'Bleiburg' massacres of fleeing Ustasha, Chetniks, and Slovene Home Guard and communal cohorts

1945 Kosovo, Drenica region, Titoist suppression of Albanian uprising, renewed Albanian 'repatriations' to Turkey, paralleled by comparable Bulgarian policy with regard to Bulgarian Muslims

1945–50 Soviet borderlands, NKVD extirpation of West Ukrainian, Moldovan, and Baltic resistance, followed by mass deportations to east

1945–6, Central and Eastern Europe, mass violent deportations by Poland, Czechoslovakia, and Rumania—and subsequently Hungary—of ethnic Germans to Germany. Projected Czech deportations of Hungarians vetoed by Allies

1945–8 Soviet borderlands/western Polish borderlands, Poles in newly assigned Soviet territory removed to new (formerly German) territories in west in 'exchange' for Ukrainians, Belorussians, and others removed to western Soviet republics

1946–8 Poland, mass flight of majority of remaining Polish Jews following Kielce and other communal anti-Jewish pogroms

1947 Polish south-eastern borderlands, Operation Vistula, Polish military extirpation of UPA as pretext for final wave of anti-Ukrainian ethnic cleansing, including against Lemkos

1949 Black Sea region, Moldavia and borderlands, NKVD deportation of Pontic Greeks and other social and ethnic groups, including Jehovah's Witnesses

1952–3 USSR, projected mass deportation of Soviet Jews to far east

Notes

CHAPTER 1

1. Here quoted on basis of Lochner's original report in Richard Breitman, *The Architect of Genocide: Himmler and the Final Solution* (London: The Bodley Head, 1991), 43. Also 258, n. 47, for further commentary on its authenticity. See Alexander B. Rossino, *Hitler Strikes Poland: Blitzkrieg, Ideology and Atrocity* (Lawrence: University Press of Kansas, 2003), 241, n. 5, for similar considerations. Margaret Lavinia Anderson, 'Who Still Talked about the Extermination of the Armenians: German Talk and German Silences', 198–217, in Ronald Grigor Suny, Fatma Müge Göçek and Norman N. Naimark, eds., *A Question of Genocide: Armenians and Turks at the End of the Ottoman Empire* (Oxford and New York: Oxford University Press, 2011), for cross-reference to the original German awareness and 'talk' of the Armenian extermination.
2. Christopher R. Browning (with Jürgen Matthaus), *The Origins of the Final Solution: The Evolution of Nazi Jewish Policy, September 1939–March 1942* (London: William Heinemann, 2004), 17–18, 21, 23.
3. One long-term consequence was that Lemkin's Białystok province birthplace in Bezwondene became a place eventually known as Volkovysk in today's Belarus. See Tanya Elder, 'What You See Before Your Eyes: Documenting Raphael Lemkin's Life by Exploring his Archival Papers, 1900–1959', *Journal of Genocide Research* (hereafter *JGR*), 7:4 (2005), 470.
4. Raphael Lemkin, *Axis Rule in Occupied Europe* (Washington DC: Carnegie Endowment for International Peace, 1944), 79.
5. See Mark Levene, *The Rise of the West and the Coming of Genocide* (London and New York: I.B.Tauris, 2005), 182–3. Also R.W. Tims, *Germanizing Prussian Poland: The H-K-T Society and the Struggle for the Eastern Marches in the German Empire, 1894–1919* (New York: Columbia University Press, 1941), esp. 35–40.
6. See Irma Kreiten, 'A Colonial Experiment in Cleansing: The Russian Conquest of Western Caucasus, 1856–65', *JGR*, 11:2/3 (2009), 213–41.
7. Pavel Polian, *Against Their Will: The History and Geography of Forced Migrations in the USSR* (Budapest and New York: Central European University Press, 2004), 30–2.
8. Götz Aly, *Final Solution: Nazi Population Policy and the Murder of the European Jews* (London: Arnold, 1999); Phillip T. Rutherford, *Prelude to the Final Solution: The Nazi Programme for Deporting Ethnic Poles, 1939–1941* (Lawrence: University Press of Kansas, 2007).
9. In this argument I depart from Timothy Snyder's important reading of this historical moment. See Snyder, *Bloodlands: Europe between Hitler and Stalin* (London: The Bodley Head, 2010), chapter 4, 'Molotov–Ribbentrop Europe'. For the emphasis on Stalinist and Nazi exclusive versions of 'order' versus ethnic 'chaos', see Jörg Baberowski and Anselm Doering Manteuffel, 'The Quest for Order and the Pursuit of Terror: National Socialist Germany and the Stalinist Soviet Union as Multiethnic Empires', in Michael Geyer and Sheila Fitzpatrick, eds, *Beyond Totalitarianism: Stalinism and Nazism Compared* (Cambridge: Cambridge University Press, 2009), 180–227.

10. See Martin van Bruinessen, 'Genocide in Kurdistan? The Suppression of the Dersim Rebellion in Turkey (1937–38) and the Chemical War Against the Iraqi Kurds (1988)', in George D. Andreopoulos, ed., *Genocide: Conceptual and Historical Dimensions* (Philadelphia: University of Pennsylvania Press, 1994), 144–54, for the most authoritative account in English.

11. Van Bruinessen, 'Genocide', quoting Dr Şivan (Sait Kirmizitoprak), originally clandestine 1970 study of the Kurdish national movement, 147–8.

12. Van Bruinessen 'Genocide', 166–7, n. 21.

13. Consul's report, 27 September 1938, quoted in van Bruinessen, 'Genocide', 144.

14. Van Bruinessen, 'Genocide', 144–7; Mehrdad R. Izady, *The Kurds: A Concise Handbook* (Washington DC: Taylor and Francis, 1992), 52.

15. See Berna Pekesen, 'The Exodus of Armenians from the Sanjak of Alexandretta', in Hans-Lukas Kieser, ed., *Turkey beyond Nationalism: Towards Post-Nationalist Identities* (London and New York: I.B. Tauris, 2006), 57–66. Even more acerbicly, see Lucien Betterlin, *Alexandrette: Le "Munich" de l'Orient* (Paris: J. Picollec, 1999). Contrast with Andrew Mango, *Atatürk* (London: John Murray, 1999), 506–11, for a celebratory view of these events.

16. Soner Çağaptay, 'Crafting the Turkish Nation: Kemalism and Turkish Nationalism in the 1930s', unpublished PhD thesis, Yale University 2003), 212.

17. See Ronald Aronson, *Dialectics of Disaster: A Preface to Hope* (London: Verso, 1983), 58.

18. Çağaptay, 'Crafting the Turkish Nation', 216.

19. Van Bruinessen, 'Genocide', 166 n. 8; Tessa Hoffmann and Gerayer Koutcharian, 'The History of Armenian–Kurdish Relations in the Ottoman Empire', *Armenian Review*, 39:4 (1986), 6.

20. Martin van Bruinessen, *Agha, Shaikh and State: The Social and Political Structure of Kurdistan* (London: Zed Books, 1990), 278, 285, 293.

21. See Volume 1, Chapter 4, 'The Lost Peace', for the 1934 resettlement law.

22. M.A. Hasretyan, *Türkiye'de Kürt Sorunu (1918–1940)* (Berlin: Weşanên, İnstîtuya Kurdî, 1995), vol. 1, 262; Kendal, 'Kurdistan in Turkey', 66–7.

23. Van Bruinessen, 'Genocide', 153.

24. Van Bruinessen, 'Genocide', 144.

25. See Vol. 1, Chapter 4, 'The Lost Peace'.

26. Breitman, *Architect*, 39–43.

27. Thus Mango, *Atatürk*, 500: 'The military governor was authorised to relocate the population and ratify death sentences. The local tribes…rose in revolt. It was suppressed ruthlessly and the area was pacified.' See Van Bruinessen, 'Genocide', 165, n. 5, for the necessary and general reprimand.

28. See Bohdan Budurowycz, 'Poland and the Ukrainian Problem, 1921–1939', *Canadian Slavonic Papers*, 25:4 (1983), 473–500; Alexander J. Motyl, 'Ukrainian Nationalist Political Violence in Inter-War Poland, 1921–1939', *East European Quarterly*, 19:1 (1985), 45–55.

29. Đorđe Stefanović, 'Seeing the Albanians through Serbian Eyes: The Inventors of the Tradition of Intolerance and their Critics, 1804–1939', *European History Quarterly*, 35:3 (2005), 482; Ryan Gingeras, *Sorrowful Shores: Violence, Ethnicity and the End of the Ottoman Empire, 1912–1923* (Oxford: Oxford University Press, 2009), 161–5.

30. Quoted in H.T. Norris, 'Kosova and the Kosovans: Past, Present and Future as Seen through Serb, Albanian and Muslim Eyes', in F.W. Carter and H.T. Norris, eds., *The Changing Shape of the Balkans* (Boulder, CO, and London: Westview Press, 1996), 15.

31. See Eric D.Weitz. 'From the Vienna to the Paris System: International Politics and the Entangled Histories of Human Rights, Forced Deportations and Civilizing Missions', *American Historical Review*, 11:3/5 (2008), 1342.

32. See Paul Robert Magocsi, *The Shaping of a National Identity: Sub-Carpathian Rus, 1848–1948* (Cambridge, MA: Harvard University Press, 1978), 237–49.

33. I.C. Butnaru, *The Silent Holocaust, Romania and its Jews* (New York and Westport, CT: Greenwood Press, 1992), 85. See Chapter 3, herein, for development.

34. See Shalom Cholawsky, *The Jews of Bielorussia During World War II* (Amsterdam: Harwood Academic Publishers, 1998), xv–xvii; John Hiden and Patrick Salmon, *The Baltic Nations and Europe: Estonia, Latvia and Lithuania in the 20th Century* (London and New York: Longman, 1991), 2.

35. Carole Fink, *Defending the Rights of Others: The Great Powers, the Jews, and International Minority Protection, 1878–1938* (New York: Cambridge University Press, 2004), 348–50; Carol Iancu, *Les Juifs en Roumanie (1866–1919): De l'exclusion à émancipation* (Aix-en-Provence: Éditions de l'Université de Provence, 1978), 303–14.

36. See Laurence Weinbaum, *A Marriage of Convenience: The New Zionist Organisation and the Polish Government, 1936–1939* (Boulder, CO: East European Monographs, 1993), 143–60.

37. Anthony Read and David Fisher, *The Deadly Embrace: Hitler, Stalin, and the Nazi-Soviet Pact, 1939–1941* (New York and London: W.W. Norton, 1988), 68–9.

38. See Leni Yahil, 'Madagascar—Phantom of a Solution for the Jewish Question', in George Mosse and Béla Vago, eds., *Jews and Non-Jews in Eastern Europe* (Jerusalem: Israel Universities Press, 1974), 315–34, for background.

39. Yehuda Bauer, *Jews for Sale? Nazi-Jewish Negotiations 1933–1945* (New Haven, CT, and London: Yale University Press, 1995), 41.

40. Ronald Zweig, *The Gold Train: The Destruction of the Jews and the Second World War's Most Terrible Robbery* (London: Penguin, 2003), 16.

41. Donald Bloxham, *The Final Solution: A Genocide* (Oxford: Oxford University Press, 2009), 122.

42. Bloxham, *The Final Solution*, 107.

43. Adam Tooze, *The Wages of Destruction: The Making and Breaking of the Nazi Economy* (London: Penguin, 2006), 293–304. Also R.J. Overy, *War and Economy in the Third Reich* (Oxford: Clarendon Press, 1994), chapter 8, 'Hitler's War and the German Economy', esp. 243–54.

44. See Gerhard L.Weinberg, 'Germany's War for World Conquest and the Extermination of the Jews', *Holocaust and Genocide Studies* (hereafter *HGS*), 10:2 (1996), 119–33.

45. Stanley G. Payne, *A History of Fascism, 1914–45* (London: UCL Press, 1995), 360.

46. Tooze, *Wages*, 322.

47. See Jan Tomasz Gross, *Revolution from Abroad: The Soviet Conquest of Poland's Western Ukraine and Western Belorussia* (Princeton, NJ: Princeton University Press, <1988> 2002), 222–4; Jürgen Zimmerer, 'Colonialism and the Holocaust: Towards an Archaeology of Genocide', in A. Dirk Moses, ed., *Genocide and Settler Society: Frontier Violence and Stolen Indigenous Children in Australian History* (New York and Oxford: Berghahn Books 2001), 55, for further commentary on Nazi spatial reordering.

48. See Ian Kershaw and Moshe Lewin, eds., *Stalinism and Nazism: Dictatorships in Comparison* (Cambridge: Cambridge University Press, 1997); Geyer and Fitzpatrick, *Beyond Totalitarianism*; Rousso, *Stalinism*; Snyder, *Bloodlands*, for different takes on the parallels and respective mortality figures. Stéphane Courtois et al., eds., *The Black Book of Communism: Crimes, Terror, Repression*, trans. Jonathan Murphy and Mark

Kramer (Cambridge, MA: Harvard University Press, 1999), for Soviet 'excess' situated within a history of communist states.

49. See Nikolai Tolstoy, *Stalin's Secret War* (London: Pan Books, 1982), 96–7, 104.
50. See Norman Davies, *Europe: A History* (London: Pimlico, 1997), for a famous study in which Warsaw, far from being part of the rimlands, is claimed as Europe's historical pivot.
51. Read and Fisher, *Deadly Embrace*, 356; Anna M. Cienciala, Natalia S. Lebedeva, and Wojciech Materski, *Katyn: A Crime without Punishment*, trans. Marian Schwartz (New Haven, CT, and London: Yale University Press, 2007), 39–41, 59–61, for texts of original and 28 September protocols.
52. See A.J.P. Taylor, *The Origins of the Second World War* (London: Penguin, 1964), 270–2, 306–7, for a notably acerbic analysis of the Polish 'sabre-rattling'.
53. See Brian Porter, *When Nationalism Begins to Hate: Imagining Modern Politics in Nineteenth-Century Poland* (Oxford and New York: Oxford University Press, 2000), esp. chapter 8, 'National Egoism'; Branimir Anzulović, *Heavenly Serbia: From Myth to Genocide* (New York: New York University Press, 1999). The notion of Poland as the Christ of Nations was a potent Polish self-image dating back to the nineteenth-century poet Adam Mickiewicz.
54. See Callum MacDonald, *The Killing of SS Obergruppenführer Reinhard Heydrich* (New York: The Free Press, 1989), 184–7, 196; Robert Gerwarth, *Hitler's Hangman: The Life of Heydrich* (New Haven, CT, and London: Yale University Press, 2011), 280–1, 285.
55. Taylor, *Origins*, 26, albeit very controversially, stated the case thus: 'Less than a 100,000 Czechs died during the war. Six and a half million Poles were killed. Which was better—to be a betrayed Czechoslovakia or a saved Poland?' Taylor also makes repeated comparative reference (263, 273, 277, 329) to the distinct leadership styles of Beneš and Beck.
56. Mark Levene, *The Meaning of Genocide* (London: I.B. Tauris, 2005), 56–65, for discussion of Warfare Types One to Three.
57. See Andrzej Paczkowski, *The Spring Will Be Ours: Poland and the Poles from Occupation to Freedom*, trans. Jane Cave (University Park, PA: The Pennsylvania State University Press, 2003), 40–1.
58. Imanuel Geiss, *Der polnische Grenzstreifen 1914–1918: Ein Beitrag zur deutschen Kriegszielpolitik im Ersten Weltkrieg* (Lübeck: Matthiesen, 1960).
59. Richard Bessel, *Political Violence and the Rise of Nazism: The Storm Troopers in Eastern Germany, 1925–1934* (New Haven, CT, and London: Yale University Press, 1984), 6, 109–10.
60. See Rossino, *Hitler Strikes*, 223–4. See also T. Hunt Tooley, *National Identity and Weimar Germany: Upper Silesia and the Eastern Border, 1918–1922* (Lincoln: University of Nebraska Press, 1997), 297, for how this was closely linked with the sense of Weimar's shame. Also Robert Jan van Pelt and Deborah Dwork, *Auschwitz: 1270 to the Present* (New Haven, CT, and London: Yale University Press, 1996), 87, on the plebiscite.
61. Philippe Burrin, *Hitler and the Jews: The Genesis of the Holocaust*, trans. Patsy Southgate (London: Edward Arnold, 1994), 60.
62. Quoted in Rossino, *Hitler Strikes*, 1; Browning, *Origins*, 438, n. 8.
63. Rossino, *Hitler Strikes*, 13.
64. Gerwarth, *Hitler's Hangman*, 135–8; Rossino, *Hitler Strikes*, 13–14. See also Baberowski and Manteuffel, 'Quest for Order', 184, n. 14, for the original programmatic formulation of *Flurbereinigung* by Ewald Banse in *Raum und Volk* (1932).
65. Hitler as reported by Bormann, 2 October 1940. Quoted in Uriel Tal, 'On the Study of the Holocaust and Genocide', in Michael R. Marrus, *The Nazi Holocaust* (Westport, CT, and London: Meckler, 1989), vol. 1, 203–4.

66. Marrus, *The Nazi Holocaust*, Himmler to camp commanders, occupied Poland, 15 March 1940; Browning, *Origins*, 69.

67. See Rossino, *Hitler Strikes*, 12–14.

68. Rossino, *Hitler Strikes*, 10–12, 98–102; Gerwarth, *Hitler's Hangman*, 143. Also Jochen, Böhler, Klaus-Michael Mallman and Jürgen Matthäus, *Einsatzgruppen in Polen: Darstellung und Dokumentation* (Warsaw: Bellona, 2009), for the full range of Einsatzgruppen atrocities.

69. Jan Tomasz Gross, *Polish Society under German Occupation: The Generalgouvernement, 1939–1944* (Princeton, NJ: Princeton University Press, 1979), 68, puts the figure at 20,000 between 1 September and 26 October. Gerwarth, *Hitler's Hangman*, 144, puts it at 40,000, by December.

70. Rossino, *Hitler Strikes*, 90–9.

71. Rossino, *Hitler Strikes*, 67–74, for the Bydgozscz events.

72. Rossino, *Hitler Strikes*, 181–3 and also 174–6, for a wider assessment of the Wehrmacht elite's response to the massacres. Also Szymon Datner, *Crimes Committed by the Wehrmacht during the September Campaign and the Period of Military Government* (Poznań: Instytut Zachodni, 1962), for close analysis of the Ciepielów and other atrocities; Browning, *Origins*, 17–21, on the September struggle for authority between Wehrmacht and SS.

73. Rossino, *Hitler Strikes*, 233. Gerwarth, *Hitler's Hangman*, 152, argues that the Heydrich order refers to western Poland only, and was precipitated by Heydrich's fear that the supersession of military jurisdiction by civil administration 'might limit his freedom of action'.

74. Michael Burleigh, *The Third Reich: A New History* (Basingstoke and Oxford: Pan Books, 2000), 441; Paczkowski, *Spring*, 52.

75. See Robert L. Koehl, *RKFVD: German Resettlement and Population Policy, 1939–1945: A History of the Reich Commission for the Strengthening of Germandom* (Cambridge, MA: Harvard University Press, 1957), esp. chapter 2, 'Birth of a Program', for the early, breakthrough study of this subject.

76. See Rutherford, *Prelude*, 8, 58–9, for population figures for the regions.

77. Aly, *Final Solution*, 37.

78. Quoted in Rutherford, *Prelude*, 206. See also Richard C. Lukas, *The Forgotten Holocaust: The Poles under German Occupation 1939–1944* (Lexington: University Press of Kentucky, 1986), 10.

79. Tooze, *Wages*, 366.

80. Gross, *Polish Society*, 72.

81. Jan Erik Schulte, *Zwangsarbeit und Vernichtung: Das Wirtschaftsimperium der SS: Oswald Pohl und das SS-Wirtschaft-Verwaltungshauptamt 1933–1945* (Paderborn: F. Schoningh, 2001), 248.

82. See Joachim C. Fest, 'Hans Frank—Imitation of a Man of Violence,' in his *The Face of the Third Reich* trans., Michael Bullock (London: Penguin, 1970), 318–31, for a revealing portrait.

83. See Gross, *Polish Society*, chapter 3, 'The Pattern of Unlimited Exploitation'; Götz Aly and Susanne Heim, 'Forced Emigration War, Deportation and Holocaust', in Jonathan Frankel, ed., *The Fate of the European Jews, 1939–1945: Continuity or Contingency? Studies in Contemporary Jewry XIII* (New York and London: Oxford University Press, 1997), 56–73.

84. See Breitman, *Architect*, 98–9; Browning, *Origins*, 61–2.

85. See Herbert S. Levine, 'Local Authority and the SS State: The Conflict over Population Policy in Danzig-West Prussia, 1939–1945', *Central European History*, 2 (1969), 531–55.

86. Rutherford, *Prelude*, 191–3.
87. Browning, *Origins*, 31–3; Gerwarth, *Hitler's Hangman*, 152; Rutherford, *Prelude*, 74.
88. See Tooze, *Wages*, 364–6. Also Lukas, *Forgotten Holocaust*, 9.
89. See Antony Polonsky, ed., *My Brother's Keeper?: Recent Polish Debates on the Holocaust* (London: Routledge, 1990), for intense debates on this issue.
90. Paczkowski, *Spring*, 61.
91. Jan T. Gross, 'A Tangled Web: Confronting Stereotypes Concerning Relations between Poles, Germans, Jews, and Communists', in István Deák, Jan T. Gross and Tony Judt, eds., *The Politics of Retribution in Europe: World War II and its Aftermath* (Princeton, NJ: Princeton University Press, 2000), 120, n. 250.
92. See Czesław Madajczyk, *Die Okkupationspolitik Nazisdeutschlands in Polen, 1939–1945* (Cologne: Pahl-Rugenstein, 1988), for the detailed picture.
93. Van Pelt and Dwork, *Auschwitz*, chapter 6, 'A Concentration Camp'.
94. Jan T. Gross, 'Themes for a Social History of War Experience and Collaboration', in Deák, *The Politics*, 33, n. 14.
95. Gross, *Revolution from Abroad*, 228–9.
96. Gross, *Revolution from Abroad*. Also xiv, for Soviet archival figures; Polian, *Against Their Will*, 118–19. Alexander Statiev, 'Soviet Ethnic Deportations: Intent versus Outcome', in *JGR*, 11:2/3 (2009), 244, for further commentary. By comparison, see Norman Davies, *God's Playground* (Oxford: Clarendon Press, 1981), vol. 2, 451, for overwrought figures—though these abound in many books and films. See, for further example, Jagna Wright, 'A Forgotten Odyssey: The Untold Story of 1,700,000 Poles Deported to Siberia in 1940', *Lest We Forget Productions* (2003).
97. Paczkowski, *Spring*, 48. For the experience of Polish deportation to Soviet central Asia, see Matthew Kelly, *Finding Poland: From Tavistock to Hruzdowa and Back Again* (London: Jonathan Cape, 2010).
98. Gross, *Revolution from Abroad*, 155.
99. See Alexander V. Prusin, *The Lands Between: The East European Frontiers in Wars, Revolutions and Nationality Conflicts, 1900–1992* (Oxford: Oxford University Press, 2010), 212–15.
100. Quoted in Geoffrey Hosking, *Russia, People and Empire, 1552–1917* (London: HarperCollins, 1997), 372–3. See also Cienciala, *Katyn*, 3–4.
101. Cienciala, *Katyn*, 25–6.
102. See Norman Davies, *White Eagle, Red Star: The Polish-Soviet War, 1919–20* (London: MacDonald, 1972), for a comprehensive account.
103. See Manus I. Midlarsky, 'Territoriality and the Onset of Mass Violence: The Political Extremism of Joseph Stalin', *JGR*, 11:2/3 (2009), 275–6, 280, for the significance of the humiliation-shame motif. Also Robert Service, *Stalin: A Biography* (Cambridge, MA: Belknap Press, 2005), 180–2, for close analysis of Stalin's personal role in these events.
104. See Kate Brown, *A Biography of No Place: From Ethnic Borderland to Soviet Heartland* (Boston, MA: Harvard University Press, 2005), 98. Also Cienciala, *Katyn*, 417.
105. Quoted in Robert C. Tucker, *Stalin in Power: The Revolution from Above, 1929–1941* (New York and London: Norton, 1990), 602; Norman M. Naimark, *Fires of Hatred: Ethnic Cleansing in Twentieth Century Europe* (Cambridge, MA, and London: Harvard University Press, 2001), 70.
106. See Cienciala, *Katyn*, 212, doc. 3. 42–4.
107. Prusin, *Lands Between*, esp. 192–4, for wider discussion; 213. See also Gross, *Revolution from Abroad*, 18–21, 35–9 and Cienciala, *Katyn*, 21, for estimates of Poles killed

in the Soviet occupied area in September 1939, generally put at 200 to 300 military and 1,000 to 2,500 civilians—mostly at the hands of roving bands.

108. Gross, *Revolution from Abroad*, 35–6.

109. See Gross, *Revolution from Abroad*, 86, for analysis.

110. Madajczyk, *Die Okkupationspolitik*, 412; Rutherford, *Prelude*, 95.

111. Polian, *Against Their Will*, 116. Polian's reference here to *osadniki* as a 'Polish equivalent to Cossacks' surely tells us more about Soviet perception than Polish reality.

112. See Wright, 'Forgotten Odyssey'.

113. See Sarah Meiklejohn Terry, *Poland's Place in Europe: General Sikorski and the Origins of the Oder-Neisse Line, 1939–1943* (Princeton, NJ: Princeton University Press, 1983), chapter 6, 'The Eastern Boundary', chapter 9, Retreat from Rapprochement', the latter for the tortuous negotiations around the evacuation.

114. See J.K. Zawodny, *Death in the Forest: The Story of the Katyn Forest Massacre* (London: Macmillan, 1962), on the early detective work before the opening up of the Soviet archives.

115. Adam Hochschild, foreword to Michael Parrish, *The Lesser Terror: Soviet State Security, 1939–1953* (Westport, CT: Praeger, 1996), xii.

116. Claudia Weber, ' "The Export of Terror"—On the Impact of the Stalinist Culture of Terror on Soviet Foreign Policy during and after World War II', *JGR*, 11:2/3 (2009), 293. Recent documents released by the US National Archives confirm that Roosevelt and Churchill were complicit in Stalin's cover-up story. See *BBC News Europe*, 'US "hushed up" Soviet guilt over Katyn', 11 September 2011, <http://www.bbc.co.uk/news/world-europe-19552745>.

117. The Zakopane conference is referred to in the Laurence Rees documentary *World War II Behind Closed Doors: Stalin, The Nazis and the West*, BBC/PBS, 2008, episode 1.

118. Cienciala, *Katyn*, 145–6.

119. Read and Fisher, *Deadly Embrace*, 410; Jeffrey Burds, 'The Soviet War against "Fifth Columnists": The Case of Chechnya, 1942–4', *Journal of Contemporary History*, 42:2 (2007), 286.

120. See Cienciela, *Katyn*, 143–4, for different views on the significance of the Polish brigade as a smoking gun. Also NKVD UPV (prisoner of war administration) report to Merkulov, 22 April 1940, on mood of Polish POWs, 177–82.

121. Read and Fisher, *Deadly Embrace*, 414.

122. Cienciala, *Katyn*, Beria memorandum, 5 March 1940, 118–20. See also Weber, 'Export of Terror', 290, for commentary.

123. Tolstoy, *Stalin's Secret War*, 10.

124. See Joan McGuire Mohr, *The Czech and Slovak Legion in Siberia, 1917–1922* (Jefferson, NC: McFarland and Company, 2012).

125. Cienciala, *Katyn*, 136. Much less has been pieced together about these victims.

126. See Parrish, *Lesser Terror*, 56.

127. Tolstoy, *Stalin's Secret War*, 188.

128. Cienciala, *Katyn*, 26.

129. Statiev, 'Soviet Ethnic Deportations', 244, is notable for his refutation of the western rimlands deportations being on any grounds other than class affiliation.

130. Gross, *Revolution from Abroad*, 224.

131. Prusin, *Lands Between*, 218.

132. Polian, *Against Their Will*, 118–19.

133. Cited in Prusin, *Lands Between*, 222.

134. Prusin, *Lands Between*, 1.

135. Prusin, *Lands Between*, 224. See also Gross, *Revolution from Abroad*, 178, 226–9.
136. See Aly, *Final Solution*, 18–19.
137. Geiss, *Der polnische Grenzstreifen*; 128; Kitchen, *Silent Dictatorship*, 193–4.
138. Browning, *Origins*, 69–70; Peter Longerich, *Heinrich Himmler*, trans. Jeremy Noakes and Lesley Sharpe (Oxford and New York: Oxford University Press, 2012), 450–1. See also Burleigh, *Third Reich*, 443–4, on the Goral issue; Rutherford, *Prelude*, 137, 207–10, on the *Volkliste* screening process.
139. Valdis O. Lumans, *Himmler's Auxiliaries: The Volksdeutsche Mittelstelle and the German National Minorities of Europe, 1933–1945* (Chapel Hill and London: University of North Carolina Press, 1993), 185; Rutherford, *Prelude*, 104.
140. Gross, *Revolution from Abroad*, 155.
141. Polian, *Against Their Will*, 120; Hiden and Salmon, *Baltic Nations*, 114–15.
142. See Henning Heske, 'Karl Haushofer: His Role in German Geopolitics and in Nazi Politics', *Political Geography Quarterly* 6:2 (1987), 136: Mark Bassin 'Race Contra Space: The Conflict between German *Geopolitik* and National Socialism', *Political Geography Quarterly*, 6:2 (1987), 127.
143. See Read and Fisher, *Deadly Embrace*, esp. 351–2, 63–73; Rutherford, *Prelude*, 51.
144. See Polian, *Against Their Will*, 121–3; Hiden and Salmon, *Baltic Nations*, 114–15, for various figures for these deportations. In Estonia, recent downgraded estimates of the number of deportees—35,000 (compared with Hiden and Salmon's figure of 60,000)—have not deterred researchers from claiming a 60 per cent mortality from the deportations. See Olaf Mertelsmann and Aigi Rahi-Tamm, 'Soviet Mass Violence in Estonia Revisited', *JGR*, 11:2/3 (2009), 309–10. This in turn has led to a bitter division between those, particularly nationalist Baltic commentators, who read the 1941 deportations as a case of ethnic cleansing, or genocide, and those who argue that they were first and foremost 'security operations', even, as in the case of Alexander Statiev, *The Soviet Counter-Insurgency in the Western Borderlands* (Cambridge: Cambridge University Press, 2010), 167–71, a precautionary NKVD pre-emption of a pro-German 'fifth column'. For support of the Statiev assessment, see also Aldis Purs, 'Soviet in Form, Local in Context: Elite Repression and Mass Terror in the Baltic States, 1940–1953', in Kevin McDermott and Matthew Stibbe, eds., *Stalinist Terror in Eastern Europe: Elite Purges and Mass Repressions* (Manchester: Manchester University Press, 2010), 22–9.
145. Van Pelt and Dwork, *Auschwitz*, 126–30.
146. See Michael Barutciski, 'Lausanne Revisited: Population Exchanges in International Law and Policy', in Renée Hirschon, ed., *Crossing the Aegean: An Appraisal of the 1923 Compulsory Population Exchange between Greece and Turkey*, Studies in Forced Migration, vol. 12 (New York and Oxford: Berghahn, 2003), 25.
147. Götz Aly, ' "Jewish Resettlement": Reflections on the Political Prehistory of the Holocaust', in Ulrich Herbert, ed., *National Socialist Extermination Polices: Contemporary German Perspectives and Controversies* (New York and Oxford: Berghahn, 2000), 61. See also Rutherford, *Prelude*, 263, n. 9.
148. Lumans, *Himmler's Auxiliaries*, 163–4.
149. See, for instance, Doris L. Bergen, 'The Nazi Concept of "Volksdeutsche" and the Exacerbation of Anti-Semitism in Eastern Europe 1939–45', *Journal of Contemporary History*, 29:4 (1994) 569–82.
150. Lumans, *Himmler's Auxiliaries*, 165–70.
151. Zygmunt Bauman, *Modernity and the Holocaust* (Oxford: Blackwell, 1989), 91–2; Gross, 'Tangled Web', 74–129.

152. Ben Kiernan, *Blood and Soil: A World History of Genocide and Extermination from Sparta to Darfur* (New Haven, CT, and London: Yale University Press, 2007), 428–30.
153. Rutherford, *Prelude*, 59–60; Lumans, *Himmler's Auxiliaries*, 151.
154. Burleigh, *Third Reich*, 449; Longerich, *Himmler*, 455.
155. Aly and Heim, 'Forced Emigration', 63.
156. Browning, *Origins*, 96–7; Hans Safrian, *Eichmann's Men*, trans. Ute Stargardt (Cambridge and New York: Cambridge University Press, 2010), chapter 2, 'The Unsuccessful Beginning: The Deportations to Nisko on the River San'.
157. Isabel Heinemann, ' "Another Type of Perpetrator": The SS Racial Experts and Forced Population Movements in the Occupied Regions', *HGS*, 15:3 (2001), 404, n. 17.
158. The emergence and paroxysm of the Łódź ghetto was notably well documented by its own secret archivists and diarists, and has been closely studied in the more recent historiography of the Holocaust. See, among other sources, Lucjan Dobroszycki, ed., *The Chronicle of the Lodz Ghetto, 1941–1944*, trans. Richard Lourie et al. (New Haven, CT, and London: Yale University Press, 1984); Michal Unger, *The Last Ghetto: Life in the Lodz Ghetto, 1940–1944* (Jerusalem: Yad Vashem, 1995).
159. Rutherford, *Prelude*, 9,117, 211.
160. Browning, *Origins*, 36–43.
161. David Cesarani, *Eichmann, His Life and Crimes* (London: Vintage, 2004), 82.
162. Henry R. Huttenbach, 'The Romani Porajmos: The Nazi Genocide of Gypsies in Germany and Eastern Europe', in David Crowe and John Kolsti, eds., *The Gypsies of Eastern Europe* (New York and London: M.E. Sharpe, 1991), 38.
163. Quoted in Browning, *Origins*, 56.
164. Dobroszycki, *Chronicle*, 420–1.
165. Michael Zimmerman, 'The National Socialist "Solution of the Gypsy Question": Central Decisions, Local Initiative and their Interrelation', *HGS*, 15:3 (2001), 416.
166. See Bloxham, *Final Solution*, 178–9.
167. The comment of one of the SS officials involved in the Łódź deportations. Quoted in Rutherford, *Prelude*, 95.
168. See Michael Burleigh, *Death and Deliverance: 'Euthanasia' in Germany, 1900–1945* (Cambridge: Cambridge University Press, 1994), for the full story; Henry Friedlander, *The Origins of Nazi Genocide: From Euthanasia to Final Solution* (Chapel Hill: University of North Carolina Press, 1995), 296–8, for the redeployment of T-4 personnel to the 'final solution'. For a view which contests that freeing up space—essentially the Aly, *Final Solution*, argument—was the first 'utilitarian' cause of these killings, see Peter Longerich, *Holocaust: The Nazi Persecution and Murder of the Jews* (Oxford: Oxford University Press, 2010), 57–60.
169. Burleigh, *Death*, 130; Browning, *Origins*, 188.
170. Browning, *Origins*, 187–90.
171. See Aly, *Final Solution*, 84, n. 49.
172. Browning, *Origins*, 188–9; Aly and Heim, 'Forced Emigration', 67. Friedlander, *Origins*, 140, questions whether Lange actually received his 'rent'. There was certainly a squabble over money.
173. Aly and Heim, 'Forced Emigration', 67. However, Aly and Heim's number are at variance with the close research of Volker Riess, *Die Anfänge der Vernichtung "Lebensunwerten Lebens" in den Reichsgauen Danzig-Westpreussen und Wartheland 1939/40* (Frankfurt: Peter Lang, 1995), 355, who puts the number of borderland patients killed in this phase at 7,700.

174. See Aly and Heim, 'Forced Emigration', 66.

175. Aly, *Final Solution*, 75; Browning, *Origins*, 186, 64–5.

176. Read and Fisher, *Deadly Embrace*, 421.

177. Misha Glenny, *The Balkans 1804–1999: Nationalism, War and the Great Powers* (London: Granta Books, 1999), 469–71; Read and Fisher, *Deadly Embrace*, 503–5, 521, for the developing friction over the Balkans.

178. Bassin, 'Race', 115–34.

179. For key critical studies following on from Hannah Arendt, *Eichmann in Jerusalem: A Report on the Banality of Evil* (London: Penguin, 1965), see Safrian, *Eichmann's Men*; Cesarani, *Eichmann*.

180. The quote on Serov comes from Alan Fisher, *The Crimean Tatars* (Stanford, CA: Hoover Institute Press, 1978), 165. However, there is no Western-language study of Serov per se. Some aspects of Serov's Chekist career can be garnered in Viktor Suvorov, *Inside Soviet Military Intelligence* (New York: Macmillan, 1984).

181. See Peter Holquist, ' "Information is the Alpha and Omega of Our Work": Bolshevik Surveillance in its Pan-European Context', *Journal of Modern History*, 69:3 (1997), 415–50.

182. Lemkin, *Axis Rule*, 23.

183. *World War II Behind Closed Doors*, episode 1, for corroboration.

184. Alexander Dallin, *German Rule in Russia 1941–1945: A Study of Occupation Politics* (London: Macmillan, 1957), 260.

185. See Herbert, 'Extermination Policy', 26. For closer analysis, Michael Wildt, *An Uncompromising Generation: The Nazi Leadership of the Reich Security Main Office*, trans. Tom Lampert (Madison: University of Wisconsin Press, 2009); Ruth Bettina Birn, *Die Höheren SS-und Polizeiführer* (Düsseldorf: Droste Verlag, 1986); Ulrich Herbert, *Best: Biographische Studien uber Radikalismus, Weltanschauung und Venunft* (Bonn: Dientz, 1996), part III, chapter 4.

186. See Wendy Lower, ' "Anticipatory Obedience" and the Nazi Implementation of the Holocaust in the Ukraine: A Case Study of Central and Peripheral Forces in the Generalbezirk Zhytomyr 1941–1944', *HGS*, 16:1 (2002), 1–22, for discussion.

187. Charles W. Syndor Jr, 'Executive Instinct: Reinhard Heydrich and the Planning for the Final Solution', in Michael Berenbaum and Abraham J., Peck, eds., *The Holocaust and History: The Known, The Unknown, The Disputed and The Reexamined* (Bloomington and Indianapolis: Indiana University Press, 1998), 159–86.

188. Karl Dietrich Bracher, *The German Dictatorship: The Origins, Structure and Consequences of National Socialism*, trans. Jean Steinberg (London: Penguin, 1973), esp. 440–3. Also Jens Banach, *Heydrichs Elite: Das Führerkorps der Sicherheitspolizei und des SD 1936–1945* (Paderborn: F. Schoningh, 1998).

189. See Michael Mann, *The Dark Side of Democracy: Explaining Ethnic Cleansing* (Cambridge and New York: Cambridge University Press, 2005): 200; Franciszek Piper, 'The System of Prisoner Exploitation', in Yisrael Gutman and Michael Berenbaum eds., *Anatomy of the Auschwitz Death Camp* (Bloomington and Indianapolis: Indiana University Press, 1998), 36. For the Gulag mortality comparison, see Parrish, *Lesser Terror*, 2.

190. Himmler instructions to Hoess (1940), quoted in Ben Kiernan, 'Twentieth Century Genocides: Underlying Ideological Themes from Armenia to East Timor', in Ben Kiernan and Robert Gellately, eds., *The Spectre of Genocide: Mass Murder in Historical Perspective* (Cambridge and New York: Cambridge University Press, 2003), 43. More generally, van Pelt and Dwork, *Auschwitz*, 174–82.

191. There is a huge, largely sensational literature on this subject. See, however, Robert J. Lifton and Amy Hackett, 'Nazi Doctors', in Gutman and Berenbaum, *Anatomy*, 301–16, for a terse overview.

192. See Paul Weindling, *Epidemics and Genocide in Eastern Europe, 1890–1945* (Oxford: Oxford University Press, 2000), esp. 246–59. Also Bettina Arnold, 'Justifying Genocide: Archaeology and the Construction of Difference', and Gretchen E. Schafft, 'Scientific Racism in Service of the Reich: German Anthropologists in the Nazi Era', in Alexander Laban Hinton, *Annihilating Difference: The Anthropology of Genocide* (Berkeley: University of California Press, 2002), 95–116 and 117–34, respectively.

193. Van Pelt and Dwork, *Auschwitz*, 138–43, 307–10; Longerich, *Himmler*, 578–80.

194. Breitman, *Architect*, 5.

195. Fest, *Face*, 173; Longerich, *Himmler*, chapter 10, 'Ideology and Religious Cult', also 368–76. For more on the *Lebensborn*, see Catrine Clay and Michael Leapman, *Master Race: The Lebensborn Experiment in Nazi Germany* (London: Hodder and Stoughton, 1995).

196. See Götz Aly and Susanne Heim, *Vordenker der Vernichtung, Auschwitz und die Deutschen Pläne für eine Neue Europäische Ordnung* (Hamburg: Hoffman and Campe, 1991), for the middle order technocrats.

197. Parrish, *Lesser Terror*, 32.

198. Ronald Hingley, *The Russian Secret Police: Muscovite, Imperial Russian and Soviet Political Security Operations, 1565–1970* (London: Hutchinson, 1970), 185–6; Tolstoy, *Stalin's Secret War*, 200–1.

199. Matthew Kott, 'Stalin's Great Terror (1937–38) as Antecedent and Other Aspects of the Recent Historiography of Soviet Genocide', *Yearbook of the Museum of the Occupation of Latvia* 8 (2007), 42–54. With thanks to Dr Kott for a copy of the original MS. Herein 8–10 (original MS), for wider NKVD anxieties about ethnic group danger as centred on Murmansk.

200. Parrish, *Lesser Terror*, 32.

201. Mertelsmann and Rahi-Tamm, 'Soviet Mass Violence', 310; Tolstoy, *Stalin's Secret War*, 201–2. Prusin, *Lands Between*, 143, for confirmation of the extensive torture.

202. Simon Sebag Montefiore, *Stalin: The Court of the Red Tsar* (London: Phoenix, 2004), 342.

203. See Parrish, *Lesser Terror*, chapter 1. By comparison, with regard to the RHSA's 'imperfect organizational structure', see Gerwarth, *Hitler's Hangman*, 165–8.

204. Sebag Montefiore, *Stalin*, 79. Also 330–2, on the fall of the Ezhov.

205. Cienciala, *Katyn*, 124; Sebag Montefiore, *Stalin*, 201, 214, 332.

206. Jared Diamond, *Collapse: How Societies Choose to Fail or Survive* (London: Penguin, 2005), 432, for discussion.

207. Sebag Montefiore, *Stalin*, 79.

208. Parrish, *Lesser Terror*, 10–13; Mann, *Dark Side*, 223–8.

209. Parrish, *Lesser Terror*, 45–6. Longerich, *Himmler*, 632–4, 684–9, 703–4, for Himmler's repeated failures to wrest control of major technological and other aspects of Germany's military-industrial complex.

210. Longerich, *Himmler*, 696–7, on the transparent security service failure in face of the attempted coup.

211. See Mark Roseman, *The Villa, The Lake, the Meeting: Wannsee and the Final Solution*, (London: Penguin, 2002), 83–7, for discussion.

212. See, for example, Himmler to Berger, 28 July 1942, quoted in Martin Dean, *Local Collaboration in the Holocaust: Crimes of the Local Police in Belorussia and Ukraine, 1941–44* (Basingstoke: Macmillan, 2000), 92.

213. Burleigh, *Death*, 119.

214. Breitman, *Architect*, 152–3.
215. Aly, *Final Solution*, 215–16.
216. Bauer, *Jews for Sale*, 56; Fest, *Face*, 'Heinrich Himmler—Petty Bourgeois and Grand Inquisitor', 177–8.
217. Fest, *Face*, 185; Breitman, *Architect*, 194–6.
218. Burleigh, *Death*, 132.
219. Breitman, *Architect*, 197.
220. See Aly, *Final Solution*, 195–8, for ongoing Nazi estimates of Jewish numbers.
221. See Max Domarus, ed., *Hitler, Reden und Proklamationen 1932–45* vol. 1 (Würzburg: Edition Schmidt, 1962), 1058, for original.
222. Tooze, *Wages*, 282–3, 324. Also Shlomo Aronson, *Hitler, the Allies and the Jews* (Cambridge: Cambridge University Press, 2004), 33.
223. Tooze, *Wages*, 280; Michael Marrus, *The Unwanted: European Refugees in the Twentieth Century* (New York and Oxford: Oxford University Press, 1985), 216–17.
224. Quoted in Naimark, *Fires*, 70, referring to *Völkisher Beobachter* report, 9 February 1939.
225. Bauer, *Jews for Sale*, 35–43.
226. Quoted in David Vital, *A People Apart: A Political History of the Jews in Europe, 1789–1939* (Oxford: Oxford University Press, 1999), 894–5. FO memo and minute, 19 October 1938.
227. Tony Kushner, *The Persistence of Prejudice: Antisemitism in British Society during the Second World War* (Manchester: Manchester University Press, 1989), 12.
228. Gordon Thomas and Max Morgan-Witts, *Voyage of the Damned* (London: Hodder and Stoughton, 1974).
229. See Aronson, *Hitler*, for the thesis of the Holocaust as a multiple trap.
230. André Gerrits, *The Myth of Jewish Communism: A Historical Interpretation* (Brussels: P.I.E. Peter Lang, 2009), 50–1 and 129–30, which offer some intriguing pointers for this discussion. He refers to Harold Kaplan's (*Conscience and Memory: Meditations in a Museum of the Holocaust*, Chicago, University of Chicago Press,1994), assessment that in Hitler's mind 'the Jew' was more closely identified 'with democracy, not Bolshevism as well as with internationalism, "cosmopolitanism"', liberalism and pacifism', adding for good measure that 'Hitler regarded bourgeois democracy as his natural enemy (or victim) to be destroyed, and that Bolshevism, though surely to be destroyed, was less a moral antithesis than a dangerous rival which shared the same ultimate goals of power.' Later on, Gerrits refers to a Hitler speech (21 January 1941) to military experts in which he stated, 'As long as Stalin lives, there is no threat, he is clever and cautious. But when he will be gone, the Jews, who are now in the second and third echelons of power might return again.'
231. Quoted in Browning, *Origins*, 25–6.
232. Noakes and Pridham, *Nazism*, vol. 3, 1051–3, for *Schnellbrief* details.
233. Aly, *Final Solution*, 15.
234. Noakes and Pridham, *Nazism*, vol. 3, 927. The new order threw into further disarray Heydrich's plans from just a few days earlier, predicated as they had been on the assumption that the Cracow, not Lublin region, would be the temporary or more semi-permanent holding area pending a Jewish 'exit'. See Gerwarth, *Hitler's Hangman*, 154–7.
235. Browning, *Origins*, 37; Longerich, *Holocaust*, 153–4.
236. See Levene, *Rise*, 56–8.

237. Safrian, *Eichmann's Men*, chapter 2, 'The Unsuccessful Beginning: The Deportations to Nisko'.
238. Browning, *Origins*, 30.
239. Bauer, *Jews for Sale*, 50–1. More broadly, see Francis R. Nicosia, *The Third Reich and the Palestine Question* (London: I.B. Tauris, 1986).
240. Polian, *Against Their Will*, 30.
241. See Longerich, *Holocaust*, 160–1, for the anti-Jewish measures in Poland; Avraham Barkai, *From Boycott to Annihilation: The Economic Struggle of German Jews 1933–1943*, trans. William Templar (Hanover, NH: Brandeis Press and University Press of New England, 1989), 168, for Germany.
242. See Aronson, *Hitler*, 4; Nicosia, *Third Reich*, 150. See also Peter Longerich, 'The Wannsee Conference in the Development of the "Final Solution"', trans. Ian Gronbach and Donald Bloxham, *Holocaust Education Trust Research Papers* 1:2 (London: Holocaust Educational Trust,1999–2000), 7, for emphasis on Nazi proclivities vis-à-vis the hostage card.
243. Franz Rademacher, the FO expert responsible for the new Madagascar plan, put it thus: 'the Jews should be set up as a bargaining counter under German control to ensure the future good behaviour of their racial associates in America'. Quoted in Peter Longerich, *The Unwritten Order: Hitler's Role in the Final Solution* (London: Tempus, 2001), 93.
244. See Browning, *Origins*, 81–9, for succinct assessment of the plan; and Hans Jansen, *Madagaskar-Plan: Die beabsichtigte Deportation der europäischen Juden nach Madagaskar* (Munich: Herbig, 1997), for the full story.
245. Hilberg, *Destruction*, 161.
246. Hilberg, *Destruction*, 90.
247. Tooze, *Wages*, 366.
248. Raul Hilberg, *The Destruction of the European Jews* (New York: Holmes and Meier, unabridged 3 volume edition, 1985), vol. 1, 269, vol. 3, 1212. See also Martin Broszat, 'Hitler and the Genesis of the "Final Solution": An Assessment of David Irving's Theses', *Yad Vashem Studies*, 13 (1970) 73–125, for the deliberateness of Nazi planning within a process of 'cumulative radicalisation'.
249. See Christopher R. Browning, *The Path to Genocide: Essays on Launching the Final Solution* (Cambridge and New York: Cambridge University Press, 1992), chapter 2, 'Nazi Ghettoisation Policy in Poland, 1939–1941'.
250. Browning, *The Path to Genocide*, 35–7, 42–7.
251. See Sybille Steinbecher, 'In the Shadow of Auschwitz: The Murder of the Jews of East Upper Silesia', in Herbert, *National Socialist Extermination Policies*, 283–7.
252. Burleigh, *Third Reich*, 583–4; Longerich, *Holocaust*, 154.
253. See Longerich, *Himmler*, 348–51, on Globocnik's peculiarly 'dog-like' dependency on Himmler. Also Breitman, *Architect*, 103–4; Birn, *Die Höheren SS-und Polizeiführer*, 350–62.
254. Syndor, 'Executive Instinct', 173.
255. See Schmuel Krakowski, 'The Fate of Jewish Prisoners of War in the September 1939 Campaign', *Yad Vashem Studies*, 12 (1977), 297–323. Also Vejas Gabriel Liulevicius, *War Land on the Eastern Front: Culture, National Identity and German Occupation in World War 1* (Cambridge and New York: Cambridge University Press, 2000), 73–4.
256. Peter Black, 'Rehearsal for "Reinhard"?: Odilo Globocnik and the Lublin *Selbschutz*', *Central European History*, 25:2 (1993), 204–26.
257. Aly, *Final Solution*, 195–6.

258. See Domarus, *Hitler, Reden, 1941–45*, vol. 2, 1663. Significantly, Hitler, in reminding his audience of the original prophecy, falsely claimed that it had been made on 1 September (the date of the invasion of Poland), rather than in the backwash of the aborted Schacht-Rublee talks.

CHAPTER 2

1. Quoted from Isaac Babel, *Sochineniia*, vol. 2, in Yuri Slezkine, *The Jewish Century* (Princeton, NJ, and Oxford: Princeton University Press, 2004), 131.

2. See Hilberg, *Destruction*, 339, for the lower-end estimate of 5.1 million; Poliakov and Wulf, *Das Dritte Reich* (1955), reprinted in Paul R. Mendes-Flohr and Jehuda Reinharz, eds., *The Jew in the Modern World: A Documentary History* (New York: Oxford University Press, 1980), 520, for the upper end figure of 5,978,000. On the death-toll of children, Eric Markusen and David Kopf, *The Holocaust and Strategic Bombing: Genocide and Total War in the 20th Century* (Boulder, CO, San Francisco, and Oxford: Westview Press, 1995), 13.

3. Again, see Hilberg, *Destruction*, 339, and Poliakov and Wolf (in Mendes-Flohr and Reinharz, *The Jew*), 520, for slightly different statistical interpretations.

4. The subject represents a book in itself. See Dan Stone, *Constructing the Holocaust: A Study in Historiography* (London and Portland, OR: Vallentine Mitchell, 2003), chapter 5, 'The Uniqueness of the Holocaust: A Historiographical Case-Study', for a critically rigorous overview of many of the arguments. More recent elaborations of this theme have been developed, particularly with reference to Donald Bloxham's attempt in his *Final Solution* to situate the Holocaust within a broader historical context of modern European genocide. See, among others, Robert Rozett, 'Diminishing the Holocaust: Scholarly Fodder for a Discourse of Distortion', *Israel Journal of Foreign Affairs*, 6:1 (2012), 53–64; Dan Michman, 'The Jewish Dimension of the Holocaust in Dire Straits? Current Challenges of Interpretation and Scope', 'Rewriting the History of the Holocaust' Conference, University of Florida, 17–19 March 2012, unpublished paper; Omer Bartov, 'Genocide and the Holocaust: What Are We Arguing About?' in Uffa Jensen et al., *Gewalt und Gesellschaft: Klassiker modernen Denkens neu gelesen* (Göttingen: Wallstein Verlag, 2011), 381–93.

5. Key examples include A. Dirk Moses, ed. *Genocide and Settler Society*, esp. Jürgen Zimmerer, 'Colonialism and the Holocaust', 49–76; Moses, ed., *Empire, Colony, Genocide, Conquest: Occupation and Subaltern Resistance in World History*, (Oxford and New York: Berghahn 2008); Moses, 'Conceptual Blockages and Definitional Dilemmas in 'The "Racial Century": Genocides of Indigenous Peoples and the Holocaust', *Patterns of Prejudice*, 36:4 (2002), 7–36; Isabel V. Hull, *Absolute Destruction: Military Culture and the Practices of War in Imperial Germany* (Ithaca, NY: Cornell University Press, 2005); Tony Barta, 'Discourses of Genocide in Germany and Australia: A Linked History', *Aboriginal History*, 25 (2001), 37–56. Also see the critique of the colonial 'turn' in Robert Gerwarth and Stephan Malinowski, 'Hannah Arendt's Ghosts: Reflections on the Disputable Path from Windhoek to Auschwitz', *Central European History*, 42:2 (2009), 279–300. On Armenia as forerunner to the Holocaust, see Hans-Lukas Kieser and Dominick Schaller, eds., *Der Völkermord an den Armeniern und die Shoah* (Zurich: Chronos Publishing, 2002), as well as the many works of Vahakn N. Dadrian, exemplified by Dadrian, 'The Convergent Aspects of the Armenian and Jewish Cases of Genocide: A Reinterpretation of the Concept of Holocaust', *HGS*, 3:2 (1988), 151–70.

6. See Jeffrey C. Alexander, 'On the Social Construction of Moral Universals: The "Holocaust" from War Crime to Trauma Drama', *European Journal of Social Theory*, 5:1 (2002), 5–85.

7. See the advocacy of Saul Friedländer, on this point, as in, for instance, Friedländer, ed., *Probing the Limits of Representation: Nazism and the Final Solution* (Cambridge, MA: Harvard University Press, 1992). It is thus ironic, perhaps, that one leading Holocaust and genocide historian has assessed Friedländer's *Nazi Germany and the Jews* as 'a major contribution to the historicisation of the Holocaust, despite his early warnings about the risk of such an attempt'. See Dan Stone, 'Nazi Germany and the Jews and the Future of Holocaust Historiography', in Christian Wiese and Paul Betts, eds., *Years of Persecution, Years of Extermination: Saul Friedländer and the Future of Holocaust Studies* (London and New York: Continuum, 2010), 343.

8. See Michael Burleigh, 'Nazi Europe: What if Nazi Germany had Defeated the Soviet Union?', in Niall Ferguson, ed., *Virtual History: Alternatives and Counterfactuals* (London and Basingstoke: Macmillan, 1998), 321–47, for an attempt at counterfactual analysis. Significantly, Burleigh hardly explores the Jewish dimension.

9. Hitler, 'political testament', 29 April 1945, available at <http://www.ess.uwe.ac.uk/documents/poltest.htm>.

10. Burrin, *Hitler*.

11. Some of the analysis here will agree and some will disagree with the diverse and exhaustive existing scholarship. Readers may note, for instance, that while closely following Browning's trajectory, I dispute his explanation for a leap into mass Russian Jewish killing as a consequence of a euphoric expectation of Nazi victory.

12. Levene, *Meaning*, 41.

13. Bauman, *Modernity*, 12.

14. Mark Levene, 'Is the Holocaust Simply Another Example of Genocide?', *Patterns of Prejudice*, 28:2 (1994), 22.

15. Glenny, *Balkans*, 473–7, however, disputes that the British-abetted coup would have actually extricated Yugoslavia from falling into the Tripartite Pact.

16. Walter Manoschek, *'Serbien ist judenfrei': Militärische Besatzungspolitik und Judenvernichtung in Serbien 1941/42* (Munich: R. Oldenbourg, 1995), 19.

17. Jozo Tomasevich, *The Chetniks: War and Revolution in Yugoslavia, 1941–1945* (Stanford, CA: Stanford University Press, 1975); Marko Attila Hoare, *Genocide and Resistance in Hitler's Bosnia: The Partisans and Chetniks 1941–1943* (Oxford: Oxford University Press, 2006).

18. Walter Manoschek, 'The Extermination of the Jews in Serbia', in Herbert, *National Socialist Extermination Policies*, 167.

19. Mark Mazower, 'Two Wars: Serbia 1914–1918 and 1941–1944', unpublished paper, 'Cultures of Killing' Conference, Birkbeck College (July 2000). With thanks to Prof. Mazower for a copy of this paper. Also Levene, *Rise*, 323, 334–5.

20. Quoted in Manoschek, 'Extermination', 170.

21. Manoschek, 'Extermination', 163–4. The most notable Jewish partisan was Moša Pijade.

22. Mara Jovanović, ' "Wir Packen, Wir auspacken" ': Tragična Sudbina Jevreja Izbeglica u Šapcu 1941', *Zbornik*, (Belgrade), 4 (1979), 245–65.

23. Glenny, *Balkans*, 498. See also Zdenko Lowenthal, ed., *The Crime of the Fascist Occupants and Their Collaborators against Jews in Yugoslavia* (Belgrade: Federation of Jewish Communities, 1957).

24. Manoschek, 'Extermination', 167–8.

25. Manoschek, '*Serbien ist judenfrei*', 63.
26. Christopher R. Browning, 'Wehrmacht Policy and the Murder of the Male Jews in Serbia', in Browning, *Fateful Months: Essays on the Emergence of the Final Solution* (New York: Holmes and Meier, 1978), 50.
27. Manoschek, 'Extermination', 177.
28. Christopher R. Browning, *The Final Solution and the German Foreign Office: A Study of Referat DIII of Abteilung Deutschland, 1940–43* (New York and London: Holmes and Meier, 1978), 59–60.
29. See Mark Mazower, *Inside Hitler's Greece: The Experience of Occupation 1941–1944* (New Haven, CT: Yale Nota Bene, 2001 <1993>), for the seminal study.
30. Manoschek, '*Serbien ist judenfrei*', 157.
31. See Browning, *Origins*, 343. The slowing down of anti-Serb violence, though hardly representing accommodation with the Serbs, is somewhat reminiscent of French revolutionary policy in the Vendée after the excesses of General Turreau. See Levene, *Rise*, 109.
32. Reported in Glenny, *Balkans*, 502.
33. Browning, *Origins*, 421–43; Lowenthal, *The Crime*, 30–2; Manoschek, 'Extermination', 178–80.
34. Turner to General Lohr as quoted in Manoschek, 'Extermination', 181.
35. Browning, *Origins*, 334.
36. It is worth remembering Helen Fein's second characterization of genocide as involving collective destruction 'sustained regardless of the surrender or lack of threat offered by the victim'. See Helen Fein, 'Genocide: A Sociological Perspective', *Current Sociology*, 38:1 (1990), 24.
37. Manoschek, 'Extermination', 182.
38. See, for example, Werner Maser, *Hitler's Letters and Notes*, trans. Arnold Pomerans (London: Heinemann, 1974), 233–4.
39. See Jürgen Förster, 'Operation Barbarossa as a War of Conquest and Annihilation', in Horst Boog et al., *Germany and the Second World War*, vol. 4, *The Attack on the Soviet Union* (Oxford: Clarendon Press, 1998), 482, for the notion of 'Keimzelle' (kernel or germ-cell).
40. See Förster, 'Hitlers Wendung nach Osten: Die Deutsche Kriegspolitik 1940–1941', in Bernd Wegner, ed., *Zwei Wege nach Moskau: Vom Hitler-Stalin-Pakt nach 'Unternehmen Barbarossa'* (Munich and Zurich: Piper, 1991), 113–52.
41. Hilberg, *Destruction*, 102; Browning, *Origins*, 215–16. Himmler also developed his own evolving if tortuous argument about the Asiatic threat. See Longerich, *Himmler*, 261–5.
42. See Theo J. Schulte, *The German Army and Nazi Policies in Occupied Russia* (Oxford and New York: Berg, 1989), 321–3, for full text of the Barbarossa-*Erlass*.
43. See Browning, *Origins*, 218, for text of 30 March 1941 meeting; Jürgen Förster, 'The Wehrmacht and the War of Extermination against the Soviet Union', *Yad Vashem Studies*, 14 (1981), 7–34, for the subsequent 'guidelines'.
44. Browning, *Origins*, 223.
45. Schulte, *German Army*, 322.
46. Quoted in Browning, *Origins*, 219.
47. Cholawsky, *Jews of Bielorussia*, 55–6, referring to Kube report, July 1942; Gottberg order, August 1943.
48. Browning, *Origins*, 218, referring to 30 March meeting.
49. See Jewish NKVD numbers as enumerated in Timothy Snyder, 'The Life and Death of Western Volhynian Jewry, 1921–1945', in Ray Brandon and Wendy Lower, eds.,

The Shoah in Ukraine: History, Testimony, Memorialization (Bloomington and Indianapolis: Indiana University Press, 2008), 88. Indeed, the Jewish percentage of leading NKVD cadres plummeted from 39.1 per cent in July 1934 (43 individuals) to 3.9 per cent (6 people) in September 1938. See Gerrits, *Myth* (referring to the N. Petrov and K. Skorkin 1999 study of the NKVD), 125.

50. Helmut Krausnick and Martin Broszat, *Anatomy of the SS State*, trans. Dorothy Long and Marian Jackson (London: Paladin 1970), 78–9; Browning, *Origins*, 216–17, for details of the Wehrmacht-SD discussions.
51. Dallin, *German Rule*, 69.
52. Arno Mayer, *Why did the Heavens Not Darken? The 'Final Solution' in History* (London and New York: Verso,1990), 216–22.
53. Omer Bartov, *The Eastern Front 1941–45: German Troops and the Barbarisation of Warfare* (Basingstoke: Macmillan, 1985), and Bartov, *Hitler's Army: Soldiers, Nazis and War in the Third Reich* (New York and London: Oxford University Press, 1991), esp. chapter 4, 'The Distortion of Reality'.
54. See Christian Streit, *Keine Kameraden: Die Wehrmacht und die sowjetischen Kriegsgefangenen 1941–1945* (Stuttgart: DVA, 1978); Alfred Streim, *Die Behandlung sowjetischer Kriegsgefangener im 'Fall Barbarossa'* (Karlsruhe: C.F. Müller, 1981), for the early, groundbreaking studies on this theme.
55. See Gerd Ueberschär, 'The Ideologically Motivated War in the East', in Rolf-Dieter Müller and Gerd Ueberschär, *Hitler's War in the East, 1941–1945: A Critical Assessment*, trans. Bruce D. Little (Oxford: Berghahn, 1997), 216.
56. Ueberschär, *Hitler's War in the East*, 215. Ueberschär notes that the figures for total Soviet POWs who died range from Joachim Hoffman's 2–2.8 million figure to Streit's upper limit of 3.3 million, out of a total of 5.24 million captured in the course of the war.
57. See Karel C. Berkhoff, *Harvest of Despair: Life and Death in Ukraine under Nazi Rule* (Cambridge, MA, and London: Harvard University Press, 2004), chapter 4, 'Prisoners of War', for full assessment, specifically 90; also Adam Jones, 'Gendercide and Genocide', *JGR*, 2:2 (2000), 195–6, for comment on the gendered aspect.
58. Quoted in Browning, *Origins*, 220–1.
59. Bartov, *Hitler's Army*, 129–30, for full text.
60. Lower, *Nazi Empire-Building*, 55–6; Streit, *Keine Kameraden*, 17, for more on Reichenau.
61. See Donald Bloxham, 'Punishing German Soldiers during the Cold War: The Case of Erich von Manstein', *Patterns of Prejudice*, 33:4 (1999), 25–46.
62. Bartov, *Hitler's Army*, 130–1, for text and comment.
63. For a not dissimilar assessment, see Hannes Heer, 'The Wehrmacht and the Holocaust in Belorussia', *HGS*, 11:1 (1997), 79–101.
64. See Browning, *Origins*, 226–7, following analysis in Alfred Streim's *Die Behandlung*. Also Donald Bloxham, *Genocide on Trial: War Crimes Trials and the Formation of Holocaust History and Memory* (Oxford: Oxford University Press, 2001), 89–90, for further commentary on the way so much weight was placed on Einsatzgruppen testimony in the International Military Tribunal (IMT) proceedings.
65. Browning, *Origins*, 228, felt this sufficiently significant to use italics. See Noakes and Pridham, *Nazism*, vol. 3, 1091–2, for text.
66. See Hilberg, *Destruction*, 105–6, for breakdown of units.
67. Longerich, *Unwritten Order*, 99.
68. See Lower, 'Anticipatory Obedience', 1–22, for development of this theme. See also Longerich, *Himmler*, 539; Gerwarth, *Hitler's Hangman*, 190–1, 196–7.

69. Browning, *Origins*, 262–4. See also Richard Breitman, *Official Secrets: What the Nazis Planned, What the British and Americans Knew* (New York: Hill and Wang, 1998), chapter 3, 'A Battalion Gets the Word'.

70. Burrin, *Hitler*, 106, on the role of Einsatzgruppe B. Dean, *Local Collaboration*, 28–9, notes that the unit had eliminated 'only' 45,467 by mid-November, which contrasts with Streim, *Die Behandlung*, 85–6, reporting the execution of 85,000 by 19 September 1941 and a huge tally of 229,052 Jews by January 1942.

71. Dean, *Local Collaboration*, 43.

72. Ronald Headland, 'The Einsatzgruppen: The Question of their Initial Operation', *HGS*, 4:4 (1989), 406.

73. See Adam Jones, *Crimes against Humanity: A Beginner's Guide* (Oxford: Oneworld, 2008), 35.

74. See Dan Stone, 'Modernity and Violence: Theoretical Reflections on the Einsatzgruppen', *JGR*, 1:3 (1999), 367–78; Donald Bloxham, 'Perpetrators and Perpetration', in Bloxham, *Genocide: the World Wars*, 146–54, 159.

75. Browning, *Origins*, 262–4, for a range of examples.

76. See Alexander B. Rossino, 'Polish "Neighbours" and German Invaders: Anti-Jewish Violence in the Białystok District during the Opening Weeks of Operation Barbarossa', *Polin*, 16 (2000), 435; Browning, *Origins*, 255–6; Daniel Jonah Goldhagen, *Hitler's Willing Executioners: Ordinary Germans and the Holocaust* (London: Little, Brown and Company, 1996), 188–91, for Białystok narratives, notable in their diversity of visceral vividness.

77. See Konrad Kwiet, 'From the Diary of a Killing Unit', in John Milfull, ed., *Why Germany?: National Socialist Anti-Semitism and the European Context* (Providence, RI, and Oxford: Berg, 1993), 84; Rossino, *Hitler Strikes*, 435; Browning, *Origins*, 257, offer notably different figures for the numbers killed.

78. Christian Gerlach, *Kalkulierte Morde: Die Deutsche Wirtschafts- und Vernichtungspolitik in Weissrussland 1941 bis 1944* (Hamburg: Hamburger Edition, 1999), 506–10.

79. See Slezkine, *Jewish Century*, 217.

80. Slezkine, *Jewish Century*; 216–26; Benjamin Pinkus, *The Jews of the Soviet Union: The History of a National Minority* (Cambridge and New York: Cambridge University Press, 1988), 90–9, for more on the accelerated late 1920s and 1930s modernization and urbanization of Soviet Jewry to the east of the historic Pale.

81. Dieter Pohl, 'The Murder of Ukraine's Jews under German Military Administration and in the Reich Commissariat Ukraine', in Brandon and Lower, *The Shoah*, 25; Longerich, *Holocaust*, 208.

82. Quoted in Longerich, *Holocaust*, 208.

83. Berkhoff, *Harvest*, 98. This included, in one instance, the testing of Soviet dum-dum explosives on Jewish prisoners. See Lower, *Nazi Empire-Building*, 65.

84. See Rolf-Dieter Müller, Parts A and B, 'Policy and Strategy: The Military Campaign', in Müller and Ueberschär, *Hitler's War*, esp. 36 and 88, for overview of Hitler plans and hubris.

85. Mayer, *Why did the Heavens*, 238–9.

86. Müller and Ueberschär, *Hitler's War*, 88.

87. Matthew Cooper, *The German Army, 1933–1945: Its Political and Military Failure* (London: Macdonald and Jane's, 1978), 311. See also Omer Bartov, *Hitler's Army*, 37–9, for broader evolution of German manpower losses on the Eastern Front 1941–2.

88. See Andreas Hillgruber, *Der Zenit des Zweiten Welkrieges Juli 1941* (Weisbaden: Steiner, 1977), for full assessment of the failure. More recently, Boog, *Germany and the Second World War*, vol. 4, *The Attack*.

89. Burrin, *Hitler*, 137–8; Jodl testimony, 1946, quoted in Percy Ernst Schramm, *Hitler: The Man and the Military Leader* (London: Penguin, 1972), 204.

90. Quoted in Christoph Dieckmann, 'The War and the Killing of the Lithuanian Jews', in Herbert, *National Socialist Extermination Policies*, 264.

91. Noakes and Pridham, *Nazism*, vol. 3, 1103–4, for text.

92. Roseman, *The Villa*, 35.

93. Browning, *Origins*, 265–7, 309–10.

94. See Breitman, *Architect*, 184–7, for Himmler's immediate post-meeting planning. Also Longerich, *Himmler*, 528–9; Gerwarth, *Hitler's Hangman*, 195–6, who mirror each other in arguing that Himmler's mid-July radicalization of the war against the Jews was closely tied to demonstrating to Hitler that the SS *Apparat* were capable of making the dream of a new ethnic order in the East a practical proposition through a grand project of ethnic cleansing.

95. Quoted in Browning, *Origins*, 315.

96. Roseman, The *Villa*, 62.

97. See Broszat, 'Hitler and the Genesis', 88.

98. Cited in Naimark, *Fires*, 92. See Roseman, *The Villa*, 62, for further commentary.

99. See Stone, *Constructing the Holocaust*, 66–9, for succinct overview; Herbert, *National Socialist Extermination Policies* for a major functionalist collection emphasizing the importance of periphery actors.

100. Mann, *Dark Side*, 7–8.

101. Browning, *Path to Genocide*, 111, 113.

102. Noakes and Pridham, *Nazism*, vol. 3, 1104; Cesarani, *Eichmann*, 128.

103. Browning, *Origins*, 319.

104. Longerich, *Holocaust*, 247.

105. Quoted in David Bankier, 'The Use of Antisemitism in Nazi Wartime Propaganda', in Berenbaum and Peck, *The Holocaust and History*, 37.

106. Ueberschär, 'The Ideologically Motivated War', 215–16.

107. See Yehoshua Büchler, 'Kommandostab Reichsführer-SS: Himmler's Personal Murder Brigades in 1941', *HGS*, 1:1 (1986) 13–14.

108. See Gerlach, *Kalkulierte Morde*, 2002–21, and Dean, *Local Collaboration*, 33–6, for different emphases on the nature of the events at Pinsk and the degree to which the massacre embraced women and children.

109. Dieckmann, 'War and Killing', 240–6, for details and analysis. Also Konrad Kwiet, 'Rehearsing for Mass Murder: The Beginning of the Final Solution in Lithuania in 1941', *HGS*, 12:1 (1998), 3–26.

110. Browning, *Origins*, 281; Lower, *Nazi Empire-Building*, 76.

111. See Longerich, *Himmler*, 530–3; Gerlach, *Kalkulierte Morde*, 545.

112. Manoschek, 'Extermination', 178.

113. See Herbert, 'New Answer and Questions', 31. See also Dieckmann, 'War and Killing', and Christian Gerlach, 'German Economic Interests, Occupation Policy, and the Murder of the Jews in Belorussia, 1941/43', also Herbert, *National Socialist Extermination Policies*, 210–23, for similar lines of inquiry.

114. See Berkhoff, *Harvest*, chapter 7, 'Famine in Kiev'. Significantly, Longerich *Holocaust*, 209–10, considers the Gerlach 'hypothesis' about feeding and housing Jews as the basis for the expansion of the programme of shooting as insufficiently 'adequate explanation of what took place'.

115. Noakes and Pridham, *Nazism*, vol. 3, 1199–200.

116. Noakes and Pridham, *Nazism*, vol. 3, 1200. There was an even more explicit speech Himmler made to Wehrmacht senior officers at the Adolf Hitler school, Sonthofen, on 5 May 1944. Here, speaking of the murder of Jewish children, he proposed that 'we as Germans however deeply we may feel in our hearts are not entitled to allow a generation of avengers filled with hatred to grow up with whom our children and grandchildren will have to deal because we were too weak and cowardly'. For further consideration (and a slightly different rendition) of this speech, see also 'Himmler, Hitler and the End of the Reich', BBC *Timewatch* (2001).

117. See Breitman, *Architect*, 192, for the directive and commentary.

118. Browning, *Origins*, 334–5, 397; Aly, *Final Solution*, 223.

119. See Kwiet, 'From the Diary', 88, for commentary.

120. Kwiet, 'From the Diary', 86–8. See also Christopher R. Browning, *Ordinary Men: Reserve Police Battalion 101 and the Final Solution in Poland* (New York: HarperPerennial, 1993), esp. 63–70, for the 'confusion' and 'agitation' among battalion members during and after their initiation into mass killing at the Józefów massacre, July 1942.

121. See Raul Hilberg, *Perpetrators, Victims, Bystanders: The Jewish Catastrophe, 1933–1945* (London: Lime Tree, 1993), 58–61, for the full story.

122. Pohl, 'Murder of Ukraine's Jews', 33–4. See also Shmuel Spector, *The Holocaust of Volhynian Jewry, 1941–1944* (Jerusalem: Yad Vashem, 1990), 76–7, 86.

123. Glenny, *Balkans*, 505.

124. Pohl, 'Murder of Ukraine's Jews', 32. See also Lower, *Nazi Empire-Building*, 75–8, for more on Jeckeln.

125. See Lower, *Nazi Empire-Building*, 73–5.

126. Pohl, 'Murder of Ukraine's Jews', 30–2.

127. Dieckmann, 'War and Killing', 260–2. It should be added that Dieckmann puts the emphasis on military and food security rather than 'resettlement' as the primary motivation for the Lithuanian killings.

128. Thomas Sandkühler, 'Anti-Jewish Policy and the Murder of the Jews in the District of Galicia, 1941/42', in Herbert, *National Socialist Extermination Policies*, 113.

129. Hilberg, *Perpetrators*, 21–2.

130. Browning, *Origins*, 349. More fully, Dieter Pohl, 'Hans Krüger and the Murder of the Jews in the Stanislawow region (Galicia)', *Yad Vashem Studies*, 26 (1994), 239–64.

131. Quoted in Förster, 'Complicity or Entanglement', 277.

132. Hilberg, *Destruction*, 126.

133. Berkhoff, *Harvest*, 65–9. For some of the key participating units in the massacre, see Alexander V. Prusin, 'A Community of Violence: The SiPo/SD and its role in the Nazi Terror System in Generalbezirk Kiew', *HGS* 21:1 (2007), 1–30.

134. The celebrated Yevgeny Yevutshenko poem 'Babi Yar' (1961) has been most famously followed by an eponymous Shostakovich symphony (1962) and the later, Soviet censured, Anatoli Kuznetsov novel (1966). For a wide bibliography, see notes in Karel C. Berkhoff, 'Dina Pronicheva's Story of Surviving the Babi Yar Massacre: German, Jewish, Soviet, Russian and Ukrainian Records', in Brandon and Lower, *The Shoah*, 310–17.

135. See Hilberg, *Destruction*, 110–11, for emphasis on Jeckeln. Also Pohl, 'Murder of Ukraine's Jews', 43–4, on the Rovno (Rivne) mass murders.

136. Andrej Angrick, 'Einsatzgruppe D', in Peter Klein, ed., *Die Einsatzgruppen, in der Besetzten Sowjetunion, 1941/42—die Tätigkeits- und Lageberichte des Chefs der Sicherheitspolizei und des SD* (Berlin: Edition Hentrich, 1997), 88–110; Fisher, *Crimean Tatars*, 156; Dallin, *Nazi Rule*, 260, for the debate on the Karaim.

137. Spector, *The Holocaust*, 114. Longerich, *Holocaust*, chapter 13, 'Enforcing the Annihilation Policy: Extending the Shootings to the Whole Jewish Population', for a much fuller inventory of Einsatzgruppen killings in Soviet Russia to the end of 1941.

138. Burrin, *Hitler*, 84.

139. See, among many other studies, Klaus Reinhardt, *Moscow—The Turning Point: The Failure of Hitler's Strategy in the Winter of 1941–42*, trans Karl. B. Keenan (Oxford and Providence, RI: Berg, 1992).

140. Referred to in Bloxham, *Final Solution*, 207.

141. Roseman, *The Villa*, 41. See also Longerich, *Holocaust*, 267–9, for further assessment and linkage to the wider geopolitical situation, more especially the growing US 'alliance' with Britain.

142. For instance, Hitler's 'table talk comments', 25 October 1941, quoted in Longerich, *Unwritten Order*, 129.

143. Browning, *Origins*, 196–7, 176–7. On the ongoing German use of Jewish labour, see Wolf Gruner, *Die Geschlossene Arbeitseinsatz deutscher Juden: Zur Zwangsarbeit als Element der Verfolgung, 1938–1943* (Berlin: Metropol, 1997).

144. Longerich, *Unwritten Order*, 133–4. More generally, see Ulrich Herbert, 'The German Military Command in Paris and the Deportation of the French Jews', in Herbert, *National Socialist Extermination Policies*, 128–62.

145. Longerich, *Unwritten Order*, 130: Longerich, *Holocaust*, 269.

146. See Raul Hilberg, *Documents of Destruction: Germany and Jewry, 1933–1945* (London: W.H. Allen: London, 1972), 87, for full text.

147. As quoted here in Aly, *Final Solution*, 220–1.

148. See Ian Kershaw, 'Improvised Genocide? The Emergence of the "Final Solution" in the Warthegau', *Transactions of the Royal Historical Society*, 2 (1992), 51–78.

149. Pohl, 'Murder of Ukraine's Jews', 42.

150. See Breitman, *Official Secrets*, 81–4, for the lead-up to the Riga events.

151. Quoted in Dallin, *Nazi Rule*, 208, n. 3.

152. See Ian Kershaw, 'The Persecution of the Jews and German Popular Opinion in the Third Reich', *Leo Baeck Year Book*, 26 (1981), 261–89. See also Dan Michman, 'Understanding the Jewish Dimension of the Holocaust', in Frankel, *Fate*, 237, Gerlach, 'Wannsee Conference', 114–15, for further discussion.

153. This necessarily contrasts with the Czech Jewish transport *from* Terezin sent on 15 January 1942 to Riga, which was liquidated on arrival. See Browning, *Origins*, 396.

154. Breitman, *Official Secrets*, 85–6.

155. See Kwiet, 'From the Diary', 84, for Himmler's orders to Rear Army Centre, 11 July 1941, on method and follow-through for executions.

156. Quoted in Mark Edele and Michael Geyer, 'States of Exception: The Nazi-Soviet War as a System of Violence', in Geyer and Fitzpatrick, *Beyond Totalitarianism*, 379.

157. Browning, *Origins*, 396.

158. Longerich, *Holocaust*, 291.

159. Aly, *Final Solution*, 223. Also 23–33; Browning, *Origins*, 416–21.

160. Christian Gerlach, 'Failure of Plans for an SS Extermination Camp in Mogilev, Belorussia', *HGS*, 7:1 (1999), 60–78.

161. Aly, *Final Solution*, 224–5.

162. Browning, *Origins*, 397.

163. See Longerich, *Wannsee*, 9.

164. Dallin, *Nazi Rule*, 208, n. 3.

165. Spector, *The Holocaust*, 173.
166. Aly, *Final Solution*, 223; van Pelt and Dwork, *Auschwitz*, 292–3.
167. Roseman, *The Villa*, 51; Browning, *Origins*, 403–6.
168. Browning, *Origins*, 407–8. My paraphrase and emphasis.
169. Gerlach, 'Wannsee Conference', 108–61.
170. As quoted in Roseman, *The Villa*, 61.
171. There is, of course, a more concrete instance of revenge, when Hitler launched V-1 and more specifically V-2 rockets against Britain in late 1944–45. See n. 226 below.
172. Breitman, *Official Secrets*, chapter 6, 'British Restraint'.
173. Quoted in Browning, *Path to Genocide*, 83; Breitman, *Architect*, 215–19, for background.
174. See Bloxham, *Genocide on Trial*, 215–16. Also Trude Levi, *A Cat Called Adolf* (London and Portland, OR: Vallentine Mitchell, 1995), for the experience through the victims' prism and ironically where sabotage *was* an element of the equation.
175. Gerlach, 'German Economic Interests', 223–4; Andrej Angrick, 'Annihilation and Labour: Jews and Thoroughfare IV in Central Ukraine', in Brandon and Lower, *The Shoah*, 194.
176. Liulevicius, *War Land*, 68.
177. See Spector, *The Holocaust*, 86, 110–11.
178. See Roseman, *The Villa*, 1–6, for overview.
179. Gerlach, 'Wannsee Conference', esp. 127–8, 137–40.
180. Roseman, *The Villa*, appendix for full text.
181. Roseman, *The Villa*, 74.
182. Browning, *Origins*, 413, Cesarani, *Eichmann*, 113–14, commentaries by reference to Eichmann trial transcripts.
183. Cesarani, *Eichmann*, 114.
184. Quoted in Roseman, *The Villa*, 70.
185. See Angrick, 'Annihilation and Labour', esp. 193–4, 208–9.
186. Sandkühler, 'Anti-Jewish Policy', 111–12; Angrick, 'Annihilation and Labour', 201–3.
187. Angrick, 'Annihilation and Labour', 203–8.
188. Angrick, 'Annihilation and Labour', 214.
189. Longerich, *Holocaust*, 309; Gerwarth, *Hitler's Hangman*, 213–14, who adds 'Bühler and Meyer thus placed an alternative on the table that rendered Heydrich's deportation programme largely superfluous'.
190. See Gerwarth, *Hitler's Hangman*, chapter 8, 'Reich Protector'; MacDonald, *The Killing*, 107–12.
191. Van Pelt and Dwork, *Auschwitz*, 300.
192. Shmuel Krakowski, 'The Satellite Camps', in Gutman and Berenbaum, *Anatomy*, 51.
193. Burrin, *Hitler*, 107.
194. Van Pelt and Dwork, *Auschwitz*, 302–6.
195. Hilberg, *Destruction*, tables, 339.
196. Franciszek Piper, 'Auschwitz Concentration Camp: How it was Used in the Nazi System of Terror and Genocide and in the Economy of the Third Reich', in Berenbaum and Peck, *The Holocaust and History*, 374. Raul Hilberg, 'Auschwitz and the "Final Solution"', in Gutman and Berenbaum, *Anatomy*, 86.
197. Hilberg, *Destruction*, 153. See also Pohl, 'Murder of Ukraine's Jews', 47–52.
198. Browning, *Path to Genocide*, ix.
199. Lucy Dawidowicz, *The War Against the Jews, 1933–45* (London: Penguin, 1975), 363–75, for a graphic overview of Warsaw Jewry's paroxysm. Dawidowicz puts the

figure at 45,000 Jews remaining in Warsaw at the end of this sequence. See also Yitzhak Arad, *Belzec, Sobibor, Treblinka: The Operation Reinhard Death Camps* (Bloomington: Indiana University Press, 1986), for the camps themselves.

200. Browning, *Ordinary Men*, esp. 53, 95; Goldhagen *Hitler's Willing Executioners*, 232–4.
201. Longerich, *Himmler*, 563–4.
202. Longerich, *Holocaust*, 332–5, for background.
203. Longerich, *Holocaust*, 309.
204. See Christopher R. Browning, 'German Technocrats, Jewish Labor, and the Final Solution: A Reply to Gotz Aly and Susanne Heim', in Browning, *Path*; 59–76. Also Browning, *Origins*, 165.
205. Longerich, *Wannsee*, 22.
206. Angrick, 'Annihilation and Labour', 194–5, However, see also Donald Bloxham, 'Jewish Slave Labour and the Economics of the Final Solution', in Bloxham, *Genocide, the World Wars*, 184, who questions the usefulness of the very term 'annihilation through work' as 'a broad analytical tool', not least given that later in the war, it could equally represent an SS rationalization for prolonging the lives of Jewish and gentile slave labourers.
207. Angrick, 'Annihilation and Labour', 198, n. 16, for the estimated 300 to 400 ZALs in the General Government alone.
208. Goldhagen, *Hitler's Willing Executioners*, chapter 11, 'Life in the "Work" Camps'.
209. See Dawidowicz, *War*, chapters 13 and 14; Isaiah Trunk, *Judenrat: The Jewish Councils in Eastern Europe under Nazi Occupation* (New York: Macmillan, 1972); Trunk, *Łódź Ghetto: A History*, trans. Robert Moses Shapiro (Bloomington and Indianapolis: Indiana University Press, 2006); Israel Gutman, *The Jews of Warsaw, 1939–1943: Ghetto, Underground, Revolt* (Bloomington and Indianapolis: Indiana University Press, 1982), for major overviews of the ghettos' last days.
210. See Donald Bloxham, 'Jewish Slave Labour', 167–90, for an excellent overview.
211. Bloxham, 'Jewish Slave Labour', 177–80.
212. Lower, 'Anticipatory Obedience', 8–9; Lower, *Nazi Empire-Building*, 150–61.
213. There is an extensive literature on Jewish armed resistance. In addition to Dawidowicz, *War*, chapter 15, see particularly Shmuel Krakowski, *The War of the Doomed: Jewish Armed Resistance in Poland, 1942–1944* (New York: Holmes and Meier, 1984); Arad, *Belzec*, Part 3, 'Escape and Resistance', for the revolts at Sobibor and Treblinka; Hermann Langbein, 'The Auschwitz Underground', in Gutman and Berenbaum, *Anatomy*, 485–502, for the Auschwitz rebellion.
214. Bartov, *Mirrors*, 109; Stargardt, 'Speaking in Public', 14–42.
215. See Browning, *Ordinary Men*, chapter 15, 'The Last Massacres: Harvest Festival'; Arad, *Belzec*, 365–9.
216. Bloxham, *Final Solution*, 244–5.
217. Levene, *Meaning*, 41.
218. Patrick Hands, ed., *Collins English Dictionary* (London and Glasgow: Collins, 1979), 1546.
219. Bauman, *Modernity*, 17.
220. Raul Hilberg, 'In Search of Special Trains', *Midstream* (October 1979), 32–8; Hilberg, *Destruction*, 168–86.
221. See, for instance, Bauman, *Modernity*, 197; Browning, *Fateful Months*, 64–5, for full rendition of the 'Sauer' document; Bloxham, *Final Solution*, 27–9, for further commentary.
222. Steven T. Katz, *Historicism, The Holocaust and Zionism: Critical Studies in Modern Jewish Thought and History* (New York and London: New York University Press,

1992), 212–13; Andrzej Strzelecki, 'The Plunder of Victims and Their Corpses', in Gutman and Berenbaum, *Anatomy*, 261. For the overall picture, see Jean-Claude Pressac with Robert-Jan van Pelt, 'The Machinery of Murder at Auschwitz', also in Gutman and Berenbaum, *Anatomy*, 183–245.

223. Pressac, 'The Machinery', 201.
224. Michael R. Marrus, 'Auschwitz: New Perspectives on the Final Solution', in Frankel, *Fate*, 82.
225. There is, of course, a whole issue for development here on the actual or perceived convergence of 'Jewish' and 'German' science. But that will have to wait for another book.
226. See Dennis Pizkiewicz, *The Nazi Rocketeers: Dreams of Space and Crimes of War* (Westport, CT: Praeger, 1995).
227. See Daniel Pick, *War Machine: The Rationalization of Slaughter in the Modern Age* (New Haven, CT, and London: Yale University Press, 1993), 178–88, for discussion.
228. See Robert-Jan van Pelt, 'A Site in Search of a Mission', in Gutman and Berenbaum, *Anatomy*, 128–34.
229. Pressac, 'The Machinery', 214–15.
230. Pressac, 'The Machinery', 215–16.
231. Browning, *Ordinary Men*, 95–6; Hilberg, *Destruction*, 229; Arad, *Belzec*, 87–9.
232. Arad, *Belzec*, 128.
233. Michael Berenbaum, 'Foreword', in Randolph L. Braham, and Scott Miller, eds., *The Nazis' Last Victims: The Holocaust in Hungary* (Detroit, MI: Wayne State University Press, 1998), 9; Pressac, 'The Machinery', 238; van Pelt and Dwork, *Auschwitz*, 342–3.
234. Andrzej Strzelecki, 'The Plunder of Victims and Their Corpses', in Gutman and Berenbaum, *Anatomy*, 262.
235. Spector, *The Holocaust*, 97–8, 100.
236. Strzelecki, 'The Plunder', 259–61. See also Eric D. Weitz, *A Century of Genocide: Utopias of Race and Nation* (Princeton, NJ, and Oxford: Princeton University Press, 2003).138, for an additional line of enquiry on the shaving of victims' genital hair.
237. Proctor, *Nazi War on Cancer*, quoted in Weitz, *Century*, 140.
238. See Uli Linke, 'Archives of Violence: The Holocaust and the German Politics of Memory', in Hinton, *Annihilating Difference*, 229–72, for a suggestive and, in the best sense of the word, controversial exploration.
239. Strzelecki, 'The Plunder', 250–6, for full details.
240. Strzelecki, 'The Plunder', 258.
241. See Cholawksy, *Jews of Bielorussia*, 64–5, for the dispute.
242. Strzelecki, 'The Plunder', 256.
243. See Frank Bajohr, *Parvenus und Profiteure: Korruption in der NS-Zeit* (Frankfurt-am-Main: S. Fischer, 2001), 75–89; Lower, *Nazi Empire-Building*, 114, for the case of Erwin Göllner, the district commissioner for Berdichev.
244. Aleksander Lasik, 'Rudolf Hoess: Manager of Crime', in Gutman and Berenbaum, *Anatomy*, 294–5; Strzelecki, 'The Plunder', 257. See also Raphael Gross, '"The Ethics of a Truth-Seeking Judge": Konrad Morgen, SS Judge and Corruption Expert', in Weise and Betts, *Years of Persecution*, 193–209, for the mindset of the supposedly 'moral' (*sic*) incorruptible Nazi investigating the matter.
245. Strzelecki, 'The Plunder', 254–5, 259.
246. Van Pelt and Dwork, *Auschwitz*, 197–211.
247. See Karin Orth, 'The Concentration Camp SS', esp. 316–19, for the emerging significance of WVHA.

248. Weindling, *Epidemics*, 92–6, 120–6.
249. See Lifton and Hackett, 'Nazi Doctors'; Helena Kubica, 'The Crimes of Josef Mengele', in Gutman and Berenbaum, *Anatomy*, 317–37.
250. Hilberg, *Perpetrators*, 34; Franciszek Piper, 'Gas Chambers and Crematoria', in Gutman and Berenbaum, *Anatomy*, 162.
251. Browning, *Ordinary Men*, 137–9, See also Andrew Charlesworth, 'The Topography of Genocide', in Dan Stone, ed., *The Historiography of the Holocaust* (Basingstoke and New York: Palgrave, 2004), 237.
252. See Hilberg, *Destruction*, 243–9.
253. Ian Traynor, 'Death and its Detail', *Guardian Weekend*, 21 January 1995, 17.
254. Traynor, 'Death and its Detail'. See also the centrality of maps in van Pelt and Dwork, *Auschwitz*, in situating Auschwitz in its exact imperial and post-imperial geographical context. Also Paul R. Magocsi, *Historical Atlas of East Central Europe* (Seattle: University of Washington Press, 2002), 90 and accompanying map, 91. Also cross-reference with Second World War map, 178.
255. Franciszek Piper, 'The Number of Victims', in Gutman and Berenbaum, *Anatomy*, 61–76 (esp. 71–2), for extrapolation of mortality figures of up to 1.5 million people, of which 1.35 million were Jewish.
256. See for instance, Guenter Lewy, *The Nazi Persecution of the Gypsies* (Oxford and New York: Oxford University Press, 2000), esp. 221–8.
257. Huttenbach, 'Romani Porajmos', 45; Donald Kenrick and Grattan Puxon, *Gypsies under the Swastika* (Hatfield: University of Hertfordshire Press, 1995), 150, for the upper figure. Michael Zimmerman, 'The National Socialist "Solution of the Gypsy Question"', in Herbert, *National Socialist Extermination Policies*, 186–209, is notably circumspect about offering figures. Also see the caution in Lewy, *Nazi Persecution*, 222.
258. Yehuda Bauer, 'Gypsies', in Gutman and Berenbaum, *Anatomy*, 446.
259. Figures vary on exact numbers. Bauer, 'Gypsies', 449, puts the figure at 20,946 registered; Zimmerman, 'National Socialist Solution', in Herbert, *National Socialist Extermination Policies*, 203, puts it at 22,600; Lewy, *Nazi Persecution*, 165, proposes 'about' 23,000.
260. Isabel Fonseca, *Bury Me Standing: The Gypsies and their Journey* (London: Chatto and Windus, 1995), 266.
261. Zimmerman, 'National Socialist Solution', in Herbert, *National Socialist Extermination Policies*, 203. Lewy, *Nazi Persecution*, 166, puts the total Roma death-toll in Auschwitz at over 20,000, including the further consignment of 800 to 1,000 young Romani too weak to work who were railroaded two months later from Buchenwald for gassing.
262. Kenrick and Puxon, *Gypsies*, 142–3; Fonseca, *Bury Me*, 262–6.
263. Fonseca, *Bury Me*, 267–71.
264. See Lewy, *Nazi Persecution*, 140–3.
265. See *Crisis of Genocide*, Vol. 1, Chapter 5, p. xx.
266. Zimmerman, 'National Socialist Solution', 418–19.
267. Zimmerman, 'National Socialist Solution', 419.
268. Anton Weiss-Wendt, 'Extermination of the Gypsies in Estonia during World War II: Popular Images and Official Policies', *HGS*, 17:1 (2003), 43–4, 46–7.
269. Lewy, *Nazi Persecution*, 142.
270. Lewy, *Nazi Persecution*, 135–40.
271. Kenrick and Puxon, *Gypsies*, 40–1.

272. Some 170,000 German and 40,000 Austrian Jews were killed in the Holocaust according to Poliakov and Wulf, and as cited in Mendes-Flohr and Reinharz, *The Jew*, 520.

273. See Mathieu Pernot, *Un camp pour les Bohémiens: mémoires du camp d'internement pour nomades de Saliers* (Arles: Actes Sud, 2001).

274. Huttenbach, 'Romani Porajmos', 44.

275. Huttenbach, 'Romani Porajmos', 42.

276. Kenrick and Puxon, *Gypsies*, 78–9; Huttenbach, 'Romani Porajmos', 44.

277. See Weiss-Wendt, 'Extermination', 37, for further commentary.

278. Kenrick and Puxon, *Gypsies*, 95–8.

279. Kenrick and Puxon, *Gypsies*, 98.

280. Weiss-Wendt, 'Extermination', 40.

281. Kenrick and Puxon, *Gypsies*, 98.

282. Weiss-Wendt, 'Extermination', 44–8; Kenrick and Puxon, *Gypsies*, 93.

283. Fonseca, *Bury Me*, 276.

284. Fonseca, *Bury Me*, 276.

285. See Lewy, *Nazi Persecution*, 202–4; Fonseca, *Bury Me*, 274–5.

286. Günter Grass, 'What have you done to my country?', *Independent Weekend*, 13 February 1993.

287. Katz, *Historicism*, 126.

288. Quoted in Lewy, *Nazi Persecution*, 140.

289. See Goldhagen, *Hitler's Willing Executioners*, part 1, 'Understanding German Antisemitism: The Eliminationist Mind-Set'.

290. Huttenbach, 'Romani Porajmos', 38; Kenrick and Puxon, *Gypsies*, 54.

291. Zimmerman, 'National Socialist Solution', in Herbert, *National Socialist Extermination Policies*, 201.

292. Here quoted in Lewy, *Nazi Persecution*, 224.

293. The point is well made in Bauer, *Jews for Sale*, 247–8.

294. See Noakes and Pridham, *Nazism*, vol. 3, 1200, for Himmler's Sonthofen speech (as above, n. 113).

295. Goebbels diary, quoted in Jonathan Steinberg, *All or Nothing: The Axis and the Holocaust 1941–43* (London and New York: Routledge, 1990), 50.

296. Quoted in Gerald Fleming, *Hitler and the Final Solution* (Oxford: Oxford University Press, 1986), 22–3.

297. See Jeffrey Herf, *The Jewish Enemy: Nazi Propaganda during World War II and the Holocaust* (Cambridge, MA: Harvard University Press, 2006), and Herf, 'Comparative Perspectives on Anti-Semitism, Radical Anti-Semitism in the Holocaust and American White Racism', *JGR*, 9:4 (2007), 581–95. For a brilliantly penetrating recent assessment, see Nicholas Stargardt, 'Speaking in Public About the Murder of the Jews: What did the Holocaust Mean to the Germans?', in Wiese and Betts, *Years of Persecution*, 133–55.

298. See Nathan Stoltzfus, *Resistance of the Heart: Intermarriage and the Rosenstrasse Protest in Nazi Germany* (New York: W.W. Norton, 1996), esp. 245.

299. Arad, *Belzec*, chapter 25, 'The Erasure of the Crimes'.

300. Piper, 'Gas Chambers', 163.

301. Breitman, *Official Secrets*, chapter 6, 'British Restraint'; Fleming, *Hitler*, 22 for the Jodl comment.

302. Walter Laqueur, *The Terrible Secret: Suppression of the Truth about Hitler's 'Final Solution'* (London: Penguin, 1982), 48–50; Hilberg, *Perpetrators*, 218–21.

303. Laqueur, *Terrible Secret*, chapter 4, 'The News from Poland'; Jozef Lewandowski, 'Early Swedish Information About the Nazis' Mass Murder of the Jews', *Polin*, 13 (2000),

113–27. Also, Hilberg, *Perpetrators*, 221–3, for a more critical reading of Karski's visit to Bełzec which, Hilberg believes, may have been to a neighbouring slave camp.

304. Browning, *The Final Solution and the German Foreign Office*, 152.

305. Quoted in Tony Kushner, *The Holocaust and the Liberal Imagination: A Social and Cultural History* (Oxford: Blackwell, 1994), 171.

306. See Stargardt, 'Speaking in Public', 136–47. There is a notable parallel here with the Rwandan genocide, namely in the insistence that if one fails to stand with the state, by joining in or accepting its killings, one's fate will be to be murdered by the Jewish (or, in the Rwandan case, Tutsi) 'liquidation' squads.

307. David Engel, *In the Shadow of Auschwitz: The Polish Government-in-Exile and the Jews, 1939–1942* (Chapel Hill: University of North Carolina Press, 1987), 183, 200.

308. Bauer, *Jews for Sale*, 84.

309. Kushner, *Holocaust and the Liberal Imagination*, 198, adds to the contradiction, by noting that Goebbels, at the time of the Allied declaration, claimed that the Allies actually supported Germany's anti-Jewish policies.

310. See Aronson, *Hitler*.

311. Among others, see Bernard Wasserstein, *Britain and the Jews of Europe, 1939–1945* (Oxford and New York: Oxford University Press, 1978); David Wyman, *The Abandonment of the Jews: America and the Holocaust, 1941–1945* (New York: Pantheon Books, 1984); Monty Noam Penkower, *The Jews were Expendable: Free World Diplomacy and the Holocaust* (Urbana: University of Illinois Press, 1983).

312. Kushner, *Holocaust and the Liberal Imagination*, chapter 6, 'The Rules of the Game: Britain, the United States and the Holocaust, 1943 to 1945'.

313. Kushner, *Holocaust and the Liberal Imagination*, 194.

314. See John Klier, 'The Holocaust and the Soviet Union', in Stone, *Historiography*, 280–1; Shimon Redlich, *Propaganda and Nationalism in Wartime Russia: The Jewish Antifascist Committee in the USSR, 1941–1948* (Boulder, CO: East European Monographs, 1982), for the full background.

315. Kushner, *Holocaust and the Liberal Imagination*, 195–7. Kushner particularly emphasizes the ambivalence of (not just wartime) liberal politics and society towards the Jews and their suffering. Also Wyman *Abandonment*, esp. chapter 10.

316. For assessments and analysis on the possibility of bombing, see 'Auschwitz—The Forgotten Evidence', dir. Lucy Carter (Channel 4, 2004), For a notable apologia (by one of the talking heads in the documentary), see William Rubinstein, *The Myth of Rescue: Why the Democracies Could Not Have Saved More Jews from the Nazis* (London: Routledge, 1997).

317. Stargardt, 'Speaking in Public', 137, for the interesting manner in which the work of *Aktion* 1005 made its way into German public consciousness.

318. Bauer, *Jews for Sale*, 113–14.

319. See Randolph L. Braham, *The Politics of Genocide: The Holocaust in Hungary* (New York: Columbia University Press, 1981), vol. 2, chapter 23, 'The Conspiracy of Silence'; Jean-Claude Favez, *The Red Cross and the Holocaust* (Cambridge: Cambridge University Press, 1999), 14–15, 43–4, 73–4; Rudolf Vrba, 'The Preparations for the Holocaust in Hungary: An Eyewitness Account', in Braham and Miller, *The Nazis' Last Victims*, 86–7.

320. See Bloxham, *Final Solution*, 241–3.

321. Bloxham, *Final Solution*, 243–4. For an important alternative interpretation, see Longerich, *Holocaust*, 397–401, who put the onus for the Danish Jewish escape on Best, not Himmler, but goes on to argue that the case suggests the limits of

Nazi *Judenpolitik* where it 'threatened to lose its function within the system of occupation'.

322. Bauer, *Jews for Sale*, 103; Breitman, *Architect*, 241.

323. Randolph L. Braham, 'The Holocaust in Hungary: A Retrospective Analysis', in Braham and Miller, *The Nazis' Last Victims*, 38: Asher Cohen, 'Pétain, Horthy, Antonescu and the Jews, 1942–1944, Toward a Comparative View', in Marrus, *The Nazi Holocaust*, vol. 4:1, 86.

324. Braham, 'The Holocaust in Hungary: A Retrospective Analysis', 36.

325. See Longerich, *Holocaust*, 405–6, for critical analysis.

326. Vrba, 'Preparations', 57, 87–95; Yehuda Bauer, 'Conclusion: The Holocaust in Hungary: Was Rescue Possible?', in David Cesarani, ed., *Genocide and Rescue: The Holocaust in Hungary 1944* (Oxford and New York: Berg, 1997), 204–5.

327. Vrba, 'Preparations', 57.

328. Bauer, *Jews for Sale*, chapter 7, 'Himmler's Indecision, 1942–1943'.

329. Richard Breitman, 'Nazi Jewish Policy in 1944', in Cesarani *Genocide and Rescue*, 86; see Bauer, *Jews for Sale*, 104–7, for more on Schellenberg and his third party contacts with the West.

330. Bauer, *Jews for Sale*, chapters 9 and 10.

331. Hilberg, *Destruction*, 330.

332. Goldhagen, *Hitler's Willing Executioners*, chapters 13 and 14.

333. Fleming, *Hitler*, 177.

334. Fleming, *Hitler*, 182; Bauer, *Jews for Sale*, 246–7; Longerich, *Himmler*, 727–8.

335. Breitman, 'Nazi Jewish Policy', 85; Bauer, 'Conclusion: The Holocaust in Hungary', 205; Piper, 'Gas Chambers', 174.

336. See in Paul A. Levine, 'Bureaucrats, Resistance and the Holocaust: Understanding the Success of Swedish Diplomacy in Budapest 1944–1945', in Berenbaum and Peck, *The Holocaust and History*, 518–35, for the key Swedish role.

337. Fleming, *Hitler*, 178.

338. Cesarani, *Eichmann*, 193.

339. See Goldhagen, *Hitler's Willing Executioners*, 356–7. However, see Richard Bessel, 'Murder amidst Collapse: Explaining the Violence of the Last Months of the Third Reich', in Weise and Betts, *Years of Persecution*, 259–61, for an assessment of the unravelling of Nazi Jewish policy within the context of wider collapse and mass violence.

340. Shlomo Aronson, 'The "Quadruple Trap" and the Holocaust in Hungary', in Cesarani, *Genocide and Rescue*, 112–16.

341. See Timewatch, 'Himmler, Hitler and the End of the Reich', for the last secret Himmler approaches to the Western Allies—and their unravelling. Also, Longerich, *Himmler*, 728–31.

342. See Joanne Reilly, *Belsen: The Liberation of a Concentration Camp* (London and New York: Routledge, 1998).

CHAPTER 3

1. Quoted in Porter, *When Nationalism*, 177.

2. See Ian Kershaw, *The Nazi Dictatorship: Problems and Perspectives of Interpretation* (London and New York: Edward Arnold, 1985), chapter 5, 'Hitler and the Holocaust', for a perfectly sound but entirely Germanocentric summary.

3. Joseph Rothschild, *Return to Diversity: A Political History of East Central Europe since World War II* (New York and Oxford: Oxford University Press, 1990), 9.

4. Helen Fein, *Accounting for Genocide: National Responses and Jewish Victimization during the Holocaust* (Chicago, IL: University of Chicago Press, 1984).

5. For more on these themes, see Birnbaum and Katznelson, *Paths;* Jonathan Frankel and Steven J. Zipperstein eds., *Assimilation and Community: The Jews in 19th Century Europe* (Cambridge and New York: Cambridge University Press, 1992).

6. Quoted in Levene, *War*, 150.

7. Quoted in Fink, *Defending the Rights*, 26.

8. Iancu, *Les Juifs*, 186–9.

9. Norman Cohn, *Warrant for Genocide: The Myth of the Jewish World-Conspiracy and the Protocols of the Elders of Zion* (London: Penguin, 1967), 60–5.

10. See Eugene C. Black, *The Social Politics of Anglo-Jewry, 1880–1920* (Oxford: Blackwell, 1998); Paula E. Hyman, *From Dreyfus to Vichy: The Remaking of French Jewry, 1906–1939* (New York: Columbia University Press, 1979); Jack Wertheimer, *Unwelcome Strangers: East European Jews in Imperial Germany* (New York: Oxford University Press, 1987); Steven E. Aschheim, *Brothers and Strangers: The East European Jew in German and German Jewish Consciousness, 1800–1923* (Madison: University of Wisconsin Press, 1982), for critical, country by country analyses.

11. Levene, *Meaning*, 182–96.

12. See Florint Lobont, 'Antisemitism and Holocaust Denial in Post-Communist Eastern Europe', in Stone, *Historiography*, 441. See also his referent Vladimir Tismaneanu, *Fantasies of Salvation: Democracy, Nationalism and Myth in Post-Communist Europe* (Princeton, NJ: Princeton University Press, 1998).

13. Michael Marrus and Robert O. Paxton, *Vichy France and the Jews* (New York: Basic Books, 1981), 40.

14. Leo Pinsker, 'Auto-emancipation', (1882), quoted in Arthur Hertzberg, ed., *The Zionist Idea: A Historical Analysis and Reader* (New York: Atheneum, 1959), 184.

15. Cited in Moshe Davis, *Israel: Utopia Incorporated* (London: Zed Books, 1977), 24. See also Jonathan Frankel, *Prophecy and Politics: Socialism, Nationalism and the Russian Jews, 1862–1917* (Cambridge and New York: Cambridge University Press, 1981), chapter 8, 'The Revolutionary Ethos in Transition: Russian-Jewish Youth in Palestine, 1904–1914'. For a further variation on this theme, see Gerrits, *Myth*, 35–6, for the US joint fact-finding mission to the Jewish communities of the sub-Carpathian region in 1926. The mission reported on the 'unbelievable' and 'pathetic backwardness of our people', the milieu 'an Eastern one of the year 1500'. The subtext, as clearly denoted by Gerrits, is 'a Western Jewish' combination of sympathy, pity, contempt, and suspicion for 'never really welcome' Jews of the East.

16. See *Der Ewige Jude* ('The Eternal Jew'), dir. Fritz Hippler, Deutsche Film Gesellschaft: (1940), for the classic Nazi film exploitation of the trope.

17. Renée Poznanski, *Jews in France during World War II*, trans. Nathan Bracher (Hanover, NH, and London: Brandeis University Press and United States Holocaust Memorial Museum, 2001), 255.

18. See Frederic Cople Jaher, *The Jews and the Nation: Revolution, Emancipation, State Formation, and the Liberal Paradigm in America and France* (Princeton, NJ, and Oxford: Princeton University Press, 2002), chapters 2 and 3, for further development and analysis.

19. Paula E. Hyman, *The Jews of Modern France* (Berkeley: University of California Press, 1998), 145–9. See also Paul J. Kingston, *Anti-Semitism in France during the 1930s: Organisations, Personalities, Propaganda* (Hull: University of Hull Press, 1983).

20. Poznanski, *Jews*, 1.
21. See David Weinberg, *A Community on Trial: The Jews of Paris in the 1930s* (Chicago, IL: University of Chicago Press, 1977), for closer analysis.
22. Marrus, *Unwanted*, 149.
23. Robert Paxton, *Vichy France: Old Guard and New Order* (New York: Knopf, 1972) is the key breakthrough study of Vichy. More recently, see particularly Julian Jackson, *France: The Dark Years, 1940–1944* (Oxford: Oxford University Press, 2001), 380.
24. Marrus and Paxton, *Vichy France and the Jews*, 3–9, 76.
25. Browning, *Origins*, 200.
26. Poznanski, *Jews*, 131–2.
27. Hyman, *Jews*, 164–5.
28. Paxton, *Vichy France*, 353, 356.
29. Poznanski, *Jews*, 71.
30. Joan Tumblety, review of Michael Curtis, *Verdict on Vichy: Power and Prejudice in the Vichy France Regime* (London: Weidenfeld & Nicolson, 2002*), Journal of Jewish Studies*, 54:2 (2003), 350–2.
31. See J. Kaplan, 'French Jewry under the Occupation', *American Jewish Year Book*, 47 (1945), 116.
32. Susan Zuccotti, *The Holocaust, The French, and the Jews* (Lincoln and London: University of Nebraska Press, 1993) 53, 57, 98. It is also notable too that soon after the *Statut des Juifs*, the Jews of Algeria—then part of metropolitan France—were all divested of their French citizenship.
33. David Weinberg, 'France', 10, in David S. Wyman, ed., *The World Reacts to the Holocaust* (Baltimore and London: Johns Hopkins University Press, 1996).
34. Zuccotti, *Holocaust*, 87–9.
35. Poznanski, *Jews*, 254–5.
36. See Herbert, 'The German Military Command', 130, 154.
37. István Deák, 'Introduction', in Deák, *Politics of Retribution*, 6.
38. Zuccotti, *Holocaust*, 98–9.
39. Quoted in Poznanski, *Jews*, 256. Interestingly, Zuccotti, *Holocaust*, 99, attempts (rather unsuccessfully) to give Laval the benefit of the doubt for this action.
40. See Zuccotti, *Holocaust*, chapter 6, 'The July Roundup, Paris, 1942'.
41. Poznanski, *Jews*, 237–45.
42. Jackson, *France*, 380.
43. Zuccotti, *Holocaust*, 145–8, and Poznanski, *Jews*, 295–9, both note the significance of the clamour coming from leading bishops and cardinals.
44. Zuccotti, *Holocaust*, 175–6; Steinberg, *All or Nothing*, 157.
45. Quoted in Cohen, 'Pétain, Horthy', 74.
46. Zuccotti, *Holocaust*, 169–70.
47. Marrus and Paxton, *Vichy France*, 330; Cohen, 'Pétain, Horthy', 76.
48. Weinberg, 'France', 14.
49. Weinberg, 'France', 13.
50. Michael R. Marrus, *The Holocaust in History* (London: Penguin, 1987), 73.
51. Zuccotti, *Holocaust*, 176, 180–7.
52. See Zuccotti, *Holocaust*, 206–8, for analysis.
53. Weinberg, 'France', 16, 18–19.

54. See Henry Rousso, *The Vichy Syndrome: History and Memory in France since 1944*, trans. Arthur Goldhammer (Cambridge, MA: Harvard University Press, 1991), for *the* consideration of French post-war amnesia and its long-term consequences.

55. See Livia Rothkirchen, 'Czechoslovakia', in Wyman, *The World Reacts*, 159–62. See also Roman Vishniac, *A Vanished World* (London: Allen Lane, 1983), for a remarkable visual insight into the lost pre-war milieu of rural Transcarpathian and Subcarpathian Jewry.

56. Bloxham, *Final Solution*, 121.

57. Rothkirchen, 'Czechoslovakia', 160.

58. Roger D. Petersen, *Understanding Ethnic Violence: Fear, Hatred and Resentment in Twentieth Century Eastern Europe* (Cambridge and New York: Cambridge University Press, 2002), 198.

59. See Chapter 2, p. 118.

60. Browning, *The Final Solution and the German Foreign Office*, 96–9.

61. Laqueur, *Terrible Secret*, 140–1; Rothkirchen, 'Czechoslovakia', 169.

62. Bauer, *Jews for Sale*, chapter 6, 'What Really Did Happen in Slovakia?'

63. Payne, *History*, 402.

64. See Yeshayahu Jelinek, *The Parish Republic: Hlinka's Slovak People's Party, 1939–1945* (Boulder, CO: East European Quarterly, 1976), chapter 4, 'Party Factions', for close analysis on the internal fractures within the regime. For the shift in Jewish policy, see also Jelinek, 'The Vatican, the Catholic Church, the Catholics and the Persecution of the Jews during World War II: The Case of Slovakia', in Mosse and Vago, *Jews and Non-Jews*, 221–5; Livia Rothkirchen, 'The Slovak Enigma: A Reassessment of the Halt to the Deportations', in Marrus, *The Nazi Holocaust*, vol. 4:2, 473–83.

65. Kenrick and Puxon, *Gypsies*, 120–3; Jiri Lipa, 'The Fate of Gypsies in Czechoslovakia under Nazi Domination', in Michael Berenbaum, ed., *A Mosaic of Victims: Non-Jews Persecuted and Murdered by the Nazis* (London and New York: I.B. Tauris, 1990), 210.

66. Bloxham, *Final Solution*, 122–3; Lipa, 'The Fate', 212.

67. Frederick B. Chary, *The Bulgarian Jews and the Final Solution, 1940–1944* (Pittsburgh: University of Press, Pittsburgh 1972), chapters 4 and 5.

68. Slawomir Kapralski, 'Ritual of Memory in Constructing the Modern Identities of Eastern European Romanies', in Nicholas Saul and Susan Tebbutt, eds., *The Role of the Romanies: Images and Counter-Images of 'Gypsies'/Romanies in European Cultures* (Liverpool: Liverpool University Press. 2004), 214–15.

69. Frederick B. Chary, 'Bulgaria', in Wyman, *The World Reacts*, 258–62.

70. Stefan Troebst, 'Triangling Bulgarian Jewry: Between Nation-State, Socialism and Zionist Utopia' (unpublished paper) given at 'Between Trieste, Salonika and Odessa' conference Simon Dubnow Institute, Leipzig, 4–6 November 2000.

71. See Chary, 'Bulgaria', 278–87, for discussion.

72. Chary, 'Bulgaria', 264.

73. Chary, *Bulgarian Jews*, 69–84.

74. Chary, *Bulgarian Jews*, 188–93; Glenny, *Balkans*, 509.

75. Chary, *Bulgarian Jews*, 127–8.

76. See Alexander Matkovski, *A History of the Jews in Macedonia*, trans. David Arney (Skopje: Macedonian Review Editions 1985), 132–43, for more on these events.

77. Browning, *The Final Solution and the German Foreign Office*, 164; Glenny, *Balkans*, 510–11.

78. Mark Levene, '"Ni grec, ni bulgare, ni turc": Salonika Jewry and the Balkan Wars, 1912–13', *Jahrbuch des Simon-Dubnow Instituts*, 2 (2003), 87–90.

79. See Marshall Lee Miller, *Bulgaria during the Second World War* (Stanford, CA: Stanford University Press, 1975), for the necessary overview.

80. See Steven B. Bowman, *The Agony of Greek Jews, 1940–1945* (Stanford, CA: Stanford University Press, 2009), 80–92, and Mazower, *Inside Hitler's Greece*, 238–46, for detailed surveys of the operation of destruction. Also Andrew Apostolou, 'The Exception of Salonika: Bystanders and Collaborators in Northern Greece', *HGS*, 14:2 (2000), 165–96. The degree to which elements of the Greek population connived in Jewish destruction is also corroborated in Mark Mazower, *Salonica, City of Ghosts: Christians, Muslims and Jews, 1430–1950* (London: Harper Perennial, 2004), chapter 22, 'Genocide'. On the ironies surrounding the Baron de Hirsch railway station, see Glenny, *Balkans*, 515–16. The further irony, of course, is that the community would have collectively survived if it had been deported from Greece to Turkey after the Balkan wars, or Lausanne. See Volume 1, Chapter 3.

81. Mark Biondich, *The Balkans: Revolution, War, and Political Violence since 1878* (Oxford: Oxford University Press, 2011), 152.

82. Roseman, *The Villa*, 114.

83. Biondich, The *Balkans*, 128–9, 140–1; Edmond Paris, *Genocide in Satellite Croatia, 1941–1945: A Record of Racial and Religious Persecutions and Massacres*, trans. Lois Perkins (Chicago, IL: American Institute for Balkan Affairs, 1961), 116–17; Glenny, *Balkans*, 500–1.

84. Menachem Shelah, 'Genocide in Satellite Croatia during the Second World War', in Berenbaum, *Mosaic*, 78; Kenrick and Puxon, *Gypsies*, 114–20.

85. Braham, *Politics of Genocide*, vol. 1, 208–15, notes that sentences passed on senior officers in December 1943 were then revoked by the pro-Nazi Sztójay government. See also Mark Mazower, *Hitler's Empire: Nazi Rule in Occupied Europe* (London: Penguin, 2009), 329.

86. Stella Alexander, *The Triple Myth: A Life of Archbishop Alojzije Stepinac* (Boulder, CO: East European Monographs, 1987), 101.

87. Mazower, *Hitler's Empire*, 349–50, and Davide Rodogno, *Fascism's European Empire: Italian Occupation during the Second World War*, trans. Adrian Belton, (Cambridge: Cambridge University Press, 2006), 400–7, are both notably robust on this point.

88. Levene, *Rise*, 275–6.

89. Mann, *Dark Side*, 309–10. See also Angelo Del Boca (and Giorgio Rochat et al.), *I gas di Mussolini: il fascismo e la guerra d'Etiopa* (Rome: Editori Riuniti, 1996).

90. Rodogno, *Fascism's European Empire*, chapter 10, 'Repression'.

91. See L. Picciotto Fargion, 'The Jews during the German Occupation and Italian Social Republic', in Ivo Herzer et al., ed., *The Italian Refuge: Rescue of Jews during the Holocaust* (Washington DC: Catholic University of America Press, 1989), 109–38; Meir Michaelis, *Mussolini and the Jews: German-Italian Relations and the Jewish Question in Italy, 1922–1945* (Oxford: Clarendon Press, 1978), 342–406; Susan Zuccotti, *The Italians and the Holocaust: Persecution, Rescue and Survival* (New York: Basic Books, 1987).

92. See, for instance, Michele Sarfatti, *Mussolini contro gli ebrei: cronaca dell'elaborazione delle leggi del 1938* (Turin: S. Zamorani, 1994), for the view that Mussolini embraced ideological racism. Compare with Georg Zachariae, *Mussolini si confessa* (Milan:

Garzanti, 1966), 167–70, for the argument that he provided conditions for the 'Final Solution' in Italy but was not himself anti-Semitic.

93. Meir Michaelis, 'Italy', in Wyman, *The World Reacts*, 519.

94. Michaelis, 'Italy'. See also Alexander Stille, *Benevolence and Betrayal: Five Jewish Families under Fascism* (London: Vintage, 1992), for layers of regional and national interaction between Italian Jews and Gentiles.

95. See Browning, *The Final Solution and the German Foreign Office*, 164–70.

96. Bloxham, *Final Solution*, 118.

97. Steinberg, *All or Nothing*, 76.

98. Massimo Legnani, 'Il 'ginger' del generale Roatta: le direttive della 2a Armata sulla repressione antipartigiana in Slovenia e Croazia', *Italia Contemporanea*, 209/10 (1997/1998), 155–74; Rodogno, *Fascism's European Empire*, 333–8.

99. Poznanski, *Jews*, 387–9; Steinberg, *All or Nothing*, 108–9; Dennis Reinhartz, 'Damnation of the Outside: The Gypsies of Croatia and Serbia in the Balkan Holocaust, 1941–1945', in Crowe and Kolsti, *Gypsies*, 84; Kenrick and Puxon, *Gypsies*, 106–8.

100. See Rodogno, *Fascism's European Empire*, 379, for close analysis of what this 'Italian bureaucratic parlance' actually meant.

101. Mann, *Dark Side*, 242.

102. Steinberg, *All or Nothing*, 3, 57. See also Browning, *The Final Solution and the German Foreign Office*, 134–41, for the scope of Italian actions.

103. Curtis, *Verdict*, quoted in Tumblety, review (n. 30).

104. Rodogno, *Fascism's European Empire*, 363.

105. Rodogno, *Fascism's European Empire*, 365–6; Mazower, *Hitler's Empire*, 400; Steinberg, *All or Nothing*, 116–19.

106. Quoted in Longerich, *Holocaust*, 396.

107. Hoare, *Genocide*, 134–5, 143.

108. Kenrick and Puxon, *Gypsies*, 114–15.

109. Biondich, *Balkans*, 133–5.

110. Hoare, *Genocide*, 342–5.

111. Poznanski, *Jews*, 390–3; Marc D. Angel, *The Jews of Rhodes: The History of a Sephardic Community* (New York: Sepher-Hermon Press, 1980), 151–2.

112. See Jan T. Gross, *Neighbours: The Destruction of the Jewish Community in Jedwabne, Poland, 1941* (London: Arrow, 2003), for the seminal study; Antony Polonsky and Joanna B. Michlic, eds., *The Neighbors Respond: The Controversy over the Jedwabne Massacre in Poland* (Princeton, NJ: Princeton University Press, 2003), for critical commentary. The controversy has revolved around not just the degree of German responsibility for the pogrom but the exact numbers killed, with Gross's figure of 1,600 disputed by Polish state reports (2002–4), which opt for a much lower *c.*340 killed.

113. See Spector, *The Holocaust*, 64–9, for details.

114. Dov Levin, 'Lithuania', in Wyman, *The World Reacts*, 33. See also Martin Gilbert, ed., Avraham Tory, *Surviving the Holocaust: The Kovno Ghetto Diary*, trans. Jerzy Michalowicz (Cambridge, MA: Harvard University Press, 1990), 8–9. Also Petersen, *Understanding Ethnic Violence*, 97.

115. See Radu Ioanid, *The Holocaust in Romania: The Destruction of Jews and Gypsies under the Antonescu Regime, 1940–1944* (Chicago, IL: Ivan R. Dee, 2000), 63–90, for a full account. However, see also Vladimir Solonari, *Purifying the Nation: Population Exchange and Ethnic Cleansing in Nazi-Allied Romania* (Washington DC and Baltimore: Woodrow Wilson Center Press and Johns Hopkins University Press, 2010),

164–7, for critical commentary on the origins, scope, and top-down *halting* of the massacres.

116. See David Kahane, *Lvov Ghetto Diary*, trans. Jerzy Michalowicz (Amherst: University of Massachusetts Press, 1990), 13.
117. Petersen, *Understanding Ethnic Violence*, 7.
118. Hilberg, *Destruction*, 120; Dean, *Local Collaboration*, 37–8. For a range of readings which dispute local instigation, see notably Andrew Ezergailis, 'Neighbours did not Kill Jews!', in David Gaunt, Paul A. Levine, and Laura Palosuo, eds., *Collaboration and Resistance during the Holocaust: Belarus, Estonia, Latvia, Lithuania* (Bern and Oxford: Peter Lang, 2004), 187–222; Paul R. Magocsi, *A History of the Ukraine* (Washington DC: University of Washington Press, 1996), 631; Rossino, *Hitler Strikes*, 452; Hiden and Salmon, *Baltic Nations*, 118–19.
119. Spector, *The Holocaust*, 74.
120. Spector, *The Holocaust*, 68–70.
121. Alexander Victor Prusin, *Nationalizing a Borderland: War, Ethnicity, and Anti-Jewish Violence in East Galicia, 1914–1920* (Tuscaloosa: University of Alabama Press, 2005), 26–7.
122. See Bloxham, *Final Solution*, 121–2.
123. Andrzej Zbikowski, 'Jewish Reaction to the Soviet arrival in the Kresy in September 1939', *Polin*, 13 (2000), 63. Also, more generally, Prusin, *Lands Between*, chapter 5, 'Redrawing Ethno-Social Boundaries'.
124. Frank Golczewski, 'Shades of Grey: Reflection on Jewish-Ukrainian and German-Ukrainian Relations in Galicia', in Brandon and Lower, *The Shoah*, 132–3.
125. Petersen, *Understanding Ethnic Violence*; John-Paul Himka, 'Ukrainian Collaboration in the Extermination of the Jews during the Second World War: Sorting Out the Long-Term and Conjunctural Factors', in Frankel, *Fate*, 170–89, esp. 182.
126. See Nechama Tec, *When Light Pierced the Darkness: Christian Rescue of Jews in Nazi-Occupied Poland* (New York: Oxford University Press, 1986), for one notable analysis.
127. Gross, *Neighbours*, 65, testimony of Menachem Finkelsztayn.
128. Amir Weiner, *Making Sense of War: The Second World War and the Fate of the Bolshevik Revolution* (Princeton, NJ, and Oxford: Princeton University Press, 2001), 268. Lower, *Nazi Empire*, 93, cites the example of the service at Khmil'nyk, Zhytomir district.
129. See Shimon Redlich, 'Metropolitan Andrii Sheptyts'kyi and the Complexities of Ukrainian-Jewish Relations', in Zvi Y. Gitelman, ed., *Bitter Legacy: Confronting the Holocaust in the USSR* (Bloomington and Indianapolis: Indiana University Press, 1997), 70–2, on Sheptyts'kyi's 'rescue' efforts in what Redlich describes as an increasingly 'impossible situation'. For a more negative assessment, by way of Sheptyts'kyi's consistently pro-German stance, see Statiev, *Soviet Counter-Insurgency*, 72–3.
130. Weiner, *Making Sense*, 280–1. The Dorohoi witness was Meyer Teich, head of the Jewish community of Suceava.
131. Polian, *Against Their Will*, 121–3.
132. See Gross, *Neighbours*, 47–53; Rossino, *Hitler Strikes*, 438–9.
133. See Gross, *Revolution from Abroad*, 181–2, for the nature of some of the atrocities committed. However, as a caveat, Prusin, *Lands Between*, 157, rather plausibly notes that the Soviets would not have been able to engage in such 'time-consuming practices' at a moment of head-long retreat, thus implying that it was 'the Germans and

militiamen (who) deliberately disfigured and defiled corpses before opening the prisons'. For corroboration of this argument, see also Bogdan Musiał, *'Konterrevolutionäre Elemente sind zu erschießen': Die Brutalisierung der deutsch-sowjetischen Krieges im Sommer 1941* (Berlin: Propyläen, 2000), esp. 262–9. Musiał's study offers the most extensive discussion of the massacres.

134. Prusin, *Lands Between*, 151. Significantly, the official figures are much smaller. Statiev, *Soviet Counter-Insurgency*, 55, for instance, cites a total of 11,319 prisoners killed and 141,527 evacuated across the entirety of the rimlands.

135. Golczewski, 'Shades of Grey', 130; Gross, *Revolution from Abroad*, 181. See also Shimon Redlich, *Together and Apart in Brzezany: Poles, Jews, and Ukrainians, 1919–1945* (Bloomington and Indianapolis: Indiana University Press, 2002), 104–5, 115–16, for the knock-on sequence of NKVD massacres and anti-Jewish massacres in a small eastern Galician town.

136. Spector, *The Holocaust*, 75.

137. Golczewski, 'Shades of Grey', 131.

138. See Ross Brann, *Power in the Portrayal: Representations of Jews and Muslims in Eleventh-and Twelfth-Century Islamic Spain* (Princeton, NJ: Princeton University Press, 2002), chapters 1–3.

139. Quoted in Zbikowski, 'Jewish Reaction', 70. See also Gerrits, *The Myth*, 89–93, for further analysis of the actual, complex, Jewish response to Soviet invasion.

140. As quoted in Petersen, *Understanding Ethnic Violence*, 127.

141. Petersen, *Understanding Ethnic Violence*, 40.

142. See Spector, *The Holocaust*, 64–7, for the Hanna Berenstein narrative.

143. Zbikowski, 'Jewish Reaction', 70–1; Himka, 'Ukrainian Collaboration', 142; Levene, *Meaning*, 140, for the 'Gerwani' comparison.

144. A. Zuvinites memoir (1989) quoted in Petersen, *Understanding Ethnic Violence*, 109.

145. See Michael MacQueen, 'Nazi Policy towards the Jews in the Reichskommissariat Ostland, June-December 1941: From White Terror to Holocaust in Lithuania', in Gitelman, *Bitter Legacy*, 97–100; Hiden and Salmon, *Baltic Nations*, 120.

146. The 254,000 figure constitutes about 96 per cent of the community. See Dina Porat, 'The Holocaust in Lithuania: Some Unique Aspects', in David Cesarani, ed., *The Final Solution: Origins and Implementation* (London: Routledge, 1994), 160–3.

147. Cesarani, *The Final Solution*, 164. Lithuanian enthusiasm in the killing of Jews contrasts with what one commentator sees as rather lukewarm support in fighting *for* the Germans. See Statiev, *Soviet Counter-Insurgency*, 69–70.

148. Michael MacQueen, 'The Context of Mass Destruction: Agents and Prerequisites of the Holocaust in Lithuania', *HGS*, 12:1 (1998), 37–9; Anton Weiss-Wendt and Uğur Ümit Üngör, 'Collaboration in Genocide: The Ottoman Empire, 1915–16, the German-occupied Baltic States and Rwanda, 1994', *HGS* 25:3 (2011), 419.

149. See Dov Levin, 'The Jews and the Socio-Economic Sovietisation of Lithuania, 1940–41', *Soviet Jewish Affairs*, 17 (1987), 17–30.

150. See Solomonas Atamukas, 'The Hard Long Road toward the Truth: On the Sixtieth Anniversary of the Holocaust in Lithuania', *Lituanus* 47:4 (winter 2001), here accessed at <http://www.lituanus.org/2001/01_4_03.htm>, for the necessary corrective.

151. Šarunas Liekis, 'The Patterns of Anti-Jewish Violence Prior to 1941: "The Lithuanian Case"-Prelude to the Holocaust?', Unpublished paper for 'The Mass Dynamics of Anti-Jewish Violence in Eastern and East-Central Europe' International

Conference, Parkes Institute Southampton, 18–19 March 2007. With thanks to Dr Liekis for a copy.

152. See Alex Faitelson, *The Truth and Nothing but the Truth: Jewish Resistance in Lithuania 1941–44* (Jerusalem: Gefen Publishing House, 2006), 13, for full text of the LAF (22 June 1941) proclamation.
153. Petersen, *Understanding Ethnic Violence*, 108.
154. Mann, *Dark Side*, 283–4.
155. Mazower, *Hitler's Empire*, 456–7.
156. Dina Porat, 'The Holocaust in Lithuania', 165.
157. Andrew Ezergailis, 'Latvia', in Wyman, *The World Reacts*, 368.
158. Weiss-Wendt and Üngör, 'Collaboration in Genocide', 418–19; Weiss-Wendt, 'Extermination', 38–9, 47.
159. Ezergailis, 'Latvia', 367.
160. My argument here has further Turkish-Armenian parallels, not least as explored by Taner Akçam in his understanding of the Turkish elite mindset during its Ottoman crisis years. See Taner Akçam, *From Empire to Republic: Turkish Nationalism and the Armenian Genocide* (London and New York: Zed Books, 2004), esp. 39.
161. See Weiss-Wendt and Üngör, 'Collaboration in Genocide', 420–1, for critical discussion of the Saulius Sužiedėlis analysis, the latter proposing that in the case of Lithuania the most extreme collaborators emulated the value system, rhetoric, and behaviour of the Nazis.
162. See Golczewski, 'Shades of Grey', 124–7, for the background.
163. Lower, *Nazi Empire-Building*, 95; see Weiner, *Making Sense*, 244, for further contemporary statements suggesting the OUN's aim was to create a 'clean page'.
164. Golczewski, 'Shades of Grey', 116–17.
165. Golczewski, 'Shades of Grey', 139.
166. Browning, *Origins*, 274; Dean, 'Local Collaboration in the Holocaust in Eastern Europe', in Stone, *Historiography*, 126–7.
167. Golczewski, 'Shades of Grey', 139.
168. Kazimierz Sakowicz, quoted in Mazower, *Hitler's Empire*, 451.
169. Berkhoff, 'Dina Pronicheva's Story', esp. 305.
170. See Nicholas A. Robins and Adam Jones, eds., *Genocides by the Oppressed: Subaltern Genocide in Theory and Practice* (Bloomington and Indianapolis: Indiana University Press, 2009), for wider exploration of this theme, though interestingly not of groups acting as Nazi subalterns.
171. See, for instance, Berkhoff, *Harvest*, 66, for how bystanders' filching was a standard accompaniment to Kievan Jewry's stations to the cross, at Babi Yar. For further sober assessment, see also Cholawsky, *Jews of Bielorussia*, chapter 14, 'The Non-Jewish Population's Attitude Towards the Jews During the Holocaust'.
172. At the back of my mind here are Philip Zimbardo's 1971 Stanford prison experiments. See Zimbardo, *The Lucifer Effect: Understanding how Good People Turn Evil* (New York: Random House, 2007), for updated analysis with reference also to the Abu Ghraib prison abuses in Iraq.
173. Browning, *Origins*, 203–4; Bob Moore, *Victims and Survivors: The Nazi Persecution of the Jews in the Netherlands* (London and New York: Arnold, 1997), 201–3, for a somewhat more circumspect view of Dutch police enthusiasm for the task.
174. See Kevin Brownlow and Andrew Mollo, dir., *It Happened Here* (1966), for a highly creative, fictive film portrayal of British collaborationist paramilitaries operating

under German rule in a 1940s Nazi-occupied Britain. The film received a stormy reception as a consequence. That said, British colonial style parallels with (as well as distinctions from) Nazi policing are themselves worthy of further exploration, not least with respect to Ireland's pre-1921 British experience. See Charles Townshend, *The British Campaign in Ireland, 1919–1921: The Development of Political and Military Policies* (Oxford: Oxford University Press, 1975).

175. See Dean, *Local Collaboration*, 44–8, for a full account.
176. See Bernhard Chiari, *Alltag hinter der Front: Besatzung, Kollaboration und Widerstand in Weissrussland 1941–1944* (Düsseldorf: Droste, 1998), esp. 170–84, 247–67, for fuller analysis of police collaboration in Belorussia.
177. See Mark Roseman, 'Holocaust Perpetrators in Victims' Eyes', in Wiese and Betts, *Years of Persecution*, esp. 84–5, for a notable recent examination of victim testimonies in which Jewish police are portrayed as particular figures of hate. Also, Saul Friedländer, 'An Integrated History of the Holocaust: Possibilities and Challenges', 27, also in Wiese and Betts, for a succinct reminder of the more general breakdown of Jewish solidarity, more broadly pursued in his *Years of Extermination*, in critical part with reference to the contemporary Warsaw (Oneg Shabbat) archive of Emmanuel Ringelblum. Equally revealingly, see Calel Perechodnik, *Am I a Murderer?: Testament of a Jewish Ghetto Policeman* (Boulder, CO: Westview, 1996), for something of the thought processes of one such police recruit.
178. See Martin Dean, 'Soviet Ethnic Germans and the Holocaust in the Reich Commissariat Ukraine, 1941–1944', in Brandon and Lower, *The Shoah*, 248–71, for further background and incisive commentary. The ethnic German predicament as more broadly representative of all rimlands peoples under Nazi rule brings to mind a comment by Stathis N. Kalyvas, *The Logic of Violence in Civil War* (Cambridge: Cambridge University Press, 2006), 12: 'Irrespective of their sympathies (and everything else being equal) most people prefer to collaborate with the political actor that best guarantees their survival.'
179. Dean, 'Soviet Ethnic Germans', 264–5.
180. Dean, *Local Collaboration*, 106; Cholawsky, *Jews of Bielorussia*, 51, and most especially Dallin, *Nazi Rule*, 217–25, for commentary.
181. See Prusin, *Lands Between*, 184; Weiss-Wendt, 'Extermination', 38–9.
182. Berkhoff, 'Dina Pronicheva's Story', 303. See also Solonari, *Purifying the Nation*, 177–8, for confirmation of the importance of OUN-style nationalism among the majority Ukrainian population of north Bukovina. Solonari, 194–6, further makes important distinctions between anti-Jewish pogroms motivated by venality and the usually much more extreme form, in which nationalist ideology was the core driver.
183. See Erich Koch, Reich Commissar for the Ukraine's comment, as quoted in Mazower, *Hitler's Empire*, 458.
184. Golczewski, 'Shades of Grey', 136–7.
185. Mazower, *Hitler's Empire*, 458–60; David. Cesarani, *Justice Delayed* (London: Heinemann, 1992), 31.
186. Lukas, *Forgotten Holocaust*, 118, 156.
187. Gunnar S. Paulssohn, *Secret City: The Hidden Jews of Warsaw 1940–1943* (New Haven, CT: Yale University Press, 2002), 224–5. Also Paulssohn, 'The Demography of Jews in Hiding in Warsaw, 1943–1945', *Polin*, 13 (2000), 97–9.
188. Lukas, *Forgotten Holocaust*, 141.

189. Jan T. Gross, 'Opportunistic Killings and Plunder of Jews by Neighbours—a Norm or an Exception in German Occupied Europe?', in Wiese and Betts, *Years of Persecution*, 269–86.
190. Engel, *In the Shadow*, 50–1, 80.
191. Engel, *In the Shadow*, esp. 'Conclusion', 203–13, for Engel's overall assessment.
192. Engel, *In the Shadow*, 17–18. See also Antony Polonsky, 'Introduction', *Polin*, 13 (2000), 1, for more on the origins of this aspect of Polish national paranoia.
193. Quoted in Andrzej Brink, 'The Hidden Complex of the Polish Mind: Polish–Jewish Relations during the Holocaust', in Polonsky, *My Brother's Keeper*, 166–7. Fuller text also in Polonsky, 'Introduction', 20.
194. Engel, *In the Shadow*, 38. For the Czech position, see Jan Laníček, 'The Czechoslovak Government-in-Exile and the Jews during World War 2 (1938–1948)', unpublished PhD thesis, Southampton University, 2010.
195. Lukas, *Forgotten Holocaust*, 170.
196. Quoted from Polonsky, 'Introduction', 14, 13.
197. See Gross, 'Tangled Web', 110, for NKVD intelligence report on pogromist tendencies in July 1945 and their repeated justification: 'Poland is ruled by the Jews'.
198. Quoted in Lukas, *Forgotten Holocaust*, 178; see Joshua D. Zimmerman, 'The Attitude of the Polish Home Army (AK) to the Jewish Question during the Holocaust: the Case of the Warsaw Ghetto Uprising', in Murray Baumgarten, Peter Kenez, and Bruce Thompson, eds., *Varieties of Antisemitism: History, Ideology, Discourse* (Newark, NJ: University of Delaware Press, 2009), 105–26, esp. 122, for a detailed study confirming this interpretation.
199. Engel, *In the Shadow*, 65.
200. Quoted in Gross, 'Tangled Web', 81–2.
201. See Jean Ancel, *Documents Concerning the Fate of Romanian Jewry during the Holocaust* (New York: Beate Klarsfeld Foundation, 1986), vol. 10, SSI report, 4 July 1940, 29–34; also Solonari, *Purifying the Nation*, 158–64.
202. Solonari, *Purifying the Nation*, 1–3.
203. See Butnaru, *Silent Holocaust*, 85, for the nature of the assault on Bucharest Jewry; Solonari, *Purifying the Nation*, 125–36, for the background to the National Legionary state's rise and fall.
204. See Solonari, *Purifying the Nation*, 32.
205. Carol Iancu, *L'émancipation des juifs de Roumanie (1913–1919): De l'inégalité civique aux droits de minorité* (Montpelier: Université Paul-Valéry, 1992), 31.
206. Jean Ancel, 'Antonescu and the Jews', in Berenbaum and Peck, *The Holocaust and History*, 464–6.
207. Radu Ioanid, 'Romania', in Wyman, *The World Reacts*, 229.
208. Ioanid, *Holocaust*, 170.
209. Ancel, 'Antonescu', 467.
210. Solonari, *Purifying the Nation*, 54–5.
211. Solonari, *Purifying the Nation*, 54.
212. Ancel, 'Antonescu', 469; Solonari, *Purifying the Nation*, 132.
213. Ancel, 'Antonescu'; see Solonari, *Purifying the Nation*, 117–20, for a further concise portrait.
214. Jean Ancel, 'The Romanian Way of Solving the "Jewish Problem" in Bessarabia and Bukovina, June-July 1941', *Yad Vashem Studies* 29 (1988), 190, for the full protocol of government meeting, 8 July 1941.

215. See Mark Levene, 'The Experience of Genocide: Armenia 1915–16, Romania, 1941–42', in Kieser and Schaller, *Der Völkermord*, 423–62, for both broad contours of the programme and Ottoman parallels.
216. Ancel, 'Romanian Way', 190–1, 210.
217. Solonari, *Purifying the Nation*, 170–3; Ioanid, *The Holocaust*, chapter 3, 'The Massacres at the Beginning of the War', for fuller detail.
218. Ancel, 'Romanian Way', 227.
219. Solonari, *Purifying the Nation*, 176–7.
220. Ancel, *Documents*, vol. 6, 470–7, warrant for arrest of Capt. Adamovici and others (1950).
221. Julius S. Fisher, *Transnistria: The Forgotten Cemetery* (South Brunswick, NY: T. Yoseloff, 1969), 25.
222. Hilberg, *Destruction*, 131. Also Ancel, 'Romanian Way', 229, for the direct complaints made to the Rumanians by Wöhler's superior, General von Schobert.
223. Ancel, *Documents*, vol. 5, 17, 19, and 31 July 1941 reports, 15–16, 23–4, 25–6. Also vol. 8, 595–6, testimony of Marian Michael.
224. See Fisher, *Transnistria*, 53; Solonari, *Purifying the Nation*, 200–4.
225. Ancel, *Documents*, vol. 5, 59–63, vol. 9, 188–9, for further details of the Tighina agreement.
226. Mazower, *Hitler's Empire*, 333.
227. Significantly, Lemkin, *Axis Rule*, 237–8, picked up on the genocidal significance of this expropriation project.
228. Ancel *Documents*, vol. 5, 91–4, 98, 182–3, 187.
229. Fisher, *Transnistria*, p. 57, 100.
230. Ioanid, *Holocaust*, pp. 111–12, 143–4.
231. Quoted in Solonari, *Purifying the Nation*, 206.
232. Solonari, *Purifying the Nation*, 184–90.
233. Figures for the numbers who died at Dalnik differ. Ancel, 'Antonescu', 470, opts for a figure of 20,500. Dora Litani, 'The Destruction of the Jews of Odessa in the Light of Rumanian Documents', *Yad Vashem Studies*, 6 (1967), 139, puts the figure at 16,000 within an overall 40,000 total from the two days of Odessa massacres. See Ioanid, *Holocaust*, 177–82, for further assessment.
234. Jean Ancel, 'The Romanian Campaigns of Mass Murder in Transnistria, 1941–1942', in Randolph L. Braham, ed., *The Destruction of Romanian and Ukrainian Jews during the Antonescu Era* (Boulder, CO: Social Science Monographs, 1997), 110–11.
235. Ancel, 'The Romanian Campaigns', 117–19; Fisher, *Transnistria*, 122–3.
236. Ancel, *Documents*, vol. 5, 204.
237. Lieberman, *Terrible Fate*, 201–2; Solonari, *Purifying the Nation*, 239.
238. Ioanid, *Holocaust*, 142.
239. Solonari, *Purifying the Nation*, 273–6.
240. Dennis Deletant, 'Transnistria and the Romanian Solution to the 'Jewish Problem', in Brandon and Lower, *The Shoah*, 170–2. See more generally Solonari, *Purifying the Nation*, chapter 14, 'Deporting Roma'.
241. Ancel, *Documents*, vol. 10, Saraga speech, 322–8; Ministry of Interior report, 10 November 1943, 510–14.
242. Fisher, *Transnistria*, chapter 7, 'Relief, Repatriation and Rescue Efforts'; Ioanid, *Holocaust*, chapter 6, 'Life in Transnistria'.
243. Ioanid, *Holocaust*, 155–7, 165–8.
244. Solonari, *Purifying the Nation*, 222–6.

245. Deletant, 'Transnistria', 174–5, for Mihai Antonescu's speech. See also Solonari, *Purifying the Nation*, 283, on the Roma element of the suspension.
246. Deletant, 'Transnistria', 172–3, 177–8.
247. Béla Vago, 'Jewish Leadership Groups in Hungary and Romania during the Holocaust', 'International Scholars Conference on the Holocaust—A Generation After', unpublished March 1975 conference paper, YIVO, New York. Cited in Fein, *Accounting*, 324.
248. See Solonari, *Purifying the Nation*, 292–3.
249. See the perspicacious comments of Aureliu Weiss, quoted in Ioanid, *Holocaust*, 248. Also the secret German diplomatic communiqués, 240–1.
250. Solonari, *Purifying the Nation*, 294–5.
251. Solonari, *Purifying the Nation*, 299–300, referring to Sebastian Balta's *Rumänien und die Grossmächte in der Ära Antonescu, 1940–1944* (Bucharest: Editura Eminescu, 2005).
252. Ioanid, *Holocaust*, 214.
253. Ioanid, *Holocaust*, 264–70; Solonari, *Purifying the Nation*, 302.
254. Solonari, *Purifying the Nation*, 287.
255. Solonari, *Purifying the Nation*, 300–1.
256. Marrus, *Unwanted*, 290–1; Fisher, *Transnistria*, 130–1.
257. Ioanid, *Holocaust*, 256–7; Favez, *The Red Cross*, 109–14, for the key role of the ICRC in these negotiations.
258. See Tony Barber, 'Romanians Cherish Memories of their Genocidal Dictator', *The Independent*, 23 August 1994; Ioanid, 'Romania', 251–2, and Ioanid, 'When Mass Murderers Become Good Men', *Journal of Holocaust Education*, 4:1 (1995), 92–104.
259. Ancel, 'Antonescu', 476. More recently, Mazower, *Hitler's Empire*, 339, offers figures of 300,000 dying in Transnistria, including between 115,000 and 180,000 from the region itself.
260. See Holly Case, 'The Holocaust in Regional Perspective: Antisemitism, and the Holocaust in Hungary, Romania and Slovakia', in Baumgarten, *Varieties*, 79, 81.
261. Ioanid, *Holocaust*, 266–7.
262. See William O. McCagg, *Jewish Nobles and Geniuses in Modern Hungary* (Boulder, CO: East European Quarterly, 1972).
263. See Victor Karady, 'Religious Divisions, Socio-Economic Stratification and the Modernisation of Hungarian Jewry after the Emancipation', in Michael K. Silber, ed., *Jews in the Hungarian Economy, 1760–1945: Studies Dedicated to Moshe Carmilly-Weinberger on his Eightieth Birthday* (Jerusalem: Magnes Press 1992), 170, and table 3, 182. The caveat is that Jewish adherence to Budapest, in 'outer' areas such as Transylvania or Slovakia, did not necessarily translate into having Magyar as mother tongue.
264. István Deák, 'Hungary and the Holocaust', in Baumgarten, *Varieties*, 96.
265. See Attila Pók, 'Germans, Hungarians, and the Destruction of Hungarian Jewry', in Braham and Miller, *The Nazis' Last Victims*, 48–9, for the emerging articulation of an anti-Jewish discourse. See also István I. Mócsy, *The Effect of World War I: The Uprooted: Hungarian Refugees and their Impact on Hungary's Domestic Politics, 1918–1921* (New York: Brooklyn College Press, 1983).
266. Braham, *Politics of Genocide*, vol. 1, 76–8, for a breakdown of the figures, which also included 100,000 'converted' Jews.
267. Cohen, 'Pétain, Horthy', 86.
268. Cesarani, *Eichmann*, 162–4.
269. István Deák, 'Could the Hungarian Jews have Survived?', in Marrus, *The Nazi Holocaust*, 4:2, 647.

270. Arendt, *Eichmann*, 125; Nicholas M. Nagy-Talavera, 'Làszló Endre: The Frontrunner of the Final Solution in Hungary', in Randolph L. Braham, and Attila Pók, eds., *The Holocaust in Hungary: Fifty Years Later* (New York: Columbia University Press, 1997), 367.

271. Braham, *Politics of Genocide*, vol. 1, 82–3. Also Thomas L. Sakmyster, *Hungary's Admiral on Horseback: Miklós Horthy, 1918–1944* (Boulder, CO: East European Monographs, 1993), 251, for further evidence.

272. See Braham, *Politics of Genocide*, vol. 1, 142, for instance, for the views of the former Prime Minister, Pál Teleki, and vol. 1, 226–9, for Braham's assessment of Kállay.

273. Braham, 'Hungary', in Wyman, *The World Reacts*, 204. There were some 401,000 Jews in post-Trianon Hungary, the acquired territories adding an estimated 324,000 more.

274. This stands in contrast to Budapest's early 1943 abandonment of Hungarian Jews abroad to the demands of German 'resettlement' to the east, albeit with 'selected' exceptions. See Browning, *The Final Solution and the German Foreign Office*, 155.

275. Nagy-Talavera, 'Làszló Endre', 370, for Veesenmayer's 1948 trial recollection; Braham, *Politics of Genocide*, vol. 1, 379; Mann, *Dark Side*, 300, for further commentary.

276. Braham, *Politics of Genocide*, vol. 1, 373–4, 596–600.

277. See Braham, *Politics of Genocide*, vol. 1, 528–690, for detailed examination.

278. See Nicholas M. Nagy-Talavera, *'The Green Shirts' and the Others: A History of Fascism in Hungary and Romania*, 2nd ed. (Iaşi and Oxford: Centre for Romanian Studies, 2001), chapter 8, 'The Hungarianist Empire'; Làszló Karsai, 'The Last Phase of the Hungarian Holocaust: The Szálasi Regime and the Jews', in Braham and Miller, *The Nazis' Last Victims*, 103–4.

279. Deak, 'Fatal Compromise', 67.

280. See Levine, 'Bureaucrats', which among other things, places Raoul Wallenberg, the most high profile of the Legation 'rescuers', in a wider and more measured diplomatic context. See also Robert Rozett, 'International Intervention: The Role of Diplomats in Attempts to Rescue Jews in Hungary', in Braham and Miller, *The Nazis' Last Victims*, 136–52.

281. See Zweig, *Gold Train*, 40, 97; more generally, Braham, *Politics of Genocide*, vol. 2, chapter 26, 'The Szálasi Era'.

282. See Braham, *Politics of Genocide*, vol. 2, 873–5, for the January 1945 incident. See also Karsai, 'The Last Phase', 103–16.

283. Asher Cohen, 'The Dilemma of Rescue or Revolt', in Braham and Miller, *The Nazis' Last Victims*, 132.

284. Braham, *Politics of Genocide*, vol. 1, 200–3; Judit Fejes, 'On the History of the Mass Deportations from Carpatho-Ruthenia in 1941', in Braham and Pók, *The Holocaust in Hungary*, 309–10.

285. Fejes, 'On the History', 15–16; Cohen, 'Pétain, Horthy', 83.

286. Bauer, 'Conclusion', 194; Braham, *Politics of Genocide*, vol. 1, 277–9, 282; Browning, *The Final Solution and the German Foreign Office*, 128.

287. See Randolph L. Braham, 'The Kamenets Podolsk and Délvidék Massacres: Prelude to the Holocaust in Hungary', *Yad Vashem Studies*, 9 (1973) 133–56.

288. Braham, *Politics of Genocide*, vol. 1, 330–7; Bauer, 'Conclusion', 195.

289. Braham, *Politics of Genocide*, vol. 1, 320–1, 328, 348–9.

290. Zweig, *Gold Train*, 40, 42. It is also noteworthy that Jaross himself was a native of the Subcarpathian region (Felvidék), to which he had been previously appointed as special minister under the Imrédy regime. See Braham, *Politics of Genocide*, vol. 1, 174.

291. Braham, *Politics of Genocide*, vol. 1, 406.
292. Braham, *Politics of Genocide*, vol. 1, 403. Also Nagy-Talavera', Làszló Endre', 367–8.
293. Braham, *Politics of Genocide*, vol. 1, 403.
294. Braham, *Politics of Genocide*, vol. 1, 588.
295. Tim Cole, *Traces of the Holocaust: Journeying In and Out of Ghettos* (London and New York: Continuum, 2011), chapter 9, 'Narrating Concentration and Deportation 1: Làszló Ferenczy's reports'. With thanks to Dr Cole for providing a pre-publication copy of this chapter.
296. Cole, *Traces of the Holocaust*, 105. Interestingly, these figures are at variance with those supplied by Veesenmayer, who proposed 289,357 deportees for zones 1 and 2 and a complete list to 7 June of 437,402. See Braham, *Politics of Genocide*, vol. 1, 607.
297. See Braham, 'Hungary', in Wyman, *The World Reacts*, 207.
298. Cited in Zweig, *Gold Train*, 57.
299. Nagy-Talavera, 'Làszló Endre', 366; Braham, *Politics of Genocide*, vol. 1, 569.
300. Nagy-Talavera, 'Làszló Endre', 366.
301. Zweig, *Gold Train*, 54.
302. Zweig, *Gold Train*, 57.
303. Cole, *Traces*, 111–13.
304. Nagy-Talavera, 'Làszló Endre', 369.
305. Zweig, *Gold Train*, 51–2.
306. Zweig, *Gold Train*, for the whole, sorry, sordid story.
307. Dean, 'Local Collaboration in the Holocaust', 133; see Götz Aly and Christian Gerlach, *Das Letze Kapitel: Realpolitik, Ideologie und der Mord in den Ungarischen Juden 1944/5* (Stuttgart: Deutsche Verlags-Anstalt, 2002), for a full analysis.
308. Nagy-Talavera, 'Làszló Endre', 373; Braham, *Politics of Genocide*, vol. 2, 707.
309. Zweig, *Gold Train*, 63–4.
310. Zweig, *Gold Train*, 217–18.
311. See Martin Dean, *Robbing the Jews: The Confiscation of Jewish Property in the Holocaust* (Cambridge and New York: Cambridge University Press, 2008). Also Götz Aly, *Hitler's Beneficiaries: Plunder, Racial War and the Nazi Welfare State* (New York: Metropolitan Books, 2006), who argues more forcefully for the *primacy* of economics as the Nazi driving force to genocide.
312. Braham, 'Hungary', 308.

CHAPTER 4

1. Markusen and Kopf, *The Holocaust*, 70, and more generally chapter 4, 'The Relationship between Genocide and Total War'. Levene, *Meaning*, 52–3, for commentary.
2. Martin Shaw, *War and Genocide: Organised Killing in Modern Society* (Cambridge: Polity Press, 2003), 4–6.
3. See Raffael Scheck, *Hitler's African Victims: The German Army Massacres of Black French Soldiers in 1940* (New York: Cambridge University Press, 2006). Numerous studies of the Oradour massacre include most recently Jean-Jacques Fouché, *Massacre at Oradour France 1944: Coming to Grips with Terror*, trans. David Sices and James B. Atkinson (Dekalb: Northern Illinois University Press, 2005). On the mass killing of surrendered US troops at Malmédy and environs, see James J. Weingartner, *Crossroads of Death: The Story of the Malmédy Massacre and Trial* (Berkeley: University of California Press, 1979).

4. Richard Bessel, 'Murder Amidst Collapse', 255.
5. Levene, *Meaning*, 57–65.
6. Markusen and Kopf, *The Holocaust*, 161–3, 175–80. Paul Addison and Jeremy A. Crang, eds., *Firestorm: The Bombing of Dresden* (London: Pimlico, 2006), among the more recent contributions to the voluminous literature on Dresden.
7. See Jörg Friedrich, *Der Brand Deutschland im Bombenkrieg, 1940–1945* (Berlin: Propyläen, 2002), esp. 74–7, for an albeit controversial reading.
8. See Ina Zweiniger-Bargielowska, 'Bread Rationing in Britain, July 1946–July 1948', *Twentieth Century British History* 4:1 (1993): 57–85; Richard Storry, *A History of Modern Japan* (London: Penguin, 1960), 238–9.
9. Lemkin, *Axis Rule*, 196–7, for this Western European arena does proffer the case of the Luxembourgers (Letzeburgesch) on grounds of cultural emasculation. I have generally held out against cultural pressures, however severe, being *sufficient on their own* to constitute genocide. See, however, A. Dirk Moses, 'Raphael Lemkin: Culture and the Concept of Genocide', in Donald Bloxham and A. Dirk Moses, eds., *The Oxford Handbook of Genocide Studies* (Oxford: Oxford University Press, 2010), 19–41, esp. 22–30, 37, for a view which more strongly foregrounds culture.
10. James Holland, *Italy's Sorrow: A Year of War 1944–45* (London: HarperPress, 2008). The Marzabotto massacres over three days in September–October 1944, in which over 1,800 men, women, and children were killed, were the height of this sequence. See Jack Olsen, *Silence on Monte Sole* (London: Pan Books, 1968). See Mazower, *Inside Hitler's Greece*, chapter 16, 'Anatomy of a Massacre: 16 August 1943', for a single but not singular Hellenic comparison—the destruction of the village of Komeno in western Greece.
11. Vojtech Mastny, *The Czechs under Nazi Rule: The Failure of National Resistance 1939–1942* (New York and London: Columbia University Press, 1971), 12, 126–32, 216–20.
12. Dallin, *German Rule*, 427, for the conservative estimate; Schulte, *German Army*, 181, for a table of estimates which include those of Hans Adolf Jacobsen as well as Streit.
13. Berkhoff, *Harvest*, 93–106, for close analysis.
14. Streit, *Keine Kamaraden*, 128; Schulte, *German Army*, 209.
15. Lower, *Nazi Empire*, 65 also 231–2, n. 106.
16. Dallin, *German Rule*, 68–70; Berkhoff, *Harvest*, 92.
17. Adam Jones, *Genocide: A Comprehensive Introduction* (London and New York: Routledge, 2nd ed. 2011), 271, reads this as a direct case of genocide. See also his further gendered commentary in Jones, 'Gendercide and Genocide', 195–6.
18. Here quoted in Bracher, *German Dictatorship*, 522.
19. Christopher Kobrak and Andrea H. Schneider, 'Big Business and the Third Reich', in Stone, *Historiography*, 158, offer a figure of *c.*13.5 million forced or slave labourers in Reich areas—both Jew and Gentile—by the end of the war.
20. Schulte, *German Army*, 278; Berkhoff, *Harvest*, 301.
21. Berkhoff, *Harvest*, 35–6, 45, 164–5. One might note that Backe was another Russian, more precisely Georgian-born, ethnic German with seemingly murderous Nazi views harboured against his once compatriots. During the Great War, he was interned by the tsarist authorities as an enemy alien. See Gerwarth, *Hitler's Hangman*, 188.
22. See Alan Kramer, 'Mass Killing and Genocide from 1914 to 1945: Attempting a Comparative Analysis', in Wiese and Betts, *Years of Persecution*, 221, for these specific figures. See also Polian, *Against Their Will*, 242–75, for a fuller breakdown of the German civilian deportations.

23. Kramer, 'Mass Killing', 221. Red Army atrocities against Germans are more fully explored in Rüdiger Overmans, 'Das Schicksal der deutschen Kriegsgefangenen des Zweiten Weltkrieges', in Rolf-Dieter Müller, *Das deutsche Reich und der Zweite Weltkrieg* (Munich: Deutsche Verlags-Anstalt, 2008), vol. 10:2, esp. 404–5, 502–3.

24. Kramer, 'Mass Killing', 221.

25. See Norman M. Naimark, *The Russians in Germany: A History of the Soviet Zone of Occupation, 1945–1949* (Cambridge, MA: Harvard University Press, 1995), chapter 2, 'Soviet Soldiers, German Women, and the Problem of Rape'.

26. Antony Beevor, *Berlin: The Downfall 1945* (London: Viking, 2007), 30.

27. Alexander M. Yakovlev, *A Century of Violence in Soviet Russia*, trans. Anthony Austin (New Haven, CT, and London: Yale University Press, 2002), 174. Cross-reference with the Parrish, *Lesser Terror* figures for those arrested in chapter 1, n. 115.

28. See Callum MacDonald, '"Kill All, Burn All, Loot All": The Nanking Massacre of December 1937 and Japanese Policy in China', in Mark Levene and Penny Roberts eds., *The Massacre in History* (Berghahn: Oxford, 1999), esp. 237–41.

29. Naimark, *The Russians in Germany*, 70–1.

30. Mark James, 'Remembering Rape: Divided Social Memory and the Red Army in Hungary', *Past and Present* 188:1 (2005), 133–61.

31. MacDonald, 'Kill All', 240.

32. Edele and Geyer, 'States of Exception', 356.

33. See Nicholas Bethell, *The Last Secret: Forcible Repatriation to Russia, 1944–7* (London: Futura Publications, 1976).

34. Edward N. Peterson, *The American Occupation of Germany: Retreat to Victory* (Detroit, MI: Wayne State University Press, 1978), 42, 116.

35. Polian, *Against Their Will*, 241–9.

36. Michael R. Beschloss, *The Conquerors: Roosevelt, Truman and the Destruction of Hitler's Germany, 1941–1945* (New York and London: Simon and Schuster, 2003), 144–5.

37. Beschloss, *The Conquerors*, 273, 277–8.

38. Yakovlev, *Century*, 174.

39. See Catherine Merridale, *Ivan's War: The Red Army, 1939–1945* (London: Faber and Faber, 2005), 136–7.

40. Yakovlev, *Century*, 174–8. See Alexander Solzhenitsyn, *The Gulag Archipelago, 1918–1956: An Experiment in Literary Investigation*, trans. Thomas P. Whitney (New York: New York University Press, 1992), 3 volumes, for the classic first-hand study of these peoples' fate.

41. Mazower, *Hitler's Empire*, 524.

42. Bessel, 'Murder Amidst Collapse', 262–3. Also Michael Geyer, 'Endkampf of 1918 and 1945: German Nationalism, Annihilation and Self-Destruction', in Alf Lüdtke and Bernd Weisbrod, eds., *No Man's Land of Violence: Extreme Wars in the 20th Century* (Gottingen: Wallstein, 2006), 36–67, for Hitler's apocalyptic mentality at the end.

43. Anthony Read and David Fisher, *The Fall of Berlin* (New York: W.W. Norton, 1992), 421–4.

44. R.J. Rummel, 'Democide in Totalitarian States: Mortacracies and Megamurders', in Israel W. Charny, ed., *Genocide, A Critical Bibliographical Review*, vol. 3, *The Widening Circle of Genocide* (New Brunswick, NJ, and London: Transaction Publishers, 1994), 3.

45. Gerlach, *Kalkulierte Morde*, 57.

46. Dallin, *German Rule*, 278.

47. See Lower, *Nazi Empire-Building*, 111–12; Heinemann, 'Another Type', 397.

48. Gross, *Polish Society*, 39.
49. Inspector of Armaments for the Ukraine, 2 December 41, quoted in Schulte, *German Army*, 103.
50. Berkhoff, *Harvest*, 47–9; 167. Schulte, *German Army*, 95–9.
51. See Kenneth Slepyan, 'The Soviet Partisan Movement and the Holocaust', *HGS*, 14:1 (2000), 8, for a Ukrainian ditty which neatly summarizes popular sentiment: 'The Germans have come *gut*, For the Jews *kaput*, For the Gypsies *tozhe* [as well], For the Ukrainians *pozhe* [later].'
52. Leonid D Grenkevich, The *Soviet Partisan Movement 1941–1944: A Critical Historiographical Analysis* (London: Frank Cass, 1999), 189–90.
53. See Ben Shepherd, *War in the Wild East: The German Army and Soviet Partisans* (Cambridge, MA, and London: Harvard University Press, 2004), 35–40, for further discussion. Also, more generally, Ian F.W. Beckett, *Modern Insurgencies and Counter-Insurgencies* (London: Routledge, 2001).
54. Dallin, *German Rule*, 667.
55. See Kenneth Slepyan, 'Soviet Partisan Movement', 8, for examples of openly exterminatory Nazi anti-Jewish propaganda and positive indigenous responses.
56. See Slepyan, *Stalin's Guerrillas: Soviet Partisans in World War Two* (Lawrence: University Press of Kansas 2006), for further analysis. Also Mazower, *Hitler's Empire*, 167–70, 487–91.
57. Here quoted from Dean, *Local Collaboration*, 27. Also Levene, *Rise*, 396, n. 165, on the Boxer reference.
58. Shepherd, *War in the Wild East*, 125–6; Chalowsky, *Jews of Bielorussia*, 53–4.
59. Gerlach, *Kalkulierte Morde*, 957–8, 1158.
60. Snyder, *Bloodlands*, 250–1, offers some of his own extrapolations at occasional variance from the Gerlach figures.
61. Snyder, *Bloodlands*, 241.
62. Dallin, *German Rule*, 211; Prusin, *Lands Between*, 181.
63. Quoted in Dallin, *German Rule*, 210. Stalin had already affirmed the mutual nature of the threat when, in early November 1941, he had proclaimed, 'The German invaders want a war of extermination with the peoples of the USSR. Well, then, if the Germans want a war of extermination, they will get it.' Quoted in Edele and Geyer, 'States of Exception', 368.
64. Gerlach, 'German Economic Interests', 227.
65. Nechama Tec, *Defiance: The Bielski Partisans* (New York: Oxford University Press, 1993), though not the only work on the subject, provided the basis for an eponymous 2009 Hollywood feature film.
66. Slepyan, 'Soviet Partisan Movement', 4–7, 13–16.
67. See Shepherd, *War in the Wild East*, chapter 5, 'More of the Sugar, Less of the Whip'.
68. Snyder, *Bloodlands*, 244–6.
69. Schulte, *German Army*, 122, n. 22.
70. Prusin, *Lands Between*, 182.
71. Snyder, *Bloodlands*, 251.
72. Cholawsky, *Jews of Bielorussia*, 50; Dallin, *German Rule*, 219.
73. Slepyan, *Stalin's Guerillas*, 209.
74. Grenkevich, *Soviet Partisan Movement*, 299.
75. Cholawsky, *Jews of Bielorussia*, 54.
76. Prusin, *Lands Between*, 182.
77. Gerlach, *Kalkulierte Morde*, 705, 919; Dean, *Local Collaboration*, 127.

78. Gerlach, *Kalkulierte Morde*, 938–41, 967–8; Berkhoff, *Harvest*, 280–1.
79. Snyder, *Bloodlands*, 242. For Vietnam parallels, see Bernd Greiner, *War without Fronts: The USA in Vietnam*, trans. Anne Wyburn and Victoria Fern (London: Bodley Head, 2009); Deborah Nelson, *The War behind Me: Vietnam Veterans Confront the Truth about U.S. War Crimes* (New York: Basic Books, 2008).
80. Shepherd, *War in the Wild East*, 121. The term actually comes from the nineteenth-century British operations against the tribes of India's North-West Frontier.
81. Snyder, *Bloodlands*, 241–2; Black, 'Rehearsal', 205–6; Burleigh, *Third Reich*, 585, 754; Per Anders Rudling, 'The Khatyn Massacre in Belorussia: A Historical Controversy Revisited', *HGS*, 26:1 (2012) 29–58, for a detailed analysis of one well-known massacre in March 1943, in which Dirlewanger's unit alongside a *Schutzmannshaft* battalion (118) played a particularly vicious role. More generally, see Christian Ingrao, *The SS Dirlewanger Brigade: The History of the Dark Hunters*, trans. Phoebe Green (New York: Skyhouse, 2011).
82. Mazower, *Hitler's Empire*, 465.
83. Schulte, *German Army*, 172–9; also Alexander Dallin, *The Kaminski Brigade, 1941–1944: A Case Study of German Military Exploitation of Soviet Disaffection* (Maxwell, AL: Air University, 1952).
84. Snyder, *Bloodlands*, 244–6.
85. Daniel Marston and Carter Malkasian, *Counter-Insurgency in Modern Warfare* (Oxford and New York: Osprey, 2008), 83–90, for discussion. Recent research on the efficacy of the Himmler-founded 'werewolf' units, left to fight after the Nazi state had been overwhelmed, suggests, however, that many hundreds of Allied soldiers and German 'collaborators' did fall victim to their attacks and those of fellow-travellers, even if this campaign failed to carry German popular support. See Longerich, *Himmler*, 714–15.
86. See Levene, *Meaning*, 55.
87. Lukas, *Forgotten Holocaust*, 14–15.
88. Koehl, *RKFDV*, 87; Paczkowski, *The Spring*, 51–2.
89. See Paczkowski, *The Spring*, 61, for the case of Wacław Krzeptowski. Also Burleigh, *Third Reich*, 443–4. One might add that the majority of highlanders were not amused. Gorals played a significant role in the Polish resistance.
90. See Polonsky, 'Introduction', 26–7, 23–4, for commentary.
91. Quoted in Lukas, *Forgotten Holocaust*, 5. See also Gerwarth, *Hitler's Hangman*, 230–44, 255, in which Gerlach notes that in spite of Heydrich's early 1942 daydreams of 'unGermanizable' Czechs being shipped to Siberia to 'supervise' the 11 million European Jews who would supposedly be deposited there, Heydrich himself was actually authorizing food rations for Czech arms workers to be increased.
92. Gerwarth, *Hitler's Hangman*, 110–15; Gross, *Polish Society*, 126–7.
93. Mazower, *Hitler's Empire*, 494–5.
94. Dean, *Local Collaboration*, 100.
95. Lukas, *Forgotten Holocaust*, 21–3; Czesław Madajczyk, 'Deportations in the Zamość Region in 1942 and 1943 in the Light of German Documents', *Acta Poloniae Historica* (1958), 75–106.
96. See Bruno Wasser, 'Die "Germanisierung" im Distrikt Lublin als Generalprobe und erste Realisierungphase des Generalplans Ost', in Mechtild Rössler, Sabine Schleiermacher, and Cordula Tollmien, eds., *Der 'Generalplan Ost': Hauptlinien der Nationalsozialistischen Planungs- und Vernichtungpolitik* (Berlin: Akademie Verlag, 1993), 271–93, for the Zamość project in context.
97. Dallin, *German Rule*, 282.

98. Lukas, *Forgotten Holocaust*, 13. Mazower, *Hitler's Empire*, 215, puts the figure at 25 per cent.
99. Mazower, *Hitler's Empire*, 208–9.
100. Heinemann, 'Another Type', 396; Sybil Milton, 'Non-Jewish Children in the Camps', in Berenbaum, *Mosaic*, 153.
101. Lukas, *Forgotten Holocaust*, 36–7; Paczowski, *The Spring*, 53; Snyder, *Bloodlands*, 295.
102. Mazower, *Hitler's Empire*, 461.
103. Lukas, *Forgotten Holocaust*, 193–4.
104. Paczowski, *The Spring*, 121–2.
105. Paczowski, *The Spring*, 123; Włodzimierz Borodziej, *The Warsaw Uprising of 1944*, trans. Barbara Harshav (Madison: University of Wisconsin Press 2006), 62, 64, for commentary.
106. Joanna K.M. Hanson, *The Civilian Population and the Warsaw Uprising of 1944* (Cambridge and New York: Cambridge University Press, 1982), 90–2.
107. Lukas, *Forgotten Holocaust*, 199; Hanson, *Civilian Population*, 87–90, including eyewitness testimonies.
108. Mazower, *Hitler's Empire*, 513. Hanson, *Civilian Population*, 96, confirms that German ultra-violence *prolonged* the uprising.
109. Lukas, *Forgotten Holocaust*, 203–4.
110. Hanson, *Civilian Population*, 92, 193–4.
111. Lukas, *Forgotten Holocaust*, 201, 205. Hanson, *Civilian Population*, 90, notes that the 4–5 August Wola killings alone may have reached 30,000 to 40,000.
112. Lukas, *Forgotten Holocaust*, 218.
113. Cited in Andrew Borowiec, *Destroy Warsaw: Hitler's Punishment, Stalin's Revenge* (Westport, CT, and London: Prager, 2001), 178.
114. Borodziej, *Warsaw Uprising*, 141–2.
115. Snyder, *Bloodlands*, 308–9.
116. See the various essays, Graham's (and Martin Shaw's) included, in Stephen Graham, ed., *Cities, War, and Terrorism: Towards an Urban Geopolitics* (London: Blackwell, 2004).
117. See Stephen Graham, *Cities under Siege: The New Military Urbanism* (London and New York: Verso, 2010), and Mike Davis, *Planet of Slums* (London: Verso, 2006), 202–6, for further commentary.
118. Paczowski, *The Spring*, 132; Snyder, *Bloodlands*, 306.
119. Mazower, *Inside Hitler's Greece*, chapters 15 and 16, more specifically 150, on the massacre of Italians on Cefalonia and elsewhere.
120. Mazower, *Inside Hitler's Greece*, 37–41. Mazower estimates 300,000 Greek dead as a consequence of 'food scarcity' by war's end. Also Steinberg, *All or Nothing*, 95–6.
121. Isabel Heinemann, '"Until the Last Drop of Blood": The Kidnapping of "Racially Valuable" Children and Nazi Racial Policy in Occupied Eastern Europe', in Moses, *Genocide and Settler Society*, 253; Longerich, *Himmler*, 626, for the perceived seriousness of the 'bandit' threat in Upper Carniola and Lower Styria.
122. Hoare, *Genocide*, 273.
123. Tomislav Dulić, 'Mass Killing in the Independent State of Croatia, 1941–1945: A Case Study for Comparative Research', *JGR*, 8:3 (2006), 263.
124. Hugh Seton-Watson, *Eastern Europe between the Wars, 1918–1941* (Cambridge: Cambridge University Press, 1945), 239–40; Noel Malcolm, *Bosnia: A Short History* (London and Basingstoke: Macmillan, 1994), 171–3.

125. Malcolm, *Bosnia*, 174.
126. See Jozo Tomasevich, *War and Revolution in Yugoslavia, 1941–1945: Occupation and Collaboration* (Stanford, CA: Stanford University Press, 1975), 47–57.
127. The figures are culled here from a variety of sources at slight variance with one another. See Jonathan Steinberg, 'Types of Genocide, Croatians, Serbs and Jews, 1941–5', in Cesarani, *Final Solution*, 80; Shelah, 'Genocide in Satellite Croatia', 74; Mazower, *Hitler's Empire*, 346–7.
128. Jonathan E. Gumz, 'Wehrmacht Perceptions of Mass Violence in Croatia', *Historical Journal*, 44:4 (2001), 1028; Steinberg, 'Types', 181.
129. Dulić, 'Mass Killing', 260; Paris, *Genocide*, 102.
130. Biondich, *Balkans*, 136; Mazower, *Hitler's Empire*, 347–8.
131. See Hoare, *Genocide*, 22–3; Steinberg, 'Types', 180; Tomasevich, *War and Revolution*, 342–5, on the fundamental weakness of the Pavelić regime.
132. Dulić, 'Mass Killing', 264–5, 268; Mazower, *Hitler's Empire*, 348.
133. Kiernan, *Blood and Soil*, 2.
134. Payne, *History*, 405; Glenny, *Balkans*, 433–4.
135. Biondich, *Balkans*, 24–6, 126–7.
136. Dulić, 'Mass Killing', 261–2, Fein, *Accounting*, 102. See also Michael Ignatieff, *Blood and Belonging: Journeys into the New Nationalism* (London: Vintage, 1994), 14–16, for what amounted to a 'narcissism of minor difference'.
137. Ben Kiernan, *The Pol Pot Regime: Race Power and Genocide in Cambodia under the Khmer Rouge, 1975–79* (New Haven, CT, and London: Yale University Press, 1996), 1–4.
138. Steinberg, 'Types', 188.
139. Bauman, *Postmodernity*, 18.
140. Payne, *History*, 404.
141. Glenny, *Balkans*, 434; Jill A. Irvine, *The Croat Question: Partisan Politics in the Formation of the Yugoslav Socialist State* (Boulder, CO: Westview Press, 1993), 50.
142. Steinberg, 'Types', 177.
143. Biondich, *Balkans*, 127.
144. Mann, *Dark Side*, 297.
145. Palmer, *Lands Between*, 263.
146. Biondich, *Balkans*, 128–9; Mann, *Dark Side*, 296–7.
147. Dulić, 'Mass Killing', 260.
148. See, for instance, Dennis Reinhartz, 'Unmarked Graves: The Destruction of the Yugoslav Roma in the Balkan Holocaust, 1941–1945', *JGR* 1:1 (1999), 84–6.
149. Glenny, *Balkans*, 498–9.
150. Mann, *Dark Side*, 296.
151. Both Steinberg 'Types', 175, and Mann *Dark Side*, 295, cite the figure of 487,000 Serbs killed in the totality of the 1941–5 conflict, with the implication that most of these deaths were the responsibility of the NDH. However, this figure may be considerably too high. Tomasevich, *War and Revolution*, 367, puts it at a minimum of 350,000; Robin Okey, 'The Legacy of Massacre: The "Jasenovac Myth" and the Breakdown of Communist Yugoslavia', in Levene and Roberts, *The Massacre*, 268–70, refers to the careful calculations of Boglijub Kocovic, which put Serb wartime losses, albeit in the NDH, at 334,000. This figure, incidentally, is less than half the 'received totemic wisdom' from the Tito years that 700,000 people, mostly Serbs, were killed at Jasenovac *alone*.
152. Alexander, *Triple Myth*, 71, for the reference; Dulić, 'Mass Killing', 264, n. 54, for its disavowal.

153. *Hrvatska Krajina*, 30 May 1941. Quoted here in Paris, *Genocide*, 80–1.
154. Dulić, 'Mass Killing', 262.
155. Quoted in Paris, *Genocide*, 98.
156. Biondich, *Balkans*, 137.
157. Paris, *Genocide*, 82–3; Shelah, 'Genocide in Satellite Croatia', 75; Biondich, *Balkans*, 137.
158. See Paris, *Genocide*, esp. 82–3, 108.
159. Alexander, *Triple Myth*, 80.
160. Dulić, 'Mass Killing', 267; Steinberg, *All or Nothing*, 30.
161. Okey, 'Legacy', 264–5; Biondich, *Balkans*, 140–1.
162. See Paris, *Genocide*, chapter 6, 'The Death camps', more esp. 132, 136–9.
163. Quoted in Mann, *Dark Side*, 297.
164. Again, there is controversy about these 'low' numbers set against the received Titoist wisdom. That said, Okey, 'Legacy', 270, notes that Kočović and another cautious non-partisan observer, Vladimir Žerjavić, offer figures of no more than 50,000 killed in the Jasenovac complex. Biondich, *Balkans*, 141, referring to the estimates of Mirko Persen, suggests 120,000 killed in all the Ustasha camps, of which some 80,000 were in Jasenovac. Mann, *Dark Side*, 296, quotes a further 'conservative' estimate of 85,000 Jasenovac dead, about 60 per cent of whom were Serbs.
165. Biondich, *Balkans*, 138–9.
166. Irvine, *Croat Question*, 97, 100–1.
167. Alexander, *Triple Myth*, 69.
168. See Steinberg, 'Types', 186–7.
169. Steinberg, 'Types'.
170. Mann, *Dark Side*, 297, referring to a Damir Mirković, *HGS* (1993) study on victims and perpetrators in wartime Yugoslavia. Also Paris, *Genocide* 107–15, for an inventory of Franciscan priest-*génocidaires*.
171. Paris, *Genocide*, 41.
172. Payne, *History*, 136.
173. Paris, *Genocide*, 105–6. One should note, however, that the figure of 2,000 reported as killed by this author is tendentious. Other reports suggest closer to 250–300 deaths.
174. Paris, *Genocide*, 89; Steinberg, 'Types', 178.
175. Dulić, 'Mass Killing', 268, 264–5.
176. Alexander, *Triple Myth*, 58. See also Guberina's comments quoted in Steinberg, 'Types', 178.
177. The 350,000 figure was probably Croat rhetoric. See Steinberg, 'Types', 178. For lower estimates, see Shelah, 'Genocide', 77; Alexander, *Triple Myth*, 58.
178. Quoted in Paris, *Genocide*, 89.
179. Biondich, *Balkans*, 141.
180. Hoare, *Genocide*, 33–4.
181. See Tomasevich, *War and Revolution*, chapter 5, 'The Puppet Government of Serbia', more esp. 214–17, for the counterpoint and convoluted relationships between the Chetniks and Nedić regime. Also Simon Trew, *Britain, Mihailović and the Chetniks, 1941–42* (Basingstoke: Macmillan, 1998), for the change in the British alignment.
182. Hoare, *Genocide*, 95.
183. See Todor Kuljić, 'Was Tito the Last Habsburg? Reflections on Tito's Role in the History of the Balkans', *Balkanistica*, 20 (2007), 85–100, for thoughtful commentary.
184. Hoare, *Genocide*, 123.

185. Quoted in Hoare, *Genocide*, 218.
186. See Malcolm, *Bosnia*, 163–8; Tomasevich, *War and Revolution*, 488–510.
187. Biondich, *Balkans*, 143. Also Tomasevich, *War and Revolution*, 500, who notes the rapidity of desertion from the 'Handzar' division by October 1944, to either Ustasha or Partisans, again underscoring the dilemma of where active, young Bosnian Muslims ought best to turn.
188. Malcolm, *Bosnia*, 185–6; Dulić, 'Mass Killing', 266, n. 70; Paris, *Genocide*, 122–4.
189. Hoare, *Genocide*, 145–7; Malcolm, *Bosnia*, 187–8; Malcolm, *Kosovo: A Short History* (London and Basingstoke: Macmillan, 1998), 298.
190. Hoare, *Genocide*, 106–8.
191. Hoare, *Genocide*, 295.
192. Dulić, 'Mass Killing', 269.
193. Hoare, *Genocide*, 201, 222, for the Borač massacre; 274, for the Sanski Most massacre; 209–11, for the possibility of a Partisan truce with the Ustasha.
194. Hoare, *Genocide*, 148–56.
195. Hoare, *Genocide*, 143.
196. Hoare, *Genocide*, 143–4.
197. See Stefanović, 'Seeing the Albanians', 468; Cathie Carmichael, *Genocide before the Holocaust* (New Haven, CT, and London: Yale University Press, 2009), 11, 90, 98–9.
198. Quoted in Dulić, 'Mass Killing', 266.
199. Dulić, 'Mass Killing', 267.
200. See Benjamin Lieberman, *Terrible Fate: Ethnic Cleansing in the Making of Modern Europe* (Chicago, IL: Ivan R. Dee, 2006), 191; Carmichael, *Genocide*, 90.
201. Malcolm, *Bosnia*, 192. Carmichael, *Genocide*, 116, as derived from the work of Nusret Šehic, offers figures of between 86,000 and 103,000 Slav Muslim deaths in Bosnia and the Sanjak. Inevitably, the ethnic numbers themselves continue to be a subject of intense scrutiny followed by further re-examination. See Okey, 'Legacy', 267–8, and Dulić, 'Mass Killing', 270–4, both extrapolating from the work of Žerjavić and Kočović.
202. Lemkin, *Axis Rule*, 264, 260.
203. Berkhoff, *Harvest*, 292.
204. See Dean, *Local Collaboration*, 145; Timothy Snyder, *The Reconstruction of Nations: Poland, Ukraine, Lithuania, Belarus, 1569–1999* (New York and London: Yale University Press, 2003), 170–2, for the example of the fate of the village of Głęboczyca; Berkhoff, *Harvest*, 295–6.
205. Alexander V. Prusin, 'Revolution and Ethnic Cleansing in Western Ukraine: The OUN-UPA Assault against Polish Settlements in Volhynia and Eastern Galicia, 1943–1944', in Steven Bela Vardy and T. Hunt Tooley, eds., *Ethnic Cleansing in Twentieth Century Europe* (Boulder, CO: Social Science Monographs, 2003), 526–8, 534. Also see Statiev, *Soviet Counter-Insurgency*, 86–7, for an OUN inventory of anti-Polish 'actions' in the Przemyśl district, Tarnopol province, during the single month of April 1944.
206. Prusin, *Lands Between*, 199.
207. See Henry Huttenbach, 'Locating the Holocaust on the Genocide Spectrum: Towards a Methodology of Definition and Categorisation', *HGS* 3:3 (1988), 289–303.
208. Prusin, *Lands Between*, 186–7.
209. Prusin, *Lands Between*, 193; Berkhoff, *Harvest*, 289, 298; Dean, *Local Collaboration*, 145.
210. Himka, 'Ukrainian Collaboration', 179.
211. Berkhoff, *Harvest*, 276–7; Prusin, *Lands Between*, 197.

212. Prusin, *Lands Between*, 198.
213. Snyder, *Reconstruction*, 169, for these figures. Berkhoff, *Harvest*, 286, suggests even lower Polish numbers: a quarter of a million of a 1.5 million regional total.
214. Prusin, *Lands Between*, 195.
215. See Himka, 'Ukrainian Collaboration', 184.
216. See John A. Armstrong, *Ukrainian Nationalism, 1939–1945* (New York: Columbia University Press, 1955), 22–3.
217. Prusin, 'Revolution', 520; Statiev, *Soviet Counter-Insurgency*, 44–6.
218. Weiner, *Making Sense*, 241.
219. Snyder, *Reconstruction*, 143.
220. See Motyl, 'Ukrainian Nationalistic Political Violence'.
221. Anton Shekhovtsov, 'By Cross and Sword: Clerical Fascism in Inter-War Ukraine', *Totalitarian Movements and Political Religions*, 8:2 (2007), 271–85.
222. Bohdan Budurowycz, 'Sheptyts'kyi and the Ukrainian National Movement after 1914', in Paul Robert Magocsi and Andrii Krawchuk, eds., *Morality and Reality: The Life and Times of Andrei Sheptyts'kyi* (Edmonton: Canadian Institute of Ukrainian Studies, University of Alberta Press, 1989), 63–4.
223. Anna Reid, *Borderland: A Journey through the History of Ukraine* (London: Weidenfeld and Nicolson, 1997), 158–9.
224. Dallin, *German Rule*, 115; Armstrong, *Ukrainian Nationalism*, 74; Gross, *Polish Society*, 187.
225. Golczewski, 'Shades of Grey', 125–7.
226. Solonari, *Purifying the Nation*, 177–84.
227. Armstrong, *Ukrainian Nationalism*, 77–9; Lower, *Nazi Empire-Building*, 38–9; Berkhoff, *Harvest*, 51–3.
228. Snyder *Reconstruction*. 164; Prusin, 'Revolution', 523; Mazower, *Hitler's Empire*, 458.
229. See Armstrong, *Ukrainian Nationalism*, 59–63, 67–70, for the historic and contemporary divisions between the two factions.
230. Prusin, 'Revolution', 525.
231. See Régis Debray, *Revolution in the Revolution* (London: Penguin, 1967), for the concept of revolutionary *foco*.
232. Berkhoff, *Harvest*, 289–91; Armstrong, *Ukrainian Nationalism*, 99.
233. Prusin, *Lands Between*, 190.
234. Berkhoff, *Harvest*, 291, 297–8. David R. Marples, *Heroes and Villains: Creating National History in Contemporary Ukraine* (Budapest: Central European University Press, 2007), 178, proposes that UPA control at its height while not necessarily contiguous extended across 150,000 square kilometres, embracing some 15 million inhabitants.
235. Berkhoff, *Harvest*, 291; Prusin, *Lands Between*, 196; Prusin, 'Revolution', 528; Statiev, *Soviet Counter-Insurgency*, 86.
236. Weiner, *Making Sense*, 263; Berkhoff, *Harvest*, 297.
237. Berkhoff, *Harvest*, 297; Armstrong, *Ukrainian Nationalism*, 157. Statiev, *Soviet Counter-Insurgency*, 84, cites UPA seepage to the Soviet partisans from late autumn 1943 as one possible catalyst for the swathe of SB executions. East Ukrainians were almost by definition considered militarily second rate, and suspect (108–9).
238. Berkhoff, *Harvest*, 297–8; Prusin, *Lands Between*, 197.
239. Snyder *Reconstruction*, 172–4.
240. Marek Jasiak, 'Overcoming Ukrainian Resistance: The Deportation of Ukrainians within Poland in 1947', in Phillip Ther and Ana Siljak, eds., *Redrawing Nations:*

Ethnic Cleansing in East-Central Europe 1944–1948 (Oxford and Lanham NY: Rowman and Littlefield, 2001), 174.

241. Timothy Snyder, 'The Life and Death of Western Volhynian Jewry, 1921–1945', in Brandon and Lower, *The Shoah*, 101–2; Lower, *Nazi Empire-Building*, 198–9.

242. Prusin, *Lands Between*, 198.

243. See Omer Bartov, 'White Spaces and Black Holes: Eastern Galicia's Past and Present', in Brandon and Lower, *The Shoah*, 318–53, for wider exploration and sober commentary on contemporary Ukrainian narcissism and historical avoidance. Also Marples, *Heroes*, chapter 6, 'The Ukrainian-Polish Conflict', for detailed analysis of more contemporary Ukrainian apologias.

244. Prusin, 'Revolution', 532; Marples, *Heroes*, 214–15.

245. It is notable that in Armstrong's 1955 study, long before the accessibility of Soviet archives (not to say at a juncture when for mainstream Western scholars Ukrainian nationalists stood in positive juxtaposition to the Soviet 'enemy'), there is almost no reference to the massacres at all.

246. Berkhoff, *Harvest*, 292–3; Marples, *Heroes*, 203–14, for a Ukrainian nationalist historiography which largely continues to read the events of 1943–4 in these terms.

247. See Snyder, *Reconstruction*, 178, for perceptive commentary.

248. Prusin, 'Revolution', 533; Snyder, *Bloodlands*, 526–7.

CHAPTER 5

1. Slezkine, *Jewish Century*, 365–6.

2. See Sebag Montefiore, *Stalin*, 360–90, for the sometimes farcical bungling of Stalin and his entourage in the days and weeks both preceding and succeeding 22 June 1941. See also the verdict of Martin Malia, *The Soviet Tragedy: A History of Socialism in Russia, 1917–1991* (New York: The Free Press, 1994), 284: 'Never in modern European military history had an army in the field lost such a high proportion of its men with so little resistance.'

3. Berkhoff, *Harvest*, 12–13.

4. David Brandenberger, ' "It Is Imperative to Advance Russian Nationalism as the First Priority": Debates within the Stalinist Ideological Establishment, 1941–1945', in Ronald Grigor Suny, and Terry Martin, eds., *A State of Nations: Empire and Nation-Making in the Age of Lenin and Stalin* (Oxford: Oxford University Press, 2001), 277; Dallin, *German Rule*, 678.

5. Berkhoff, *Harvest*, 23–34.

6. Mazower, *Hitler's Empire*, 462; Polian, *Against Their Will*, 25.

7. See Catherine Andreyev, *Vlasov and the Russian Liberation Movement: Soviet Reality and Émigré Theories* (Cambridge: Cambridge University Press, 1987).

8. Ann Sheehy and Bohdan Nahalyo, *The Crimean Tatars: Volga Germans and Meshketians: Soviet Treatment of some National Minorities*, 3rd ed. (London: Minority Rights Group, 1981), 9; Polian, *Against Their Will*, 152–3.

9. *Voprosy istorii*, 3 (1954), 3, quoted in Alexander Y, Yurchenko, 'Genocide through Destruction of National Culture and Sense of Nationality', in Nikolai K. Deker and Andrei Lebed, eds., *Genocide in the USSR: Studies in Group Destruction* (New York: Scarecrow Press 1958), 9.

10. Weiner, *Making Sense*, 136–7.

11. See Weitz, *Century*, 83.

12. Robert Conquest, *The Nation Killers: The Soviet Deportation of Nationalities* (London: Macmillan, 1970), 119.
13. D.L. Brandenberger and A.M. Dubrovsky, ' "The People Need a Tsar": The Emergence of National Bolshevism as Stalinist Ideology, 1931–1941', *Europe-Asia Studies*, 50:5 (1998), 878, also notes 47 and 48.
14. Andreas Kappeler, *The Russian Empire: A Multiethnic History*, trans. Alfred Clayton (Harlow: Longman, 2001), 381.
15. See Levene, *Rise*, 293–302.
16. See, for instance, Peter Holquist, 'The Politics and Practice of the Russian Occupation of Armenia, 1915–February 1917', in Suny, *A Question*, 158–63.
17. However, see Peter A. Blitstein, 'Nation-Building or Russification? Obligatory Russian Instruction in the Soviet Non-Russian School, 1938–1953', in Suny and Martin, *State of Nations*, 253–74, for the debate on the degree to which Stalin consciously promoted active Russification. Also Terry Martin, 'An Affirmative Action Empire: The Soviet Union as the Highest Form of Imperialism', also in Suny and Martin, *State of Nations*, 67–90.
18. See Statiev, 'Soviet Ethnic Deportations', 246, for the official numbers of each group deported.
19. As cited in Weitz, *Century*, 80.
20. See James Wilson, *The Earth Shall Weep: A History of Native America* (London: Picador, 1998), chapter 10, 'Kill the Indian, Save the Man'.
21. See front cover of *American Historical Review*, 104: 4 (1999), as accompaniment to Amir Weiner, 'Nature, Nurture and Memory in a Socialist Utopia: Delineating the Soviet Socio-Ethnic Body in the Age of Socialism', *American Historical Review*, 104:4 (1999), 1114–55.
22. Naimark, *Fires*, 105.
23. Statiev, 'Soviet Ethnic Deportations', 258.
24. See Volume 1, 119–21.
25. Statiev, 'Soviet Ethnic Deportations', esp. 246–54.
26. Conquest, *Nation-Killers*, 71.
27. Robert Seely, *Russo-Chechen Conflict, 1800–2000: A Deadly Embrace* (London and Portland, OR: Frank Cass, 2001), 85.
28. Sheehy and Nahalyo, *Crimean Tatars*, 9.
29. Sheehy and Nahalyo, *Crimean Tatars*, 8.
30. See Yakovlev, *Century*, 193; Alan Fisher, *The Crimean Tatars* (Stanford, CA: Hoover Institute Press, 1978), 172; Conquest, *Nation-Killers*, 67.
31. Yakovlev, *Century*, 193–4.
32. Sheehy and Nahalyo, *Crimean Tatars*, 9–17; Fisher, *Crimean Tatars*, 150.
33. J. Otto Pohl, 'Stalin's Genocide against the "Repressed Peoples"', *JGR*, 2:2 (2000), 268–9.
34. Pohl, 'Stalin's Genocide', 289.
35. Aleksandr Nekrich, *The Punished Peoples: The Deportation and Tragic Fate of Soviet Minorities at the End of the Second World War* (New York: W.W. Norton, 1978), 107. The 194,000 Crimean Tatar figure, according to Statiev, is 14,000 too many. See n. 45, below.
36. Quoted in Pohl, 'Stalin's Genocide', 267–8.
37. Pohl, 'Stalin's Genocide', tables 2, 3, and 4, 283, 285, 286; Statiev, 'Soviet Ethnic Deportations', tables 5 and 6, figures 1–3, 256–8.
38. Nekrich, *Punished Peoples*, 88; Birgit Brauer, 'Chechens and the Survival of their Cultural Identity in Exile', *JGR*, 4:3 (2002), 389.

39. Polian, *Against Their Will*, 146; Fisher, *Crimean Tatars*, 166.
40. Yakovlev, *Century*, 188–90.
41. Yakovlev, *Century*, 191.
42. Polian, *Against Their Will*, 141.
43. Walter Comins-Richmond, 'The Deportation of the Karachays', *JGR*, 4:3 (2002), 433.
44. Pohl, 'Stalin's Genocide', 284.
45. Statiev, 'Soviet Ethnic Deportations', 246.
46. Nekrich, *Punished Peoples*, 108–10.
47. Yakovlev, *Century*, 189; Edige Kirimal, 'The Crimean Turks', in Deker and Lebed, *Genocide in the USSR*, 26–7; Pohl, 'Stalin's Genocide', 275; Naimark, *Fires*, 97.
48. Polian, *Against Their Will*, 147.
49. Pohl, 'Stalin's Genocide', 272. See also 'New Facts about the Mass Deportation of the Crimean Tatars', *The Crimean Review: Voice of the Crimean Tatar Human Rights Movement*, 5:2 (31 December 1990), 13–14; Polian, *Against Their Will*, 147, also 176–7, n. 102.
50. Yakovlev, *Century*, 192; Polian, *Against Their Will*, 147. Burds, 'Soviet War', 305, also cites, in addition to 'untransportability', anxiety about the spread of typhus as a factor in the killings.
51. Yakovlev, *Century*, 192–3.
52. Polian, *Against Their Will*, 176–7, n. 102. As Statiev, 'Soviet Ethnic Deportations', 249, himself notes, part of the problem in providing a clear and concise picture of the NKVD atrocities which took place in the North Caucasus resides in the ongoing classified status of the deportation records.
53. Cited in Naimark, *Fires*, 102.
54. Statiev, 'Soviet Ethnic Deportations', 250.
55. Naimark, *Fires*, 97; Statiev, 'Soviet Ethnic Deportations', 250.
56. Naimark, *Fires*, 102.
57. Conquest, *Nation-Killers*, 162.
58. Quoted in Sheehy and Nahalyo, *Crimean Tatars*, 8.
59. See Brian Glyn Williams, 'Hidden Ethnocide in the Soviet Muslim Borderlands: The Ethnic Cleansing of the Crimean Tartars', *JGR*, 4:3 (2002), 362. See also Comins-Richmond, 'The Deportation', 431–9, for similar Karachai experiences.
60. Statiev, 'Soviet Ethnic Deportations', 252–4.
61. Statiev, 'Soviet Ethnic Deportations', 252–3.
62. See Polian, *Against Their Will*, 142–3, for the full text of the Soviet Presidium decree on the abolition of the Karachai republic, 12 October 1943. On the internal NKVD appellation of 'bandit nations', see Burds, 'Soviet War', 283–4.
63. Polian, *Against Their Will*, 134.
64. Pohl, 'Stalin's Genocide', 281. See also Eric J. Schmaltz and Samuel D Sinner, '"You will die under ruins and snow": The Soviet Repression of Russian Germans as a Case Study of Successful Genocide', *JGR*, 4:3 (2002), 332, who further argue (328) that, considered in a wider 1914–53 time frame, some 1 million Germans perished by violent means. More specifically in the Stalin years, the group's excess mortality rate reached 'about one-fourth to one-third of the total'.
65. Polian, *Against Their Will*, 137–9. See also Pohl, 'Stalin's Genocide', 280–1, for the not unique example of the Bogoslav corrective labour camp, where 12,000 out of 15,000 ethnic German inmates perished in 1942.
66. See Roger Daniels, *Concentration Camps USA: Japanese Americans and World War II* (New York: Holt, Rinehart and Winston, 1971).

67. Louise Burletson, 'The State, Internment and Public Criticism in the Second World War', in David Cesarani and Tony Kushner, *The Internment of Aliens in Twentieth Century Britain* (London and Portland, OR: Frank Cass, 1993), 102–24.
68. Polian, *Against Their Will*, 139.
69. See Volume 1, p.359 for the Korean deportation.
70. Polian, *Against Their Will*, 128–9.
71. George Vvedensky, 'The Volga Germans and Other German Groups', in Deker and Lebed, *Genocide in the USSR*, 49–50; Nicholas Werth, 'The Mechanism of a Mass Crime: The Great Terror in the Soviet Union 1937–38', in Kiernan and Gellately, *Spectre of Genocide*, 237.
72. Polian, *Against Their Will*, 127.
73. Polian, *Against Their Will*, 132–4; Pohl, 'Stalin's Genocide', 280; Sheehy and Nahalyo, *Crimean Tatars*, 19.
74. Pohl, 'Stalin's Genocide', 279, notes the number rose to over 1.2 million by 1945.
75. Nekrich, *Punished Peoples*, 41; Dallin, *German Rule*, 244–50; Ramazan Karcha, 'Peoples of the North Caucasus', in Deker and Lebed, *Genocide in the USSR*, 42.
76. Dallin, *German Rule*, 257–8; Fisher, *Crimean Tatars*, 154–7.
77. Nekrich, *Punished Peoples*, 74–80, for the sometimes intense historians' debate as to the degree of Kalmyk collaboration. Also Dallin, *German Rule* 252, n. 1, 258, n. 5; Lukas, *Forgotten Holocaust*, 199.
78. Dallin, *German Rule*, 251, referring to Hitler meeting with Wehrmacht chiefs, 12 December 1942, regarding possible creation of Caucasian formations.
79. Fisher, *Crimean Tatars*, 154, referring to the research of the German writer Patrik von Mühlen.
80. Nekrich, *Punished Peoples*, 98.
81. The 'secret' speech was famously reprinted in the *New York Times*, 5 June 1956.
82. Burds, 'Soviet War', 289.
83. See Abdurahman Avtorkhanov, 'The Chechens and Ingush during the Soviet Period and its Antecedents', in Marie Beningsen Broxup, ed., *The North Caucasus Barrier: The Russian Advance towards the Muslim World* (London: Hurst and Co., 1992), 184, 180.
84. Nekrich, *Punished Peoples*, 83–5; Polian, *Against Their Will*, 125, who also cites a figure of 137,000 Crimean Tatars mobilized, 57,000 of whom were killed.
85. Fisher, *Crimean Tatars*, 160.
86. While clearly Cold War warrior in tone, the various chapters of Deker and Lebed, *Genocide in the USSR*, are illuminating on this score. See esp. Nikolaus Imnaishvili, 'The Georgians'; Dorzha Arbakov, 'Kalmyks'; Mirza Bala, 'The Azerbaidzhanis'; Murat Tachmurat and Aman Berdimut, 'The Turkestanis'; Edige Kirimal, 'The Crimean Turks'.
87. Arbakov, 'Kalmyks', 39.
88. See Brauer, 'Chechens', 388.
89. Susan Layton, 'Nineteenth-Century Russian Mythologies of Caucasian Savagery', in Daniel R. Brower and Edward J. Lazzerini, eds., *Russia's Orient, Imperial Borderlands and Peoples, 1700–1917* (Bloomington and Indianapolis: Indiana University Press, 1997), 90–1, 95–6; Burds, 'Soviet War', 283, on the way in which Chechen society defied 'class-based paradigms'.
90. Solzhenitsyn, *Gulag Archipelago*, vol. 3, 402.
91. Quoted in Seely, *Russo-Chechen Conflict*, 85–6. The academician specifically cited was K.G. Adzhemyan.

92. See Moshe Gammer, *Muslim Resistance to the Tsar: Shamil and the Conquest of Chechnia and Daghestan* (London: Frank Cass, 1994); Anna Zelinka, *In Quest for God and Freedom: The Sufi Response to the Russian Advance in the North Caucasus* (London: Hurst, 2000), for critical background. Levene, *Rise*, 295–6, for cross-reference to the Circassian genocide.

93. Avtorkhanov, 'The Chechens', 182–4.

94. Avtorkhanov, 'The Chechens', 192, n. 10.

95. Quoted in Nekrich, *Punished Peoples*, 99.

96. See Martin Kitchen, *The Silent Dictatorship: The Politics of the German High Command under Hindenburg and Ludendorff, 1916–1918* (London: Croom Helm, 1976), 239–42, for Ludendorff's plans.

97. Kappeler, *Russian Empire*, 235, 337; Aviel Roshwald, *Ethnic Nationalism and the Fall of Empires: Central Europe, Russia and the Middle East, 1914–1923* (London and New York: Routledge, 2001), 56–7. Also Fisher, *Crimean Tatars*, chapter 10, 'The Crimean Tatar National Awakening', and Layton, 'Nineteenth-Century Russian Mythologies', on the seminal role of Ismail Bey Gaspirali (Gasprinsky).

98. Fisher, *Crimean Tatars*, 118. See also Milan Hausner, 'Russia's Geopolitical and Ideological Dilemmas in Central Asia', in Robert L. Canfield, ed., *Turko-Persia in Historical Perspective* (Cambridge: Cambridge University Press, 1991), 212, for further exploration of an evolving Soviet thinking back towards a tsarist geopolitical default position.

99. Kirimal, 'Crimean Turks', 24, 27; Fisher, *Crimean Tatars*, 154.

100. Hausner, 'Russia's Geopolitical and Ideological Dilemmas', 212–13.

101. See Dallin, *German Rule*, 234, 135–6. Also William Hale, *Turkish Foreign Policy, 1774–2000* (London: Frank Cass, 2000), 90–1. Prominent in these exchanges was Nuri, the brother of Enver Pasha, while among participants in the Hotel Adlon conference the GFO organized, in April 1942, to showcase their plans, was Shamil's grandson. For more on Nuri's covert 'Turanian' war and possibly post-war intrigues, see also Burds, 'Soviet War', 286–7, inc. n. 10, and 309–10, inc. n. 127.

102. Dallin, *German Rule*, 135–6.

103. Hale, *Turkish Foreign Policy*, 90–1.

104. Conquest, *Nation Killers*, 99–100; Nekrich, *Punished Peoples*, 97–8; Karcha, 'Peoples', 42.

105. Sheehy and Nahalyo, *Crimean Tatars*, 6.

106. Çagaptay, 'Crafting the Turkish Nation', 437–8.

107. See Michael Khodarkovsky, *Where Two Worlds Met: The Russian State and the Kalmyk Nomads 1600–1771* (Ithaca, NY: Cornell University Press, 1992), chapter 7, 'Russian Colonization and the Kalmyks' Decline and Exodus'.

108. Kappeler, *Russian Empire*, 181–2.

109. Burds, 'Soviet War', 280.

110. Fisher, *Crimean Tatars*, 169; see also Polian, *Against Their Will*, 155.

111. Sheehy and Nahalyo, *Crimean Tatars*, 29.

112. Polian, *Against Their Will*, 155; Hovann H. Simonian, 'The Vanished Khemshins: Return from the Brink', *JGR*, 4:3 (2002), 379.

113. Kappeler, *Russian Empire*, 350; Martin, 'Origins', 829.

114. Simonian, 'Vanished Khemshins', 379; Polian, *Against Their Will*, 156.

115. Salahi Sonyel, *The Great War and the Tragedy of Anatolia* (Ankara: Turkish Historical Printing House, 2000), 183. In fact, some Dashnak Armenians were later specifically targeted for deportation. See Polian, *Against Their Will*, 169. There is also a further

murky irony in that Tiemuraz Shavdia, Beria's own nephew by marriage, was involved in the putative formation of a German 'Georgian' Legion out of Soviet POWs like himself, and was personally implicated in Wehrmacht atrocities in France, but at the war's end was brought back to the USSR under his uncle's protection. See Arkady Vaksberg, *Stalin Against The Jews*, trans. Antonina W. Bouis (New York: Alfred A. Knopf, 1994), 275–6.

116. Polian, *Against Their Will*, 154.
117. Polian, *Against Their Will*. Also Eric Lohr, *Nationalizing the Russian Empire: The Campaign against Enemy Aliens during World War One* (Cambridge, MA, and London: Harvard University Press, 2003), 152.
118. Gerard J. Libaridian, *Modern Armenia: People, Nation, State* (New Brunswick, NJ, and London: Transaction Publishers, 2005), 24–5; Joanne Laycock, 'The Repatriation of Armenians to Soviet Armenia 1945–1949', in Peter Gatrell and Nick Baron, eds., *Warlands: Population Resettlement and State Reconstruction in the Soviet-East European Borderlands, 1945–50* (Basingstoke: Palgrave-Macmillan, 2009), 144–5.
119. Pohl, 'Stalin's Genocide', 268; Polian, *Against Their Will*, 155–6.
120. Polian, *Against Their Will*, 162, for the Daghestani settlers' experience in Chechen and Ingush auls.
121. Sheehy and Nahalyo, *Crimean Tatars*, 26–7.
122. See Nekrich, *Punished Peoples*, 24–40.
123. Polian, *Against Their Will*, 153.
124. Polian, *Against Their Will*.
125. Conquest, *Nation Killers*, 110–11. The figure of 100,000 cited by Neal Ascherson, *Black Sea: The Birthplace of Civilisation and Barbarism* (London: Vintage, 1996), 188, is probably an overestimate.
126. See Ascherson, *Black Sea*, 188–9, for further ruminations on the causes of the Greek deportations.
127. Nekrich, *Punished Peoples*, 104.
128. Polian, *Against Their Will*, 157, 166–71; Igor Casu, 'Stalinist Terror in Soviet Moldavia, 1940–1953', in McDermott and Stibbe, *Stalinist Terror*, 49, for the Moldavian Operation South; Purs, 'Soviet in Form', 32, for the Baltic equivalent.
129. Karcha, 'Peoples', 43–5.
130. Fisher, *Crimean Tatars*, 162–3; Nekrich, *Punished Peoples*, 28–9.
131. Hiden and Salmon, *Baltic Nations*, 128; Keith Lowe, *Savage Continent: Europe in the Aftermath of World War II* (London: Viking, 2012), chapter 27, 'The Resistance of the Forest Brothers'. By contrast, Statiev, *Soviet Counter-Insurgency*, 111–15, takes a much more cautious view on the strength of Baltic resistance, proposing that insurgent numbers and capacity in Estonia and Latvia, if not necessarily in Lithuania, have been inflated by *its* latter-day partisans.
132. Statiev, *Soviet Counter-Insurgency*, chapter 8, 'Red *Rurales*: The Destruction Battalions', and also 334, 336, is at pains to emphasize that Soviet force was held in check and that there were no 'unsanctioned atrocities' on the Soviet side. For a less forgiving view on the counter-insurgency, including the evolution of the destruction battalions, see Prusin, *Lands Between*, 208–11.
133. Nicholas Werth, 'Forms of Autonomy, in "Socialist" Society', in Henry Rousso, ed., *Stalinism and Nazism: History and Memory Compared*, trans. Lucy B. Golsan et al. (Lincoln and London: University of Nebraska Press, 2004), 122.
134. Werth, 'Forms', 123, including n. 32.

135. See Statiev, *Soviet Counter-Insurgency*, 192–3, for a notably forceful repudiation of standard Baltic nationalist arguments that these deportations were tantamount to genocide. Statiev's view is that these were security operations, not conducted on an ethnic basis but against 'class enemies'.

136. See Prusin, *Lands Between*, 231–4, including table 9.1 for regional demographic changes.

137. Werth, 'Forms', 122.

138. Prusin, *Lands Between*, 206; Weiner, *Making Sense*, 173; Statiev, *Soviet Counter-Insurgency*, 110, table 4.4, for GUBB figures on all rimlands insurgent deaths, 1944–6.

139. Prusin, *Lands Between*, 207. This was in spite of over 67,000 security actions mounted against them in 1946 alone. See Jasiak, 'Overcoming', 176. Statiev, *Soviet Counter-Insurgency*, 246, offers a particular gruesome example of an SB killing of informers and families, underscoring his case that the resort to extreme violence largely emanated from the OUN.

140. Weiner, *Making Sense*, 179; Werth, 'Forms', 122; Brown, *Biography*, 215, particularly makes the point that the attraction of OUN-style Ukrainian nationalism to its Soviet-born intelligentsia, both rural and urban, derived from an education in which 'they had been trained to think... in the *national* taxonomies of both Soviet progressive reform and repression'.

141. Weiner, 'Nature, Nurture', 1136.

142. Statiev, *Soviet Counter-Insurgency*, 266–7; Prusin, *Lands Between*, 214.

143. Prusin, *Lands Between*, 212–17.

144. Marta Craveri and Nikolai Formozov, 'La Résistance au Goulag: Grèves, révoltes, évasions dans les camps de travail sovietiques de 1920 à 1956', *Communisme*, 42/43/44 (1995), 197–209; Anne Applebaum, *Gulag: A History of the Soviet Camps* (London: Penguin, 2003), 439–40, 443–8.

145. Weiner, *Making Sense*, 173; Prusin, *Lands Between*, 221. Marples, *Heroes*, 179, notes that in the mid-1950s there were, according to official records, still 136,762 OUN members and their families designated as 'special settlers'.

146. The argument is fundamental to Weiner, *Making Sense*.

147. See Andrew Wilson, 'Ukraine, Between Eurasia and the West', in Seamus Dunn and T.G. Fraser, *Europe and Ethnicity: The First World War and Contemporary Ethnic Conflict* (London and New York: Routledge, 1996), 124–5, for details.

148. Prusin, *Lands Between*, 213.

149. See, however, Orest Subtelny, 'Expulsion, Resettlement, Civil Strife: The Fate of Poland's Ukrainians, 1944–1947', in Ther and Siljak, *Redrawing Nations*, 157, for an opposing view. Subtelny argues that Russian migration into the Ukraine underscored Moscow's interest in not ethnic homogeneity but ethnic heterogeneity.

150. Snyder, *Reconstruction*, 183; Prusin, *Lands Between*, 201–2; Naimark, *Fires*, 132, cites figures of 480,000 Ukrainians actually transferred from south-east Poland to the Ukraine, compared with 2.1 million Poles erected from the *kresy* to Poland.

151. Weiner, *Making Sense*, 351.

152. Peter Gatrell and Nick Baron, 'Introduction', in Gatrell and Baron, *Warlands*, 4, note that the exchange 'far from being carefully administered, became a chaotic, hasty and brutal business'. For confirmation, see Kateryna Stadnik, 'Ukrainian-Polish Population Transfers, 1944–46: Moving in Opposite Directions', in Gatrell and Baron, *Warlands*, 165–87. Also Catherine Gousseff, 'Evacuation versus Repatriation: The Polish-Ukrainian Population Exchange, 1944–6', in Jessica Reinisch and Elizabeth White, eds., *The Disentanglement of Populations: Migration, Expulsion*

and Displacement in Postwar Europe, 1944–49 (Basingstoke: Palgrave Macmillan, 2011), 81–111.

153. Snyder, *Reconstruction*, 196.
154. Snyder, *Reconstruction*, 194. Also Lowe, *Savage Continent*, 212–14, including survivor testimony of the atrocities committed in the village by the Polish 34th Infantry Regiment. One might add that the official Polish and Soviet forces were not the only perpetrators of such massacres. Residual AK units and possibly those of the more right wing Polish National Armed Forces (NSZ) were also culpable. See Jasiak, 'Overcoming', 178.
155. Subtelny, 'Expulsion', 161–2; Snyder, *Reconstruction*, 194.
156. Snyder, *Reconstruction*, 189.
157. Subtelny, 'Expulsion', 188–9.
158. Paczowski, *The Spring*, 170–3; Davies, *Heart*, 80–1.
159. Neal Ascherson, *The Struggles for Poland* (London: Pan, 1987), 136.
160. Snyder, *Bloodlands*, 314. In Snyder, *Reconstruction*, 189, 'multinational principle' reads as the 'principle of nationalities'.
161. Snyder, *Reconstruction*, 196; Norman Davies, *Heart of Europe: A Short History of Poland* (Oxford: Oxford University Press, 1984), 32, for figures.
162. Snyder, *Reconstruction*, 207.
163. Snyder, *Reconstruction*, 197; Subtelny, 'Expulsion', 167.
164. To be sure, the results have in the long term been mixed, many of the deportees assimilating to their 'Polish' surroundings, while others, today, are fiercely conscious of their Ukrainian connections, or, alternatively, their specifically Rusyn 'national' origins. See Susyn Yvonne Mihalsky, 'Ethno-National Orientation among Lemkos in Poland', in Ray Taras, ed., *National Identities and Ethnic Minorities in Eastern Europe: Selected Papers from the Fifth World Congress of Central and East European Studies 1995* (New York: St Martin's Press, 1998); Olena Duc' Fajfer, 'The Lemkos in Poland', in Paul R. Magocsi, ed. *The Persistence of Regional Cultures: Rusyns and Ukrainians in their Carpathian Homeland and Abroad* (Fairview, NJ: East European Monographs, 1993).
165. Snyder, *Reconstruction*, 198–201, and 332, n. 84. See also Jasiak, 'Overcoming', 178, for total estimates of Ukrainian civilian deaths in Polish actions, 1944–7, which according to government sources were *c.* 4,000 but which Ukrainian commentators put at between 8,000 and 10,000. With thanks also to my Lublin friends, Hanka and Wojciech Samolinski, for first alerting me to the Lemko tragedy.
166. Polian, *Against Their Will*, 169; Yoram Gorlicki and Oleg Khlevniuk, *Cold Peace, Stalin and the Soviet Ruling Circle, 1945–1953* (New York: Oxford University Press, 2004), 98. Given that the 1951 deportations of Jehovah's Witnesses extended beyond the USSR, certainly to embrace Poland, a serious, comparative study of their twentieth-century persecution is overdue. See Casu, 'Stalinist Terror', 53; Lukasz Kaminiski, 'Stalinism in Poland 1944–1956', also in McDermott and Stibbe, *Stalinist Terror*, 92.
167. Vaksberg, *Stalin*, 83–96, who notes that one further casualty of these events was the leading Soviet Jewish writer Isaac Babel. See also Weiner, *Making Sense*, 274, n. 119, for corroboration of Vaksberg's argument. Also Slezkine, *Jewish Century*, 254–55, 301, who describes the Soviet foreign service as 'an almost exclusively Jewish speciality', and for further confirmation of the attack on the Jewish elite, beginning May 1939.
168. See Sebag Montefiore, *Stalin*, 310–12; Svetlana Alliluyeva, *Only One Year* (New York: Harper and Row, 1969), 153; Isaac Deutscher, *Stalin: A Political Biography*

(London: Oxford University Press, 1961 <1949>), 372; Weiner, *Making Sense*, 369–70, for various considerations on this theme.

169. Vaksberg, *Stalin*, 51–8, for an entirely unflattering portrait.
170. Vaksberg, *Stalin*, 49–51.
171. Vaksberg, *Stalin*, 70.
172. Gorlicki and Khlevniuk, *Cold Peace*, 98.
173. Redlich, *Propaganda and Nationalism*, chapter 2, 'The Ehrlich-Alter Affair'; Vaksberg, *Stalin*, 4–6, 106–16.
174. Weiner, *Making Sense*, chapter 4, 'Memory of Excision: Excisionary Memory'; see Shimon Redlich, *War, Holocaust and Stalinism: A Documented Study of the Jewish Anti-Fascist Committee in the USSR* (Luxembourg: Harwood Academic Publishers, 1995), chapter 5, 'The Black Book', for documents and extended discussion. For the English version of the Black Book itself, see Ilya Ehrenburg and Vassily Grossman, *The Complete Black Book of Russian Jewry*, trans. David Patterson (New Brunswick, NJ: Transaction Publishers, 2002).
175. Weiner, *Making Sense*, 114–22, 207–9; Redlich, *War, Holocaust*, 246–63. Also Frank Gruner, 'Did Anti-Jewish Violence Exist in the Soviet Union?: Anti-Semitism and Collective Violence in the USSR During the War and Post-War Years', *JGR*, 11:2/3 (2009), 361–6.
176. Weiner, 'Nature, Nurture', 1151.
177. Robert Weinberg, 'Jews into Peasants?: Solving the Jewish Question in Birobidzhan', in Yaacov Ro'i, ed., *Jews and Jewish Life in Russia and the Soviet Union* (Ilford, Essex, and Portland, OR: Frank Cass, 1995), 87–102.
178. Vaksberg, *Stalin*, 114–6, 120–7. Vaksberg's speculations include consideration of the role of the NKVD minder, Sergei Shpigelgaz, as one possible conduit between the Kremlin and the JAC on Crimean possibilities. Redlich, *War, Holocaust*, 264–7 (doc. 64), for text of the 15 February 1944 letter.
179. John Klier, 'The Holocaust and the Soviet Union', in Stone, *Historiography*, 286; also Hale, *Turkish Foreign Policy*, 111–16, for the emergence of the Truman Doctrine with respect to Turkey.
180. Yakovlev, *Century*, 202; Snyder, *Bloodlands*, 341.
181. See Yaacov Ro'i, *Soviet Decision-Making in Practice: The USSR and Israel, 1947–1954* (New Brunswick, NJ: Transaction Books, 1980), chapters 2–5. Also Albert Kaganovich, 'Stalin's Great Power Politics: The Return of Jewish Refugees to Poland and Continued Migration to Palestine, 1944–1946', *HGS*, 26:1 (2012), 59–94.
182. Snyder, *Bloodlands*, 346.
183. Sebag Montefiore, *Stalin*, 599–601; Gorlicki and Khlevniuk, *Cold Peace*, 75–6; Larisa Nikolaevna Vasilieva, *Kremlin Wives*, ed. and trans. Cathy Porter (London: Weidenfeld and Nicolson, 1994), 137, for Stalin's long-standing animosity towards Zhemchuzhina.
184. Vaksberg, *Stalin*, chapter 8, 'The Murder of Solomon Mikhoels'; Redlich, *Propaganda and Nationalism*, 162–4, for details and commentary.
185. See Levene, *War*, 141–2, for the debate around the degree to which Russian Zionism really did 'take off' in 1917.
186. Snyder, *Bloodlands*, 221–2, iterates that of these 2.6 million, 1.6 million had only been under Soviet rule since 1939.
187. Slezkine *Jewish Century*, 216–26; Pinkus, *Jews of the Soviet Union*, 89–98, for the demographic tendencies.

188. Hans Rogger, *Jewish Policies and Right-Wing Politics in Imperial Russia* (London: Macmillan, 1985), 26–7.

189. Slezkine, *Jewish Century*, 224.

190. Sebag Montefiore, *Stalin*, 311; Slezkine, *Jewish Century*, 254; Gerrits, *Myth*, 124–6.

191. Vaksberg, *Stalin*, 154–6: Gennadi Kostrychenko, 'The Genesis of Establishment Anti-Semitism in the USSR, 1948–1953', in Zvi Y. Gitelman and Yaacov Ro'i, eds., *Revolution, Repression and Revival: The Soviet Jewish Experience* (Lanham, NY: Rowman and Littlefield, 2007), 181–3, for confirmation. Also Vasily Grossman, *Life and Fate*, trans. Robert Chandler (London: Collins Harvill, 1985), for *the* masterful literary evocation of how this wartime campaign developed, particularly through the character of Grossman's alter ego, Victor Shtrum.

192. Vaksberg, *Stalin*, 192; Gorlicki and Khlevniuk, *Cold Peace*, 157, 159.

193. Yakovlev, *Century*, 207, for extract from the 13 January 1953 *Pravda* text.

194. Yakovlev, *Century*, 203; Tony Judt, *Postwar: A History of Europe since 1945* (London: Heinemann, 2005), 183.

195. Judt, *Postwar*, 178–81; more generally McDermott and Stibbe, *Stalinist Terror*.

196. Slezkine, *Jewish Century*, 301; Levene, *Rise*, 129, for the converso 'threat'.

197. Quoted in David Brion Davis, ed., *The Fear of Conspiracy: Images of Un-American Subversion from the Revolution to the Present* (Ithaca, NY, and London: Cornell University Press, 1971), 307. See also Mark Levene, 'Battling Demons or Banal Exterminism? Apocalypse and Statecraft in Modern Mass Murder', *Journal of Human Rights*, 3:1 (2004), 70–1, for more on the comparison.

198. Sebag Montefiore, *Stalin*, 646; Gorlicki and Khlevniuk, *Cold Peace*, esp. 26–9, 74–9, 148–51, for Stalin's ongoing efforts to divide, rule, emasculate, and destroy his potential successors.

199. Sebag Montefiore, *Stalin*, 626–7; Gorlicki and Khlevniuk, *Cold Peace*, 154–5.

200. Yakovlev, *Century*, 207, quoting *Pravda* text.

201. Service, *Stalin*, 581. Also see front cover of *American Historical Review*, 104:4 (1999).

202. Vaksberg, *Stalin*, 222–5, 244–7.

203. Vaksberg, *Stalin*, 247.

204. Quoted in Yakovlev, *Century*, 203–4.

205. Quoted in Judt, *Postwar*, 183.

206. Paczkowski, *The Spring*, 240–1; Gerrits, *Myth*, 154–72, for broad, incisive analysis of the emergent anti-Jewish 'party' turn.

207. Judt, *Postwar*, 186; Ro'i, *Soviet Decision-Making*, 357–71.

208. Judt, *Postwar*, 186. See also François Fejtö, *A History of the People's Democracies*, trans. Daniel Weissbort (London: Pelican, 1974 <1969>), 14–25, for a thoughtful examination of the Slansky affair in its wider East European communist context. Also Heda Margolius Kovaly, *Prague Farewell*, trans. Franci and Helen Epstein (London: Victor Gollancz, 1988), for what it was like as one of the wives of the accused caught up in the affair.

209. Shlomo Lambroza, 'The Pogroms of 1903–1906', in John D. Klier and Shlomo Lambroza, eds., *Pogroms: Anti-Jewish Violence in Modern Russian History* (Cambridge: Cambridge University Press, 1991), 195–247.

210. Judt, *Postwar*, 187.

211. Vaksberg, *Stalin*, 259–63; Snyder, *Bloodlands*, 367–8, for slightly different emphases. The letter appears to have gone through several drafts, the last on 20 February. Some celebrity Jews, notably Ehrenburg, attempted to resist or prevaricate against signing.

212. Vaksberg, *Stalin*, 258–9. Vaksberg's evidence is based primarily on written or oral testimony from various intelligence and other sources garnered thirty or more years after these events. However, much of the narrative would appear to be independently corroborated by Iakov Ettinger, a personal victim and survivor of the Doctors' Plot, largely by way of the testimony of leading Praesidium member and post-Stalin premier Nicolai Bulganin, in the 1970s. See Iakov Ettinger, 'The Doctors' Plot: Stalin's Solution to the Jewish Question', in Ro'i, ed., *Jews and Jewish Life*, 117–18.
213. Judt, *Postwar*, 43, 182.
214. See Joanna Michlic-Coren, 'Anti-Jewish Violence in Poland, 1918–1939 and 1945–1947', 34–61, and Michlic-Coren, 'Polish Jews during and after the Kielce Pogrom: Reports from the Communist Archives', *Polin* 13 (2000), 53–67, for broader background. Paczkowski, *The Spring*, 183, firmly rules out of court that Kielce was a PPR provocation, a repeated claim of nationalist apologists.
215. Michlic-Coren, 'Anti-Jewish Violence', 43; Michlic-Coren, 'Polish Jews', 263, 266. See also Padraic Kenny, 'Whose Nation, Whose State?: Working-Class Nationalism and Antisemitism in Poland, 1945–1947', *Polin* 13 (2000), 224–35, for further supporting evidence.
216. See Yehoshua Robert Buchler, *Topol'cany: The Story of a Perished Ancient Community* (Jerusalem: Yad Vashem, 1989).
217. Weiner, *Making Sense*, 291–3; Gruner, 'Anti-Jewish Violence', 372–3.
218. Vaksberg, *Stalin*, 257; Ettinger, 'Doctor's Plot', 118, adds that for good measure as the deportations got under way 'a series of train crashes were also to be devised'.
219. Sebag Montefiore, *Stalin*, 655, among others, queries whether Beria might have had a hand in his death, ironically, by spiking his wine 'with a blood-thinning drug such as warfarin'.
220. Service, *Stalin*, 593; Ettinger, 'Doctors' Plot', 119–21.
221. Weiner, *Making Sense*, 297.
222. Slezkine, *Jewish Century*, 308–9, n. 147, referring to the research of Prof. Gennadi Kostyrchenko.
223. Gorlicki and Khlevniuk, *Cold Peace*, 158–9.
224. Samson Madievski, '1953: la déportation des juifs soviétiques était-elle programmée?', *Cahiers du monde russe*, 41:4 (2000), 561–8, for the archival evidence for and against.
225. Yakovlev, *Century*, 209.
226. Sebag Montefiore, *Stalin*, 624, not least for the impact on the Jewish managers of the 'prestigious' Stalin automobile plant that made his limousines.
227. Vaksberg, *Stalin*, 270–1, for personal recollection.
228. See Zvi Y. Gitelman, *Jewish Nationality and Soviet Politics: The Jewish Sections of the CPSU 1917–1930* (Princeton, NJ: Princeton University Press, 1972), for the intense debates around this subject; Naomi Blank, 'Redefining the Jewish Question from Lenin to Gorbachev: Terminology or Ideology?', in Ro'i, *Jews and Jewish Life*, 51–66.
229. Gerrits, *Myth*, 177–8; Benjamin Pinkus, *The Soviet Government and the Jews, 1948–1967: A Documented Study* (Cambridge: Cambridge University Press, 1984), for the wider context.
230. See Darius Stola, 'The Hate Campaign of March 1968; How did it become Anti-Jewish?' *Polin*, 21 (2008), 16–36.
231. See Walter Laqueur, *Black Hundred: The Rise of the Extreme Right in Russia* (New York: Harper Perennial, 1993); Lev Gudkov, 'Attitudes towards Jews in Post-Soviet Russia and the Problem of Anti-Semitism', in Gitelman and Ro'i, *Revolution*, 193–217.

232. One is reminded here of how Tim Kirk, *Nazi Germany* (Basingstoke: Palgrave Macmillan, 2007), 7, describes a plebiscitary democracy: 'a political system which employs techniques of mass mobilisation to elicit acclaim and consent without genuine political participation'.

233. See Noah Lewin-Epstein, Yaacov Ro'i, and Paul Ritterband eds., *Russian Jews on Three Continents: Emigration and Resettlement* (London: Frank Cass, 1997).

CHAPTER 6

1. Quoted in Matthew Frank, *Expelling the Germans: British Opinion and Post-1945 Population Transfer in Context* (Oxford: Oxford University Press, 2008), 70–1.

2. Quoted in Alfred-Maurice de Zayas, *A Terrible Revenge: The Ethnic Cleansing of the East European Germans* (Basingstoke: Palgrave, 2006 <1986>), 88.

3. Tony Judt, 'The Past is Another Country: Myth and Memory in Postwar Europe', in Deák, *Politics of Retribution*, 298.

4. William A. Schabas, *Genocide in International Law: The Crime of Crimes* (Cambridge: Cambridge University Press, 2000), 168, 196, 200, for intriguing commentary on international legal debates during and after the UNC formulation.

5. Marrus, *Unwanted*, 297, 299.

6. Marrus, *Unwanted*, 299.

7. Primo Levi, *The Truce*, trans. Stuart Woolf (London: Bodley Head, 1965 <1963>). For the general chaos of Europe at the end of war, see Lowe, Savage Continent.

8. Panikos Panayi and Pippa Virdee, 'Preface: Key Themes, Concepts and Rationale', in Panayi and Virdee, *Refugees and the End of Empire: Imperial Collapse and Forced Migration during the Twentieth Century* (Basingstoke: Palgrave, 2011), viii.

9. Levene, Meaning, 196–201. See also A. Dirk Moses, 'Genocide and the Terror of History', *Parallax* 17:4 (2011), 90–108, for a more sustained development of this theme, as prelude to his forthcoming book of the same title.

10. See Kushner and Knox, *Refugees*, 10–12, for the 1951 UN Convention and the ongoing disputes as to the 'refugee' definition.

11. Naimark, *Fires*, 14; de Zayas, *Terrible Revenge*, 156.

12. Mark Kramer, 'Introduction', in Ther and Siljak, *Redrawing Nations*, 2 and 27, n. 6.

13. Rüdiger Overmans, 'Personelle Verluste der Deutschen Zivil Bevölkerung durch Flucht und Vertreibung', *Dzieje Najnowsze*, 26 (1994), 51–65.

14. Cathie Carmichael, 'Genocide and Population Displacement in Post-Communist Eastern Europe', in Bloxham and Moses, *Oxford Handbook*, 523, for instance, opts for the conservative figure of c. 100,000 military and civilian dead plus 2 million displaced people. See 'Bosnian Genocide Case', <http://en.wikipedia.org/wiki/Bosnian_Genocide_Case>, for the ongoing ICJ trials.

15. See William A. Schabas, 'Genocide and the International Court of Justice: Finally, a Duty to Prevent the Crime of Crimes', and David Scheffer, 'The World Court's Fractured Ruling on Genocide', *Genocide Studies and Prevention* (hereafter *GSP*), 2:2 (2007), 101–22 and 123–36, respectively.

16. See notably Andrew Bell-Fialkoff and Andrew Villen Bell, *Ethnic Cleansing*, 2nd ed. (Basingstoke: Palgrave Macmillan, 1999); Naimark, *Fires*, chapter 5, 'The Wars of Yugoslav Succession'; Lieberman, Terrible Fate, chapter 8, 'A Kind of Second Reality'.

17. Pertti Ahonen et al., *People on the Move: Forced Population Movements in Europe in the Second World War and its Aftermath* (Oxford and New York: Berg, 2008), 89–90.

18. See member of British relief team, and Robert Murphy testimonies: respectively Frank, *Expelling*, 133–4, and de Zayas, *Terrible Revenge*, 149–50.
19. Ugur Ümit Üngör, 'Fresh Understanding of the Armenian Genocide: Mapping New Terrain with Old Questions', in Adam Jones, ed., *New Directions in Genocide Research* (New York and London: Routledge, 2012), 199–200.
20. Estimates inevitably vary. Frank, *Expelling*, 1, puts the range at between 10 and 15 million expellees. Ahonen, *People*, 87, opts for total German displacement from Poland and Czechoslovakia at 10.5 million, but with more open-ended figures for those from Hungary, Rumania, and Yugoslavia. De Zayas, *Terrible Revenge*, 156, offers a table enumerating 14,447,000 ethnic Germans expelled in toto (including 72,000 civilians deported to the USSR), but excluding another 2,111,000 killed or missing in flight or expulsion.
21. Marrus, *Unwanted*, 314–17; more generally, Bethell, *The Last Secret*.
22. Lower, *Nazi Empire-Building*, 200–1.
23. De Zayas, *Terrible Revenge*, 41–3; Ahonen, *People*, 135.
24. Ahonen, *People*, 87.
25. Marrus, *Unwanted*, 326.
26. De Zayas, *Terrible Revenge*, 66–79.
27. Ahonen, *People*, 87.
28. Ahonen, *People*, 74.
29. Polian, *Against their Will*, 259–63.
30. Polian, *Against their Will*, 293. Compare with de Zayas, *Terrible Revenge*, 118. However, for the true human impact on the Silesians deported and those they left behind, see Ewa Ochman, 'Population Displacement and Regional Reconstruction in Post-War Poland: The Case of Upper Silesia', in Gatrell and Baron, *Warlands*, 210–28.
31. Polian, *Against their Will*, section: 'Internment and Deportation of German Civilians from European Countries to the USSR', 241–75.
32. Ahonen, *People*, 74–7.
33. Eagle Glassheim, 'The Mechanics of Ethnic Cleansing: The Expulsion of Germans from Czechoslovakia', in Ther and Siljak, *Redrawing Nations*, 43; de Zayas, *Terrible Revenge*, 90, for *Daily Mail* report, 6 August 1945.
34. See Frank, *Expelling*, 98–115.
35. Glassheim, 'Mechanics', 211, referring to Tomás Staněk's 1991 Czech-language study of the 'transfer' movement.
36. Naimark, *Fires*, 116.
37. Frank, *Expelling*, 184–8.
38. Naimark, *Fires*, 116–17.
39. Ahonen, *People*, 87.
40. Ahonen, *People*, 91; Stanisław Jankiowak, '"Cleansing" Poland of Germans: The Province of Pomerania, 1945–1949', in Ther and Siljak, *Redrawing Nations*, 89, cites 274,206 Germans expelled from territory east of the Oder in the period 19–30 June 1945 *alone*. Ana Siljak, 'Conclusion', 331, in the same volume puts the Czech figures at 870,000 expellees, but confirms the Jankiowak figure for Poland.
41. Article XIII of Potsdam agreement.
42. Naimark, *Fires*, 119–20; Ahonen, *People*, 140.
43. Ahonen, *People*, 79, gives figures of 15,000 to 20,000 Hungarians killed and something in the region of 10,000 Germans, though the Ahonen team note other sources which claim the latter figure may have been as high as 60,000 to 70,000.
44. Ahonen, *People*, 71, 77–8, 83.

45. The complexities of Istria's war and post-war violence and population losses are well examined in Pamela Ballinger, 'Who Defines and Remembers Genocide after the Cold War? Contested Memories of Partisan Massacre in Venezia Giulia in 1943–1945', *JGR*, 2:1 (2000), 11–30; Ballinger, 'At the Borders of Force: Violence, Refugees, and the Reconfiguration of the Yugoslav and Italian States', in Mark Mazower, Jessica Reinisch, and David Feldman, eds., *Post-War Reconstruction: International Perspectives 1945–1948* (Oxford: Oxford University Press, 2011), 158–76; Gustavo Corni, 'The Exodus of Italians from Istria and Dalmatia, 1945–1956', in Reinisch and White, *Disentanglement of Populations*, 71–90; Ahonen, *People*, 104–9.

46. Malcolm, *Kosovo*, 311–12. Malcolm, however, doubts Albanian figures of 47,300 (including 28,400 within Kosovo) killed by the communists in the course of war and post-war conflict.

47. Malcolm, *Kosovo*, 316–17.

48. Mark Mazower, *After The War Was Over: Reconstructing the Family, Nation and State in Greece, 1943–1960* (Princeton, NJ: Princeton University Press, 2000), 25–6. Also Andrew Rossos, 'Macedonianism and Macedonian Nationalism on the Left', in Ivo Banac and Katherine Vedery, eds., *National Character and National Ideology in Interwar Europe* (New Haven, CT: Yale Center for International and Area Studies, 1995), 219–54, for Slavophone political alignments.

49. See Thanos Veremis, '1922: Political Continuations and Realignments in the Greek State', in Hirschon, *Crossing*, 61; Çagaptay, 'Crafting the Turkish Nation', 299, for further commentary.

50. The Sudeten reference as cited in Donald Bloxham and A. Dirk Moses, 'Genocide and Ethnic Cleansing', in Donald Bloxham and Robert Gerwarth, *Political Violence in Twentieth-Century Europe* (Cambridge: Cambridge University Press, 2011), 125.

51. Polian, *Against Their Will*, 36. See also Joseph B. Schechtman, *European Population Transfers, 1939–1945* (New York: Oxford University Press, 1946), 404–14; Solonari, *Purifying the Nation*, chapter 6, 'The Population Exchange with Bulgaria', for the practice.

52. Lieberman, *Terrible Fate*, 277.

53. Hale, *Turkish Foreign Policy*, 92–3.

54. See Speros Vyronis, *The Mechanism of Catastrophe* (New York: Greekworks, 2005), for detailed analysis of the pogrom.

55. Alfred de Zayas, 'The Istanbul Pogrom of 6–7 September 1955 in the Light of International Law', *GSP*, 2:2 (2007), 137–8.

56. Marrus, *Unwanted*, 331–9.

57. Ahonen, *People*, 97.

58. Biondich, *Balkans*, 181. Tomasevich, *War and Revolution*, 774–5, for a much lower figure of 20,000 based on Žerjavić estimates, and with the issue of the women and children somewhat elided. Glenny, *Balkans*, 530, by contrast, cites 80,000 killed *including* 30,000 women and children executed in a five-day sequence of killing from 20 May near the village of Tezna. Glenny's narrative suggests this was only part of the overall death toll.

59. Quoted in Mastny, *Czechs*, 119; see Lowe, *Savage Continent,* chapters 13 and 14, for the scope, scale, and extent of post-liberation revenge across the continent.

60. See Glassheim, 'Mechanics', 206; Naimark, *Fires*, 115.

61. See Zimbardo, *Lucifer Effect*.

62. Quoted in de Zayas, *Terrible Revenge*, 97.

63. Naimark, *Fires*, 129; Lowe, *Savage Continent*, 135–8, 226. Morel also seems to have been a perpetrator in the ill-treatment of Lemkos in Jaworzno: see chapter 5 and <http://en.wikipedia.org/wiki/Zgoda_labour_camp>.

64. Naimark, *Fires*,130; Snyder, *Bloodlands*, 321–2; Lowe, *Savage Continent*, 141–4, for more on Gęborski and similar examples.

65. De Zayas, *Terrible Revenge*, 89.

66. See Glassheim, 'Mechanics', 204–5, for the tensions between the two entities.

67. Lieberman, *Terrible Fate*, 230.

68. Gordon Dean to Robert Jackson, 11 August 1945. Quoted in Bloxham, *Genocide on Trial*, 17.

69. Bloxham, *Genocide on Trial*, 10; Ahonen, *People*, 61–2.

70. Kazimierz Wyka, quoted in Polonsky, 'Introduction', *Polin*, 13, 31.

71. Glassheim, 'Mechanics', 204.

72. Glassheim, 'Mechanics', 208.

73. Lieberman, *Terrible Fate*, 231.

74. See Jankowiak, ' "Cleansing" Poland', 89.

75. Ahonen, *People*, 77.

76. Ahonen, *People*, 67–9. See Vaso Cubrilović, 'The Minority Problem in the New Yugoslavia' [3 November 1944], in K. Elsie, ed., *Kosovo: In the Heart of the Powder Keg* (New York: East European Monographs, 1997), 449–64 for full text.

77. See Stefanović, 'Seeing the Albanians', 482; Ahonen, *People*, 69.

78. Glenny, *Balkans*, 530–2; Mann, *Dark Side*, 386; Ahonen, *People*, 79.

79. Ahonen, *People*, 66, 88–9.

80. Paczkowski, *The Spring*, 89–90.

81. See Claudia Kraft, 'Who is a Pole, and Who is a German?: The Province of Olsztyn in 1945', in Ther and Siljak, *Redrawing Nations*, 111–12.

82. Frank, *Expelling*, 245, 253.

83. Kraft, 'Who is a Pole?', 112.

84. Frank, *Expelling*, 242.

85. Ahonen, *People*, 102–3.

86. Kraft, 'Who is a Pole?', 107–9, 116–17; Naimark, *Fires*, 131.

87. See Bernard Linek, ' "De-Germanization" and "Re-Polonization" in Upper Silesia, 1945–1950', in Ther and Siljak, *Redrawing Nations*, 121–34. Also Naimark, *Fires*, 14–15, 124.

88. Glassheim, 'Mechanics', 200–1; Ahonen, *People*, 62–6.

89. Ahonen, *People*, 81.

90. Glassheim, 'Mechanics', 213: Frank, *Expelling*, 95–6, 109.

91. See Naimark, *Fires*, 115, for examples.

92. Naimark, *Fires*, 112–13; Ahonen, *People*, 66.

93. Kramer, 'Introduction', 5; Ahonen, *People*, 81.

94. Fein, 'Sociological Perspective', 36.

95. Ahonen, *People*, 91–2.

96. Kramer, 'Introduction', 14–15; Ahonen *People*, 81–3.

97. Kramer, 'Introduction', 15.

98. See Matthew Frank, 'Reconstructing the Nation-State: Population Transfer in Central and Eastern Europe, 1944–8', in Reinisch and White, *Disentanglement of Populations*, 36–42, for the piece by piece derailing of Prague's Hungarian transfer scheme, at Allied, including—eventually—Soviet hands.

99. Benjamin Frommer, 'To Prosecute or to Expel?: Czechoslovak Retribution and the "Transfer" of Sudeten Germans', in Ther and Siljak, *Redrawing Nations*, 230–4.

100. Naimark, *Fires*, 121–2.
101. Lemkin, *Axis Rule*, 79.
102. Ahonen, *People*, 84–6, 69–70.
103. See Mazower, *Hitler's Empire*, 568.
104. De Zayas, *Terrible Revenge*, 84.
105. Quoted in Ahonen, *People*, 61.
106. See Mark Mazower, *No Enchanted Palace: The End of Empire and the Ideological Origins of the United Nations* (Princeton, NJ, and Oxford: Princeton University Press, 2009), 62–3.
107. Frank, *Expelling*, 78.
108. Quoted in Ahonen, *People*, 61.
109. As quoted in Naimark, *Fires*, 110; Frank, *Expelling*, 75.
110. Frank, *Expelling*, 75–6. Or, put another way, the US-British position was for 'selective' transfers, not 'general' ones. See Frank, 'Reconstructing the Nation-State', 33–4.
111. Frank, *Expelling*, 9–10, 17, 8–9.
112. Frank, *Expelling*, 50–1, 54–5. See Volume One, 27 for more on Macartney.
113. Frank, *Expelling*, 50; Arnold J. Toynbee, *The Western Question in Greece and Turkey: A Study in the Contact of Civilisations* (London: Constable and Co. 1923), xv.
114. Mazower, *No Enchanted Palace*, 111–13; Marrus, *Unwanted*, 298–9.
115. De Zayas, *Terrible Revenge*, 86; Frank, *Expelling*, 162.
116. Frank, *Expelling*, 78–9.
117. Frank, *Expelling*, 152.
118. Frank, *Expelling*, 140–53.
119. Gerhard Weinberg, *A World at Arms: A Global History of World War II* (Cambridge: Cambridge University Press, 1994), 895.
120. See Frank, *Expelling*, 157–60.
121. Marrus, *Unwanted*, 300, 312; Weindling, *Epidemics*, 373–5, 396–8.
122. Frank, *Expelling*, 245–61.
123. Marrus, *Unwanted*, 317–24, not least on UNRRA's early structural problems. See also Jessica Reinisch, 'Internationalism in Relief: The Birth (and Death) of UNRRA', in Mazower, *Post-War Reconstruction*, 258–89, on the different conceptions of international cooperation underlying UNRRA's fraught European DP operation.
124. Judt, *Postwar*, 141–2.
125. See Krystyna Kersten, 'Forced Migration and the Transformation of Polish Society in the Post-War Period', in Ther and Siljak, *Redrawing Nations*, 81.
126. Kramer, 'Introduction', 5; Snyder, *Bloodlands*, 324.
127. Frank, 'Reconstructing the Nation-State', 35.
128. Sir Halford J. Mackinder, *Democratic Ideals and Reality: A Study in the Politics of Reconstruction* (London: Constable and Co. 1919), 179.
129. See Winston Churchill, 'The Sinews of Peace', in Mark A. Kishlansky, ed., *Sources of World History* (New York: Harper Collins, 1995), 298–302, for the full text of Churchill's Fulton, MO, speech, 5 March 1946.
130. Peter Gatrell and Nick Baron, 'Introduction', in Gatrell and Baron, *Warlands*, 3.
131. Judt, *Postwar*, 110–11.
132. See Mary Kaldor, *The Disintegrating West* (London: Pelican Books, 1979), for incisive development of this argument. The 'largely' in the text comes with some caveats of the present author, as a full-time peace campaigner operating in the context of the heightened tensions of the 1980s.

133. Quoted in Kramer, 'Introduction', 7.

134. Judt, *Postwar*, 9.

135. See Kramer, 'Introduction', 8–9, for commentary on these tendencies.

136. Donald Bloxham and Devin O. Pendas, 'Punishment as Prevention? The Politics of Punishing Génocidaires', in Bloxham and Moses, *Oxford Handbook*, 622.

137. See Special Issue: 'Raphael Lemkin: The "Founder of the United Nation's Genocide Convention" as a Historian of Mass Violence', *JGR*, 7:4 (2005), and '60 years after the Ratification of the Genocide Convention: Critical Reflections on the State and Future of Genocide Studies', *GSP*, 6:3 (2011), for examples.

138. A. Dirk Moses, 'Raphael Lemkin: Culture and the Concept of Genocide', in Bloxham and Moses, *Oxford Handbook*, 37. For text of the resolution, see Leo Kuper, *Genocide: Its Political Use in the Twentieth Century* (New Haven, CT, and London: Yale University Press, 1981), 23.

139. See A. Dirk Moses, 'The Holocaust and Genocide', in Stone, *Historiography*, 541, for further discussion.

140. Schabas, *Genocide*, 37–8, including quote from French IMT prosecutor, Champetier de Ribes.

141. Schabas, *Genocide*, 48–9.

142. Moses, 'Raphael Lemkin', 36; Bloxham, *Genocide on Trial*, 67.

143. William A. Schabas, 'Law and Genocide', in Bloxham and Moses, *Oxford Handbook*, 126–7; Samantha Power, *'A Problem from Hell': America and the Age of Genocide* (New York: Basic Books, 2002), 50–1.

144. Schabas, 'Law and Genocide', 127–8.

145. Schabas, *Genocide*, 36–7.

146. See Judt, *Postwar*, 58; Weindling, *Epidemics*, 408–12.

147. At least, that is, until the ending of the Cold War. See Kramer, 'Introduction', 23, for the Czech–German declaration of January 1997, and its attempts to try to come to terms with the legacy of Nazi occupation *and* subsequent Czech expulsions.

148. See Mark Levene, *War, Jews and the New Europe: The Diplomacy of Lucien Wolf, 1914–1919* (Oxford: Littman Library of Jewish Civilization and Oxford University Press, 1992), chapter 15, 'The New States Committee and Peace Settlement'.

149. Quoted in Schabas, *Genocide*, 195.

150. Schabas, *Genocide*, 196.

151. Schabas, *Genocide*, 196–7. The Syrian amendment read: 'Imposing measures intended to oblige members of a group to abandon their homes in order to escape the threat of subsequent ill-treatment.' This reads like a response to the ethnic cleansing then taking place in Palestine, though, significantly, it fails to grasp the full import of compulsory deportation or expulsion.

152. Schabas, *Genocide*, 195–6. Schabas refers to Georges Scelle as the one vocal dissenter.

153. Mazower, *No Enchanted Palace*, 113–16.

154. Mazower, *No Enchanted Palace*, 116–18.

155. Mazower, *No Enchanted Palace*, 8.

156. Mazower, *No Enchanted Palace*, 25.

157. Article VI, quoted here in Kuper, *Genocide*, 211.

158. Mazower, *No Enchanted Palace*, 130; Moses, 'Raphael Lemkin', 37.

159. Kuper, *Genocide*, 23, for the text.

160. See Mark Levene, 'The Limits of Tolerance: Nation-State Building and What it Means for Minority Groups', *Patterns of Prejudice*, 34:2 (2000), 40, for original reference.

161. Quoted in Nur Masalha, *Expulsion of the Palestinians: The Concept of 'Transfer' in Zionist Political Thought 1882–1948* (Washington DC: Institute for Palestinian Studies,1992), 29. See also Mazower, *No Enchanted Palace*, 117–19, 136–7.
162. Quoted in Masalha, *Expulsion*, 128.
163. Mazower, *No Enchanted Palace*, 135. Intriguingly, the April 1941 conversation was with the Russian ambassador in London.
164. Marrus, *Unwanted*, 339, for the 30,000 figure. Yehuda Bauer, *Flight and Rescue: Brichah* (New York: Random House, 1970) is the classic study.
165. Yosef Grodzinsky, *In the Shadow of the Holocaust: The Struggle between Jews and Zionists in the Aftermath of World War II* (Monroe, ME: Common Courage Press, 2004). Also see Idith Zertal, *Israel's Holocaust and the Politics of Nationhood*, trans. Chaya Galai (Cambridge and New York: Cambridge University Press, 2005), for a searching critique, among other things, of the emerging Jewish state utilization of diasporic Holocaust anxieties in its own political interests.
166. Gerrits, *Myth*, esp. 107–16, for fuller rendition of this analysis.
167. See Ada Aharoni, 'The Forced Migration of Jews from Arab Countries', *Peace Review*, 15 (2003), 53–60. A comprehensive study of the Middle Eastern-wide Jewish exodus is awaited.
168. See, for example, Francesca Klug, 'Lessons from History', in Anne Karpf et al., eds, *A Time to Speak Out: Independent Jewish Voices on Israel, Zionism and Jewish Identity* (London: Verso, 2008), 175–81.
169. See Zertal, *Israel's Holocaust*, chapter 5, 'Yellow Territories'.
170. Mazower, *No Enchanted Palace*, 129.
171. Paczkowski, *The Spring*, 147.
172. Brown, *Biography*, esp. chapter 2, 'Ghosts in the Bathhouse', is unusually sensitive as a historian to the issue of people in their 'place'.
173. Ahonen, *People*, 133.
174. See Redlich, *Together and Apart*, for further sensitive reading of communities living together, and its limits.
175. See Norman Davies and Roger Moorhouse, *Microcosm: Portrait of a Central European City* (London: Jonathan Cape, 2002), for the Breslau/Wrocław metamorphosis. Günter Grass, *The Tin Drum*, trans. Ralph Mannheim (London: Secker and Warburg, 1962), is a classic literary account of Danzig's mid-twentieth-century paroxysm; and see Per Brodersen, *Die Stadt im Westen: Wie Königsberg Kaliningrad wurde* (Gottingen: Vandenhoeck and Ruprecht, 2008), for Soviet archive-based analysis of Königsberg's fate.
176. Ahonen, *People*, chapter 5, 'Forced Migrations and Mass Movements in the Memorialisation Processes since the Second World War', for wider examination.
177. Kersten, 'Forced Migration', 84.
178. However, see Rifat N. Bali, 'The Politics of Turkification during the Single Party Period', in Kieser, *Turkey*, 43–9, for a brief case study in how Turkification was applied to the Jews.
179. Quoted in Naimark, *Fires*, 135. See also Linek, ' "De-Germanization" ', 124; Konrad Zielinski, 'To Pacify, Populate and Polonise: Territorial Transformations and the Displacement of Ethnic Minorities in Communist Poland, 1944–49', in Gatrell and Baron, *Warlands*, 193–6.
180. Judt, *Postwar*, 26.
181. Judt, 'The Past', 297. For more focused discussion, see Charles P. Kindleberger, *Europe's Postwar Growth: The Role of Labor Supply* (Cambridge, MA: Harvard University Press, 1967).

182. As one standard sociological study puts it, 'The Jewish community of Israel is a total society.' See Calvin Goldscheider and Alan S. Zukerman, *The Transformation of the Jews* (Chicago, IL: University of Chicago Press, 1984), 205. Also S.N. Eisenstadt, *Israeli Society* (London: Weidenfeld and Nicolson, 1967); Maurice M. Roumani, *From Immigrant to Citizen: The Contribution of the Army to National Integration in Israel—The Case of the Oriental Jews* (The Hague: Foundation for the Study of Plural Societies, 1979)

183. Subtelny, 'Expulsion', 169.

184. See Wim Willems, *In Search of the True Gypsy: From Enlightenment to Final Solution* (London: Frank Cass, 1997), 270–3. See also Josef Kalvoda, 'The Gypsies of Czechoslovakia', in Crowe and Kolsti, *The Gypsies*, 96, 107–8, for parallel Czech examples of anti-Roma continuity.

185. See Polonsky, 'Introduction', *Polin*, 13, 29, for the example of Bishop Stefan Wyszyński of Lublin, who, in July 1946, not only stated that 'The Germans murdered the Jewish nation because the Jews were the propagators of communism' but also refused to condemn either the Kielce pogrom or the accompanying charge of blood libel.

186. Readers may recognize the congruence here between my assessment and that in A. Dirk Moses, 'Paranoia and Partisanship: Genocide Studies, Holocaust Historiography and the "Apocalyptic Conjuncture"', *The History Journal*, 54:2 (2011), 553–83. I venture to add that we have come to very similar conclusions by our own independent routes.

187. Judt, *Postwar*, 58 (emphases mine).

188. See Hosking, *Russia*, xix, for the distinction between imperial and national formulations.

189. Quoted in Dallin, *German Rule*, 184.

190. See István Deák, 'A Fatal Compromise? The Debate over Collaboration and Resistance in Hungary', in Deák, *The Politics*, 68.

191. Peter Kenez, *Hungary from the Nazis to the Soviets: The Establishment of the Communist Regime in Hungary, 1944–1948* (Cambridge and New York: Cambridge University Press, 2006), 45, 47; Weiner, *Making Sense*, 135; Payne, *History*, 396.

192. Levene, 'Battling Demons', 78–9.

193. Judt, *Postwar*, 5.

194. Mark Mazower, *Dark Continent: Europe's Twentieth Century* (London: Penguin Press, 1998), 269, 273–4.

195. See Paul Preston, *The Spanish Holocaust: Inquisition and Extermination in Twentieth-Century Spain* (London: W.W. Norton, 2012), chapter 13, 'No Reconciliation: Trials, Executions, Prisons'; Jean Grugel and Tim Rees, *Franco's Spain* (London: Arnold, 1997), 165–8.

196. Mazower, *Hitler's Empire*, 553–6, for acute analysis of Goebbels' 'Das Jahr 2000', 25 February 1945.

197. Judt, *Postwar*, 104. See also George F. Kennan, *Russia and the West under Lenin and Stalin* (New York: New American Library, 1961), for the classic study.

198. Weindling, *Epidemics*, 403, 410.

199. Michael J. Neufeld, *The Rocket and the Reich: Peenemünde and the Coming of the Ballistic Missile Age* (New York: The Free Press, 1995); Mazower, *Hitler's Empire*, 573–4.

200. Christopher Simpson, *Blowback: The First Full Account of America's Recruitment of Nazis, and its Disastrous Effect on our Domestic and Foreign Policy* (London and New York: Weidenfield and Nicholson, 1988), 163–71. Also Jeffrey Burds, *The Early Cold*

War in the Soviet West Ukraine, 1944–1948, Carl Beck Papers, 1505 (Pittsburgh: University of Pittsburgh, 2001), 13, 16–18, for both initially Bandera's and then Lebed's interest to the CIA as anti-Soviet 'assets'.
201. Simpson, *Blowback*, 176.
202. Glenny, *Balkans*, 544.
203. Mazower, *No Enchanted Palace*, 145.
204. See Aimé Cesaire, *Discourse on Colonialism*, trans. Joan Pinkham (New York and London: Monthly Review Press, 1972 <1955>), for the classic critique.

Select Bibliography

This bibliography lists the principal works that supported this study. For fuller references see the endnotes.

Addison, Paul, and Jeremy A. Crang, eds., *Firestorm: The Bombing of Dresden* (London: Pimlico, 2006).

Aharoni, Ada, 'The Forced Migration of Jews from Arab Countries', *Peace Review*, 15 (2003), 53–60.

Ahonen, Pertti, et al., *People on the Move: Forced Population Movements in Europe in the Second World War and its Aftermath* (Oxford and New York: Berg, 2008).

Akçam, Taner, *From Empire to Republic: Turkish Nationalism and the Armenian Genocide* (London and New York: Zed Books, 2004).

Alexander, Jeffrey C., 'On the Social Construction of Moral Universals: The "Holocaust" from War Crime to Trauma Drama', *European Journal of Social Theory*, 5:1 (2002), 5–85.

Alexander, Stella, *The Triple Myth: A Life of Archbishop Alojzije Stepinac* (Boulder, CO: East European Monographs, 1987).

Alliluyeva, Svetlana, *Only One Year* (New York: Harper and Row, 1969).

Aly, Götz, *Final Solution: Nazi Population Policy and the Murder of the European Jews* (London: Arnold, 1999).

Aly, Götz, *Hitler's Beneficiaries: Plunder, Racial War and the Nazi Welfare State* (New York: Metropolitan Books, 2006).

Aly, Götz, and Christian Gerlach, *Das Letze Kapitel: Realpolitik, Ideologie und der Mord in den Ungarischen Juden 1944/5* (Stuttgart: Deutsche Verlags-Anstalt, 2002).

Aly, Götz, and Susanne Heim, *Vordenker der Vernichtung: Auschwitz und die Deutschen Pläne für eine Neue Europäische Ordnung* (Hamburg: Hoffman and Campe, 1991).

Ancel, Jean, *Documents Concerning the Fate of Romanian Jewry during the Holocaust* (New York: Beate Klarsfeld Foundation, 1986).

Ancel, Jean, 'The Romanian Way of Solving the "Jewish Problem" in Bessarabia and Bukovina June–July 1941', *Yad Vashem Studies*, 29 (1988), 187–232.

Andreopoulos, George D., ed., *Genocide: Conceptual and Historical Dimensions* (Philadelphia: University of Pennsylvania Press, 1994).

Andreyev, Catherine, *Vlasov and the Russian Liberation Movement: Soviet Reality and Émigré Theories* (Cambridge: Cambridge University Press, 1987).

Angel, Marc D., *The Jews of Rhodes: The History of a Sephardic Community* (New York: Sepher-Hermon Press, 1980).

Anzulović, Branimir, *Heavenly Serbia: From Myth to Genocide* (New York: New York University Press, 1999).

Apostolou, Andrew, '"The Exception of Salonika": Bystanders and Collaborators in Northern Greece', *Holocaust and Genocide Studies*, 14:2 (2000), 165–96.

Applebaum, Anne, *Gulag: A History of the Soviet Camps* (London: Penguin, 2003).

Arad, Yitzhak, *Belzec, Sobibor, Treblinka: The Operation Reinhard Death Camps* (Bloomington: Indiana University Press, 1986).

Arendt, Hannah, *Eichmann in Jerusalem: A Report on the Banality of Evil* (London: Penguin, 1965).

Armstrong, John A., *Ukrainian Nationalism 1939–1945* (New York: Columbia University Press, 1955).

Aronson, Ronald, *Dialectics of Disaster: A Preface to Hope* (London: Verso, 1983).

Aronson, Shlomo, *Hitler, the Allies and the Jews* (Cambridge: Cambridge University Press, 2004).

Ascherson, Neal, *The Struggles for Poland* (London: Pan, 1987).

Ascherson, Neal, *Black Sea: The Birthplace of Civilisation and Barbarism* (London: Vintage, 1996).

Aschheim, Steven E., *Brothers and Strangers: The East European Jew in German and German Jewish Consciousness 1800–1923* (Madison, WI: University of Wisconsin Press, 1982).

Atamukas, Solomonas, 'The Hard Long Road toward the Truth: On the Sixtieth Anniversary of the Holocaust in Lithuania', trans. M. Gražina Slavėnas, *Lituanus*, 47:4 (winter 2001). <www.lituanus.org//2001/01_4_03%20htm>

Bajohr, Frank, *Parvenus und Profiteure: Korruption in der NS-Zeit* (Frankfurt-am-Main: S. Fischer, 2001).

Ballinger, Pamela, 'Who Defines and Remembers Genocide after the Cold War?: Contested Memories of Partisan Massacre in Venezia Giulia in 1943–1945', *Journal of Genocide Research*, 2:1 (2000), 11–30.

Banac, Ivo, and Katherine Vedery, eds., *National Character and National Ideology in Interwar Europe* (New Haven, CT: Yale Center for International and Area Studies, 1995).

Banach, Jens, *Heydrich's Elite: Das Führerkorps der Sicherheitspolizei und des SD 1936–1945* (Paderborn: F. Schoningh, 1998).

Barkai, Avraham, *From Boycott to Annihilation: The Economic Struggle of German Jews 1933–1943*, trans. William Templar (Hanover, NH: Brandeis Press and University Press of New England, 1989).

Barta, Tony, 'Discourses of Genocide in Germany and Australia: A Linked History', *Aboriginal History*, 25 (2001), 37–56.

Bartov, Omer, *The Eastern Front 1941–45: German Troops and the Barbarisation of Warfare* (Basingstoke: Palgrave Macmillan, 1985).

Bartov, Omer, *Hitler's Army: Soldiers, Nazis and War in the Third Reich* (New York and London: Oxford University Press, 1991).

Bassin, Mark, 'Race Contra Space: The Conflict between German *Geopolitik* and National Socialism', *Political Geography Quarterly*, 6:2 (1987), 115–34.

Bauer Yehuda, *Flight and Rescue: Brichah* (New York: Random House, 1970).

Bauer Yehuda, *Jews for Sale? Nazi–Jewish Negotiations 1933–1945* (New Haven, CT, and London: Yale University Press, 1995).

Bauman, Zygmunt, *Modernity and the Holocaust* (Oxford: Blackwell, 1989).

Baumgarten, Murray, Peter Kenez, and Bruce Thompson, eds., *Varieties of Antisemitism: History, Ideology, Discourse* (Newark, NJ: University of Delaware Press, 2009).

Beckett, Ian F.W., *Modern Insurgencies and Counter-Insurgencies* (London: Routledge, 2001).

Beevor, Antony, *Berlin: The Downfall 1945* (London: Viking, 2007).

Bell-Fialkoff, Andrew, and Andrew Villen Bell, *Ethnic Cleansing* (2nd ed., Basingstoke: Palgrave Macmillan, 1999).

Berenbaum, Michael, ed., *A Mosaic of Victims: Non-Jews Persecuted and Murdered by the Nazis* (London and New York: I.B.Tauris, 1990).

Berenbaum, Michael, and Abraham J., Peck, eds., *The Holocaust and History: The Known, the Unknown, the Disputed and the Reexamined* (Bloomington and Indianapolis: Indiana University Press, 1998).

Bergen, Doris L., 'The Nazi Concept of "Volksdeutsche" and the Exacerbation of Anti-Semitism in Eastern Europe 1939–45', *Journal of Contemporary History*, 29:4 (1994), 569–82.

Berkhoff, Karel C., *Harvest of Despair: Life and Death in Ukraine under Nazi Rule* (Cambridge, MA, and London: Harvard University Press, 2004).

Beschloss, Michael R., *The Conquerors: Roosevelt, Truman and the Destruction of Hitler's Germany 1941–1945* (New York and London: Simon and Schuster, 2003).

Bessel, Richard, *Political Violence and the Rise of Nazism: The Storm Troopers in Eastern Germany 1925–1934* (New Haven, CT, and London: Yale University Press, 1984).

Bethell, Nicholas, *The Last Secret: Forcible Repatriation to Russia 1944–7* (London: Futura Publications, 1976).

Betterlin, Lucien, *Alexandrette: Le 'Munich' de l'orient* (Paris: J. Picollec, 1999).

Biondich, Mark, *The Balkans: Revolution, War, and Political Violence since 1878* (Oxford: Oxford University Press, 2011).

Birn, Ruth Bettina, *Die Höheren SS-und Polizeiführer* (Düsseldorf: Droste Verlag, 1986).

Black, Eugene C., *The Social Politics of Anglo-Jewry 1880–1920* (Oxford: Blackwell, 1998).

Black, Peter, 'Rehearsal for "Reinhard"?: Odilo Globcnik and the Lublin *Selbschutz*', *Central European History*, 25:2 (1993), 204–26.

Bloxham, Donald, 'Punishing German Soldiers during the Cold War: The Case of Erich von Manstein', *Patterns of Prejudice*, 33:4 (1999), 25–46.

Bloxham, Donald, *Genocide on Trial: War Crimes Trials and the Formation of Holocaust History and Memory* (Oxford: Oxford University Press, 2001).

Bloxham, Donald, *The Final Solution: A Genocide* (Oxford: Oxford University Press, 2009).

Bloxham, Donald, and A. Dirk Moses, eds., *The Oxford Handbook of Genocide Studies* (Oxford: Oxford University Press, 2010).

Bloxham, Donald, and Robert Gerwarth, *Political Violence in Twentieth-Century Europe* (Cambridge: Cambridge University Press, 2011).

Boca, Angelo Del (and Giorgio Rochat), *I gas di Mussolini: Il fascismo e la guerra d'Etiopa* (Rome: Editori Riuniti, 1996).

Böhler, Jochen, Klaus-Michael Mallman, and Jürgen Matthäus, *Einsatzgruppen in Polen: Darstellung und Dokumentation* (Warsaw: Bellona, 2009).

Boog, Horst, et al., *The Attack on the Soviet Union* [vol. 4 of *Germany and the Second World War*] (Oxford: Clarendon Press, 1998).

Borodziej, Włodzimierz, *The Warsaw Uprising of 1944*, trans. Barbara Harshav (Madison, WI: University of Wisconsin Press, 2006).

Borowiec, Andrew, *Destroy Warsaw: Hitler's Punishment, Stalin's Revenge* (Westport, CT, and London: Prager, 2001).

Bowman, Steven B., *The Agony of Greek Jews 1940–1945* (Stanford, CA: Stanford University Press, 2009).

Bracher, Karl Dietrich, *The German Dictatorship: The Origins, Structure and Consequences of National Socialism*, trans. Jean Steinberg (London: Penguin, 1973).

Braham, Randolph L., 'The Kamenets Podolsk and Delvidek Massacres: Prelude to the Holocaust in Hungary', *Yad Vashem Studies*, 9 (1973), 133–56.

Braham, Randolph L., *The Politics of Genocide: The Holocaust in Hungary* (New York: Columbia University Press, 1981).

Braham, Randolph L., ed., *The Destruction of Romanian and Ukrainian Jews during the Antonescu Era* (Boulder, CO: Social Science Monographs, 1997).

Braham, Randolph L., and Scott Miller, eds., *The Nazis' Last Victims: The Holocaust in Hungary* (Detroit, MI, Wayne State University Press, 1998).

Braham, Randolph L., and Attila Pók, eds., *The Holocaust in Hungary: Fifty Years Later* (New York: Columbia University Press, 1997).

Brandenberger, D.L., and A.M. Dubrovsky, ' "The People Need a Tsar": The Emergence of National Bolshevism as Stalinist Ideology 1931–1941', *Europe–Asia Studies*, 50:5 (1998), 871–90.

Brandon, Ray, and Wendy Lower, eds., *The Shoah in Ukraine: History, Testimony, Memorialization* (Bloomington and Indianapolis: Indiana University Press, 2008).

Brann, Ross, *Power in the Portrayal: Representations of Jews and Muslims in Eleventh- and Twelfth-Century Islamic Spain* (Princeton, NJ: Princeton University Press, 2002).

Brauer, Birgit, 'Chechens and the Survival of their Cultural Identity in Exile', *Journal of Genocide Research*, 4:3 (2002), 387–400.

Breitman, Richard, *The Architect of Genocide: Himmler and the Final Solution* (London: Bodley Head, 1991).

Breitman, Richard, *Official Secrets: What the Nazis Planned, What the British and Americans Knew* (New York: Hill and Wang, 1998).

Brodersen, Per, *Die Stadt im Westen: Wie Königsberg Kaliningrad Wurde* (Göttingen: Vandenhoeck and Ruprecht, 2008).

Broszat, Martin, 'Hitler and the Genesis of the "Final Solution": An Assessment of David Irving's Theses', *Yad Vashem Studies*, 13 (1970), 73–125.

Brower, Daniel R., and Edward J. Lazzerini, eds., *Russia's Orient: Imperial Borderlands and Peoples 1700–1917* (Bloomington and Indianapolis: Indiana University Press, 1997).

Brown, Kate, *A Biography of No Place: From Ethnic Borderland to Soviet Heartland* (Boston, MA: Harvard University Press, 2005).

Browning, Christopher R., *Fateful Months: Essays on the Emergence of the Final Solution* (New York: Holmes and Meier, 1978).

Browning, Christopher R., *The Final Solution and the German Foreign Office: A Study of Referat DIII of Abteilung Deutschland 1940–43* (New York and London: Holmes and Meier, 1978).

Browning, Christopher R., *The Path to Genocide: Essays on Launching the Final Solution* (Cambridge and New York: Cambridge University Press, 1992).

Browning, Christopher R., *Ordinary Men: Reserve Police Battalion 101 and the Final Solution in Poland* (New York: Harper Perennial, 1993).

Browning, Christopher R. (with Jurgen Matthaus), *The Origins of the Final Solution: The Evolution of Nazi Jewish Policy September1939–March 1942* (London: William Heinemann, 2004).

Broxup, Marie Beningsen, ed., *The North Caucasus Barrier: The Russian Advance towards the Muslim World* (London: Hurst and Co., 1992).

Bruinessen, Martin van, *Agha, Shaikh and State: The Social and Political Structure of Kurdistan* (London: Zed Books, 1990).

Büchler, Yehoshua, 'Kommandostab Reichsführer-SS: Himmler's Personal Murder Brigades in 1941', *Holocaust and Genocide Studies*, 1:1 (1986), 11–25.

Büchler, Yehoshua, *Topol'čany: The Story of a Perished Ancient Community* (Jerusalem: Yad Vashem, 1989).

Budurowycz, Bohdan, 'Poland and the Ukrainian Problem 1921–1939', *Canadian Slavonic Papers*, 25:4 (1983), 473–500.

Burds, Jeffrey, *The Early Cold War in the Soviet West Ukraine 1944–1948*, Carl Beck Papers, 1505 (Pittsburgh: University of Pittsburgh, 2001).

Burleigh, Michael, *Death and Deliverance: 'Euthanasia' in Germany 1900–1945* (Cambridge: Cambridge University Press, 1994).

Burleigh, Michael, *The Third Reich: A New History* (Basingstoke and Oxford: Pan Books, 2000).

Burrin, Phillipe, *Hitler and the Jews: The Genesis of the Holocaust*, trans. Patsy Southgate (London: Edward Arnold, 1994).

Butnaru, I.C., *The Silent Holocaust: Romania and its Jews* (New York and Westport, CT: Greenwood Press, 1992).

Canfield, Robert L., ed., *Turko-Persia in Historical Perspective* (Cambridge: Cambridge University Press, 1991).

Çağaptay, Soner, 'Crafting the Turkish Nation: Kemalism and Turkish Nationalism in the 1930s', unpublished PhD dissertation, Yale University, 2003.

Carmichael, Cathie, *Genocide before the Holocaust* (New Haven, CT, and London: Yale University Press, 2009).

Carter, F.W., and H.T. Norris, eds., *The Changing Shape of the Balkans* (Boulder, CO, and London: Westview Press, 1996).

Césaire, Aimé, *Discourse on Colonialism*, trans. Joan Pinkham (New York and London: Monthly Review Press, 1972 <1955>).

Cesarani, David, *Justice Delayed* (London: Heinemann, 1992).

Cesarani, David, ed., *The Final Solution: Origins and Implementation* (London: Routledge, 1994).

Cesarani, David, ed., *Genocide and Rescue: The Holocaust in Hungary 1944* (Oxford and New York: Berg, 1997).

Cesarani, David, *Eichmann: His Life and Crimes* (London: Vintage, 2004).

Cesarani, David, and Tony Kushner, *The Internment of Aliens in Twentieth Century Britain* (London and Portland, OR: Frank Cass, 1993).

Charny, Israel W., ed., *The Widening Circle of Genocide* [vol. 3 of *Genocide: A Critical Bibliographical Review*] (New Brunswick, NJ, and London: Transaction Publishers, 1994).

Chary, Frederick B., *The Bulgarian Jews and the Final Solution 1940–1944* (Pittsburgh: University of Press, Pittsburgh 1972).

Chiari, Bernhard, *Alltag hinter der Front: Besatzung, Kollaboration und Widerstand in Weissrussland 1941–1944* (Düsseldorf: Droste Verlag, 1998).

Cholawsky, Shalom, *The Jews of Bielorussia During World War II* (Amsterdam: Harwood Academic Publishers, 1998).

Cienciala, Anna M., Natalia S. Lebedeva, and Wojciech Materski, *Katyn: A Crime without Punishment*, trans. Marian Schwartz (New Haven, CT, and London: Yale University Press, 2007).

Clay, Catrine, and Michael Leapman, *Master Race: The Lebensborn Experiment in Nazi Germany* (London: Hodder and Stoughton, 1995).

Cohn, Norman, *Warrant for Genocide: The Myth of the Jewish World-Conspiracy and the Protocols of the Elders of Zion* (London: Penguin, 1967).

Cole, Tim, *Traces of the Holocaust: Journeying In and Out of Ghettos* (London and New York: Continuum, 2011).

Comins-Richmond, Walter, 'The Deportation of the Karachays', *Journal of Genocide Research*, 4:3 (2002), 431–9.

Conquest, Robert, *The Nation Killers: The Soviet Deportation of Nationalities* (London: Macmillan, 1970).

Cooper, Matthew, *The German Army 1933–1945: Its Political and Military Failure* (London: Macdonald and Jane's, 1978).

Courtois, Stéphane, et al., eds., *The Black Book of Communism: Crimes, Terror, Repression*, trans. Jonathan Murphy and Mark Kramer (Cambridge, MA: Harvard University Press, 1999).

Craveri, Marta, and Nikolai Formozov, 'La Résistance au Goulag: Grèves, révoltes, évasions dans les camps de travail soviétiques de 1920 à 1956', *Communisme*, 42/43/44 (1995), 197–209.

Crowe, David, and John Kolsti, eds., *The Gypsies of Eastern Europe* (New York and London: M. Armonk and M.E. Sharpe, 1991).

Dadrian, Vahakn N., 'The Convergent Aspects of the Armenian and Jewish Cases of Genocide: A Reinterpretation of the Concept of Holocaust', *Holocaust and Genocide Studies*, 3:2 (1988), 151–70.

Dallin, Alexander, *The Kaminski Brigade 1941–1944: A Case Study of German Military Exploitation of Soviet Disaffection* (Maxwell, AL: Air University, 1952).

Dallin, Alexander, *German Rule in Russia 1941–1945: A Study of Occupation Politics* (London: Macmillan, 1957).

Daniels, Roger, *Concentration Camps USA: Japanese Americans and World War II* (New York: Holt, Rinehart and Winston, 1971).

Datner, Szymon, *Crimes Committed by the Wehrmacht during the September Campaign and the Period of Military Government* (Poznań: Instytut Zachodni, 1962).

Davies, Norman, *White Eagle, Red Star: The Polish-Soviet War 1919–20* (London: MacDonald, 1972).

Davies, Norman, *God's Playground*, vol. 2 (Oxford: Clarendon Press, 1981).

Davies, Norman, *Heart of Europe: A Short History of Poland* (Oxford: Oxford University Press, 1984).

Davies, Norman, *Europe: A History* (London: Pimlico, 1997).

Davies, Norman, and Roger Moorhouse, *Microcosm: Portrait of a Central European City* (London: Jonathan Cape, 2002).

Davis, David Brion, ed., *The Fear of Conspiracy: Images of Un-American Subversion from the Revolution to the Present* (Ithaca, NY, and London: Cornell University Press, 1971).

Davis, Mike, *Planet of Slums* (London: Verso, 2006).

Davis, Moshe, *Israel: Utopia Incorporated* (London: Zed Books, 1977).

Dawidowicz, Lucy, *The War against the Jews 1933–45* (London: Penguin, 1975).

Deák, István, Jan T. Gross, and Tony Judt, eds., *The Politics of Retribution in Europe: World War II and its Aftermath* (Princeton, NJ: Princeton University Press, 2000).

Dean, Martin, *Local Collaboration in the Holocaust: Crimes of the Local Police in Belorussia and Ukraine 1941–44* (Basingstoke: Palgrave Macmillan, 2000).

Dean, Martin, *Robbing the Jews: The Confiscation of Jewish Property in the Holocaust* (Cambridge and New York: Cambridge University Press, 2008).

Debray, Régis, *Revolution in the Revolution* (London: Penguin, 1967).

Deker, Nikolai K., and Andrei Lebed, eds., *Genocide in the USSR: Studies in Group Destruction* (New York: Scarecrow Press, 1958).

Deutscher, Isaac, *Stalin: A Political Biography* (London: Oxford University Press, [1949] 1961).

Diamond, Jared, *Collapse: How Societies Choose to Fail or Survive* (London: Penguin, 2005).

Dobroszycki, Lucjan, ed., *The Chronicle of the Lodz Ghetto 1941–1944*, trans. Richard Lourie et al. (New Haven, CT, and London: Yale University Press, 1984).

Domarus, Max, ed., *Hitler: Reden und Proklamationen 1932–45*, vol. 1 (Würzburg: Edition Schmidt, 1962).

Dulić, Tomislav, 'Mass Killing in the Independent State of Croatia 1941–1945: A Case Study for Comparative Research', *Journal of Genocide Research*, 8:3 (2006), 255–81.

Dunn, Seamus, and T.G. Fraser, *Europe and Ethnicity: The First World War and Contemporary Ethnic Conflict* (London and New York: Routledge, 1996).

Ehrenburg, Ilya, and Vassily Grossman, *The Complete Black Book of Russian Jewry*, trans. David Patterson (New Brunswick, NJ: Transaction Publishers, 2002).

Eisenstadt, S.N., *Israeli Society* (London: Weidenfeld and Nicolson, 1967).

Elder, Tanya, 'What You See Before Your Eyes: Documenting Raphael Lemkin's Life by Exploring his Archival Papers, 1900–1959', *Journal of Genocide Research*, 7:4 (2005), 469–99.

Elsie, K., ed., *Kosovo: In the Heart of the Powder Keg* (New York: Columbia University Press, 1997).

Engel, David, *In the Shadow of Auschwitz: The Polish Government-in-Exile and the Jews 1939–1942* (Chapel Hill: University of North Carolina Press, 1987).

Faitelson, Alex, *The Truth and Nothing but the Truth: Jewish Resistance in Lithuania 1941–44* (Jerusalem: Gefen Publishing House, 2006).

Favez, Jean-Claude, *The Red Cross and the Holocaust* (Cambridge: Cambridge University Press 1999).

Fein, Helen, *Accounting for Genocide: National Responses and Jewish Victimization during the Holocaust* (Chicago: University of Chicago Press, 1984).

Fein, Helen, 'Genocide: A Sociological Perspective', *Current Sociology*, 38:1 (1990), 1–120.

Fejtö, François, *A History of the People's Democracies*, trans. Daniel Weissbort (London: Pelican, 1974 <1969>).

Ferguson, Niall, ed., *Virtual History: Alternatives and Counterfactuals* (London and Basingstoke: Palgrave Macmillan, 1998).

Fest, Joachim C., *The Face of the Third Reich* (London: Penguin, 1970).

Fink, Carole, *Defending the Rights of Others: The Great Powers, the Jews, and International Minority Protection 1878–1938* (New York: Cambridge University Press, 2004).

Fisher, Alan, *The Crimean Tatars* (Stanford, CA: Hoover Institute Press, 1978).

Fleming, Gerald, *Hitler and the Final Solution* (Oxford: Oxford University Press, 1986).

Fonseca, Isabel, *Bury Me Standing: The Gypsies and their Journey* (London: Chatto and Windus, 1995).

Förster, Jürgen, 'The Wehrmacht and the War of Extermination against the Soviet Union', *Yad Vashem Studies*, 14 (1981), 7–34.

Fouché, Jean-Jacques, *Massacre at Oradours France 1944: Coming to Grips with Terror*, trans. David Sices and James B. Atkinson (Dekalb: Northern Illinois University Press, 2005).

Frank, Matthew, *Expelling the Germans: British Opinion and Post-1945 Population Transfer in Context* (Oxford: Oxford University Press, 2008).

Frankel, Jonathan, *Prophecy and Politics: Socialism, Nationalism and the Russian Jew, 1862–1917* (Cambridge and New York: Cambridge University Press, 1981).

Frankel, Jonathan, ed., *The Fate of the European Jews 1939–1945: Continuity or Contingency?*, Studies in Contemporary Jewry XIII (New York and London: Oxford University Press, 1997).

Frankel, Jonathan, and Steven J. Zipperstein, eds., *Assimilation and Community: The Jews in 19th Century Europe* (Cambridge and New York: Cambridge University Press, 1992).

Friedlander, Henry, *The Origins of Nazi Genocide: From Euthanasia to Final Solution* (Chapel Hill: University of North Carolina Press, 1995).

Friedländer, Saul, ed., *Probing the Limits of Representation: Nazism and the Final Solution* (Cambridge, MA.: Harvard University Press, 1992).

Friedrich, Jörg, *Der Brand Deutschland im Bombenkrieg 1940–1945* (Berlin: Propyläen, 2002).

Gammer, Moshe, *Muslim Resistance to the Tsar: Shamil and the Conquest of Chechnia and Daghestan* (London: Frank Cass, 1994).

Gatrell, Peter, and Nick Baron, eds., *Warlands: Population Resettlement and State Reconstruction in the Soviet-East European Borderlands 1945–50* (Basingstoke: Palgrave Macmillan, 2009).

Gaunt, David, Paul A. Levine and Laura Palosuo, eds., *Collaboration and Resistance during the Holocaust: Belarus, Estonia, Latvia, Lithuania* (Bern and Oxford: Peter Lang, 2004).

Geiss, Imanuel, *Der polnische Grenzstreifen 1914–1918: Ein Beitrag zur deutschen Kriegszie-politik im Ersten Weltkrieg* (Lubeck: Matthiesen, 1960).

Gerlach, Christian, 'Failure of Plans for an SS Extermination Camp in Mogilev, Belorussia', *Holocaust and Genocide Studies*, 7:1 (1999), 60–78.

Gerlach, Christian, *Kalkulierte Morde: Die Deutsche Wirtschafts- und Vernichtungspolitik in Weissrussland 1941 bis 1944* (Hamburg: Hamburger Edition, 1999).

Gerrits, André, *The Myth of Jewish Communism: A Historical Interpretation* (Brussels: P.I.E. Peter Lang, 2009).

Gerwarth, Robert, *Hitler's Hangman: The Life of Heydrich* (New Haven, CT, and London: Yale University Press, 2011).

Gerwarth, Robert, and Stephan Malinowski, 'Hannah Arendt's Ghosts: Reflections on the Disputable Path from Windhoek to Auschwitz', *Central European History*, 42:2 (2009), 279–300.

Geyer, Michael, and Sheila Fitzpatrick, eds., *Beyond Totalitarianism: Stalinism and Nazism Compared* (Cambridge: Cambridge University Press, 2009).

Gingeras, Ryan, *Sorrowful Shores: Violence, Ethnicity and the End of the Ottoman Empire 1912–1923* (Oxford: Oxford University Press, 2009).

Gitelman, Zvi Y., *Jewish Nationality and Soviet Politics: The Jewish Sections of the CPSU 1917–1930* (Princeton, NJ: Princeton University Press, 1972).

Gitelman, Zvi Y., ed., *Bitter Legacy: Confronting the Holocaust in the USSR* (Bloomington and Indianapolis: Indiana University Press, 1997).

Gitelman, Zvi Y., and Yaacov Ro'i, eds., *Revolution, Repression and Revival: The Soviet Jewish Experience* (Lanham, NY: Rowman and Littlefield, 2007).

Glenny, Misha, *The Balkans 1804–1999: Nationalism, War and the Great Powers* (London: Granta Books, 1999).

Goldhagen, Daniel Jonah, *Hitler's Willing Executioners: Ordinary Germans and the Holocaust* (London: Little, Brown and Company, 1996).

Goldscheider, Calvin, and Alan S. Zukerman, *The Transformation of the Jews* (Chicago: University of Chicago Press, 1984).

Gorlicki, Yoram, and Oleg Khlevniuk, *Cold Peace: Stalin and the Soviet Ruling Circle 1945–1953* (New York: Oxford University Press, 2004).

Graham, Stephen, ed., *Cities, War, and Terrorism: Towards an Urban Geopolitics* (London: Blackwell, 2004).

Graham, Stephen, *Cities under Siege: The New Military Urbanism* (London and New York: Verso, 2010).

Grass, Günter, *The Tin Drum*, trans. Ralph Mannheim (London: Secker and Warburg, 1962).

Greiner, Bernd, *War without Fronts: The USA in Vietnam*, trans. Anne Wyburn and Victoria Fern (London: Bodley Head, 2009).

Grenkevich, Leonid D., *The Soviet Partisan Movement 1941–1944: A Critical Historiographical Analysis* (London: Frank Cass, 1999).

Grodzinsky, Yosef, *In the Shadow of the Holocaust: The Struggle between Jews and Zionists in the Aftermath of World War II* (Monroe, ME: Common Courage Press, 2004).

Gross, Jan Tomasz, *Polish Society under German Occupation: The Generalgouvernement 1939–1944* (Princeton, NJ: Princeton University Press, 1979).

Gross, Jan Tomasz, *Revolution from Abroad: The Soviet Conquest of Poland's Western Ukraine and Western Belorussia* (Princeton, NJ: Princeton University Press, [1988] 2002).

Gross, Jan Tomasz, *Neighbours: The Destruction of the Jewish Community in Jedwabne, Poland 1941* (London: Arrow, 2003).

Grossman, Vasily, *Life and Fate*, trans. Robert Chandler (London: Collins Harvill, 1985).

Grugel, Jean, and Tim Rees, *Franco's Spain* (London: Arnold, 1997).

Gruner, Frank, 'Did Anti-Jewish Violence Exist in the Soviet Union? Anti-Semitism and Collective Violence in the USSR during the War and Post War Years', *Journal of Genocide Research*, 11:2/3 (2009), 355–79.

Gruner, Wolf, *Die Geschlossene Arbeitseinsatz deutscher Juden: Zur Zwangsarbeit als Element der Verfolgung 1938–1943* (Berlin: Metropol, 1997).

Gumz, Jonathan E., 'Wehrmacht Perceptions of Mass Violence in Croatia', *Historical Journal*, 44:4 (2001), 1015–38.

Gutman, Israel, *The Jews of Warsaw 1939–1943: Ghetto, Underground, Revolt* (Bloomington and Indianapolis: Indiana University Press, 1982).

Gutman, Israel, and Michael Berenbaum, eds., *Anatomy of the Auschwitz Death Camp* (Bloomington and Indianapolis: Indiana University Press, 1998).

Hale, William, *Turkish Foreign Policy 1774–2000* (London: Frank Cass, 2000).

Hanson, Joanna K.M., *The Civilian Population and the Warsaw Uprising of 1944* (Cambridge and New York: Cambridge University Press, 1982).

Hasretyan, M. A., *Türkiye'de Kürt Sorunu (1918–1940)*, vol. 1 (Berlin: Weşanên, Înstîtuya Kurdî, 1995).

Headland, Ronald, 'The Einsatzgruppen: The Question of their Initial Operation', *Holocaust and Genocide Studies*, 4:4 (1989), 401–12.

Heer, Hannes, 'The Wehrmacht and the Holocaust in Belorussia', *Holocaust and Genocide Studies*, 11:1 (1997), 79–101.

Heinemann, Isabel, ' "Another Type of Perpetrator": The SS Racial Experts and Forced Population Movements in the Occupied Regions', *Holocaust and Genocide Studies*, 15:3 (2001), 387–411.

Herbert, Ulrich, *Best: Biographische Studien über Radikalismus, Weltanschauung und Venunft* (Bonn: Dientz, 1996).

Herbert, Ulrich, ed., *National Socialist Extermination Polices: Contemporary German Perspectives and Controversies* (New York and Oxford: Berghahn, 2000).

Herf, Jeffrey, *The Jewish Enemy: Nazi Propaganda during World War II and the Holocaust* (Cambridge, MA: Harvard University Press, 2006).

Herf, Jeffrey, 'Comparative Perspectives on Anti-Semitism, Radical Anti-Semitism in the Holocaust and American White Racism', *Journal of Genocide Research*, 9:4 (2007), 581–95.

Hertzberg, Arthur, ed., *The Zionist Idea: A Historical Analysis and Reader* (New York: Atheneum, 1959).

Herzer, Ivo, et al., eds., *The Italian Refuge: Rescue of Jews during the Holocaust* (Washington DC: Catholic University of America Press, 1989).

Heske, Henning, 'Karl Haushofer: His Role in German Geopolitics and in Nazi Politics', *Political Geography Quarterly*, 6:2 (1987), 135–44.

Hiden, John, and Patrick Salmon, *The Baltic Nations and Europe: Estonia, Latvia and Lithuania in the 20th Century* (London and New York: Longman, 1991).

Hilberg, Raul, ed., *Documents of Destruction: Germany and Jewry 1933–1945* (London: W.H. Allen, 1972).

Hilberg, Raul, *The Destruction of the European Jews*, 3 vols., unabridged (New York: Holmes and Meier, 1985).

Hilberg, Raul, *Perpetrators, Victims, Bystanders: The Jewish Catastrophe 1933–1945* (London: Lime Tree, 1993).

Hillgruber, Andreas, *Der Zenit des Zweiten Weltkrieges: Juli 1941* (Wiesbaden: Steiner, 1977).

Hingley, Ronald, *The Russian Secret Police: Muscovite, Imperial Russian and Soviet Political Security Operations 1565–1970* (London: Hutchinson, 1970).

Hinton, Alexander Laban, *Annihilating Difference: The Anthropology of Genocide* (Berkeley: University of California Press, 2002).

Hirschon, Renée, ed., *Crossing the Aegean: An Appraisal of the 1923 Compulsory Population Exchange between Greece and Turkey* (New York and Oxford: Berghahn, 2003).

Hoare, Marko Attila, *Genocide and Resistance in Hitler's Bosnia: The Partisans and Chetniks 1941–1943* (Oxford: Oxford University Press, 2006).

Hofmann, Tessa, and Gerayer Koutcharian, 'The History of Armenian-Kurdish Relations in the Ottoman Empire', *Armenian Review*, 39:4 (1986), 1–45.

Holland, James, *Italy's Sorrow: A Year of War 1944–45* (London: HarperPress, 2008).

Holquist, Peter, ' "Information is the Alpha and Omega of Our Work": Bolshevik Surveillance in its Pan-European Context', *Journal of Modern History*, 69:3 (1997), 415–50.

Hosking, Geoffrey, *Russia: People and Empire 1552–1917* (London: HarperCollins, 1997).

Hull, Isabel V., *Absolute Destruction: Military Culture and the Practices of War in Imperial Germany* (Ithaca, NY: Cornell University Press, 2005).

Huttenbach, Henry, 'Locating the Holocaust on the Genocide Spectrum: Towards a Methodology of Definition and Categorization', *Holocaust and Genocide Studies*, 3:3 (1988), 289–303.

Hyman, Paula E., *From Dreyfus to Vichy: The Remaking of French Jewry 1906–1939* (New York: Columbia University Press, 1979).

Hyman, Paula E., *The Jews of Modern France* (Berkeley: University of California Press, 1998).

Iancu, Carol, *Les Juifs en Roumanie (1866–1919): De l'exclusion à l'émancipation* (Aix-en-Provence: Éditions de l'Université de Provence, 1978).

Iancu, Carol, *L'émancipation des juifs de Roumanie (1913–1919): De l'inégalité civique aux droits de minorité* (Montpelier: Université Paul-Valéry, 1992).

Ignatieff, Michael, *Blood and Belonging: Journeys into the New Nationalism* (London: Vintage, 1994).

Ingrao, Christian, *The SS Dirlewanger Brigade: The History of the Dark Hunters*, trans. Phoebe Green (New York: Skyhouse, 2011).

Ioanid, Radu, 'When Mass Murderers Become Good Men', *Journal of Holocaust Education*, 4:1 (1995), 92–104.

Ioanid, Radu, *The Holocaust in Romania: The Destruction of Jews and Gypsies under the Antonescu Regime 1940–1944* (Chicago: Ivan R. Dee, 2000).

Irvine, Jill A., *The Croat Question: Partisan Politics in the Formation of the Yugoslav Socialist State* (Boulder, CO: Westview Press, 1993).

Izady, Mehrdad R., *The Kurds: A Concise Handbook* (Washington DC: Taylor and Francis, 1992).

Jackson, Julian, *France: The Dark Years 1940–1944* (Oxford: Oxford University Press, 2001).

Jaher, Frederic Cople, *The Jews and the Nation: Revolution, Emancipation, State Formation, and the Liberal Paradigm in America and France* (Princeton, NJ, and Oxford: Princeton University Press, 2002).

James, Mark, 'Remembering Rape: Divided Social Memory and the Red Army in Hungary', *Past and Present*, 188:1 (August 2005), 133–61.

Jansen, Hans, *Madagaskar-Plan: Die beabsichtigte Deportation der europäischen Juden nach Madagaskar* (Munich: Herbig, 1997).

Jelinek, Yeshayahu, *The Parish Republic: Hlinka's Slovak People's Party 1939–1945* (Boulder, CO: East European Quarterly, 1976).

Jensen, Uffa, et al., *Gewalt und Gesellschaft: Klassiker modernen Denkens neu gelesen* (Göttingen: Wallstein Verlag, 2011).

Jones, Adam, 'Gendercide and Genocide', *Journal of Genocide Research*, 2:2 (2000), 185–211.

Jones, Adam, *Crimes against Humanity: A Beginner's Guide* (Oxford: Oneworld, 2008).

Jones, Adam, *Genocide: A Comprehensive Introduction* (2nd ed., London and New York: Routledge, 2011).

Jones, Adam, ed., *New Directions in Genocide Research* (New York and London: Routledge, 2012).

Jovanović, Mara, ' "Wir packen, Wir auspacken": Tragična Sudbina Jevreja Izbeglica u Šapcu 1941', *Zbornik*, 4 (Belgrade: Federation of Jewish Communities 1979), 246–79.

Judt, Tony, *Postwar: A History of Europe since 1945* (London: Heinemann, 2005).

Kaganovich, Albert, 'Stalin's Great Power Politics: The Return of Jewish Refugees to Poland and Continued Migration to Palestine 1944–1946', *Holocaust and Genocide Studies*, 26:1 (2012), 59–94.

Kahane, David, *Lvov Ghetto Diary*, trans. Jerzy Michalowicz (Amherst: University of Massachusetts Press, 1990).

Kaldor, Mary, *The Disintegrating West* (London: Pelican Books, 1979).

Kalyvas, Stathis N., *The Logic of Violence in Civil War* (Cambridge: Cambridge University Press, 2006).

Kaplan, J., 'French Jewry under the Occupation', *American Jewish Year Book*, 47 (1945), 71–118.

Kappeler, Andreas, *The Russian Empire: A Multiethnic History*, trans. Alfred Clayton (Harlow: Longman, 2001).

Karpf, Anne, et al., eds., *A Time to Speak Out: Independent Jewish Voices on Israel, Zionism and Jewish Identity* (London: Verso, 2008).

Katz, Steven T., *Historicism, the Holocaust and Zionism: Critical Studies in Modern Jewish Thought and History* (New York and London: New York University Press, 1992).

Kelly, Matthew, *Finding Poland: From Tavistock to Hruzdowa and Back Again* (London: Jonathan Cape, 2010).

Kenez, Peter, *Hungary from the Nazis to the Soviets: The Establishment of the Communist Regime in Hungary 1944–1948* (Cambridge and New York: Cambridge University Press, 2006).

Kennan, George F., *Russia and the West under Lenin and Stalin* (New York: New American Library, 1961).

Kenny, Padraic, 'Whose Nation, Whose State?: Working-Class Nationalism and Antisemitism in Poland 1945–1947', *Polin*, 13 (2000), 224–35.

Kenrick, Donald, and Grattan Puxon, *Gypsies under the Swastika* (Hatfield: University of Hertfordshire Press, 1995).

Kershaw, Ian, 'The Persecution of the Jews and German Popular Opinion in the Third Reich', *Leo Baeck Year Book*, 26 (1981), 261–89.

Kershaw, Ian, *The Nazi Dictatorship: Problems and Perspectives of Interpretation* (London and New York: Edward Arnold, 1985).

Kershaw, Ian, 'Improvised Genocide? The Emergence of the "Final Solution" in the Warthegau', *Transactions of the Royal Historical Society*, 2 (1992), 51–78.

Kershaw, Ian, and Moshe Lewin, eds., *Stalinism and Nazism: Dictatorships in Comparison* (Cambridge: Cambridge University Press, 1997).

Khodarkovsky, Michael, *Where Two Worlds Met: The Russian State and the Kalmyk Nomads 1600–1771* (Ithaca, NY: Cornell University Press, 1992).

Kiernan, Ben, *The Pol Pot Regime: Race Power and Genocide in Cambodia under the Khmer Rouge 1975–79* (New Haven, CT, and London: Yale University Press, 1996).

Kiernan, Ben, *Blood and Soil: A World History of Genocide and Extermination from Sparta to Darfur* (New Haven, CT, and London: Yale University Press, 2007).

Kiernan, Ben, and Robert Gellately, eds., *The Spectre of Genocide: Mass Murder in Historical Perspective* (Cambridge and New York: Cambridge University Press, 2003).

Kieser, Hans-Lukas, ed., *Turkey beyond Nationalism: Towards Post-Nationalist Identities* (London and New York: I.B. Tauris, 2006).

Kieser, Hans-Lukas, and Dominick Schaller, eds., *Der Völkermord an den Armeniern und die Shoah* (Zürich: Chronos Verlag, 2002).

Kindleberger, Charles P., *Europe's Postwar Growth: The Role of Labor Supply* (Cambridge, MA: Harvard University Press, 1967).

Kingston, Paul J., *Anti-Semitism in France during the 1930s: Organisations, Personalities, Propaganda* (Hull: University of Hull Press, 1983).

Kirk, Tim, *Nazi Germany* (Basingstoke: Palgrave Macmillan, 2007).

Kishlansky, Mark A., ed., *Sources of World History* (New York: Harper Collins, 1995).

Kitchen, Martin, *The Silent Dictatorship: The Politics of the German High Command under Hindenburg and Ludendorff 1916–1918* (London: Croom Helm, 1976).

Klein, Peter, ed., *Die Einsatzgruppen, in der Besetzen Sowjetunion, 1941/42—die Tätigkeits- und Lageberichte des Chefs der Sicherheitspolizei und des SD* (Berlin: Edition Hentrich, 1997).

Klier, John D., and Shlomo Lambroza, eds., *Pogroms: Anti-Jewish Violence in Modern Russian History* (Cambridge: Cambridge University Press, 1991).

Koehl, Robert L., *RKFVD: German Resettlement and Population Policy 1939–1945: A History of the Reich Commission for the Strengthening of Germandom* (Cambridge, MA: Harvard University Press, 1957).

Kott, Matthew, 'Stalin's Great Terror (1937–38) as Antecedent and Other Aspects of the Recent Historiography of Soviet Genocide', *Yearbook of the Museum of the Occupation of Latvia*, 8 (2007), 42–54.

Kovaly, Heda Margolius, *Prague Farewell*, trans. Franci and Helen Epstein (London: Victor Gollancz, 1988).

Krakowski, Schmuel, 'The Fate of Jewish Prisoners of War in the September 1939 Campaign', *Yad Vashem Studies*, 12 (1977), 297–323.

Krakowski, Schmuel, *The War of the Doomed: Jewish Armed Resistance in Poland 1942–1944* (New York: Holmes and Meier, 1984).

Krausnick, Helmut, and Martin Broszat, *Anatomy of the SS State*, trans. Dorothy Long and Marian Jackson (London: Paladin, 1970).

Kreiten, Irma, 'A Colonial Experiment in Cleansing: The Russian Conquest of Western Caucasus 1856–65', *Journal of Genocide Research*, 11:2/3 (2009), 213–41.

Kuljić, Todor, 'Was Tito the last Habsburg?: Reflections on Tito's Role in the History of the Balkans', *Balkanistica*, 20 (2007), 85–100.

Kuper, Leo, *Genocide: Its Political Use in the Twentieth Century* (New Haven, CT, and London: Yale University Press, 1981).

Kushner, Tony, *The Persistence of Prejudice: Antisemitism in British Society during the Second World War* (Manchester: Manchester University Press, 1989).

Kushner, Tony, *The Holocaust and the Liberal Imagination: A Social and Cultural History* (Oxford: Blackwell, 1994).

Kwiet, Konrad, 'Rehearsing for Mass Murder: The Beginning of the Final Solution in Lithuania in 1941', *Holocaust and Genocide Studies*, 12:1 (1998), 3–26.

Láníček, Jan, 'The Czechoslovak Government-in-Exile and the Jews during World War 2 (1938–1948)', unpublished PhD thesis, Southampton University, 2010.

Laqueur, Walter, *The Terrible Secret: Suppression of the Truth about Hitler's 'Final Solution'* (London: Penguin, 1982).

Laqueur, Walter, *Black Hundred: The Rise of the Extreme Right in Russia* (New York: Harper Perennial, 1993).

Legnani, Massimo, 'Il "ginger" del generale Roatta: le direttive della 2a armata sulla repressione antipartigiana in Slovenia e Croazia', *Italia contemporanea*, 209/10 (1997/1998), 155–74.

Lemkin, Raphael, *Axis Rule in Occupied Europe* (Washington DC: Carnegie Endowment for International Peace, 1944).

Levene, Mark, *War, Jews and the New Europe: The Diplomacy of Lucien Wolf, 1914–1919* (Oxford: Littman Library of Jewish Civilisation and Oxford University Press, 1992).

Levene, Mark, 'Is the Holocaust Simply Another Example of Genocide?', *Patterns of Prejudice*, 28:2 (1994), 3–26.

Levene, Mark, 'The Limits of Tolerance: Nation-State Building and What it Means for Minority Groups', *Patterns of Prejudice*, 34:2 (2000), 19–40.

Levene, Mark, ' "Ni grec, ni bulgare, ni turc", Salonika Jewry and the Balkan Wars, 1912–13', *Jahrbuch des Simon-Dubnow Instituts*, 2 (2003), 65–97.

Levene, Mark, Battling Demons or Banal Exterminism?: Apocalypse and Statecraft in Modern Mass Murder', *Journal of Human Rights*, 3:1 (2004), 67–81.

Levene, Mark, *The Meaning of Genocide* (London: I.B. Tauris, 2005).

Levene, Mark, *The Rise of the West and the Coming of Genocide* (London and New York: I.B. Tauris, 2005).

Levene, Mark, and Penny Roberts, eds., *The Massacre in History* (Oxford: Berghahn, 1999).

Levi, Primo, *The Truce*, trans. Stuart Woolf (London: Bodley Head, [1963] 1965).

Levi, Trude, *A Cat Called Adolf* (London and Portland, OR: Valentine Mitchell, 1995).

Levin, Dov, 'The Jews and the Socio-Economic Sovietization of Lithuania 1940–41', *Soviet Jewish Affairs*, 17 (1987), 17–30.

Levine, Herbert S., 'Local Authority and the SS State: The Conflict over Population Policy in Danzig-West Prussia 1939–1945', *Central European History*, 2 (1969), 531–55.

Lewandowski, Jozef, 'Early Swedish Information about the Nazis' Mass Murder of the Jews', *Polin*, 13 (2000), 113–27.

Lewin-Epstein, Noah, Yaacov Ro'i and Paul Ritterband, eds., *Russian Jews on Three Continents: Emigration and Resettlement* (London: Frank Cass, 1997).

Lewy, Guenter, *The Nazi Persecution of the Gypsies* (Oxford and New York: Oxford University Press, 2000).

Libaridian, Gerard J., *Modern Armenia: People, Nation, State* (New Brunswick, NJ, and London: Transaction Publishers, 2005).

Lieberman, Benjamin, *Terrible Fate: Ethnic Cleansing in the Making of Modern Europe* (Chicago: Ivan R. Dee, 2006).

Liekis, Šarūnas, 'The Patterns of Anti-Jewish Violence Prior to 1941: The Lithuanian Case—Prelude to the Holocaust?', unpublished paper, 'The Mass Dynamics of Anti-Jewish Violence in Eastern and East-Central Europe', Parkes Institute Conference, Southampton, 18–19 March 2007.

Litani, Dora, 'The Destruction of the Jews of Odessa in the Light of Rumanian Documents', *Yad Vashem Studies*, 6 (1967), 135–54.

Liulevicius, Vejas Gabriel, *War Land on the Eastern Front: Culture, National Identity and German Occupation in World War 1* (Cambridge and New York: Cambridge University Press, 2000).

Lohr, Eric, *Nationalizing the Russian Empire: The Campaign against Enemy Aliens during World War One* (Cambridge, MA, and London: Harvard University Press, 2003).

Longerich, Peter, *The Wannsee Conference in the Development of the 'Final Solution'* (London: Holocaust Education Trust Research Papers 1:2, 1999–2000).

Longerich, Peter, *The Unwritten Order: Hitler's Role in the Final Solution* (London: Tempus, 2001).

Longerich, Peter, *Holocaust: The Nazi Persecution and Murder of the Jews* (Oxford: Oxford University Press, 2010).

Longerich, Peter, *Heinrich Himmler*, trans. Jeremy Noakes and Lesley Sharpe (Oxford and New York: Oxford University Press, 2012).

Lowe, Keith, *Savage Continent: Europe in the Aftermath of World War II* (London: Viking, 2012).

Lowenthal, Zdenko, ed., *The Crime of the Fascist Occupants and Their Collaborators against Jews in Yugoslavia* (Belgrade: Federation of Jewish Communities, 1957).

Lower, Wendy, ' "Anticipatory Obedience" and the Nazi Implementation of the Holocaust in the Ukraine: A Case Study of Central and Peripheral Forces in the Generalbezirk Zhytomyr 1941–1944', *Holocaust and Genocide Studies*, 16:1 (2002), 1–22.

Lüdtke, Alf, and Bernd Weisbrod, eds., *No Man's Land of Violence: Extreme Wars in the 20th Century* (Göttingen: Wallstein, 2006).

Lukas, Richard C., *The Forgotten Holocaust: The Poles under German Occupation 1939–1944* (Lexington, KY: University Press of Kentucky, 1986).

Lumans, Valdis O., *Himmler's Auxiliaries: The Volksdeutsche Mittelstelle and the German National Minorities of Europe 1933–1945* (Chapel Hill and London: University of North Carolina Press, 1993).

McCagg, William O., *Jewish Nobles and Geniuses in Modern Hungary* (Boulder, CO: East European Quarterly, 1972).

McDermott, Kevin, and Matthew Stibbe, eds., *Stalinist Terror in Eastern Europe: Elite Purges and Mass Repressions* (Manchester: Manchester University Press, 2010).

MacDonald, Callum, *The Killing of SS Obergruppenführer Reinhard Heydrich 27 May 1942* (New York: The Free Press, 1989).

Mackinder, Sir Halford J., *Democratic Ideals and Reality: A Study in the Politics of Reconstruction* (London: Constable and Co., 1919).

MacQueen, Michael, 'The Context of Mass Destruction: Agents and Prerequisites of the Holocaust in Lithuania', *Holocaust and Genocide Studies*, 12:1 (1998), 27–48.

Madajczyk, Czesław, 'Deportations in the Zamość Region in 1942 and 1943 in the Light of German Documents', *Acta Poloniae Historica*, 1 (1958), 75–106.

Madajczyk, Czesław, *Die Okkupationspolitik Nazisdeutschlands in Polen, 1939–1945* (Cologne: Pahl-Rugenstein, 1988).

Madievski, Samson, '1953: La déportation des juifs soviétiques était-elle programmée?' *Cahiers du monde russe*, 41:4 (2000), 561–8.

Magocsi, Paul Robert, *The Shaping of a National Identity: Sub-Carpathian Rus 1848–1948* (Cambridge, MA: Harvard University Press, 1978).

Magocsi, Paul Robert, ed., *The Persistence of Regional Cultures: Rusyns and Ukrainians in their Carpathian Homeland and Abroad* (Fairview, NJ: East European Monographs, 1993).

Magocsi, Paul Robert, *A History of the Ukraine* (Washington DC: University of Washington Press, 1996).

Magocsi, Paul Robert, *Historical Atlas of East Central Europe* (Seattle: University of Washington Press, 2002).

Magocsi, Paul Robert, and Andrii Krawchuk, eds., *Morality and Reality: The Life and Times of Andrei Sheptyts'kyi* (Edmonton: Canadian Institute of Ukrainian Studies, University of Alberta Press, 1989).

Malcolm, Noel, *Bosnia: A Short History* (London and Basingstoke: Palgrave Macmillan, 1994).

Malcolm, Noel, *Kosovo: A Short History* (London and Basingstoke: Palgrave Macmillan, 1998).

Malia, Martin, *The Soviet Tragedy: A History of Socialism in Russia 1917–1991* (New York: The Free Press, 1994).

Mango, Andrew, *Atatürk* (London: John Murray, 1999).

Mann, Michael, *The Dark Side of Democracy: Explaining Ethnic Cleansing* (Cambridge and New York: Cambridge University Press, 2005).

Manoschek, Walter, *'Serbien ist judenfrei': Militärische Besatzungspolitik und Judenvernichtung in Serbien 1941/42* (Munich: R. Oldenbourg, 1995).

Markusen, Eric, and David Kopf, *The Holocaust and Strategic Bombing: Genocide and Total War in the 20th Century* (Boulder, CO, San Francisco, CA, and Oxford: Westview Press, 1995).

Marples, David R., *Heroes and Villains: Creating National History in Contemporary Ukraine* (Budapest: Central European University Press, 2007).

Marrus, Michael, *The Unwanted: European Refugees in the Twentieth Century* (New York and Oxford: Oxford University Press, 1985).

Marrus, Michael, *The Holocaust in History* (London: Penguin, 1987).

Marrus, Michael, *The Nazi Holocaust*, 4 vols (Westport and London: Meckler, 1989).

Marrus, Michael, and Robert O. Paxton, *Vichy France and the Jews* (New York: Basic Books, 1981).

Marston, Daniel, and Carter Malkasian, *Counter-Insurgency in Modern Warfare* (Oxford and New York: Osprey, 2008).

Masalha, Nur, *Expulsion of the Palestinians: The Concept of 'Transfer' in Zionist Political Thought 1882–1948* (Washington DC: Institute for Palestinian Studies, 1992).

Maser, Werner, *Hitler's Letters and Notes*, trans. Arnold Pomerans (London: Heinemann, 1974).

Mastny, Vojtech, *The Czechs under Nazi Rule: The Failure of National Resistance 1939–1942* (New York and London: Columbia University Press, 1971).

Matkovski, Alexander, *A History of the Jews in Macedonia*, trans. David Arney (Skopje: Macedonian Review Editions 1985).

Mayer, Arno, *Why did the Heavens Not Darken?: The 'Final Solution' in History* (London and New York: Verso, 1990).

Mazower, Mark, *Dark Continent: Europe's Twentieth Century* (London: Penguin Press, 1998).

Mazower, Mark, *After the War Was Over: Reconstructing the Family, Nation and State in Greece 1943–1960* (Princeton, NJ: Princeton University Press, 2000).

Mazower, Mark, 'Two Wars: Serbia 1914–1918 and 1941–1944', unpublished paper, 'Cultures of Killing' Conference, Birkbeck College, London, July 2000.

Mazower, Mark, *Inside Hitler's Greece: The Experience of Occupation 1941–1944* (New Haven, CT: Yale Nota Bene, [1993] 2001).

Mazower, Mark, *Salonica, City of Ghosts: Christians, Muslims and Jews 1430–1950* (London: HarperPerennial, 2004).

Mazower, Mark, *Hitler's Empire: Nazi Rule in Occupied Europe* (London: Penguin, 2009).

Mazower, Mark, *No Enchanted Palace: The End of Empire and the Ideological Origins of the United Nations* (Princeton, NJ, and Oxford: Princeton University Press, 2009).

Mazower, Mark, Jessica Reinisch, and David Feldman, eds., *Post-War Reconstruction: International Perspectives 1945–1948* (Oxford: Oxford University Press, 2011).

Mendes-Flohr, Paul R., and Jehuda Reinharz, eds., *The Jew in the Modern World: A Documentary History* (New York: Oxford University Press, 1980).

Merridale, Catherine, *Ivan's War: The Red Army 1939–1945* (London: Faber and Faber, 2005).

Mertelsmann, Olaf, and Aigi Rahi-Tamm, 'Soviet Mass Violence in Estonia Revisited', *Journal of Genocide Research*, 11:2/3 (2009), 307–22.

Michaelis, Meir, *Mussolini and the Jews: German-Italian Relations and the Jewish Question in Italy 1922–1945* (Oxford: Clarendon Press, 1978).

Michlic-Coren, Joanna, 'Polish Jews during and after the Kielce Pogrom: Reports from the Communist Archives', *Polin,* 13 (2000), 53–67.

Michman, Dan, 'The Jewish Dimension of the Holocaust in Dire Straits?: Current Challenges of Interpretation and Scope', unpublished paper, 'Rewriting the History of the Holocaust' Conference, University of Florida, 17–19 March 2012.

Midlarsky, Manus I., 'Territoriality and the Onset of Mass Violence: The Political Extremism of Joseph Stalin', *Journal of Genocide Research,* 11:2/3 (2009), 265–83.

Milfull, John, ed., *Why Germany? National Socialist Anti-Semitism and the European Context* (Providence, RI, and Oxford: Berg, 1993).

Miller, Marshall Lee, *Bulgaria during the Second World War* (Stanford, CA: Stanford University Press, 1975).

Mócsy, István I., *The Effect of World War I: The Uprooted: Hungarian Refugees and their Impact on Hungary's Domestic Politics 1918–1921* (New York: Brooklyn College Press, 1983).

Mohr, Joan McGuire, *The Czech and Slovak Legion in Siberia 1917–1922* (Jefferson, NC: McFarland and Company, 2012).

Moore, Bob, *Victims and Survivors: The Nazi Persecution of the Jews in the Netherlands* (London and New York: Arnold, 1997).

Moses, A. Dirk, ed., *Genocide and Settler Society: Frontier Violence and Stolen Indigenous Children in Australian History* (New York and Oxford: Berghahn, 2001).

Moses, A. Dirk, 'Conceptual Blockages and Definitional Dilemmas in the "Racial Century": Genocides of Indigenous Peoples and the Holocaust', *Patterns of Prejudice,* 36:4 (2002), 7–36.

Moses, A. Dirk, ed., *Empire, Colony, Genocide, Conquest: Occupation and Subaltern Resistance in World History* (Oxford and New York: Berghahn, 2008).

Moses, A. Dirk, 'Genocide and the Terror of History', *Parallax,* 17:4 (2011), 90–108.

Moses, A. Dirk, 'Paranoia and Partisanship: Genocide Studies, Holocaust Historiography and the "Apocalyptic Conjuncture"', *The History Journal,* 54:2 (2011), 553–83.

Mosse, George, and Bela Vago, eds., *Jews and Non-Jews in Eastern Europe* (Jerusalem: Israel Universities Press, 1974).

Motyl, Alexander J., 'Ukrainian Nationalist Political Violence in Inter-War Poland 1921–1939', *East European Quarterly,* 19:1 (1985), 45–55.

Müller, Rolf-Dieter, *Das deutsche Reich und der Zweite Weltkrieg,* vol.10:2 (Munich: Deutsche Verlags-Anstalt, 2008).

Müller, Rolf-Dieter, and Gerd Ueberschär, *Hitler's War in the East 1941–1945: A Critical Assessment,* trans. Bruce D. Little (Oxford: Berghahn, 1997).

Musiał, Bogdan, *'Konterrevolutionäre Elemente sind zu erschießen': die Brutalisierung der deutsch-sowjetischen Krieges im Sommer 1941* (Berlin: Propyläen, 2000).

Nagy-Talavera, Nicholas M., *The Green Shirts and the Others': A History of Fascism in Hungary and Romania* (2nd ed., Iaşi and Oxford: Centre for Romanian Studies, 2001).

Naimark, Norman M., *The Russians in Germany: A History of the Soviet Zone of Occupation, 1945–1949* (Cambridge, MA: Harvard University Press, 1995).

Naimark, Norman M., *Fires of Hatred: Ethnic Cleansing in Twentieth Century Europe* (Cambridge, MA, and London: Harvard University Press, 2001).

Nekrich, Aleksandr, *The Punished Peoples: The Deportation and Tragic Fate of Soviet Minorities at the End of the Second World War* (New York: W.W. Norton, 1978).

Nelson, Deborah, *The War Behind Me: Vietnam Veterans Confront the Truth about U.S. War Crimes* (New York: Basic Books, 2008).

Neufeld, Michael J., *The Rocket and the Reich: Peenemünde and the Coming of the Ballistic Missile Age* (New York: The Free Press, 1995).

Nicosia, Francis R., *The Third Reich and the Palestine Question* (London: I.B. Tauris, 1986).

Olsen, Jack, *Silence on Monte Sole* (London: Pan Books, 1968).

Overmans, Rüdiger, 'Personelle Verluste der deutschen Bevölkerung durch Flucht und Vertreibung', *Dzieje Najnowsze*, 26 (1994), 51–65.

Overy, R.J., *War and Economy in the Third Reich* (Oxford: Clarendon Press, 1994).

Paczkowski, Andrzej, *The Spring Will Be Ours: Poland and the Poles from Occupation to Freedom*, trans. Jane Cave (University Park: The Pennsylvania State University Press, 2003).

Panayi, Panikos, and Pippa Virdee, *Refugees and the End of Empire: Imperial Collapse and Forced Migration during the Twentieth Century* (Basingstoke: Palgrave, 2011).

Paris, Edmond, *Genocide in Satellite Croatia 1941–1945: A Record of Racial and Religious Persecutions and Massacres*, trans. Lois Perkins (Chicago: American Institute for Balkan Affairs, 1961).

Parrish, Michael, *The Lesser Terror: Soviet State Security 1939–1953* (Westport, CT: Praeger, 1996).

Paulsson, Gunnar S., 'The Demography of Jews in Hiding in Warsaw 1943–1945', *Polin*, 13 (2000), 78–103.

Paulsson, Gunnar S., *Secret City: The Hidden Jews of Warsaw 1940–1943* (New Haven, CT: Yale University Press, 2002).

Paxton, Robert, *Vichy France: Old Guard and New Order* (New York: Knopf, 1972).

Payne, Stanley G., *A History of Fascism 1914–45* (London: UCL Press, 1995).

Pelt, Robert Jan van, and Deborah Dwork, *Auschwitz: 1270 to the Present* (New Haven, CT, and London: Yale University Press, 1996).

Penkower, Monty Noam, *The Jews were Expendable: Free World Diplomacy and the Holocaust* (Urbana, IL: University of Illinois Press, 1983).

Perechodnik, Calel, *Am I a Murderer?: Testament of a Jewish Ghetto Policeman* (Boulder, CO: Westview, 1996).

Pernot, Mathieu, *Un camp pour les Bohémiens: mémoires du camp d'internement pour nomades de saliers* (Arles: Actes Sud, 2001).

Petersen, Roger D., *Understanding Ethnic Violence: Fear, Hatred and Resentment in Twentieth Century Eastern Europe* (Cambridge and New York: Cambridge University Press, 2002).

Peterson, Edward N., *The American Occupation of Germany: Retreat to Victory* (Detroit: Wayne State University Press, 1978).

Pick, Daniel, *War Machine: The Rationalization of Slaughter in the Modern Age* (New Haven, CT, and London: Yale University Press, 1993).

Pinkus, Benjamin, *The Soviet Government and the Jews 1948–1967: A Documented Study* (Cambridge: Cambridge University Press, 1984).

Pinkus, Benjamin, *The Jews of the Soviet Union: The History of a National Minority* (Cambridge and New York: Cambridge University Press, 1988).

Pizkiewicz, Dennis, *The Nazi Rocketeers: Dreams of Space and Crimes of War* (Westport, CT: Praeger, 1995).

Pohl, Dieter, 'Hans Krüger and the Murder of the Jews in the Stanisławów Region (Galicia)', *Yad Vashem Studies*, 26 (1994), 239–64.

Pohl, J. Otto, 'Stalin's Genocide against the "Repressed Peoples"', *Journal of Genocide Research*, 2:2 (2000), 267–93.

Polian, Pavel, *Against Their Will: The History and Geography of Forced Migrations in the USSR* (Budapest and New York: Central European University Press, 2004).

Polonsky, Antony, ed., *My Brother's Keeper? Recent Polish Debates on the Holocaust* (London: Routledge, 1990).

Polonsky, Antony, 'Introduction', *Polin*, 13 (2000), 3–33.

Polonsky, Antony, and Joanna B. Michlic, eds., *The Neighbors Respond: The Controversy over the Jedwabne Massacre in Poland* (Princeton, NJ: Princeton University Press, 2003).

Porter, Brian, *When Nationalism Begins to Hate: Imagining Modern Politics in Nineteenth-Century Poland* (Oxford and New York: Oxford University Press, 2000).

Power, Samantha, *'A Problem from Hell': America and the Age of Genocide* (New York: Basic Books, 2002).

Poznanski, Renée, *Jews in France during World War II*, trans. Nathan Bracher (Hanover, NH, and London: Brandeis University Press and United States Holocaust Memorial Museum, 2001).

Preston, Paul, *The Spanish Holocaust: Inquisition and Extermination in Twentieth-Century Spain* (London: W.W. Norton, 2012).

Prusin, Alexander Victor, *Nationalizing a Borderland: War, Ethnicity, and Anti-Jewish Violence in East Galicia 1914–1920* (Tuscaloosa, AL: University of Alabama Press, 2005).

Prusin, Alexander Victor, 'A Community of Violence: The SiPo/SD and its Role in the Nazi Terror System in Generalbezirk Kiew', *Holocaust and Genocide Studies*, 21:1 (2007), 1–30.

Prusin, Alexander Victor, *The Lands Between: The East European Frontiers in Wars, Revolutions and Nationality Conflicts 1900–1992* (Oxford: Oxford University Press, 2010).

Read, Anthony, and David Fisher, *The Deadly Embrace: Hitler, Stalin, and the Nazi–Soviet Pact 1939–1941* (New York and London: W.W. Norton, 1988).

Read, Anthony, *The Fall of Berlin* (New York: W.W. Norton, 1992).

Redlich, Shimon, *Propaganda and Nationalism in Wartime Russia: The Jewish Antifascist Committee in the USSR 1941–1948* (Boulder, CO: East European Monographs, 1982).

Redlich, Shimon, *War, Holocaust and Stalinism: A Documented Study of the Jewish Anti-Fascist Committee in the USSR* (Luxembourg: Harwood Academic Publishers, 1995).

Redlich, Shimon, *Together and Apart in Brzezany: Poles, Jews, and Ukrainians 1919–1945* (Bloomington and Indianapolis: Indiana University Press, 2002).

Reid, Anna, *Borderland: A Journey through the History of Ukraine* (London: Weidenfeld and Nicolson, 1997).

Reilly, Joanne, *Belsen: The Liberation of a Concentration Camp* (London and New York: Routledge, 1998).

Reinhardt, Klaus, *Moscow–The Turning Point? The Failure of Hitler's Strategy in the Winter of 1941–42*, trans Karl. B. Keenan (Oxford and Providence, RI: Berg, 1992).

Reinhartz, Dennis, 'Unmarked Graves: The Destruction of the Yugoslav Roma in the Balkan Holocaust 1941–1945', *Journal of Genocide Research*, 1:1 (1999), 81–9.

Reinisch, Jessica, and Elizabeth White, eds., *The Disentanglement of Populations: Migration, Expulsion and Displacement in Postwar Europe 1944–49* (Basingstoke: Palgrave Macmillan, 2011).

Riess, Volker, *Die Anfänge der Vernichtung 'Lebensunwerten Lebens' in den Reichsgauen Danzig-Westpreussen und Wartheland 1939/40* (Frankfurt: Peter Lang, 1995).

Robins, Nicholas A., and Adam Jones, eds., *Genocides by the Oppressed: Subaltern Genocide in Theory and Practice* (Bloomington and Indianapolis: Indiana University Press, 2009).

Rodogno, Davide, *Fascism's European Empire: Italian Occupation during the Second World War*, trans. Adrian Belton (Cambridge: Cambridge University Press, 2006).

Rogger, Hans, *Jewish Policies and Right-Wing Politics in Imperial Russia* (London: Palgrave Macmillan, 1985).

Ro'i, Yaacov, *Soviet Decision-Making in Practice: The USSR and Israel 1947–1954* (New Brunswick, NJ: Transaction Books, 1980).

Ro'i, Yaacov, ed., *Jews and Jewish Life in Russia and the Soviet Union* (Ilford, Essex, and Portland, OR: Frank Cass, 1995).

Roseman, Mark, *The Villa, the Lake, the Meeting: Wannsee and the Final Solution* (London: Penguin, 2002).

Roshwald, Aviel, *Ethnic Nationalism and the Fall of Empires: Central Europe, Russia and the Middle East 1914–1923* (London and New York: Routledge, 2001).

Rossino, Alexander B., *Hitler Strikes Poland: Blitzkrieg, Ideology and Atrocity* (Lawrence: University Press of Kansas, 2003).

Rossino, Alexander B., 'Polish "Neighbours" and German Invaders: Anti-Jewish Violence in the Białystok District during the Opening Weeks of Operation Barbarossa', *Polin*, 16 (2003), 431–52.

Rössler, Mechtild, Sabine Schleiermacher and Cordula Tollmien, eds., *Der 'Generalplan Ost': Hauptlinien der Nationalsozialistischen Planungs- und Vernichtungpolitik* (Berlin: Akademie Verlag, 1993).

Rothschild, Joseph, *Return to Diversity: A Political History of East Central Europe since World War II* (New York and Oxford: Oxford University Press 1990).

Roumani, Maurice M., *From Immigrant to Citizen: The Contribution of the Army to National Integration in Israel: The Case of the Oriental Jews* (The Hague: Foundation for the Study of Plural Societies, 1979).

Rousso, Henry, *The Vichy Syndrome: History and Memory in France since 1944*, trans. Arthur Goldhammer (Cambridge, MA: Harvard University Press, 1991).

Rousso, Henry, ed., *Stalinism and Nazism: History and Memory Compared*, trans. Lucy B Golsan et al. (Lincoln, NE, and London: University of Nebraska Press, 2004).

Rozett, Robert, 'Diminishing the Holocaust: Scholarly Fodder for a Discourse of Distortion', *Israel Journal of Foreign Affairs*, 6:1 (2012), 53–64.

Rubinstein, William, *The Myth of Rescue: Why the Democracies Could Not Have Saved More Jews from the Nazis* (London: Routledge, 1997).

Rudling, Per Anders, 'The Khatyn Massacre in Belorussia: A Historical Controversy Revisited', *Holocaust and Genocide Studies*, 26:1 (2012), 29–58.

Rutherford, Phillip T., *Prelude to the Final Solution: The Nazi Programme for Deporting Ethnic Poles 1939–1941* (Lawrence: University Press of Kansas, 2007).

Safrian, Hans, *Eichmann's Men*, trans. Ute Stargardt (Cambridge and New York: Cambridge University Press, 2010).

Sakmyster, Thomas L., *Hungary's Admiral on Horseback: Miklos Horthy 1918–1944* (Boulder, CO: East European Monographs, 1993).

Sarfatti, Michele, *Mussolini contro gli ebrei: Cronaca dell'elaborazione delle leggi del 1938* (Turin: S. Zamorani, 1994).

Saul, Nicholas, and Susan Tebbutt, eds., *The Role of the Romanies: Images and Counter-Images of 'Gypsies'/Romanies in European Cultures* (Liverpool: Liverpool University Press, 2004).

Schabas, William A., *Genocide in International Law: The Crime of Crimes* (Cambridge: Cambridge University Press, 2000).

Schabas, William A., 'Genocide and the International Court of Justice: Finally, a Duty to Prevent the Crime of Crimes', *Genocide Studies and Prevention*, 2:2 (2007), 101–22.

Schaller, Dominik J., and Jürgen Zimmerer, eds., 'Special Issue: Raphael Lemkin: The "Founder of the United Nation's Genocide Convention" as a Historian of Mass Violence', *Journal of Genocide Research*, 7:4 (2005), 441–78.

Schechtman, Joseph B., *European Population Transfers 1939–1945* (New York: Oxford University Press, 1946).

Scheck, Raffael, *Hitler's African Victims: The German Army Massacres of Black French Soldiers in 1940* (New York: Cambridge University Press, 2006).

Scheffer, David, 'The World Court's Fractured Ruling on Genocide', *Genocide Studies and Prevention*, 2:2 (2007), 123–36.

Schmaltz, Eric J., and Samuel D Sinner, ' "You will die under ruins and snow": The Soviet Repression of Russian Germans as a Case Study of Successful Genocide', *Journal of Genocide Research*, 4:3 (2002), 327–56.

Schramm, Percy Ernst, *Hitler: The Man and the Military Leader* (London: Penguin, 1972).

Schulte, Jan Erik, *Zwangsarbeit und Vernichtung: Das Wirtschaftsimperium der SS: Oswald Pohl und das SS-Wirtschaft-Verwaltungshauptamt 1933–1945* (Paderborn: F. Schoningh, 2001).

Schulte, Theo J., *The German Army and Nazi Policies in Occupied Russia* (Oxford and New York: Berg, 1989).

Seely, Robert, *Russo–Chechen Conflict 1800–2000: A Deadly Embrace* (London and Portland, OR: Frank Cass, 2001).

Service, Robert, *Stalin: A Biography* (Cambridge, MA: Belknap Press, 2005).

Seton-Watson, Hugh, *Eastern Europe between the Wars 1918–1941* (Cambridge: Cambridge University Press, 1945).

Shaw, Martin, *War and Genocide: Organised Killing in Modern Society* (Cambridge: Polity Press, 2003).

Sheehy, Ann, and Bohdan Nahalyo, *The Crimean Tatars, Volga Germans and Meshketians: Soviet Treatment of some National Minorities*, (3rd ed., London: Minority Rights Group, 1981).

Shekhovtsov, Anton, 'By Cross and Sword: Clerical Fascism in Inter-War Ukraine', *Totalitarian Movements and Political Religions*, 8:2 (2007), 271–85.

Shepherd, Ben, *War in the Wild East: The German Army and Soviet Partisans* (Cambridge, MA, and London: Harvard University Press, 2004).

Silber, Michael K., ed., *Jews in the Hungarian Economy 1760–1945: Studies Dedicated to Moshe Carmilly-Weinberger on his Eightieth Birthday* (Jerusalem: Magnes Press, 1992).

Simonian, Hovann H., 'The Vanished Khemshins: Return from the Brink', *Journal of Genocide Research*, 4:3 (2002), 375–85.

Simpson, Christopher, *Blowback: The First Full Account of America's Recruitment of Nazis, and its Disastrous Effect on our Domestic and Foreign Policy* (London and New York: Weidenfield and Nicholson, 1988).

Slepyan, Kenneth, 'The Soviet Partisan Movement and the Holocaust', *Holocaust and Genocide Studies*, 14:1 (2000), 1–27.

Slepyan, Kenneth, *Stalin's Guerrillas: Soviet Partisans in World War Two* (Lawrence: University Press of Kansas, 2006).

Slezkine, Yuri, *The Jewish Century* (Princeton, NJ, and Oxford: Princeton University Press, 2004).

Snyder, Timothy, *The Reconstruction of Nations: Poland, Ukraine, Lithuania, Belarus 1569–1999* (New York and London: Yale University Press, 2003).

Snyder, Timothy, *Bloodlands: Europe between Hitler and Stalin* (London: Bodley Head, 2010).

Solonari, Vladimir, *Purifying the Nation: Population Exchange and Ethnic Cleansing in Nazi-Allied Romania* (Washington DC and Baltimore: Woodrow Wilson Center Press and Johns Hopkins University Press, 2010).

Solzhenitsyn, Alexander, *The Gulag Archipelago, 1918–1956: An Experiment in Literary Investigation*, 3 vols, trans. Thomas P. Whitney (New York: New York University Press, 1992).

Sonyel, Salahi, *The Great War and the Tragedy of Anatolia* (Ankara: Turkish Historical Printing House, 2000).

Spector, Shmuel, *The Holocaust of Volhynian Jewry 1941–1944* (Jerusalem: Yad Vashem, 1990).

Statiev, Alexander, 'Soviet Ethnic Deportations: Intent versus Outcome', in *Journal of Genocide Research*, 11:2/3 (2009), 243–64.

Statiev, Alexander, *The Soviet Counter-Insurgency in the Western Borderlands* (Cambridge: Cambridge University Press, 2010).

Stefanović, Đorđe, 'Seeing the Albanians through Serbian Eyes: The Inventors of the Tradition of Intolerance and their Critics 1804–1939', *European History Quarterly*, 35:3 (2005), 465–92.

Steinberg, Jonathan, *All or Nothing: The Axis and the Holocaust 1941–43* (London and New York: Routledge, 1990).

Stille, Alexander, *Benevolence and Betrayal: Five Jewish Families under Fascism* (London: Vintage, 1992).

Stola, Darius, 'The Hate Campaign of March 1968: How did it become Anti-Jewish?' *Polin*, 21 (2008), 16–36.

Stoltzfus, Nathan, *Resistance of the Heart: Intermarriage and the Rosenstrasse Protest in Nazi Germany* (New York: W.W. Norton, 1996).

Stone, Dan, 'Modernity and Violence: Theoretical Reflections on the Einsatzgruppen', *Journal of Genocide Research*, 1:3 (1999), 367–78.

Stone, Dan, *Constructing the Holocaust: A Study in Historiography* (London and Portland, OR: Vallentine Mitchell, 2003).

Stone, Dan, ed., *The Historiography of the Holocaust* (Basingstoke and New York: Palgrave, 2004).

Storry, Richard, *A History of Modern Japan* (London: Penguin, 1960).

Streim, Alfred, *Die Behandlung sowjetischer Kriegsgefangener im 'Fall Barbarossa'* (Karlsruhe: C.F. Müller, 1981).

Streit, Christian, *Keine Kameraden: Die Wehrmacht und die sowjetschen Kriegsgefangenen 1941–1945* (Stuttgart: DVA, 1978).

Suny, Ronald Grigor, and Terry Martin, eds., *A State of Nations: Empire and Nation-Making in the Age of Lenin and Stalin* (Oxford: Oxford University Press, 2001).

Suny, Ronald Grigor, Fatma Müge Göçek and Norman N. Naimark, eds., *A Question of Genocide: Armenians and Turks at the End of the Ottoman Empire* (Oxford and New York: Oxford University Press, 2011).

Suvorov, Viktor, *Inside Soviet Military Intelligence* (New York: Palgrave Macmillan, 1984).

Taras, Ray, ed., *National Identities and Ethnic Minorities in Eastern Europe: Selected Papers from the Fifth World Congress of Central and East European Studies 1995* (New York: St Martin's Press, 1998).

Taylor, A.J.P., *The Origins of the Second World War* (London: Penguin, 1964).

Tec, Nechama, *When Light Pierced the Darkness: Christian Rescue of Jews in Nazi-Occupied Poland* (New York: Oxford University Press, 1986).

Tec, Nechama, *Defiance: The Bielski Partisans* (New York: Oxford University Press, 1993).

Terry, Sarah Meiklejohn, *Poland's Place in Europe: General Sikorski and the Origins of the Oder-Neisse Line 1939–1943* (Princeton, NJ: Princeton University Press, 1983).

Ther, Phillip, and Ana Siljak, eds., *Redrawing Nations: Ethnic Cleansing in East-Central Europe 1944–1948* (Oxford and Lanham, NY: Rowman and Littlefield, 2001).

Theriault, Henry, and Samuel Totten, eds., '60 years after the Ratification of the Genocide Convention: Critical Reflections on the State and Future of Genocide Studies, Part I', *Genocide Studies and Prevention*, 6:3 (2011), 207–304.

Thomas, Gordon, and Max Morgan-Witts, *Voyage of the Damned* (London: Hodder and Stoughton, 1974).

Tims, R.W., *Germanizing Prussian Poland: The H-K-T Society and the Struggle for the Eastern Marches in the German Empire 1894–1919* (New York: Columbia University Press, 1941).

Tismaneanu, Vladimir, *Fantasies of Salvation: Democracy, Nationalism and Myth in Post-Communist Europe* (Princeton, NJ: Princeton University Press, 1998).

Tolstoy, Nikolai, *Stalin's Secret War* (London: Pan Books, 1982).

Tomasevich, Jozo, *The Chetniks: War and Revolution in Yugoslavia 1941–1945* (Stanford, CA: Stanford University Press, 1975).

Tomasevich, Jozo, *War and Revolution in Yugoslavia 1941–1945: Occupation and Collaboration* (Stanford, CA: Stanford University Press, 2001).

Tooley, T. Hunt, *National Identity and Weimar Germany: Upper Silesia and the Eastern Border 1918–1922* (Lincoln, NE: University of Nebraska Press, 1997).

Tooze, Adam, *The Wages of Destruction: The Making and Breaking of the Nazi Economy* (London: Penguin, 2006).

Tory, Avraham, *Surviving the Holocaust: The Kovno Ghetto Diary*, trans. Jerzy Michalowicz (Cambridge, MA: Harvard University Press, 1990).

Townshend, Charles, *The British Campaign in Ireland 1919–1921: The Development of Political and Military Policies* (Oxford: Oxford University Press, 1975).

Toynbee, Arnold J., *The Western Question in Greece and Turkey: A Study in the Contact of Civilisations* (London: Constable and Co., 1923).

Trew, Simon, *Britain, Mihailović and the Chetniks 1941–42* (Basingstoke: Palgrave Macmillan, 1998).

Troebst, Stefan, 'Triangling Bulgarian Jewry: Between Nation-State, Socialism and Zionist Utopia', unpublished paper, 'Between Trieste, Salonika and Odessa', Simon Dubnow Institute Conference, Leipzig, 4–6 November 2000.

Trunk, Isaiah, *Judenrat: The Jewish Councils in Eastern Europe under Nazi Occupation* (New York: Palgrave Macmillan, 1972).

Trunk, Isaiah, *Łódź Ghetto: A History*, trans. Robert Moses Shapiro (Bloomington and Indianapolis: Indiana University Press, 2006).

Tucker, Robert C., *Stalin in Power: The Revolution from Above 1929–1941* (New York and London: W.W. Norton, 1990).

Tumblety, Joan, 'Review of *Verdict on Vichy: Power and Prejudice in the Vichy France Regime* by Michael Curtis', *Journal of Jewish Studies*, 54:2 (2003), 350–2.

Unger, Michal, *The Last Ghetto: Life in the Łódź Ghetto 1940–1944* (Jerusalem: Yad Vashem, 1995).

Vaksberg, Arkady, *Stalin against The Jews*, trans. Antonina W. Bouis (New York: Alfred A. Knopf, 1994).

Vardy, Steven Bela and T. Hunt Tooley, eds., *Ethnic Cleansing in Twentieth Century Europe* (Boulder, CO: Social Science Monographs, 2003).

Vasilieva, Larisa Nikolaevna, *Kremlin Wives*, ed. and trans. Cathy Porter (London: Weidenfeld and Nicolson, 1994).

Vishniac, Roman, *A Vanished World* (London: Allen Lane, 1983).

Vital, David, *A People Apart: A Political History of the Jews in Europe 1789–1939* (Oxford: Oxford University Press, 1999).

Vyronis, Speros, *The Mechanism of Catastrophe* (New York: Greekworks, 2005).

Wasserstein, Bernard, *Britain and the Jews of Europe 1939–1945* (Oxford and New York: Oxford University Press, 1978).

Weber, Claudia, ' "The Export of Terror": On the Impact of the Stalinist Culture of Terror on Soviet Foreign Policy during and after World War II', *Journal of Genocide Research*, 11:2/3 (2009), 285–306.

Wegner, Bernd, ed., *Zwei Wege nach Moskau: Vom Hitler-Stalin-Pakt nach 'Unternehmen Barbarossa'* (Munich and Zürich: Piper, 1991).

Weinbaum, Laurence, *A Marriage of Convenience: The New Zionist Organisation and the Polish Government 1936–1939* (Boulder, CO: East European Monographs, 1993).

Weinberg, David, *A Community on Trial: The Jews of Paris in the 1930s* (Chicago: University of Chicago Press, 1977).

Weinberg, Gerhard, *A World at Arms: A Global History of World War II* (Cambridge: Cambridge University Press, 1994).

Weinberg, Gerhard, 'Germany's War for World Conquest and the Extermination of the Jews', *Holocaust and Genocide Studies*, 10:2 (1996), 119–33.

Weindling, Paul, *Epidemics and Genocide in Eastern Europe 1890–1945* (Oxford: Oxford University Press, 2000).

Weiner, Amir, 'Nature, Nurture and Memory in a Socialist Utopia: Delineating the Soviet Socio-Ethnic Body in the Age of Socialism', *American Historical Review*, 104:4 (1999), 1114–55.

Weiner, Amir, *Making Sense of War: The Second World War and the Fate of the Bolshevik Revolution* (Princeton, NJ, and Oxford: Princeton University Press, 2001).

Weingartner, James J., *Crossroads of Death: The Story of the Malmédy Massacre and Trial* (Berkeley: University of California Press, 1979).

Weiss-Wendt, Anton, 'Extermination of the Gypsies in Estonia during World War II: Popular Images and Official Policies', *Holocaust and Genocide Studies,* 17:1 (2003) 31–61.

Weiss-Wendt, Anton, and Uğur Ümit Üngör, 'Collaboration in Genocide: The Ottoman Empire 1915–16, the German-occupied Baltic States and Rwanda 1994', *Holocaust and Genocide Studies*, 25:3 (2011), 203–45.

Weitz, Eric D., *A Century of Genocide: Utopias of Race and Nation* (Princeton, NJ, and Oxford: Princeton University Press, 2003).

Weitz, Eric D., 'From the Vienna to the Paris System: International Politics and the Entangled Histories of Human Rights, Forced Deportations and Civilizing Missions', *American Historical Review*, 113:5 (2008), 1313–43.

Wertheimer, Jack, *Unwelcome Strangers: East European Jews in Imperial Germany* (New York: Oxford University Press, 1987).

Wiese, Christian, and Paul Betts, eds., *Years of Persecution, Years of Extermination: Saul Friedländer and the Future of Holocaust Studies* (London and New York: Continuum, 2010).

Wildt, Michael, *An Uncompromising Generation: The Nazi Leadership of the Reich Security Main Office*, trans. Tom Lampert (Madison, WI: University of Wisconsin Press, 2009).

Willems, Wim, *In Search of the True Gypsy: From Enlightenment to Final Solution* (London: Frank Cass, 1997).

Williams, Brian Glyn, 'Hidden Ethnocide in the Soviet Muslim Borderlands: The Ethnic Cleansing of the Crimean Tatars', *Journal of Genocide Research*, 4:3 (2002), 357–73.

Wilson, James, *The Earth Shall Weep: A History of Native America* (London: Picador, 1998).

Wyman, David S., ed., *The World Reacts to the Holocaust* (Baltimore and London: Johns Hopkins University Press, 1996).

Wyman, David S., *The Abandonment of the Jews: America and the Holocaust 1941–1945* (New York: Pantheon Books, 1984).

Yakovlev, Alexander M., *A Century of Violence in Soviet Russia*, trans. Anthony Austin (New Haven, CT, and London: Yale University Press, 2002).

Zachariae, Georg, *Mussolini si confessa* (Milan: Garzanti, 1966).

Zawodny, J.K., *Death in the Forest: The Story of the Katyn Forest Massacre* (London: Macmillan, 1962).

Zayas, Alfred-Maurice de, *A Terrible Revenge: The Ethnic Cleansing of the East European Germans* (Basingstoke: Palgrave, [1986] 2006).

Zayas, Alfred-Maurice de, 'The Istanbul Pogrom of 6–7 September 1955 in the Light of International Law', *Genocide Studies and Prevention*, 2:2 (2007), 137–54.

Zbikowski, Andrzej, 'Jewish Reaction to the Soviet Arrival in the Kresy in September 1939', *Polin*, 13 (2000), 62–72.

Zelinka, Anna, *In Quest for God and Freedom: The Sufi Response to the Russian Advance in the North Caucasus* (London: Hurst, 2000).

Zertal, Idith, *Israel's Holocaust and the Politics of Nationhood*, trans. Chaya Galai (Cambridge and New York: Cambridge University Press, 2005).

Zimbardo, Philip, *The Lucifer Effect: Understanding How Good People Turn Evil* (New York: Random House, 2007).

Zimmerman, Michael, 'The National Socialist "Solution of the Gypsy Question": Central Decisions, Local Initiative and their Interrelation', *Holocaust and Genocide Studies*, 15:3 (2001), 412–27.

Zuccotti, Susan, *The Italians and the Holocaust: Persecution, Rescue and Survival* (New York: Basic Books, 1987).

Zuccotti, Susan, *The Holocaust, The French, and the Jews* (Lincoln, NE, and London: University of Nebraska Press, 1993).

Zweig, Ronald, *The Gold Train: The Destruction of the Jews and the Second World War's Most Terrible Robbery* (London: Penguin, 2003).

Zweiniger-Bargielowska, Ina, 'Bread Rationing in Britain, July 1946–July 1948', *Twentieth Century British History*, 4: 1 (1993), 57–85.

Index

Index   517

Black Book of Soviet Jewry, The 346
Black Hundreds, pogroms
    orchestrated by 356
Black Legion militia 179
Blackshirts *see* SS (*Schutzstaffel*)
Bleiburg, killings between Maribor and 379
Blobel, Paul 104, 105, 141
Bloch, Ernst 15
Blokhin, V. M. 62–3
Bloxham, Donald 123, 145
Blue Police Poland 34
Blum, Léon 163
Böhme, Franz 82, 83
Bolsheviks and Bolshevism 42, 58, 86, 97, 139,
    154, 251, 328
Boris, III, Tsar of Bulgaria 175, 176–7
Bormann, Martin 135, 137, 140
Borovets, 'Taras Bulba' 297
Borysław, Ukraine 189
Bosnia-Herzegovina 179, 239, 269, 275, 276,
    289, 364–5
    Banjia 276
    Bosanka Krajina 276, 285
        Mount Kozara region 268
    Herzegovina 277
        eastern 276
        western 274
    karst 277
    Muslim death toll in 289
    Muslim support for Germans 284
    Muslim vulnerability in 184, 284
    Partisan behaviour towards 285
    north-west region 276
Bosniaks 379
Bosquet, René 167
Bouhler, Philipp 65
Brack, Victor 65
Braham, Randolph 229
Brand, Joel 148
Bratislava 118
Brauchitsch, Field Marshal Walther
    von 27
Braun, Jerzy 203
Braun, Wernher von 125, 413
Breslau (Wrocław) 406
Brest, killings in 254
Brest-Litovsk 139, 411
Britain 75, 366, 378, 396
    Balkan strategy shift from Chetniks towards
        Tito 282
    bombing raids to wreak
        vengeance on Japanese
        and Germans 237
    internment programme of Italian and
        German 'aliens' 322
    Jewish communities in 157
British Guyana 21
Brno/Brünn 371
Brody 202

Browning, Christopher 50, 73, 120, 164
Brownshirts (*Sturmabteilung*) 58
Bruinessen, Martin van 13
Brzica, Petar 278
Buchenwald 151, 366
Budak, Mile 276
Budapest 360
    Jewish community 148
    Russian army entry into 243
Bug river 405
Bugai, N. F. 308, 313, 344
Bühler, Josef 117, 120
Bukovina 47, 185, 208, 218
    Jews 220, 364
    Rumanians 370
Bulgaria 54, 124, 153, 174–7, 377
    anti-semitism in 175
    Commissariat of Jewish Affairs 175
    joins Axis 174
    Law for the Protection of
        the Nation 175
    Orthodox Church 174
    Roma 175
    Sephardi community 175
    Sobranje 174
Bulgarians 268
    eructed from Crimea 333
Burrin, Jacques 78
Burzio, Giuseppe 172, 173
Bydgoszcz (Bromberg) massacres 29,
    30, 33

Calotescu, Corneliu 214
Cambodia 251, 273, 409
    as Democratic Kampuchea 275
Canaris, Admiral Wilhelm 97, 295
Carol II, King, of Rumania 20, 209
'Carpatho-Ukraine',
    'Republic of' 295
Casablanca conference 139
Catholic clergy
    involvement in Ustasha massacres of
        Serbs 280
    in Jewish destruction 188
Caucasus 5, 14, 56, 106, 304, 326,
    327, 348
    mountain peoples of 350
    see also North Caucasus
Central Asia 14, 71, 313, 326, 330
    conquest and consolidation under Russian
        rule 307
    deportation of Georgian border peoples
        towards 332
    nomads of 350
    west Ukrainians deported to 338
Cernowitz 405
Chamberlain, Neville 15, 396
Chams post-war massacres of 376
Channel Islands 116

Printed and bound by CPI Group (UK) Ltd, Croydon, CR0 4YY